How Monetary Policy Works

For monetary policymakers worldwide, developing a practical understanding of how monetary policy transmits to the economy is a day-to-day challenge. The data such policymakers have are imperfect and the maps they use are continually redrawn. With such uncertainty, understanding this complicated issue is rarely straightforward.

This book, a collaboration between practitioners of monetary policy across the world, helps to provide a foundation for understanding monetary policy works in all its complex glory. Using models, case studies and new empirical evidence, the contributors to this book help readers on many levels develop their technical expertise.

Students of macroeconomics, money and banking and international finance will find this to be a good addition to their reading lists. At the same time, policymakers and professionals within banking will learn valuable lessons from a thorough read of this book's pages.

Lavan Mahadeva is a Monetary Policy Committee Research Advisor to the Bank of England, UK. His previous book, *Monetary Policy Frameworks in a Global Context*, co-edited with Gabriel Sterne, is also available from Routledge. **Peter Sinclair** was recently, for three years, Director of the Bank of England Centre for Central Banking Studies and Professor of Economics at the University of Birmingham, UK.

Central banks governors' symposium
Published in association with the Bank of England

Previous titles in this series include:

1 **Financial Regulation**
Why, how and where now
Charles Goodhart, Philipp Hartmann, David Llewellyn, Liliana Rojas Suàrez and Steven Weisbrod

2 **Monetary Policy Frameworks in a Global Context**
Edited by Lavan Mahadeva and Gabriel Sterne

3 **Financial Stability and Central Banks**
Edited by Peter Sinclair and Juliette Healey

4 **How Monetary Policy Works**
Edited by Lavan Mahadeva and Peter Sinclair

How Monetary Policy Works

Edited by Lavan Mahadeva and Peter Sinclair

Routledge
Taylor & Francis Group
LONDON AND NEW YORK

First published 2005
by Routledge
2 Park Square, Milton Park, Abingdon, Oxon OX14 4RN

Simultaneously published in the USA and Canada by Routledge
270 Madison Ave, New York, NY 10016

Routledge is an imprint of the Taylor & Francis Group

Typeset in Baskerville by Wearset Ltd, Boldon, Tyne and Wear
Printed and bound in Great Britain by MPG Books Ltd, Bodmin

British Library Cataloguing in Publication Data
A catalogue record for this book is available from the British Library

Library of Congress Cataloging in Publication Data
A catalog record for this book has been requested

ISBN 0-415-34351-8

Contents

Figures

Tables

Contributors

Velimir Bole is Professor at the Economic Institute at the School of Law, University of Ljubljana, Slovenia.

Shaun de Jager currently heads the forecast group in the Macro Models Unit of the South African Reserve Bank.

David Dodge is the Governor of the Bank of Canada.

Charles Freedman was, at the time of writing, the Deputy Governor of the Bank of Canada. Currently, he is Scholar in Residence in the Department of Economics at Carleton University and a Research Fellow at the C.D. Howe Institute.

Áron Gereben was, at the time of writing, with the Monetary Policy Department of the National Bank of Hungary. Currently he is a Senior Analyst at the Reserve Bank of New Zealand.

Javier Gómez is a senior researcher at the Department of Economic Studies of the Banco de la República (the central bank of Colombia).

Toni Gravelle was, at the time of writing, a Principle Researcher in the Financial Markets Department of the Bank of Canada. He is currently an economist in the International Capital Markets Department of the IMF.

Bimal Jamal was, at the time of writing, the Governor of the Reserve Bank of India.

Juan Manuel Julio was, at the time of writing, an econometrician at the Department of Economic Studies of the Banco de la República (the central bank of Colombia).

Tomasz Łyziak is a chief specialist at the Bureau of Macroeconomic Research at the National Bank of Poland.

Lavan Mahadeva is a Research Advisor for the Monetary Policy Committee of the Bank of England.

Richhild Moessner is an economist at the Bank of England.

Judit Neményi is Senior Economist at the Financial Research Ltd. (Budapest). At the time of writing she was Managing Director of the Economics and Research Department and member of the executive board of directors of the Magyar Nemzeti Bank (National Bank of Hungary).

Gülbin Şahinbeyoğlu is a manager at the Research Department at the Central Bank of the Republic of Turkey.

Peter Sinclair is Professor of Economics at the University of Birmingham. He was Director of the Centre for Central Banking Studies from 2000 to 2002.

Daleen Smal is Deputy Head of the Research Department at the South African Reserve Bank.

John Vickers was, at the time of writing, the Chief Economist of the Bank of England and is now Chairman of the Office of Fair Trading, on leave from the Drummond Professorship of Political Economy at the University of Oxford.

Marion Williams is the Governor of the Central Bank of Barbados.

Acknowledgments

The editors are grateful to the Centre of Central Banking Studies at the Bank of England. They would also like to acknowledge their debt to the many economists from central banks around the world that have taken part in its workshops and training courses on modelling for monetary policy at the Centre of Central Banking Studies; this book arose from these collaborations. They would like to thank Dan Huynh and Bojan Markovic for research assistance, and are also grateful to Lucy Clary for administrative help and to Tony Ison for bibliographical research. All errors and opinions are entirely the responsibility of the authors and not the Bank of England or any other central bank institution.

1 Introduction

Lavan Mahadeva and Peter Sinclair

> *Confucius said: Research without thought is a mere net and entanglement; thought without gathering data, a peril.*[1]

This book is about developing a practical understanding of how monetary policy transmits to the economy. For monetary policymakers worldwide, this is a day-to-day challenge. The structure of their economies is evolving. The data they have are imperfect. The map they use needs to be continually re-drawn. With such uncertainty, the Chinese analect explains that our understanding must be built through a mixture of theory and empiricism, and the chapters contained in this book are written very much in that spirit.

That spirit divulges its origin: the book was developed at the Centre of Central Bank Studies in the Bank of England and builds on the collaboration of many central banks in understanding how monetary policy actually operates, and comparing that across a wide range of economies.[2]

Chapters 2 and 3, in Part 1, provide an overview of the theory of monetary transmission from the early stages of identifying what monetary policy is reacting to, tracing the effects on market rates, the exchange rate, consumption and investment and on to the effect of monetary policy on inflation and output. That overview is related to the experience of monetary policy worldwide: charts and estimations are used both to bring out the systematic features of transmission and also to highlight wide divergences.

Part 2 focuses on building formal models of the transmission mechanism. Chapters 4 and 5 discuss the role of the output gap and the Phillips curve in monetary policy models. The aim here is not to be limited to the familiar territory of comparing different estimates of these relationships, but rather to put some rigorous thought into what these concepts could mean for other types of economies. Each of the following four chapters in this section presents a simple model of the transmission mechanism for an emerging market economy, and uses that model to analyse the idiosyncratic features of those transmission mechanisms. Chapter 6 examines how monetary policy should be used to disinflate in Colombia. In Chapter 7, Aron Gereben's model is used to analyse the relevance of having both tradable and non-tradable sectors in Hungary. Chapter 8 tackles the importance of credit frictions in Poland, whilst Chapter 9 focuses on the interaction between fiscal policy and monetary policy in Turkey.

When today's monetary policymakers construct their views of the transmission mechanism, they must remember that they will be called upon to explain those views. Many central banks now publish an inflation report in which they say what they think is happening to the economy and how their instruments are aligned to respond to those developments. Part 3 (Chapter 10) is about what this great drive for transparency has meant for the transmission mechanism itself, looking at data from the US, the UK and Canada. Do agents respond more to data releases or central banks' announcements?

Part 4 collects the views and opinions of those who need to apply this knowledge to make policy decisions. Much of the work in this book was discussed at the Central Bank Governors' Symposium in the Bank of England in 2001, and the views of the discussants (Governor Marion Williams of Barbados, Governor David Dodge of Canada and Governor Bimal Jamal of India) are given in Chapters 11, 12 and 13 respectively, alongside those of other senior central bankers, Velimir Bole (Slovenia), Daleen Smal and Shaun de Jager (South Africa), Judit Neményi (Hungary), Charles Freedman (Canada) and John Vickers (UK) in Chapters 14–18 respectively. As with the models in Part 2, the issues that are faced by different economies are varied, but the formal thinking that goes into understanding how monetary policy works is in many ways strikingly similar.

Addressing those varied issues properly calls for good models; and good models must marry available data with good thinking. It is only when they are armed with these that policymakers can hope to escape Confucius's two pitfalls – and square up to the unending and vital task of safeguarding people's livelihoods and monetary environment.

Notes

1 Ancient Chinese analect (5–4 BC), translated by Ezra Pound (Mair 2000: 42).
2 http://boe-intra-w2s/internet/ccbs/index htm.

Part 1

An overview of the transmission mechanism of monetary policy

2 The transmission of monetary policy through interest rates

Policy rate effects on other interest rates, asset prices, consumption and investment

Peter Sinclair

2.1 Introduction

Section 2.2 of this chapter is concerned with how and why central banks change their policy rates, and what happens when they do. An overview of those effects is presented in section 2.3. Impacts on other interest rates are explored in section 2.4, while sections 2.5 and 2.6 look at repercussions on consumption and investment. The analysis is extended to other variables in Chapter 3.

2.2 The prompts for official interest rate changes

Most monetary policy decisions mean changes in central bank interest rates. Much of this book is concerned with tracing their effects. It helps to begin by studying those interest rate changes. This section gives, first, a statistical picture of *how* these interest rates have moved in as large a spectrum of countries as available data allow. The next step is to ask *why* they moved. Thus most of this section is devoted to uncovering information about central banks' reaction functions. However, interest rates change for a reason – often, to stabilise the macroeconomy in the face of shocks – and therefore it is useful to see *why* they change. Hence the first paradox of monetary policy: perfectly successful stabilisation would mean that the instruments of monetary policy looked completely powerless and unnecessary!

As Figures 2.1–2.6 reveal, the modal event is for the central bank interest rate not to change. When changes occur, looking at the 21 years studied, they usually exceed 100 basis points. Quarterly changes of at least 300 basis points seem the rule in much of Latin America, and in transition countries too. Many African and Asian countries, on the other hand, appear loath to change interest rates at all.

Short-term official interest rates are the main instrument of monetary policy. In some countries these are set by the central bank; in others by the finance ministry; and in some, by the two institutions in concert or at

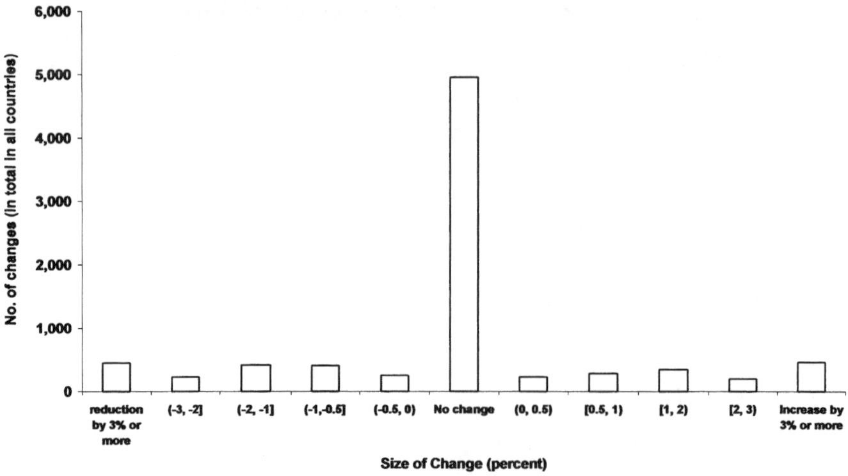

Figure 2.1 Quarterly changes in central bank official interest rates – all countries (1980–2000).

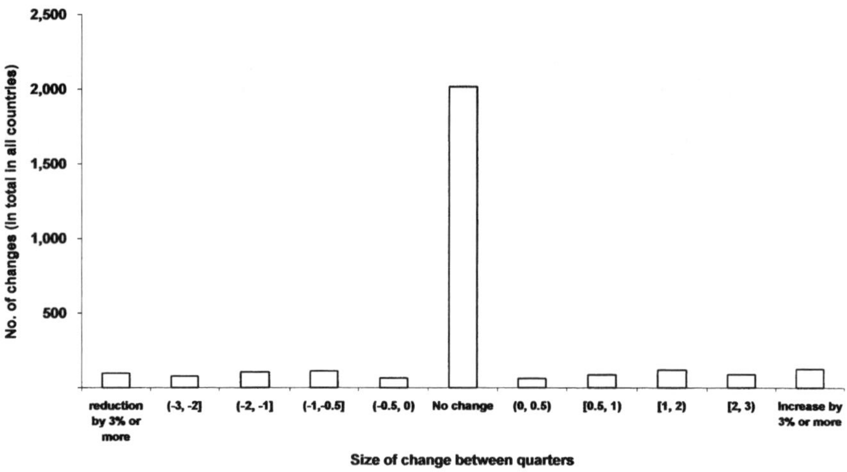

Figure 2.2 Quarterly changes in central bank official interest rates – African countries (1980–2000).

least in consultation with each other. Chapters 2 and 3 examine the consequences of such interest rate changes: what happens to other interest rates, to key elements of aggregate demand, and to inflation. The dependability, magnitude and speed of these repercussions will be explored, with analysis and some econometric evidence drawn from a wide variety of countries' experiences.

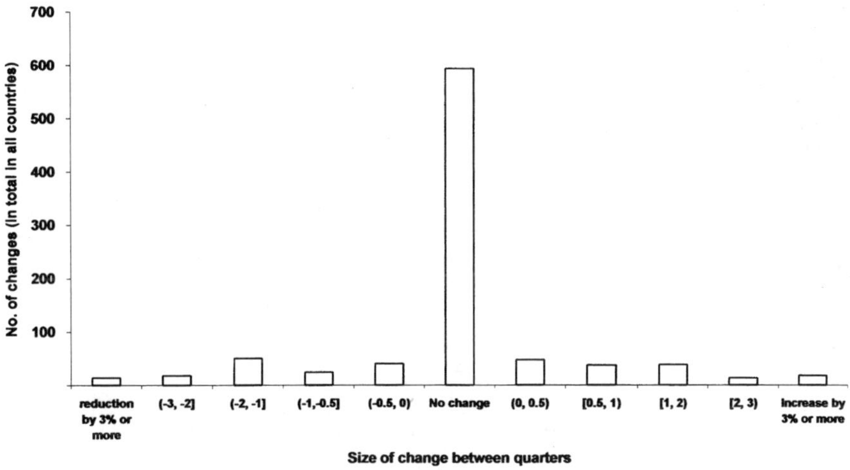

Figure 2.3 Quarterly changes in central bank official interest rates – Asian countries (1980–2000).

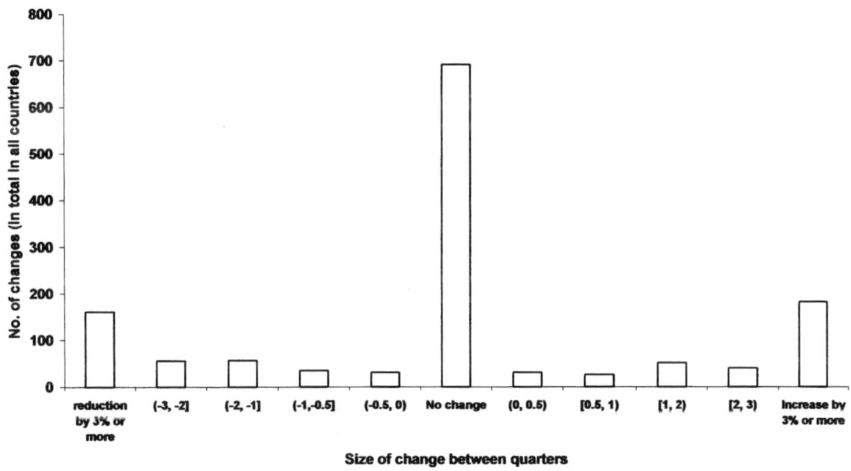

Figure 2.4 Quarterly changes in central bank official interest rates – Latin American and Caribbean countries (1980–2000).

So what prompts changes in official interest rates? There are really four main influences here. These are current levels, or forecasts, of inflation; current levels, or forecasts, of the output gap (that is, the difference between the economy's level of real income, and its estimated potential); where available, the market's expectations of future policy rates; and official interest rate changes abroad.

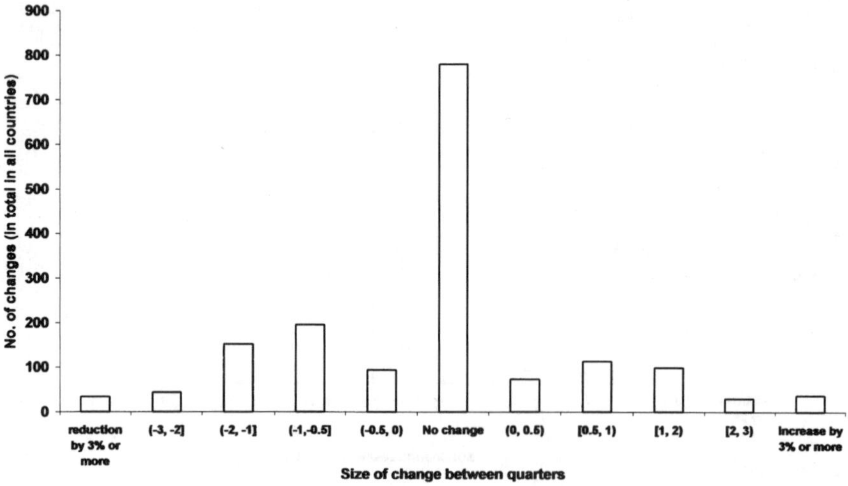

Figure 2.5 Quarterly changes in central bank official interest rates – OECD countries (1980–2000).

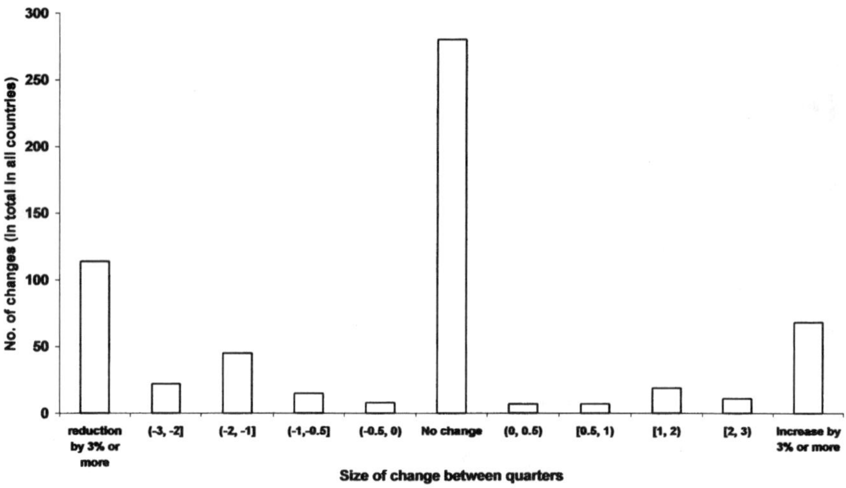

Figure 2.6 Quarterly changes in central bank official interest rates – transition countries (1980–2000).

Nominal, official short-term interest rates ('policy rates') are raised primarily to moderate the rate of inflation. This is especially true for central banks with an explicit inflation target. With inflation above target, or thought soon to climb above it, interest rate increases are needed to dampen inflation by squeezing domestic expenditure. This is the second paradox of monetary policy. If nominal interest rates are now too high (because inflation and inflation expectations are too high), central banks may need to raise them further, to reduce inflation (and interest rates too) later on. So, in the war against inflation, high nominal interest rates are both an admission of defeat – recognising the unwelcome reality of excessive inflation – and the key weapon that can lead to eventual victory.

Inflation matters, too, for central banks which target other variables, such as the exchange rate or some measure of the supply of money. Domestic macro-stability is the final aim of money and exchange-rate targeters just as for inflation targeters. Keeping the exchange rate on track will become increasingly difficult if domestic inflation persistently outpaces inflation abroad (by a larger margin than could be ascribed to other developments, at least). Adhering to a monetary target will also prove harder and harder if inflation is too rapid, because the demand for monetary aggregates will run away. In both cases, higher policy rates are needed. With output above potential, the monetary authorities will seek to stabilise it, both for its own sake and because a positive output gap threatens inflation – or indeed increasing inflation.

The third likely influence on official interest rates is the market's expectation of future policy rates. In many countries, something about these expectations can be gleaned from term structure data for treasury bill and money market interest rates (and government bond markets). When markets anticipate a policy rate rise in the near future, a decision to leave them unchanged, contrary to these expectations, may have numerous effects – some undesirable, some deliberately sought. There may be sudden negative pressure on the exchange rate. The prices of other assets, such as equities and long-term bonds, may jump. The demand for domestic dwellings may strengthen, reflecting the unexpectedly generous supply and terms of credit. Domestic aggregate demand will be buoyed up, with positive effects on labour demand, money wage rates, and the prices of goods and services in the medium term.

A fourth and final possible prompter for higher official interest rates at home is changes in policy rates (now, and expected in the future) abroad. In countries that attempt to target the exchange rate, the monetary authorities will watch international interest rate differences keenly. If rates rise abroad but not at home, and with no controls on international capital movements, capital may flee overseas, possibly in vast amounts. Even countries that maintain a freely floating exchange rate will not be indifferent to the domestic inflation and output consequences of large exchange-rate depreciation (or appreciation), operating through the home-currency prices of traded goods and those sectors' labour demand and pay settlements. Furthermore, when a major central bank abroad increases its policy rate, it reveals something about its own intentions, expectations and information. The domestic authorities may draw inferences about world trading conditions affecting many of its domestic firms. A rate cut abroad could signal a downward revision in expected world trade growth.

Stabilising domestic output and inflation may call for a domestic official rate reduction in those circumstances.

The probability and size of an official interest rate change at home are largest when all four prompts point in the same direction. If interest rates abroad have just risen, if treasury bill and money market term structure data (where available) point to market expectations of interest rate rises in the near future, and if domestic output and inflation appear abnormally high, the monetary authorities at home will usually wish to raise rates. A combination of recent rate cuts abroad, a downward-sloping term structure at the short end, and abnormally low inflation and output will point to the need for an official interest rate cut. Sometimes the prompts may point in different directions, and decisions will then be challenging and less easy to predict. The character of target regime, if there is one, will become important: inflation targeters are likely to pay most attention to inflation out-turns and predictions, while for exchange-rate targeters it is probable that official interest-rate developments abroad will matter most.

2.2.1 Econometric evidence

What do these interest-rate data tell us? Some impression of the monetary authorities' reaction functions can be conveyed by econometric evidence. We ran regressions for changes in official interest rates against changes in inflation, changes in the current output growth rate relative to trend, and interest rate changes by the US Fed (in the case of Austria, Belgium and the Netherlands, the Bundesbank rate). The main results for the largest available sample of 37 countries, estimated on quarterly data from the start of 1983 to the end of 2000, are as follows.

- Changes in inflation are found to have a positive effect upon interest rate changes in all but 6 countries. In 12, this effect is significant. It is highest in Chile and Israel, the only countries where nominal interest rates rise more than one-for-one with current inflation, and about a half (and significant) in Britain, Portugal, Australia, New Zealand, Mexico and Thailand. Changes in current inflation have a smaller, but still significantly positive, effect in the US, Finland, Germany and Turkey. The measured effect of inflation on official interest rates may be weak, as pre-emptive action may already have been taken. This observation also holds for output growth.
- Output growth has a significantly positive impact in Australia, Costa Rica, the Netherlands, Switzerland and the US, and nearly so in Belarus, Britain, South Africa and Spain. The effect is positive but insignificant in many others. However, in half the sample it is negative. Of these, three countries, Germany, Peru and Turkey, display significantly negative coefficients. What could explain this? In some cases at least it may be that the onset of a financial crisis triggers a

simultaneous fall in output and rise in interest rates. The same responses would follow a serious, adverse, domestic supply shock (and that could of course easily prompt a financial crisis, too).

Thus far, our results match those of many other recent empirical investigations of the hypothesis that central banks follow some reaction function, such as a Taylor Rule. The studies by Clarida *et al.* (1998, 1999, 2000) are celebrated examples. Our canvas, however, is as broad as possible. Another thing that is new in this report is the inclusion of other central banks' interest rates in the regressions. We find that the US rate (or, for Austria, Belgium and the Netherlands, the German rate) has a significantly positive effect for fourteen countries. In some cases, such as Costa Rica, Latvia and South Africa, it is the lagged foreign rate that works this way; for others, the foreign rate appears to exert an immediate effect. For Canada, the coefficient on the US rate exceeds unity. This exposes two possibilities, not mutually exclusive. One is that, for much of the period, the Bank of Canada was reluctant to see sharp changes in the exchange rate with her overwhelmingly preponderant trading partner. The other is that the Canadian and US business cycles are so closely integrated that the shocks prompting the Fed to change interest rates south of the border have a simultaneous appearance (and effect) north of it.

Finally, we take a brief look at the distribution of real central bank rates in recent years. Two samples are examined: first, an unvarying population of 56 countries with continuous reporting from 1976 to 1998 (supplemented with occasional interpolation), and second, a varying population of 116 countries from 1970 to 1999. Median and other quantile data are reported for these two samples in Figures 2.7 and 2.8. The constant population group displays a positive time trend, flattening off in the 1990s. The median central bank's policy rate fluctuated between 1 per cent and 4 per cent below the rate of inflation in the later 1970s and early 1980s, but then climbed to some 3–4 per cent above inflation by the late 1980s, where it remained. There is minimal evidence of convergence. The distribution points to a negative skew, with volatile but heavily negative real interest rates for the bottom tail, at least until the late 1990s. The varying population group presents a more complex picture of apparently growing divergence for much of the period. The negative real rates for the whole distribution in 1974–75 betray the effects of the first oil shock. About one-quarter of the distribution exhibits negative real rates in all but the last few years, suggesting that financial repression has been widespread in many emerging economies.

The climb in most central bank real interest rates from the later 1970s reflects a variety of influences. Four stand out. First, the normally positive level of real interest rates was restored after the 1970s oil price shocks. Second, the 1980s (and the 1990s) saw serious attempts to cut inflation in many countries, broad success in achieving this aim, and yet

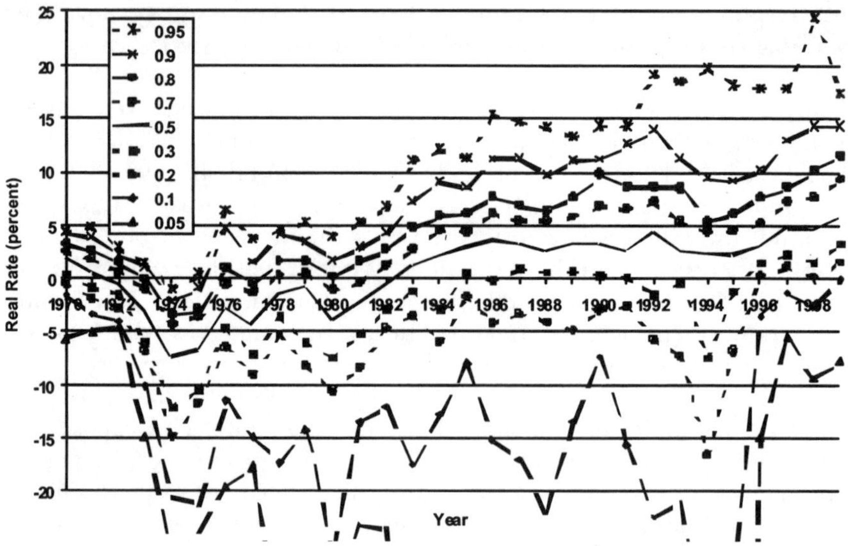

Figure 2.7 Quantiles of real central bank interest rates of 116 countries, 1970–1999 (varying population).

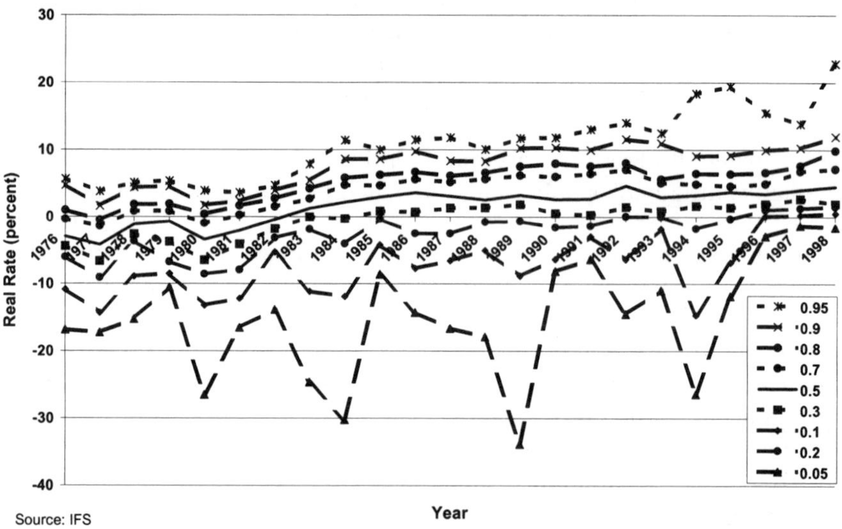

Figure 2.8 Quantiles of real central bank interest rates of 56 countries, 1976–1998.

some lingering fears (in official quarters as well as the financial markets) that higher inflation might return. Third, several developing countries' central banks became increasingly aware of the drawbacks of policies of financial repression, which had usually held official real interest rates to negative values. Finally, economic growth rates increased, particularly in much of Asia and, at least after 1992, the US. Although growth and real interest rates are often interdependent, faster given increases in labour productivity and in the labour force should both exert a positive long-run effect on real interest rates. Armed with some impression of how central bank interest rates have moved across the world, and why they moved when and where they did, we are now ready to examine what effects these interest rate changes had. The rest of this chapter explores different facets of this.

2.3 Interest rates and prices: an overview of effects

Section 2.2 examined what prompts official interest rate changes. It is now time to look at their effects. The first stage involves the repercussions that official interest rate changes have on other interest rates, and the demand for, and prices of, various assets.

At the core of *Stage 1* is the close link that official interest rates display with other market interest rates. In many countries there are bills issued by government (the finance ministry, or Treasury) or, in certain cases, by central banks themselves. The typical bill carries no coupon; it matures for a certain sum, say \$100 or £100, 3 months or 90 days after it is issued. It is sold below par at a price of $\mathbf{x}$, perhaps in an auction, and if its term to maturity is the fraction θ of 1 year, the annualised rate of interest on the bill, r_T, is calculated from the formula $(1 + r_T)^\theta = V/x$, where V is the price on redemption. Statistically this rate of interest is usually very close to the official interest rate, call it r_O. To be precise, the expected average value of r_O over the bill's life, call it Er_O, will be given by the approximation $Er_O \approx r_T + n$, where n equals the 'normal' excess of r_O over r_T. This might lie between about 10 to 30 basis points. The gap between Er_O and r_O should be modest.

Thus r_T will generally be very close to r_O. Newly issued treasury bills, sold after r_O has altered, will usually respond about one-for-one. The only cases where they will not are when the rise or fall in r_O has already been anticipated, or when the market expects the latest change in r_O to be reversed very quickly. In many economies, money market interest rates can be observed. These rates will behave very much like r_T, varying a little if terms differ. Money market rates will respond to r_O in similar ways. Funds placed in money markets are very close substitutes for treasury bills.

Financial institutions borrow or lend in money markets. Most also hold treasury bills, which they can augment or run down at will. Retail banks set interest rates on various classes of deposits and loans. These loans consist, in the main, of secured loans to companies, often at variable interest rates, and mortgages, some at fixed interest and some at variable interest, issued to households purchasing property. For retail banks, r_T (or its money market equivalent) reflects the marginal cost of issuing a loan. The expected marginal revenue from loans will equal the interest rate on loans, r_L, with adjustment for management costs, any monopoly power, and a margin for expected default. When r_O rises r_T rises too, and we should expect r_L to rise quite soon as well, though not always quite one-for-one. A profit-maximising retail bank will seek to equate the expected marginal revenue from its variable-rate loans with r_T (or its money market equivalent).

Analogous links can be derived between r_T and r_D, the interest rate offered on a typical deposit. Generally r_D will be somewhat lower than r_T, and particularly so for modest deposits or deposits with chequing rights. Part of the gap can be explained by deposit management costs, and part by the extent of any monopsony power the retail bank enjoys.

The links between r_D, r_L and r_O are examined in more detail below. They form a key element in the transmission mechanism for monetary policy, because they represent the financial system's main monetary interface with firms and households determining their expenditure plans.

There are other links that matter too, in this connection. In many developing countries, government and public corporations typically conduct most of their borrowing abroad, usually in the medium of US dollars. However, in a growing number of both developing and transition economies, and in advanced industrial countries, public agents issue some bonds in domestic currency to domestic portfolio-holders, such as insurance companies. Conditions vary, but most such bonds will be repaid in nominal terms at a specified future date, perhaps 5 or 10 years ahead. Setting aside risks, tax complications and the possibility of illiquidity in thin markets, there should exist a close association between bond yields and the average rates of interest expected on a sequence of 3-month treasury bills held over the bond's life.

If r_O is raised by 100 basis points now, and this comes as a complete surprise, the current r_T on the next issue of treasury bills will rise, by something close to 100 basis points if the change of Er_O is close to the change of r_O. What will happen to the price of a 5-year bond, x_B? Suppose market's expectations of future values of r_T, in 3, 6, 9 and up to 57 months' time, are unchanged. In that case, the average value of r_T expected over the full 5 years will have risen by roughly 5 basis points (i.e. 100/20). Ignoring coupons, the market price of the 5-year bond will be related to the annualised 5-year bond interest rate, r_5, by the formula $(1 + r_5)^5 = V_B/x_B$, where V_B is the bond's future value at redemption. In this case, r_B will have risen by 5 basis points, so that x_B should fall by about a quarter of 1 percent. The longer the term to maturity, the less sensitive the bond's price will be to the current r_T.

At the other extreme, market participants may think that the treasury bill rate will stay up at its new high level throughout the next 5 years. In this admittedly rather unlikely case, r_5 will jump by some 100 basis points, not the mere 5 basis points in the previous case when all future r_T's were unaffected by the rise in r_O. With r_5 up by 100 basis points, x_B will fall by 20 times as much as in the previous case – by very nearly 5 per cent. So how much bond prices react to changes in r_O depends on two things above all: on how long the new higher official interest rates are expected to persist, on average; and on the bond's life. They will also react to changes in expected inflation. If an official interest rate increase is interpreted as a major assault on inflation, which is expected to succeed, bond interest rates would rise at the shorter end and fall at the long end of a maturity spectrum.

Similar observations apply to the price of equities. The equity–interest rate link is explored further below. One key to unlock them, in the simplest case, tax and risk considerations aside, is the equation

$$P_E\,(1 + R_1) = d^e{}_1 + P^e{}_{E1} \tag{2.2.1}$$

Here, $P^e{}_{E1}$ is the current expectation of the (real) price of equities is in the next period, say a year's time; $d^e{}_1$ is the current expectation of the (real) dividend payment then; and R_1 is the current real interest rate over the period. This equation suggests that the proportionate fall in P_E now approximates to the rise in the expected value of all future real interest rates, and the proportionate change in all future ratios of d to P_E. How much today's official policy rate rise reduces current equity prices depends on the extent to which this raises *real* interest rates, and how long for. The impact may well be modest, particularly if *ex-ante* real interest rates at home have to match those abroad with free international capital mobility. Equities are internationally traded assets in that case. Real estate is different. Here, international trade is usually negligible. Domestic official interest rate decisions, and the supply of domestic credit to which they are often (negatively) linked, can make for powerful repercussions. A closer look at this relationship is provided in section 2.5.

When policy rate changes alter the values of real estate, equity and bonds, they change aggregate net wealth. Bonds may play a rather weak role here, because bonds usually represent a claim by one domestic resident against another (often the taxpayer whose taxes have to service public sector debt). Bonds can matter though, perhaps because most taxpayers are unaware of how government borrowing affects their future net income, but more particularly when the country's net bond holdings are non-zero. Countries with net obligations, public or private, to the rest of the world are impoverished to some degree if the real value of those obligations goes up. The final asset price to consider in Stage 1 is the price of foreign currency. Here a rise in domestic official nominal interest rates should lead, all else equal, to an appreciation under free floating, or perhaps a reduced risk of a devaluation under a regime of adjustable pegs.

Stage 2 is the effect that asset price changes have on expenditure. A fall in $\boldsymbol{P_E}$ implies a higher cost of equity capital for firms. A fall in bond prices raises the cost of debenture (corporate bond) external finance. Firms are likely to react, all else equal, by revising their investment plans downward. Investment expenditure is liable to fall, with a lag. Working capital decisions will be sensitive to short interest rates, and fixed investment to longer interest rates, because prudence enjoins firms to match the maturity structure of obligations with the maturity structure of the assets those obligations finance. For consumers, a fall in net wealth will inevitably constrain consumption spending, but often with a lag (or a phased set of lags) to reflect perception delays, commitments and adjustment costs. There is also some direct impact on consumption plans, through intertemporal substitution, but evidence provided below suggests that this effect is far from robust or large, at least for non-durable spending. Changes in the market value of real estate should have a large and quite protracted effect upon construction outlays by both the household sector (dwellings) and the corporate sector (structures investment).

Summing these effects, together with those on the trade balance emanating from any appreciation in the exchange rate, gives us the impact upon aggregate nominal demand. This should certainly be adverse, all else equal. However, it may be modest, and a distributed lag of several quarters, of up to 2 years, could fit the data. One important qualification relates to the factors that triggered the policy rate rise. If it responds to overseas rates, a larger impact may be expected than if the policy rate is raised in the face of a rise in domestic inflation, actual or expected. When an policy rate rise matches a rise in inflation, expected real interest rates will be unaffected – and in this case there is little reason for expecting firms and households to vary their spending plans. To squeeze private sector demand, policy rates have to go up by *more* than the rise in anticipated inflation.

Stage 3 is the impact on prices and wage rates. If money wage rates are given, and the prices of goods and services are freely flexible, there will be some reduction in prices as demand turns down. The factors determining the magnitude of this are examined below. Money wage rates are also liable to change, but probably after lags reflecting pay revision patterns (the frequency of which will depend positively on inflation). Money wage changes, when they occur, will tend to match changes in the prices of goods and services, current and anticipated, after allowance for changes in productivity. But absolute money wage reductions are exceptionally rare, even in a low-inflation environment (Nickell and Quintini 2002; Crawford 2001). The pace of money wage increases is reduced when the supply of labour, in aggregate, outstrips labour demand.

A rise in policy rates that translates into changes in real interest rates is liable to raise labour supply for intertemporal substitution reasons. Higher real interest rates offer a stronger inducement to postpone the pleasure from consumption; equally, they may persuade economic actors to advance pain. However, the size of this effect is likely to be small, partly because intertemporal substitution effects are modest, and partly because there are sizeable costs of, and practical obstacles to, variations in hours of work. The demand for labour should react much more than its supply. If firms face a weakened demand for their products in domestic or overseas markets, their labour requirements will drop. There is also a direct interest rate channel on labour demand, in the case of industries where labour is engaged before the product is completed and sold. Here a higher policy rate should weaken the demand for labour straightaway, because it lowers the discounted present value of the proceeds of output on sale. This effect is explored below. With labour demand down, partly in the near future and partly later on, and the supply of labour if anything possibly increased, unemployment should tend to go up. As it rises, unemployment should exert a dampening effect on pay settlements, and the rate of price inflation should edge downwards in response. A schematic representation of these four stages is shown in Figure 2.9. Stage 0 depicts the triggers for official interest rate changes.

In Figure 2.9, links 1 and 2 depict the operation of a Taylor Rule on the authorities' behaviour. Both should be positive. Links 3 and 4 arise because market participants may expect changes in the official rate, r_0 soon the central bank may take implicit market expectations into account (link 5). Link 6 is a reverse causation channel, from the policy to the money market rate. Link 7 is the influence from foreign interest rates. Evidence on links 3 and 6 is explored on daily data by Haldane and Read (1999), Joyce and Read (1999) and, following them, by Gravelle, Moessner and Sinclair included in this volume, among others. A central bank with highly transparent policy should display money market rates (and other asset prices) reacting to economic data announcements that could herald imminent central bank interest rate changes – and much less, if at all, to those subsequent policy rate changes. Some of the evidence of recent UK and Canadian experience is consistent with this view. At lower frequencies, links 5 and 6 are impossible to tell apart: they are simultaneous.

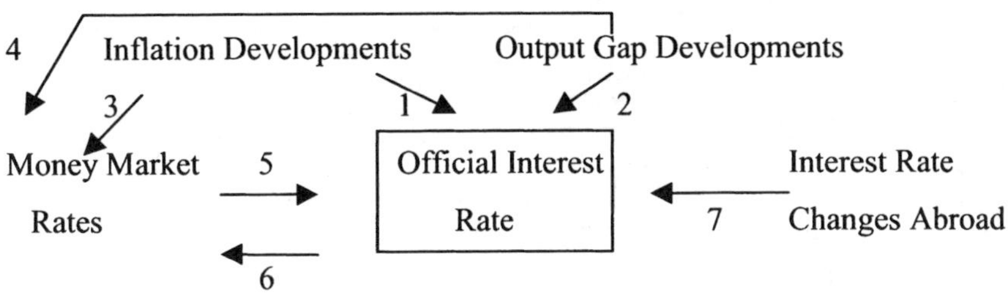

Figure 2.9 Stage 0: the triggers for official interest rate changes.

Some new multi-country evidence of the strength of links 1, 2 and 7 is reported here. Influence 1 is well attested. Current quarterly inflation changes invariably exert a positive effect on policy rate changes for all countries. However, the size of the coefficient varies widely. It is often significant, but usually quite modest in size – well below Taylor's original hypothesis of 1.5. Link 2, by contrast, is often much larger. Almost nowhere is it negative. Official interest rates are highly procyclical. Abnormally rapid growth in output is taken as a signal to put on the brakes, and abnormally slow growth leads to interest rate cuts. Scrutiny reveals that it is deseasonalised growth-rate abnormalities that tend to exert more effect than deviation in actual growth rates from trend. Turning to influence 7, we proxy foreign interest-rate changes by changes in the US Fed rate. The evidence points to a much stronger effect for some countries than others. In Canada and Mexico, where the US accounts for an overwhelming share of overseas trade, the coefficient is large and highly significant. It is also large and significant for some other countries that have maintained a peg to the US dollar for most of the period studied (Argentina, Hong Kong). For many other countries, influence 7 is rather weaker. Some of these, like Australia, appear to respond to US rates rapidly; in some others, such as Sri Lanka, there is clear evidence of a lag. Some non-American economies (such as Ireland) displayed stronger influence from US rates in the later 1990s than earlier. Stage 1 (Figure 2.10) traces the repercussions of policy rate changes on other interest rates or asset yields. Policy rates exert a direct effect on r_T (link 8), and expectations of future policy rates (link 9). When the new value of r_O is expected to be maintained over the next 3 months, links 8, 9 and 10 will make r_T respond virtually one-for-one with r_O. If the exchange rate floats, and the interest rate change was unexpected, some appreciation should result (link 11). Under an exchange rate peg, the rise in r_O should reduce the risk of a forced devaluation. As the equilibrium exchange rate will be sensitive

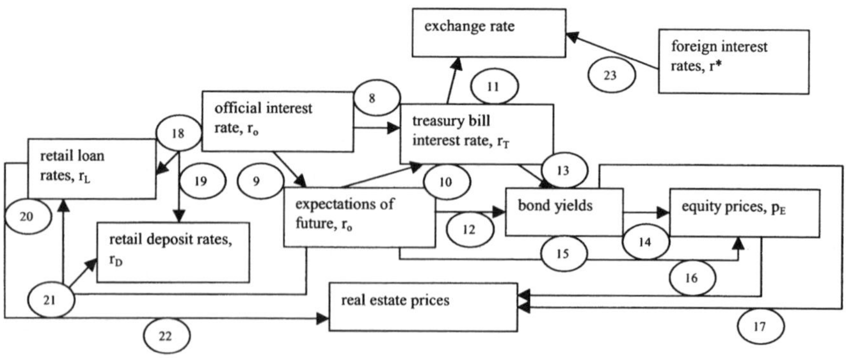

Figure 2.10 Stage 1: the repercussions on other interest rates and asset prices and yields.

to the gap between home and foreign interest rates, link 23 matters here, too.

How bond yields react depends on their term to maturity, and on how expectations of future values of r_O over the bond's life vary with a change in r_O (links 12 and 13). Bond yields and beliefs about future r_O impact on equity prices, P_E, (links 14 and 15). Retail rates on bank deposits r_D and loans, r_L react swiftly to r_O (links 18 and 19). They are strongest, and quickest, if the new value of r_O is expected to last. So links 20 and 21 matter, too. Mortgage interest rates, and responses of bond and equity yields, affect real estate markets (links 22, 16 and 17). Stage 2 (Figure 2.11) looks at how all interest rates affect expenditure. There are direct interest-rate effects on consumer spending, particularly on durables, (link 24, discussed in section 2.5). Real-estate prices are associated with construction (link 25: section 2.6), and consumption (link 28), via direct wealth effects. Consumers can take out loans secured on property (higher house prices enhance their willingness to do this, and lenders' preparedness to lend). Equity prices also affect consumption via wealth effects (link 26). Non-construction investment spending should react to equity prices (link 27) and interest rates (link 29): equity and bond yields are two key elements in firms' external finance costs. Any change in the exchange rate will affect the external trade surplus (link 30): appreciation would lower it, though possibly after a perverse initial response. If the country has large net overseas assets or debts which are denominated in foreign currency,

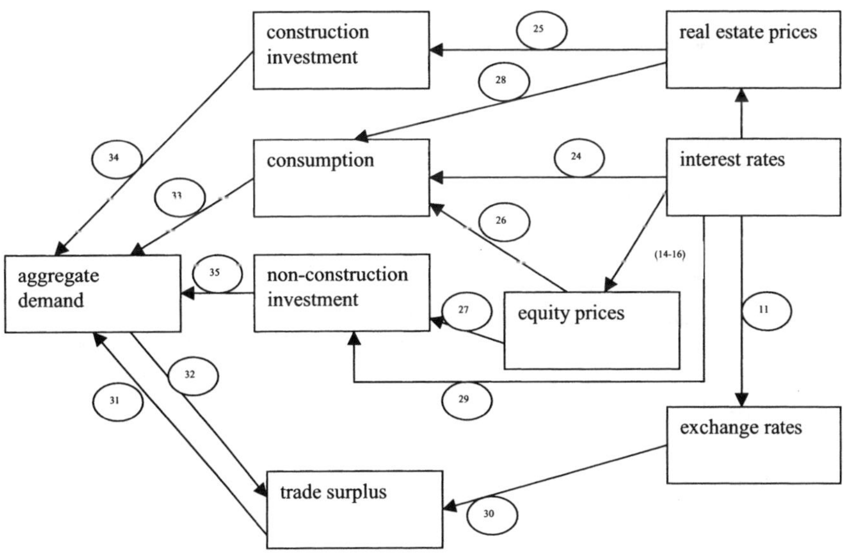

Figure 2.11 Stage 2: the effects of changes in interest rates and asset prices on aggregate demand.

an exchange rate change alters balance sheets and service income flows. The trade surplus is an element in aggregate demand (link 31). The trade surplus depends upon aggregate demand, as lower domestic spending reduces imports (link 32). So the trade surplus–aggregate demand links run both ways. Links 33, 34 and 35 testify to the fact that consumption, and both construction and non-construction investment, are part of aggregate demand.

Stage 3 (Figure 2.12) involves the last phase of the transmission mechanism of monetary policy. This runs from aggregate demand, interest rates and other affected variables to the rate of inflation. A key element here is the repercussions, direct and indirect, that interest rates have on labour markets, and hence on wage rates. Running through the links, we begin with links 36 and 37, which refer to the direct impact of interest rates on firms' demand for labour, and households' labour supply. These are examined in section 3.2. The main effect of interest rates on labour markets comes, though, through aggregate demand, operating upon the demand for labour (link 38). Changes in aggregate demand imply some direct change in the price level, to the extent that it is free to adjust (link 39, in section 3.1). Links 40 and 41 refer to the two-way interaction between the exchange rate and the domestic prices, while link 42 pinpoints the role of foreign prices in affecting domestic prices. This matters for two reasons: first, an import price shock is an example of the kind of shock domestic monetary policy has to contend with; and second, changes in foreign prices may reflect the actions of overseas

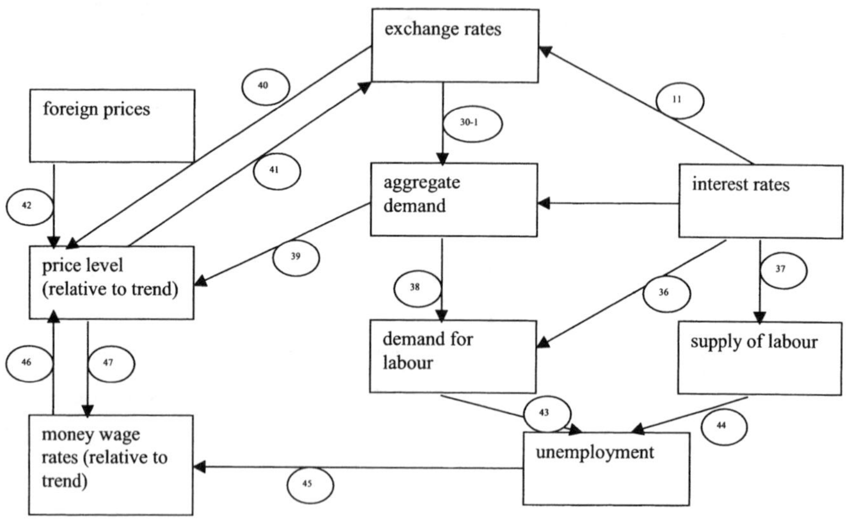

Figure 2.12 Stage 3: the effects of changes in interest rates, aggregate demand and other variables on unemployment, wage rates and prices.

central banks. Links 43 and 44 identify the impact that the demand for and supply of labour have on the level of unemployment, which affects the rate of money wage increases (link 45). Links 46 and 47 refer to the two-way interaction of the price level and the money price of labour.

2.4 Policy rates and retail interest rates

When the central bank alters its policy rate, variable rates on retail financial products should move in sympathy. However, they will not necessarily change at once, nor one-for-one with official rates. The transmission mechanism for monetary policy depends critically upon how firms' and households' spending decisions react to the interest rates they face. The short-term interest rates that confront them are not central bank policy rates, but retail rates on loans and deposits set by commercial banks. Unless competition is strong, a retail bank is unlikely to be an interest rate taker in its deposit and loan markets. However, no commercial bank could exert any appreciable influence on the interest rates on treasury bills or short-term government bonds, nor on policy rates. These rates, usually close, represent a benchmark, a guaranteed marginal revenue that a commercial bank can earn on assets.

Ignoring tax and risk and transaction costs, a profit-maximising bank should equate the marginal revenue from other assets (loans, advances and mortgages) to this benchmark rate. If marginal revenues were higher on loans than on treasury bills, for example, the bank could raise its total revenue at no cost by switching from the latter to the former, and would continue to do so until the marginal revenue gap had closed. The benchmark is also a target for the marginal cost of deposits for the profit-maximising bank. If marginal deposit costs were above (below) the benchmark marginal revenue on treasury bills, a reduction (rise) in deposits could add to profits.

Loan rates exceed the benchmark rate for several reasons. There are initial costs of processing loan applications and monitoring borrower creditworthiness, and continuing costs of managing loans that have been granted and monitoring interest receipts and repayments of principal. The possibility of default has to be allowed for. On the deposit side, the marginal cost of deposits includes costs of managing deposits, issuing cheque books, cards and statements, effecting transfers and clearing cheques when these activities are, as is usual, not separately charged for. These various costs help to explain why deposit rates typically fall some way short of official central bank interest rates, and why loan rates typically exceed them.

On top of these costs, imperfect competition may be present. If there were just one commercial bank, or a set of banks that colluded as one, loan rates would be surcharged (under profit maximisation) by a premium inversely proportional to the interest elasticity of loan demand (**e**, defined positive) that the bank or group of banks believed it faced. Deposit rates would be reduced by a discount inversely proportional to the interest elasticity of deposit supply (**E**). With **n** similar banks taking independent quantity decisions on deposits and loans, believing that their rivals' quantities are given, the mark-ups on loan rates become 1/**en**, and the discounts on deposit rates fall to 1/**En**. If each bank set its own interest rates on loans and deposits, treating rivals' rates as given, the perfectly competitive outcome should follow, but collusion would enlarge spreads between the two. Market segmentation, all too likely if customers face appreciable costs of switching from one financial intermediary to another, is another force that could increase spreads. At least tacit collusion may be fostered, particularly on the loan side, if a unilateral decision on the part of one bank to cut rates is thought to attract poor-quality extra business. Some new loan applicants would have been denied credit by other banks with superior, private knowledge of the greater risks they pose.

As it is costly to change prices, banks may delay before responding to policy rate changes. If they had any reason to expect a reversal in the policy rate change in coming weeks, they might leave their own rates unchanged. There may also be a narrow range within which official rates can move while provoking no retail interest rate response. Also, in an oligopoly where each bank is always looking over its shoulder to what its rivals are doing, there may be some reluctance, at least for smaller institutions, to initiate an interest rate change – particularly upwards on deposits, or downwards on loans – for fear of triggering a price war. Imperfect competition has recently been introduced into many analyses of international trade and exchange rates, growth, macroeconomics and labour economics; retail banks are not immune from this shift away from the perfect competition paradigm.

Imperfect competition, and other sources of friction, could, therefore, impede the transmission of central bank interest rate changes to the wider economy. So it is valuable to explore the statistical link between official interest rates on the one side, and interest rates on loans and deposits on the other. Here we are following the recent work on British retail interest rates by Heffernan (1997). A wide sample of countries was chosen – all the countries for which International Financial Statistics present data. This was the source employed; occasionally there are discrepancies in definition, as for example in the United States, where deposit rates are on relatively well-remunerated certificates of deposit, as opposed to standard rates on (some definition of) interest-bearing bank deposits reported by most other countries. For deposit rates there are 133, and 10 fewer in the case of loan rates. Our period runs from the start of 1980 to the end of 2000, or the longest sub-period for which figures are available.

Table 2.1 presents results from the long-run relationship linking deposit rates to a variable we call G-int. This is an unweighted average of the largest available subset of policy, treasury bill and money market rates.

Table 2.1 Estimate of the long-run passthrough from the policy interest rate (G-int) to deposit rates. Quarterly data, 1980Q1–2000Q4

	Constant	*Trend (98.1)*	*Policy rate (G-int)*	*No.obs*
USA	–0.048 (–0.316)	–0.001 (–0.304)	1.096 (33.118)***	82
GBR	–1.803 (–3.447)***	–0.036 (–2.488)**	0.915 (12.574)***	76
AUT	1.205 (1.145)	–0.023 (–1.701)*	0.216 (1.69)*	72
BEL	0.651 (0.905)	0.026 (1.033)	0.743 (3.628)***	84
DNK	1.437 (1.454)	–0.088 (–2.725)***	0.283 (1.197)	78
FRA	0.986 (1.271)	–0.012 (–0.458)	0.409 (2.539)**	84
DEU	–0.257 (–1.783)*	–0.005 (–2.335)**	0.953 (39.45)***	84
ITA	–3.975 (–2.053)**	0.091 (1.98)*	1.148 (4.3)***	73
LUX	2.78 (6.005)***	–0.061 (–2.106)**	0.178 (1.366)	35
NLD	1.581 (0.777)	0.013 (0.483)	0.421 (1.01)	70
NOR	–2.744 (–2.756)***	0.079 (3.718)***	1.288 (8.659)***	80
SWE	0.929 (1.832)*	–0.087 (–5.223)***	0.434 (3.564)***	83
CHE	–0.277 (–1.417)	–0.016 (–3.362)***	0.991 (16.056)***	78
CAN	–0.436 (–1.146)	0.029 (3.551)***	1.124 (16.75)***	84
JPN	–0.048 (–0.658)	0.014 (1.905)*	0.742 (10.465)***	83
FIN	–0.337 (–1.494)	–0.048 (–7.268)***	0.579 (12.735)***	69
GRC	–18.907 (–0.71)	–0.059 (–0.155)	1.724 (1.233)	84
ISL	–7.372 (–1.345)	–0.55 (–2.502)**	0.025 (0.062)	63
IRL	–0.173 (–0.057)	–0.145 (–1.69)*	0.001 (0.002)	84
MLT	7.085 (0.769)	0.011 (0.221)	–0.395 (–0.274)	82
PRT	3.892 (1.743)*	–0.311 (–2.253)**	–0.039 (–0.078)	81
ESP	0.869 (0.942)	–0.028 (–1.29)	0.598 (4.993)***	73
TUR	–9.067 (–0.328)	–0.043 (–0.188)	1.217 (3.102)***	83
AUS	0.022 (0.033)	–0.004 (–0.409)	0.87 (10.365)***	84
NZL	2.114 (3.773)***	–0.024 (–1.834)*	0.611 (8.336)***	71
ZAF	0.459 (0.336)	0.002 (0.126)	0.935 (11.094)***	83
ARG	545.385 (0.961)	–9.676 (–1.063)	0 (1.217)	84
BOL	4.546 (2.847)***	0.016 (0.275)	0.674 (7.102)***	41
BRA	440.443 (1.307)	–1.222 (–0.198)	0.571 (7.138)***	70
CCL	1.897 (0.441)	–0.036 (–0.875)	0.804 (5.664)***	58
CRI	–10.551 (–2.069)**	–0.104 (–4.081)***	0.754 (5.142)***	74
DOM	–2.572 (–0.574)	–0.182 (–0.86)	1.213 (3.893)***	17
ECU	76.163 (1.645)	0.701 (1.311)	–0.639 (–0.753)	66
SLV	8.183 (2.265)*	–0.079 (–0.574)	0.272 (0.898)	13
GTM	3.147 (5.236)***	0.38 (18.205)***	0.331 (4.693)***	14
HTI	1.233 (0.946)	0.166 (2.034)*	0.702 (8.315)***	13
MEX	–5.252 (–2.335)**	–0.24 (–4.508)***	0.781 (8.666)***	75
NIC	9.05 (6.157)***	0.107 (2.62)**	0.365 (3.34)***	20
PRY	1.282 (0.231)	–0.041 (–0.576)	0.898 (3.016)***	41
PER	–4.442 (–1.831)*	–0.02 (–0.034)	1.004 (70.38)***	49
URY	12.09 (3.071)***	–0.838 (–2.802)***	0.125 (1.383)	76
VEN	6.673 (1.483)	0.055 (0.609)	0.617 (6.217)***	65
BHS	2.523 (6.647)***	–0.009 (–1.353)	0.495 (5.852)***	82
ABW	18.234 (3.31)***	–0.072 (–4.433)***	–1.546 (–2.483)**	54
BPB	1.698 (5.174)***	–0.004 (–0.84)	0.387 (9.976)***	78
DMA	–46.475 (–1.021)	–0.018 (–1.091)	7.807 (1.098)	74
GUY	–0.232 (–0.097)	–0.03 (–1.072)	0.805 (5.518)***	77

continued

Table 2.1 Continued

	Constant	*Trend (98.1)*	*Policy rate (G-int)*	*No.obs*
BLZ	5.22 (2.142)**	–0.028 (–0.549)	0.338 (1.026)	82
JAM	–5.499 (–1.077)	–0.149 (–2.857)***	0.898 (4.502)***	83
ANT	2.856 (4.558)***	–0.028 (–5.969)***	0.128 (1.212)	59
LCA	84.028 (5.043)***	0.087 (3.311)***	–10.858 (–4.64)***	74
TTO	6.061 (3.817)***	0.011 (0.566)	0.114 (0.948)	70
BHR	0.326 (0.619)	0.024 (2.229)**	0.88 (7.844)***	53
ISR	4.009 (2.639)**	0.074 (0.673)	0.719 (12.901)***	62
JOR	–5.192 (0)	0.304 (4.846)***	1.879 (0)	20
KWT	–3.415 (–1.398)	–0.038 (–5.531)***	1.318 (3.847)***	76
LBN	–0.059 (–0.024)	–0.063 (–2.754)***	0.724 (5.435)***	73
EGY	6.561 (11.43)***	–0.021 (–3.959)***	0.274 (6.157)***	83
BGD	–0.744 (–0.737)	0.008 (0.727)	1.258 (8.683)***	83
MMR	1.723 (3.482)***	0.029 (6.208)***	0.72 (20.739)***	38
LKA	–1.59 (–0.65)	–0.103 (–5.667)***	0.91 (6.03)***	82
HKG	0.354 (0.037)	–0.075 (–1.057)	0.752 (0.449)	26
IDN	11.779 (2.686)***	0.089 (1.293)	0.499 (2.195)**	79
KOR	4.636 (3.919)***	0.024 (0.925)	0.709 (3.901)***	83
LAO	42.319 (3.048)***	0.227 (1.548)	–0.958 (–2.119)**	30
MYS	0.049 (0.034)	–0.042 (–1.988)*	0.964 (3.83)***	83
PHL	3.911 (1.225)	–0.084 (–2.789)***	0.516 (1.933)*	79
SGP	–0.794 (–1.238)	0.017 (1.12)	1.11 (6.86)***	83
THA	3.065 (2.999)***	–0.032 (–2.444)**	0.621 (6.51)***	84
DZA	8.86 (2.766)***	0.1 (2.284)**	0.187 (0.694)	61
AGO	–22.743 (–0.981)	–7.923 (–4.437)***	1.043 (3.939)***	22
BWA	–3.66 (–3.615)***	–0.066 (–7.778)***	1.031 (12.996)***	81
CMR	1.422 (2.478)**	–0.032 (–12.348)***	0.496 (7.265)***	84
CAF	1.436 (1.934)*	–0.033 (–9.85)***	0.487 (5.387)***	84
TCD	–1.018 (–0.858)	0.007 (1.241)	0.776 (5.589)***	84
COG	2.197 (1.182)	–0.039 (–3.89)***	0.385 (1.617)	84
BEN	–1.622 (–2.244)**	0.029 (2.137)**	0.917 (7.614)***	68
GNQ	1.416 (1.289)	–0.035 (–1.931)*	0.482 (3.391)***	62
ETH	3.409 (5.033)***	0.007 (0.39)	0.701 (9.068)***	57
GAB	2.928 (1.494)	–0.041 (–5.033)***	0.31 (1.251)	84
GMB	6.266 (4.418)***	0.036 (3.119)***	0.506 (5.582)***	73
GHA	5.199 (0.852)	0.045 (0.631)	0.673 (4.661)***	76
GNB	4.968 (1.503)	–0.691 (–3.67)***	0.531 (2.028)**	50
GIN	0.699 (0.066)	–0.328 (–3.182)***	0.647 (1.027)	37
CIV	–1.712 (–2.176)**	0.03 (2.079)**	0.931 (7.141)***	68
KEN	–5.756 (–4.356)***	–0.103 (–9.83)***	0.92 (13.508)***	67
LSO	2.384 (0.52)	–0.058 (–1.538)	0.472 (1.647)	71
MDG	7.414 (1.285)	–0.33 (–2.763)**	0.405 (1.37)	15
MWI	2.223 (0.46)	–0.038 (–0.584)	0.675 (4.569)***	81
MLI	–1.74 (–2.17)**	0.03 (2.068)**	0.936 (7.035)***	68
MUS	0.815 (0.55)	0.015 (1.065)	0.956 (6.502)***	79
MAR	–0.067 (–0.053)	0.006 (0.428)	1.004 (8.732)***	47
MOZ	14.508 (2.933)***	–1.158 (–2.178)**	0.106 (0.574)	25
NER	–2.003 (–2.099)**	0.034 (1.916)*	0.976 (6.13)***	68
NGA	–2.783 (–0.553)	–0.049 (–1.116)	1.029 (3.553)***	75
ZWE	3.135 (0.992)	–0.033 (–0.606)	0.696 (7.966)***	81

Table 2.1 Continued

	Constant	*Trend (98.1)*	*Policy rate (G-int)*	*No.obs*
RWA	5.135 (0.626)	0.027 (0.463)	0.255 (0.406)	75
STP	12.799 (2.638)**	0.066 (0.475)	0.575 (3.846)***	44
SYC	–6.887 (–0.167)	–0.542 (–0.358)	–0.809 (–0.262)	77
SEN	–1.697 (–2.127)**	0.03 (2.037)**	0.929 (7.026)***	68
SLE	–4.447 (–0.677)	–0.206 (–2.422)**	0.651 (2.595)**	83
NAM	–3.568 (–3.66)***	0.011 (1.146)	0.972 (15.3)***	35
SWZ	–0.825 (–1.802)*	0.016 (4.095)***	0.951 (25.507)***	84
TZA	–3.732 (–0.637)	–0.135 (–1.376)	1.006 (2.765)***	64
TGO	–1.907 (–2.16)**	0.032 (2.013)**	0.96 (6.574)***	68
UGA	–0.607 (–0.139)	–0.028 (–0.375)	0.71 (5.969)***	78
BFA	–1.589 (–2.369)**	0.029 (2.285)**	0.914 (8.154)***	68
ZMB	5.421 (0.442)	0.033 (0.198)	0.61 (2.246)**	76
SLB	10.265 (0.471)	–0.344 (–0.81)	–1.246 (–0.367)	77
FJI	1.025 (1.8)*	–0.055 (–4.333)***	0.253 (2.745)***	83
VUT	3.237 (1.359)	–0.1 (–5.846)***	–0.07 (–0.192)	58
PNG	–0.326 (–0.353)	–0.038 (–3.545)***	0.752 (10.07)***	68
ARM	19.047 (3.368)***	–0.296 (–1.031)	0.166 (1.125)	22
BLR	17.177 (5.592)***	–1.013 (–2.674)**	0.297 (8.828)***	29
ALB	4.044 (1.144)	–0.121 (–1.041)	0.591 (3.745)***	31
GEO	7.791 (1.989)*	–0.546 (–3.11)**	0.248 (2.261)**	17
KGZ	21.745 (4.46)***	–0.535 (–2.567)**	0.289 (2.402)**	17
BGR	3.272 (2.96)***	–0.509 (–5.599)***	0.58 (17.858)***	37
MDA	–0.405 (–0.017)	0.59 (1.242)	0.851 (1.033)	19
RUS	6.416 (1.179)	–1.134 (–1.6)	0.371 (5.497)***	23
CHN	0.291 (0.255)	–0.059 (–2.14)**	0.858 (4.221)***	38
UKR	–13.541 (–1.441)	–0.221 (–0.255)	0.921 (6.897)***	29
CZE	1.406 (4.346)***	–0.077 (–8.238)***	0.525 (14.642)***	29
SVK	–161.137 (–0.317)	4.09 (0.385)	19.662 (0.345)	29
EST	1.889 (0.618)	–0.189 (–1.3)	0.528 (1.33)	24
LVA	4.914 (1.421)	–0.295 (–0.618)	0.314 (0.797)	27
HUN	–8.71 (–2.195)**	0.022 (0.435)	1.338 (7.121)***	61
LTU	1.828 (2.687)**	–0.125 (–1.389)	0.508 (8.458)***	25
MNG	20.011 (5.362)***	–0.564 (–1.222)	0.137 (9.469)***	27
HRV	1.903 (0.189)	–3.522 (–1.154)	0.36 (5.117)***	33
SVN	3.698 (2.608)**	–0.194 (–2.003)*	0.769 (7.298)***	31
MKD	1.519 (6.32)***	0.048 (2.557)**	1.109 (57.715)***	25
POL	6.151 (1.371)	–0.558 (–3.152)***	0.595 (2.82)***	42

Source: IFS.

Notes
Estimated using Pesaran Shin and Smith (1996) methodology; t-stats in brackets.
*, **, *** represent significance at 10, 5 and 1 per cent respectively.

The long-run relationship is recovered from the equilibrium-correction terms in regressions of monthly changes in deposit rates (results are given in Table 2.3 in the Appendix at the end of this chapter). We applied Pesaran–Shin–Smith estimation procedures to obtain these results. What do they tell us?

The long-run effect of G-int on deposit rates is positive for all but 10 countries, and significantly so for a large majority (97 out of 133). This is evident from the data in the third column of Table 2.1. The coefficient is significantly less than unity, however, for just over half the sample, including France, Germany, Japan, Spain, Argentina, Brazil, Mexico, the Czech Republic, Russia, Indonesia and Thailand. Among Commonwealth countries, Gambia, Ghana, Mozambique, New Zealand, Uganda and all the Caribbean islands except for Jamaica are in the minority where deposit rates move *significantly* less than one-to-one with G-int. Where these coefficients are significantly less than unitary, testifying perhaps to some form of imperfect competition among retail banks, the monetary policy transmission mechanism channel running from deposit interest rates to saving by households will be undeniably weakened. We included a time trend, to pick up possible long-run changes in the intensity of competition. It is noticeable that there are just six advanced countries (Belgium, Canada, Italy, Japan, the Netherlands and Norway) which do not display a significantly negative time trend in the constant term (which is defined at 1998). For those countries with G-int coefficients close to unity (Britain, Germany, Switzerland) and also for some others, this suggests a rise in banks' gross margins on deposits, and hints at a possible decline in the intensity of competition between them.

The short-term results on deposit interest rates are presented in Table 2.3 in the Appendix. They reveal that most countries have a well-determined coefficient on the 'long-run adjustment' variable (column 2). Adjustment is really rapid in Canada and Trinidad and Tobago (and also in several other countries, Argentina, Israel and Peru among them, that have witnessed big inflation swings). In these cases, more than half the discrepancy in deposit rates from their long-run equilibrium relation to G-int is eliminated in a single month. Macedonia's large negative coefficient suggests instability, but it is unique in this respect, and not reliable given the short sample period. Elsewhere, the coefficient on long-run adjustment is quite modest, suggesting half-lives of 2 or 3 months or even longer. In France, Germany, Italy and Japan, for example, discrepancies are very long lived indeed.

As for loan rates, G-int has a significantly positive coefficient for all but 34 of the 123 countries for which data were available (and most of these 34 are at least correctly signed). Table 2.2 refers. The G-int coefficient only exceeds unity significantly in seven countries, Belgium, the Netherlands and Nigeria among them. Loan rates were predictably above G-int at almost all times and in almost all countries. Bulgaria and Uruguay are alone in displaying a significantly positive time trend for the constant (again defined for 1998). Elsewhere it is often significantly negative. This suggests that competition in lending between retail financial institutions could have been increasing.

The rather modest coefficients on G-int in some countries, such as Bar-

Table 2.2 Estimate of the long-run passthrough from policy interest rate (G-int) to lending rates. Quarterly data, 1980Q1–2000Q4

	Constant	*Trend (98.1)*	*Policy rate (G-int)*	*No.obs*
USA	2.37 (4.798)***	0.022 (1.631)	1.19 (11.81)***	84
GBR	0.434 (2.411)**	–0.003 (–0.911)	0.98 (45.261)***	84
BEL	3.292 (14.96)***	0.05 (7.783)***	1.222 (26.857)***	63
DNK	6.236 (12.809)***	–0.083 (–5.295)***	0.429 (3.735)***	78
FRA	5.046 (23.452)***	–0.037 (–5.042)***	0.413 (8.337)***	84
DEU	4.12 (1.856)*	0.027 (1.988)*	1.418 (2.871)***	84
ITA	–2.268 (–0.561)	0.118 (1.415)	1.696 (2.993)***	71
LUX	4.368 (9.668)***	–0.063 (–2.083)**	0.264 (1.893)*	34
NLD	2.779 (13.756)***	–0.003 (–1.043)	1.128 (30.864)***	74
NOR	0.784 (0.903)	–0.027 (–1.667)*	1.066 (8.503)***	80
SWE	3.394 (12.802)***	–0.032 (–3.515)***	0.923 (15.052)***	83
CHE	3.358 (22.4)***	–0.005 (–1.581)	0.554 (11.753)***	78
CAN	1.125 (3.407)***	0.015 (2.406)**	1.078 (18.248)***	84
JPN	1.858 (14.956)***	0 (0.037)	0.856 (6.797)***	83
FIN	–0.236 (–0.156)	0.062 (2.041)**	1.349 (5.344)***	81
GRC	–3.561 (–0.236)	0.053 (0.202)	1.583 (1.374)	84
ISL	7.355 (4.537)***	–0.047 (–0.298)	0.668 (2.551)**	74
IRL	1.238 (3.001)***	–0.027 (–2.137)**	0.804 (9.977)***	84
MLT	9.45 (10.463)***	–0.012 (–1.719)*	–0.325 (–1.859)*	82
PRT	12.225 (1.144)	–0.507 (–0.826)	–0.829 (–0.364)	81
ESP	2.51 (1.999)**	–0.033 (–1.172)	0.775 (4.107)***	73
AUS	4.54 (4.021)***	0.008 (0.322)	0.847 (4.939)***	84
NZL	4.884 (9.615)***	0.01 (0.627)	0.805 (12.231)***	54
ZAF	4.134 (3.063)***	0.018 (2.195)**	1.006 (10.296)***	83
ARG	–14.666 (–1.017)	–0.025 (–0.21)	3.521 (1.835)*	29
BOL	17.523 (1.274)	0.297 (0.931)	1.357 (2.083)**	41
COL	18.87 (7.568)***	–0.034 (–0.957)	0.608 (6.985)***	58
CRI	37.261 (1.396)	0.146 (1.042)	–0.236 (–0.302)	74
DOM	3.463 (1.515)	–0.025 (–0.745)	1.357 (9.046)***	17
ECU	11.409 (0.594)	0.175 (0.724)	0.855 (2.231)**	78
SLV	32.147 (3.117)**	–0.393 (–2.319)*	–1.448 (–1.585)	13
GTM	15.497 (13.501)***	0.23 (2.889)**	0.285 (1.806)	14
HTI	21.024 (15.917)***	0.202 (3.064)**	0.117 (1.559)	13
MEX	3.042 (8.45)***	–0.119 (–10.891)***	1.016 (88.542)***	30
NIC	22.087 (9.459)***	–0.049 (–0.639)	–0.265 (–1.223)	20
PRY	3.712 (0.525)	0.08 (1.101)	1.444 (3.774)***	41
PER	–23.081 (–0.431)	10.183 (0.727)	2.577 (3.197)***	58
URY	47.61 (5.902)***	0.008 (0.025)	0.404 (3.449)***	76
VEN	11.936 (3.333)***	0.239 (2.973)***	0.781 (14.588)***	65
BHS	5.392 (17.733)***	–0.059 (–11.679)***	0.221 (3.687)***	84
ABW	16.396 (19.502)***	–0.004 (–0.802)	–0.634 (–6.75)***	54
BRB	6.464 (10.263)***	0.005 (0.527)	0.462 (5.399)***	77
DMA	–9.717 (–0.315)	0.01 (0.927)	3.14 (0.652)	70
GUY	8.458 (2.529)**	0.077 (1.87)*	0.813 (7.176)***	77
BLZ	252.372 (0.051)	–3.473 (–0.048)	–31.964 (–0.048)	60
JAM	0.407 (0.095)	–0.078 (–1.526)	1.215 (7.453)***	83
ANT	11.792 (4.148)***	0.027 (0.685)	0.131 (0.215)	73

continued

Table 2.2 Continued

	Constant	*Trend (98.1)*	*Policy rate (G-int)*	*No.obs*
LCA	80.034 (1.861)*	0.022 (0.622)	–9.926 (–1.623)	74
TTO	6.918 (2.288)**	–0.017 (–0.469)	0.786 (3.172)***	68
BHR	14.008 (14.307)***	0.078 (4.347)***	–0.328 (–1.884)*	58
CYP	8.646 (8.218)***	–0.009 (–2.599)**	–0.017 (–0.112)	68
ISR	35.137 (0.758)	3.266 (0.729)	2.068 (1.951)*	69
KWT	–0.599 (–0.097)	–0.01 (–0.967)	1.281 (1.437)	78
LBN	–20.255 (–1.612)	–0.221 (–2.375)**	2.216 (3.456)***	70
EGY	4.555 (1.004)	0.009 (0.197)	0.972 (2.158)**	79
BGD	9.995 (7.395)***	0.061 (3.304)***	0.711 (4.069)***	83
MMR	–69.351 (–0.557)	–0.888 (–0.452)	5.49 (0.698)	31
LKA	–7.054 (–1.958)*	–0.141 (–5.769)***	0.987 (4.945)***	82
HKG	2.463 (3.688)***	–0.001 (–0.157)	1.086 (9.477)***	33
IND	7.122 (8.161)***	–0.052 (–10.955)***	0.695 (7.403)***	83
IDN	12.687 (11.335)***	–0.093 (–3.265)***	0.455 (9.537)***	55
KOR	1.467 (0.299)	0.046 (0.594)	1.253 (1.344)	79
LAO	63.902 (5.859)***	0.599 (6.304)***	–1.116 (–3.162)***	30
MYS	2.555 (1.228)	–0.034 (–1.874)*	0.943 (2.502)**	83
NPL	4.144 (0.406)	–0.051 (–1.187)	1.001 (0.813)	64
PHL	3.7 (1.674)*	–0.077 (–3.455)***	0.927 (5.34)***	83
SGP	2.571 (3.988)***	0.03 (1.725)*	1.129 (5.899)***	83
THA	5.448 (11.125)***	–0.018 (–2.295)**	0.721 (11.902)***	84
AGO	–40.794 (–3.049)***	–8.474 (–5.89)***	1.725 (9.174)***	22
BWA	–6.237 (–1.118)	–0.097 (–1.701)*	1.511 (3.674)***	81
BDI	8.786 (4.424)***	0.016 (1.238)	0.599 (2.976)***	69
CMR	25.217 (14.581)***	0.132 (7.853)***	–0.431 (–2.092)**	84
CAF	23.69 (6.776)***	0.165 (8.351)***	–0.228 (–0.588)	84
TCD	23.135 (4.622)***	0.188 (7.35)***	–0.113 (–0.205)	84
COG	23.307 (6.322)***	0.179 (8.854)***	–0.151 (–0.363)	84
ZAR	37.702 (1.068)	–2.813 (–0.348)	0.927 (2.019)*	23
GNQ	23.316 (15.099)***	0.156 (10.191)***	–0.206 (–1.169)	62
ETH	7.459 (23.105)***	0.111 (11.375)***	0.788 (12.2)***	57
GAB	24.775 (5.566)***	0.156 (5.673)***	–0.347 (–0.682)	84
GMB	11.172 (5.152)***	0.079 (4.206)***	1.082 (6.736)***	73
GNB	108.017 (1.526)	1.444 (1.028)	–1.673 (–1.028)	43
GIN	–15.052 (–4.899)***	–0.281 (–6.61)***	1.936 (13.238)***	39
KEN	8.731 (2.319)**	0.059 (1.279)	0.78 (5.135)***	83
LSO	6.865 (2.262)**	0.009 (0.492)	0.747 (3.531)***	81
MDG	22.448 (1.362)	0.227 (0.505)	0.722 (0.85)	15
MWI	8.252 (4.643)***	0.009 (0.413)	0.97 (13.92)***	81
MUS	14.904 (15.764)***	0.131 (12.627)***	0.562 (5.372)***	79
MAR	10.154 (2.194)**	0.081 (4.234)***	0.354 (0.561)	50
MOZ	16.62 (2.874)*	–0.8 (–1.211)	0.849 (4.011)**	10
NGA	–1.089 (–0.352)	0.009 (0.239)	1.424 (8.882)***	75
ZWE	–7.958 (–1.181)	–0.245 (–2.21)**	1.455 (6.365)***	82
STP	22.237 (11.846)***	0.638 (11.58)***	0.705 (12.09)***	44
SYC	12.407 (7.772)***	–0.229 (–2.158)**	–0.322 (–1.045)	45
SLE	8.133 (1.883)*	–0.049 (–0.737)	0.857 (6.359)***	83
NAM	5.206 (7.015)***	–0.01 (–1.174)	0.893 (18.023)***	35
SWZ	6.101 (9.726)***	0.046 (8.765)***	0.983 (19.488)***	84

Table 2.2 Continued

	Constant	*Trend (98.1)*	*Policy rate (G-int)*	*No.obs*
TZA	11.413 (1.742)*	–0.055 (–0.492)	0.852 (2.644)**	71
UGA	13.197 (8.162)***	0.051 (1.794)*	0.608 (15.143)***	68
ZMB	8.378 (3.031)***	0.071 (1.739)*	0.988 (18.206)***	79
FJI	7.208 (3.655)***	0.012 (0.236)	1.065 (1.544)	73
VUT	–0.123 (–0.018)	–0.173 (–4.709)***	1.555 (1.577)	58
PNG	9.151 (2.451)**	0.009 (0.198)	0.374 (1.537)	68
ARM	50.351 (12.377)***	–2.054 (–13.87)***	–0.032 (–0.281)	22
AZE	–1.539 (–0.155)	–0.45 (–0.807)	1.053 (47.803)**	8
BLR	29.825 (5.969)***	–0.255 (–0.372)	0.572 (11.563)***	30
ALB	14.269 (4.827)***	0.17 (1.398)	0.485 (4.194)***	24
GEO	50.162 (22.538)***	–1.752 (–12.489)***	–0.104 (–1.543)	17
KGZ	51.713 (6.194)***	0.181 (0.51)	0.213 (1.099)	17
BGR	8.88 (13.909)***	0.002 (0.029)	0.97 (43.332)***	37
MDA	21.937 (4.727)***	0.261 (1.536)	0.365 (2.533)**	19
RUS	–25.38 (–1.172)	1.285 (0.665)	1.743 (8.298)***	23
CHN	2.956 (5.866)***	0.001 (0.138)	0.803 (11.072)***	38
UKR	18.68 (2.623)**	–0.672 (–1.016)	0.951 (9.465)***	29
CZE	5.77 (20.126)***	–0.174 (–22.177)***	0.588 (21.05)***	29
SVK	46.854 (0.939)	–0.44 (–0.369)	–3.296 (–0.573)	29
EST	0.221 (0.016)	–0.146 (–0.225)	1.393 (1.056)	24
LVA	11.117 (3.102)***	–0.212 (–0.41)	0.773 (2.468)**	27
HUN	–0.93 (–0.302)	–0.264 (–5.039)***	1.048 (6.741)***	46
LTU	7.024 (17.994)***	0.116 (3.519)***	0.668 (23.026)***	25
MNG	32.308 (7.51)***	–0.305 (–0.633)	0.508 (15.772)***	27
HRV	4.858 (6.099)***	–0.324 (–1.165)	1.172 (143.69)***	33
SVN	8.581 (7.339)***	–0.294 (–2.76)**	0.908 (11.189)***	31
MKD	–6.569 (–5.766)***	0.175 (1.554)	2.986 (35.235)***	25
POL	–100.569 (–1.507)	–1.569 (–1.617)	5.27 (1.968)*	69

Source: IFS.

Notes
Estimated using Pesaran Shin and Smith (1996) methodology; t-stats in brackets.
*, **, *** represent significance at 10, 5 and 1 percent respectively.

bados, Denmark, France, India, Indonesia, Luxembourg and Switzerland, hints at the possibility of deliberate long-run loan-rate smoothing by banks. A possible explanation for this is fear that higher interest rates on loans have adverse incentive and selection effects, as powerfully argued by Stiglitz and Weiss (1981, 1983). In these economies, the monetary policy transmission channel that runs from loan rates to private sector investment and consumption spending will be correspondingly weaker than where G-int coefficients are higher.

The short-run loan results, in Appendix Table 2.4, testify, in the main, to well-identified and significant coefficients, of the expected negative sign, on the long-run adjustment variable (the second column). Only a handful of these coefficients is either perverse or unstable. Adjustment is notably rapid in Ireland, and rather fast in Canada, France, Sweden and the UK. It is much slower in China, Germany, India and the United States, and very sluggish in, among others, Egypt and Greece.

2.5 Interest rates and consumption

The main purpose of this section is to study how interest rates affect consumption. The section starts with an analysis of the reasons for expecting such effects to be present. It concludes by scrutinising evidence, both from econometric investigations conducted specially for this report and from the findings of other studies, on how large and how dependable these effects are in practice. This is a controversial and unsettled subject. The debate between Bernanke and Gertler (1995) and Taylor (1995) reveals the width of the range of opinions and findings on the key issue of how much impact interest rates have on consumers' spending. Countries differ greatly in this respect, we find.

Interest rewards postponed consumption. A higher interest rate makes future consumption more attractive, relative to present consumption: future consumption has become cheaper. The higher the interest is, the likelier it is that consumption displays a positive time trend, starting low and climbing later. The relevant interest rate here is a *real* one. Impatience is a psychological trait that makes people value consumption more heavily, the earlier it is enjoyed. Impatience encourages people to advance pleasure. Higher impatience makes it likelier that consumption is initially high, falling later. The degree of impatience is the rate of time preference, the rate at which future utility from consumption is discounted. Impatience and interest are forces in opposition. When interest exceeds impatience, consumption will grow over time. If impatience exceeds interest, consumption will start high but recede. In the simplest economy, where population and technology are unchanging, everyone has an infinite time horizon, preferences are similar, and information and capital markets are perfect, the real interest rate will eventually converge on the rate of impatience.

If population and technology keep advancing, real interest should exceed the rate of impatience in the long run. The gap between the two will tend to $\boldsymbol{n} + \boldsymbol{ax}$, where $\boldsymbol{n}$ is the population growth rate, $\boldsymbol{x}$ is the rate of technological progress (taken here to denote the rate of advance in the efficiency of labour) and $\boldsymbol{a}$ is a parameter, called the coefficient of relative risk aversion, that reflects the extent to which consumers are prepared to substitute between consumption at different dates. If $\boldsymbol{a}$ is high, this suggests that consumers are fussy about the timing of consumption, enjoying consumption in broadly similar amounts in all periods, substituting little between consumption at different periods. A high value of $\boldsymbol{a}$ tends to keep consumption up in bad times and down in good times.[1]

It is the role of the real rate of interest on the time path of consumption spending that is of particular interest here. Suppose there is a given rate of impatience, β. Preferences over consumption are such that the parameter a is a constant. We shall assume that capital markets are perfect, and that there are no costs of adjusting consumption at once. The one-period real rate of interest is r_t at date **t**. If individuals are to choose their consumption spending plans optimally, to do as well as they can for themselves, and are perfectly informed, facing perfect capital markets with no taxation, the following relationship will hold:

$$c^{p}_{t+1,t} = c_t + [r_t - \beta] / a \qquad (2.1)$$

Here, $c^{p}_{t+1,t}$ is the log of consumption spending planned at date t for the next date, $t + 1$, and c_t is the log of consumption at date t. One period earlier, consumers will also have laid plans about c_t and c_{t+1} (and chosen c_{t-1} as well). Back then, those plans will have implied $c^{P}_{t+1,t-1} = c^{P}_{t,t-1} + [E_{t-1}r_t - \beta]/a$ and $c^{P}_{t,t-1} = c_{t-1} + [r_{t-1} - \beta]/a$. Here, $c^{p}_{t,t-1}$ is the log of consumption planned at t–1 for date t, and $c^{P}_{t+1,t-1}$ is the log of consumption planned at $t-1$ for the following date, $t + 1$. Linking equation (2.1) with those previous plans gives a relationship between c_t and c_{t-1}, actual consumption levels (in logs) for these two dates:

$$c_t = c_{t-1} - (r_t - E_{t-1}r_t) / a + (r_{t-1} - \beta) / a + [c^{P}_{t+1,t} - c^{P}_{t+1,t-1}] \qquad (2.2)$$

There are many insights to be gained from equation (2.2). One is the fact that consumption will largely tend to repeat itself. When the other terms vanish, c_t will equal c_{t-1}. A second feature, evident from the second term on the right-hand side, is that present consumption c_t will respond adversely to an unexpected rise in the real rate of interest at date t. The term $r_t - E_{t-1}\, r_t$ is the difference between r_t and what it had been expected to be, one period earlier. When consumers are fussy, a is high, and only really large real interest-rate surprises affect consumption much. Parameter a exerts a similar effect on the third term. This expression tells us that a higher real interest rate in the previous period has a positive influence on consumption now. This is because consumption grows over time when real interest exceeds impatience. To repeat, the *previous* period's real interest rate exerts a positive impact on present consumption, while an unexpected jump in the *current* real interest rate has the opposite effect. The fourth term, in square brackets, is the revision made, between $t-1$ and t, in the planned value of consumption spending at the next date, $t + 1$. This could be positive or negative, mainly reflecting things like revised expectations of future income.

If monetary policy tightens between t and $t - 1$ unexpectedly, it will exert two principal effects. First, a higher nominal interest rate at t, increasing by more than any rise in expected inflation at least, will raise r_t above what it was predicted to be one period earlier, E_{t-1}, r_t. As equation (2.2) shows, consumption at date t must be squeezed by this, although not by much if a is large. There is a second possible effect, too. The fourth term on the right-hand side of equation (2.2) might be negative. An unexpected real interest-rate jump now may make consumers gloomier about their real income prospects in the following period, than they were before. Some workers – for example, those employed in the construction and capital goods sectors – may suddenly fear for their jobs if policy rates rise unexpectedly. Thus far, we have identified two main channels running from a monetary policy change upon consumption spending. First, an *unanticipated* rise in the real interest rate will lower consumption now. Second, it may make households more pessimistic about their future income, lowering present consumption relative to previous plans for it. An *anticipated* monetary policy change, though it has no effect on $c_t - c_{t-1}$, will already have reduced the level of consumption when it first came to be expected, thereby tending to lower current consumption, too.

To all these effects we must now add another. In practice, capital markets display numerous imperfections. One of these is illustrated by the adage, 'you can always get a loan if you can prove you do not need it'. Potential borrowers are usually subject to constraints on what they can borrow. Collateral may be needed. An unexpected rise in interest rates will cut the value of collateral, and borrowing limits tighten. A fall in consumption spending by such borrowers must ensue. Financial institutions may predict a rise in defaults on existing loans, and become more selective in granting new credit. Credit will be harder to obtain; credit gets dearer and scarcer. Borrowers may be forced to curtail their outlays. Even if not required to cut spending by their lenders, they may think they should. Any expectation that credit will tighten later on, though it may encourage greater pre-emptive borrowing arrangements now, will tend to lower current consumption. When policy rates drop, equation (2.2) shows that consumption rises. If the rate cut is unanticipated, the second term on the right-hand side is positive. That raises c_t relative to c_{t-1}. Real income prospects later on may improve, making the fourth term on the right-hand side of equation (2.2) positive. Had the rate cut been predicted back at date $t - 1$, neither of these effects operates, but instead c_{t-1} will already have received a stimulus – and so c_t should recover too. In addition, collateral requirements are eased, and the value of collateral offered increases as well; a credit expansion should follow, with a favourable impact on borrowers' consumption.

All effects operating via equation (2.2) should work symmetrically in both directions – higher interest should deter consumption, and lower interest encourage it. However, credit effects could be asymmetric. Higher interest can starve new (or renegotiating) borrowers of credit. Lower collateral values may force spending cuts. But cheaper interest is only permissive: being allowed to borrow more need not mean that you will borrow more. That may be why Peermans and Smets (2002) find that, in eight Euroland countries, interest rate changes have quantitatively different effects in booms and recessions. Equation (2.2) also confirms the results obtained about interest rates in the long run. In a long-run steady state, devoid of shocks, r_t and r_{t-1} will both settle down at the value of β (assuming no trend in population or technology). So the third term on the right-hand side of equation (2.2) vanishes. With no shocks, so will the other terms. Consumption will be steady.

Does evidence confirm these ideas, drawn from the hypotheses underlying our discussion – namely that consumers optimise over an infinite horizon, and face perfect capital markets? Our empirical analysis of quarterly changes in the real value of consumption per head related these to:

- i A constant, reflecting any trend;
- ii The previous quarter's change in consumption;
- iii Changes in central bank nominal interest rates, in the current quarter and the previous quarter;
- iv The level of real central bank interest rates, a quarter ago;
- v The proportionate change in the real value of the stock market price index;
- vi The real value of consumption per head a year ago; and
- vii The level of real income per head a year ago.

Regressions were run on 25 countries (the largest number for which data were available) on IFS data. The period under study ran from the start of 1980 to the end of 2000. Full results are presented in the Table 2.5 in the Appendix. The main points are as follows. Our key interest rate terms (iii) and (iv) performed rather unsatisfactorily in the main, with insignificant coefficients and even perverse signs in several cases. Above all, there were big differences in countries' experiences. There is a negative effect, statistically significant, of (iii) in the US, the UK, Sweden, Japan, New Zealand, Mexico and Peru. Sometimes, as in Sweden and New Zealand, it is current interest rate changes that display the predicted effect. In other cases, higher interest rates depress consumption only with a lag. There could be reverse causation – policy rates may rise if consumption grows fast in the current quarter.

The predicted positive effect of the lagged real interest rate, (iv), was well displayed in the US, the UK, France, Japan and the Philippines, in each of which it was significant. Elsewhere, the results for this term were disappointing and mostly uninformative. Only Germany, the Netherlands and the US generated significant, correctly-signed coefficients on share prices (the sixth term). The coefficients on the last two regressors (lagged consumption and income) are well determined and of appropriate sign and relative magnitude for several (mostly European) countries, but not all.

The main inference, then, is that the speed, size and predictability of interest rate effects on consumption vary widely across countries. In some, there appears no dependable evidence about them at all. But is this a surprise? Central banks change interest rates for a reason. Usually it is to counter the effects of a shock; or to alter aggregate spending if it seems to be too strong or sluggish; or to stabilise future inflation at a target level, declared or tacit. The impact of policy rate changes may be buried by the shocks or deviation that prompted them. Shocks calling for policy rate rises are likely to be linked to rapid consumption growth, witnessed or foreseen; a positive relationship. However, interest rate increases are designed to lower consumption growth, among other objectives. It is a consoling thought that if interest rates were moved with the objective of stabilising consumption growth, and if perfect stabilisation were achieved, econometric results would imply that interest rates had no effect. (This is the first paradox of the transmission mechanism, mentioned in section 2.2 above).

Cross-country diversity in the impact of interest rates upon consumption is not a new finding. Figure 2.13 displays estimates of the semi-elasticities of real interest rates (annualised) on real quarterly consumption or real quarterly GDP for different countries, obtained from various other sources.[2] It is interesting how the diversity of these results is matched by the diversity of our own results, even if details differ.

There are strong reasons for expecting consumers' spending on durables to be interest-sensitive. The data we have examined draw no distinction between durables and non-durables spending. It may well be that the evidence we have found, that interest rate increases do reduce total consumer spending significantly in several countries, either at once or with a brief lag, is primarily driven by their effects on durables expenditure. Furthermore, the simplest two-period models (from which our analysis has generalised) suggest that although *savers*' non-durable spending could in principle rise or fall in response to interest rate changes, *borrowers*' spending should drop when interest rates go up. It should also be emphasised that a sizeable minority of consumers appears to be credit-

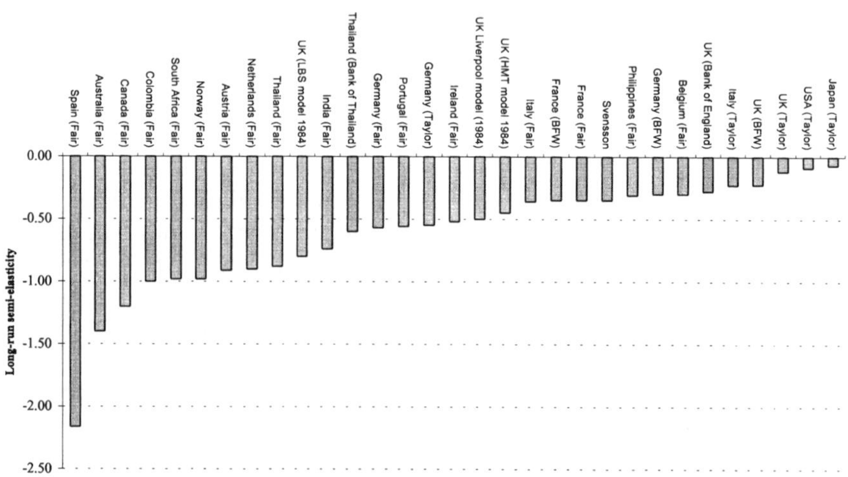

Figure 2.13 Long-run semi-elasticities in consumption equations.

rationed. This suggests that a relaxation of monetary policy, which increases the supply of credit, should stimulate aggregate consumer spending even when interest rates facing consumers are sticky, or actually rise as credit restrictions are liberalised.

This section gives mixed evidence on the effect of interest rate effects upon consumption. It shows that choice by rational long-lived consumers should predict a negative effect of a nominal interest rate increase on the growth of consumption, but a positive effect from previous real interest rate levels. So *high* (real) interest rates in the recent past should make consumption grow faster, while *rising* (nominal or real) interest rates should have the opposite effect. Cross-country evidence gives highly diverse results from different countries. Our hypothesis receives no support from some countries' experience, but data for Britain, Japan and the United States in particular, and from several other countries to a reduced extent, provide an encouraging degree of support for it.

2.6 Interest rates and investment

When studying the impact that monetary policy exerts on investment and construction, it is helpful to begin with a number of relevant observations.

First, new capital goods and buildings are supplied. We should not simply focus on the demand side. Producers typically need a higher selling price, or the prospect of it, to induce them to raise output. The output of the machine-producing and construction sectors should therefore increase with the relative price of those products, actual or expected. These sectors' output is of two kinds: there is output to replace assets as they wear out (replacement investment); and there is net investment, the rise in the stock. So writing q as the relative price of the physical investment product, in terms of consumption goods, δ as the rate of depreciation, and S as the stock of the asset in question, supply will be given by an equation of the form

$$\delta S + \dot{S} = f(q) \tag{2.3}$$

Here, δS is replacement investment, and $\dot{S}$ is net investment. So the left-hand side of equation (2.3) is the total output of capital goods. The positive link between this expression for the total output of the sector on the one side, and its relative price q on the other, means that $f'(q)$ is positive. If the stock is to be steady, a bigger stock will imply more replacement investment, and so a higher price. If q is higher than needed to keep a given stock steady, the stock will climb (and decline if less).

Second, an asset becomes more attractive to buy if it is expected to rise in value. Company executives are often besieged by requests from their IT experts to buy the latest computers. An executive anxious to resist such pressures can react with the following argument: 'I agree that these latest computers are better than what we have at present. But why do we need to replace our existing stock now? In a few months' time, new ones will be cheaper – and possibly superseded by still better ones at the cutting edge. So should we not wait?' The negative trend in q for computers, which fall in price on a quality-adjusted basis by some 40 per cent per year on average, restrains demand for them, and increases the cost of renting them. A computer-leasing agency must cover its costs to survive, and a big component of those costs is the anticipated rate of value depreciation. Rentals must be high: a year's rental might be 60 per cent of the purchase price. Assets expected to appreciate in price, such as houses in sought-after areas with strict zoning regulations, antiques, and shares in companies with excellent profit growth forecasts, are correspondingly attractive and expensive.

A third point is that those engaged in the sale or purchase of large or valuable assets have strong incentives to be well informed. A corollary of good, up-to-date information is that systematic forecasting errors should be few and far between; it is simplest to assume there are none. The future is unknowable; random events may exert big effects on asset markets. Economists are unhappy constructing models of a market where there is a difference between the model proposed and the perceptions of participants in that market as to how it works. If there is a good model, should it not fit in with the perceptions of those involved in the market? So rational expectations are likely to form part of that model.

The fourth point is that the value of any asset is inextricably linked to the real rate of interest, R. This link is the key point of contact with monetary policy, and the analysis of the transmission mechanism. Complications like tax and capital market imperfections aside, the demand for the stock of an asset like housing will be negatively related to the 'rental cost of capital', $q(R + \delta - E\dot{q}/q)$. Here, $E\dot{q}/q$ is the anticipated growth rate for q. For computers it is negative – explaining why rental rates are high; for housing, it could be positive, at least it will be in a growing economy.

If expectations are rational (the third point), and with no unanticipated disturbances or trends in supply or demand, q and S should evolve together towards a long-run equilibrium where both are steady. There will be just one path, the 'saddle path', to that equilibrium, and rational expectations and foresight should place the market on it. If S is climbing to long-run equilibrium, q should be declining (and climbing if S is slipping). Suppose we start in long-run equilibrium, say in the housing market, then perturb it with an unexpected permanent rise in R. In the new long-run equilibrium, perhaps not attained for many years, S and q will be lower than before. S only changes very slowly. The approach to long-run equilibrium sees S slipping and q climbing, along the saddle path. Thus the monetary policy change that raised R will mean that, on impact, house prices must drop sharply. They overshoot. They fall not just by the anticipated long-run fall, but by more, to make room for their gradual recovery in the adjustment phase.

In practice, though, monetary policy affects real interest rates only temporarily. Suppose the central bank raises the (nominal) policy rate now, unexpectedly, by 100 basis points. Two years later, it is expected to bring the rate down again to the old level. The real interest rate rises straightaway by 100 basis points, then climbs a little (as inflation recedes), and is then expected to drop back after two years to something close to its previous level. We may now identify three phases for the housing market: phase 1 is the immediate drop in house prices, when the policy surprise occurs, and before *S* has had any time to react; phase 2 lasts for 2 years, and ends with the policy rate reversal; phase 3 then starts, and concludes – eventually – when the initial long-run equilibrium is restored. Working backwards, phase 3 is quite straightforward – here, *S* will be rising, and *q* slipping slightly, along the saddle path. Phase 2 should see *q* climbing a bit and *S* dropping (at least initially). In the very brief phase 1, *q* takes a bit of a tumble, to create room for the amount by which phase 2's rise in house prices exceeds phase 3's slight decline. Phase 2, incidentally, sees the building trades in recession, with some knock-on effects on spending elsewhere in the economy, which are amplified by the drop in consumers' housing wealth that occurred in phase 1. In a closed economy at least, what happened to house prices and residential construction would be qualitatively similar to the effects on machine prices and equipment investment, for example. And because *q* is not just the price of a new machine, but also the market value of a little company whose sole asset was one new machine, the analysis just described could be extended easily to share prices. If monetary policy affects share prices, it will affect consumer spending (see Poterba 2000 for an analysis of the empirics of this link for the United States), and also corporate investment, too. The collateral that a bank is likely to request in return for a loan falls in value if *q* drops; banks respond by tightening credit and raising loan rates, triggering the 'financial accelerator' effects described by Bernanke and Gertler (1995).

Figure 2.14 depicts the time-paths of nominal and real short-term interest rates, asset prices and gross investment during the three phases. It is noteworthy that there is no jump or crash in *q*, except at Phase 1. This is because we have assumed that the date – 2 years on – at which the monetary authorities are expected to reverse the initial rise in nominal interest rates has been correctly predicted. If it had not been, what would have happened? If the interest rate rise is reversed unexpectedly early – in less than the 2 years we assumed – Phase 2 would be truncated, and *q* would jump upwards, by at least a little, as soon as the decision to reverse was announced. If Phase 2 lasted longer than expected, *q* would slip at the end of the 2 years, and keep slipping until lower interest rates were introduced.

Equities are internationally traded. Many big companies are quoted on stock exchanges in different countries. Even for those with a single quotation, profits often come at least as much from overseas subsidiaries and affiliates as from operations at home. Crucially, stock market price

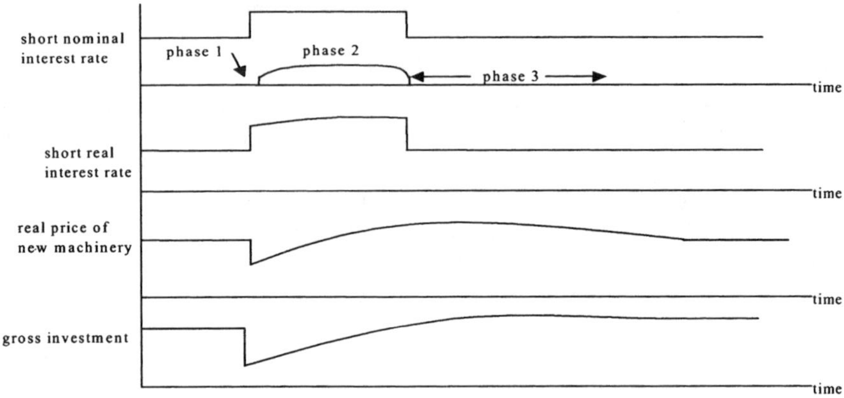

Figure 2.14 The time-paths of key variables in response to a correctly perceived temporary rise in interest rates.

movements are closely correlated across countries. Put simply, US stock market prices drive world equity prices. To the extent monetary policy affects share prices, US monetary policy matters most, outside the US almost as much as inside it. Furthermore, machinery is also usually traded internationally, so our analysis of the q and S should perhaps best be thought of as a global story, not a national one.

Real-estate prices are very different. International trade in titles to buildings and land is still very modest. Dwellings are mostly non-traded assets. Monetary policy decisions in a small open economy should therefore have much bigger effects on house prices and construction than on share prices and machinery investment. It is noteworthy that most econometric studies of plant and machinery investment (such as Bean 1981) find interest rates to have at best a limited effect on investment. Other variables, such as changes in sales (or changes in real GDP at the aggregate level) appear considerably more powerful. This is not to say that monetary policy exerts *no* direct impact on corporate investment. A rival tradition, associated with Jorgenson and his co-authors, suggests the opposite. Rather, the impact of interest rates on investment is unclear, controversial, and usually subordinate to other factors.

Establishing the exact empirical relationship between interest rates and investment is challenging. First, policy rates change for a reason. Inflation has just climbed unexpectedly, perhaps, or the latest central bank forecasts have just detected a probable rise in inflation in the near future that was not previously predicted, or some shock has appeared that threatens higher inflation in the near future. Econometricians find it really hard to separate the investment effect of the higher interest rates from the investment consequences of the phenomena that led the central bank to introduce them.

Second, the time profiles of interest rates and investment are highly complex, pointing to spells of rising as well as falling investment during the period when interest rates are held above their long-run values. Third, there are lags, a factor our analysis has ignored in the interest of simplicity: capital projects simply cannot be switched on and off like a tap. Fourth, from the standpoint of equities at least, share price and interest rate movements in the United States may dominate the impact of domestic monetary policy.

In the case of housing, however, monetary conditions play a very powerful role. Easy money during competition and credit control (mid-1971–73) and the DM-shadowing period (1986–87) were swiftly followed by a near-doubling of UK house prices. The spell of high interest rates before and after ERM entry in November 1990 saw house prices in South East England fall by some 40 per cent in real terms, peak-to-trough. Hendry's (1984) econometric model of UK house prices, probably the most sophisticated to date, testifies to the potency of credit and monetary variables in causing large, sharp house-price changes.

In conclusion, a tightening of monetary policy should cut asset values and, at least temporarily, reduce investment. These effects should be stronger, and more easily discerned, in real-estate prices and construction activity than in equity prices and non-construction investment. Yet monetary factors form only one of several influences affecting all these variables. Furthermore, since interest rates are normally changed for a reason – to try to offset the inflation effects of some shock – it is hard in practice to disentangle the consequences of interest rate changes from those of the shock that precipitated them. This applies to investment no less than to consumption.

2.7 Conclusion

This chapter has examined how and why policy interest rates changed, and then turned to key initial aspects of the transmission mechanism for policy rates – their impact on other interest rates, other asset prices, and the major components of aggregate demand, consumption and investment. The next stages of the transmission mechanism concern how a change in the level of aggregate demand translates into changes in output and prices, and labour markets. These questions, together with the special features of the open economy, statistical features of inflation, and evidence on interest rates and disinflation, are examined in Chapter 3.

Appendix

This Appendix begins with the short run econometric results tracing the links from central banks' policy rates to retail deposit rates (Table 2.3) and retail lending rates (Table 2.4). This is followed by regression statistics for changes in real consumption growth against changes in nominal rates, levels of real rates, and other regressors (Table 2.5).

Table 2.3 Dynamic regressions of short-run adjustment from central bank rates through to deposit rates.

	c	ECM_{-1}	$D(cb\_intn)$	$D(cb\_intn_{-1})$	$D(dep\_intn_{-1})$	$D(dep\_intn_{-2})$	*No. Obs*
USA	0.137 (2.17)**	–0.09 (–2.11)**	0.65 (5.55)***	0.207 (1.66)*	0.259 (1.89)*		203
GBR	0.03 (0.26)	–0.071 (–1.58)	0.898 (10.16)***	0.106 (1.73)*			228
AUT	0.088 (1.11)	–0.017 (–1.64)	0.064 (2.19)**	0.074 (1.83)*			243
BEL	–0.011 (–0.23)	–0.07 (–2.59)**	0.002 (0.03)	–0.004 (–0.05)	0.332 (3.44)***		124
DEU	0.05 (1.97)*	–0.019 (–1.42)	0.176 (3.31)***	0.156 (2.46)**	0.474 (8.63)***		251
ITA	–0.111 (–2.21)**	–0.045 (–3.52)***	0.049 (1.78)*	0.199 (3.65)***	0.174 (1.74)*		106
NLD	0.051 (1.15)	–0.035 (–2.94)***		0.022 (0.62)			83
SWE	–0.005 (–0.03)	0 (0)	0.797 (7.25)***	0.263 (2.13)**	–0.238 (–2.59)**	–0.051 (–1.94)*	113
CHE	–0.018 (–0.25)	–0.083 (–2.35)**	0.609 (3.06)***	0.352 (3.23)***	0.132 (1.71)*		238
CAN	–0.129 (–1.31)	–0.112 (–2.55)**	1.044 (15.32)***	0.377 (4.55)***	–0.489 (–5.94)***		251
JPN	–0.015 (–0.48)	–0.098 (–3.65)***	0.084 (1.3)	0.457 (6.59)***			248
FIN	0.051 (0.7)	–0.018 (–0.96)	0.631 (4.23)***				172
GRC	–0.326 (–1.99)*	–0.017 (–0.64)	0.198 (1.42)	0.122 (2.17)**	0.14 (2.12)**		95
ISL	0.095 (0.33)	–0.016 (–1.69)*	0.469 (5.37)***				191
IRL	–0.255 (–2.43)**	–0.048 (–2.3)**	0.455 (5.47)***	0.34 (3.69)***	–0.206 (–2.91)***		246
MLT	0.063 (1.64)	–0.005 (–1.63)	0.095 (0.97)				246
PRT	–0.204 (–2.27)**	–0.175 (–2.32)**	0.187 (2.51)**			0.315 (2.05)**	66
ESP	–0.142 (–2.37)**	–0.058 (–2.6)**	0.262 (4.92)***	0.277 (4.51)***			130
TUR	0.888 (0.73)	–0.051 (–1.68)*	0.919 (2.32)**		0.196 (3.68)***		241
AUS	0.057 (1.12)	–0.06 (–1.74)*	0.331 (4.47)***	0.193 (2.35)**	0.163 (2.07)**		155
NZL	0.47 (3.46)***	–0.258 (–5.27)***	0.23 (4.68)***		0.187 (2.55)**	0.341 (4.21)***	129
ZAF	0.16 (0.8)	–0.096 (–2.72)***	0.251 (1.83)*	0.432 (3.94)***			249
BOL	4.245 (1.09)	–0.379 (–1.28)	0.048 (1.48)	0.781 (3.86)***			106
BRA	1.712 (1.66)	–0.317 (–4.54)***	0.805 (22.31)***				47
COL	0.126 (1.03)	–0.071 (–2.9)***	0.703 (5.04)***	0.122 (2.69)***			179
CRI	–0.413 (–1.95)*	–0.041 (–2.21)**	0.52 (4.51)***				225
ECU	1.959 (2.36)**	–0.027 (–2.14)**	0.522 (3.23)***			–0.374 (–5.68)***	201
NIC	0.607 (0.81)	–0.108 (–0.98)	0.186 (2.38)**	0.579 (3.22)***	–0.144 (–3.22)***		64

PRY	2.617 (1.77)*	–0.122 (–1.58)	0.113 (2.02)**		–0.358 (–2.72)***		128
PER	51.489 (1.31)	–0.435 (–3.39)***	0.037 (2.2)**	0.538 (3.58)***	0.152 (4.32)***		153
URY	1.67 (2.59)**	0.01 (1.92)*			0.297 (1.82)*		171
VEN	0.283 (0.64)	–0.054 (–1.56)	0.21 (3.35)***	0.31 (3.26)***			200
BHS	0.064 (1.53)	–0.07 (–2.81)***	0.267 (2.79)***	0.27 (3.31)***	–0.193 (–2.39)**		190
ABW	0.349 (1.21)	–0.012 (–0.95)	0.11 (8.13)***	0.137 (6.37)***			175
BRB	0.149 (1.93)*	–0.086 (–2.41)**	0.095 (2.65)***	0.071 (3.34)***		0.136 (3.82)***	232
GUY	0.06 (0.39)	–0.109 (–1.61)	0.729 (17.29)***	0.236 (2.81)***	–0.345 (–2.74)***		237
BLZ	0.107 (1.17)	–0.029 (–1.36)	0.081 (3.05)***		0.316 (5.59)***	0.203 (4.35)***	201
ANT	0.004 (0.06)	–0.011 (–0.79)			–0.599 (–5.54)***	–0.262 (–2.34)**	187
TTO	1.9 (2.26)**	–0.279 (–2.29)**		0.246 (2.71)***			124
ISR	3.721 (1.03)	–0.661 (–4.06)***	0.423 (5.19)***				146
JOR	–0.086 (–1.28)	–0.006 (–0.97)					29
KWT	–0.027 (–0.57)	–0.033 (–1.65)	0.371 (4.92)***	0.234 (1.98)**	0.081 (1.79)*		240
LBN	–0.05 (–0.51)	–0.017 (–1.43)	0.062 (2.45)**	0.048 (2.04)**	0.266 (3.2)***		223
EGY	0.339 (1.92)*	–0.053 (–2.1)**					249
BGD	–0.08 (–2.57)**	–0.083 (–3.43)***	1.044 (2.19)**				249
MMR	0.109 (1.51)	–0.075 (–1.53)					119
LKA	0.022 (0.13)	–0.014 (–0.84)					247
HKG	0.119 (0.37)	0.008 (0.64)	0.677 (2.05)**	0.638 (2.78)***			83
IDN	1.27 (3.61)***	–0.214 (–4.55)***			0.495 (4.23)***		128
KOR	0.584 (1.93)*	–0.098 (–1.81)*	0.588 (2.12)**		0.162 (1.64)	0.095 (2.19)**	246
LAO	–0.25 (–2.43)**	–0.03 (–1.97)*	–0.039 (–0.66)				103
MYS	0.056 (0.46)	–0.016 (–1.11)	0.263 (1.68)*	0.26 (2.78)***			203
PHL	0.379 (0.83)	–0.04 (–1.19)	0.154 (1.72)*				235
THA	0.081 (0.63)	–0.029 (–1.45)	0.275 (2.98)***		0.167 (2.09)**		251
DZA	0.053 (1.03)	–0.021 (–1.03)					193
AGO	1.434 (0.42)	–0.01 (–0.26)	1.275 (4.41)***				71
BWA	–0.031 (–0.39)	–0.041 (–2.34)**	0.359 (1.96)*	0.282 (1.69)*	–0.204 (–1.68)*	0.17 (2.9)***	248
CMR	–0.045 (–0.7)	–0.02 (–1.73)*	0.246 (2.68)***				251
CAF	–0.049 (–0.64)	–0.029 (–1.82)*	0.256 (3.03)***				251

continued

Table 2.3 Continued

	c	ECM_{-1}	*D(cb_intn)*	$D(cb\_intn_{-1})$	$D(dep\_intn_{-1})$	$D(dep\_intn_{-2})$	*No. Obs*
TCD	–0.151 (–1.37)	–0.067 (–1.73)*	0.369 (2.56)**				251
COG	–0.077 (–1.04)	–0.013 (–1.41)	0.265 (3.22)***				251
BEN	–0.252 (–2.63)***	–0.144 (–3.11)***	0.514 (3.42)***				208
GNQ	–0.06 (–0.49)	–0.045 (–1.14)	0.319 (3.72)***				191
ETH	0.15 (0.85)	–0.12 (–2.01)**	0.979 (5.48)***	–0.095 (–1.98)*	0.059 (2.16)**		125
GAB	–0.075 (–0.9)	–0.011 (–1.24)	0.26 (2.36)**				251
GMB	0.885 (1.51)	–0.148 (–1.47)					189
GHA	0.336 (1.25)	–0.031 (–1.37)		0.231 (3.56)***	0.23 (3.6)***		233
GNB	–0.677 (–1.19)	–0.364 (–3.3)***	0.994 (4.24)***		0.11 (1.57)		125
GIN	–0.009 (–0.09)	0.001 (0.09)	1.169 (2.79)***				130
CIV	–0.229 (–2.41)**	–0.122 (–2.84)***	0.556 (3.61)***				208
KEN	0.151 (1.2)	–0.014 (–1.02)	0.131 (3.47)***	0.221 (3.13)***			208
LSO	0.114 (0.51)	–0.039 (–1.86)*	0.048 (1.23)	0.077 (1.9)*			185
MWI	0.062 (0.11)	–0.088 (–2.51)**	0.66 (5.18)***	0.102 (2.94)***			249
MLI	–0.223 (–2.36)**	–0.12 (–2.78)***	0.55 (3.75)***				208
MUS	–0.034 (–0.5)	–0.091 (–2.92)***	0.495 (1.97)*		–0.088 (–1.65)*		220
MAR	–0.007 (–0.9)	–0.049 (–2.1)**	0.933 (6.17)***				151
MOZ	1.236 (1.4)	–0.07 (–1.59)					82
NER	–0.167 (–2.18)**	–0.104 (–2.56)**	0.587 (3.78)***				208
NGA	0.253 (1.33)	–0.063 (–1.87)*	0.564 (3.87)***	0.201 (3.14)***	–0.243 (–2.65)***		226
ZWE	–0.068 (–0.26)	–0.042 (–1.95)*	0.125 (2.09)**	0.425 (9.41)***			250
RWA	0.032 (0.39)	–0.013 (–0.69)	0.351 (4.05)***			0.076 (1.98)**	226
STP	0.384 (0.98)	–0.047 (–1.64)	0.38 (2.87)***				139
SYC	–0.165 (–1.99)**	0.008 (1.71)*					149
SEN	–0.229 (–2.41)**	–0.122 (–2.84)***	0.556 (3.61)***				208
NAM	–0.482 (–3.67)***	–0.077 (–3.23)***	0.252 (2.66)***	0.262 (3.99)***			109
SWZ	–0.098 (–1.59)	–0.049 (–2.2)**	0.614 (7.57)***	0.094 (1.77)*			251
TZA	–0.026 (–0.27)	–0.011 (–1.04)	0.111 (2.04)**			0.186 (1.89)*	202

TGO	–0.229 (–2.41)**	–0.122 (–2.84)***	0.556 (3.61)***				208
UGA	0.192 (0.73)	–0.106 (–2.23)**	0.433 (3.63)***				239
BFA	–0.229 (–2.41)**	–0.122 (–2.84)***	0.556 (3.61)***				208
ZMB	0.451 (0.7)	–0.071 (–2.03)**	0.341 (4.59)***	0.185 (2.4)**	0.173 (1.75)*		189
FJI	–0.029 (–1.41)	0.005 (0.96)					250
ARM	16.666 (4.14)***	–0.503 (–11.79)***	0.102 (1.74)*	–0.571 (–3.7)***	–0.297 (–5.32)***		35
BLR	2.343 (2.22)**	–0.109 (–2.19)**			0.344 (3.32)***		60
ALB	–0.025 (–0.1)	–0.103 (–1.64)	0.379 (3.83)***	0.206 (2.42)**			99
BGR	2.977 (0.97)	–0.086 (–1.06)		0.705 (5.81)***	–0.312 (–7.5)***		77
RUS	3.819 (1.62)	–0.168 (–3.81)***			0.35 (2.81)***		69
CHN	–0.003 (–0.06)	–0.042 (–1.68)*	0.917 (4.75)***				117
UKR	–7.179 (–1.82)*	–0.099 (–1)		0.249 (3.25)***			95
CZE	0.229 (1.34)	–0.087 (–1.7)*	0.488 (2.3)**				94
SVK	0.038 (0.07)	–0.001 (–0.41)	–0.274 (–2.27)**				94
LVA	0.669 (0.87)	–0.065 (–1.11)			–0.21 (–6.32)***		87
HUN	0.39 (1.4)	–0.021 (–1.5)	0.56 (3.32)***	0.323 (2.59)**	0.332 (3.39)***		188
MNG	2.746 (2.66)***	–0.083 (–2.45)**	–0.026 (–2.73)***				82
HRV	1.482 (2.11)**	–0.493 (–4.46)***	0.374 (24.96)***				94
SVN	1.725 (2.37)**	–0.181 (–2.3)**	0.719 (4.09)***	0.218 (2.83)***			69
MKD	0.8 (0.66)	–1.312 (–7.25)***	1.215 (27.36)***		–0.177 (–3.77)***		75
POL	0.489 (1.5)	–0.094 (–1.84)*	0.837 (6.8)***		0.209 (1.78)*	–0.136 (–2.95)***	129

Notes

Regression of the change in deposit rates on a constant, ECM_{-1}, change in the central bank rate (non-lagged and one lag), the change in deposit rates (one lag and two lags).

Monthly data. Sample period is 1980. 1 to 2000. 12 unless adjusted to match that of quarterly estimate; long run equilibrium correction mechanism (ECM) series constructed using co-efficient from quarterly data estimate. ***, **, *:significance of estimate at 1%, 5%, and 10% respectively; t-statistics in brackets; data source: International Financial Statistics.

Table 2.4 Dynamic regressions of short-run adjustment from central bank interest rates through to lending rates.

	c	ECM_{-1}	*D(cb_intn)*	*D(cb_intn(–1))*	*D(Ind_intn(–1))*	*D(Ind_intn(–2))*	*No. Obs*
USA	0.32 (3.3)***	–0.077 (–2.86)***	0.602 (6.59)***	0.396 (5.74)***	0.122 (1.86)*	0.136 (2)**	203
GBR	0.078 (0.88)	–3.199 (–2.08)**					251
AUT	0.014 (0.19)	–0.023 (–1.53)				0.608 (3.11)***	32
BEL	0.202 (2.38)**	–0.071 (–2.4)**	0.021 (0.14)	0.153 (1.44)			83
DNK	0.398 (1.92)*	–0.102 (–3.3)***	1.113 (8.66)***		0.134 (4.23)***	0.134 (1.92)*	115
DEU	0.169 (2.31)**	–0.039 (–3.18)***	0.175 (2.78)***	0.275 (2.68)***	0.177 (2.11)**	0.125 (2.01)**	251
ITA	–0.154 (–3.6)***	–0.007 (–0.61)		0.185 (3.59)***	0.669 (6.81)***		82
NLD	0.054 (1.03)	–0.046 (–2.31)**		0.127 (1.23)			83
SWE	0.47 (2.2)**	–0.077 (–2.19)**	1.057 (22.57)***			0.1 (1.95)*	80
CHE	0.199 (2.98)***	–0.069 (–3.37)***				0.184 (2.63)***	237
CAN	0.111 (1.01)	–0.2 (–5.66)***	0.842 (17.67)***				251
JPN	0.082 (1.6)	–0.044 (–2.12)**	0.11 (7.22)***	0.118 (7.45)***	0.361 (2.52)**		249
FIN	0.03 (1.11)	–0.017 (–1.72)*	0.6 (5.29)***			0.135 (2.72)***	242
GRC	0.011 (0.09)	–0.005 (–0.55)	0.439 (2.44)**				251
ISL	0.64 (1.69)*	–0.064 (–2.87)***	0.642 (6.09)***				173
IRL	0.154 (2.2)**	–0.155 (–2.94)***	0.764 (6.96)***	0.69 (3.71)***	–0.315 (–3.05)***		246
MLT	0.204 (1.31)	–0.025 (–1.32)			0.066 (2.06)**		246
PRT	–0.023 (–0.14)	–0.036 (–1.59)	0.129 (0.77)				70
ESP	0.002 (0.01)	–0.093 (–2.08)**	0.069 (1.48)	0.032 (0.9)	0.14 (1.43)		222
AUS	0.218 (2.77)***	–0.047 (–3.19)***	0.451 (6.28)***	0.318 (5.25)***			131
NZL	0.957 (5.26)***	–0.189 (–5.04)***	0.127 (4.61)***	0.085 (3.14)***	0.16 (2.19)**	0.122 (1.91)*	165
ZAF	1.496 (4.98)***	–0.408 (–5.65)***	0.587 (5.22)***	0.163 (2.59)**		0.11 (2.26)**	249
BOL	–2.554 (–0.82)	0.01 (0.14)		0.929 (8.34)***			107
COL	1.826 (2.43)**	–0.105 (–2.33)**	0.662 (4.22)***				179
CRI	0.059 (0.21)	–0.023 (–1.88)*	0.313 (3.66)***	0.064 (2.45)**	0.217 (2.63)***		218
ECU	1.13 (1.97)**	–0.052 (–1.2)	0.445 (6.27)***				239
NIC	22.615 (42.22)***	–0.969 (–11547)***			–0.004 (–3.19)***		67
PRY	3.918 (2.81)***	–0.156 (–2.99)***					129

PER	78.518 (1.9)*	–0.08 (–1.37)	0.202 (3.59)***	1.34 (7.33)***	0.398 (7.92)***		147
URY	1 (0.94)	0.006 (0.17)				0.196 (2.56)**	234
VEN	–0.053 (–0.11)	–0.061 (–1.24)	0.164 (2.66)***	0.325 (5.16)***			200
BHS	0 (0)	–0.002 (–0.39)	0.463 (2.57)**				251
ABW	2.102 (1.64)	–0.125 (–1.67)*	–0.309 (–3.86)***				176
BRB	0.609 (2.03)**	–0.109 (–2.32)**	0.205 (3.16)***	0.063 (1.76)*			237
GUY	0.255 (2.03)**	–0.055 (–1.59)	0.739 (31.3)***				238
BLZ	0.037 (0.38)	–0.002 (–0.37)	0.064 (10.54)***	0.031 (5.04)***			194
ANT	0.161 (1.04)	–0.033 (–1.69)*					235
TTO	0.632 (2.42)**	–0.062 (–2.36)**					210
CYP	0.051 (0.96)	–0.006 (–0.96)					203
ISR	–4.168 (–0.72)	–0.191 (–1.71)*	0.833 (8.82)***			0.077 (2.54)**	167
KWT	0.207 (1.57)	–0.049 (–1.84)*	0.237 (7.95)***		0.139 (2.53)**		241
LBN	0.311 (0.68)	–0.038 (–1.3)	0.169 (1.48)				222
EGY	–0.069 (–1.12)	–0.019 (–1.69)*	0.72 (4.02)***	0.383 (2.8)***	–0.243 (–2.06)**		243
BGD	0.148 (1.25)	–0.016 (–1.33)					249
MMR	–0.051 (–1.13)	–0.001 (–1.13)	0.135 (2.12)**				103
LKA	0.34 (1.23)	–0.023 (–1.64)		0.316 (2.53)**	–0.185 (–1.77)*		247
HKG	–0.108 (–1.55)	–0.005 (–0.43)	0.823 (8.42)***		0.125 (2.14)**		90
IND	0.266 (1.61)	–0.019 (–1.62)	0.134 (0.51)	0.341 (2.89)***		0.089 (2.71)***	249
IDN	1.127 (3.16)***	–0.077 (–3.39)***	0.117 (5.05)***		0.249 (3.69)***		128
KOR	0.526 (3.27)***	–0.055 (–1.72)*			0.266 (1.8)*		239
LAO	0.472 (0.86)	–0.015 (–0.86)					103
MYS	0.376 (1.62)	–0.032 (–2.51)**		0.174 (2.25)**			204
NPL	0.402 (1.45)	–0.067 (–1.51)					200
PHL	0.824 (1.91)*	–0.032 (–1.05)	0.491 (5.95)***				250
THA	0.689 (1.18)	–0.132 (–1.43)	0.404 (4.23)***	0.284 (3.86)***	–0.347 (–2.97)***		251
AGO	–5.104 (–0.43)	–0.178 (–1.63)	1.893 (4.21)***				71
BWA	2.814 (0.44)	–0.933 (–16)***	0.61 (2.61)***				250
BDI	0.491 (1.56)	–0.051 (–1.35)	0.189 (1.94)*		–0.42 (–4.91)***		214
CMR	0.172 (1.88)*	–0.005 (–1.31)	0.514 (3.54)***				251

continued

Table 2.4 Continued

	c	ECM_{-1}	*D(cb_intn)*	*D(cb_intn(–1))*	*D(Ind_intn(–1))*	*D(Ind_intn(–2))*	*No. Obs*
TCD	0.092 (1.16)	–0.002 (–0.57)	0.631 (2.57)**				251
COG	0.105 (1.37)	–0.003 (–0.82)	0.627 (2.65)***				251
ZAR	6.02 (1.71)*	–0.048 (–1.36)	0.48 (1.78)*				74
GNQ	0.305 (1.69)*	–0.012 (–1.25)	0.496 (3.15)***				191
ETH	0.328 (1.81)*	–0.063 (–1.17)	0.805 (8.17)***				126
GAB	0.11 (1.07)	–0.004 (–0.89)	0.605 (2.39)**				251
GMB	1.958 (2.29)**	–0.209 (–2.36)**			0.09 (1.69)*		187
GNB	0.734 (1.51)	–0.088 (–0.75)	1.255 (8.87)***				80
GIN	–0.007 (–0.09)	–0.001 (–0.09)	1.034 (4.79)***				138
KEN	0.444 (2.7)***	–0.053 (–3.23)***	0.059 (4.08)***		0.175 (1.85)*		250
LSO	0.66 (1.68)*	–0.148 (–3.01)***	0.276 (2.07)**		–0.215 (–2.43)**		247
MWI	1.127 (1.36)	–0.165 (–2.11)**	0.667 (3.57)***		0.076 (2.72)***		249
MUS	0.141 (1.1)	–0.024 (–1.83)*	0.371 (3.66)***	0.278 (2.49)**	–0.081 (–2.07)**		217
MAR	0.014 (1.43)	–0.004 (–1.39)	0.179 (1.13)				162
NGA	0.168 (0.8)	–0.114 (–2.97)***	0.815 (4.08)***	0.244 (1.9)*	–0.322 (–3.59)***		226
ZWE	0.003 (0.03)	–0.041 (–2.68)***	0.321 (4.88)***		–0.172 (–1.79)*		250
STP	0.034 (0.15)	–0.014 (–0.86)	0.773 (5.82)***				139
SYC	0.277 (0.61)	–0.02 (–0.69)					54
NAM	1.482 (3.49)***	–0.313 (–3.38)***		0.409 (2.95)***	–0.322 (–3.82)***	–0.111 (–1.79)*	109
SWZ	0.621 (4.3)***	–0.233 (–4.29)***	0.679 (8.43)***		0.047 (1.04)		247
TZA	0.036 (0.12)	–0.018 (–0.98)	0.1 (1.8)*		–0.059 (–0.86)		220
UGA	1.281 (2.73)***	–0.096 (–2.67)***	0.378 (2.36)**	0.162 (2.27)**	–0.161 (–2.75)***		216
ZMB	0.139 (0.37)	–0.141 (–2.63)***	0.559 (4.85)***		0.378 (3.45)***	–0.212 (–3.02)***	191
FJI	0.659 (1.39)	–0.109 (–1.4)			0.065 (2.04)**		226
ARM	18.44 (1.86)*	–0.336 (–8.29)***		–0.221 (–2.1)**	–0.587 (–5.67)***	–0.483 (–3.3)***	35
BLR	1.801 (1.01)	–0.008 (–0.27)	0.062 (1.75)*		0.593 (3.96)***		60
ALB	2.084 (1.16)	–0.059 (–1.16)	0.524 (2.78)***		–0.176 (–2.85)***		85
BGR	1.254 (0.49)	–0.05 (–0.65)	0.256 (3.19)***	0.781 (19.4)***	–0.189 (–6.23)***	0.103 (4.16)***	75

RUS	–7.702 (–2.35)**	–0.131 (–1.67)					70
CHN	0.311 (1.87)*	–0.112 (–1.95)*	0.674 (7.68)***				117
UKR	–5.035 (–1.23)	–0.109 (–1.19)	0.14 (2.43)**	0.332 (3.28)***	0.295 (2.53)**		94
CZE	0.148 (0.51)	–0.02 (–0.75)	0.615 (2.44)**				94
SVK	1.032 (0.66)	–0.024 (–0.79)	0.264 (1.01)		–0.27 (–1.72)*		93
LVA	–0.963 (–0.6)	–0.088 (–1.89)*			–0.449 (–4.02)***		87
HUN	0.169 (0.91)	–0.016 (–1.67)*	0.453 (5.55)***	0.271 (2.68)***	0.204 (2.76)***	0.183 (3.66)***	143
MNG	5.701 (1.25)	–0.265 (–2.07)**		–0.112 (–2.26)**			80
HRV	–2.07 (–0.69)	–0.132 (–1)	1.332 (41.49)***	0.705 (1.83)*	–0.526 (–1.85)*		93
SVN	2.117 (2.31)**	–0.082 (–2.19)**	0.688 (3.8)***	0.199 (2.35)**			69
MKD	2.336 (2.78)***	0.271 (96.38)***		0.662 (4.31)***	–0.526 (–3.75)***		75
POL	2.766 (3.86)***	–0.876 (–1088)***			–0.01 (–18.12)***	–0.014 (–33.6)***	130

Notes

Regression of the change in lending rates on a constant, ECM_{-1}, change in the central bank rate (non-lagged and one lag), the change in lending rates (one lag and two lags).

Regression period is 1980. 1 to 2000. 12 unless adjusted to match that of quarterly estimate; long run ECM series constructed using co-efficient from quarterly data estimate. ***, **, *, significance of estimate at 1%, 5%, and 10% respectively; t-statistics in brackets; data source: International Financial Statistics.

Table 2.5 Consumption equation estimates

	Constant	*dlog(cons₋₁)*	*D(interest)*	*D(interest₋₁)*	*Real interest₋₁*	*Dlog(stock price)*	*Log(income per cap₋₁)*	*Log(cons per cap₋₄)*	*No. Obs*
USA	0.007 (0.161)	0.188 (1.54)	0.196 (1.754)*	–0.435 (–4.71)***	0.117 (2.115)**	0.031 (2.247)**	0.002 (0.038)	0.003 (0.056)	72
GBR	0.006 (0.013)	–0.052 (–0.43)	0.025 (0.182)	–0.323 (–2.39)**	0.146 (2.219)**	0.011 (0.439)	–0.005 (–0.042)	0.001 (0.01)	72
AUT	–1.191 (–0.958)	–0.605 (–7.046)***	–0.155 (–0.1)	1.12 (0.699)	–0.996 (–1.552)	–0.106 (–1.334)	0.458 (1.218)	–0.125 (–0.364)	72
BEL	0.253 (0.768)	–0.007 (–0.038)	0.038 (0.181)	0.358 (1.946)*	–0.142 (–1.633)	–0.004 (–0.222)	–0.11 (–0.733)	0.072 (0.467)	42
DNK	–0.373 (–0.274)	–0.796 (–6.429)***	0.069 (0.131)	–0.616 (–1.404)	0.201 (0.897)	–0.014 (–0.165)	0.163 (0.483)	0.068 (0.249)	36
FRA	–0.005 (–0.018)	–0.086 (–0.694)	–0.006 (–0.038)	–0.008 (–0.049)	0.137 (1.741)*	–0.032 (–1.828)*	–0.045 (–0.345)	–0.013 (–0.11)	72
DEU	0.134 (1.643)	–0.084 (–1.117)	–0.543 (–1.187)	0.392 (0.935)	0.051 (0.294)	0.106 (11.232)***	0.019 (1.799)*	0.05 (1.724)*	72
ITA	–0.895 (–3.185)***	0.141 (1.158)	–0.031 (–0.151)	–0.014 (–0.083)	–0.145 (–1.893)*	–0.024 (–1.773)*	0.304 (3.317)***	–0.24 (–3.201)***	72
NLD	–1.147 (–3.198)***	–0.431 (–3.771)***	–0.115 (–0.416)	0.259 (0.948)	0.131 (1.346)	0.051 (2.382)**	0.228 (3.388)***	–0.243 (–3.064)***	72
NOR	3.42 (6.008)***	–0.343 (–4.119)***	0.995 (1.296)	–0.84 (–1.184)	–0.147 (–0.689)	–0.053 (–0.803)	–0.624 (–5.106)***	1.081 (6.95)***	72
SWE	–2.262 (–5.478)***	–0.557 (–8.253)***	–1.555 (–4.363)***	0.066 (0.205)	–0.255 (–1.574)	–0.089 (–2.049)**	0.652 (6.266)***	–0.507 (–4.14)***	68
CHE	0.235 (0.396)	–0.376 (–2.67)**	–0.316 (–1.237)	0.911 (3.651)***	–0.296 (–2.585)**	0.017 (0.978)	–0.07 (–0.809)	0.017 (0.106)	35
CAN	–0.543 (–1.944)*	0.106 (0.841)	–0.022 (–0.254)	0.094 (1.131)	–0.073 (–1.04)	0.012 (0.7)	0.154 (1.886)*	–0.197 (–1.999)**	72
JPN	–0.229 (–0.529)	–0.468 (–4.058)***	0.43 (1.412)	–0.622 (–1.882)*	0.264 (1.994)*	–0.014 (–0.737)	–0.064 (–0.553)	0.069 (0.533)	72
FIN	1.12 (1.981)*	–0.744 (–8.35)***	–0.296 (–0.468)	–0.143 (–0.262)	–0.338 (–1.97)*	–0.031 (–0.976)	–0.198 (–1.703)*	0.259 (2.193)**	72
ESP	0.013 (1.407)	0.048 (0.352)	–0.01 (–0.122)	–0.053(–0.701)	–0.016 (–0.337)	–0.004 (–0.351)	0.188 (2.6)**	–0.178 (–2.538)**	72
AUS	–0.058 (–0.289)	–0.12 (–0.928)	0.114 (1.17)	–0.095 (–0.966)	–0.036 (–0.869)	0.001 (0.049)	0.019 (0.382)	–0.018 (–2.578)	72
NZL	–0.126 (–0.542)	–0.09 (–0.675)	–0.549 (–2.266)**	0.21 (0.923)	–0.769 (–5.821)***	–0.067 (–3.432)***	0.016 (0.154)	0.035 (0.245)	34
ZAF	0.209 (0.75)	0.039 (0.326)	0.156 (0.644)	0.13 (0.535)	–0.017 (–0.234)	0.032 (2.952)***	0 (–0.011)	–0.048 (–0.747)	72
MEX	0.071 (0.233)	–0.403 (–2.625)**	–0.079 (–1.594)	–0.115 (–1.987)*	0.01 (0.249)	–0.01 (–0.356)	0.042 (0.15)	0.035 (0.252)	55
PER	8.973 (3.964)***	–0.606 (–3.865)***	–0.002 (–1.53)	–0.003 (–1.867)*	–0.002 (–2.63)**	0.053 (1.489)	0.73 (3.055)***	–0.989 (–3.958)	33
ISR	0.009 (0.036)	–0.398 (–3.593)***	0.002 (0.294)	–0.001 (–0.153)	–0.019 (–1.783)*	–0.01 (–0.269)	–0.618 (–3.571)***	0.414 (2.266)***	62
HKG	–0.21 (–0.187)	–0.539 (–2.334)*	2.51 (0.0954)	1.73 (0.6)	–0.063 (–0.092)	0.099 (1.054)	0.336 (1.328)	0.553 (1.383))	15
KOR	0.446 (6.058)***	–0.374 (–4.261)***	–0.618 (–1.507)	0.487 (1.134)	–0.099 (–0.76)	–0.061 (–1.398)	0.318 (6.439)***	–0.28 (–5.943)***	72
PHL	3.386 (10.267)***	–0.475 (–8.569)***	0.326 (0.828)	0.044 (0.113)	0.348 (4.603)***	–0.061 (–1.767)*	–0.153 (–1.583)	1.114 (10.711)***	64

Notes

Regression of change in consumption per head (in logs) on a constant, lagged change in consumption per head, change in nominal interest rate (current and lagged), the lagged real interest rate, change in the stock market price index, the level of real income per head (lagged one year) and consumption per head (lagged one year)

Sample period is 1980, quarter 1 to 2000, quarter 4; ***, **, *, significance of estimate at 1%, 5%, and 10% respectively, t-statistics in brackets; data source: International Financial Statistics, IMF.

Acknowledgment

Regarding Chapters 2 and 3, the author thanks Dan Huynh very warmly for very substantial research assistance. I also thank Peter Stebbing of the Reserve Bank of Australia for supplying data for the Australian Money Market Rate from 1986, which were used as a proxy for Australia's policy rates in this study. From January 1999, the Austrian, Belgian, Dutch, Finnish, French, German, Greek, Irish, Italian, Portuguese and Spanish Central Bank rates were set equal to the European Central Bank rate. For Brazil, Malaysia and Mexico, the Central Bank rate is proxied by the country's money market rate; for Chile, by the geometric mean of lending and deposit rates; and for France until December 1998, by the geometric mean of money market and treasury rates. Further details about the statistics and econometric tests will be supplied on request: please email peter.sinclair@bankofengland.co.uk, or p.j.n.sinclair@bham.ac.uk.

Notes

1 If savings and capital income are not exempt from income tax it is the *after-tax* real rate of interest that equals the rate of impatience in the long run (plus $\boldsymbol{n} + \boldsymbol{ax}$ if technology or population is growing). When all nominal interest payments are subject to tax, inflation and income tax rate interact. They reduce an economy's long-run stock of capital, and potential output. Inflation can exert adverse effects on long-run output for other reasons, too. For example, if real money holdings save their owners time that would otherwise be wasted on making transactions, sustained inflation tends to lower the supply of labour, and eventually output, capital and consumption have to fall in step, too.

2 Fair 1984; Giovannini 1985; Easton and Patterson 1987; Taylor 1993b; Britton *et al.* 1997; McCallum and Nelson 1998; Svensson 1999; Bank of England 2000; Bank of Thailand 2001.

3 How policy rates affect output, prices and labour, open economy issues, and inflation and disinflation

Peter Sinclair

3.1 Introduction

This chapter extends the analysis of Chapter 2 to output and prices (section 3.2), labour (section 3.3) and exchange rates (section 3.4). Section 3.5 looks at interest rates under money targets, while section 3.6 explores inflation dynamics, and section 3.7 looks at how these are affected by interest rates in practice.

3.2 Interest rates, output and prices

Changes in monetary conditions will lead to a change in nominal aggregate demand – that is, the total demand for goods at a given level of prices. But will a change in nominal aggregate demand lead to a change in output and employment? Or will it cause prices to change? Shall we see changes in both aggregate output and the price level, and, if so, what determines the exact mix of price and output responses? Will the pattern of responses change over time? These are the main questions discussed in this section.

Answering these questions involves exploring four separate issues. One is the extent to which the prices of goods are sticky. The second issue concerns the response of goods prices to the extent that they are flexible. The third is the reaction of costs, chief among them the cost of labour. The fourth and final issue is the role of overseas trade and the exchange rate in the open economy.

If we start with a closed economy, where the time-path of money wage rates is given, at least initially, and there is no stickiness in the prices of goods, we focus on the second issue. Goods prices are fully flexible, but money wage rates, for the time being at least, are not. The prices of goods will presumably be set, jointly with their levels of production, at points of equilibrium where demand and supply are in balance. Aggregate nominal demand has changed in response to a monetary policy initiative, such as a change in the policy rates set by the central bank. Determining the reaction of prices and outputs involves analysing the shape of the 'aggregate supply curve'. If aggregate supply is highly elastic, output will change, but prices will hardly change at all; if highly inelastic, the opposite. The ratio of the change in aggregate output to the change in the aggregate price level will be given by the elasticity of aggregate supply – call this $\boldsymbol{E_s}$.

Under perfectly competitive conditions, where labour is the only variable factors of production and the money wage rate is given, $\boldsymbol{E_s}$ will be given by the formula:

$$\boldsymbol{E_s} = \left[\text{elasticity of substitution between labour and other factors}\right] \left[\frac{\text{wages}}{\text{other costs}}\right] \quad (3.1)$$

In an economy with many sectors, $\boldsymbol{E_s}$ in the aggregate will be determined by the average values of the terms in brackets for each sector, weighted by each sector's share in total output. The ratio of wages to other costs in the economy as a whole will equal the ratio of labour's share in income to one minus that share. Employee compensation amounts to about two-thirds of national income in most advanced economies, and a little less, on average, in most developing countries, so the wages/other costs ratio is approximately 2. Estimates of the elasticity of substitution between labour and other factors of production vary somewhat; in the United States, many cluster around unity, while in Europe many are a little lower. If this elasticity can be assumed to be approximately 1, this means that our formula predicts a value for $\boldsymbol{E_s}$ of 2. A cut in policy rates that raises nominal aggregate demand by $\boldsymbol{x}$ per cent will, on that basis, be expected to raise output levels twice as much as it increases prices. Equation (3.1) gives us a useful way of decomposing the likely output and price responses to a change in monetary policy.

There are several important qualifications, however. One concerns the extent to which the change in monetary conditions had been predicted beforehand. Equation (3.1) describes the case where the policy change comes as a surprise. Had it been predicted far ahead, before the money wage rates currently ruling were determined or negotiated, nominal labour costs would reflect those predictions. It is quite possible that prior wage increases will have matched the anticipated increase in prices that the policy change would bring about. Then $\boldsymbol{E_s}$ would be zero. All else equal, perfectly competitive firms will only take on extra labour, and produce more output, if real wage rates drop. If the time-path of money wage rates matches that of prices, real wage rates stay the same, so neither employment nor output will respond.

It is not just a question of whether the monetary policy initiative is a surprise or not that matters. If it has been predicted, how far ahead it was predicted matters, too, and by whom. Suppose all market observers, including employers and labour representatives, expect relaxation in monetary policy a month before it happens, and money wage rates we set annually, let us say, with almost 2 per cent of rates of pay being reset each week. Money wage rates would have been set in about 88 per cent of the economy's industries before the policy change was predicted. In the week after the policy change, equation (3.1) will apply to between 85 per cent and 88 per cent of the economy, and in the remainder it will be price, not output, that responds. For the latter group, E_s will be (approximately) zero. Five months later a zero value of E_s should apply to half the economy; and a full year after the expectations were formed, money wage rates and prices should have responded in full, leaving us with an overall average value of zero for E_s.

So the frequency of nominal wage resetting affects the pattern of output and price responses to a monetary policy change. Whose expectations and predictions change matters too. The financial press frequently speculates on whether the authorities will raise or cut policy rates. This may not filter through to employers. They may also ignore it. Even if employers follow this discussion closely, employees and their representatives at the bargaining table may not. If an employer says, 'We must go for a moderate pay increase this year because everyone is predicting monetary policy to tighten', employees may retort, 'They would say that, wouldn't they?'

A second qualification for equation (3.1) relates to the assumptions on which it is based, and, in particular, to the notion that labour is a fully variable factor of production and that all other factors are fixed. There are costs of hiring and firing. Adjustment costs for labour are rarely negligible, especially for skilled and specialised labour. New recruits have to be trained. Dismissals may disturb productivity and morale. There may be lengthy and expensive legal processes to go through. There may also be reluctance to release labour in response to any policy change expected to have only temporary effects: any labour now released may well have to be rehired later on. If labour and other factors really are fixed, the ratio of wages to other costs no longer matters: E_s will be zero, because that term in equation (3.1) relates only to the ratio of payments to a freely variable factor to other costs.

If skilled labour were fixed and unskilled labour freely variable, up and down, the formula in equation (3.1) would replace 'labour' by 'unskilled labour' and 'wages' by 'total unskilled pay'. This would bring down the value of E_s. If capital is the only variable factor of production, and nominal capital costs were given, E_s would change again: we would replace 'labour' and 'wages' by 'capital' and 'capital costs' respectively. With capital costs about one-third of value added on most definitions in most economies, and with the elasticity of substitution taken to be unitary, our new formula would cut E_s to about one-half, much lower than implied by equation (3.1).

A third qualification for equation (3.1) arises when we probe further the initial assumption that money wage rates are (temporarily) given. If labour markets are in equilibrium, all else equal, it is only a *fall* in real wage rates that makes employers increase employment and output. All else equal, for given utility, it is only a *rise* in real wage rates that prompts workers to offer more labour. If a relaxation in monetary conditions is to raise output in such conditions, it can only work by persuading firms that real wage rates have dropped, and employees that they have risen. At least one group's beliefs must be false. In the long run, in full equilibrium, a change in monetary conditions can exert no significant effect on any variable – output, employment real wage rates or relative prices. Any output response to altered monetary conditions can only be brief, based on the unsatisfactory foundation of inconsistent expectations and perceptions. In most contemporary economies, up-to-date and dependable information about key price indices is freely available. These arguments suggest that the long-run value of $\boldsymbol{E_s}$, in response to changes in monetary conditions, really should be zero; and even for a short period (of a year or less perhaps) any confidence in a robustly positive value of $\boldsymbol{E_s}$ is undermined by serious doubts. Further, a history of monetary turbulence in the past may well make output less sensitive to monetary policy changes in the future.

In some economies, money wage rates are indexed to prices. This is particularly evident in countries with a record of rapid and/or unpredictable inflation. For many decades Italy applied its *scala mobile* to rates of pay for most categories of workers. Indexation has also been widespread in, for example, Israel and Brazil. Allowing for this possibility causes equation (3.1) to change to

$$\boldsymbol{E_s} = [\text{elasticity of substitution}]\left[\frac{\text{wages}}{\text{other costs}}\right] [1 - \text{elasticity of money wage rates to prices}] \tag{3.2}$$

Full indexation makes the new third term vanish. $\boldsymbol{E_s}$ is zero. Even partial indexation of money wage rates will reduce $\boldsymbol{E_s}$. There is clearly a link between money wage indexation and a high frequency of wage renegotiations. They are both methods of insulating real wages from the force of shocks, particularly monetary shocks. Risk aversion will strengthen their appeal, and perhaps for employers (and their creditors) as well as for employees. Both tend to reduce the elasticity of aggregate supply in response to monetary policy changes. They tend to increase the variance of prices, and reduce variance in output and employment.

The main inferences to draw for the effects of monetary policy at this point are as follows:

1 The output and employment effects of monetary policy changes will be smaller and briefer in countries with a record of rapid and/or

unpredictable inflation. Here there will be a greater tendency for frequent revisions to nominal pay, and for implicit or formal indexation of pay to prices.

2 Monetary policy changes should have smaller output and employment effects, and larger effects upon prices, in economies where the monetary authorities' behaviour is more transparent and predictable.
3 Monetary policy will exert weaker effects on output and employment in economies where firms are subject to restrictions, or substantial costs, in hiring and firing, since these will transform labour from a freely variable factor into a largely fixed one.
4 When policy rates have been revised in the past only by small amounts, and/or relatively rarely, any given policy change is likely to have larger output effects, and smaller (initial) price effects.

So far, firms have been assumed to revise goods prices immediately in response to shocks. Money wage rates are temporarily or partially fixed. This brings us to the first issue of whether goods prices are rigid or flexible, and to the question of what happens when competition is less than perfect. Under perfect competition, firms are price-takers. Under imperfect competition, a firm will not see its market vanish if it raises its product selling-prices unilaterally. Imperfectly competitive firms are price-setters, which usually adjust prices to maximise expected profits – sometimes in concert with other firms, sometimes on their own, taking rival firms' output levels (or prices) as given. What difficulties does such a firm encounter if it alters its price? One problem is gauging rivals' reactions, unless they are acting together, and even then there is the possibility of someone breaking ranks to undercut, particularly in oligopolistic tendering. A price revision sends a message to the firms' customers; and it also sends a message to its rivals. Another difficulty is the fact that many people believe 'You get what you pay for'. A price cut might be taken as indicating lower quality. Department stores often sell 'seconds' in sales. Frequent price revisions might also erode firms' goodwill and reputation, and reduce the value of information gained from past searching by consumers. Price discrimination can have this effect, too.

Then there are the actual costs of changing prices. A firm sets (and resets) its prices in terms of a unit of account: money. It is not relative prices that are set. The real costs of altering nominal prices are called menu costs. The faster the rate of inflation, the more frequently prices will have to be revised. The bearing this has for the transmission mechanism for monetary policy is that the temporary real effects of policy changes are largest when the trend of inflation is zero. The greater the rate of inflation, the more quickly firms reprice in reaction to it, and the smaller the transitory gain to output and employment following a monetary policy relaxation. For output, monetary policy changes are most powerful when policy is at its most conservative. There is a close pharmacological parallel:

a drug works best if used little. In a country with rapid inflation, output changes in the wake of an alteration in nominal interest rates will be brief and small.

After addressing the first three issues identified in the second paragraph of this section, we now look at the fourth – the question of how the open economy differs from the closed one, from the standpoint of the responsiveness of prices and output to monetary policy changes. The open economy differs from the closed economy in several ways. Many firms sell their goods abroad, not just at home, and imports become a potential source of supply. Two kinds of industrial sector are distinguished: industries supplying traded goods whether abroad or at home, and those producing non-traded goods for the domestic market only. The analysis above will hold, with minor modifications described below, for the non-traded firms. However, for the traded goods sector, it is wholly recast.

Competition from imports makes for a close link between domestic-currency import prices, and the local prices charged by home firms offering close substitutes. So long as a monetary policy change leads to no change in the exchange rate, domestic import prices will be largely given. Home firms supplying import-substitutes will not be led to alter their selling prices in response to a monetary policy change. Nor should they vary output or employment. If the monetary policy change raises aggregate demand, the variable that responds most is the volume of imports. Similar conclusions apply to exports. For a given exchange rate, monetary policy changes at home have little direct effect on prices. Competition abroad should ensure this, especially for smaller economies and for goods where close foreign substitutes are numerous. However, the supply of exports is liable to change. Monetary expansion at home raises home demand for exportables, leaving less to export.

Monetary relaxation will therefore worsen a country's trade balance, at a given exchange rate. Some exports are redirected to the more buoyant home market, and imports meet increased demand for importable products. To these developments we must add subsequent effects on wage rates, and also the effect of the home consumers' reaction to rising non-traded goods prices – substitution into traded goods. The worsening of the trade balance will transmit expansionary pressures into overseas economies, and significantly so if the monetary relaxation occurs in a very large economy such as the United States. For the domestic open economy, this leakage in additional spending power abroad will betoken a much smaller set of inflationary pressures at home than would be expected in a closed one.

These repercussions follow if exchange rate is given. Monetary relaxation at home will make it hard to hold the exchange rate, barring parallel developments abroad. A cut in home policy rates, from previous equality with foreign rates let us assume, opens a gap that prompts exports of financial capital. Domestic residents will be tempted to transfer funds to foreign centres, if free to do so. Foreigners will also respond this way, and they will find it more attractive to borrow from the country that has lowered its policy rates. International capital movements are sensitive to interest rate gaps (at least to gaps corrected for risk premia). Their magnitude can dwarf official reserves.

If monetary relaxation at home leads to a fall in the exchange rate, a free-float fall or a crisis-induced devaluation under fixed but adjustable rates, there will be immediate impacts on the domestic-currency prices of traded goods. These should rise. However, passthrough here may not be one-for-one. There is widespread recent evidence that many exchange rate depreciations in the 1990s had surprisingly limited general short-run effects on prices. Yet the direction of the effect is unambiguous. The prices of traded goods are bid up in home currency, and, if they rise relative to nominal labour costs at least, this will stimulate additional production and employment in traded sectors. The split between higher prices and higher output will be determined by the elasticity of supply – which will depend upon the factors identified in equation (3.1) above, and its subsequent variants. Under a freely floating exchange rate regime, when passthrough is large, the open economy will react to a change in monetary conditions at home in ways similar to the closed one. Non-traded goods prices will climb in direct response to higher nominal aggregate demand; home-currency traded goods prices will respond similarly, through the exchange rate mechanism.

These effects arise when the exchange rate floats, or monetary policy changes force the authorities to lower its peg. If the exchange rate is fixed, and the authorities can hold it, quite a different set of results ensues. Monetary expansion at home erodes foreign exchange reserves, as a result of the balance of payments effects noted earlier. If sterilisation is impractical or incomplete, monetary conditions at home will now steadily tighten. The previous nominal interest rate cut will have to be reversed, and domestic monetary aggregates will slide back towards their original value. Such developments would accord with Hume's price–specie–flow mechanism.

3.3 Interest rates and labour markets

The interest rate is sometimes called the price of capital. It is certainly a key element in the cost of capital. Under the simplest conditions, where competition is perfect, the buying price of a new capital asset is q and is expected to remain constant in real terms, and there is no depreciation or taxation, the rate at which a machine can be leased will be rq per period. Here, r is the real rate of interest. Allowing for depreciation at the rate of δ, and an anticipated trend in q of α, the leasing rate will be $q_t(r + \delta - \alpha)$. A higher real interest rate makes capital dearer. Competitive firms will lease capital (or buy it) up to the point where its marginal return balances the explicit (or imputed) cost of leasing it. At this point the rate of profit and the cost of capital will equate. Labour, too, is engaged up to the level where the wage rate balances the value of its marginal product.

The higher the cost of capital, the lower the wage a firm can afford to pay to labour, when the price of its product and the level of technology are given. A rise in the cost of capital lowers the demand for labour when all else is equal. When the monetary authorities increase the nominal interest rate, at a given rate of inflation, they increase the cost of capital. So firms' demand for labour must fall. A drop in labour demand will lower the real wage if labour supply is given and the labour market is in continuous equilibrium. If the real wage is fixed, and there are many different reasons for thinking that it should adjust only slowly to a shock of this kind, it will be the level of employment that responds. It can only fall.

Monetary tightening that involves higher nominal interest rates should therefore lead to a weakening in labour demand, and, all too likely, at least a temporary increase in the level of unemployment. As unemployment rises, the pace of increase in money wage rates should slacken. Pay increases may also fall because employers and employees tend to lower their expectations of future inflation, in response to the monetary authorities' restrictive actions. The first of these two effects may well work faster than the second, but both may be quite gradual, given the pattern of wage settlements.

There are reasons for suspecting that there are more links between the demand and the rate of interest. Consider a firm that produces a product that will be sold after the bulk of the work has been done. Examples abound: films, ships, buildings, pharmaceuticals, food. To simplify, imagine the following time sequence. At date 1, the firm commits itself to lease capital for date 2. At date 2, a year later, it engages labour at a wage rate W to work with the leased capital. It is then that production occurs. The product is available for sale, at a price P, a year after that, at date 3. Let technology be Cobb-Douglas, with a labour weight of b. The firm borrows from a bank at a rate r_1 for the first year, and r_2 for the second year. Banks' loan rates move one-for-one with the central bank's policy rate, let us suppose.

At date 1, W, P and r_2 are unknown. Suppose the firm has point expectations of them at that date, of E_1W, E_1P and E_1r_2. A year later, W and r_2 become known, and the new prediction of P is E_2P. At date 1, it plans the profit-maximising level of labour – call it E_1N. That will depend on E_1W, E_1P and E_1r_2.

If r_2 and E_1r_2 turn out equal, all well and good. However, imagine that the central bank's policy rate is raised unexpectedly by 100 basis points. This may well mean that P is now predicted at date 2 to be less than previously anticipated: a macroeconomic squeeze should lower the demand for the product, and if the good is traded internationally, any exchange rate appreciation could amplify this. W might possibly turn out unexpectedly low, but money wage stickiness would prevent that.

The unanticipated tightening of monetary policy should result in lower employment at date 2. Under our assumptions, the unplanned job cuts will be given by the approximation

$$\frac{E_1N - N}{E_1N} \approx \frac{1}{1-b}\left[\frac{E_1P - E_2P}{E_1P} + \left(r_2 - E_1r_2\right) - \frac{W - E_1W}{E_1W}\right] \tag{3.3}$$

Here, N is labour actually engaged at date 2. In words, equation (3.3) says that cuts in labour, relative to plans, will be some three times larger than the sum of: (i) the interest rate surprise change and (ii) the fall in the final sale price, relative to the wage rate, that this induces. (The parameter b will presumably be about two-thirds, its economy wide average). Thus in our example a rise in the expected product real wage of 0.1 per cent, together with the 100 basis point jump in the interest rate, would entail a cut in labour demand of 0.33 per cent.

There is another way in which monetary policy can affect the demand for labour in this framework. Suppose the supply of credit is unexpectedly tightened mid-way through the project, at date 2. We previously assumed that the firm could borrow as much as it wished at this point, at a rate of interest r_2. This may not be true. If it is forced to borrow less than anticipated at this stage, the level of employment the firm can afford is cut back. Less will be produced for sale at date 3 as a result. Even worse, if all credit is subject to roll-over period by period, a very tight credit squeeze might lead to the project's cancellation, and the firm's bankruptcy.

We saw in Chapter 2 (section 2.5) that consumption should grow slowest when interest rates are low and rising. For workers able to choose their hours of work, similar findings should hold, except that, for labour supply, they run in the opposite direction. We should expect labour supply to increase most when real interest rates have been low, and are now raised (in both nominal and real terms).

Not all unemployment represents an imbalance between the demand and supply of labour. Some jobs terminate and some workers quit, and it takes time for employers and employees to match. Turnover in the job market establishes an equilibrium level of unemployment, often called the natural rate, which may depend upon the level and duration of benefit and other factors. If unemployment exceeds the natural rate, the supply of labour exceeds the demand for labour. Therefore, if we begin at a point of labour market equilibrium and interest rates now rise, unemployment should increase as a result of the labour demand and supply responses just discussed. On top of these comes the indirect labour demand effect operating through aggregate demand, which will be powerful and negative in this case.

With unemployment above its natural level, downward pressure is then transmitted on the pace of money wage increases. The size of this response may be smaller when inflation is low: there is evidence from Canada (Crawford 2001) and the UK (Nickell and Quintini 2002) that money wage changes are only very rarely negative.

A reduced rate of increase in money wages implies a fall, relative to trend, in firms' unit labour costs. To the extent that labour is a variable factor of production, marginal cost drops relative to trend. Profit-maximising firms' product prices will always reflect marginal cost. In perfect competition, the two are equal. In imperfect competition, price is marked up above marginal cost, the size of the mark-up inversely proportional, in simple cases at least, to the elasticity of demand for the firm's product. So slower growth in money wage rates leads to a drop in the rate of inflation, all else equal. Taylor (2000) offers evidence, however, that the size of this effect has become somewhat weaker at low rates of inflation. This gives rise to a third paradox of monetary policy: when monetary decisions succeed in reducing inflation, monetary decisions may subsequently have a diminished impact. There is some recent evidence which accords perfectly with this: Boivin and Giannoni (2001) find that exogenous interest rate fluctuations in the United States have been exerting diminished effects, and that changes in the systematic elements of monetary policy are an important factor in this.

3.4 Interest rates and exchange rates

Actual holding period returns on different assets vary widely. *Expected* holding period returns vary too. Some assets are thought safer than others, some more convenient, some with more favourable tax status, or greater liquidity. Setting aside any difference in such features, two otherwise identical assets should display the same anticipated rate of return. If those trading in the markets for them are assumed to make no systematic forecasting errors, the actual returns on these assets should not differ systematically.

These arguments will apply not just to a pair of assets traded in the same country or denominated in the same currency. They should be no less true of cross-country comparisons as well. The only provisos are that the countries should have abjured any controls on international capital movements or restrictions on currency convertibility. This suggests that assets with very similar characteristics (such as 3-month default-free treasury bills, issued in two different national currencies) should have similar holding period yields. Suppose this instrument, issued by country *i*'s treasury in its own currency, gives an annualised yield over 3 months of x_i, given that $(1 + x_i)^{1/4}$ equals the ratio of price at redemption to price at issue. If everyone were convinced that there was no chance whatever of any rise or fall in the value of country *j*'s currency in term of *i*'s, then a similar treasury bill issued by *j*'s government in *j*'s currency should also bear an annualised return of x_i. More generally, if x_j is the annualised rate of return on this second bill, expressed in *j*'s currency, we should observe the following approximation:

$$x_i \sim x_i + Ez_{ji} + p_{ij} \tag{3.4}$$

Here, Ez_{ji} is the anticipated rate of appreciation of *i*'s currency in terms of *j*'s, over the 3-month period, expressed at an annual rate, and p_{ij} is a risk premium attaching to this prediction.

When p_{ij} is assumed negligible, approximation (3.4) is known as the *uncovered interest parity condition* (UIP). It states that any difference in interest rates between similar assets expressed in different currencies should reflect one-for-one expectations of exchange rate changes over that period. UIP is a condition of portfolio equilibrium, at least if all risks can be ignored. If it failed to hold, agents could increase expected portfolio returns by shifting funds out of one currency into another. In an efficient market, this should not be possible.

Traditionally, the analysis of the transmission mechanism of monetary policy in an open economy has relied on two pillars: One of these is UIP, and the other is a condition for arbitrage in traded goods rather than assets. This is the commodity arbitrage condition (CAC), which states that internationally traded goods should broadly cost the same at home as abroad.

Let us suppose that the central bank raises its policy rate, and that its currency is freely floating against other countries. Assume for the moment that the two conditions given above (UIP and CAC) both hold perfectly. How does the exchange rate respond? This depends on how the domestic yield curve moves in relation to a weighted average of foreign yield curves; and on the extent to which the change in nominal rates alters real rates (i.e. what has happened to inflation expectations at home and abroad). In the short run, with given inflation, we assume that a change in nominal rates is equivalent to a change in real rates. Continuing the example above, suppose that home and foreign central banks' rates were previously equal and expected to remain equal, and that they are now expected to be equal after m months, at the end of a period where they are 100 y basis points apart.

What these assumptions mean is that the market is expecting exchange rates to stay unchanged from m months onwards. Until then, however, the home currency will be expected to slide. Meantime, the monthly rate of decline, according to the UIP condition, is approximately $y/12$ per cent. So if $y = 2$ and $m = 6$, a slide of 1/6 of 1 per cent per month can be anticipated for 6 months, implying a total decline of 1 per cent. If y had been 3 and $m = 12$, the slide would expected to last a year and amount to 3 per cent in all (1/4 per cent per month over 12 months). Our assumptions about home and foreign interest rates before the policy change, and now expected from m months' time onwards, imply that the market should be predicting that the exchange rate, at the end of m months, should return to what it had been before the policy change.

Putting these items of information together, we may deduce that the spot exchange rate has to appreciate now. It must do this, to create room for the subsequent depreciation now anticipated. With $y = 2$ and $m = 6$ (a 200 per cent bp interest rate rise, to last 6 months), the spot exchange rate has to jump by 1 per cent, because that is the foreseen decline over the next half-year. With $y = 3$ and $m = 12$ (a 300 per cent bp interest rate rise, to last a year), the spot exchange rate must now jump by 3 per cent. To see what this means for inflation, we now invoke the CAC and ask to what proportion of domestic expenditure it applies. Suppose this is 40 per cent. Then, in the case of the 200 per cent bp 6-month hike, we would predict an impact effect (doubtless phased over time) of a 0.4 per cent reduction in the price index for domestic expenditure. With the 300 bp 12-month rise, the price index impact effect would treble to 1.2 per cent. These are only the impact effects, however. The exchange rate is not expected to stay up. Quite the contrary: it is only jumping now, in order to create room for the anticipated decline predicted by the UIP condition. Consequently, all the price index effects will be reversed. The appreciation of the exchange rate puts a purely temporary dent in the price index, because the subsequent depreciation will cancel it later on.

The conclusion to be drawn from the traditional theory, then, and the examples we have considered, is this. So long as the CAC and UIP conditions hold, we may use an estimate of the proportion of traded goods in total spending to predict the impact of interest rate changes on inflation quite precisely. Inflation should drop initially, then slowly climb for a while in compensation, and, after that, end up unaffected. The size of these exchange rate effects on inflation will vanish if all central banks alter interest rates in unison. When not, they will be very small if the home interest rate rise is expected to be reversed soon afterwards, and correspondingly larger if this is not so. And if the market has *anticipated* the interest rate rise, the exchange rate will have risen already, with a slide predicted (by the UIP condition) to begin after the forecast like takes place. So the key inference is – provided UIP and CAC hold – that the open economy transmission mechanism for monetary policy makes for a faster set of repercussions from unilateral interest rate changes on inflation when the exchange rate is freely floating, than when it is fixed.

Do UIP and CAC hold, however? On UIP, the verdict is mixed. The prediction that the *actual* change in an exchange rate between two currencies is approximately equal to the relevant policy rate differential fares very badly over short periods. Over a time-span of 1, 3, 6 or even 12 months, the UIP conditions turns out to be a very poor predictor of exchange rate evolution, at least between the currencies of advanced countries. A random walk usually performs much better. Lengthen the time span to a decade or more, however, and the picture changes completely. The average interest-differential becomes a highly significant and correctly signed regressor for actual exchange rate changes over longer periods.

We took the (other) OECD countries' exchange rates against the US dollar over the period 1981–98, and regressed their annual average rate of change against that country's nominal interest differential against the US, imposing commonality on the interest rate differential coefficient. This resulted in a resounding confirmation of UIP. The coefficient on the interest differential is 1.039. This is insignificantly different from unity. The constant term, 0.0013, is insignificantly different from zero. Figure 3.1 illustrates the close relationship between these two variables. Appendix Table 3.1 gives the econometric results.

We conducted a similar regression for all non-OECD countries, over the same period (or subperiods necessitated by data limitations), where the results are almost equally encouraging. Figure 3.2 presents the scatter plot of observations, and Appendix Table 3.2 gives the regression results. The coefficient on the interest differential is 1.001, and is insignificantly different from unity. The constant term is significant, and positive. This cannot be interpreted as a risk premium, unless the US dollar is deemed riskier than the average non-OECD currency. A reasonable interpretation of the positive constant is that it captures the effect of financial repression in some economies.

Appendix Table 3.3 shows how very different things are in the short run. Separate annual time series regressions were run for each of the advanced countries' exchange rates against the US dollar, upon a constant and the previous year's average interest differential. Results were

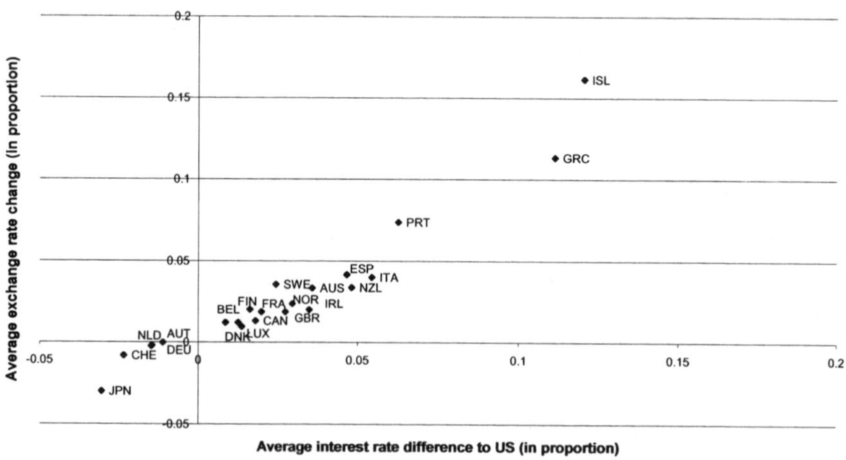

Figure 3.1 Average exchange rate changes versus average interest rate difference for 22 OECD countries (1990–98).

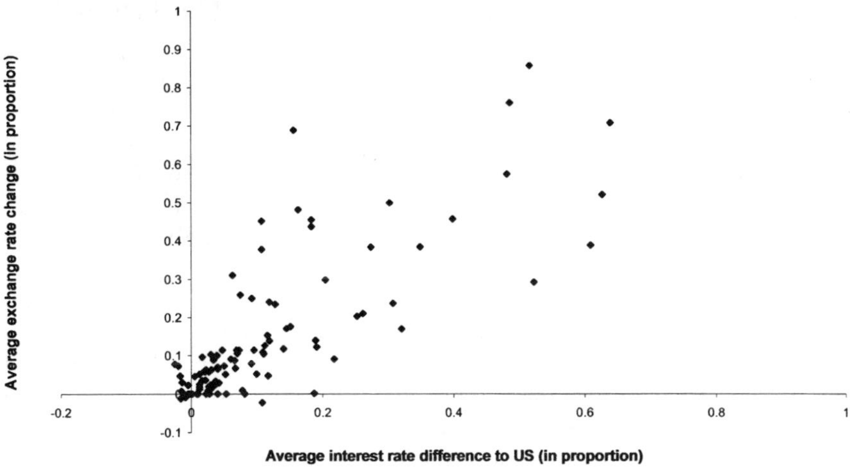

Figure 3.2 Average exchange rate changes versus average interest rate difference (1980–1999, depending on data availability).

poor: the coefficients are rarely significant or close to unity, and usually incorrectly signed. What these results tell us, therefore, is that although UIP performs very poorly in the short run, it works (almost) exactly as predicted in the long run, at least for the *generality* of OECD and non-OECD countries, as two large groups. What is most in doubt is when the drift in the exchange rate predicted, under UIP, by the interest differential actually happens. Eventually it will, but we can have no confidence at all about timing.

How can we reconcile the long-run evidence with the short-run evidence? For a start, relatively few currencies are floating freely. Some have fixed parities, with periodic discrete changes. Many others are managed. For those that float freely, two kinds of exchange rate movement are observed – jumps and drifts. Drift, or trend, movements are at least to some degree foreseeable. Jumps are not. Jumps result from news, some of it – but not all – news about interest rate decisions. UIP can be defended, as Meredith (2002) emphasises, as a statement about drift. The longer the time span, the broader the canvas, the more the trends predominate over the jumps, which should have a broad tendency to cancel out over time and across currencies. We shall return to this point below.

Quite similar findings emerge about CAC. The passthrough from the exchange rate to prices was notably smaller in the 1990s than in the previous two decades. This was true for the UK's depreciation in late 1992, and its appreciation in the late 1990s. The same phenomenon, of surprisingly low passthrough, has been evident in Australia, Chile, the Czech Republic, Indonesia, Italy, New Zealand, Spain and Thailand. The first clear evidence of it came in the United States in the mid–1980s, and prompted the hysteresis theories of Baldwin (1988) and Dixit (1989a).

There is some long-term tendency for deviations in purchasing power parity (or infringements of CAC) to decay over time. As Taylor (2001) writes, 'the present consensus is that these price differences have a half-life of five years at best, and infinity at worst'. Taylor goes on to argue that this consensus may lead to a downward bias in the speed of convergence, because prices are observed discretely and linear methods are employed. Nonetheless, deviations do not vanish overnight. What causes them?

The CAC may be undermined by several factors. Indirect tax differences, retailers' mark-ups, tariffs and international transport costs all drive wedges between consumer prices in different countries for a given traded good, expressed in a common currency. Binding import quotas can be particularly insidious, because any tariff-equivalent is amplified by the effects of imperfect competition among home producers of substitutes. Imperfect competition can also create discrepancies when cross-border arbitrage is costly, and particularly so when degrees of competition, or product demand elasticities, differ. On top of these come the effects of sunk costs faced by importers, which, as Dixit (1989b) shows, may make them reluctant to quit or alter local currency prices in the wake of adverse exchange rate changes viewed as temporary.

How may we explain the empirical short-run failure of UIP? A simple model may help to illustrate this. Consider a country that permits free international movement of capital between itself and the rest of the world, and for which the responsiveness of capital flows is perfect. In the rest of the world there is no inflation, and the nominal interest rate is given at r^*. The home country's central bank sets its policy rate, n, by the rule

$$n = r^* + \sigma[p - p_0 - \theta] \tag{3.5}$$

where $p_0 + \theta$ is an implicit price level target. (The variables p and p_0 represent the actual and target values of the logarithm of the domestic price level, and σ is positive). Aggregate demand, y in logarithms, responds to the level of external competitiveness (in logs), c, and to the domestic short-term real interest rate:

$$y = \alpha_1 c - \alpha_2 (n - \pi) \tag{3.6}$$

Here, α_1 and α_2 are both positive: an overvalued real exchange rate, implying $c < 0$, worsens the trade balance and reduces aggregate demand, while a high real interest rate lowers it by squeezing domestic investment and consumption. Inflation at home responds to the output gap

$$\dot{p} = \gamma (y - \bar{y}) \tag{3.7}$$

where $\bar{y}$ is normal potential output, again in logs. The real exchange rate, c, is related to the nominal home currency price of foreign exchange, s, and the logarithms of the home and foreign price levels by

$$c = s + p^{*} - p \tag{3.8}$$

So there is real undervaluation of the home currency when c is positive. Lastly, UIP is assumed to hold, so that

$$E\dot{s} = n - r^{*} \tag{3.9}$$

Figure 3.3 illustrates the dynamics of the exchange rate and domestic prices. The vertical axis depicts $-c$, so the currency is overvalued above and undervalued below long equilibrium at the origin. The horizontal axis variable is the gap between home prices and their target value. If domestic inflation is zero, domestic aggregate demand must equal normal potential output. The locus for zero inflation, $\dot{p} = 0$, slopes down, because if prices are above target, the interest rate rule prescribes a higher real interest rate, and the deflationary consequences of this must be offset by the stimulus to demand from currency undervaluation. There is positive inflation below the $\dot{p} = 0$ locus (the economy is overheating here) and negative inflation above. If external competitiveness is to be constant, the nominal

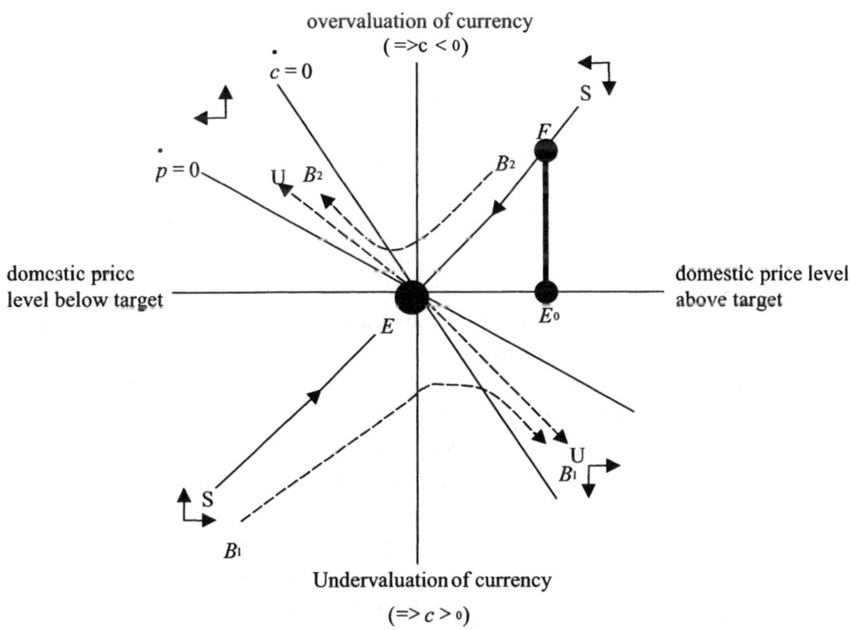

Figure 3.3 The dynamics of domestic prices and the real exchange rate.

exchange rate must drift down to offset any domestic inflation. If $\beta\gamma < 1$, the $\dot{c} = 0$ locus, which slopes down, is steeper than the $\dot{p} = 0$ locus. Competitiveness will be drifting downwards above and upwards below the $\dot{c} = 0$ locus.

To the right of the $\dot{c} = 0$ locus and above the $\dot{p} = 0$ locus, currency overvaluation and the price gap $p - p_0 - \theta$ will both be declining: hence the arrows in this region which point south and west. Below the $\dot{p} = 0$ locus and to the left of the $\dot{c} = 0$ locus, the currency will be becoming less undervalued (so c will be falling), and domestic prices will be climbing. That explains the arrows in this region, which point north and east. A unique upward-sloping saddle path SS points towards long-run equilibrium at the origin, E. The broken, downward-sloping line labelled UU depicts the system's unstable eigenvector. Had it been the case that $\beta\gamma > 1$, the $\dot{c} = 0$ locus would have been flatter than the $\dot{p} = 0$ locus, and the system would have been globally unstable.

The horizontal variable, the domestic price level, is sluggish, while, under free floating, the nominal (and real) exchange rate can jump instantaneously. With fully rational expectations, the exchange rate must jump to the unique saddle path taking the system eventually to *E*. If the domestic authorities were suddenly to reduce θ, the nominal interest rate would jump. Starting at an old long-run equilibrium at E_0, foreign exchange market participants – once they had understood what had happened – would drive the exchange rate up to point *F*, in response to the higher domestic nominal interest rate the central bank had set. We should then observe a drift downwards towards the new long-run equilibrium at *E:* domestic prices would be falling, and the exchange rate would slip back, faster initially than later on because n would be lowered gradually towards its long-run equilibrium value of r^*.

In any given period where the authorities revise θ (or any other parameter in the system changes), we should witness both jumps and slides in the exchange rate. Actual exchange rate movements would display a complex written pattern of sudden movements and subsequent reversals. It is hardly surprising if UIP is found to fail in conditions such as these. Shocks (to θ, or other variables) contaminate the actual data for exchange rate changes and interest differentials so much that the UIP mechanism, even if operates perfectly, cannot readily be discerned. Meredith (2002) offers important reflections on this point.

The model depicted in Figure 3.3 can easily be adapted to admit inflation trends at home and abroad, and to changes in foreign nominal interest rates. If there is a persistent gap between rates of inflation in two countries, this should be matched, approximately one-to-one, in the average short-run nominal interest differential between them – and in the nominal exchange rate trend, as well. This should become increasingly apparent as the length of period under study increases. For this reason, longer run tests of UIP should be more successful. We can therefore reconcile the two sets of results presented in Tables 3.1 and 3.2. Further reasons can be advanced to explain short-term discrepancies between actual exchange rate changes and relevant cross-country nominal interest differentials. One is that there could be bubbles. A bubble path is an unsustainable route that eventually diverges from long-run equilibrium by ever-increasing amounts. Two examples are exhibited in Figure 3.3. by the dashed paths labelled B_1, and B_2. If either is present, the unstable eigen-vector UU rotates clockwise slightly. Bubbles are very hard to reconcile with economic rationality. The thinking behind Figure 3.3, and the saddle path SS, is that market participants try first to calculate the long-run equilibrium for the system as a whole. Then they work out, for any given current value of p, the logarithm of the domestic price level, what the current exchange rate should be in order eventually to attain it. This is one way of formalising the thought processes of those market participants known as 'fundamentalists'.

Fundamentalists focus above all on the long run, and then on how history could evolve to reach it. They are opposed, in popular parlance, by 'chartists' whose gaze is fixed, instead, upon what may happen in the near future. Chartists predict short-term price movements on the basis of recent past movements, and what data drawn from a less recent past seem to suggest about the profile of gradual and sharp price movements. Chartists look closely at the balance of portfolio flows in and out of particular assets. At certain times they may hold extrapolative expectations, believing that what has recently been rising should continue to go up, at least for a while. They look closely at what assets seem to be in fashion. Chartist behaviour can indeed generate bubbles. At any point in time, two things can happen to a bubble: it can burst or it can survive. If it survives, it must grow. Further movement in the wrong direction is needed when it does not burst, in order to provide the capital gain that must be offered to compensate for the possibility of loss if and when it bursts.

McCallum (1994) attributes the empirical failure of UIP, in short-run tests, to the combination of bubbles and the tendency of central banks to lean against them. A central bank facing a bubble path B_1 may start to raise interest rates cautiously after undervaluation begins increasing (the ECB and the Euro in late 2000 provides a possible example). A central bank that believes the foreign exchange market is driving it along path B_2 may try to lower its interest rate as the overvaluation begins to grow (the USA in late 1984 and January 1985 is another possible instance). Either of the two things how happens: the bubble path may continue, after a slight dislodgement towards the horizontal axis; alternatively, the bubble is punctured. Bubble punctures, as in the case of the US dollar in January 1985, lead to a large crash (which might be all the way towards the saddle path SS, or even further). They will reveal a combination of interest rate changes in one direction, and exchange rate jumps in the same direction.

A few incidents of bubble puncturing will generate huge disturbances to the relationship between exchange rate changes and interest differentials.

Whether the authorities *should* attempt to puncture perceived bubbles is a fascinating question, recently addressed by Cecchetti *et al.* (2000) in the context of equity prices. Bubbles are hard to identify. The sharp movements associated with punctures are very costly: output and financial stability are imperilled. However, the case for 'wait and see' is undermined by the fact that postponing the burst of a correctly perceived bubble may involve still greater costs later (a point stressed by Kent and Lowe 1997). This is because a bubble should grow if it does not burst. Had the stock market bubble in the later 1920s in the United States been pricked earlier than it was, the resulting crash in equity prices, and perhaps the Great Depression that followed it, would have been less severe. Similar inferences may be drawn for the property and equity booms in Japan in the late 1980s, which form the basis of the powerful credit and land-price cycles model of Kiyotaki and Moore (1997) and its application to the 1997 Asian crisis by Miller *et al.* (2000). The most prominent example of a foreign exchange rate bubble is the sharp rise in the US dollar during 1984. The case for leaning against a bubble in the foreign exchange market is stronger when the bubble is of the type described in Allen and Gale (2000) rather than a mechanical bubble inserted (for example) into the UIP equation. This is because, in contrast to the former, the latter will tend to grow faster when squashed as opposed to pricked, leading to (foreseeable) difficulties later on if it does not burst in the meantime.

In the very long run, on average across countries, UIP does indeed hold. So too does CAC, wrinkles aside. However, short-term departures are so widespread that we can, alas, have very little confidence indeed about precisely how much exchange rate appreciation a given domestic nominal interest rate change will induce, let alone when. Nor can we have any clear idea about how quickly, and when, the exchange rate will tend to drift back. The impact of exchange rate changes upon domestic inflation is, unfortunately, open to similar uncertainties. Lastly, we should expect the inflation response to exchange rate changes to vary country by country. It should be fastest and largest where inflation is rapid, and exports and imports are large in relation to national income.

3.5 Interest rates under money targeting

In most economies with well-developed domestic financial markets, interest rates are key policy instruments. In some, they are deployed to keep inflation close to a pre-announced track. In others, where monetary aggregates are subject to targets, nominal interest rates may still be the month-by-month instrument of choice, revised and reset to keep the demand for monetary aggregates and their supply in balance, in the context of their pre-announced time-paths. But there are transmission mechanism questions to address, in the latter case at least, relating to the supply of money.

As in countries with less-developed financial systems, the evolution of the monetary base is unquestionably sensitive to budget deficits and (under fixed exchange rates) to balance of payments surpluses. The monetary base will tend to rise automatically in response to either, but it can be blocked. The monetary base can be insulated from the government's budgetary position if deficits are matched in full by sales of bonds to the domestic non-bank public. External payments surpluses need have no impact upon the monetary base if sterilised by bond sales on the same basis. For a variety of reasons full blockage may be hard to achieve, but partial blockage should not prove an insurmountable challenge.

Open market operations are the principal weapon at the central bank's disposal for affecting both the monetary base and the pyramid of inside money built upon it. Open market purchases will involve raising the market price of bonds. Market interest rates at the maturity of bonds purchased will fall directly, and adjacent maturities should display similar changes very quickly. Commercial banks will experience a rise in cash reserves, presumably surplus to requirements; money market interest rates and treasury bill rates should slip somewhat, and there may be some consequential easing in deposit and loan rates set by the retail banks. From this point, the transmission mechanism will display the sequence of changes in aggregate nominal demand, prices and wages similar to that studied above. The key difference between the transmission mechanism relating to a change in (some definition of) the supply of money, and the transmission mechanism for a change in interest rates, is that the former introduces a prior stage. This prior stage is the set of effects stemming directly from the money supply change. In the case of open market operations, these direct effects take the primary form of alterations in the prices and yields of the bonds that the authorities have bought and sold. Various other interest rates move in response.

When the money supply change emanates from budget deficits or payments surpluses that are less than fully offset by bond sales to the domestic non-bank public, the initial consequences differ somewhat. The larger the proportion of the budget deficit or payments surpluses covered by bond sales, the likelier it is that bond prices will fall rather than rise (unless larger bond sales and the associated lower monetary growth cause inflation expectations to be lower). Pressure on interest rates will be upward if this is so. When the proportion is small, so that substantial monetisation occurs, short interest rates are likely to fall, transmitting muted downward pressure on other interest rates.

This is one reason for uncertainty about the pattern of interest rate changes consequent upon a rise in the money supply. There are others. The benefits that holders derive from balances stem from real holdings, not nominal holdings. Thus if the money supply increase is matched by inflation, real money is unchanged, and there is no 'excess supply of money' to exert effects in other markets. Even when real money holdings do increase, the direction of interest rate changes is not necessarily downward. Real money demand might have risen in response to higher wealth or income; greater uncertainty; financial innovation; changes in intermediation patterns, transactions technology or the character of structure; or degree of competition in the provision of financial services. In such cases there may again be 'no excess supply of money'.

Furthermore, when money is initially in excess supply, there could be reasons for increases rather than reductions in nominal interest rates. One such is the traditional (if somewhat suspect) idea of real balance effects. These postulate a direct link between real money holdings and consumption. An unanticipated increase in the real level of currency or bank deposits, surplus to needs, could lead directly to higher consumption spending on the part of agents experiencing it. Additional outlays on consumer durables (like money, an asset) are particularly likely; and for households restricted by credit limits from spending what they would like, higher spending may well follow. Extra general consumption spending by a fringe of hitherto unsatisfied borrowers, or on durables by recipients of what are treated as windfall gains, will tend to raise equilibrium interest rates all else being equal, and not to lower them. There is also the possibility that market observers may raise their expectations of future growth of nominal money. That should lead them to predict faster inflation, and hence higher equilibrium nominal rates of interest. This should show up in some rise in at least long-term nominal interest rates now. Finally, there is the point that untoward or unexpected rises in nominal or real monetary aggregates may prompt the authorities to increase official interest rates, and that even if they do not do so immediately, the market may expect them to do so later on.

All this leads to the conclusion that it is perilous to draw inferences about how interest rates should respond to a rise in the supply of money. They could fall; they could also rise. The initial stage in the transmission mechanism for a change in the supply of money – its impact on interest rates – is therefore far from certain, even in direction, let alone magnitude or timing. These considerations also reinforce the case for concentrating on the official rate of interest as the key instrument of monetary policy.

3.6 Inflation dynamics – some facts

Table 3.4 in the Appendix reports evidence about inflation for 135 countries. It explores the link between the change in inflation from one year to the next on one side, and an earlier level of inflation, 1 or 2 years previously, on the other. If monetary policy stabilises the rate of inflation, we would expect the coefficient on earlier inflation to be negative. In all the countries reported it is indeed negative, and often significantly so, especially for advanced countries. Data relate to the period from 1981 to 2000, sampled at quarterly frequencies, and in some cases restricted to a more recent span of years. The constant terms are invariably positive, though often not significantly. The ratio of the estimated constant to the estimated coefficient on the lagged level of inflation gives a figure for the *equilibrium* rate of inflation. This is an equilibrium in a purely statistical sense: it is the average level of inflation that would have emerged for the country and period under inquiry, had it been constant throughout the period. In some cases the change in inflation between years 2 and 3 captures the influence of the level of inflation in year 1; in others it is the influence of inflation in year 0 that is given. The choice between the two was made on the basis of relative statistical significance.

The equilibrium rate of inflation for a country is not the same thing as the average rate of inflation over the given period. It is better treated as the core rate of inflation which monetary policy succeeded in restoring, after disturbances. It covers both the 1980s and the 1990s for most countries. In certain cases a narrower span, later in the period, had to be chosen because of data limitations, the need to obtain correct signs for the coefficients, or the creation of new states within formerly communist countries. Furthermore, the aims of monetary policy were not necessarily stable over these decades. So the equilibrium inflation estimates do not tell us about the countries' monetary policy objectives now, at the start of the new millennium, but rather what they appear to have been, on average, over the 1980s and 1990s as a whole. In the developed world, the English-speaking Caribbean (Jamaica aside), Chile, and a group of mostly smaller Asian economies, statistical equilibrium inflation rates are close to 2 per cent or 3 per cent per year. In Japan and Singapore, they are around 1 per cent; in Korea, Portugal and Trinidad and Tobago, nearer to 6 or 7 per cent. In Latin America, most statistical equilibrium inflation rates lie in one of two ranges. The lower one, from 9 to 46 per cent, embraces the majority, but in Argentina, Bolivia, Brazil and Peru, they are close to 500–600 per cent, with Nicaragua heading the list at over 2,000 per cent. Africa is diverse, varying from 2 per cent or less in Niger and Tunisia to over 1,400 per cent in Angola.

Equilibrium inflation rates implied by our regressions make an interesting contrast with the results for the average speed with which implied inflation disequilibria were corrected. We calculated implicit half-lives for inflation disequilibria (IHID) for all sampled countries, and regressed implied equilibrium inflation (IEI) rates upon them, and upon real GDP per head. The results were interesting. Richer countries tended to have lower inflation and/or more short-lived inflation disequilibria than poorer ones. There proved to be a reasonably robust negative association between the level of inflation and how quickly inflation discrepancies were removed (see the scatter plot in Figure 3.4). The faster the rate of inflation, then, the more quickly inflation adjusted back to its econometrically determined equilibrium value. This fits with the idea that the transmission mechanism for monetary policy works faster at high rates of inflation. This said, a word of caution is appropriate. These results tell us nothing about what *caused* inflation. Hendry's (2000) study of British inflation from 1875 to 1991 shows that the causation of inflation is a very complex issue, in practice as much as in theory. In the next section, we shall try to throw light on just one influence on changing inflation: interest rate policy.

3.7 Interest rates and disinflation

Bringing down the rate of inflation is not an easy task. When inflation is very rapid, the challenge is to set up a new framework for monetary policy that people can trust. A credible counter-inflation strategy is the key. When this is in place, disinflation can be very rapid. When inflation has recently been very high, firms and workers have learnt, painfully, to reprice goods, services and labour frequently, and many contracts will have become indexed or denominated in foreign currency. The crucial thing is to lower inflation expectations. Once this is achieved, disinflation can proceed swiftly and almost costlessly. This has long been known: Sargent (1982) provides compelling evidence of this. A sharp reduction in inflation expectations can be brought about by currency reform (as in Germany in November 1923), the adoption of a currency board (as in Argentina, Bosnia, Bulgaria, Estonia and Lithuania in the 1990s), or when a new legal framework for the central bank is

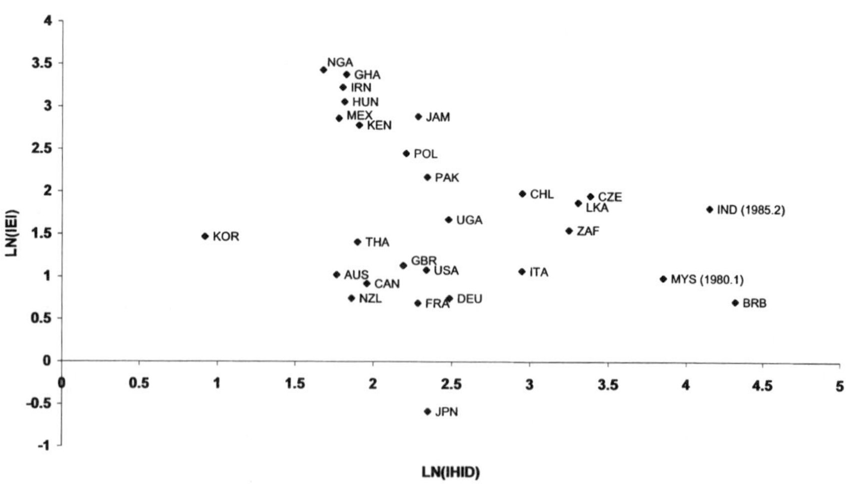

Figure 3.4 Inflation equilibrium vs half life (subgroup) 1990–2000.

imposed (Peru, 1994). Not all reforms have lasting or even initial success, but many do.

Reducing the rate of inflation poses different difficulties when it is proceeding at a modest rate. Paradoxically, the lower the rate of inflation, the harder it appears to reduce it further. The intervals of time between pay settlements or price revisions are long. Expectations of inflation are sticky, and often appear to need a substantial drop in output, relative to trend, to knock them down. Granting operational independence to the central bank, and the adoption of a regime of inflation targeting, may bring substantial benefits, particularly, perhaps, when these changes are combined. The alternative of tying the domestic currency to another, with a superior record of inflation containment, has often proved valuable, too.[2]

Short of radical measures of this kind – or after they or something similar have been done – the task of trimming an inflation regarded as excessive is usually done most appropriately by raising official nominal interest rates temporarily. The sequence of events already described should ensue. Interest rates will edge upwards on mortgages, loans, advances, deposits and government bills and bonds. The prices of real estate and equities should recede. Through a variety of mechanisms, private sector spending on consumption (particularly on durables), and investment should start to decline or at least rise at reduced rates. Exchange rates, if free to float, are liable to appreciate, and the trade balance will tend to worsen as and when this happens. The reduction in aggregate demand will translate into a weakening in the demand for labour, reducing the rate of pay increases. Goods and services prices should rise more slowly as a result. Meanwhile, product market developments should lead directly to some trimming of price rises, particularly in traded goods sectors if the exchange rate has appreciated.

However, merely raising policy rates may not be enough. For one thing, inflation expectations may have risen already. Raising policy rates by the amount of any rise in the rate of expected inflation will merely keep them steady in real terms, contributing no net disinflationary impulse. Raising them by less than any rise in inflation expectations will actually exert a counter-disinflationary effect. The critical point is that policy rates will only start to generate disinflation if they are held above a neutral value that matches the sum of relevant real rates, expected inflation and any risk premium. Bringing them up to this neutral level will only succeed in preventing further inflationary impacts. To achieve disinflation, policy rates must exceed their neutral value.

These ideas are illustrated in a simplified form in Figure 3.5. In the lower left quadrant, year 2001's central bank nominal interest rate, 'Bank Rate', is measured downwards from the origin O. Year 2001's expectations of year 2002's inflation are measured leftwards. Two lines appear in this quadrant. Both slope up. The line FF gives the Fisher condition that an equilibrium value of the nominal interest rate rises one-for-one with

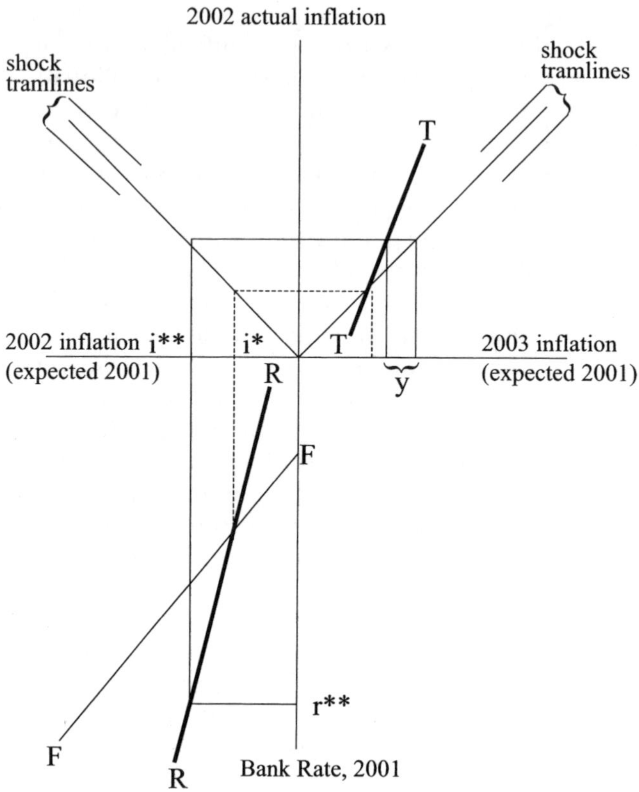

Figure 3.5 Interest rates and disinflation.

expected inflation. Its intercept on the vertical axis captures the real (1-year) rate of interest. The steeper line, RR, depicts the central bank's interest rate rule. The FF and RR lines cross at a presumed ideal rate of inflation, i^*. If the bank rate were set at the Fisher level, which we can identify with Wicksell's natural rate of interest, there will be no systematic tendency for inflation to rise or fall. (The relation between the Taylor rule and the Wicksellian natural rate of interest is quite a complex one; see Woodford (2000) for a powerful dissection).

The upper left quadrant describes the relation between current expectations of year 2002's inflation, and what it will turn out to be. These two numbers should differ only by unanticipated shocks, indicated by the tramlines. In the upper right quadrant, the horizontal axis measures, rightwards, the rate of inflation now expected for year 2003. The line TT shows the effects of setting the bank rate according to the rule RR.

The diagram abstracts from other relevant variables, such as the output gap. If inflation in year 2002 is now expected to be i^{**}, the rule should set bank rate at r^{**}. The difference between r^{**} and i^{**} is the interest rate gap. In the diagram, year 2001's gap is assumed to lower inflation between 2002 and 2003, by the distance y. The linearity embedded in the diagram implies that y will be proportional to the gap. It is important that the rule line RR should be steeper than FF – if it were flatter, inflation would diverge from its ideal value. (Clearly there will also be a problem if RR is steeper than FF, in circumstances when expected inflation is below its ideal value – this is the challenge posed by the zero bound to bank rate). In what follows in this section, we shall attempt to quantify the size of the sensitivity of y to the interest rate gap for a large group of countries.

To gain a quantitative impression of how inflation responds to the gap between actual official rates and their neutral levels, the following procedure was adopted. First, a 'world' real short-term interest rate series was constructed. This involved averaging up to three relevant short-term interest rates within 20 advanced countries, then subtracting the annual rate of change of that country's GDP deflator, and weighting the ensuing estimated real rates by the country's share of total GDP in 1998. The world real-rate series was then smoothed by a 3-year moving average. The average difference between each country's actual nominal interest series, and the sum of its GDP-deflator inflation rate and the world real-rate series, was then obtained. This gives a measure of the average implicit risk premium on short-term nominal assets denominated in the country's currency, and was calculated for the period 1980–2000. The neutral rate of country i in year t was then defined as this average country-i risk premium, in addition to the sum of: (a) a moving average world short ex post real interest rate, and (b) a moving average of the rate of inflation in country i.

When relevant policy rates exceeded their neutral value, the difference should be expected to lower inflation subsequently. When the gap is negative, the opposite could be predicted. The evidence from regressions of inflation changes on previous values of the 'interest rate gap' is somewhat mixed. Statistically significant and correctly-signed coefficients are obtained for the United States and for Japan, and for a few other countries as well. However, in the main, results for individual countries are not significant. There is also some disparity in the timing of effects, with the change in inflation between years $t + 2$ and $t + 1$ sometimes being more responsive to the interest gap in year t, and sometimes to the gap a year earlier. Pooling groups of countries and imposing a common coefficient on the gap that individual country regressions revealed to be more promising resulted, however, in some statistically significant results.

As a broad rule of thumb, an interest rate gap of 1 per cent – so that the central bank rate is 1 per cent on average above its neutral value for 1 year – reduces inflation by about 0.36 per cent either 2 or 3 years later. This was the average finding for a group of industrialised countries.

In the United States, the coefficient on the interest rate gap in year t

was smaller (0.212), and for Japan it was 0.427. Israel's (0.765) and Australia's (0.517) were higher, and Singapore's rather lower (0.343). Of these five countries, the gap coefficient was significant in all except the United States. The poor significance and low coefficient for the United States might testify to its large role in determining world real rates.

For some countries, confining the sample period to the decade 1990–2000 produced better results. For Canada, for example, it produced a statistically significant coefficient on the interest rate gap of 0.762, almost as high as Israel's for the full 20 years. There were, somewhat disturbingly, however, quite a few countries for which the interest rate gap coefficient was wrongly signed. For Madagascar, it was large and significant, as well as perverse. The likely reason for this and similar anomalies for some other developing countries is the fact that the risk premium is in practice not stationary. When a debt or foreign exchange crisis afflicts a country, for example, the risk premium is liable to rise suddenly, and a quickening of the rate of inflation may well ensue too. Official interest rates will of course go up in circumstances such as these, but probably not by enough to match the risk premium, and if this is so, the stance of monetary policy will not be disinflationary.

These regressions attempt to pinpoint the amount of disinflation that a country can achieve on its own, by holding interest rates above the value implied by the sum of world real rates, domestic inflation and the country's own long-run risk premium. It does not take account of the disinflation resulting from abnormally high world real rates resulting from similar actions undertaken by other central banks, which will form another part of the story. Disinflation proceeds from two channels. The domestic channel involves holding domestic policy rates above their neutral value at current values of world real interest rates. There is also a foreign channel of disinflation, if other central banks around the world are acting similarly. It is only the first of these channels upon which our results throw light.

Appendix

In this appendix, regression results for the long-run tests of uncovered interest parity appear in Tables 3.1 and 3.2 (which relate to OECD and non-OECD currencies respectively). The much less successful short run tests of UIP follow in Table 3.3. After these, the reader will find Table 3.4, which presents data on inflation persistence, country by country.

This leaves one final table, which aims to throw empirical light on the all-important question, does monetary policy actually seem to work? To test the effect a tightening or loosening of monetary policy has on inflation later on, it was necessary to begin by constructing a 'neutral' value of each country's nominal interest rate. This was defined as the sum of three components: (i) the country's actual 5-year backward-looking moving

Table 3.1 Long-run UIP between the US and other OECD currencies

Ordinary Least Squares regression of the annual average change in the value of 22 other OECD currencies against the United States Dollar, on a constant and that country's annual average interest differential vis-à-vis the United States. Period of cross country estimation: 1981 to 1998.

$$\Delta\text{Exchange rate} = \underset{(0.384)}{0.001^*\text{constant}} + \underset{(14.143)^{***}}{1.039^*\text{int diff}}$$

R^2	0.909
Adj. R^2	0.905
Std of reg.	0.013
No. obs.	22

Notes
t-stats in brackets
*** represent significance at 1% level

Table 3.2 Long-run UIP between the US and non-OECD currencies

OLS regression of the annual average change in the value of 115 non-OECD currencies against the United States Dollar, on a constant and that country's annual average interest differential vis-à-vis the United States. Period of cross country estimation: 1980 to 1999, adjusted according to most recent available complete data.

$$\Delta\text{Exchange rate} = \underset{(2.810)^{***}}{0.035^*\text{constant}} + \underset{(14.218)^{***}}{1.001^*\text{int diff}}$$

R^2	0.6414
Adj. R^2	0.638
Std of reg.	0.108
No. obs	115

Notes
t-stats in brackets.
*** represent significance at 1% level.

average rate of inflation; (ii) the 5-year backward-looking moving average of the GDP-weighted average real (annual, *ex post*) rate of interest for the OECD area; and (iii) the period average risk premium (the average excess, for the entire period, of the annual real interest rate in the country in question, over the OECD rate).

The next task was to identify deviations of each country's policy rate from this neutral rate. A positive deviation suggests that monetary policy is restrictive, and therefore that inflation should fall subsequently. A negative deviation suggests that policy is expansionary, and that inflation should rise. The deviation can be called 'the policy rate gap'.

The change in inflation (between years 1 and 2) was then regressed on the policy rate gap in years 0 and –1. Separate regressions were conducted for each country for which data were available; Table 3.4 presents the results for 88 countries. All countries for which at least 14 observations

Table 3.3 UIP test using annual data

	Constant	*Interest differential*	*90% confidence interval*		*Number of observations*
GBR	5.021 (1.45)	–0.977 (–1)	–2.679	0.725	19
AUT	–1.04 (–0.33)	–1.036 (–1.06)	–2.74	0.667	18
BEL	3.874 (1.09)	–1.795 (–1.15)	–4.53	0.94	18
DNK	2.886 (0.86)	–0.757 (–0.61)	–2.924	1.41	19
FRA	4.1 (0.94)	–0.659 (–0.47)	–3.097	1.779	18
DEU	–0.733 (–0.23)	–0.876 (–0.86)	–2.654	0.902	18
ITA	–1.276 (–0.14)	1.062 (0.7)	–1.578	3.703	18
LUX	4.181 (1.07)	–1.508 (–0.95)	–4.273	1.258	18
NLD	–0.716 (–0.23)	–1.314 (–1.22)	–3.19	0.561	18
NOR	6.051 (2.32)**	–1.097 (–1.87)*	–2.115	–0.079	19
SWE	5.447 (1.34)	–0.451 (–0.42)	–2.327	1.425	19
CHE	–2.768 (–0.92)	–1.223 (–1.8)*	–2.403	–0.043	19
CAN	2.621 (1.95)*	–0.71 (–1.29)	–1.667	0.247	19
JPN	–12.829 (–3.3)***	–3.247 (–3.06)***	–5.096	–1.399	19
FIN	3.141 (0.88)	–0.222 (–0.21)	–2.104	1.66	18
GRC	23.599 (2.27)**	–1.09 (–1.21)	–2.663	0.482	19
ISL	5.477 (0.49)	1.05 (1.38)	–0.272	2.373	19
IRL	1.083 (0.22)	0.43 (0.4)	–1.458	2.318	18
PRT	12.535 (1.93)*	–0.623 (–0.78)	–2.022	0.775	18
ESP	5.163 (0.8)	–0.02 (–0.02)	–1.935	1.894	18
AUS	5.954 (2.01)*	–0.718 (–1.2)	–1.759	0.324	19
NZL	10.471 (3.74)***	–1.398 (–3.32)***	–2.131	–0.666	19

Notes

Regression of percentage change in exchange rate (vis-à-vis US dollar) on a constant, and the interest differential between that country and the US.

Annual data; sample period: 1980 2000;***, **, *, significance of estimate at 1%, 5%, and 10% respectively; t-statistics in brackets; data source: International Financial Statistics.

were available were included, as were two other countries with fewer observations (China and Indonesia), because of their importance. Table 3.4 presents the full results for the coefficients on the policy rate gap, or its lagged value, with t ratios in brackets.

The GDP-weighted average value of the coefficient on the policy rate gap was also calculated for groups of countries. These were:

Whole world (105 countries):	–0.1828
OECD area (16 countries):	–0.1937
Commonwealth area (34 countries):	–0.2459
Asia (9 countries):	–0.282
Africa (33 countries):	–0.0039
Transition (2 countries):	–0.0298.

Table 3.4 Estimates of the impact a non-neutral central bank rate has on the rate of inflation 2 or 3 years later

	x	x_{-1}	*Number of observations*
USA	–0.23 (–1.763)*		19
UK	–0.14 (–0.86)		19
Austria		–0.1 (–0.768)	18
Belgium		–0.163 (–1.832)*	18
Denmark		–0.015 (–0.142)	18
France		–0.039 (–0.315)	18
Germany		–0.202 (–1.505)	18
Italy		0.166 (1.073)	18
Luxembrg		–0.255 (–2.682)**	18
Netherlds		–0.126 (–0.88)	14
Norway	0.009 (0.051)		19
Sweden	–0.233 (–0.727)		19
Switzerld	–0.394 (–2.253)**		19
Canada	–0.369 (–2.867)**		19
Japan	–0.266 (–2.065)*		19
Finland	0.163 (0.858)		19
Greece	0.007 (0.028)		19
Ireland		0.103 (0.566)	18
Malta		0.115 (0.426)	18
Portugal	–0.193 (–1.059)		19
Spain	0.138 (1.474)		19
Turkey	0.188 (0.766)		19
Australia	–0.628 (–3.073)***		19
New Zeald		–0.223 (–0.844)	18
S Africa		–0.009 (–0.072)	18
Argentina		0 (–0.019)	18
Brazil	–0.077 (–0.764)		14
Chile		–0.157 (–1.71)	18
Colombia		–0.128 (–0.561)	18
Costa R'a		–0.181 (–0.563)	18
Ecuador		0.731 (2.038)*	18
Mexico		–0.209 (–0.613)	16
Peru	–0.087 (–0.265)		19
Uruguay	–0.306 (–4.409)***		18
Venezuela	0.421 (0.688)		19
Bahamas		–0.084 (–0.466)	18
Barbados	–0.124 (–0.443)		19
Dominica	0.202 (2.317)**		19
Grenada		0.09 (1.035)	16
Jamaica		–0.746 (–1.173)	18
Antigua		–0.011 (–0.033)	18
Kitts Nevis		–0.449 (–0.705)	14
St Lucia		0.019 (0.071)	17
St Vincent		0.134 (0.747)	18
Trinidad	0.024 (0.173)		19
Cyprus		0.147 (0.806)	18

continued

Table 3.4 Continued

	x	x_{-1}	*Number of observations*
Israel	–0.359 (–3.651)***		15
Jordan		–0.05 (–0.109)	18
Kuwait		0.171 (0.933)	18
Syria		0.039 (0.125)	18
Egypt	0.046 (0.153)		19
Sri Lanka	–0.361 (–0.812)		19
India		–0.076 (–0.172)	18
Indonesia	–0.745 (–0.989)		9
Korea		–0.114 (–0.812)	18
Malaysia		–0.211 (–0.965)	17
Nepal	–0.189 (–0.428)		19
Pakistan	–0.422 (–1.784)*		19
Philippines		–0.234 (–0.337)	18
Singapore	–0.324 (–2.679)**		19
Thailand	–1.012 (–1.847)*		19
Botswana	–0.152 (–0.702)		19
Burundi		–0.113 (–0.185)	18
Cameroon		–0.039 (–0.068)	18
Congo (Z)	0.183 (0.176)		14
Gabon		–0.067 (–0.101)	16
Gambia	0.15 (0.349)		19
Ghana	0.169 (0.546)		19
IvoryCoast		–0.074 (–0.166)	18
Kenya	–0.66 (–2.653)**		19
Lesotho	–0.159 (–0.838)		19
Malawi	–0.856 (–0.935)		14
Mauritius		0.221 (0.921)	18
Niger		0.2 (0.427)	18
Nigeria	–0.299 (–0.249)		19
Zimbabwe		0.135 (0.208)	15
Rwanda	0.287 (0.346)		19
Seychelles		0.146 (0.693)	17
Senegal		0.102 (0.207)	18
Sierra L'e	0.101 (0.227)		19
Tanzania	–0.067 (–0.727)		17
Togo		0.14 (0.232)	18
Solomons	–0.06 (–0.095)		17
Fiji		0.064 (0.143)	18
Papua NG	–0.355 (–0.916)		19
China	–0.237 (–0.361)		8
Hungary	–0.11 (–0.182)		14
Poland	–0.003 (–0.004)		15

Notes

Regression of the change in inflation (forward two years) on current or lagged x, where x = nominal interest rate – country inflation rate – (world interest rate + country risk premium) Annual data. Sample period 1980–2000. ***, **, *, significance of estimate at 1%, 5%, and 10% respectively.

t-statistics in brackets.

Data source: International Financial Statistics, International Monetary Fund.

Part 2

Building structural models of the monetary policy transmission

4 Model-building in theory and practice

The output gap

Lavan Mahadeva

4.1 Introduction

When demand rises above supply, an output gap may open up, indicating an upward pressure on inflation. In monetary policy models it is common to see this effect captured by a Phillips curve where an output gap term is linked to inflation. That the Phillips curve is so common, though, belies that in practice it can be difficult to find an output gap measure that both shows a systematic relation to inflation on past data and can also be used to produce a satisfactory forecasts of future inflation. The practical difficulties to be overcome in estimating output gaps are also more challenging in developing countries, where output data is less timely and less reliable.[1]

The aim of this chapter is to clarify what the output gap means and why it is needed, and then link that to the practice of measurement. The purpose is therefore *not* to survey or evaluate the many different techniques for estimating the output gap that are available in the literature. As different measures tend to give different results, a model-builder who wants to work with an output gap measure will have to choose among these techniques. However, we would argue that much is to be gained by first understanding what in essence a measure of the output gap aims to capture, before going on to evaluate why or why not any particular strategy might work for a particular country or given data set.

From the outset we base out analysis squarely on one concept of the output gap. Here we adopt the premise that, for monetary policy purposes, the output gap should be thought of as the deviation of actual from the flexible-price level of output,[2] where the flexible-price level of output is that which would hold if there were no costs to adjusting nominal variables.

The output gap is often described in other terms in the literature. Reference is made to the output gap as the deviations of actual from 'full-capacity output'; or deviations from the 'non-inflationary level of output', and, sometimes, deviations from 'trend output'. Of course, any or all of these alternative definitions may in principle be consistent with the flexible-price definition. But they would need to be formalised with economic theory if we were to judge, and typically this rigorous underpinning of the empirical measure with theory is lacking.

Nelson (1989) provides a formal definition of an output gap concept that differs from the flexible-price concept that we adopt. He describes the output gap as deviations from the level of output that would hold in the absence of rigidities in adjusting the capital stock. His flexible-capital measure is similar to the microeconomic definition of the short run as a state where the capital stock is taken to be fixed.[3] However, we argue that only the flexible-price output gap concept is aimed directly at what matters for monetary policy: the deviation of actual output from the long-run level where capital is free to adjust is a different measure of output disequilibrium to that which we are interested in.

Why then are monetary policymakers (at least in principle) interested in measuring the deviation of actual output from its flexible-price level? A primary monetary policy interest in output gap measurement is the purpose of shock identification. As price developments resulting from nominal shocks can be very different to responses to 'real-side' shocks (shocks that affect flexible-price output), reference to a flexible-price output measure can in principle help in minimising output losses of pursuing price stability.[4] The potentially useful feature of the flexible-price state for this purpose is that it is defined by an absence of nominal rigidities: real decisions are independent of nominal values. In particular, as nominal shocks will leave flexible-price output untouched, the hope is that monetary policymakers can identify nominal shocks by observing what happens to an accurate measure of flexible-price output.

In formalisations of the monetary policy problem, it is typical to see the objectives of monetary policy stated in terms of both current and expected deviations of inflation from target and the output gap. A separate, deeper question we then tackle is whether we can go on to focus on just the volatility of the output gap rather than that of output as a whole when capturing output costs in monetary policy objectives. Would a flexible-price measure of potential output serve also for the purpose of more sharply defining objectives? We show that a key assumption needed here is nominal neutrality – that actual output will on average be equal to its flexible-price level when we abstract from nominal shocks – implying that there is no danger of permanently affecting actual output with nominal monetary policy actions. But what we also show to be important is a stronger restriction, that shocks that move flexible-price output are expected to affect the short-run path of actual output by the same proportion, leaving their proportionate difference – the output gap – untouched. By way of example, we show that many models in use (such as those with significant non-linearities) do not satisfy these latter restrictions.

Whether or not it is the output gap rather than output that matters for objectives, our ultimate interest in measuring flexible-price output is that, in principle at least, it can help us to understand what shocks are happening to output and inflation, and how monetary policy actions should be lined up against them. It follows that central banks are interested in forecasting and not just estimating flexible-price output. The distinction between estimating a model and forecasting with it is important. Forecasting involves a broader campaign to model the flexible-price level of output and not just to derive a data series of past values for it.

It follows from this that to measure the output gap we may need to look beyond output data itself. We should recognise that not only output but also other macroeconomic variables have their flexible-price values; values that are consistent with no nominal stickiness in the economy. For example, the real exchange rate has a fundamental equilibrium value; the unemployment rate has a NAIRU; and the equilibrium real interest rate, a 'Wicksellian'[5] value.[6] Much monetary policy research has proposed that deviations of other variables from their flexible-price values can inform us about inflationary pressure. We suggest that it is useful to understand how flexible-price output is related to the flexible-price values of other variables, if only because there may be more data available on these other parts of the economy. To take us further in this direction, we develop a small, dynamic general equilibrium model of a developing country that distinguishes between the flexible-price and actual economy. The model helps us to understand the link between the output gap and the 'real disequilibria'[7] (the difference between the actual values and the flexible-price values) of other variables, as well as bringing out some practical messages for output gap measurement.

4.2 A definition of flexible-price output and the role of nominal rigidities

The output gap is the difference between actual output and its potential level, and to define the output gap one must define potential output. Our favoured definition of potential output is *the flexible-price level of output*: the hypothetical level of GDP that would hold at time t if nominal variables, such as wages, prices or the nominal exchange rate, were always fully flexible now and in the past, and would be so in the future.[8] Understanding the output gap helps identify the appropriate monetary policy stance; i.e. that is consistent with achieving the monetary policy target without incurring excessive output costs.

Our aim in this section is to formalise these intuitions about the purpose of potential output measurement in monetary policy forecasting. Later on in this section we derive analytic solutions for a simple theoretical model of an economy from micro-foundations to demonstrate our understanding of the output gap. However, here we summarise the transmission mechanism in a more general form; describing it as the reduced form solutions for the log of real output (y_t); inflation (π_t); all the other endogenous variables ($\mathbf{Z}_{1t}$, $\mathbf{Z}_{2t}$) as a function of their past values; the current, past and expected future values of the exogenous variables ($\mathbf{q}_{1t}$, $\mathbf{q}_{2t}$); and the nominal interest rates (i_t).

Writing $\mathbf{X}_{rt} \equiv (\{y_s\}_{s=-\infty}^{t-1}, \{Z_{1s}\}_{s=-\infty}^{t-1})$ as the vector of all past values of endogenous real variables and $\mathbf{X}_{nt} \equiv (\{\pi_s\}_{s=-\infty}^{t-1}, \{\mathbf{Z}_{2s}\}_{s=-\infty}^{t-1})$ as the vector of all past values of all endogenous nominal values, the transmission mechanism in reduced form and conditional on interest rates is given by equations (4.1)–(4.6)

$$y_t = f_y\left(\varphi, \mathbf{X}_{rt}, \mathbf{E}_{\varphi,t}\left\{\mathbf{q}_{1s}\right\}_{s=-\infty}^{\infty} \middle| \mathbf{X}_{nt}, E_{\varphi,t}\left\{\mathbf{q}_{2s}\right\}_{s=-\infty}^{\infty}, E_{\varphi,t}\left\{i_s\right\}_{s=t}^{\infty}\right) \tag{4.1}$$

$$\pi_t = f_\pi\left(\varphi, \mathbf{X}_{rt}, E_{\varphi,t}\left\{\mathbf{q}_{1s}\right\}_{s=-\infty}^{\infty} \middle| \mathbf{X}_{nt}, E_{\varphi,t}\left\{\mathbf{q}_{2s}\right\}_{s=-\infty}^{\infty}, E_{\varphi,t}\left\{i_s\right\}_{s=t}^{\infty}\right) \tag{4.2}$$

$$\mathbf{Z}_{1t} = \mathbf{f}_{z1}\left(\varphi, \mathbf{X}_{rt}, E_{\varphi,t}\left\{\mathbf{q}_{1s}\right\}_{s=-\infty}^{\infty} \middle| \mathbf{X}_{nt}, E_{\varphi,t}\left\{\mathbf{q}_{2s}\right\}_{s=-\infty}^{\infty}, E_{\varphi,t}\left\{i_s\right\}_{s=t}^{\infty}\right) \tag{4.3}$$

$$\mathbf{Z}_{2t} = \mathbf{f}_{z2}\left(\varphi, \mathbf{X}_{rt}, E_{\varphi,t}\left\{\mathbf{q}_{1s}\right\}_{s=-\infty}^{\infty} \middle| \mathbf{X}_{nt}, E_{\varphi,t}\left\{\mathbf{q}_{2s}\right\}_{s=-\infty}^{\infty}, E_{\varphi,t}\left\{i_s\right\}_{s=t}^{\infty}\right) \tag{4.4}$$

$$\mathbf{q}_{1t} = \mathrm{f}_{q1}\left(\theta_1, E_{\theta 1}\left\{\mathbf{q}_{1s}\right\}_{s=-\infty}^{\infty}\right) \tag{4.5}$$

and

$$\mathbf{q}_{2t} = \mathbf{f}_{q2}\left(\theta_2, E_{\theta 2}\left\{\mathbf{q}_{2s}\right\}_{s=-\infty}^{\infty}\right) \tag{4.6}$$

The system described by these equations is a general formulation of the transmission mechanism, and leaves out many interesting details. However, it serves for the purpose of defining flexible-price output because it emphasises the difference between the real and nominal sides of the economy. Defining nominal variables as those that can only be measured in contemporary units of domestic currency either in levels or as rates of change, we designate $\mathbf{Z}_{2t}$ as the vector of current values of all nominal endogenous variables except for the inflation rate (the objective) and the nominal interest rate (the policy instrument). Variables which are not nominal are all designated as real, and $\mathbf{Z}_{1t}$ is the vector of any other real endogenous variables apart from output (the objective) in the system. $\mathbf{q}_{1t}$ is the vector of real exogenous variables and $\mathbf{q}_{2t}$ is the vector of nominal exogenous variables.[9] $E_{\varphi,t}z_{t+s}$ denotes the conditional expectation of a variable, z_{t+s}, formed at time t using the information set which is conditional on parameters φ. We use this notation to be explicit about rigidities in the updating of information sets that are used to make expectations. Also note that all variable are defined in logs or as rates of change, apart from interest rates.

Nominal rigidities are what matter in defining flexible-price output. To emphasise this, we have partitioned the set of parameters of the system, φ

= (φ_1, φ_2) and θ = (θ_1, θ_2), into either one of two categories.[10] (θ_2, φ_2 describes the set of parameters that describe only the costs of adjustment of nominal variables in the economy; these are the parameters that make agents care about nominal values. (θ_1, φ_1) refers to all other parameters. That we can separate parameters into two disjoint sets means that, at least conceptually, we can distinguish the parameters that imply only nominal rigidities from other parameters, even if, as we shall show, theories of nominal rigidities often also imply real rigidities. The state of there being no costs of nominal adjustment is defined by parameter values of (θ_2, φ_2) = ($\bar{\theta}_2$, $\bar{\varphi}_2$).

We now only need to determine the policy instrument to complete our description of the economy. The nominal interest rate, i_t, is set to minimise the central bank's loss function, subject to the central bank's understanding of the transmission mechanism and whilst taking the public's expectations of the sequence of interest rates as given.[11] The central bank's one-period loss function is assumed to be composed of a weighted average of the conditional variances of output and inflation, with the inflation variance being measured around a positive target rate. The infinite horizon objective is then to minimise the sum of current and future one-period loss functions.[12]

$$E_{\varphi,t}\left\{i_s\right\}_{s=t}^{\infty} \quad \text{minimises} \quad \sum_{s=t}^{\infty} E_{\varphi,s}\left(y_s\right)^2 + \lambda E_{\varphi,s}\left(\pi_s - \pi_L\right)^2 \tag{4.7}$$

given equations (4.1)–(4.6).

That output matters in objectives is a crucial assumption in our discussion of the output gap, but not a controversial one. Svensson (2001: 65) argues that, in practice, all inflation-targeting central banks are concerned (and should be concerned), about short-run output losses as well as inflation stabilisation. What is perhaps more controversial is that we are assuming a quadratic loss function, where inflation and output are separable in objectives. As we show later, the assumption of a quadratic loss function matters if we want to reformulate objectives in terms of the output gap and inflation rather than output and inflation.[13] Note also that we are allowing for rigidities in the processing of information in the central bank's forecast; we argue later that this can constitute an important type of nominal rigidity.

Monetary policy decisions are made under uncertain conditions, so we have included the underlying sources of uncertainty – both real and nominal shocks – that make the system described by equations (4.1)–(4.7) stochastic in $\mathbf{q}_{1t}$ and $\mathbf{q}_{2t}$. For example a surprise shift in the target rate of inflation in an inflation-targeting regime that is unrelated to any other developments captured in the model would be a member of $\mathbf{q}_{1t}$ in our characterisation, and a sudden change in weather conditions would constitute a member of $\mathbf{q}_{2t}$.[14,15]

The factors that make up $\mathbf{q}_{1t}$ and $\mathbf{q}_{2t}$ are described as being 'underlying' or 'deep', in the sense that they are exogenous to the system. To be more precise, we are assuming that the parameters that govern the processes affecting each member of $\mathbf{q}_{1t}$ and $\mathbf{q}_{2t}$ do not depend on the parameters that affect any of the other variables in the system, either directly or through the influence of any other variable.[16] Given our categorisation that each parameter must either be associated with nominal rigidities or not, this implies that parameter sets (θ_1, φ_1, θ_2, φ_2) are all disjoint with each other. In particular, the real exogenous variables are assumed not to depend on nominal rigidities, even in the short run.

Even if nominal shocks are unrelated to real shocks in this deep sense, their entangled effects on endogenous variables may be all that is visible to agents. As they are unable fully to discern which is which, agents' expectations of real and nominal shocks can covary. This would constitute a nominal rigidity in the spirit of Friedman (1968) and Lucas (1972). There could also be rigidities in the updating of information sets that agents use to make expectations of future nominal variables (Sargent 1999;[17] Ball 2000; Mankiw and Reis 2001; Sims 2001). It takes resources to process and transmit economic information accurately, and so agents will not always take new releases of information at face value. Instead they prefer to rely to some extent on what they assumed in the past. For example, the central bank may announce a shift in the inflation target but it can take time for agents to update their views as to the monetary policy strategy in place. The slow convergence to a new regime could constitute a significant nominal rigidity, as in Sargent (1999: Chapter 3).[18]

With the actual economy described, we can now define what we mean by the flexible-price economy. Flexible-price output was said to be the level of output that would hold if there were no costs of adjustment of nominal variables in the past, at the current time and in the expected future. We assume that the time t value of flexible-price output (as with the flexible-price value of other variables) exists and is unique, and can then be written as:

$$y_t^* = f_y\left(\overline{\varphi}, \mathbf{X}_{rt}^*, E_{\overline{\varphi},t}\left\{\mathbf{q}_{1s}^*\right\}_{s=-\infty}^{\infty}\right) \qquad (4.8)$$

where $\overline{\varphi} = (\varphi_1, \overline{\varphi}_2)$.

Note that flexible-price output is independent of the past, current or expected future values of the nominal monetary policy instrument, inflation, and other nominal variables.[19] Property (4.8) of the flexible-price economy would follow from any standard theory as to what constitutes a nominal rigidity. For example, in the micro-founded model of nominal rigidities such as those described in Mankiw and Romer (1991a), when we abstract from all costs of adjusting nominal variables, agents' decisions over real variables, such as how much consumption or investment to undertake, would only depend on real factors such as real prices and be otherwise independent of any nominal values.

We can also derive the flexible-price levels for all the other economic variables in the economy that are consistent with this definition of flexible-price output.

$$\pi_t = f_\pi\left(\overline{\varphi}, \mathbf{X}^*_{rt}, E_{\overline{\varphi},t}\left\{\mathbf{q}^*_{1s}\right\}^{\infty}_{s=-\infty} \middle| \mathbf{X}^*_{nt}, E_{\overline{\varphi},t}\left\{\mathbf{q}^*_{2s}\right\}^{\infty}_{s=-\infty}, E_{\overline{\varphi},t}\left\{i^*_s\right\}^{\infty}_{s=t}\right) \tag{4.9}$$

$$\mathbf{Z}_{1t} = \mathbf{f}_{z1}\left(\overline{\varphi}, \mathbf{X}^*_{rt}, E_{\overline{\varphi},t}\left\{\mathbf{q}^*_{1s}\right\}^{\infty}_{s=-\infty}\right) \tag{4.10}$$

$$\mathbf{Z}_{2t} = \mathbf{f}_{z2}\left(\overline{\varphi}, \mathbf{X}^*_{rt}, E_{\overline{\varphi},t}\left\{\mathbf{q}^*_{1s}\right\}^{\infty}_{s=-\infty} \middle| \mathbf{X}^*_{nt}, E_{\overline{\varphi},t}\left\{\mathbf{q}^*_{2s}\right\}^{\infty}_{s=-\infty}, E_{\overline{\varphi},t}\left\{i^*_s\right\}^{\infty}_{s=t}\right) \tag{4.11}$$

$$\mathbf{q}^*_{1t} = \mathbf{q}_{1t} \tag{4.12}$$

and

$$\mathbf{q}^*_{2t} = \mathbf{f}_{q2}\left(\overline{\theta}, E_{\overline{\theta}2}\left\{\mathbf{q}^*_{2s}\right\}^{\infty}_{s=-\infty}\right) \tag{4.13}$$

where $\overline{\theta} = (\theta_1, \overline{\theta}_2)$.

As with output, the flexible-price levels of all other real variables are independent of current, future and past values of the nominal variables. Also, we can see that the real exogenous variables ($\mathbf{q}_{1t} = \mathbf{q}^*_{1t}$) will always be equal to their actual values because they do not depend on whether there are nominal rigidities or not. The nominal exogenous variables depend on nominal rigidities, and $\mathbf{q}_{2t}$ hence does not necessarily equal $\mathbf{q}^*_{2t}$.

Interest-rate setting in the flexible-price world is somewhat simpler than in the actual world, given the additively separable loss function. As the central bank will seek to minimise only what it can control, it will only try to minimise the conditional variance of the rate of inflation about its target path.

Hence we can write that

$$E_{\overline{\varphi},t}\left\{i^*_s\right\}^{\infty}_{s=t} \text{ minimises } \sum_{s=t}^{\infty} E_{\overline{\varphi},s}\left(\pi^*_s - \pi_L\right)^2 \tag{4.14}$$

given equations (4.8)–(4.13).

4.3 Why do we care about the output gap?

It is straightforward to answer our question about why monetary policy makers want to measure flexible-price output, given the assumptions we have used so far. As flexible-price output is independent of nominal shocks and is driven only by real shocks, measuring flexible-price output offers one route to identifying 'real' disturbances. As with many other instruments in the central bank's toolkit, this would suggest that the purpose of calculating flexible-price output is to provide useful 'conditioning' information in forecasting future output and inflation movements; information that identifies what drives future output and inflation movements.

However, flexible-price output is often regarded as being more than just one of the many indicators that a central bank produces to inform its forecast. It is said to be also valuable because it can make the policy objective on output more precise: given an accurate forecast of the flexible-price level, instruments can be set to minimise only the expected volatility of future output relative to the forecasted flexible-price level. This is formalised in descriptions of monetary policy models where the monetary policy objective function, or that instrument rule, has terms in the output gap rather than in the level or growth rate of output.

In this section, we ask what assumptions in our model of the transmission mechanism can be used to justify this focus on the output gap in place of actual output in monetary policy objectives. The answers are important because they give us some guide as to what assumptions are needed if we want a model of the transmission mechanism that features the output gap rather than output in its objectives. To summarise our findings, we show that two properties of our model are sufficient: that long-run nominal neutrality holds, and that the output gap is independent of real shocks.

4.3.1 Long-run nominal neutrality

Long-run nominal neutrality is an assumption that determines the values that variables take when we abstract from nominal shocks only. More precisely, it requires that the parameters that describe the costs of nominal adjustment are such that the expected values of all variables conditional only on the real exogenous uncertainty are their flexible-price values.[20]

Let z_t denote any member of the set of variables of the model: ($z_t \in$ (y_t, π_t, $\mathbf{Z}_{1t}$, $\mathbf{Z}_{2t}$, $\mathbf{q}_{1t}$, $\mathbf{q}_{2t}$)') and let z_t^* denote the flexible price value of z_t. In terms of our set-up, we can write that if the economy displays long-run nominal neutrality, then the parameters in (θ_2, φ_2) are such that

$$z_t^* = E\left[z_t \middle| E_{\varphi,t}\{\mathbf{q}_{1s}\}_{s=-\infty}^{\infty} \right]$$

$$\text{for any } z_t \in (y_t, \pi_t, \mathbf{Z}_{1t}, \mathbf{Z}_{2t}, \mathbf{q}_{1t}, \mathbf{q}_{2t})' \text{[21]} \tag{4.15}$$

where $E[z_t \mid I_t]$ denotes the expectation of z_t conditional on given values of the stochastic variables I_t and where the solution for z_t would be given from equations (4.1)–(4.7). As $\mathbf{q}_{1t}$, $\mathbf{q}_{2t}$ are the only sources of stochastic uncertainty, equation (4.15) describes expectations conditional on the stochastic distribution of $\mathbf{q}_{1t}$, and hence takes expectations across the nominal sources of uncertainty only.

If the equations in the model of the transmission mechanism were linear, then nominal neutrality would require that both static and dynamic homogeneity holds in all equations. To define static and dynamic homogeneity, we first must categorise all expressions involving nominal variables in our model into either dynamic or level terms. A dynamic term is one which has the same order of difference stationarity as the inflation target, e.g. interest rates, wage inflation, nominal GDP growth, nominal exchange rate depreciation. A level term is one which has the same order of difference stationarity as the long-run domestic price (log) level, and thus one more degree of difference stationarity than the inflation target. Static homogeneity means that the sum of the coefficients on all level nominal variables on the right-hand side of the equation of interest must be equal to the sum of the coefficients on all level nominal variables on the left-hand side. Dynamic homogeneity means that the sum of the coefficients on all dynamic nominal variables on the right-hand side of the equation must be equal to the sum of the coefficients on all dynamic nominal variables on the left-hand side. If we conduct experiments where the interest rate shifts temporarily, then for nominal neutrality we do not want any real variables to be affected. For this to happen, every equation in our model must satisfy static homogeneity. If we conduct experiments where the interest rate shifts permanently – a permanent disinflation, for example – then for nominal neutrality we do not want any real variables to be affected permanently. For this to happen, every equation in our model must satisfy dynamic homogeneity.

What long-run nominal neutrality implies is that after abstracting from the current, past and expected future nominal uncertainty, the expected value of output is its flexible-price value.[22] We have already assumed that a unique flexible-price state exists; neutrality implies that in the absence of nominal shocks, the economy will by itself converge to the flexible-price state. A crucial property of models that display long-run nominal neutrality follows: monetary policymakers can aim to minimise the variance of output, given that the expected value of output (an expectation that is conditional on real uncertainty only) is invariant to different settings of the nominal monetary policy instruments.

4.3.2 Independence of the output gap and flexible-price output

Long-run nominal neutrality by itself is not enough to justify focus only on the volatility of the output gap rather than output as a whole over the monetary policy horizon. It may be that the transmission of monetary policy itself can depend on what real shocks are expected to hit the economy. Thus it is also important to think about when the expected output gap is independent of expected real shocks, and when it is not.

One set of assumptions that ensures independence between the gap and real shocks is that the model (as it is written in equations (4.1)–(4:7), in logs and as a reduced form) is

1 Linear in the endogeneous variables;
2 Additively separable in the exogenous variables;
3 Such that the parameters determining the role of the endogenous variables and real variables in the system are not those that characterise nominal rigidities.[23]

We can write this set of assumptions as requiring that:

$$f_z(\varphi, \mathbf{X}_{rt}, E_{\varphi,t}, \{\mathbf{q}_{1s}\}_{s=-\infty}^{\infty} | \mathbf{X}_{nt}, E_{\varphi,t}\{\mathbf{q}_{2s}\}_{s=-\infty}^{\infty}, E_{\varphi,t}\{i_s\}_{s=t}^{\infty})$$

$$= g_z(\varphi_1, \mathbf{X}_{rt} | \mathbf{X}_{nt})(+h_{rz}(\varphi_1, E_{\varphi 1,t}\{\mathbf{q}_{1s}\}_{s=-\infty}^{\infty})$$

$$+ h_{nz}(\varphi, \mathbf{E}_{\varphi,t}\{\mathbf{q}_{2s}\}_{s=-\infty}^{\infty}) \qquad (4.16)$$

where f_z is the function determining the variable z_s, (z_s, ∈ (y_s, π_s, $\mathbf{Z}_{1s}$, $\mathbf{Z}_{2s}$); g_z is a linear function; and f_z, g_z and h_z are all well-behaved functions.

Let us denote the deviation of a variable, z, from its flexible-price value, z^*, as $\tilde{z}$; and the difference between a function of the actual values of variables, f_z ($\mathbf{x}$), and the same function of their flexible-price values, f_z ($\mathbf{x}^*$), as $\tilde{f}_z$ ($\mathbf{x}$). Using the independence assumption (4.16), we can subtract our expression for the actual value of a variable from that for the flexible-price value to show that the gap in the variable is independent of the real exogenous variables:

$$\tilde{z} = g_z\left(\varphi_1, \tilde{\mathbf{X}}_{rt} \middle| \tilde{\mathbf{X}}_{nt}\right)$$

$$+ h_{nz}(\varphi, E_{\varphi,t}\{\mathbf{q}_{2s}\}_{s=-\infty}^{\infty}) - h_{nz}(\overline{\varphi}, E_{\overline{\varphi},t}\{\mathbf{q}_{2s}^*\}_{s=-\infty}^{\infty}) \qquad (4.17)$$

Applying this to output, equation (4.18) shows that the output gap, $\tilde{y}_t = y_t - y^*_t$, is independent of the real exogenous variables:

$$\tilde{y}_t = g_y\left(\varphi_1, \tilde{\mathbf{X}}_{rt} \middle| \tilde{\mathbf{X}}_{nt}\right)$$

$$+ h_{ny}(\varphi, E_{\varphi,t}\{\mathbf{q}_{2s}\}_{s=-\infty}^{\infty}) - h_{ny}(\overline{\varphi}, E_{\overline{\varphi},t}\{\mathbf{q}_{2s}^*\}_{s=-\infty}^{\infty}) \qquad (4.18)$$

Similarly, the past, current and expected future deviations of all other endogenous variables from their flexible-price values are independent of real sources of uncertainty and only driven by the stochastic nominal shocks, given our assumption (4.16).

Comparing the equation for the output gap, (4.18), with that of flexible-price output (4.8), we can see that now each is driven by an entirely different source of uncertainty flexible-price output is driven by real shocks only, and the output gap by nominal shocks only. The expected distributions for the two variables are hence statistically independent, and, for example, the conditional covariance between the two will be zero.

Now if we turn our attention back to the loss function of the central bank, the conditional variance in actual output can be decomposed in terms of the conditional variances of the output gap, and flexible-price output and the covariance between the two:

$$E_{\varphi,t}\sum_{s=t}^{\infty}(y_s - y_s^*)^2 + E_{\varphi,t}\sum_{s=t}^{\infty}(y_s^*)^2 + E_{\varphi,t}\sum_{s=t}^{\infty}(y_s - y_s^*)(y_s^*)$$
$$+\lambda E_{\varphi,t}\sum_{s=t}^{\infty}(\pi_s - \pi_L)^2 \tag{4.19}$$

As the covariance of flexible-price output and the output gap is zero and as the central bank cannot affect the variance of flexible price output, we can now write the objectives of the central bank in terms of the conditional variance of the output gap only:

$$E_{\varphi,t}\sum_{s=t}^{\infty}(y_s - y_s^*)^2 + \lambda E_{\varphi,t}\sum_{s=t}^{\infty}(\pi_s - \pi_L)^2 \tag{4.20}$$

The objective of the central bank can therefore be equivalently written in terms of the output gap rather than output, providing the model of the economy is such that nominal neutrality holds and that the model satisfies property (1–3). Clearly this role of potential output measurement is distinct from the goal of measuring output gaps to provide conditioning information on the expected future inflation and output. Its purpose is to simplify the output objective over the uncertain horizon. The supposed advantage of concentrating on the gap rather than output would simply be that the unconditional variance of the output gap (assuming that errors in measuring and predicting it are not too large) is less than that of actual output.

4.3.3 Implications

To summarise, we will now run through what we have shown with our general framework.

(A) What is flexible-price output?

First, we have shown how the concept of flexible-price output is defined by the absence of nominal rigidities, currently, in the past and in the expected future.

(B) Why do we want to measure flexible-price output?

Second, we discussed why flexible-price output measurement is important for monetary policy. It can both serve as a shock identification device and also sharpen objectives. However, there are important conditions which our economies and hence the monetary policy models that capture them must satisfy for both to be true.

These two implications were derived from the previous section, but there are other, more practical, implications from the framework that we can now draw out.

(C) Theory versus data in measuring potential output

The schema above points to two routes to forecasting flexible-price output. The first, more data-based, method follows from the long-run nominal neutrality assumption (4.15). Neutrality implies that if we were able to measure over a long enough (or more precisely, informative enough) data set for nominal shocks to cancel out, and providing that we correctly condition on the effects of real shocks, the average value of variables would be equal to the flexible-price values. This suggests that we can use these correctly conditional averages as estimates of the process for potential output. If we can project forecasts of the effects of real shocks onto the policy horizon, this method can be used to derive a forecast for potential output.

The other, more theory-based, approach would be to build a model of our economy in which we have separately identified the nominal rigidities inherent in the economy. The path of output that would follow when we solved the model after setting the nominal rigidity parameters to values consistent with no nominal rigidities would then describe flexible-price output. With nominal effects absent, the forecast would leave us with having to model real shocks and their dynamic effects.

In principle, both methods can be consistent with each other, and both crucially depend on accurate understanding and assumptions about real shocks and effects. However, the first method builds on the assumption that the effects of nominal rigidities 'cancel out' within the sample of data that we have, whilst the second favours, using more theory on sticky nominal adjustments.

Broadly speaking, the data-based method lends itself to using statistical methods to deal with nominal shocks. The emphasis is here on estimating the output gap by depending on only a few broad assumptions about how the cyclical and secular nature of the output gap differs from that potential output. Typically, only a single time-series of GDP or other output data is used.

The danger with these data-based methods is that estimates of the output gap based on single time-series estimations are highly sensitive to what we assume about the cyclical properties of potential output, as Quah (1992) formally demonstrated. They can also depend on what sample of data is used. For this reason, output gap researchers following data-based techniques frequently find that the most recent measured output gap is highly sensitive to seemingly innocuous changes in the technique used.

This need not be as disheartening as it first sounds: many of the econometric estimates that policymakers work with are sensitive to the assumptions that are used to derive them. However, what is particularly disconcerting with data-based potential output forecasting is that methodological differences that drive results tend to have little economic content.

The second theory-based route relies more on imposing theory in estimating the output gap and correspondingly placing less weight on the single time-series of output data. A seemingly inevitable and indeed desirable side-effect of bringing more theory on board is that the output gap is estimated utilising information on what is happening to inflation, even to the extent that potential output is estimated jointly in a system with the Phillips curve. According to the more theory-based approaches, a system that explains real output and inflation (and possibly other important variables) is estimated and identified, and the scrutiny is directed towards explaining how underlying shocks affect inflation, output and other variables differently.[24]

The framework in the previous section explained that the theories that matter when we want to separate actual from potential (flexible-price) output movements are those that refer to nominal rigidities. It follows that the theory-based approach to measuring potential output depends critically on our ability to quantify theories of nominal rigidities. The major challenge here is to be able separately to identify and understand short-run fluctuations in flexible-price output from those due to nominal shocks.[25] Both types of fluctuations can be present at a similar frequency in the data. For example, developing countries tend to be more dependent on the production conditions of particular commodities and therefore more sensitive to temporary supply-side shocks caused by weather conditions. Local circumstances must then matter in drawing out differences between the fluctuations in output and inflation that are due to nominal rigidities alone, and those that are due to supply-side shocks.

It would therefore seem sensible to vary the relative influence of theory and data depending on the economic conditions and data available. The chosen measure of flexible-price output could then be judged from both points of view. Data-based methods can often be justified by some theory, even if that assumption is simple. For example, we can construct motivations for using actual unemployment to determine the natural or potential rate by referring to hysteresis in equilibrium unemployment (Cross 1995; Ball 1999). Conversely, if the output gap measure is derived from a theory-based strategy, it would seem sensible to validate the model against data (Quah 1995; Canova 2000; Favero and Maffezzoli 2001). It would be most valuable to tease out the predictions that the estimated output gap models makes for other variables on which we also have data. Models can be tested on cross-sectional data, or used to derive controlled experiments that compare to event studies of identified shocks rather than just on the aggregate output series on which they were formulated.

(D) The balanced growth path versus flexible-price output

We have conceived of the output gap as the deviation from flexible-price output. Many monetary policy researchers follow the real business cycle literature in considering the output gap in terms of deviations from a balanced-growth path equilibrium, which is often referred to as a steady state. The balanced-growth equilibrium is itself an equilibrium of the flexible-price economy, one in which there are not only no nominal rigidities but also there is the restriction that, when we abstract from the uncertainty in real exogenous variables, all real variables are expected either to be constant or to grow at a constant rate.

When compared to what is required to model the flexible-price state, it seems relatively straightforward to calculate and forecast the balanced-growth state. The defining assumption of constant growth rates of output and capital and labour supply lends itself easily to producing forecasts for these variables, once we assume that technical progress is either a smooth exponential process or a random walk.[26] Modelling the (more general) flexible-price state would require us separately to identify and quantify real frictions: the adjustment costs that would affect real variables even in the absence of nominal rigidities.

However, even if they are easier to produce, forecasts based on balanced growth assumptions may be inappropriate. That is because over the horizons that monetary policy operates, the actual economy can be far from the balanced growth path. In particular, during many decades of economic development growth seems to be punctuated by intermittent shifts and phases that take a number of years to work through and which can be explained by disequilibrium dynamics.

Typical examples of factors that especially impact on developing countries and make the process of development unsteady include:

1 The production conditions of primary and agricultural commodities, which may have to do with climate;
2 Administered price changes which, like any other relative price movement, influence the composition of the consumers' basket and can induce changes in real income;[27]
3 Changes in the world prices of important imported inputs and exported goods;
4 Shifts in world demand for exports;

5 International financial markets' appetite for investment in emerging market economies.

We can be of course be cheered by reminding ourselves that the first-round effects of many of these real or these supply-side processes are observable (Pesaran and Smith 1999). For example, we know about current weather conditions and may even have reliable forecasts of future weather. For primary commodity producing countries, forecasts of the world price of their exports are also available, as are oil prices for oil-importing manufacturers, for example. Institutions such as the IMF and the OECD produce forecasts of US GDP, and world real interest rate and emerging market-risk premium can to some extent be measured from available data.

That task becomes more complicated when these flexible-price developments can feed through to have 'second round effects' on price and output. For example, if the primary commodity export is produced under a government monopoly, the government may alter its spending plans when the world price for that good changes.[28] If this then threatens price stability, a monetary policy response may be appropriate, making the modelling of the second-round effect a crucial issue. Often the second-round effects of even those shocks that have very apparent first-round effects may have to be traced as they reverberate through the transmission mechanism, and it may require a model to do so.

One useful tactic could be to decompose potential output into its inputs by using an assumption as to how they are combined in production. This is the essence of the production function approach to potential output measurement.[29] The advantage is that we can separate the effect of technical progress on output from the contributions of flexible-price values of marketable inputs, say labour and capital. By isolating technical progress and assuming that is exogenous, it may then be adequately modelled by a smooth trend or random walk.

However, this still begs the question of how to determine the flexible-price quantities of the other production inputs, in particular capital and labour. Time series approaches may not help if the quantities of these inputs are off the balanced growth path in much of the sample, and if the slow adjustment to the balanced growth path is not exogenous but rather depends on other economic factors.

To begin with, investment dynamics can be related to other economic factors, because of the sunk costs and lumpiness involved.[30] For example, if firms can vary the intensity with which they use that capital to maximise profits (Basu 1995; Neiss and Nelson 2001; Chadha and Nolan 2002b) the path that the flexible-price capital stock takes to return to the balanced growth state can depend on output and employment adjustment.

A separate important consideration is that as physical capital investment has to be financed in imperfect capital markets, factors that shape the access to financial capital and bank credit may become important inputs for the running of the firm. The state of the financial system and its interaction with macroeconomic variables can affect flexible-price output, especially if these financial markets are subject to significant imperfections. The flexible-price prices and quantities of financial flows may require explicit treatment if the flexible-price capital stock is to be modelled.[31]

Analogously, in the flexible-price state, labour supply (in heads or hours or effort) may also depend on factors that determine the wage bargainers' choices over the share of real wages, such as labour market legislation and unemployment benefits.[32] More generally, the different components of flexible-price labour input (working population, hours, effort and human capital) can be affected by war, immigration, demographics, health, development in the informal sector and education for example. These circumstances really do seem to matter for a monetary policy understanding of the developments of labour input in developing countries, and deserve some consideration in our models.

As for other inputs, the intensity of usage of intermediate inputs in modern systems of roundabout production can vary with macroeconomic factors (Basu 1994). Models of imperfect competition also stress how barriers to entry and other real market structure factors or preferences (and not just monetary factors) affect the share of profit above costs, even in the flexible-price world.

If these adjustment costs are an important feature of the transmission mechanism, they will need to be explicitly modelled. One implication of adjustment costs is that the current value of key variables in our models depends in part on expected future information. For example, if firms face costs in adjusting, say, employment, they will need to think about future exconomic prospects when choosing how many workers to hire or to fire, because they could keep adjustment costs down by retaining staff. Thus many modern monetary policy forecasting models have both forward-looking and backward-looking variables. Moreover, the distinction between a flexible-price state and a balanced growth path can matter when we derive the terminal values of forward-looking real variables in a policy forecast. If the adjustments of the flexible-price state to the balanced growth path can last many years, the flexible-price state may need to be explicitly modelled and distinguished. Although we can expect that the effects of nominal shocks will have died out at the end of the forecast horizon,[33] the balanced growth state can typically be expected to be reached after many more years before real adjustment costs, say in investment, have washed out of the system. Hence if we were to choose terminal conditions[34] to impact close to the end of the forecast horizon, these should tie the values of real variables to their flexible-price and not to their balanced growth values. A model of the flexible-price economy can thus help tie down the terminal point of a forecast by providing a consistent basis for the treatment of the terminal values of different endogenous variables, whilst still allowing for persistence in real rigidities beyond the policy horizon

We could instead solve beyond that forecast horizon, ending our solution at terminal date where the economy can be expected to be close to its balanced growth state. The further beyond the forecast horizon we solve, the less important will the terminal condition be in determining our endogenous variable forecast during the forecast horizon. However, that terminal date can be far ahead; the common practice in policy forecasts is to solve 10 or 20 years ahead. There is also a cost to adopting a distant terminal date; an accurate model of real exogenous variables will be needed to project their values into the future, and the forecast then becomes more dependent on the process that we choose to model such variables.[35]

To summarise, we have shown that by interpreting potential output as output in the counterfactual flexible-price state, we can derive important lessons about forecasting potential output in developing countries. One benefit is that the forecast values of real variables in the flexible-price state can more realistically display non-constant growth rates. However, we would also be encouraged to make and defend assumptions about the dynamics of the flexible-price economy, tackling the implications of features such as foreign investment, financial market development, government pricing, agriculture production and trade conditions, and labour supply, to name but a few. In many cases, there would seem to be much to gain from tackling the dynamic effects of these important developmental rigidities explicitly.

(E) The flexible-price values of other real variables

The flexible-price level of output is related to the flexible-price levels of other real variables such as unemployment, money velocity or the real exchange rate. As with output, the deviations of actual from flexible-price levels of these other real variables can in principle tell us about nominal shocks independent of the effects of real disturbances if long-run neutrality holds and if the model is additively separable in real exogenous factors. For example:

1. In Chapter 3 of this volume, and also Woodford (2000), Neiss and Nelson (2001) and Chadha and Nolan (2002b), *the equilibrium* or *Wicksellian real interest rate* refers to where the real interest rate would be if prices were flexible. The gap between this, equilibrium real rate and the actual real rate may tell us about the output gap, and also more directly about where real interest rates should be heading.
2. *The fundamental equilibrium exchange rate* (and related equilibrium exchange rate concepts) tell us what the real exchange rate would be if prices were flexible, and hence where the real exchange rate should be heading.

3 Galí and Gertler (1999), Galí (2000a, 2000b), Batini *et al.* (2000b) and Sbordone (2002), for example, have argued that *the mark-up of prices on unit labour costs* may tell us about where inflation will head.
4 *The deviation of unemployment from its natural rate* should provide valuable information about wage and, presumably, inflationary pressure (Budd *et al.* 1988; Nickell, 1996 and Ball and Mankiw 2002).[36]
5 *An unsustainable balance of trade deficit* may be used as a proxy for inflationary pressure when both excessive import growth and inflation are symptoms of excess demand. In some economies, especially developing countries with fixed exchange rates, a sustainable trade balance becomes an intermediate objective in its own right, as it determines the sustainability of the exchange rate regime.[37]
6 Finally, and most importantly for traditional developing country central bank models, *the deviation of the velocity of money from the value that is compatible with growth being sustainable and inflation being at target* can, under certain conditions, tell us about whether policy should be tightened or not. As Polak (1998) and Mussa and Savastano (1999) explain, the modelling of this real disequilibria in velocity is at the heart of the IMF Monetary Programming Framework. Explicit recognition is made that real, structural factors can affect the flexible-price velocity, such as remonetisation and financial sector reform, and these are distinguished from inflationary shifts in velocity (De Broek *et al.* 1997).

The advantage of using these measures is that the data regarding these variables may be more readily available than GDP data. This is obviously an important motivation for central banks in developing countries. However, there are also reasons why we should be cautious about the use of these measures in isolation:

1 As these concepts are linked to the GDP gap, some of them – for example the equilibrium velocity of money demand – will themselves depend on having a reliable estimate of potential output (IMF 1996).
2 Many of these concepts are dogged by the same measurement problems faced in calculating the output gap. These measurement problems are common because the task is similar: we are trying to measure different aspects of a hypothetical flexible-price economy for which no direct data exist! For example, in using the balance of trade, how do we know that the growth of imports is excessive? Even large trade deficits can be sustainable – reflecting that the economy is importing capital to grow and catch up with its trading partners, or perhaps satisfying the greater consumption needs of its younger population.
3 If it is the output gap we are interested in, and if we have to allow any of these concepts to proxy the output gap, then we should make sure that the link between the two is clearly thought out. It is important to

be aware that these links are not automatic and are conditional on what shocks are expected to be taking place. Excess demand does not always imply inflationary pressure; a large trade deficit detracts from the inflationary impact of excessive domestic demand on the GDP output. Similarly, even if unemployment falls well below the natural rate, that need not always be matched by a rise in the output gap. The fall in unemployment could reflect firms changing the way their staff work, perhaps with more or less overtime. Finally, measures of demand pressure based on real money aggregates are only appropriate if the money demand function and the effect of interest rates and money on consumption – that together link this monetary proxies to the output gap – are stable. As financial markets are liberalised these monetary relationships may become unpredictable, and other ways of guessing at potential output may have to be sought out.

All real disequilibria concepts relate to how far the economy is from where it would be if prices were flexible, and all these concepts were linked to the output gap. They can certainly be useful, especially when GDP data is scarce, but they should not be seen as automatic indicators of demand pressure. The detective work of explaining what is causing recent and projected changes in any of these indicators and how they are linked cannot be neglected,[38] just as it can't be when we look at the aggregate GDP output gap.

(F) The importance of relating nominal rigidities to the flexible-price output concept

The framework shows that what is useful when it comes to calculating the output gap is a separate understanding and quantification of nominal rigidities. An interesting corollary applies to countries where there are few nominal rigidities and flexible-price output will be close to actual output so that the output gap will be relatively short-lived.[39,40] The implication is that the central bank can afford to ignore the output gap altogether in its monetary policy setting in such a country. Domestic prices, nominal wages and inflation will be quick to adjust to nominal policy movements that could be represented by exchange rate depreciations or, if the exchange rate is fixed, to movements in foreign prices, nominal interest rates, or changes in monetary aggregates. However policy is conducted, the real values of the rate of interest, asset prices and credit should not then move far from their flexible-price values. As outlined in Chapter 3 (sections 3.5, 3.6) consumption and investment decisions are sensitive to squeezes and busts in real credit, or shifts in the real rate of interest. However, if these real levers are unaffected by systematic monetary policy, then real consumption and investment plans will remain invariant to monetary policy setting.

At this point we should be careful to distinguish the situation where prices are flexible and quick to adjust, from the situation where prices are volatile and unpredictable. Volatile and unpredictable inflation rates can affect output, lowering it. There is evidence that inflation uncertainty makes investment and production decisions difficult and lowers permanently the growth rates of investment and consumption. The picture becomes complicated in reality because, as discussed in Chapter 3.10 (and as we shall return to in Chapter 5), there are reasons to suspect that, all other things being equal, volatile inflation often goes hand-in-hand with flexible inflation.

There are other practical implications that we can derive once we relate flexible-price output to the absence of nominal rigidities. For example, we can show how to simplify flexible-price output measurement by excluding sectors whose production conditions are independent of domestic nominal rigidities. This could be relevant for the many developing countries with primary commodity-producing exporting sectors for whom the economic decisions involved in the production and sale of the good (the purchase of raw materials and capital inputs and the hiring of labour) and the distribution and consumption of profit (the consumption and investment decisions of its owners) are carried out entirely in foreign currency. Production of exported primary commodities, for example mined minerals, is often licensed to international companies, which act as price-takers on world markets. As the goods are destined for the world market, the quantity produced would reflect external demand rather than domestic demand factors, as well as domestic supply factors. Any profits that are transferred to the domestic fiscal authorities are mostly spent abroad, re-invested in foreign currency or used to repay external debt. Production of these goods is often capital intensive, and the workforce's weight in costs can be small. However, even if the sector employed many workers, they could have no bargaining power and their real wages would then adjust flexibly to the real wage paid by producers (nominal wages relative to their world market output price).[41] What is interesting for our discussion of output gap measurement is that if the decisions regarding the production of this commodity are independent of domestic nominal rigidities, the output, output price, investment, wages and employment in this sector will always be equal to their flexible-price values. When calculating the output gap of the country as a whole, this sector's outputs could be excluded.[42]

We return to discuss the cross-country variation in the extent of nominal rigidities in Chapter 5, where we provide evidence with a variety of structural models for different countries. For the moment, we can summarise by concluding that it is important to bear the extent of nominal rigidities in mind when transferring potential output measurement technology from one country to another. Identifying assumptions about the properties of the output gap that are based, for example, on our understanding of the US may not be appropriate for other countries (Ball and Mankiw 2002: 8).

4.4 A dynamic general equilibrium model

In order to explain the implications discussed in section 4.3.3, it may be helpful to demonstrate them in a simple model of the transmission mechanism derived from microfoundations. The model is simplified because it describes a closed economy with only one asset, and allows only for labour as the sole marketable input into production. Monetary policymakers only care about inflation, and nominal rigidity arises only from an imperfect updating of the information used in setting wages. These assumptions are unrealistic and difficult to justify in developing countries, but we shall use them because they serve to demonstrate what more complicated and more appropriate models will also show.

4.4.1 Microeconomic foundations

There are four categories of economic decisions made in this economy: workers choose leisure, consumption and asset holdings; firms choose employment and production; the central bank chooses nominal interest rates; and wage-setters choose the nominal wage rate. We shall take each in turn, and use the first-order conditions to construct a general equilibrium model of the actual economy, which can be compared with its flexible-price state.

Consumption and leisure

The objective of the ith representative consumer/worker is to maximise his utility over an infinite horizon, where the infinite horizon utility function is given as

$$U_{it} = E_t \sum_{s=t}^{\infty} \beta^{s-t} \left(\frac{(C_{is})^{1-\vartheta}}{1-\vartheta} + \mu_s \frac{(1-N_{is})^{1-\vartheta}}{1-\vartheta} \right) \tag{4.21}$$

with $v < 1$. N_{it} is the time spent in formal employment by the ith representative worker/consumer, as opposed to leisure or informal employment. The real net income from his investments in the only asset is $(1+i_{t-1}/P_t\ B_{it-1} - B_{it}/P_{it})$ and earnings from formal employment is $(W_t/P_t\ N_{it})$.

The return (in terms of utility) of an hour of leisure or informal employment depends on technical progress, as in Correia *et al.* (1995). We can write this as

$$\mu_t = A_t^{-(1-v)} \tag{4.22}$$

where A_t is technological progress.

The budget constraint of the ith representative worker/consumer is therefore written as

$$P_tC_{it} = W_tN_{it} - B_{it} + (1 + i_{t-1})\, B_{it-1} \tag{4.23}$$

We can write the Lagrangean for this problem as

$$E_t\sum_{s=t}^{\infty}\beta^{s-t}\left(\frac{(C_{is})^{1-\vartheta}}{1-\vartheta}+\frac{(\mu_s(1-N_{is}))^{1-\vartheta}}{1-\vartheta}\right)$$
$$+\sum_{s=t}^{\infty}\lambda_s(P_sC_{is}-W_sN_{is}+B_{is}-(1+i_{s-1})B_{is-1}) \tag{4.24}$$

The first-order conditions give us an expression for labour supply,

$$\mu_s(1-N_{is})^{-\vartheta}=(C_{is})^{-\vartheta}\frac{W_t}{P_t} \tag{4.25}$$

an intertemporal equation for consumption:[43]

$$C_{it}=E_t\left(\left(\frac{1+i_t}{\beta}\right)\frac{P_t}{P_{t+1}}\right)^{\frac{1}{\vartheta}}C_{it+1} \tag{4.26}$$

and the budget constraint:

$$P_tC_{it} = W_tN_{it} - B_{it} + (1 + i_{t-1})\, B_{it-1} \tag{4.27}$$

There are L_t identical consumer/workers and the supply of labour in heads is exogenous. Aggregating across them gives as the following expression for aggregate consumption and labour effort:

$$C_t=E_t\left(\left(\frac{1+i_t}{\beta}\right)\frac{P_t}{P_{t+1}}\right)^{\frac{1}{\vartheta}}C_{t+1} \tag{4.28}$$

$$1-N_t=\frac{C_t}{L_t}\left(\frac{1}{\mu_t}\frac{W_t}{P_t}\right)^{-\frac{1}{\vartheta}} \tag{4.29}$$

and

$$P_tC_t = W_tN_tL_t - B_t + (1 + i_{t-1})B_{t-1} \tag{4.30}$$

Monetary policy setting

Our simple assumption about monetary policy is that the policymaker chooses to set the nominal rate of interest such that *expected* rate of inflation is always equal to a target path, ignoring any output losses whatsoever:[44]

$$E_t p_{t+1} = p_t + \text{target}_t \tag{4.31}$$

The choice of policy rule is dictated by convenience rather than realism. Building in a more realistic rule that is in some sense optimal, given the transmission mechanism, or that allows for concern over short-run output volatility would certainly imply different solutions. However, it would not alter the qualitative messages that this example manages to send out.

The targeted path of inflation is assumed to follow an autoregressive process about a constant mean rate, so that the planned readjustment to the long-run target ($\overline{\text{target}}$) following a shock is gradual:

$$\text{target}_t = (1-\alpha)\,\overline{\text{target}} + \alpha\,\text{target}_{t-1} + e_{nt} \tag{4.32}$$

where e_{nt} is independently normally distributed with mean of zero and a variance of σ_n^2.

Firms

Turning to production, there is one firm that produces all domestic consumption. The owner of this firm chooses to maximise profits using a simple production function that is linear in the only input of production, effective labour $(L_t N_t)$:

$$Y_t = A_t\,(L_t N_t) \tag{4.33}$$

Technological progress (A_t) follows a random walk in logs, that we can write as:

$$a_t = a_{t-1} + e_{rt} \tag{4.34}$$

where e_{rt} is normally distributed with a mean of zero and with a variance of σ_r^2.

Information and expectations

To close the model, we need to specify what information is available to agents at each moment in time. The broadest information set constructed at time t comprises the values of all variable dated at time t or earlier, including the values of the shocks e_{rt} and e_{nt}.[45]

For the large part, the broadest information set is what agents use when making decisions at time *t*. For example, central banks use this set in setting interest rates, and in the Appendix to this chapter we show that this implies a solution for inflation as:[46]

$$p_t - p_{t-1} = -e_{nt} + \overline{\text{target}} + \sum_{j=0}^{\infty} \alpha^j e_{n,t-1-j} \tag{4.35}$$

The inflation solution shows that current inflation depends negatively on the current shock to the target: as policymakers aim to raise expected inflation in line with the a sudden ratchet up in its target, current inflation will fall. However if these changes in target are persistent ($\alpha > 0$), shocks will not be immediately reversed, and current inflation will also depend positively on past shocks.

Nominal wage setting

Not all decisions are made with the broadest information set, though. The only nominal rigidity that characterises this economy arises from an imperfect updating of information that firms and workers use when they make expectations of the marginal revenue product in determining the nominal wage rate. Following Mankiw and Reis (2001), the updating of information on real variables is costly and is hence updated towards the broadest set available at the exogenous geometric rate of ς_1. On the nominal variables, updating takes place at the rate of ς_2.[47]

We can write the time *t* nominal wage rate in logs as:

$$\begin{aligned}\omega_t = {} & (1-\varsigma_1)\sum_{k=0}^{\infty} \varsigma_1^k E_{t-k}(y_t - l_t - n_t) \\ & + (1-\varsigma_2)\sum_{k=0}^{\infty} \varsigma_2^k E_{t-k}(p_t)\end{aligned} \tag{4.36}$$

Note that the parameter ς_2 by itself determines the degree of nominal rigidity in this model; if and only if $\varsigma_2 \neq 0$ will nominal values by themselves bear on real variables.

Rewriting equation (4.36) yields:

$$\begin{aligned}w_t = {} & p_t + y_t - l_t - n_t \\ & + (1-\varsigma_1)\left(\sum_{k=0}^{\infty} \varsigma_1^k [E_{t-k}(y_t - l_t - n_t) - (y_t - l_t - n_t)]\right) \\ & + (1-\varsigma_2)\left(\sum_{k=0}^{\infty} \varsigma_2^k [E_{t-k}(p_t) - p_t]\right)\end{aligned} \tag{4.37}$$

Equations (4.37), (4.34) (4.76) imply that:

$$w_t = p_t + y_t - l_t - n_t + (1-\varsigma_1)\left(\sum_{k=1}^{\infty}\varsigma_1^k\sum_{s=1}^{k} e_{r,t-k+s}\right) + \frac{(1-\varsigma_2)}{1-\alpha}\left(\sum_{k=1}^{\infty}\varsigma_2^k\sum_{i=0}^{k-1}\alpha^i e_{n,t-i}\right) \tag{4.38}$$

Equation (4.38) shows us that the real wage differs from effective labour productivity because of real rigidities and real shocks (the moving average term in the errors in predicting labour productivity) on one hand, and nominal rigidities and nominal shocks (the moving average error term in predicting the price level) on the other.

4.4.2 *The model of the actual economy*

Leaving aside the equation that determines bonds,[48] we can now rewrite the model of the actual economy in logs as:[49]

$$c_t = y_t \tag{4.39}$$

$$-n_t = y_t - l_t - \frac{1}{\vartheta}(\ln(\mu_t) + w_t - p_t) \tag{4.40}$$

$$\ln(\mu_t) = -(1-\vartheta)\,a_t \tag{4.41}$$

$$y_t = a_t + l_t + n_t \tag{4.42}$$

$$a_t = a_{t-1} + e_{rt} \tag{4.43}$$

$$E_t p_{t+1} = p_t + \overline{\text{target}} + e_{nt} \tag{4.44}$$

$$i_t = \overline{\text{target}} + e_{nt} + \vartheta E_t(y_t - y_{t+1}) + \ln\beta \tag{4.45}$$

and

$$w_t = p_t + a_t - (1-\varsigma_1)\left(\sum_{k=1}^{\infty}\varsigma_1^k\sum_{s=1}^{k} e_{r,t-k+s}\right) + \frac{(1-\varsigma_2)}{1-\alpha}\left(\sum_{k=1}^{\infty}\varsigma_2^k\sum_{i=0}^{k-1}\alpha^i e_{n,t-i}\right) \tag{4.46}$$

Assuming that the exogenous value of labour supply in heads is $\bar{l}$, we also have:

$$l_t = \bar{l} \tag{4.47}$$

4.4.3 The model of the flexible-price economy

Following implication (A) in section 4.2.3, the flexible-price state of the economy is as the above but with $\varsigma_2 = 0$. The flexible-price economy can be written as:

$$c_t^* = y_t^* \tag{4.48}$$

$$-n_t^* = y_t^* - \bar{l} - \frac{1}{\vartheta}(\ln(\mu_t) + w_t^* - p_t^*) \tag{4.49}$$

$$y_t^* = a_t + \bar{l} + n_t^* \tag{4.50}$$

$$p_t^* = p_t \tag{4.51}$$

$$i_t^* = \overline{\text{target}} + e_{nt} + \vartheta E_t\,(y_t^* - y_{t+1}^*) + \ln\beta \tag{4.52}$$

$$w_t^* = p_t^* + a_t - (1-\varsigma_1)\left(\sum_{k=1}^{\infty} \varsigma_1^k \sum_{s=1}^{k} e_{r,t-k+s}\right) \tag{4.53}$$

and

$$l_t^* = \bar{l} \tag{4.54}$$

We can combine equations (4.49), (4.50) and (4.53), to solve for the flexible-price effective labour supply as:

$$-2n_t^* = a_t - \frac{1}{\vartheta}\left(\ln(\mu_t) + a_t - (1-\varsigma_1)\left(\sum_{k=1}^{\infty} \varsigma_1^k \sum_{s=1}^{k} e_{r,t-k+s}\right)\right)$$

or, by rearranging, as

$$n_t^* = -\frac{a_t}{2}\left(1 - \frac{1}{\vartheta}\right) + \frac{1}{2\vartheta}\ln(\mu_t) - \frac{(1-\varsigma_1)}{2\vartheta}\left(\sum_{k=1}^{\infty} \varsigma_1^k \sum_{s=1}^{k} e_{r,t-k+s}\right) \tag{4.55}$$

Substituting equation (4.55) into (4.50) produces an expression for flexible-price output:

$$y_t^* = a_t + \bar{l} - \frac{a_t}{2}\left(1 - \frac{1}{\vartheta}\right) + \frac{1}{2\vartheta}\ln(\mu_t) - \frac{(1-\varsigma_1)}{2\vartheta}\left(\sum_{k=1}^{\infty} \varsigma_1^k \sum_{s=1}^{k} e_{r,t-k+s}\right) \tag{4.56}$$

Using equation (4.22) and rearranging gives us

$$y_t^* = a_t + \bar{l} - \frac{(1-\varsigma_1)}{2\vartheta}\left(\sum_{k=1}^{\infty} \varsigma_1^k \sum_{s=1}^{k} e_{r,t-k+s}\right) \tag{4.57}$$

The solutions for flexible-price output in our example economy demonstrates implication (D) in section 4.2.3.

First, the flexible-price output need not be near its balanced growth path value, which is $(a_t + \bar{l})$, because real rigidities mean that the lagged effects of past productivity shocks still matter.

Second, all other real variables also have their flexible-price values, which convey similar but not the same information as flexible-price output. For example, the flexible-price real interest rate is given in equation (4.52) by $r_t^* \equiv i_t^* - \overline{\text{target}} - e_{nt}$. Although it is related to the same real shocks that drive flexible-price output, the dynamics between the two differ. Also, in this closed economy with monetary policy entirely directed at inflation, the flexible-price interest rate depends on intertemporal preference for current consumption; flexible-price output does not.

4.4.4 The output gap

Following a similar set of substitutions on the actual economy, we can show that actual output is given by:

$$y_t = a_t + \bar{l} - \frac{(1-\varsigma_1)}{2\vartheta}\left(\sum_{k=1}^{\infty}\varsigma_1^k\sum_{s=1}^{k} e_{r,t-k+s}\right) + \frac{(1-\varsigma_2)}{2\vartheta(1-\alpha)}\left(\sum_{k=1}^{\infty}\varsigma_2^k\sum_{i=0}^{k-1}\alpha^i e_{n,t-i}\right) \tag{4.58}$$

Taking expectations of equation (4.58), conditional on real shocks, we note that:

$$E\left[y_t \middle| \{e_{rs}\}_{s=-\infty}^{\infty}\right] = a_t + \bar{l} - \frac{(1-\varsigma_1)}{2\vartheta}\left(\sum_{k=1}^{\infty}\varsigma_1^k\sum_{s=1}^{k} e_{r,t-k+s}\right) = y_t^* \tag{4.59}$$

providing that $\varsigma_2 < 1$

Clearly, the important linear restriction that ensures long-run nominal neutrality (implication (B)) in this model is simply that the updating of information on nominal variables is convergent. If there are no more nominal shocks, the information set used in wage setting will converge to the broadest set.

The output gap is given by subtracting equations (4.56) from (4.58):[50]

$$\tilde{y}_t = \frac{(1-\varsigma_2)}{2\vartheta(1-\alpha)}\left(\sum_{k=1}^{\infty}\varsigma_2^k\sum_{i=0}^{k-1}\alpha^i e_{n,t-i}\right)$$

$$= \frac{(1-\varsigma_2)}{2\vartheta(1-\alpha)}\left(\sum_{i=0}^{\infty}\frac{(\varsigma_2)^{i+1}\alpha^i}{1-\varsigma_2}e_{n,t-1}\right)$$

$$= \frac{(\varsigma_2)}{2\vartheta(1-\alpha)}\left(\sum_{i=0}^{\infty}(\varsigma_2\alpha)^i e_{n,t-i}\right) \tag{4.60}$$

Comparing equations (4.56) and (4.60), we can see that the output gap is driven only by nominal shocks and is therefore independent of flexible-price output; that is only driven by real shocks as explained in implication (B).

Note also that the smoothness of the output gap is affected both by the smoothness of the underlying monetary policy shock (α), and the rate of information updating (ς_2). This demonstrates implication (F); the cyclical properties of the output gap depend on the degree of the nominal rigidity.

4.4.5 Path-dependence of the output gap

We can also adapt this model to describe the circumstances when assumption (4.16) does not hold.

There are at least two plausible sets of circumstances under which the covariance of flexible-price output and the output gap may not be zero:

1 There may be non-linearities in the economy. One important reason for non-linear effects in the transmission mechanism is the presence of significant financial market frictions. Under endogenous models of financial market frictions, the spreads between interest rates on two assets are non-linearly related to the quantities of financial assets and physical capital, and thus to output.
2 A second reason is that the parameters that determine real rigidity may be related to parameters that determine nominal rigidity by economic theory. For example, it may be that the information updating costs on real variables are restricted to being always equal to those on nominal variables, unlike our version of the Mankiw and Reis model. Other forms of nominal rigidity that are common in the literature could make the output gap dependent on real shocks.

To illustrate the effects of non-linearity, note that when we assumed that $-n_t \approx 1 - N_t$, we acknowledged that this linear approximation would be accurate only if a small proportion of hours were spent in formal employment. Taking logs of the original equation without using this approximation gives us:

$$\ln(1-\exp(n_t)) = c_t - l_t - \frac{1}{\vartheta}\left(\ln\left(\frac{1}{\mu_t}\right) + w_t - p_t\right) \quad (4.61)$$

Rearranging and substituting in from equation (22) gives:

$$\ln(1-\exp(n_t^*)) = \frac{a_t}{\vartheta} + n_t^* - \frac{1}{\vartheta}(w_t^* - p_t^*) \quad (4.62)$$

Using equations (4.61) and (4.62) instead of (4.40) and (4.49) would lead us to depart from a world in which the path of the output gap to its new equilibrium would not depend on real shocks. Although the only real exogenous variable in this model in logs (a_t) still enter this new model additively, the disequilibria in employment, $n_t - n_t^*$, and hence the output gap no longer just depend on nominal shocks.

We could similarly allow real exogenous uncertainty to enter non-linearly, and would find that the output gap is no longer purely driven by nominal factors. For example, if the parameter θ were not a fixed parameter but instead a real exogenous stochastic variable reflecting, say, structural changes in hours of labour supply, then the output gap would be again be affected by these real shocks.

We can also illustrate the importance of our assumption of independence in the parameters determining real and nominal rigidity with a simple example. Instead of equation (4.36) assume that the time t nominal wage rate (in logs) is autoregressive:

$$w_t = \nu(y_t - l_t - n_t + p_t) + (1-\nu)\, w_{t-1} \quad (4.63)$$

The stickiness in wages. $0 < \nu < 1$, now determines the degree of nominal rigidity in the system.

Rewriting (4.63) gives us an expression for the real wage:

$$w_t - p_t = -(1-\nu)p_t + \sum_{i=1}^{\infty}\nu(1-\nu)^i p_{t-i} + \sum_{i=0}^{\infty}\nu(1-\nu)^i(y_{t-i} - l_{t-i} - n_{t-i})$$

$$= \sum_{i=1}^{\infty}\nu(1-\nu)^i(p_{t-i} - p_t) + \sum_{i=0}^{\infty}\nu(1-\nu)^i a_{t-i} \quad (4.64)$$

The real wage depends on past inflation as well as the history of technical progress when $\nu < 1$. What expression (4.64) also shows is that the rate of updating on nominal variables is related to the rate of updating on real variables. Now when we subtract the flexible-price wage, $w_t^* - p_t^* = y_t^* - l_t^*$

$- n^*_t = a_t$, from the actual wage, the real disequilibrium in wages is shown to be dependent on both nominal and real shocks:

$$\tilde{w}_t - \tilde{p}_t = \sum_{i=1}^{\infty} \nu(1-\nu)^i(p_{t-i} - p_t) + \sum_{i=0}^{\infty} \nu(1-\nu)^i(a_{t-i} - a_t) \tag{4.65}$$

As the disequilibria in the real wage affects hours worked, the output gap will also depend on productivity shocks under this nominal rigidity.

We have shown that assumption (4.16) is not 'weak'; there are good reasons why the convergence path of the output gap, and hence the expected short-run costs of monetary policy actions, depend on what is happening to the flexible-price economy. Path-dependence could be a feature in many standard monetary policy models, although it remains an empirical issue as to quantitative significance. If it is important, then the implication is that the central bank should forecast and understand potential output as well as the output gap when formulating policy, because even if potential output is independent of monetary policy actions, it can itself affect the output gap.

4.5 Conclusions

In this chapter we have detailed the problems in measuring the output gap and assessed the costs and benefits of different strategies for dealing with this in formulating monetary policy. We began by explaining what potential output is supposed to capture, making reference to a counterfactual state of the economy in which there are no nominal rigidities. Local circumstances and data issues *do* seem to matter in the practice of potential output measurement and, according to our discussion of what potential output means, they *should* matter. A key message is that as the potential output process is driven by structural economic factors, different strategies will work best in different environments – there is no globally successful technique.

The purpose of the output gap measurement is to separate the role of demand from supply-side shocks in affecting output movements, and inform policy about the trade-off between output and inflation. What we have also shown is that even if the output gap can be well measured, there are good reasons to believe that, if referred to by itself, it can mislead about expected output trade-off. Even if central banks cannot affect the flexible-price economy with their systematic monetary policy actions, what is happening to flexible-price economy can impinge on the expected path of the output gap, and so we have to be aware of what is happening to both and of how they interact. For example, financial fragility can affect the expected output gap, because when firms and consumers are excessively indebted to banks, high real interest rates can lead to large output losses than otherwise. This explains why central banks devote resources to thinking about the role of productivity shocks and financial market imperfections in monetary policy transmission. They do not only want to forecast the supply-side, they also want to understand its interaction with the effects of nominal frictions.

It follows that a crucial aspect of the potential output measurement is the extent and form of nominal rigidities. In Chapter 5 we shall draw from CCBS research team project work to discuss why nominal variables might be more or less sticky in different economies.

Appendix

Solving for inflation

The monetary policy set-up is sufficiently simple so as to make the rational expectation solution of the model straightforward. (Explicit solutions to some more complicated monetary policy set-ups in this framework may be derived using the analysis set out in Gourieroux and Montfort 1990: Chapter 12.) Taking logs of (4.31) and solving forward T periods, we have:

$$\begin{aligned} p_t &= E_t p_{t+1} - \text{target}_t \\ &= E_t p_{t+2} - E_t \text{target}_{t+1} - \text{target}_t \\ &= E_t p_{t+T} - E_t \sum_{s=0}^{T-1} \text{target}_{t+s} \end{aligned} \tag{4.66}$$

Subtracting a similar expression for the time $t-1$ log of the price level, and using:

$$\text{target}_{t+s} = \alpha^{s+1}\text{target}_{t-1} + \sum_{j=0}^{s} \alpha^j \left[(1-\alpha)\overline{\text{target}} + e_{n,s+t-j}\right] \tag{4.67}$$

gives the general solution for the rate of inflation as:

$$\begin{aligned} p_t - p_{t-1} &= -\sum_{s=0}^{T-1} \left(E_t \text{target}_{t+s} - E_{t-1}\text{target}_{t+s}\right) \\ &\quad + E_{t-1}\text{target}_{t-1} + E_t p_{t+T} - E_{t-1} - p_t + T \\ &= -\sum_{s=0}^{T-1} \left(E_t \sum_{j=0}^{s} \alpha^j \left[e_{n,s+t-j}\right] - E_{t-1} \sum_{j=0}^{s} \alpha^j \left[e_{n,s+t-j}\right] \right) \\ &\quad + E_{t-1}\text{target}_{t-1} + E_t p_{t+T} - E_{t-1} p_{t+T} \end{aligned} \tag{4.68}$$

We have assumed that agents follow rational expectations and that only time t and earlier variables are known with certainty at time t. We also assume that time $t + T$ is far enough forward such that $E_{tpt} + T = E_{t-1}p_{t+T}$.

We can then write (68) as:

$$p_t = p_{t-1} - e_{nt} + \text{target}_{t-1} \tag{4.69}$$

Equation (4.32) implies that

$$\begin{aligned}\text{target}_{t-1} &= \alpha^{-\infty}\text{target}_0 + \sum_{j=0}^{\infty}\alpha^j\left[(1-\alpha)\overline{\text{target}} + e_{n,t-1-j}\right] \\ &= \overline{\text{target}} + \sum_{j=0}^{\infty}\alpha^j e_{n,t-1-j}\end{aligned} \tag{4.70}$$

We can then write (4.69) as:

$$p_t = p_{t-1} - e_{nt} + \overline{\text{target}} + \sum_{j=0}^{\infty}\alpha^j e_{n,t-1-j} \tag{4.71}$$

Solving for the expectational error for inflation

We now wish to derive the expectation error in forecasting current prices when the broadest information set that was available k periods earlier is used.

To begin with, note that equation (4.32) implies that:

$$\text{target}_{t+s} = \alpha^{s+k}\text{target}_{t-k} + \sum_{j=0}^{s+k-1}\alpha^j\left[(1-\alpha)\overline{\text{target}} + e_{n,s+t-j}\right] \tag{4.72}$$

Substituting (4.72) into (4.66), we can write the price level as:

$$\begin{aligned}p_t &= E_t p_{t+T} \\ &- E_t\sum_{s=0}^{T-1}\left(\alpha^{s+k}\text{target}_{t-k} + \sum_{j=0}^{s+k-1}\alpha^j\left[(1-\alpha)\overline{\text{target}} + e_{n,s+t-j}\right]\right)\end{aligned} \tag{4.73}$$

Taking expectations k periods earlier gives:

$$E_{t-k}p_t = E_{t-k}p_{t+T} - E_{t-k}\sum_{s=0}^{T-1}\left(\alpha^{s+k}\text{target}_{t-k} + \sum_{j=0}^{s+k-1}\alpha^j\left[(1-\alpha)\overline{\text{target}} + e_{n,s+t-j}\right]\right) \tag{4.74}$$

Subtracting (4.73) from (4.74), we have:

$$E_{t-k}p_t - p_t = E_t\sum_{s=0}^{T-1}\sum_{j=0}^{s+k-1}\alpha^j e_{n,s+t-j} - E_{t-k}\sum_{s=0}^{T-1}\sum_{j=0}^{s+k-1}\alpha^j e_{n,s+t-j}$$

$$= \sum_{s=0}^{T-1}\sum_{j=s}^{s+k-1}\alpha^j e_{n,s+t-j}$$

$$= \sum_{s=0}^{T-1}\sum_{j=0}^{k-1}\alpha^{t+s} e_{n,t-1} \qquad (4.75)$$

Taking T to be ∞ gives an expression that can be substituted to give (4.38) in the main text:

$$E_{t-k}p_t - p_t = \frac{1}{1-\alpha}\sum_{i=0}^{k-1}\alpha^i e_{n,t-i} \qquad (4.76)$$

Notes

1 Using a cross-country panel data set. Boyd and Smith (2002) find that the source of much estimation error in the transmission mechanism in developing countries arises from difficulties in measuring important unobservables such as the output gap.

2 For definitions and implications of flexible-price output concept, see McCallum and Nelson 1998; Astley and Yates 1999; McCallum 2001; Neiss and Nelson 2001–2002; Smets and Wouters 2002.

3 See, for example, Varian (2002).

4 Note that this is consistent with the consensus view that routine monetary policy actions cannot affect flexible-price output.

5 Wicksell (1958) distinguished between the real rate of return on new capital, the 'natural rate of interest' and the actual market rate of interest. The natural rate was a 'certain rate of interest on loans which is neutral in respect to commodity prices, and tends neither to raise nor to lower them.' See also Woodford (2000).

6 For current papers measuring the equilibrium rate of interest, see for example Laubach and Williams 2001; Neiss and Nelson 2001; Chadha and Nolan 2002b.

7 For an explanation of the term, see Astley and Yates (1999).

8 This definition differs from that of Woodford (2002). Chapter 4, who allows for past nominal rigidities to determine current potential output. McCallum (2001) argues that if the capital is assumed to be given when prices are determined, the capital stock will always be equal to its flexible-price value. However Casares and McCallum (2001) show that the capital stock need not be taken as fixed in when deriving the microfoundations of price-setting. Investment and capital will depend on whether prices are flexible. See also the appendix to Neiss and Nelson (2001).

9 We explain below in which sense these variables are exogenous.

10 A strict definition would be that a parameter, as opposed to a variable, does not change according to a given process. Even though it can change and the change can be analysed by comparative statistics, the best predictor of its future values is always its past value. See Hoover (2001: 171).

11 We are assuming that the only time-consistent policy is the discretionary policy. The central bank takes the public's expectations of its own behaviour as given when setting its instrument.

12 Woodford (2002). Chapter 6, follows a more rigorous approach in deriving the central bank objectives in terms of inflation and output gap volatility from the starting point of the representative consumer's utility function. See also McCallum (1986b) Section 5 for a discussion of when consumption variability incurs excessive welfare costs.

13 Recently Al-Nowaihi and Stracca (2002) have discussed the implications of non-standard central bank loss functions.

14 It could be argued that, strictly speaking, we need to develop a better understanding of what constitutes a superexogenous monetary policy shock (McCallum, 1999).

15 We assume that the members of $\mathbf{q}_{1t}$ and $\mathbf{q}_{2t}$ that are stochastic follow zero mean-reverting distributions. That does not mean that all variables in the system are stationary members of $\mathbf{q}_{1t}$ and $\mathbf{q}_{2t}$ could affect endogenous variables that are random walks.

16 The relevant concept here is super exogeneity. See Hoover (2001: 172) for example, for a definition.

17 See also Soderstrom and Sargent (2002).

18 Out set-up leads us to conceive of these as distinct from rigidities in updating on real variables, even if, as we show, the theories of imperfect updating of information do not as yet explain any different treatment between real and nominal variables.

19 Andersen (1994) describes the flexible-price state as being characterised by a 'scaling up or down of all nominal variables [that] leaves real variables (relative prices and quantities) unaffected.' This could be equivalent to our definition that is applied to the reduced form, but we would first have to be explicit as to what the scaling up or down of a nominal variable (in levels or differences?) would mean.

20 This assumption establishes only that the economy will converge to the unique long-run nominal neutral equilibrium. We have not specified how long it would take for variables to be expected to return to their nominal neutral values following a nominal shock.

22 Grandmont (1989:5) presents this assumption as 'when demand shocks lead to multipliers that do not rely on such supply side effects'. He presents a model where neither long-run nominal neutrality nor independence holds, because of increasing returns to scale and endogenous expectations-driven fluctuations.

23 This is a sufficient assumption, but not a necessary one. Weaker conditions would refer to the bounds on the error in approximating the system with functions of the form 16 See Woodford 2002: Chapter 6.

24 See, for example Blanchard and Quah 1989; Adams and Coe 1990; Kuttner 1994; Sterne and Bayonmi 1995; Haltmaier 1996; Astley and Yates 1999.

25 In the literature, reservations have been expressed as whether currently available theoretical models of macroeconomic dynamics, many of which have real business cycle models as a distant ancestors, are adequately designed to quantify the potential output definition that is relevant for monetary policy (McCallum. 2000a).

26 For example, Church *et al.* (2000) compare the effect of developments in technical progress as described by three different models of the UK economy.

27 See, for example, Fischer (1981) for references and a discussion of the theory of relative price movements and inflation, and Mohanty and Klau (2000) for a survey of evidence in emerging market economies.

28 Tracing the effect of export price movements on output or domestic prices can

require careful modelling. An export price shock will only boost real output in so far as it boosts export volumes, and production conditions (supply elasticities) must be crucial here. For example, the nominal wage bargain and labour supply in the export sector may also depend on the terms of trade (Bean 1986). Following the export price shocks, there could even be a deflationary effect on prices if foreign investors aim to take advantage of any rise in profits and the exchange rate appreciates in response to the ensuing capital inflow. For an example of a developing country's experience, see Perera's (1984) account of Sri Lanka's response to fluctuations in the tea price. Cufer *et al.* (2000) discuss the second-round effects of administered price changes in Slovenia.

29 See Torres and Martin (1997) for an example.

30 Caballero (1999) surveys the modelling of investment.

31 A separate issue as to whether credit and financial market imperfections matter in the flexible-price state is whether they increase or decrease the sensitivity of investment and output to nominal shocks.

In a simple model of a developed economy. Bean *et al.* (2002) demonstrate that if financial frictions make the model non-linear in endogenous factors (in our set-up, this would represent a departure from assumption (4.16), then the transmission of monetary policy can be amplified. Real shocks will also distort the transmission of nominal shocks onto inflation and output.

In developing countries, financial frictions can sometimes act to diminish rather than amplify transmission.

Montiel (1991) and Green and Murinde (1993) discuss monetary transmission when unofficial curb markets for foreign exchange and loans co-exist with financially repressed (with a low real interest rate) formal markets. See also Burkett and Vogel (1992) for a discussion of how investment decisions are made in these financially repressed economies. Kamin *et al.* (1998:44) provide a broader discussion of credit market imperfections in emerging markets, and Meltzer (1995, 2001) surveys the implications of these imperfections for monetary transmission more generally. Borio and Fritz (1995) and Borio (1996) provide some evidence from industrialised countries. Finally, many theories of economic growth now emphasise the role of institutions (and investors' perceptions of a country's institutions), and not just the initial level of capital, in affecting the incorporation of financial capital originating from abroad, and thus the flows of capital in and out of national borders.

32 See, for example, Layard *et al.* 1991; Manning (1993); Nickell 1996.

33 After all, the choice of horizon (Batini and Nelson 2000) is related to the time it takes for the effects of nominal rigidities to die out.

34 Here, terminal conditions refer to the conditions imposed at the end of the solution period when solving a numerical model with forward-looking terms for forecasting. Transversality conditions refer to necessary conditions for the solutions of dynamic optimisation problems, when expressed in algebraic form. The two need not be the same: terminal conditions are often stronger. Takayama (1995) and Ekeland and Scheinkman (1986) explain the mathematics between different transversality condition assumptions.

35 See Isard (2000:7) for a discussion of alternative terminal conditions for growth and the real interest rate in the IMF's MULTIMOD, and Drew and Hunt (1998: section 4.2) for a similar discussion regarding terminal conditions for growth and the capital stock in the Reserve Bank of New Zealand Forecasting and Policy System, for example.

36 A typical assumption used to identify the natural rate in these models is that inflation is constant in the flexible-price state, hence the term 'non-accelerating inflationary rate of unemployment'. However, Nickell (1988) argues

against automatically linking a stable level of inflation with unemployment being at its natural rate in macroeconomic models.

37 Assessing the sustainability of fiscal deficits (both sovereign and private sector) is an important aspect of macroeconomic modelling on developing countries. As Hagemann (1999) points out in his explanation of the IMF methodology, we need to distinguish the role of different shocks in affecting the forecasted balance when we assess the sustainability of a country's policy mix. Separating out the role of monetary factors by forecasting the public deficit in the flexible-price state is one such potentially useful identification.

38 There are many examples of papers that show how the real disequilibria of different variables can be related – for example, see Fischer's (1988) study of disinflation in a small open economy or Joyce and Wren-Lewis (1990), linking between real exchange rate and labour market behaviour. Phelps (1994) links short-run fluctuations in flexible-price unemployment to differences in asset price evaluations.

39 See Kiley 1996; Basu and Taylor 1999; Jadresic 1999

40 The historical dimension might matter too; Gordon (1990) provides some discussion regarding whether nominal rigidities have increased or decreased over US history.

41 Agenor and Aizenman (1994) discuss the macro-economics of segmented labour markets in developing countries.

42 More generally this relates to the literature that compares alternative sectoral weighting schemes to derive optimal monetary policy indicators. The aim is to minimise the volatility of headline inflation and output by placing less or more weight on information from different sectors in formulating targets or indicators. See Aoki (2001) for an example of weighting based on relative price stickiness.

43 If employment were not constant, then this would have to be $E_t L_{t+1} C_t = E_t((1+i_t/\beta) P_t/P_{t+1})^{1/v} C_{t+1} L_t$

44 In what follows, lower-case values indicate natural logs, except for interest rates.

45 This would have to be generalised if we wanted to allow for pre-announced shocks etc.

46 We assume that $E_t p_{t+T} = E_{t-1} p_{t+T}$, for a terminal date that is far enough into the future.

47 For example, assume that information is updated at a rate ρ towards the broadest information set in forming expectations of a variable z_{t+s} at time t.

Then the time t expectations of z, $E_{t-k,\rho} z_{t+s}$, are given by $E_{t-k,\rho} z_{t+s} = \Sigma_{k=0}^{\infty} \rho^k E_{t-k} z_{t+s}$; where $E_{t-k} z_{t+s}$ denotes expectations of z_{t+s}, using the broadest set available at time t–k.

48 This would be written as $\exp(b_t) = \exp(w_t + n_t + l_t) - \exp(p_t + y_t) + (1 + i_{t-1}) * \exp(b_{t-1})$

49 We are assuming that $-n_t \approx 1 - N_t$ which would be accurate only if a small proportion of hours were spent at work. This approximation is not innocuous; we discuss its ramifications in section 4.3.5.

50 Note that the output gap is equal to the unemployment gap $(n_t - n_t^*)$, implying an elasticity of 1 in an Okun's Law relationship. This is not a general result, though, and more complicated utility functions, such as those modelled in Correia *et al.* (1995), or different production functions (Prachowny 1992) will display different elasticities.

5 Model-building in theory and practice

The Phillips curve

Lavan Mahadeva

5.1 Introduction

The purpose of the previous chapter was to explain why we might want to measure and forecast the output gap for monetary policy. The intention was to separate out the output movements that are determined by nominal (demand-side) shocks only. If we can understand how the output gap relates to inflation, we can then inform on the contribution of these shocks to inflation.

In this chapter, we examine the relationship between the output gap and inflation-commonly referred to as the Phillips curve. The contribution of nominal demand-side shocks to inflation is typically summarised by the Phillips curve relationship in macroeconomic models. What we show is that this reliance on the Phillips curve may be unwarranted. One reason is that the Phillips curve should not always be expected to be a stable phenomenon for every country nor easy to estimate on every data set. However, neither is it a necessary feature of every model of the transmission mechanism. Alternative disaggregated wage and price structures may do in better capturing how inflation and output are both affected by nominal shocks.

This is not to say that we can neglect to build nominal rigidities into our models. An understanding of nominal stickiness is of crucial importance for many policy questions and is relevant in all types of countries. For open economies, it is important in determining how quickly and how completely the exchange rate changes pass on to domestic prices. For fixed exchange-rate countries, the issue is about how changes in foreign prices affect domestic prices. For a high inflation country that wants to lower inflation without large output losses, the optimal speed of disinflation depends, at least in part, on this price passthrough.[1] However the Phillips curve is only one of many ways of capturing this feature.

We will explore why the relationship between the output gap and inflation might vary across countries, combining insights of the theoretical model described in Chapter 4 with findings from some estimated models included in the following chapters of this book. A key message from both theory and cross-country comparison is that the modeller needs to understand the specific nature of the nominal rigidities that are present in his or her country before that is built into a model. For example, in the extreme case where a country has very few nominal rigidities, we should find actual output almost always close to its flexible-price level, and any movements in the output gap short-lived.

5.2 The Phillips curve

5.2.1 What is the Phillips curve?

In the previous chapter we emphasised that one of the purposes of measuring the output gap was to quantify the contribution of demand-side shocks to inflation. How does this relate to the famous Phillips curve relationship that links the output gap to inflation?

The Phillips curve relationship – which establishes how, under certain conditions, a higher output gap predicts higher inflation – is often constructed from two theoretical steps:

1. 'Implicit collusion' theories of firms' monopolistic pricing behaviour predict that the mark-up of their prices over marginal costs (say, wages and imported inputs) rises in a recession and falls in a boom. Rotemberg and Woodford (1991), for example, show that firms can lower their mark-up when current output is high relative to future profits because there is less incentive for their competitors to undercut them.
2. Theories of the cost of nominal *price* adjustment – such as the Calvo price-setting framework[2] – predict that a low real mark-up is associated with an expected deceleration in inflation in the future. As inflation is expected to decelerate in the future, all other things being equal, inflation will rise now. A low real mark-up is therefore associated with a rise in current inflation.

Combining the two steps explains that in booms, a large positive output gap implies a low real mark-up, which in turn implies higher inflation. Conversely, in recessions negative output gaps are associated with higher mark-ups and lower inflation.

5.2.2 Difficulties with the Phillips curve

The Phillips curve, originally presented as an empirical relationship,[3] can be supported by some theory. Notwithstanding its familiarity, it has a turbulent history. It has frequently been found to be rejected by data, and these empirical failures are often attributed to deficiencies in the theory underpinning it.

Most recently, Galì (2002b), Galì and Gertler (1999) and Sbordone (2002) tested and rejected what amounts to the first step of our theoretical argument. They failed to find the predicted relationship between the output gap and inflation acceleration on the US and EU,[4] a failure which, as Galì and Gertler (1999) later went on to suggest, seems to comes about because the output gap is poorly related to the mark-up in US data. Other research questions whether the mark-up is negatively related to the output gap (or 'counter-cyclical'). For example, the 'customer markets' model of price-setting – in contrast to the theory of implicit collusion – points to a procyclical mark-up.[5]

The second step of our argument is also open to debate. Allowing for costs of adjusting inflation (or costs of updating expectations of inflation) over and above the costs of price adjustment would mean that past inflation now also matters in determining expected inflation (Smets and Wouters 2002; Steinsson 2002). Once the Phillips curve involves dynamic terms in inflation, a lower mark-up need not always be associated with a rise in current inflation.

The debate is ongoing: dissatisfaction with Phillips curve estimates continues to drive searches for a stable and better micro-founded form. However, perhaps we should not expect the Phillips curve to be a universal phenomenon: it may not manifest itself in the data for every country and for every regime, even when there are significant nominal rigidities.

One reason is that shifts in monetary policy or structural changes to the rest of the transmission mechanism can disrupt the link between the output gap and inflation. Our model in the previous chapter can be used to illustrate this point. There we derived explicit expressions for inflation and the output gap as linear combinations of demand-side shocks, given assumptions about how the demand-side shocks were expected to behave in the future. We showed that output gap, $\tilde{y}_t$, is related to nominal shocks, e_{nt}, by the following expression:

$$\tilde{y}_t = \varsigma_2 \alpha \tilde{y}_{t-1} + \frac{\varsigma_2}{2\vartheta(1-\alpha)} e_{nt} \tag{5.1}$$

and inflation is

$$p_t = p_{t-1} - e_{nt} + \overline{\text{target}} + \sum_{j=0}^{\infty} \alpha^j e_{n,t-1-j} \tag{5.2}$$

Recall that the parameter ς_2 captures by the degree of nominal rigidity in the economy: the closer ς_2 is to one, the more rigidities they were. υ is both the intertemporal elasticity of substitution and the elasticity of labour supply (we worked with a CES utility function with consumption and leisure). The nominal shock, e_{nt}, and the degree of policy gradualism, α, are defined by a simple monetary policy set-up. The policy rule was such that the expected rate of inflation is always kept equal to a target path:

$$E_t p_{t+1} = P_t + \text{target}_t \tag{5.3}$$

where the targeted path of inflation (target_t) is assumed to follow an autoregressive process about a constant mean rate ($\overline{\text{target}}$):

$$\text{target}_t = (1-\alpha)\overline{\text{target}} + \alpha \text{target}_{t-1} + e_{nt} \tag{5.4}$$

e_{nt} is independently normally distributed random shock with a mean of zero and a variance of σ_n^2.

We can re-write 1 as:

$$e_{nt} = \frac{2\vartheta(1-\alpha)}{\varsigma_2}\left(\tilde{y}_t - \varsigma_2 \alpha \tilde{y}_{t-1}\right) \tag{5.5}$$

Using equation (5.5), we can write (5.2) as a dynamic relationship relating inflation to terms in the output gap:

$$\begin{aligned} & p_t - p_{t-1} \\ &= \alpha\left(p_{t-1} - p_{t-2}\right) + (1-\alpha)\overline{\text{target}} \\ &\quad - \frac{2\vartheta(1-\alpha)}{\varsigma_2}\left(\tilde{y}_t - \alpha\tilde{y}_{t-1} - \varsigma_2\alpha\tilde{y}_{t-1} + \varsigma_2\alpha^2\tilde{y}_{t-2}\right) \\ &\quad + \frac{2\vartheta(1-\alpha)}{\varsigma_2}\left(\tilde{y}_{t-1} - \varsigma_2\alpha\tilde{y}_{t-2}\right) \\ &= \alpha\left(p_{t-1} - p_{t-2}\right) + (1-\alpha)\overline{\text{target}} \\ &\quad + \frac{2\vartheta(1-\alpha)}{\varsigma_2}\left(-\tilde{y}_t + \left(\varsigma_2\alpha + \alpha + 1\right)\tilde{y}_{t-1} - \varsigma_2\alpha(1+\alpha)\tilde{y}_{t-2}\right) \end{aligned} \tag{5.6}$$

Equation (5.6) shows that our model does predict some form of (dynamic) Phillips curve relationship. However, the coefficient depends not only on the degree of nominal rigidity – ς_2 – but also on the elasticity of labour supply – υ – and on the degree of policy gradualism – α. The 'Lucas critique' applied here means that although a trade-off between output and inflation exists, it is conditional on assumptions about the monetary policy reaction as well as those regarding other aspects of the transmission mechanism – for example, on the shock processes and the timing of information available on the shocks.[6,7] The observed inflationary impact of oil price shocks of the 1970s and early 1980s, for example, depended on the extent to which they were accommodated or resisted. Fry and Lilien (1986) show how similar economies reacted very differently to the same oil-price supply shock, and suggest that these differences were due to monetary policy stance.

Equation (6) describes a complicated dynamic relationship between the output gap and inflation. What would happen if we ignored those dynamics and estimated a simple Phillips curve on those data?[8] Would the trade-off as captured by the coefficient on the output gap in a simple ordinary least squares regression of inflation on a constant and the output gap always be positive? To answer this question, note that the asymptotic value of this OLS coefficient (derived in the appendix) is:[9]

$$\frac{2\vartheta(1-\alpha)\left(1-(\varsigma_2\alpha)^2\right)}{\varsigma_2}\left(\frac{\varsigma_2\alpha-1+\varsigma_2\alpha^2}{1-\varsigma_2\alpha^2}\right). \tag{5.7}$$

A positive value of the estimated coefficient of output on inflation emerges only under certain conditions. If changes in the target rate are not sufficiently persistent, or if there are a few nominal rigidities, such that $\varsigma_2\alpha(1 + \alpha) < 1$, shocks to expected future inflation (effectively announced with changes in the inflation target) will be quickly offset by falls in current inflation. As monetary policymakers do not care about output, the contribution of these shocks on output, the output gap, will still be positive. In this case the asymptotic coefficient in the Phillips curve can be expected to be negative. Only if target changes are sufficiently persistent such that $\varsigma_2\alpha(1 + \alpha) > 1$ would current inflation may have to rise somewhat, and the coefficient in the Phillips curve in our model be positive as is 'standard'.

The above result is model-dependent; it does not mean that the correlation between output and inflation will always be negative. The key point is that the Phillips curve is a 'reduced form' relationship. As such it depends not just on nominal rigidities but also on other aspects of the transmission mechanism and the monetary policy framework. Recall that the theoretical arguments of section 5.2.1 explained only the output gap and inflation are driven by the same nominal shocks: the theory does not go as far as asserting that the output gap causes' inflation in any deeper sense.[10] Consequently, finding a positive relationship between the two on past data does not imply that the output gap can *always* be used as a predictor of domestic sources of inflationary pressure. The output gap can be thought of rather more of a signal than a cause of inflationary pressure. There can be circumstances when that signal malfunctions.

Another problem is that we can only successfully adapt theoretical underpinnings of the Phillips curve into a practical monetary policy tool if the data permit us to do so. The requirements of the data set are substantial: it must allow us accurately to measure flexible-price output, to identify and strip out flexible-price inflation, and to model the dynamic processes that related both to underlying demand shocks. So even if a stable underlying Phillips curve exists, there could be many reasons why data (especially that available in developing countries) are not up to the task of identifying and estimating it.

A very likely source of error is in output gap measurement. Here, the main problem is that data on GDP can be available infrequently, unreliably and subject to wild revision. Industrial production measures and survey data are available with more frequency, but can be unrepresentative of the economy as a whole. For example, the September 1999 edition of the IMF's International Financial Statistics included no recent quarterly data (for any of the previous four quarters) at all for any item in the National Accounts for 80 percent of the developing and transitional economies included in our study, compared with only 15 per cent of the industrialised economies.[11]

The consequences of this lack of data are, as Fry *et al.* (2000) argued, that 'there appear to be large gaps in the analysis of the real sector in developing and transitional economies'. In their survey of central banks, only 8 per cent of respondent banks in such economies had published research on labour markets, and there had been similarly little analysis of consumption and investment. Similarly, only 6 per cent of developing and transitional economies reported having published such research on the Phillips curve and output gap, compared to 67 per cent in industrialised economies.[12]

To summarise, nominal rigidities can imply an output gap inflation trade-off but not necessarily one that implies a stable Phillips curve. Moreover, even if a stable relationship exists, that relationship can be difficult to estimate because of the quality of available data.[13]

5.2.3 Do we need to estimate Phillips curves?

The last section went through the many potentially serious problems associated with estimating Phillips curves. Can we do without an explicit Phillips curve in our monetary policy models? We now show that the answer is yes, possibly. Although the Phillips curve is one route to modelling the effect of demand shocks on inflation, there are alternative structures that may tell us more about what drives inflation than relying on a poorly measured output gap in an unreliable Phillips curve.[14]

An example can make things clear. Let us derive two different set of equations that both describe the same economy depicted in Chapter 4. Model 1, from the previous chapter, is defined by the following equations:[15]

Model 1

$$c_t = y_t \tag{5.8}$$

$$-n_t = y_t - l_t - \frac{1}{\vartheta}(\ln(\mu_t) + w_t - p_t) \tag{5.9}$$

$$\ln(\mu_t) = -(1-\vartheta)a_t \tag{5.10}$$

$$y_t = a_t + l_t + n_t \tag{5.11}$$

$$a_t = a_{t-1} + e_{rt} \tag{5.12}$$

$$E_t p_{t+1} = p_t + \overline{\text{target}} + e_{nt} \tag{5.13}$$

$$i_t = \overline{\text{target}} + e_{nt} + \vartheta E_t(y_t - y_{t+1}) + \ln\beta \tag{5.14}$$

$$\begin{aligned} w_t = {} & p_t + y_t - l_t - n_t \\ & + (1-\varsigma_1)\left(\sum_{k=0}^{\infty}\varsigma_1^k\left[E_{t-k}(y_t - l_t - n_t) - (y_t - l_t - n_t)\right]\right) \\ & + (1-\varsigma_2)\left(\sum_{k=0}^{\infty}\varsigma_2^k\left[E_{t-k}(p_t) - p_t\right]\right) \end{aligned} \tag{5.15}$$

$$l_t = \bar{l} \tag{5.16}$$

$$c_t^* = y_t^* \tag{5.17}$$

$$-n_t^* = y_t^* - \bar{l} - \frac{1}{\vartheta}\left(\ln(\mu_t) + w_t^* - p_t^*\right) \tag{5.18}$$

$$y_t^* = a_t + \bar{l} + n_t^* \tag{5.19}$$

$$p_t^* = p_t \tag{5.20}$$

$$i_t^* = \overline{\text{target}} + e_{nt} + \vartheta E_t\left(y_t^* - y_{t+1}^*\right) + \ln\beta \tag{5.21}$$

$$w_t^* = p_t^* + y_t^* - l_t^* - n_t^* + (1-\varsigma_1)\left(\sum_{k=0}^{\infty}\varsigma_1^k\left[E_{t-k}(y_t^* - l_t^* - n_t^*) - (y_t^* - l_t^* - n_t^*)\right]\right. \tag{5.22}$$

$$l_t^* = \bar{l} \tag{5.23}$$

Model 2

The purpose of another representation of the same economy, called Model 2, is to avoid using data on wages. To eliminate wages from the labour supply expression (5.9), we can subsitute (5.10), (5.11) and (5.15) into (5.9) to give an expression for hours in formal employment which does not refer to wages explicitly:

$$n_t = \frac{(1-\varsigma_1)}{2\vartheta}\left(\sum_{k=0}^{\infty}\varsigma_1^k\left[E_{t-k}a_t - a_t\right]\right) + \frac{(1-\varsigma_2)}{2\vartheta}\left(\sum_{k=0}^{\infty}\varsigma_2^k\left[E_{t-k}(p_t) - p_t\right]\right) \quad (5.24)$$

Similarly, the hours in formal employment in the flexible-price state would be as (5.24) but with $\varsigma_2 = 0$;

$$n_t^* = \frac{(1-\varsigma_1)}{2\vartheta}\left(\sum_{k=0}^{\infty}\varsigma_1^k\left[E_{t-k}a_t - a_t\right]\right) \quad (5.25)$$

We can replace the wage equation in the flexible-price economy with the Phillips curve of section 5.2.2 (5.6) and add the identity to define the output gap:

$$\tilde{y}_t = y_t - y_t^* \quad (5.26)$$

As well as equations (5.6), (5.24), (5.25) and (5.26) Model 2 would comprise:

$$c_t = y_t \quad (5.27)$$

$$y_t = a_t + l_t + n_t \quad (5.\ 28)$$

$$a_t = a_{t-1} + e_{rt} \quad (5.29)$$

$$i_t = \overline{\text{target}} + e_{nt} + \vartheta E_t\left(y_t - y_{t+1}\right) + \ln\beta \quad (5.30)$$

$$l_t = \bar{l} \quad (5.31)$$

$$c_t^* = y_t^* \quad (5.32)$$

$$y_t^* = a_t + \bar{l} + n_t^* \quad (5.33)$$

$$p_t^* = p_t \quad (5.34)$$

$$i_t^* = \overline{\text{target}} + e_{nt} + \vartheta E_t\left(y_t^* - y_{t+1}^*\right) + \ln\beta \quad (5.35)$$

and

$$l_t^* = \bar{l} \quad (5.36)$$

Note that no Phillips curve is explicit in Model 1 as it is in Model 2. However, nominal shocks affect both inflation and output identically in both models: there would still be the same short-run run trade-off in monetary policy, so we could (at least in principle) work with either structure.

Why have many modellers chosen to work with models with Phillips curves (like Model 2) instead of models with disaggregate wage and price systems (like Model 1)? After all, if wage setting contained important and distinct information for monetary policy, a structure that models the labour market explicitly would be more appropriate.[16] One reason is that wage data can be of poor quality. Another is that nominal wages in their country are near to completely flexible; nominal wage dynamics add little extra interesting information above that gained from modelling prices. In general terms, which strategy will work best for monetary policy forecasting depends on the sources and types and uncertainty faced in the economy.[17] What *is* important is to build some structure that picks up how inflation and output are affected by different underlying shocks (in our simple model, these were nominal shocks or real shocks) and that takes conscious account of local constraints such as measurement error.

5.2.4 Phillips curve when inflation is far from zero

Developing countries tend to have high or trending inflation rates. Another question that comes to mind when we consider estimating Phillips curves for developing countries then is the following: is it necessary for inflation to keep at very low levels for there to be a Phillips curve relationship? We show that the answer to this question, at least in our model, is no; the Phillips curve relationship (5.6) that arises from our model is independent of the target rate of inflation.[18]

This issue is of interest because many theoretical derivations of the Phillips curve in the literature assume that inflation is close to zero. The standard practise is to linearise an expression that describes the aggregate inflation rate implied by optimal price setting around a steady state.[19] As these are intended to be applied only to countries with low inflation, the designated steady-state value of output is usually the balanced growth path and that of inflation is zero. We derived our Phillips curve in Chapter 4 with its application to developing countries in mind, so we had to avoid linearising equations around a state where inflation was zero. Instead, we worked with the deviations of the variables about the a flexible-price state where inflation does not have to be zero (or even close to it).

This does not mean that stable Phillips curves can easily be found under high-inflation environments. Monetary policy regime changes are more frequent and more unpredictable in high-inflation countries, and there may be measurement difficulties associated with the use of deflators that worsen the quality of the real data. What we have shown is that it does not necessarily follow that a Phillips curve will not exist under high inflation. In the next section, we provide some model-based evidence of Phillips curves across such countries.

5.3 Some model-based evidence on the extent of nominal rigidities across countries

Chapters 6, 8 and 9 in this volume contain small structural models built for Colombia, Poland and Turkey respectively. These models have a similar form in so far as the supply-sides were all based on estimated wage and price relationships where in the long run prices and wages are driven by labour productivity and import prices, the latter in domestic currency terms. In the short run, dynamics and expectations of inflation play a crucial part. However, how important these dynamics have been in slowing down inflation is, as we shall see, very country-specific. To broaden the comparison, we also include a model for the Czech Republic described in Mahadeva and Smidková (2000) and one for the UK, a simple closed economy model described by Bean *et al.* (2002).

The Appendix to this chapter contains the plots of impulse responses from these models to a set of common shocks. To make the comparison as transparent as possible, we used the same standard Taylor policy rule in each model, adjusted for a foreign rate of interest.[20] Also for purposes of comparison, we include the impulse responses to the same shocks from the dynamic general equilbrium model of Hungary (Chapter 7) and from Svensson's (2000) illustrative model of an imaginary open economy in the Appendix.

We focus on the response of these models to the same shock: an unanticipated 0.25 pp increase in the nominal interest (in annualised terms) for four quarters, with nominal interest rates held fixed (the policy rule switched off) for two quarters, which can be interpreted as a temporary policy surprise. However, in the Appendix we also derive the responses of the models to other shocks: an unanticipated temporary 1 per cent increase in domestic inflation and an unanticipated temporary 1 per cent increase in real GDP (above potential). The former can be interpreted as a pricing-error shock and the latter as real-demand or government-spending shock.[21]

Figures 5.1–5.3 plot the responses of annual inflation, the annual real interest rate and the output gap following the surprise rise in the nominal interest rates.

What stands out is that the speed of transmission of this monetary policy shock varies enormously across the models. Inflation reacts immediately to policy changes in Turkey, but it takes much longer in the Czech Republic, Poland and the UK, and even longer in Colombia. One measure is that 50 per cent of the permanent fall in the price level following the shock takes place after only two quarters in the model of Turkey, whereas for that of UK and the Czech Republic it takes five quarters, for

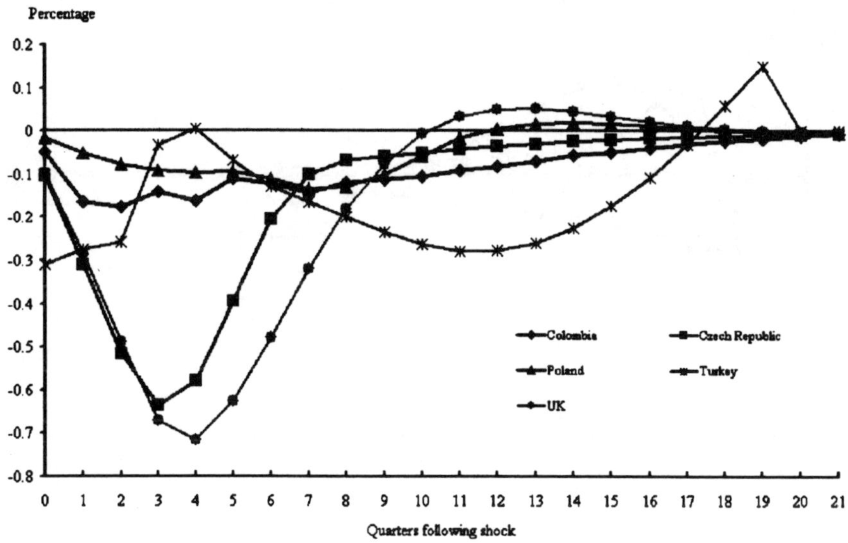

Figure 5.1 Responses of annual inflation to a nominal interest rate shock.

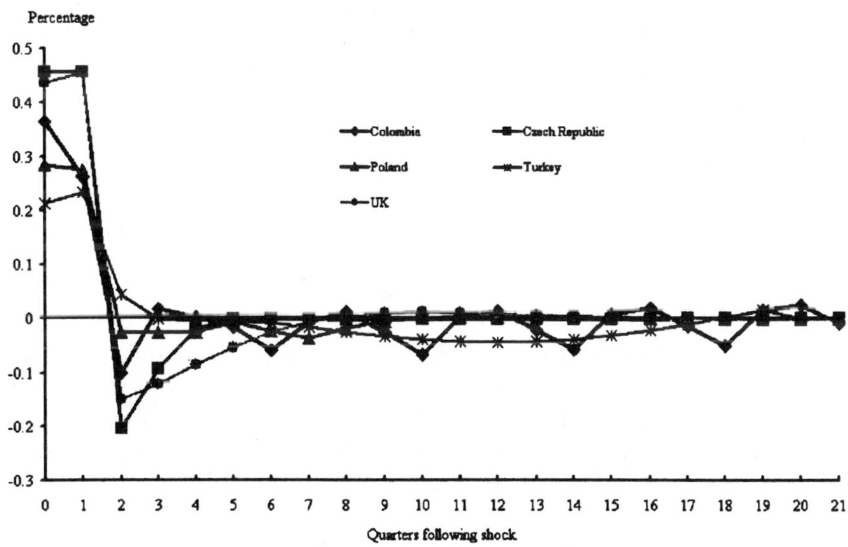

Figure 5.2 Responses of the real interest rate to a nominal interest rate shock.

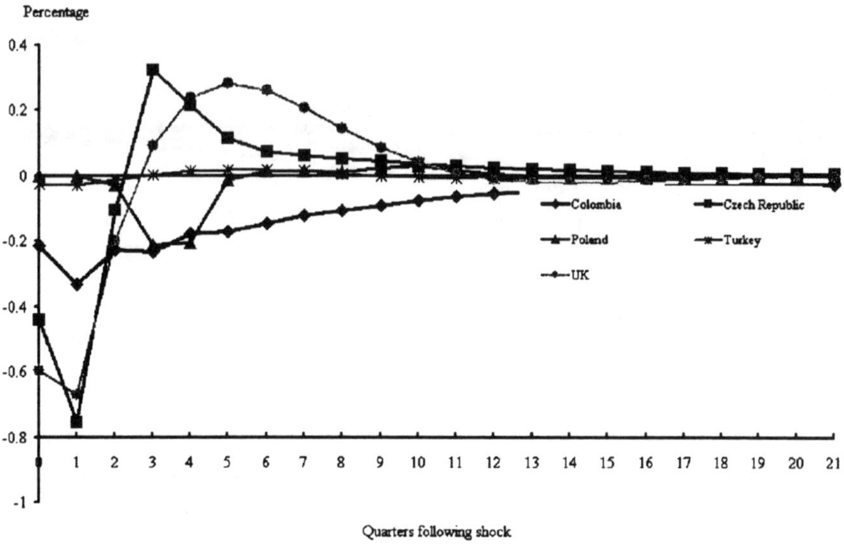

Figure 5.3 Responses of the output gap to a nominal interest rate shock.

Poland seven quarters, and for Colombia eight quarters. Figure 5.3 shows that the speed with which the output gap opens up and closes follows a similar ranking. Taken together, these results suggest that the extent of nominal rigidities matter in determining the responses of inflation and output to monetary policy shocks.

If a major factor in determining differences in the speed of transmission is the extent of nominal rigidities, can we see this reflected in significant differences in inflation processes between these countries? Figures 5.4 and 5.5 describe the different inflation series from these countries, as well as Hungary, in the 1990s for when data were available.[22]

Turkey's inflation is consistently the highest, and the most variable. By contrast, Colombian and UK inflation seem very steady. Figure 5.5 shows statistical measures of the degree of predictability of the inflationary processes in each country. This confirms that inflation in Colombia and the UK is indeed the most predictable, whilst Turkey's inflation rate is very uncertain, with the other three Central European countries in between.

When we match the predictability of inflation with speed of monetary policy transmission, it is interesting to note that for Turkey, its uncertain inflationary process seems to exhibit more flexibility in prices. The explanation would seem to be quite intuitive: if prices are very unpredictable, agents will be extremely reluctant to fix price and wage contracts in nominal terms. Whatever their reason for fixing wages and prices in nominal terms, their opportunity cost of doing so will be higher. As has

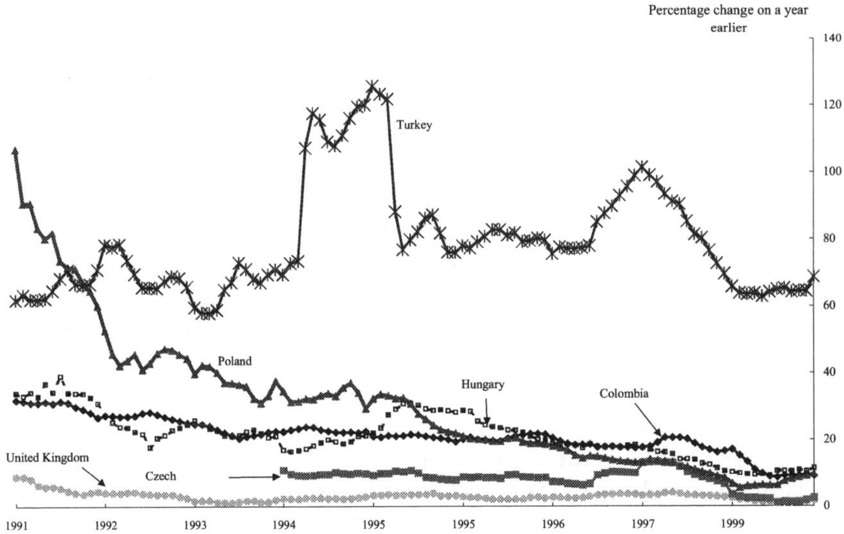

Figure 5.4 Annual consumer price inflation in the 1990s.

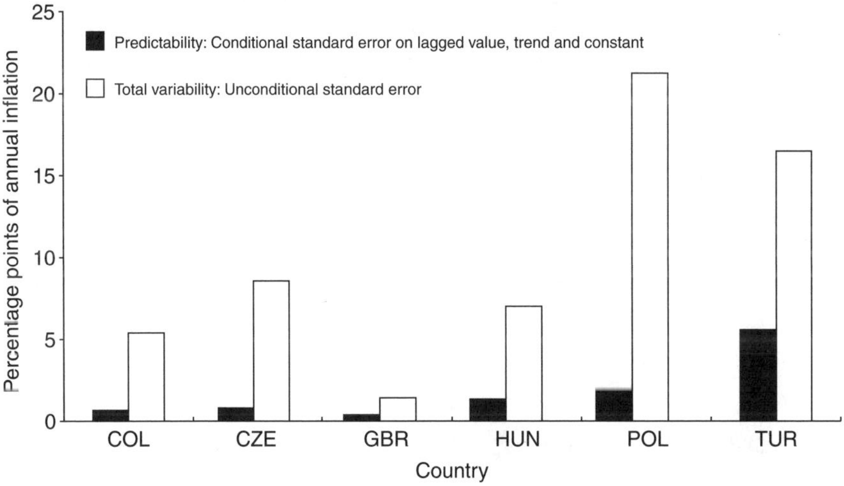

Figure 5.5 Predictability and volatility of annual consumer price inflation in the 1990s.

been pointed out in the literature, this degree of passthrough also seems to depend on the level of inflation.[23] That need not be at odds with what we have found here: high-inflation countries typically have the most variable inflation too. As with every rule they are exceptions and, at least in its past, Colombia seems to be one of these. Its inflation rate is quite high, but steady, and its degree of passthrough seems to be relatively slow.

The size of the responses of inflation and output in Figures 5.1 and 5.2 also vary enormously across the models. However, here further aspects of the transmission mechanism seem to matter other than nominal rigidities. As our theoretical results emphasised, the effects of demand shocks on inflation and output can depend on the monetary policy in place, the production process and the parameters that govern national consumption decisions, for example.

The impulse responses of the output gap confirm that with more flexible prices, therefore, the output gap will be more short-lived. As GDP data is available on, at most, a quarterly basis, this means that the output gap is hard to measure. If only annual GDP data exist, the effect of a short-lived output gap may have already been averaged out. A general intuition would be that a typical developing country would have more flexible prices and less frequent GDP data than more developed countries. In such a country, we have shown that the output gap will be difficult to measure and but also less relevant for practical policy purposes.

The intuition behind these results seems quite straightforward, but the policy implications are not. In countries with more unpredictable inflationary series, even if prices are flexible, economic agents will have to pay a price for the extra uncertainty. The simple models used in this chapter do not capture these longer-run output costs. They take no account of the adverse effects on investment and consumption of unanticipated and volatile inflation, or of shoe-leather costs.[24]

5.3.1 Asymptotic estimate of the output-gap inflation coefficient

We can write the output gap as:

$$\tilde{y}_t = \frac{\varsigma_2}{2\vartheta(1-\alpha)}\left(\sum_{i=0}^{\infty}(\varsigma_2\alpha)^i e_{n,t-i}\right) \tag{5.37}$$

and inflation as:

$$p_t - p_{t-1} = -e_{nt} + \overline{\text{target}} + \sum_{j=0}^{\infty}\alpha^j e_{n,t-1-j} \tag{5.38}$$

The unconditional variance of the output gap is:

$$\begin{aligned} E(\tilde{y}_t)^2 &= \sigma_n^2\left(\frac{\varsigma_2}{2\vartheta(1-\alpha)}\right)^2\left(\sum_{i=0}^{\infty}(\varsigma_2\alpha)^{2i}\right) \\ &= \sigma_n^2\left(\frac{\varsigma_2}{2\vartheta(1-\alpha)}\right)^2\frac{1}{1-(\varsigma_2\alpha)^2} \end{aligned} \tag{5.39}$$

The unconditional covariance between the output gap and inflation is given by:

$$Cov(\tilde{y}_t, p_t - p_{t-1}) = \frac{\sigma_n^2 \varsigma_2}{2\vartheta(1-\alpha)}\left(-1 + \left(\sum_{i=1}^{\infty} (\varsigma_2 \alpha)^i \alpha^{i-1}\right)\right)$$

$$= \frac{\sigma_n^2 \varsigma_2}{2\vartheta(1-\alpha)}\left(-1 + \frac{1}{\alpha}\left(\sum_{i=1}^{\infty} (\varsigma_2 \alpha^2)^i\right)\right)$$

$$= \frac{\sigma_n^2 \varsigma_2}{2\vartheta(1-\alpha)}\left(-1 + \frac{\varsigma_2 \alpha}{1-\varsigma_2 \alpha^2}\right)$$

$$= \frac{\sigma_n^2 \varsigma_2}{2\vartheta(1-\alpha)}\left(\frac{\varsigma_2 \alpha - 1 + \varsigma_2 \alpha^2}{1-\varsigma_2 \alpha^2}\right) \tag{5.40}$$

The asymptotic value of the coefficient on the output gap, in a regression of the output, plus a constant on inflation will then be given by:

$$\frac{Cov(\tilde{y}_t, p_t - p_{t-1})}{E(\tilde{y}_t)^2} = \frac{2\vartheta(1-\alpha)\left(1-(\varsigma_2\alpha)^2\right)}{\varsigma_2}\left(\frac{\varsigma_2 \alpha - 1 + \varsigma_2 \alpha^2}{1-\varsigma_2 \alpha^2}\right) \tag{5.41}$$

Appendix

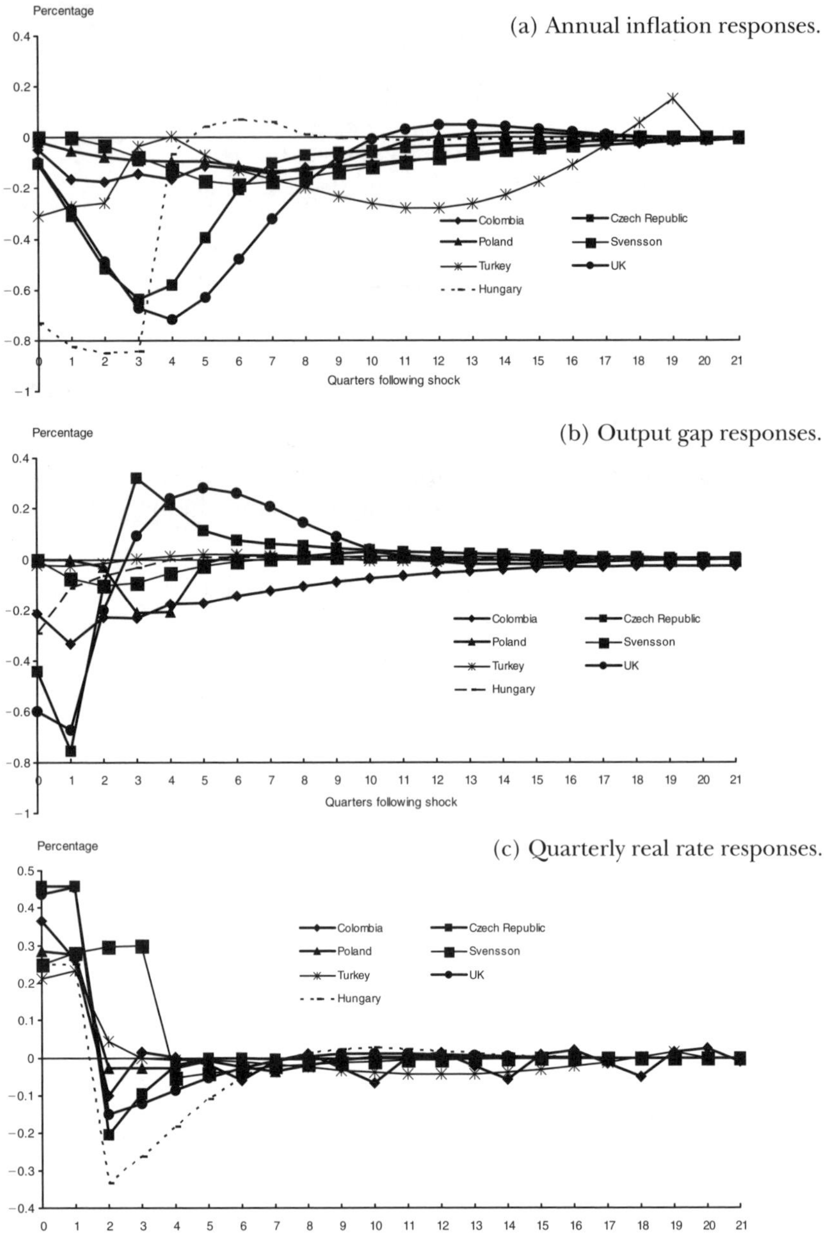

Figure 5.6 Responses for a policy rate shock*

Note

* An unanticipated 0.25 pp increase in the nominal interest (in annualised terms) for four quarters, with nominal interest rates held fixed (the policy rule switched off) for two quarters.

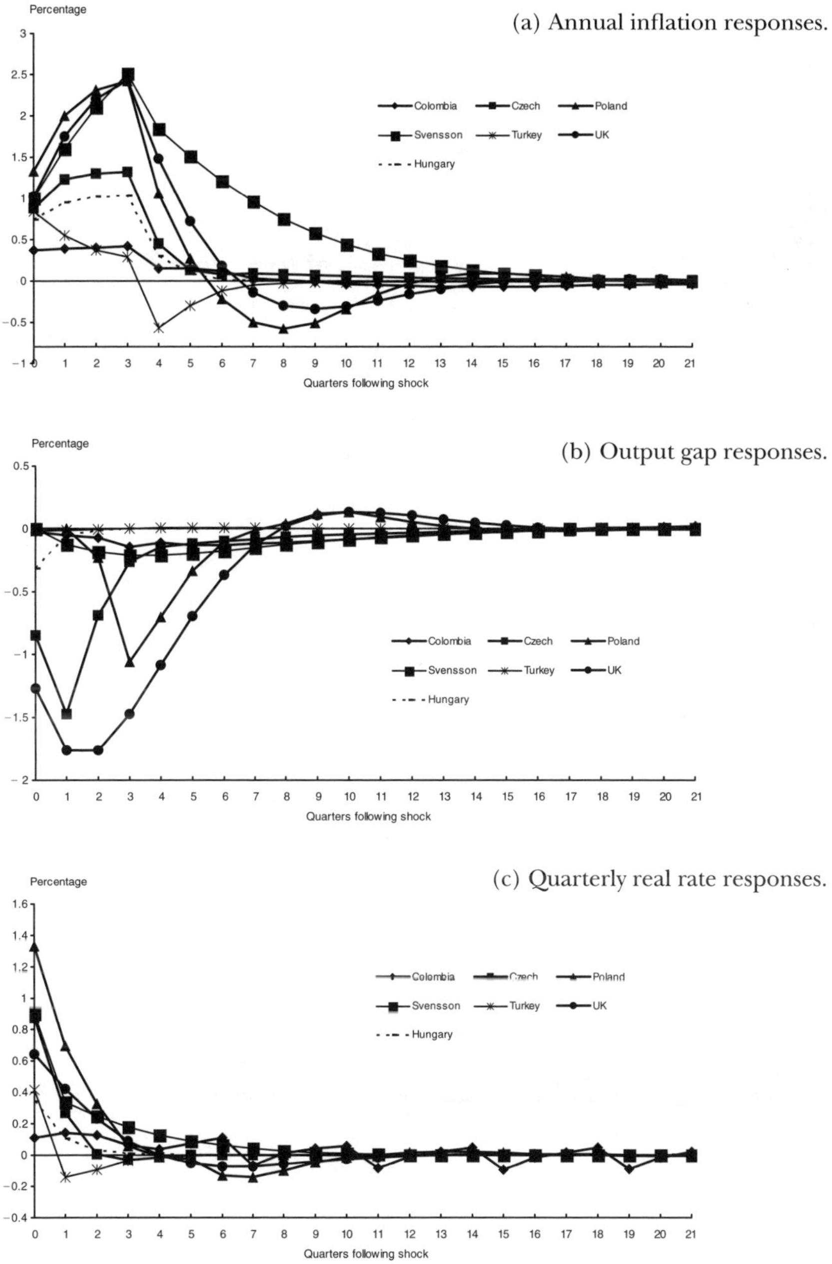

Figure 5.7 Responses for a cost-push shock to inflation**

Note

** An unanticipated 1 pp increase in quarterly inflation for one quarter, except for Colombia, for which it was a 0.25 pp on annual inflation imposed for four quarters.

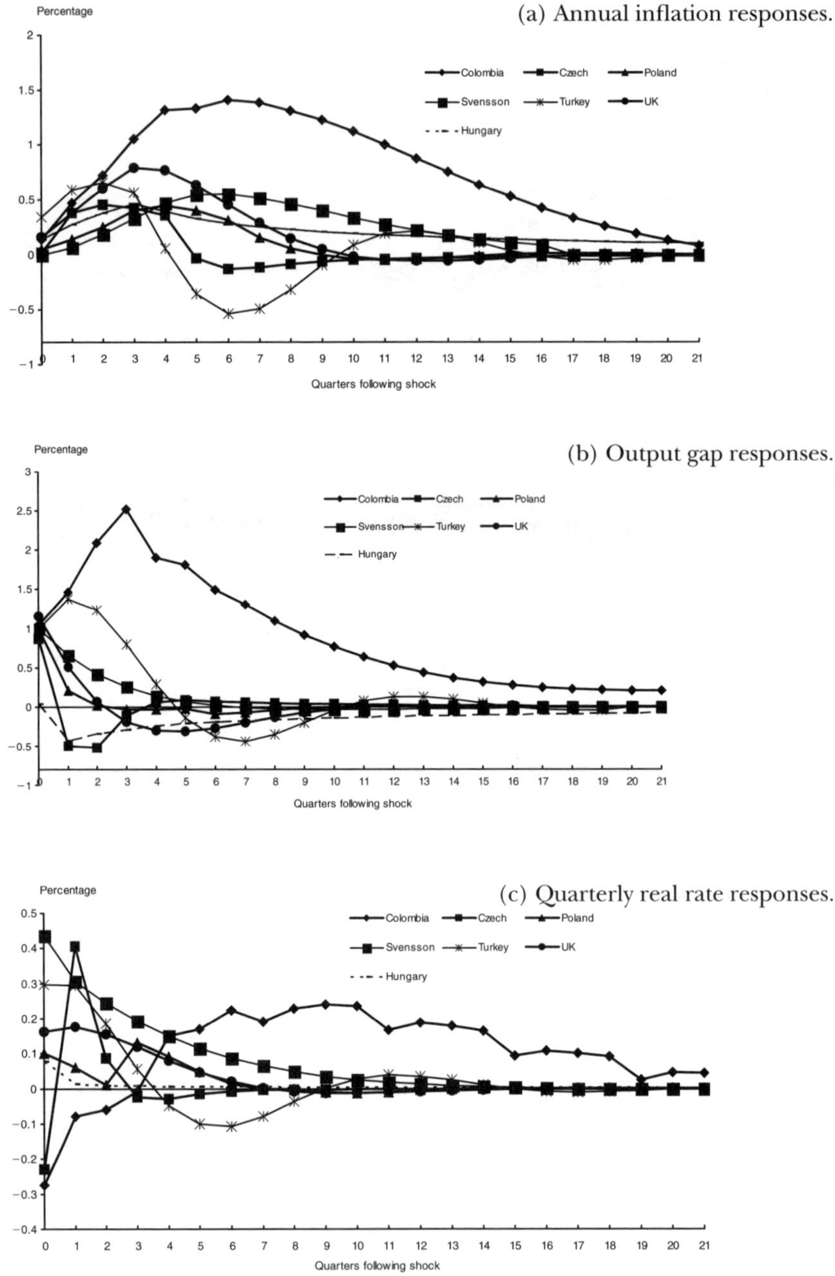

Figure 5.8 Responses for a real demand shock

Note
** An unanticipated 1 pp increase in output above potential for one quarter.

Notes

1 See Mahadeva and Sterne (2002) for a discussion of monetary policy during disinflation.
2 See Calvo (1983).
3 Phillips (1958).
4 See also Batini *et al.* (2000b) & Mavroeidis (2002).
5 See Phelps and Winter (1970) and for a recent empirical test on the UK, Britton, Larsen and Small (2000).
6 See Lucas (1972: 18), Ball and Romer (1991) or Woodford (2002) for similar derivations of the Phillips curve coefficients that relate to underlying parameters. Alogoskoufis and Smith (1991) and Devereux (2002) show how the Phillips curve can shift in between fixed and floating exchange rate regimes. Andersen and Beier (2000) stress the importance of informational and timing assumptions. Summers (1988) emphasises that the trade-off will be sensitive if there is no unique flexible-price equilibrium because of increasing returns and 'sunspot' effects.
7 A lack of identification could be the diagnosis: we have taken the headline rate of inflation as the dependent variable in our regression, and have not in any way tried to condition the inflation data on some assumptions about monetary policy.
8 It is important to note that even though the true output gap and inflation are driven by the same shocks, (6) shows that they can be driven by different dynamic linear combinations of those shocks. If the Phillips curve were estimated with mis-specified dynamics, some element of demand shocks would be excluded to contaminate the residual.
9 The calculation assumes that both inflation and output are well measured by available data, the data set is informative enough, and the shock processes are as described in Chapter 4.
10 Shadman-Mehta (1996) found that inflation was not weakly exogenous with respect to the long-run estimation of the Phillips curve, using the A.W. Phillips original data.
11 Ventures such as the General Data Dissemination System (GDDS) project – a statistical capacity building initiative of the Statistics Department of the IMF – may alleviate these constraints. For example, there is a GDDS Project for Anglophone African Countries Botswana, Eritrea, Ethiopia, Kenya, Lesotho, Liberia, Malawi, Namibia, Nigeria, Sierra Leone, Sudan, Swaziland, Zambia, and Zimbabwe (see http://dsbb.imf.org/gddsweb/whatgdds.htm).
12 To show this, we could have used our set-up to allow for measurement error in our data. The measured trade-off would then be conditional on assumptions about the variances of the measurement errors relative to the underlying shocks, as in Mavroeidis (2002).
13 See Mankiw (2001). Lucas (1972, 1973) and, more recently, Jung (1985) provide some evidence that the output inflation trade-off is more unstable in developing countries than in industrialised economies.
14 The set of micro-founded relationships that describe a model can we rewritten in many ways, any of which can be internally consistent. Therefore, the choice of what variables we should explicitly refer to (those that best capture the model) can depend on local circumstances, such as objectives, data reliability and underlying shocks. For example, de Fiore (1998) discusses whether the influence of capital inflows disturbances on domestic output in a model of transmission mechanism for Israel may be entirely captured by a real interest rate term without any need for exchange rate terms. On this point, see also Friedman's responses to questions B11 and B12 of the HMSO Treasury and Civil Service Committee (1980).

15 Here, c_t is real consumption, y_t is output, n_t is hours spent in formal employment, w_t is nominal wages, p_t is the aggregate price level and i_t is the nominal rate of interest. l_t is employment in heads and is fixed at a exogenous level $\bar{l}$. a_t is technical progress and $\overline{\text{target}}$ is the steady-state target rate of inflation. μ_t is a term which picks up how the marginal utility from time spent outside formal employment depends on technical progress. β, θ, ς_1 and ς_2 are all parameters. e_{nt} and e_{rt} are normally distributed terms whose values are not known in advance. All variables except the nominal rate of interest are in logs, and $E_{t-k}\, z_t$ denotes the expectation of z_t made with the information set available at time $t - k$. z^*_t denotes the flexible-price value of z_t. See Chapter 4 for a full explanation of terms and equations.

16 See Galí and Gertler (1999), Sbordone (2002) or Batini *et al.* (2000), for example.

17 Whether it is better to estimate the wage and price system separately or jointly is a distinct issue, since the equations can be estimated separately but then formulated into a single-equation Phillips curve. The costs and benefits of systems versus reduced-form estimation do involve some related considerations to our discussion of how best to forecast inflation, however.

18 In a more sophisticated model, the parameters α and ς_2 could become functions of the rate of inflation, or the predictability of inflation. See, for example, Edwards 1983; Ball and Mankiw 1994a: 144; Yates and Chapple 1996; Kandil 1997.

19 See Sbordone (2002) for example.

20 It could be argued that a different policy rule should have been chosen for each economy on the grounds that each policy rule should be optimal. Thus the rules chosen should have been model- (and shock-) dependent, rather than uniform. Some of the impulse responses betray that policy rule are clearly suboptimal for some of these experiments. However, changing the rules for each model and each shock would have made comparison difficult.

21 See Clarida *et al.* (1999: Section 2.1) for motivation of these shocks.

22 All annual inflation rates were based on headline consumer price series, available from the IFS.

23 See Ball *et al.* (1988, especially p. 3).

24 See Clarida *et al.* (1999: section 2.1) for references on the explicit modelling of the costs of inflation.

6 Transmission mechanisms and inflation targeting

The case of Colombia's disinflation[1]

Javier Gómez and Juan Manuel Julio

6.1 Introduction

Colombia has been on a steady disinflation path since the early 1990s. In this chapter we model the transmission mechanism of monetary policy during this disinflation. We describe how inflation evolves in response to important shocks that occurred during disinflation such as the terms of trade and to the risk premium, comparing the responses across different monetary policy rules and under different assumptions about inflation persistence. Disinflation itself is captured by a permanent shift to the inflation target. We judge to what extent a shift towards a more forward-looking wage and price-setting determines the sacrifice ratio under disinflation. We discuss the welfare gains from a lower and more stable inflation rate and estimate the degree of uncertainty surrounding inflation forecasts for Colombia.

6.2 The targets and channels of monetary policy in Colombia

Figure 6.1 depicts the turbulent history of monetary policy in Colombia. Large monetary contractions in 1983 and 1998 were interrupted by a huge expansion in 1992. During the 1990s changes in monetary policy stance became even more frequent: the real interest rate jumped from a low of zero in 1992 to a peak of 12 per cent in 1994 and from this peak to a low of 6 per cent in 1997 and back to a peak of 18 per cent in 1998.

The wild swings in interest rates reflected the authorities' attempts to stabilise output and inflation in a rapidly changing and unpredictable economic environment. The high interest rates of 1984 may be understood as an antidote to the risk of capital outflows as a balance of payments crisis loomed. The low interest rates of 1992 were intended as a treatment for the exact opposite 'malaise': an inflow of capital that, given the exchange rate objective, was jeopardising stable money growth and inflation. Interest rates scaled heights again in 1994 in order to decrease the expansion of aggregate demand and excessive credit growth. The 1999 peaks, on the

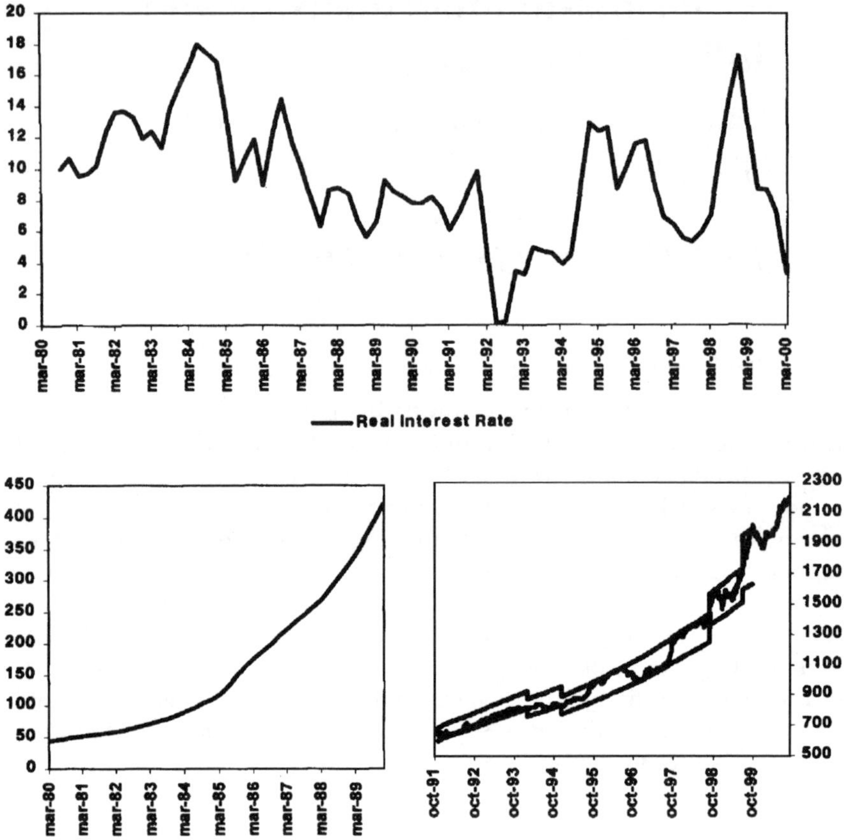

Figure 6.1 Decreasing emphasis in exchange rate targets.

other hand, were a response to a mix of underlying developments. At that time the crawling exchange rate band had to be defended in the face of a risky international environment and a deterioration of the domestic political situation. The threat to be averted was the scenario of an exchange rate crisis which leads to both a burst of inflation and (as borrowing costs mount) a deep recession, as suffered by Mexico in 1995.

Both inflation and output were important for the determination of the monetary policy stance during these years. The instruments used and intermediate targets pursued by monetary policy were also diverse. Targets for money supply, the exchange rate and the interbank interest rate were all used, often simultaneously. Even within the crawling band exchange rate regime, there was a system of 'mini' narrower bands.

All that began to change gradually as the exchange rate policy became increasingly flexible and ever more subservient to the inflation target, culminating with a float in 24 September 1999 (see Figure 6.1 shows).[2] Hence Colombia is considered by some analysts to be an early inflation-targeter.[3] Indeed, price stability was made a formal mandate of the central bank by the constitution and inflation targets first defined in 1991. However, inflation reports where the setting of interest rates based on the inflation forecast is emphasised have only been published since 1998. The point at which all other central bank policy objectives became truly subordinated to the inflation target, is open to discussion.[4]

What is remarkable about Colombian inflation is that it kept to the low double digits for the last quarter of the twentieth century (Figure 6.2). It was only during the 1990s, following the implementation of policies placing greater emphasis in monetary policy on stabilising inflation at lower levels, that inflation entered a steady downward path. This trend culminated in a major disinflationary impetus in 1999 that took inflation down to 9.2 per cent. The public's expectations of inflation were of less than 10 per cent for the year 2000, a figure that would last have been conceived as plausible in the 1960s. The inflation targets for the following years were set to decrease inflation further. If sustained, this trend would put an end to the world's longest experience of moderate inflation (Dornbusch and Fischer 1992)

How was this disinflation achieved in Colombia? The sustained falls in inflation have been associated with rises in unemployment. In Figure 6.3, we can see that the heights hit by interest rates in 1983–84 were accompanied by rapidly increasing unemployment. The behaviour of inflation suggests that these rises in unemployment were above the

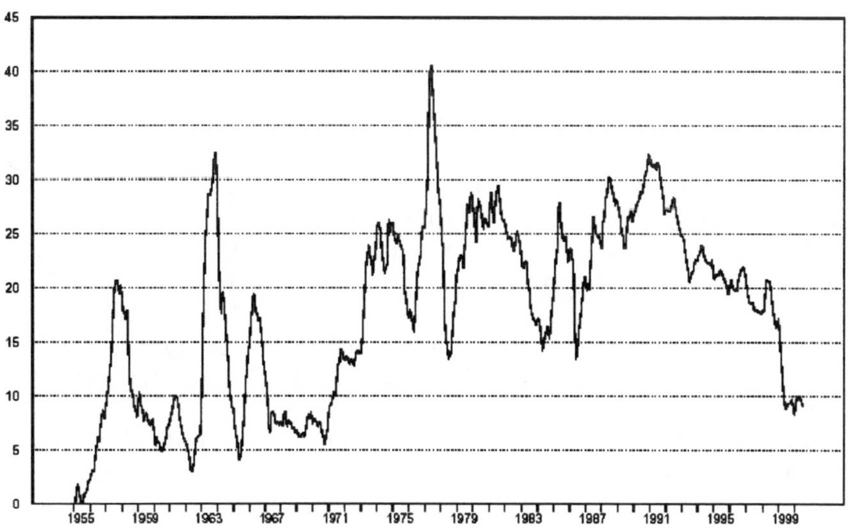

Figure 6.2 Inflation in Colombia, 1955–99.

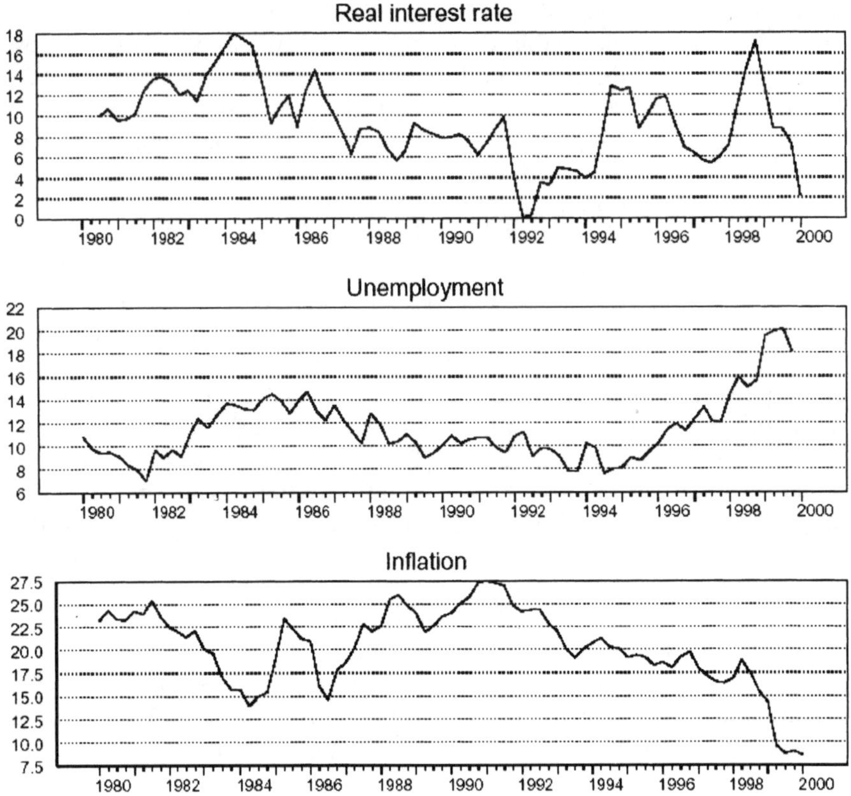

Figure 6.3 Monetary policy, economic activity and inflation.

natural rate of unemployment. Almost a decade later, the low real interest rates of 1992 may have contributed to relatively low unemployment, at levels probably below the natural rate. As a consequence, inflation peaked at over 30 per cent in 1992 and only began decreasing thereafter when high real rates pushed up unemployment again.

Monetary policy has also affected inflation through the exchange rate. In the short run, changes in the rate of nominal depreciation have important consequences for imported price inflation but not for the other parts of the CPI basket. In the longer run, exchange rate changes do spread, though. During the 1980s, when the rate of nominal devaluation was relatively high, inflation in the domestic price of imported goods was above total CPI inflation but pressures on the cost of production eventually drove up total CPI inflation (Figure 6.4). In the 1990s the pattern was reversed: the rate of nominal depreciation was smaller than CPI inflation, and this may have helped the disinflation in the long run by decreasing the cost of imported inputs.

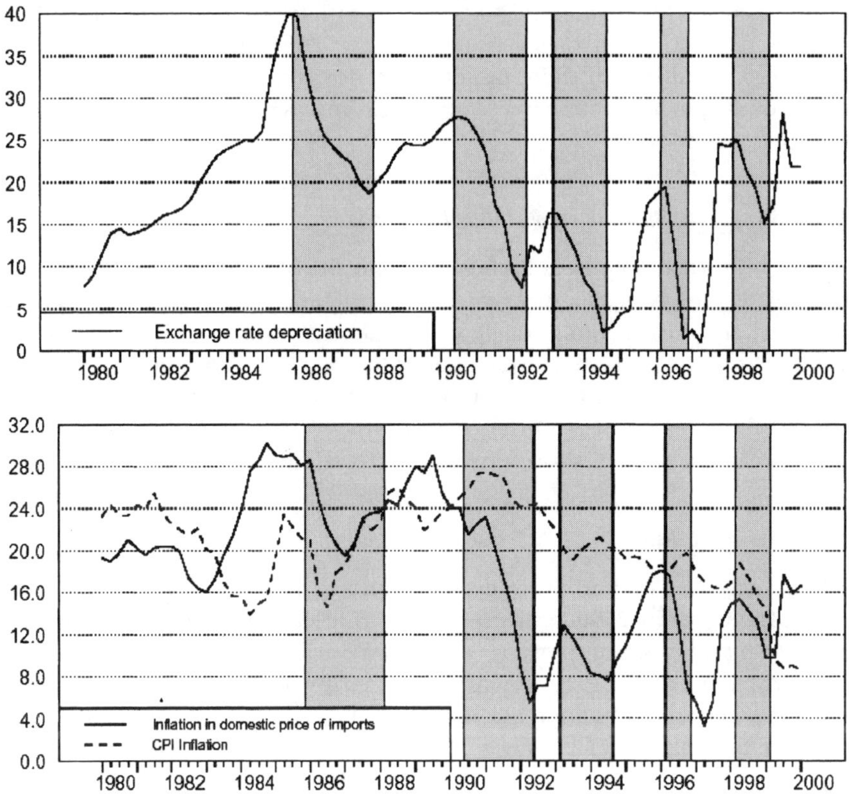

Figure 6.4 Nominal depreciation, inflation of the domestic price of imports and CPI inflation.

6.3 The main shocks to the Colombian economy in the 1990s

Since 1998, the monetary policy regime in Colombia has resembled more closely the template set by other inflation-targeting countries. A key step in this direction was the decision to have inflation reports focus on explaining the future effects on inflation and output on likely economic developments. As a contribution to this effort, in this chapter we develop an understanding of how key shocks and structural changes affect inflation in Colombia.

6.3.1 Shift in the inflation target

The Colombian disinflation is modelled as a previously unexpected permanent decline in the inflation target. Simulating the effects of this shock would help us to quantify the effect of the macro-economic programme agreed with the IMF that set an inflation target path of 10 per cent, 8 per cent, and 6 per cent for 2000, 2001 and 2002 respectively (Figure 6.5). Although these targets were not compulsory, they were part of the overall macro-economic programme and as such acted as the monetary policy anchor.

6.3.2 Supply shocks in the agricultural sector

In 1991 the weather phenomenon El Niño drove food price inflation up beyond 30 per cent (Figure 6.6). The post-Niño weather brought good harvests, and with it temporarily low food-price inflation; 10 per cent in 1993. The cycle repeated itself later with food-price inflation of 25 per cent in 1998 followed by 2.5 per cent in 1999. As food items are 30 per cent of the CPI, changes in the relative price of food may continue to be an important source of short-term shocks to inflation.

6.3.3 Terms of trade

Since coffee and oil and derivatives amounts to 11.4 per cent and 32.5 per cent of exports in 2000 respectively, the fluctuation in the international market price is an important source of variability to the Colombian economy (Figure 6.7). Movements in the terms of trade are quantitatively large; for instance, the increase in the terms of trade in the third quarter over the first quarter of 1994 was 41.3 per cent.

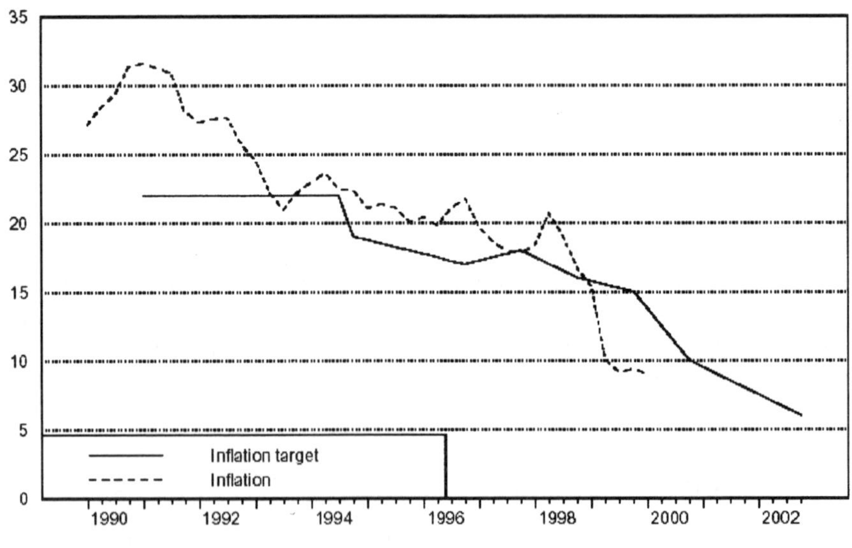

Figure 6.5 A permanent shift in the inflation target.

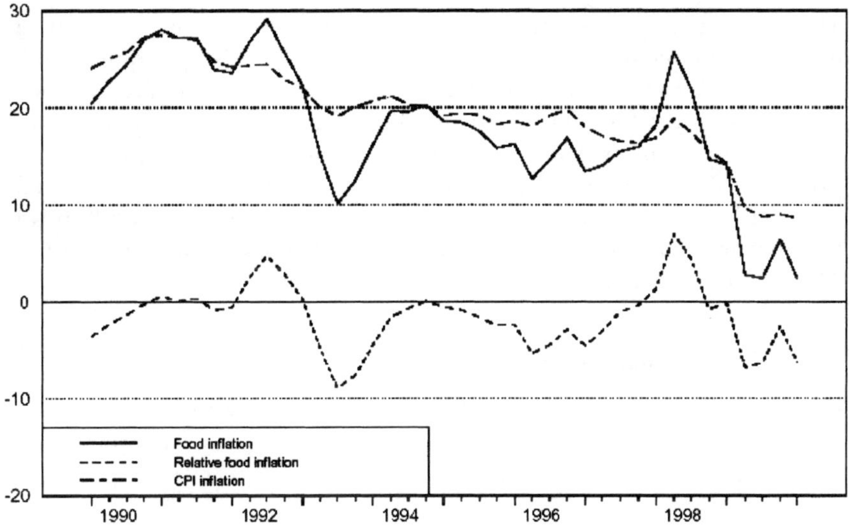

Figure 6.6 Supply shocks in agriculture.

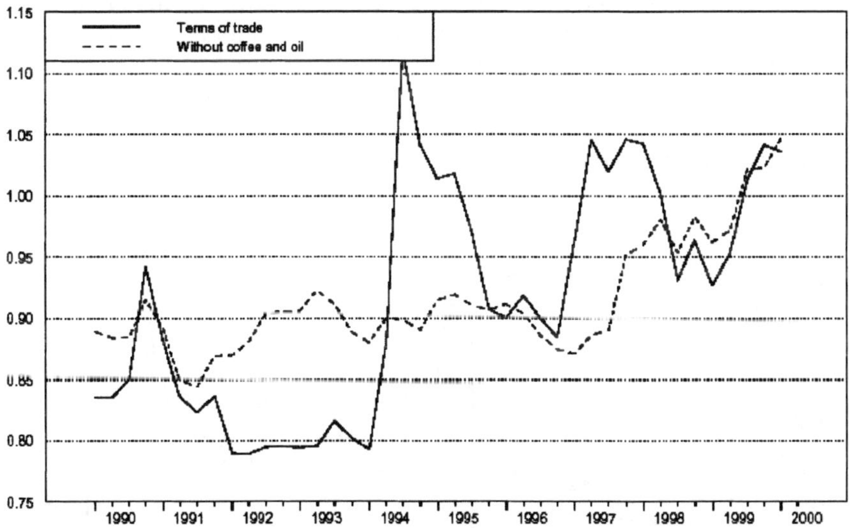

Figure 6.7 Shocks to the terms of trade.

6.3.4 Risk premium

The foreign exchange risk premium has also been, on occasion, an important source of uncertainty for Colombia. The risk premium can be swayed by domestic economic factors (such as the evolution of public finances and developments in the conflict with guerrilla groups) or external developments, (such as international financial crises). Since the risk premium affects the exchange rate, it may have important consequences for inflation. From May to June 2000, the spread of Colombian bonds in the international markets increased by about 200 basis points (Figure 6.8). This was most probably spurred by political events.

6.3.5 Changes in interest rates

Our final experiment is to simulate an unexpected temporary monetary policy impulse so that we can discuss the effects of both temporary and permanent shifts in the monetary stance.

6.4 A model of the transmission mechanisms of monetary policy in Colombia

The transmission mechanisms of monetary policy can be summarised in a flow chart (see Figure 6.9) and formalised into a model. All models are simplifications and should be used flexibly, adjusting as the economy and our understanding of it develops. In this spirit, the model in this chapter does not discuss all factors that contribute to Colombian inflation and does not necessarily correspond to the view of the Board of the Banco de la República.

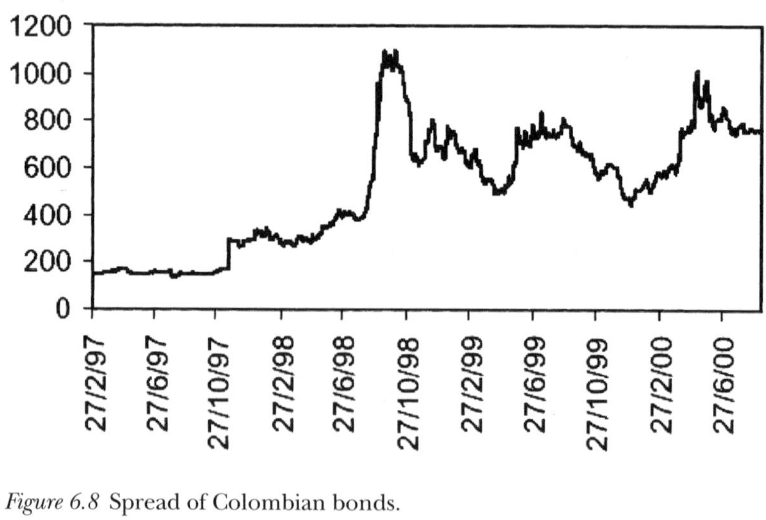

Figure 6.8 Spread of Colombian bonds.

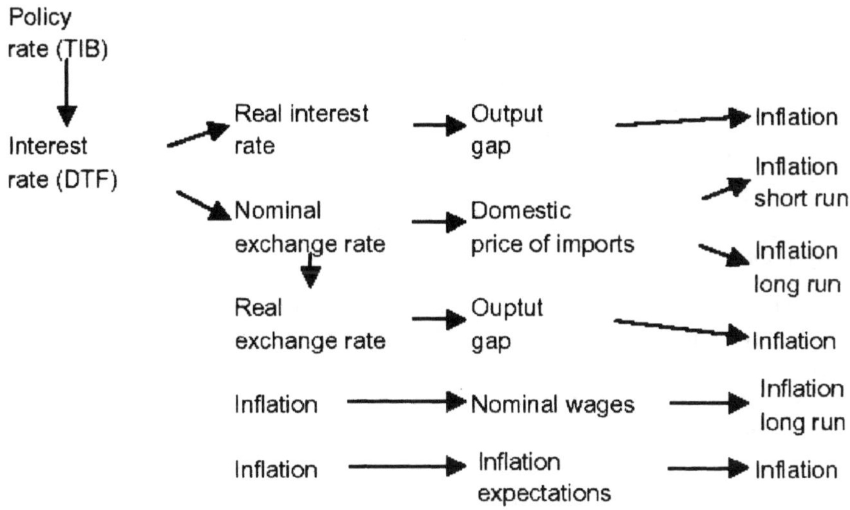

Figure 6.9 Flow chart of the transmission mechanisms of monetary policy.

We now briefly describe each transmission channel, highlighting what we estimate to be their lags and their relative strength.

Most important appears to be an *aggregate demand channel*, whereby an increase in the interest rate raises the real rate and leads, with a one-quarter lag, to a fall in investment and consumption. After a further one-quarter lag, that drop causes a fall in output below its potential level and decreases inflation.

Also in play is a *direct exchange rate channel*, whereby an increase in interest rate leads to an immediate appreciation. After a one-quarter lag the appreciation causes a decrease in inflation largely through a fall in the rate of inflation of prices of imported goods. This small immediate effect of the direct exchange rate channel on inflation may eventually build up and spread to the prices of other goods, starting with the prices of import substitutes, if the increase in the exchange rate is sustained. That would be the case for a sustained fall in the risk premium.

Monetary policy matters, too, through an *indirect exchange rate channel*, whereby the immediate appreciation affects the real exchange rate and causes a fall in net exports and so output. The decrease in output is small and only leads to a slight decrease in inflation, after a lag of one-quarter.

An *expectations channel* is also important. A credible monetary policy action lowers expectations of future inflation rate, pushing down current inflation. The size of the expectations effect on current inflation depends on the weight of expectations of future inflation expectations compared to lagged inflation on the right-hand side of the price equation.

Finally there is a *cost-push channel*, whereby final goods price inflation is dragged down by a moderation in the costs of domestic and imported inputs into production. Domestic costs are dominated by wage costs, and the incorporation of this channel requires us to model the labour market. These cost changes transmit credible, sustained monetary policy changes into final goods prices.

6.4.1 Price equation

Estimation

In what follows we present our estimates of the different equations of the model. We chose to estimate the equations of this model separately, using instrumental variables if necessary.

As part of our estimation of the price equation, we needed to calculate how expectations of future inflation affect current inflation. There are currently only eight data points available on inflation expectations data as measured by the return on nominal and real bonds, and only two data points for directly survey-based measured inflation expectations in Colombia, so we had to use actual data on future inflation. We estimated the price equation using the method proposed by McCallum (1976); lags of the explanatory variables (lagged values of inflation and the output gap) acted as instruments for expected inflation.

The price equation should be dynamically homogeneous to reflect our *a priori* assumption that permanent changes in the inflation target do not affect long-run output. Accordingly, the coefficients on right-hand side inflation terms were restricted to add up to one.

The restricted estimates of the price equation are:

$$\pi_t - \pi_{t-1} = \underset{(1.607)}{3.757} + \underset{(0.143)}{0.299}(\pi_{t+1} - \pi_{t-1}) + \underset{(0.146)}{0.287}(\pi_{t-3} - \pi_{t-1}) + \underset{(0.089)}{0.289}\, y_{t-1} + \underset{(0.028)}{0.089}\chi_{t-1} + \underset{(0.075)}{0.285}\pi_t^R - \underset{(0.014)}{0.026} z_{t-4} + \varepsilon_t^{\pi}. \tag{6.1}$$

Definitions

π_t is the annual inflation rate defined as $\pi_t = 100^*$ ($\log P_t - \log P_{t-4}$). P_t is the monthly geometric average of the CPI for the corresponding quarter; y_t is the output gap defined as y_t = 100* ($\log (Y_t) - \log(Y_t^p)$), where Y_t^p is potential output level estimated with the multivariate HP filter and Y_t is the real GDP level. χ_t is the annual change in the real exchange rate; calculated as $\chi_t = q_t - q_{t-4}$ where $q_t = P_t^M / P_t$ and P_t^M is the PPI for imports π_t^R is annual food-price inflation relative to total inflation; $\pi_t^R = 100^*$ ($\log P_t^R - \log P_t^R - 4$). $P_t^R = P_t^A / P_t$ is the relative price of food and P_t^A is the food-price component of the CPI. We will discuss the definition of the real exchange rate in section 6.3.5. z_t is the deviation of the log of the price level from its long-run value, calculated as $z_t = 100^*$ ($\log P_t - 0.7 \log W_t - 0.3 \log P_t^M + 0.004t$), where W_t is the nominal wage rate (measured in retail trade sector) and t is a time trend that take account of labour productivity.[5]

Results

This dynamic price equation has three features that make it attractive and, we would argue, more realistic for monetary policy modelling: it contains both forward-looking and backward-looking elements: it is dynamically homogeneous; and it is statically homogeneous. It is forward-looking because it takes into account the expectations of future inflation. Dynamic homogeneity is implied by the fact that coefficients on explanatory inflation terms in the price equation add to one. Static homogeneity follows because in the long-run error correction term, the sum of the coefficients on the nominal variables affecting long-run prices is one.

We estimate that the forward-looking versus backward-looking weight on inflation is about 0.3. The persistence of inflation that this indicates implies that disinflation is costly in terms of output in Colombia.[6] In our model, not only the large coefficients on past inflation terms but also the length of their lags make for costly disinflation.

Dynamic homogeneity means that, although there is a trade-off between economic activity and inflation, that is limited to the short run. The level at which inflation settles in the long run is determined entirely by the target rate of inflation, even though the path by which inflation achieves this target rate implies a particular level of cumulated output loss or gain. From low levels in the 1960s, Colombian inflation increased and became stuck at a higher level by 1973. For the near future, the goal is to make inflation return to and settle at a lower rate, reflecting the consensus view that as monetary policy cannot stimulate economic activity in the long run, it can at best aim for a low and stable inflation rate (Mishkin 2000).

In the long run, the price level is determined by wages and imported costs with coefficients that sum up to one.[7] Static homogeneity, by which the price equation is neutral in nominal variables, means that the long-run values of real variables are independent of shocks that shift the price level permanently but affect the rate of inflation only temporarily.

We estimate regressions with all avaialable data since 1983. The long-run restrictions were comfortably satisfied but the coefficient estimates only narrowly accept the dynamic homogeneity property in this full data set.[8] One reason could be that during the 1990s, the shift to more flexible exchange rates may have altered the dynamics of inflation. We decided then to restrict ourselves to regression estimates using 1990s data where dynamic homogeneity is accepted.

6.4.2 Aggregate demand

Estimation

The estimates of the equation determining aggregate output, the IS curve, are:[9]

$$y_t = \underset{(0.490)}{1.055} + \underset{(0.140)}{0.464}\, y_{t-1} + \underset{(0.140)}{0.422}\, y_{t-2} - \underset{(0.057)}{0.185} r_{t-1} + \underset{(0.053)}{0.029} q_{t-1} + \underset{(0.030)}{0.090} \tau_t + \varepsilon^y_{t+1} \qquad (6.2)$$

$$\tau_t \equiv i_t - \pi_t \qquad (6.3)$$

Definitions

r_t is the annualised real interest rate and i_t is the annualised nominal interest rate, measured on the 90-day Certificates of Term Deposits (DTF). τ_t is the deviation of terms of trade from its HP filtered value: defined as $\tau_t = 100^*$ ($\log \tau_t^{NHP} - \log \tau_t^{HP}$), where $\tau_t^{NHP} = P_t^N / P_t^M$, and P_t^X and P_t^M are the producer price indices of exports and imports respectively.

Results

Our unrestricted estimates of the IS curve implied that the sum of the estimated coefficients on lagged output (persistence) was greater than one, which would mean that aggregate demand would not converge following temporary shocks to the real interest rate. Hence it was necessary to impose the coefficient value on lagged output that Goméz and Julio (2000) calculated (0.88).

We attempted to include the US output gap in the equation, but it was not significant on the past data set. In the model as it stands, we would have to incorporate the effect of the recent shift in US economic activity on the Colombian business cycle by residual adjustment.

6.4.3 Wages

Estimation

Our estimates of the wage equation were as follows:[10]

$$\begin{aligned}\omega_t = & -\underset{(8.898)}{22.308} + \underset{(0.136)}{0.390}\,\omega_{t-1} + \underset{(0.131)}{0.528}\left(y_t - y_{t-1}\right) - \underset{(0.066)}{0.161}\left(y_{t-2} - y_{t-3}\right) \\ & - \underset{(0.066)}{0.161}\left(\log\left(W_{t-4}\right) - 0.6\left(\log\left(Y_{t-4}/L_{t-4}\right)\right)\right.\end{aligned} \qquad (6.4)$$

Definitions

ω_t is the annual growth rate of real wages, $\omega_t = 100^*$ (log W_t – log W_{t-4}). W_t is the real wage, calculated as the geometric average of retail trade and industrial sectors and L_t is the level of employment (of the seven main cities).

Results

The wage equation is estimated for real wages and nominal wages are obtained from this by identity. This implies that nominal wages follow the same pattern of persistence as prices. An alternative strategy would be to allow for nominal shocks to affect real wages by estimating a behavioural equation for nominal wages and deriving real wages as an identity, as in Gómez (2000b).

6.4.4 *Interest rate rule*

In the model, the central bank sets interest rate to affect expected future inflation, equation (6.5), with the forecast horizon set at 1 year, $k = 4$. This is only a rough approximation of the policy horizon of decisions by the Board of Directors. The optimal targeting horizon as well as the optimal weights on influences in the forecast rule should depend on the source of the inflation and output disturbance. In particular, not all decisions should be made with a 1-year horizon, and indeed in one of our experiments we used a 2-year horizon, $k = 8$. The forecast rule could in principle allow for interest-rate smoothing via the smoothing parameter ϕ, but, given the history of large changes to the interest rates in Colombia, this was set equal to zero.

$$i_t = \phi i_{t-1} + (1-\phi)(\bar{r} + \pi_t) + 0.5\pi_{t+k|t} \tag{6.5}$$

6.4.5 *Uncovered interest parity*

Equation (6.6) is the uncovered interest rate parity relationship, expressed in terms of the real interest rate:

$$q_t = q_{t+1|t} - 0.25\left(i_t - \pi_{t+1|t} - \varphi_t - r^*_{t+1|t}\right) \tag{6.6}$$

The real exchange rate is forward-looking. Hence we can derive model-consistent solutions for the path of real exchange rates and interest rate differentials that depend in part on the risk premium path and a terminal exchange rate. The latter is the expected value of the real exchange rate at the terminal date, and in our case is set equal to productivity differentials.

We have defined the real exchange rate as imported goods prices relative to the aggregate CPI level, $q_t = P_t^M/P_t$, as in McCallum (2000b). This definition is one among many alternative measures of the relationship between the prices of traded and non-traded goods. We use this definition because it is statistically significant in the price equation, and because it enables us transparently to separate the first and second stages of the exchange rate passthrough.

An alternative real exchange rate measure could be derived from defining the price of traded goods as a linear combination of the prices of imports and exports, as in García and Montes (1988) and Mundlak *et al.* (1990). From García and Montes it can be inferred that the weight of the price of imports in the traded goods price basket is as large as 80 per cent.[11] Our assumption that all the weight belongs to the import price does not seem to be too out of line with these estimates.[12]

6.4.6 Foreign real interest rate

For forecasting purposes, future foreign real interest rates can be calculated from data on futures markets, but in a model for simulations we can postulate a simple autoregressive form for the foreign real rate process. This rule can be adjusted to link foreign real rates to foreign shocks. Our rule was estimated to be:[13]

$$r^*_{r+1} = \underset{(0.530)}{2.152} + \underset{(0.082)}{0.622} r^*_t + \varepsilon^{r^*}_{t+1}; \tag{6.7}$$

where r^*_t is the annualised expected foreign real interest rate, $r^*_t{+}1 \equiv i^*_t - \pi^*_t{+}1$ and i^*_t is the foreign annualised rate on bonds of 3-month maturity

6.4.7 Risk premium

Equation (6.8) illustrates the evolution of the risk premium (φ_t) as an autoregressive process, calibrated to Svensson's (2000) parameters:

$$\varphi_{t+1} = 0.8\varphi_t + \varepsilon^{\varphi}_{t+1} \tag{6.8}$$

6.4.8 Terms of trade

Equation (6.9) simulates the evolution of the HP filtered log-level of the terms of trade also as an autoregressive process:[14]

$$\tau_t = \underset{(0.148)}{0.864}\tau_{t-1} - \underset{(0.178)}{0.460}\tau_{t-2} + \underset{(0.159)}{0.365}\tau_{t-3} - \underset{(0.121)}{0.341}\tau_{t-4} + \varepsilon^{\tau}_t \tag{6.9}$$

6.4.9 Passthrough

Calibration

The passthrough equation allows for partial adjustment for inflation of import prices (measured in domestic currency) in response to nominal exchange rate depreciation:

$$\pi_t^M = \gamma\pi_{t-1}^M + (1-\gamma)\varepsilon_t \tag{6.10}$$

where $\gamma = 0.3$.

Definitions

$\pi^M{}_t$ is the inflation of import prices in domestic currency, defined as $\pi_t^M = 100(\log P_t^M - \log P_{t-4}^M)$; ε_t is the annual rate of nominal depreciation, defined as $\varepsilon_t = 100(\log E_t - \log E_{t-4})$ where E_t is the nominal exchange rate level.

Results

The final form for equation (6.10) was derived by testing from a more general version where the current depreciation rate, three lags of depreciation and four lags of the inflation of import prices were all included as explanatory variables. The coefficients on these explanatory terms were restricted to sum to one, so that dynamic homogeneity holds. Insignificant lags were then gradually deleted and at each step a simulation of a permanent shift in the inflation target using that particular equation was carried out in the model. The specifications with implausible dynamics were rejected, leaving us with a final regression where the explanatory variables were only lagged import price inflation and the current depreciation rate, equation (6.10).

6.4.10 Money demand

In our model, real money balances do not actively affect other variables. We include them as an endogenous variable so that we can investigate their role as an indicator of underlying shocks.

Estimation

The money demand equation was estimated as.[15]

$$\begin{aligned}\mu_t = {} & \underset{(0.134)}{0.430}\mu_{t-1} - \underset{(0.017)}{0.052}\rho_t + \underset{(0.229)}{0.777}g_t \\ & - \underset{(0.042)}{0.146}\left(-1.743 - 0.442t + \log M_{t-4} + 0.5\log i_{t-4} - 0.5\log Y_{t-4}\right)\end{aligned} \tag{6.11}$$

Definitions

M_t is the real value of the adjusted monetary base; t is a time trend representing a trend shift in the velocity of circulation, taking the value of 1 in 1982Q1. μ_t is the growth of rate real balances of the monetary base: $\mu_t = 100^* (\log M_t - \log M_{t-4})$. ρ_t is the annual change in the nominal interest rate, $\rho_t = 100^* (i_t - i_{t-4})$. g_t is the annual growth rate of real GDP: $g = 100^* (\log Y_t - \log Y_{t-4})$.

Results

The Baumol (1952) model for real balances implies an interest rate semi-elasticity of – 0.5 and an income elasticity of 0.5. Using the Johansen co-integration technique with data up to 1990, we find that the coefficient values implied by the Baumol model are not rejected by the data. However, when we include date after 1990, we find that real balances, interest rates and real GDP are not co-integrated. That year marked the start of a sustained and unpredictable burst of financial innovation in Colombia. Assuming that this financial restructuring was responsible for the breakdown of co-integration, we imposed the elasticities of the Baumol model onto the long run of the money demand equation and estimated the short-run dynamics in the full data set.

6.4.11 The interest rate and the policy rate

Estimation

The estimated equation is:[16]

$$\begin{aligned} i_t - i_{t-1} = {} & \underset{(0.077)}{0.380}(i_{t-1} - i_{t-2}) - \underset{(0.069)}{0.162}(i_{t-2} - i_{t-3}) + \underset{(0.063)}{0.120}(i_{t-3} - i_{t-4}) \\ & + \underset{(0.014)}{0.169} i_t^P - \underset{(0.021)}{0.144}(i_{t-1} - 1.064 i_{t-1}^P) \end{aligned} \qquad (6.12)$$

Definitions

i_t^P is the policy rate, the annualised interbank interest rate (TIB).

Results

Econometric tests reveal that the deposit interest rate and the policy rate are cointegrated and that the policy rate is weakly exogenous to the estimate of the long-run coefficients on post-1990 data. That the policy rate is weakly exogenous in this sample is plausible because, after the 1990s, policy rates were less directed at offsetting risk premia (which would have destabilised both market rates and the exchange rate) and rather more at stabilising future inflation. As the policy rate is weakly exogenous, this does not rule out that we can estimate the above equation consistently by OLS. We use monthly data because we believe there is much information in movements that die out after a quarter.

A one percentage point increase in the policy rate results in the following increases in the deposit interest rate: 0.169 in the first month, 0.511 in the third month, 0.829 in the sixth month, 1.035 in the twelfth month and 1.064 since the second year.

6.5 Comparison with other estimates

It is interesting to compare our findings with those for the US of Rudebusch and Svensson (1998). Their estimates of the Phillips curve and aggregate demand relationship are:

$$\pi_t = \underset{(0.08)}{0.70}\pi_{t-1} - \underset{(0.10)}{0.10}\pi_{t-2} + \underset{(0.10)}{0.28}\pi_{t-3} + \underset{(0.08)}{0.12}\pi_{t-4} + \underset{(0.03)}{0.14}y_t + \varepsilon_t^{\pi} \qquad (6.13)$$

and

$$y_t = \underset{(0.08)}{1.16}y_{t-1} - \underset{(0.08)}{0.25}y_{t-2} - \underset{(0.03)}{0.10}\tau_{t-1} + \varepsilon_t^{y} \qquad (6.14)$$

The coefficient for the interest rate is also comparable across their and our equations, since both interest rates are defined in annual terms. The estimate of –0.185 for the short-run effect of real interest rates on output in Colombia is larger in absolute size than Rudebusch and Svensson's estimate of –0.10 for the US. The long-run semi-interest rate elasticities are –0.185/1–0.464–0.422 = –1.622 and –0.10/1–1.16+0.25 = – 1.11 for Colombia and the US, respectively. The multipliers suggest that the real interest rate effect on inflation via the aggregate demand channel is strong in Colombia, and stronger than would be expected for a relatively open economy.[17]

6.6 Simulating the transmission of shocks

Having outlined our model and described our econometric estimates, we now model the effect of some key shocks on Colombian output and inflation. In the Banco de la República's Inflation Report, the Board of Directors periodically publishes its views on the shocks affecting the economy and how they will affect inflation. We have chosen to model some of the important shocks that feature in this discussion.[18]

6.6.1 Permanent shift in the inflation target

As soon as the inflation target is raised, nominal interest rates are raised permanently. The increase in interest rates leads immediately to a faster nominal exchange rate appreciation. That appreciation passes very quickly, although not immediately, to lower the rate of inflation in the price of imports. Acting through the exchange rate channel, one quarter after the shock, inflation decreases. This effect of the direct exchange rate channel on inflation is, however, small.

Not only nominal but also real interest rates increase on impact. The real rate remains positive for 10 quarters. This creates a recession that lasts for several years, reaching a trough in the eighth quarter. From the fourth quarter onwards, the aggregate demand channel kicks in to accelerate the disinflation process. Inflation decreases 75 basis points by 14 quarters and 95 basis points by 19 quarters (Figure 6.10). The sacrifice ratio, or the cumulative loss of output per unit of annual inflation reduced, is 0.788.

The lowest chart on the left-hand side of Figure 6.11 compares the

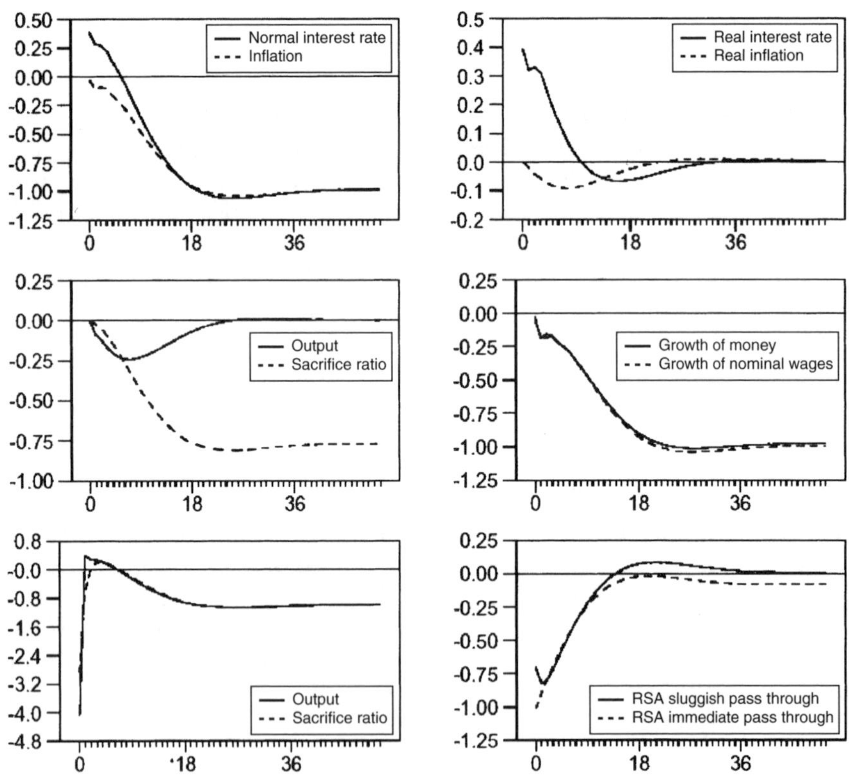

Figure 6.10 A permanent shift in the inflation target.

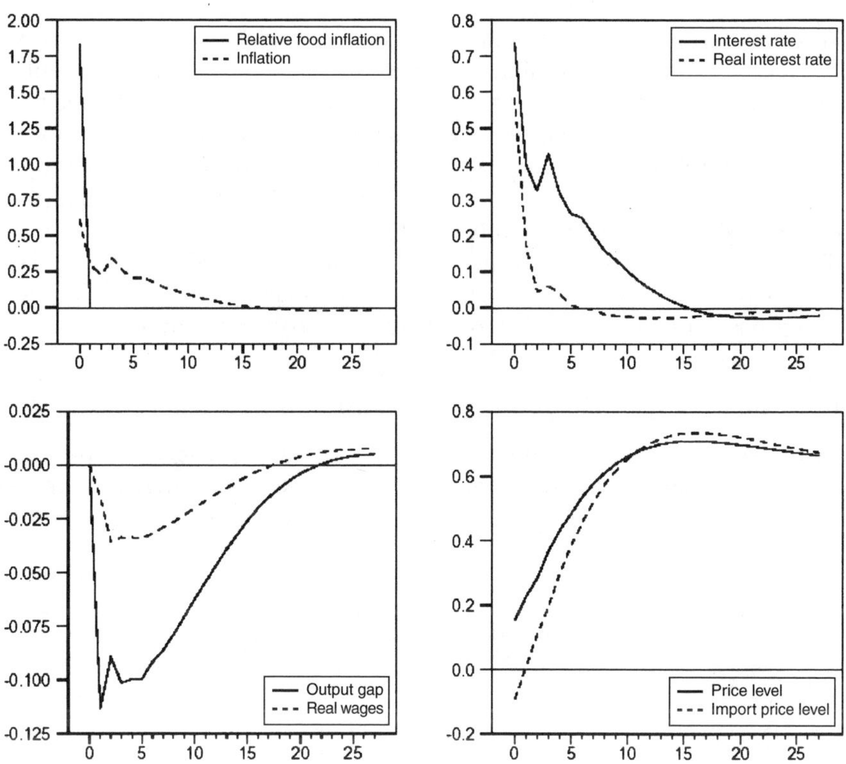

Figure 6.11 A supply shock in the agricultural sector

responses of two measures of the real exchange rate (RER). The measure that uses the domestic currency price of imports calculated with equation (10) demonstrates a sluggish passthrough. An immediate passthrough would follow if it were assumed instead that $\pi^M_t = \varepsilon_t$, that is, that the inflation of import prices is equal to the rate of depreciation. It is evident that there is not much difference between the responses of the two exchange rates.

6.6.2 A supply shock in the agricultural sector

Disturbances to relative food prices make inflation volatile (Figure 6.11). Food items are a small share of GDP but a fairly large share of CPI. As in the model, monetary policy often has to respond, at least to the second-round effect of the shocks on inflation. The extra real interest rate volatility adds some extra variability to real variables over and above those directly associated with the change in the agricultural sector's production conditions.

6.6.3 A shock to the terms of trade

More favourable relative prices boost the demand for exporting sectors' outputs. However, in our simulations we assume that potential output is slow to adjust and hence that there is an increase in the output gap. That increase in the output gap increases inflation to some extent, precipitating an interest-rate increase. Acting through all transmission channels, monetary policy dampens aggregate inflation. The direct exchange rate channel contributes with its immediate but small effect and the aggregate demand channel with its lagged and strong effect (Figure 6.12). The lower left hand side chart compares the real exchange rate calculated with sluggish and immediate passthrough, again showing no difference

6.6.4 A shock to the exchange rate risk premium

As investors demand a higher return on Colombian assets, the nominal and real exchange rates depreciate on impact. Real exchange rate depreciation leads directly to inflation. Interest rates are raised to combat future

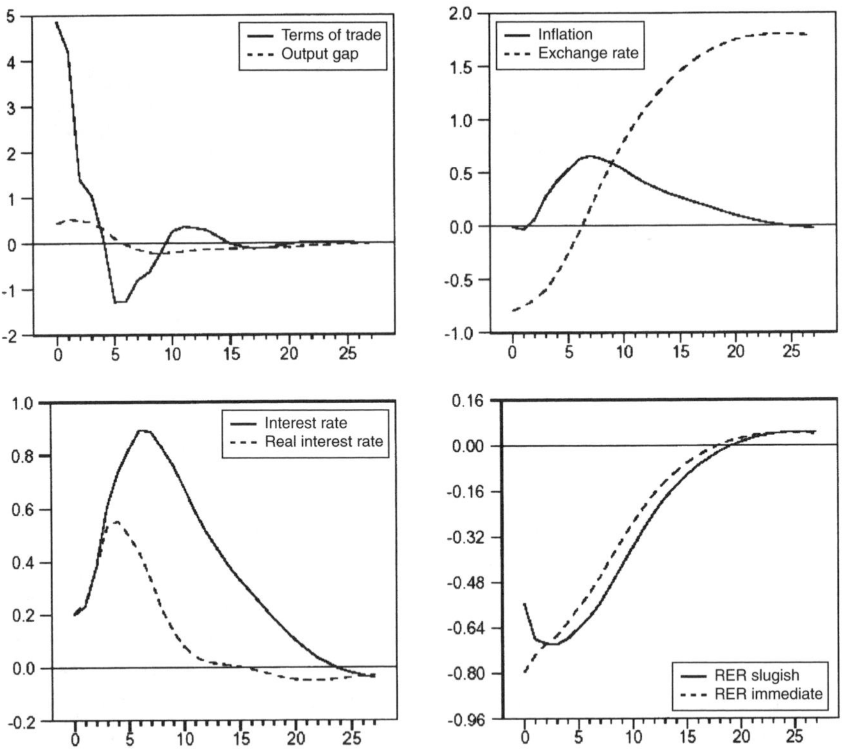

Figure 6.12 A shock to the terms of trade.

inflationary pressures, rather than to defend an exchange rate. Although trade improves on impact, eventually the higher real interest rates cause a real exchange rate appreciation and a recession. Both outcomes act to move inflation back to target (Figure 6.13).

6.7 Policy rules and the supply shock

The evolution of the terms of trade is modelled as an autoregressive process. To some extent the future evolution of the terms of trade is predictable, and it is of interest to compare how the economy behaves under forecast rules that target inflation four quarters and eight quarters ahead, and under rules that have no forward-looking terms. Our results show that long horizons are needed for this shock if we care about interest rate volatility: the forecast rule that targets inflation at eight quarters results in the smoothest path for the interest rate. The rule without forward-looking terms results in the sharpest swings in the interest rate. The difference in variability between an eight-quarter rule and a four-quarter rule, however, is not very large (Figure 6.14).

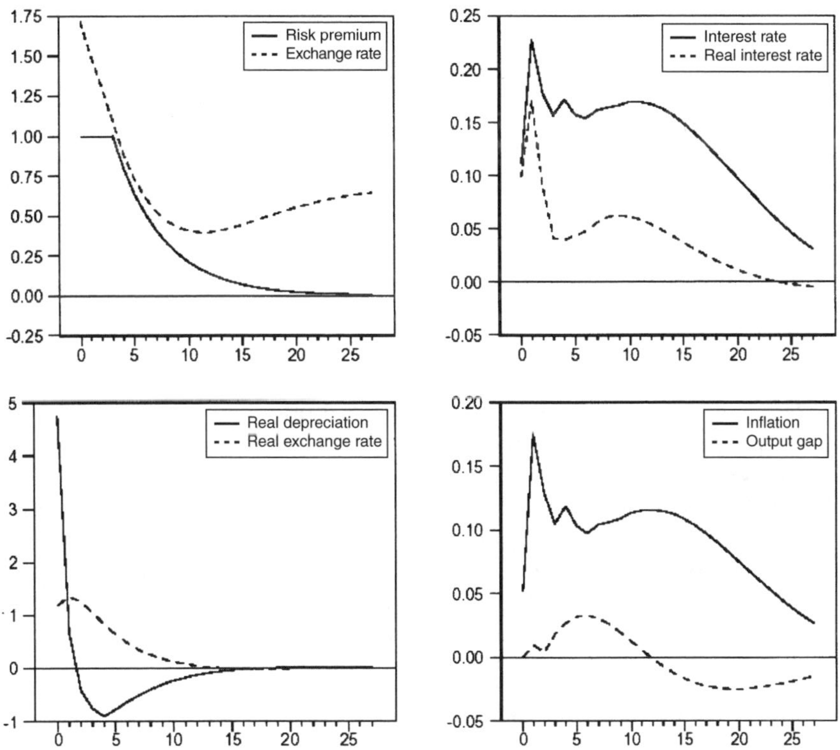

Figure 6.13 A shock to the risk premium.

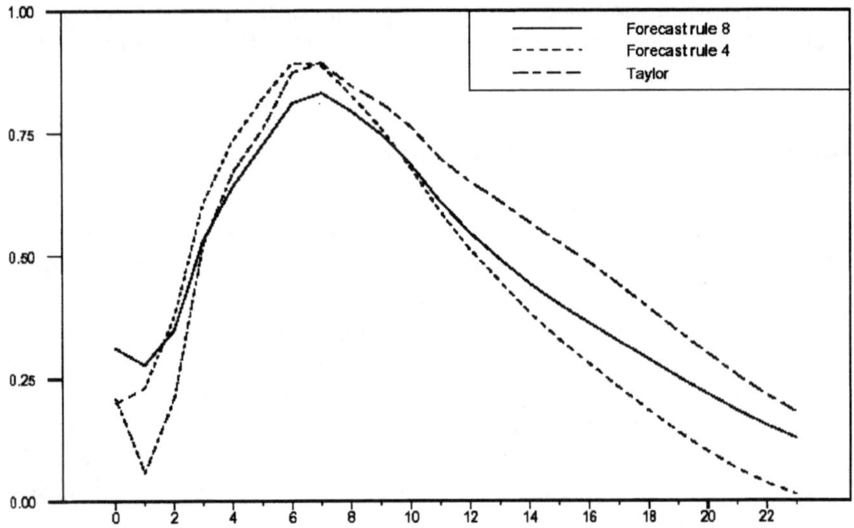

Figure 6.14 Policy rules and a shock to the terms of trade.

6.8 Monetary policy and expectations

The solid lines in Figure 6.15 present the behaviour of the economy under a percentage point shock to the nominal interest rate that is sustained for four quarters. During the period of the shock interest rates are fixed, but after the fourth quarter the interest rate is allowed to follow the policy rule (equation (5)). Acting through the direct exchange rate channel, inflation decreases immediately and by a relatively small amount. After a lag, inflation falls further following an opening of the output gap. Once the policy rule is switched on the interest rate decreases and this returns inflation back to target.[19]

The dotted line describes the response under an alternative experiment where we make the price equation more forward-looking by increasing the weight of the forward-looking lead of inflation to 0.5. To preserve dynamic homogeneity, the coefficients on the first and third lags in proportion. A more forward-looking price equation makes inflation more responsive to credible monetary policy. The interest rate decreases more in the fifth quarter than when inflation was more backward-looking. The recovery is stronger, and the economy re-establishes equilibrium sooner.

6.9 Disinflation and the sacrifice ratio

The sacrifice ratio has mostly simply been defined in the literature as $1/\alpha_y$. A more intuitive measure would be the outcome of an experiment

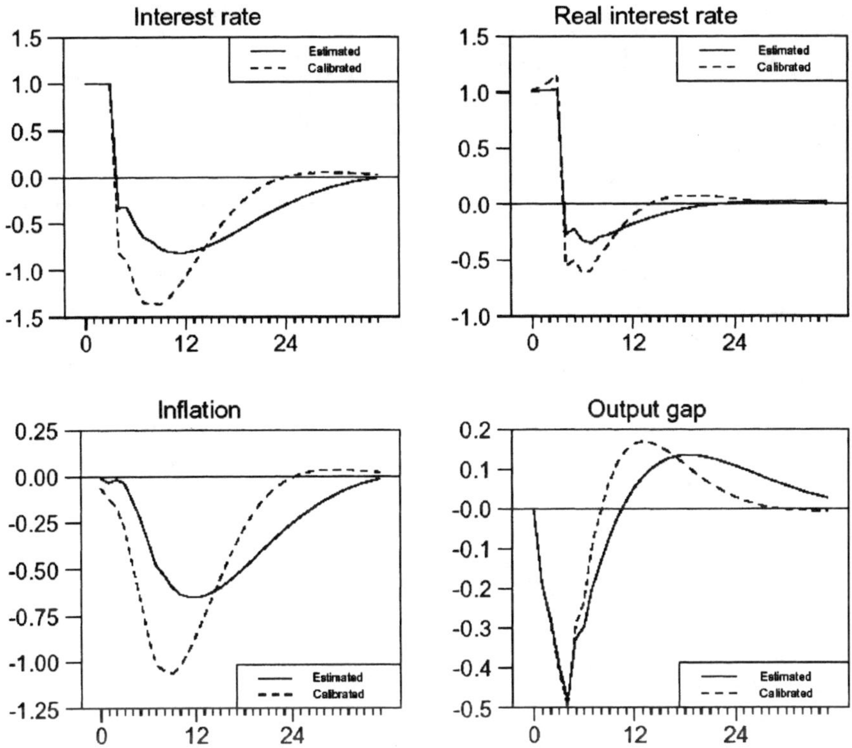

Figure 6.15 A shock to the interest rate under different expectations.

where we simulate a permanent 1 percentage point decrease in the inflation target in our model. The sacrifice ratio is calculated as the cumulated loss in the output gap per unit rate of annual inflation reduced. Using the estimated coefficient $\alpha_y = 0.289$, we estimate a sacrifice ratio of 0.786 for Colombia.[20] The estimate of α_y is associated with a 95% confidence interval (0.114, 0.464). The low end of the confidence interval, 0.114, implies a sacrifice ratio of 1.785, while the high end of the interval, 0.464, implies a sacrifice ratio of 0.500.

Figure 6.16 compares the cost of disinflation for two price equations. Simulations with our estimated price equation (with a weight of 0.3 on forward-looking versus backward-looking inflation) are described by the solid lines. The dotted lines describe the responses from the forward-looking calibrated version (with a weight of 0.5 on forward-looking versus backward-looking inflation). The sacrifice ratio decreases from 0.786 to 0.322.

Estimates of the sacrifice ratio are uncertain, and we should be cautious in placing too much emphasis on these findings. However, it does seem

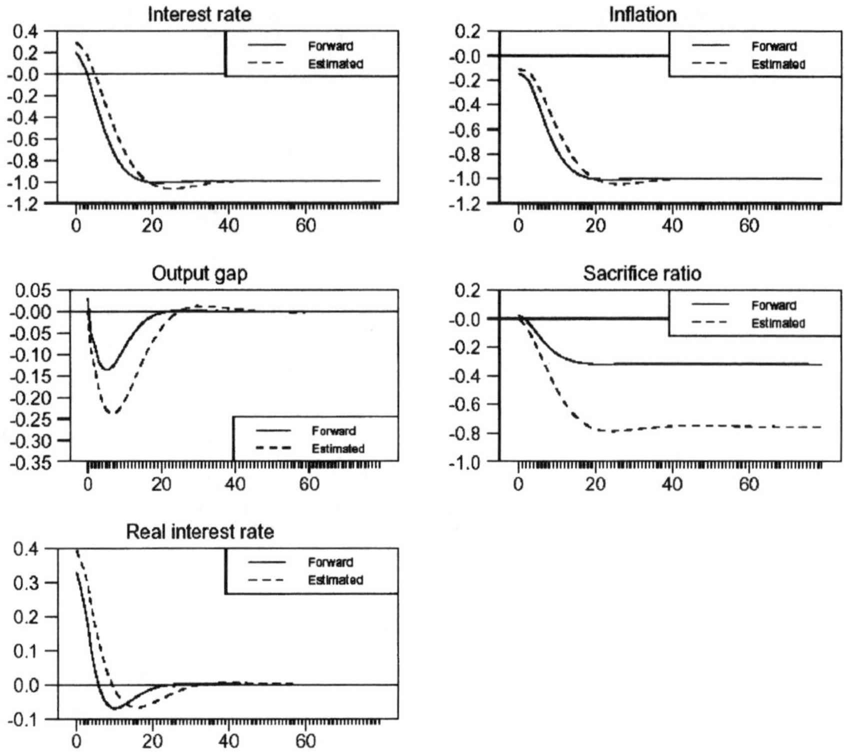

Figure 6.16 Disinflation and the sacrifice ratio for different levels of inflation stickiness.

plausible that further disinflation will be costly. Inflation in 1999 was around 9 per cent. Using our estimate of α_y, this model indicates that if inflation were taken down from 9 per cent to 2 per cent, the 7 percentage points disinflation would incur a cost of 5.6 per cent of output loss in 1992 (2.2 per cent with the calibrated more forward-looking price equation). A more comprehensive welfare evaluation would weight these losses against the welfare gains accrued from lowering and stabilising inflation.

6.10 Welfare gains from disinflation

The literature discusses two separate measures of the welfare costs of inflation: the effect on the level of output, and the effect on its rate of growth. The level effect has been considered by Bailey (1956), Sidrausky (1967), Lucas (1994) and Cooley and Hansen (1989). It is not difficult to show that the level effect in the model of Bailey is not robust to the specification of the demand for money, that is, whether it is logarithmic or semilogarithmic. Neither is it robust to the semi-interest elasticity of money demand.[21] It can be also be proved that in the models of Sidrausky, Lucas, and Cooley and Hansen, the level effect is not robust to the specification of the utility function or the transactions technology. Gómez (2000a) shows that the level welfare effect of a 20 per cent inflation rate in Colombia lies within the very wide range of 0.8 to 4.5 per cent of consumption.

The growth effect has been studied by De Gregorio (1993), Chari *et al.* (1996), Barro (1996), Fischer (1993), Levine and Renelt (1992) and Summers and Heston (1988). Of these, the first two papers help explain the effect of inflation on growth with the use of models. The last three papers are empirical and find an effect on growth that is higher than predicted in the theoretical papers. For the case of Colombia, Uribe (1994) estimated that decreasing inflation by 10 percentage points would increase the rate of growth by 0.5 per cent. This estimate of the growth effect seems to imply that large welfare gains result from disinflation.

We now compare the costs of inflation with the costs of disinflation. Junguito (1998) weighed the gains and the costs of disinflation and estimated the net internal rate of return from the project of a disinflation of 25 per cent. In this chapter, we weigh the gains and costs of disinflation following the welfare analysis in Lucas (1987). To calculate the welfare gain from disinflation, we compare two economies: Economy 1 has a given rate of inflation and a consumption growth rate of $g_1 = 0.03$; Economy 2 undergoes disinflation – there is a 10 percentage point disinflation and output enters a recession but reaches a higher output growth in the long run. The growth rate of Economy 2 becomes $g_{2T} = 0.035$ for some terminal date T. We assume that there is no investment, and both economies are closed. Hence output equals consumption and consumption grows at the same rate as output.

As mentioned, the rate of growth of consumption in Economy 1 is $g_1 = 0.03$. The rate of growth in Economy 2 is $g_{2t} = \frac{1}{2}\,\Delta\pi^{t}_{j=0} + g_1$. Potential output and consumption in the first stages of disinflation grow at a rate that increases from g_1 to $0.5 + g_1$. By the sixteenth quarter, we assume that the disinflation is nearly complete, and hence $\Delta\pi^{T}_{j=0} \simeq 1$ and $g_{2T} \simeq 0.005 + g_1$ for $t = 16$. The growth of output (consumption) increases from 0.03 to 0.035 by the sixteenth quarter.

Our welfare evaluation consists of compensating the representative consumer in the inflationary economy with a given percentage of consumption at all dates. After receiving the correct level of compensation, he or she should be indifferent to whether the economy is in a state of inflation or disinflation. Algebraically,

$$\sum_{t=0}^{\infty}\beta^{t}u((1+\lambda)c_{1t}) = \sum_{t=0}^{\infty}\beta^{t}u(c_{2t}) \tag{6.15}$$

where λ is the welfare gain from disinflation, and c_{1t} and c_{2t} are the consumption paths in the inflationary economy and in the economy that disinflates, respectively. The consumption path in the economy that disinflates enjoys a higher growth of potential output. The welfare gain from disinflation was obtained from this model by numerical methods after assuming a CES utility function and choosing appropriate values for preference parameters.[22] By this method, the welfare gain from disinflating by 10 percentage points was estimated to be equivalent to an increase in output of 3.9 per cent until perpetuity, substantially outweighing our calculation of the output loss.

6.11 The inflation forecast and the fan chart

The fan chart is a pictorial description of the subjective probability assessment of future values of inflation by the Central Bank or Board of Directors. It summarises the conclusions of the current inflation report, and shows relative weights of the factors affecting inflation as covered in the report.

One attractive feature of a fan chart is its focus on the entire probability distribution of the forecast. The fan chart also shows the balance of risks for future values of inflation – that is, it displays a non-symmetrical probability distribution that indicates how likely inflation is to lie above or below the central view.

A fan chart is thus composed of three elements: the central view, which can be the mode, or the more likely outcome of inflation; the degree of uncertainty measured in terms of the variance of the distribution; and the balance of risks, which shows how likely it is that an outcome will be above or below the central view. These three aspects are summarised in a non-symmetric distribution function of inflation outcomes at each of the forecasting periods.

It is widely recognised that the most important use of the fan chart is to provide a structured way of thinking about the inflation forecast. The basic requirements for producing a fan chart are:

1 A clear understanding of the transmission mechanisms of monetary policy and the shocks that affect the inflation rate. That seems to require a model or a linked set of models that are capable of reproducing the effect of different shocks on inflation as well as the response of inflation and output to monetary policy.
2 An understanding of the shocks that could affect the future inflation rate, evidence for which should be described in the inflation report.
3 An iterative process whereby the monetary policy committee and the technical staff of the central bank can coordinate their interpretation about how these shocks affect inflation.

The implementation of the chart in this chapter focuses on three identified shocks that are likely to affect the future inflation rate in Colombia:

a food-inflation supply shock that is thought to come from the beginning of a livestock cycle, a risk-premium shock believed to originate in the decrease in Congress's support to the economic reforms of the executive after the latter suggested the Congress's mandate could be revoked and an increase in gasoline prices in domestic currency due to an increase in the international price of oil. Table 6.1 depicts the more likely path (the mode) of the effects of these shocks obtained from the inflation report. Since in our model there is currently no disaggregation up to gasoline prices, we model this effect as a direct adjustment to the inflation rate.

The balance of risks is measured as the probability of obtaining shocks higher or lower than the more likely outcome reported in Table 6.2. We assume that the gasoline shock is symmetric, but that there is a 60 per cent chance of obtaining a higher as opposed to lower value of the risk premium or the supply shock. The scale of uncertainty may be measured either from econometric estimates, as we did, or from past deviations of monetary policy forecasts around the historical realisations. The former procedure tends to produce a higher level of uncertainty. The latter,

Table 6.1 The most likely path of the shocks

	π_t^R	ψ_t	π_t^{Oil}
2000 Q4	0.70	7.0	2.5
2001 Q1	0.35	7.0	1.4
2001 Q2	0.35	7.0	1.4
2001 Q3	0.00	7.0	0.0
2001 Q4	0.00	7.0	0.0
2002 Q1	0.00	7.0	0.0
2002 Q2	0.00	7.0	0.0
2002 Q3	0.00	7.0	0.0
2002 Q4	0.00	7.0	0.0

Table 6.2 The inflation forecast

	90%	*80%*	*70%*	*60%*	*Mode*	*60%*	*70%*	*80%*	*90%*	*Target*
2000 Q4	6.27	7.45	8.27	9.00	9.69	10.56	11.47	12.51	13.99	10.0
2001 Q1	5.86	6.93	7.68	8.34	8.97	9.78	10.62	11.59	12.97	
2001 Q2	4.92	6.08	6.90	7.61	8.29	9.18	10.10	11.16	12.66	
2001 Q3	3.96	5.07	5.85	6.54	7.19	8.06	8.97	10.00	11.47	
2001 Q4	3.27	4.38	5.17	5.85	6.51	7.40	8.32	9.37	10.87	8.0
2002 Q1	2.31	3.58	4.47	5.25	6.00	6.97	7.98	9.14	10.78	
2002 Q2	1.20	2.69	3.74	4.66	5.54	6.64	7.78	9.09	10.95	
2002 Q3	1.22	2.60	3.57	4.42	5.23	6.28	7.37	8.62	10.39	
2002 Q4	1.15	2.48	3.42	4.23	5.02	6.04	7.11	8.33	10.06	6.0
2003 Q1	0.99	2.33	3.26	4.08	4.87	5.90	6.97	8.19	9.93	

common in most other central banks that produce a fan chart, can result in a smaller degree of uncertainty because actual forecasts are made more accurate with off-model information

Figure 6.17 shows our fan chart and Table 6.2 summarises the results.

6.12 Conclusion

Despite large and frequent changes in the monetary policy stance. Colombia has experienced a long history of moderate inflation. Monetary policy has pursued targets for money and the exchange rate, and short-term targets for interest rates. The temporary defence of the exchange rate, supporting exporters' and borrowers short-term interests led to large expansions and contractions in the real interest rate. During the 1990s, the exchange rate policy gradually became more directed at stabilising inflation. The consequence was a historically unprecedented disinflation in 1999, with current plans for future decreases in inflation targets.

To explain this disinflation our model estimates identifies three key aspects of the Colombian transmission mechanism: an inflation process that it is persistent: a strong aggregate demand channel; and a relatively weak and indirect exchange rate effect.

We have shown how the model can describe plausible responses to shocks that are particular to Colombia: a permanent shift in the inflation target, a temporary surprise monetary policy action, a supply disturbance in the agricultural sector, a change in the terms of trade, and a shift in the risk premium.

We found that monetary policy has a greater effect on inflation when

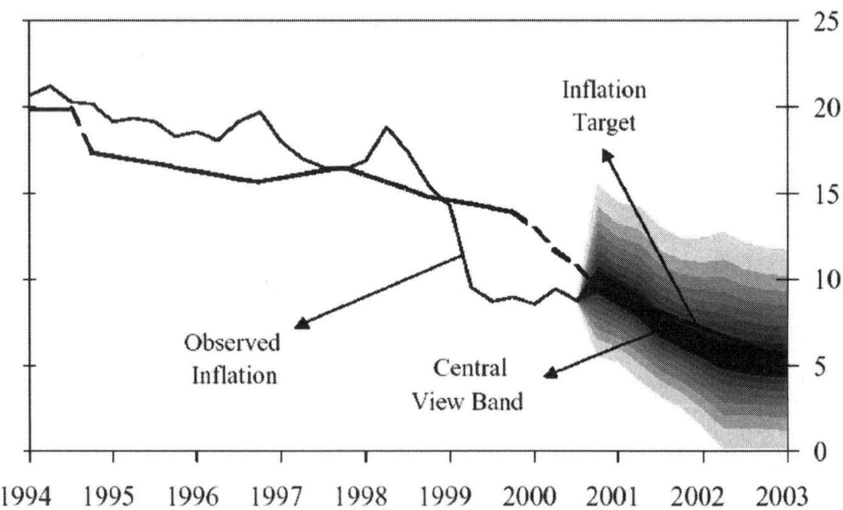

Figure 6.17 The inflation forecast.

inflation is dominated by forward-looking elements. More inertia in inflation rates, on the contrary, imposes higher demands on monetary policy.

This model's estimate of the cost of disinflation, as measured by the sacrifice ratio, is –0.788, although ratios between –0.500 and –0.786 are also plausible. Once we take account of the gains accrued from stabilising inflation, the net welfare gain from a 10 percentage point disinflation is a 3.9 per cent increase of consumption in perpetuity.

Notes

1 Prepared for the CCBS (Bank of England) Workshop on Transmission Mechanisms of Monetary Policy. jgomezpi@banrep.gov.co jjulioro@banrep.gov.co. The views expressed in this paper are those of the authors and not necessarily those of the Banco de la Republica nor its Board of Directors. The authors wish to thank Lawrence Ball, Ron Smith, Miguel Urrutia, Hernando Vargas and Adolfo Cobo for comments. Rodrigo Avella for research assistance and Lavan Mahadeva and Gabriel Sterne for their valuable suggestions and for the organisation of a most enjoyable workshop. Any errors are ours.

2 A more detailed description of the evolution of the nominal exchange rate regime is in Villar and Rincón (2000).

3 In 1997, five countries, including Colombia were selected from 150 developing and transition countries as possible candidates for future adoption of an inflation-targeting framework (Masson *et al.* 1997). Colombia may soon be fully considered an inflation-targeting country.

4 For a discussion on inflation-targeting see Masson *et al.* (1997) and Mishkin (2000b).

5 The results also hold for a geometric average of wages in the retail trade and industrial sectors. The trend is needed to approximate the change in productivity because the quarterly employment figures are not available for the entire economy but only for the main cities.

6 Chadha *et al.* (1992) show how the cost of disinflations is decreasing in the weight on future inflation.

7 Cointegration tests indicate that the CPI, import prices, nominal wages and a time trend are co-integrated.

8 As inflation is measured at an annual rate, to make the coefficients compatable to coefficients of Phillips curves estimated with quarterly inflation, the coefficient on the gap should be divided by four.

9 The estimation method is restricted OLS. The sample period is 1990Q1–2000Q3. $R^2 = 0.777$. The standard error of residuals is 1.363 and the p-value of significance of Ljung Box Q statistic is 0.458

10 The estimation method is OLS. The sample period is 1990Q1–1999Q3. $R^2 = 0.680$. The standard error of residuals is 2.133 and the p-value of significance of Ljung Box Q statistic is 0.362.

11 See García and Montes (1988: 41).

12 Another definition of the price of traded goods is a linear combination of the price levels of the main trading partners, as in Sjaastad (1998). This is one of the definitions of the Index of Real Exchange Rate (ITCR) that are calculated at the Banco de la República.

13 The estimation method is OLS. The sample period is 1982Q1–1999Q4. $R^2 = 0.453$. The standard error of the residuals is 1.669 and the p-value or significance of Ljung Box Q statistic is 0.083.

14 The estimation method is OLS, the sample period 1990Q1–2000Q1 $R^2 = 0.850$.

The standard error of the residuals is 4.850 and the p-value of significance of the Ljung Box Q statistic is 0.339.

15 The estimation method is OLS, the sample is 1992Q1–2000Q1 $R^2 = 0.883$. The standard error of the residual is 1811 and the p-value of the significance of Ljung Box Q statistic is 0.438.

16 The estimation method is OLS, the sample period is 1990M1–2000M7. $R^2 = 0.613$ the standard error of the residuals is 1.049 and the significance of Ljung Box Q statistic is 0.099.

17 The share of imports in GDP is 20.8 per cent in Colombia compared to 13.5 per cent in the US.

18 Of course there are many other types of shock to the economy that are not fully and explicitly treated in the core model. Satellite models may help us to understand the effect of these shocks on inflation, and may suggest how the aggregate model can be adjusted.

19 A positive increase in the nominal interest rate has the same qualitative impact on the economy as a negative transitory shock to the inflation target, the difference being that in the case of the shock to the target, the interest rate is endogenous.

20 This sacrifice ratio lies within the interval (0.0, 3.6) found by Ball (1994) for a sample of 28 disinflation episodes in nine countries.

21 While the level effect is not robust, the welfare gain in growth from decreasing inflation is somewhat robust to the specification of money demand and its interest elasticity. This is shown by Lucas (2000).

22 We use the same utility function that Lucas (1987) uses for the evaluation of the welfare gains from growth and the stabilisation of the business cycle

$$u(c_t) = \frac{1}{1-\sigma}(c_t^{1-\sigma} - 1).$$

When $\sigma = 0$ the representative consumer is risk neutral. For $\sigma > 0$, there is risk aversion. In the special case $\sigma \rightarrow 1$, the utility function is approximately logarithmic. We use the estimates $\beta = 0.959$ and $\sigma = 2.310$ from López (2000:10) $\sigma = 1 - (-1.310)$ where -1.310 is estimated in her paper.

7 Monetary policy and goals for external competitiveness

A dynamic general equilibrium model for Hungary

Áron Gereben

7.1 Introduction

In transition economies where econometric problems are prevalent, more weight may have to be placed on policy advice given by calibrated and more theory-based (dynamic general equilibrium) models. A two-sector open-economy optimising model with sticky prices is constructed and designed to match some characteristics of the Hungarian economy.

Domestically-owned and foreign-owned firms differ in their access to capital markets; the former have access only to domestic savings while the latter can borrow from abroad. It is assumed that monetary policy can more directly affect the costs of borrowing for foreign-owned firms, through the exchange rate, while it has only indirect effects on the borrowing costs for domestically owned firms. As Hungary began its economic transition with a relatively high level of initial external debt, monetary policy was often constrained by considerations related to external balance of payments and financing of the current account deficit. In this chapter, a profit-based measure of external balance and competitiveness is derived and the effect of monetary policy on this measure is assessed.

Simulations are performed under different monetary policy rules. Results confirm that beyond the famous short-run trade-off between inflation and output, there exists also a trade-off between faster disinflation and external competitiveness, but only insofar as prices in the domestically owned sector are sticky.

Modelling the transmission mechanism on time-series data in an economy in transition is certainly a difficult task. Data from the pre-1990 period are irrelevant from the viewpoint of an analysis that aims to describe the present. Even post-1990 data can be of limited use for econometric analysis: they are often available only in short samples and affected by the structural breaks that naturally occur during transition. In these circumstances, theory-based approaches to understanding monetary transmission may have to be relied on to a greater extent than in countries where reliable data are more abundant.

Despite these difficulties, several studies have attempted to quantify some aspects of the monetary transmission mechanism in Hungary. Világi and Vincze (1998) focused on the transmission from monetary policy instruments to the banks' lending and deposit rates. They found that between 1991 and 1995 substantial short-run rigidities were present in both deposit and lending rates. Árvai (1998) examined the transmission between market rates and the deposit and lending rates. She set up a theoretical model to explain the high observed spread, and also estimated an ECM of market rates and bank credit rates. Csermely and Varró (1998) estimated a structural VAR on five endogenous variables: output gap based on industrial production; inflation; changes in M1; the 3-month treasury bill rate; and the changes in the nominal effective exchange rate. They did not find any plausible effect of monetary policy shocks on aggregate demand. They reported a slight relationship of causality going from interest rates to inflation, but, as they pointed out, the standard errors are large and their specification did not allow for fully separating exchange rate and interest rate shocks. On the other hand, they did find evidence of a relatively high level of price stickiness. Csajbók and Varró (2000) estimated a monetary policy rule that included inflation and current account deviations as explanatory variables in a co-integrating VAR framework. They found that policy responded to both inflationary and current account developments. However, inflation and external balance did not seem to react to changes in the policy rate. Árvai and Menczel (2000) examined the consumption quarter-saving decisions of Hungarian households, and concluded that changes in real interest rates have very limited effects on savings.

Here, I follow a more theory-based approach and construct a small, calibrated, two-sector dynamic general equilibrium model that attempts to capture particular features of the Hungarian economy and can be used to tackle certain questions about monetary transmission. Open-economy general equilibrium models with similar specifications were suggested by McCallum and Nelson (1998), and are applied extensively for monetary policy analysis. Recent examples of applications for the Euro area are by Wouters and Dombrecht (2000) and Smets and Wouters (2002). The two-sector extension of this modelling framework has been used recently by Batini *et al.* (2000a) for a comparison of different policy rules in the United Kingdom, and by Devereux and Lane (2000), who analyse the choice of exchange rate regime in emerging markets.

The model presented here adds to the standard in that it emphasises the effects of monetary policy on the economy's external balance. As an alternative to the current account, a new measure of external equilibrium – a profit-based real exchange rate index – is constructed, and the behaviour of this variable is examined under different monetary policy rules.

As emphasised, an advantage of the calibrated general equilibrium modelling approach is that it relies less on time-series data and therefore circumvents the problems related to econometric estimates. A disadvantage, however, is that a theory-based approach requires the modeller to impose a large number of subjective and simplifying assumptions about the underlying macroeconomic structure. The modeller must also find plausible values for the model's unknown parameters. To validate these subjective elements – this is, to compare the real data to those generated by the model – a range of techniques is possible (see Rotemberg and Woodford 1998; Diebold *et al.* 1998; Canova 2000). Unfortunately, for the Hungarian case there is limited potential to perform such an exercise because of the lack of long and reliable time-series data. As a consequence the model discussed in this paper is not calibrated rigorously in the sense of Cooley 1997, who attempts to pin down the rules of thumb for calibration and validation of general equilibrium models.

In spite of its reliance on some arbitrary assumptions and the difficulties in matching it with economic reality, such a model has several uses. First of all, many of us who are involved to some extent in debates about monetary policy have some view about how the transmission of monetary policy works in Hungary. A calibrated general equilibrium model can be useful in checking the consistency of these intuitions, by providing a yardstick with which to measure the importance of uncertainty about numerical values of key parameters. Also, it provides qualitative results, although these results can be considered relevant only if the assumptions of the model are valid.[1]

7.2 Some characteristics of the environment in which Hungarian monetary policy operates

Before describing the model, it is useful to highlight some features of the Hungarian economic environment that are particularly relevant to monetary transmission.[2]

7.2.1 The current account and monetary policy

Exports are a significant and rapidly growing part of the GDP (Figure 7.1). Conversely, the contribution of internal demand to economic growth is relatively low, although this has started to rise recently. One implication of openness is that the competitiveness of a large part of the corporate sector is sensitive to nominal exchange rate changes in the short term. Furthermore, the share of imported goods in consumption is around 25 per cent, which means that exchange rate changes can have a significant direct impact on the level of consumer prices.

Consequently, exchange rate considerations have played an important role in the conduct of monetary policy in Hungary, especially in the short run. This reflects not only trade openness, but also the need to smooth

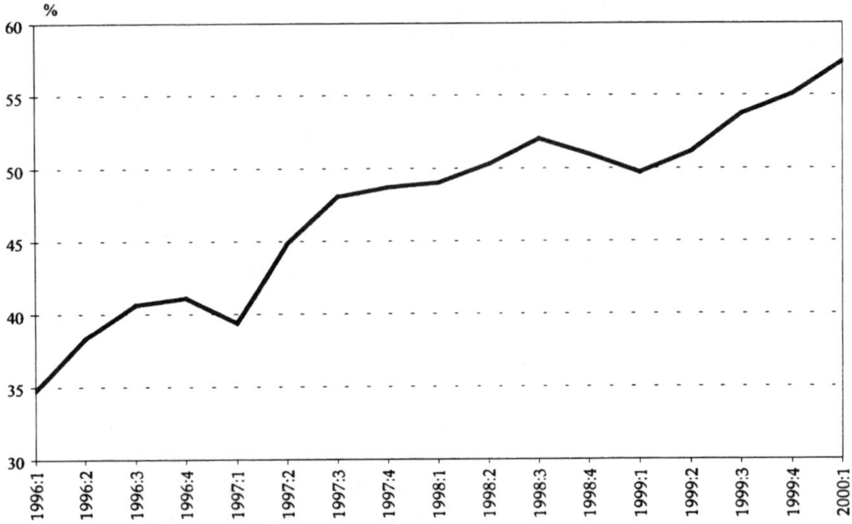

Figure 7.1 Exports as percentage of GDP.

external finance flows. As Hungary began the economic transition with a relatively high external public debt, an aggressive anti-inflationary programme could risk pushing the current account deficit to a level considered unsustainable by international lenders. The pre-announced crawling-peg regime, introduced in 1995 and maintained until May 2001, allowed the central bank to maintain a gradual path of disinflation without leading to unstable capital inflows and outflows.

Formally, within the crawling-peg regime monetary policy had two instruments: it could set both the rate of the crawl and the level of the short-term interest rates. However, the two variables were not independent. Since international capital flows were largely liberalised,[3] interest rates could not permanently deviate from the level implied by the premium-augmented uncovered interest parity (UIP). In the longer run, therefore, the rate of the crawl – together with the rather volatile risk premium and the foreign (Euro) interest rate – determined the domestic short-term rates.

The link between monetary policy and the conditions for external balance deserves some attention. First of all, a monetary tightening does not always lead to a deterioration of the current account balance – often used as the 'headline' measure of external equilibrium.[4] Furthermore, as the monetary policy is concerned about the country's ability to repay its debt, and not with the current account balance *per se*, the current account is only a rough and often inaccurate measure of external balance. The ability to repay the debt depends primarily on international competitiveness; therefore it is important to find an appropriate measure of competitiveness. In this chapter, we will use a real exchange rate measure that is based on profits and the return on capital.

7.2.2 The 'duality' of the corporate sector

A growing economy may have to depend on non-resident savings to finance its growth. Naturally, then, capital account considerations are also important for Hungarian monetary policy. Also, asymmetries in borrowers' access to funds are an important feature of the Hungarian capital markets. Because of massive privatisation and large foreign direct investment inflows a significant share of the corporate sector is in the hands of foreign strategic investors (Table 7.1); most of them are multinational corporations. This part of the economy – which is basically the driving force behind the growth observed during the previous years – is not constrained by domestic borrowing facilities. The foreign-owned sector can either borrow directly from abroad or borrow from the domestic banking sector. Banks are willing to lend to foreign firms, as they are usually considered low-risk clients (see Figure 7.2.). Since foreign ownership in the banking sector is also important and banks have access to foreign funds from their strategic owners abroad, in some cases the foreign funds are channelled to the multinational sector through the local banking system. In this respect, foreign-owned firms compete with the government for the domestic and foreign savings channelled through the banks. Since monetary policy influences market yields, it also affects the costs of bank loans to the foreign-owned sector. However, since foreign and domestic loans are substitutable, the effects of short-term domestic monetary policy on the foreign-owned firms' borrowing costs are not independent of its influence on exchange rates.[5]

The other segment of the corporate sector, which is not under foreign

Table 7.1 Foreign ownership in different sectors (as a percentage of GDP)

Sector	*1994*	*1996*	*1998*
Mining	17.8	36.1	27.8
Manufacturing	37.0	52.5	59.7
Electricity, gas, heating	0.4	21.7	31.2
Construction	32.8	40.9	28.6
Retail trade, repairing services	27.8	36.5	45.8
Tourism	30.6	38.6	31.0
Transport and telecommunications	15.5	23.1	31.0
Financial services	19.4	46.6	48.8
Real estate, rental services	19.6	22.4	26.2
Contribution of foreign-owned sector to GDP	23.0	32.8	36.6

Source: National Bank of Hungary calculations based on tax data.

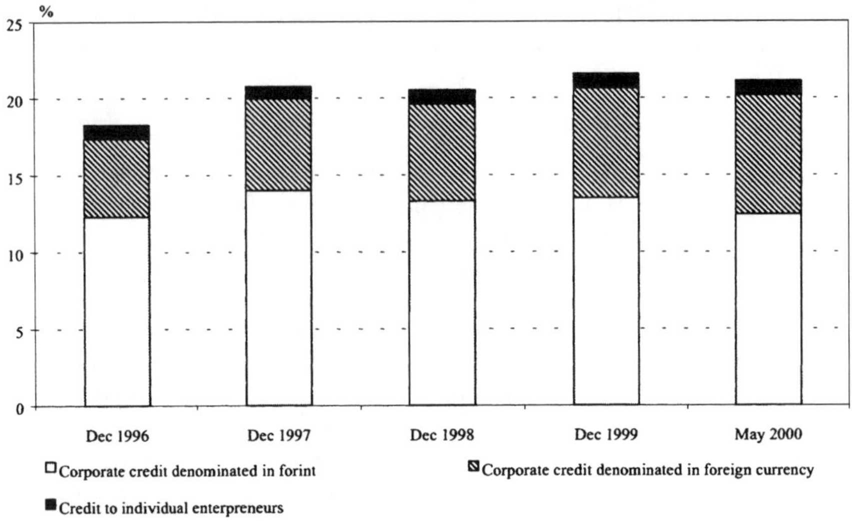

Figure 7.2 Credit from the domestic banking system to the corporate sector (as a percentage of GDP).

ownership – mainly small- and medium-sized enterprises – has limited access to bank credit. A vast proportion of these enterprises do not have a long track record, and their lenders face asymmetric information and moral hazard problems. It is not surprising that their leverage is low and most of these firms are mainly financed by equity, either through direct inflows from the owners or through retained earnings. Because of their low leverage, the direct effects of monetary policy on the borrowing costs of these firms is much weaker.

7.2.3 Monetisation of households

The net financial wealth of households is still small in Hungary, making their consumption decisions less responsive to interest rate changes. For example, the stock of credits to households is low, amounting only to 3 to 4 per cent of GDP in 1999 (see Figure 7.3). Although consumer lending has started to build up recently, the high growth rate originates from a low base. Furthermore, a market for housing loans, common to Western economies, is virtually non-existent. As to the asset side, the amount of interest rate sensitive items in household portfolios is not substantial enough to significantly affect consumption directly. Although only very limited data exists regarding the composition of households' wealth, it is widely accepted that the share of real assets – especially savings in real estate – dominates that of financial assets.

Several recent empirical studies confirm these views. Zsoldos (1997)

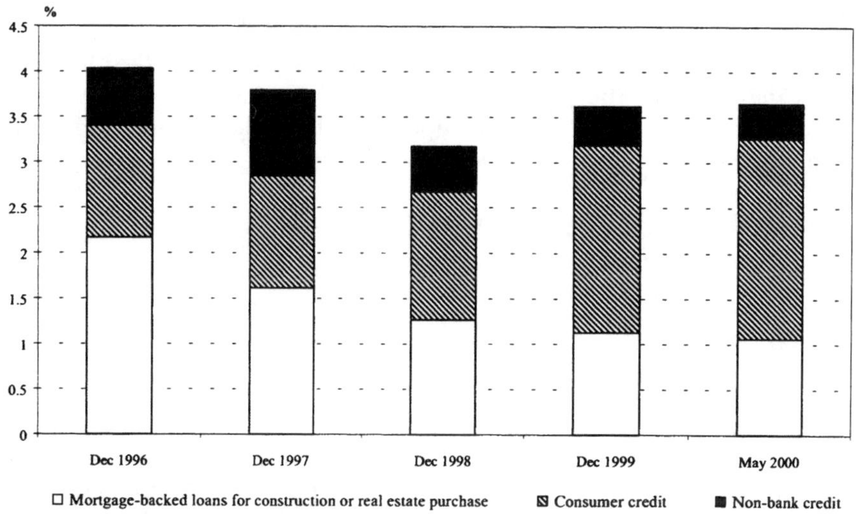

Figure 7.3 Credit to households (as a percentage of GDP).

and Menczel (2000) emphasise that, despite the recent growth in consumer credit, the majority of Hungarian households are liquidity-constrained. Árvai and Menczel (2000) also examine the transmission of monetary policy to the households' net savings position. They find that changes in real rates do not have any significant income, substitution or wealth effect on households. This, of course, does not mean that monetary policy would not influence consumption saving decisions of households, eventually or through other channels. At least in the recent past, however the evaluation of net savings was dominated by other, more influential factors that stem from the economic transition, such as the gradual abolition of liquidity constraints and the remonetisation of the whole economy.

7.2.4 Labour market[6]

Since we are planning to construct a two-sector model, it is important to know how the levels and dynamics of wages in the two sectors are connected. Evidence that wages of foreign-owned and domestic-owned sectors in Hungary are equalised independent of productivity, a key assumption in our set-up, is somewhat controversial. We can cite Ferenczi (1999), who reports no trend divergence between wages in manufacturing and services but rather a constant difference in the wage levels.

7.3 An optimising two-sector model of monetary transmission

We have constructed a model that is broadly consistent with the empirical facts described in the previous section. The model is of a small open economy, in which all agents optimise their decision-making. The economy is split into two sectors. One of the sectors;

- is owned by foreign investors;
- has access to international capital markets, and
- exports all of its output to the world market.

The other sector:

- is owned by domestic households;
- has no access to international capital markets, and therefore must finance its capital input from the savings of domestic households; and
- produces only for the domestic market, and therefore does not face international competition.

It is assumed that wages equalise between the two sectors – that is, labour is perfectly substitutable between sectors – but capital does not, which gives rise to a Balassa–Samuelson effect. With monetary policy fixed, when the foreign-owned sector experiences a (positive) shock in productivity and its workers' wages increase, firms in the other sector have to increase wages too. As domestically owned firms' productivity is independent of foreign-owned firms' productivity, domestically owned firms have to raise prices to compensate for wage increases. As a result, if one sector experiences constantly higher productivity growth over time than the other, and its prices are fixed at world levels, the other sector has continuously to increase its prices to compensate for increases in the wage level. Consequently the economy as a whole will experience a constant increase in the overall price level, providing that interest rates and exchange rates are held constant.

Households maximise their discounted utility with respect to current consumption. The choice between work and leisure is not included in the utility function for the sake of simplicity, and therefore the labour supply is constant over time. Households do not have access to international capital markets, but they are able to invest their savings in the domestic firms. As both households and domestically-owned firms are excluded from the international capital markets, the uncovered interest parity holds only for the cost of capital of the foreign-owned firms. Thus the real yield on the capital that households invest in to domestic firms does not automatically adjust to the level implied by the external factors and is determined endogenously. Nominal rigidities in domestic prices play a part in distinguishing the real rate of interest faced by households from rates faced by foreign-owned firms.

7.3.1 Firms under foreign ownership

Foreign-owned firms (FOFs) produce a single good which is exported to a perfectly competitive market and not consumed domestically. The representative FOF produces its output according to the following Cobb–Douglas technology with constant returns to scale:

$$YF_t = A_t \cdot LF_t^{\alpha 1} \cdot FK_{t-1}^{\alpha 2}, \quad \alpha_1, \alpha_2 > 0, \quad \alpha_1 + \alpha_2 = 1 \tag{7.1}$$

where A_t is a time-varying exogenous productivity scaling factor, LF_t is the labour input and FK_t is the foreign capital input. Labour is provided by the domestic households. Capital goods can be purchased at price PF_t, while funding of capital goods is carried out through local-currency borrowing from the international market at rate RFK_t. The rationale behind this formulation might be a banking system that is mainly foreign-owned and that channels funds mainly to foreign-owned firms. Such a system of financial intermediation can be considered a rough approximation of the Hungarian banking system. PF_t represents the price level of all internationally traded goods expressed in domestic currency, that is $PF_t = PW_t \cdot S_t$, where PW_t is the (exogenous) level of world prices and S_t is the nominal exchange rate.

FOFs maximise the present value of their future profits:

$$PVF_t = \sum_{t=0}^{\infty} \rho^t \, \Pi F_t \tag{7.2}$$

where the budget constraint takes the following form:

$$\Pi F_t = PF_t \cdot YF_t - WF_t \cdot LF_t - PF_{t-1} \cdot FK_{t-1} \cdot RFK_{t-1} + PF_t \cdot FK_{t-1} \,(1-\delta) \tag{7.3}$$

The first expression on the right-hand side represents the nominal sales income of the FOFs, where output is sold at price PF_t on the world market. The second expression stands for the cost of labour, where WF_t is the nominal wage level in the foreign-owned sector. The third is the total cost of capital input. It is assumed that it takes time – one period – to install capital. To obtain *FK* amount of capital goods at period t, firms thus have to borrow $FK_{t-1} \cdot PF_{t-1}$ from abroad at period t-1. As a result, in period t they will have to repay the same amount multiplied by the nominal interest rate of the previous period, RFK_{t-1}.[7] The final expression represents the gain to the FOFs in reselling the used capital at the current price (δ is the rate of depreciation).

The profit-maximisation problem of the FOFs yields the following first-order conditions:

$$PF_t \cdot \alpha_1 \cdot \frac{YF_t}{LF_t} - WF_t = 0, \qquad \text{and} \tag{7.4}$$

$$\frac{\alpha_2 E_t\left[\frac{PF_{t+1}}{PF_t} \cdot YF_{t+1}\right]}{FK_t} - RFK_t + E_t\left[\frac{PF_{t+1}}{PF_t}\right](1-\delta) = 0. \tag{7.5}$$

Equation (7.4) is the usual first-order condition for labour demand, i.e. that the marginal product of labour equals the real wage. Equation (7.5) is a similar condition for capital goods, which states that the (expected) marginal product of capital has to be equal to the real interest rate plus depreciation. Expectations are important because of the lag between the installation and the use of capital input.

7.3.2 Domestically-owned firms

Domestically-owned firms (DOFs) produce goods that are distinct from the goods produced by the foreign-owned firms, and are consumed only within the country. It is assumed that the whole sector is composed of a continuum of firms indexed by $i \in [0,1]$, each of which produces a differentiated good enabling it to have market power and sets its prices as a mark-up $1/q$ over marginal costs. This specification is similar to that of Blanchard and Kiyotaki (1987).

The aggregate output within the domestically owned sector is given by:

$$YD_t = \left[\int_0^1 YD_t(i)^q \, di\right]^{1/q} \tag{7.6}$$

The demand for the individual DOF's products is given by the standard Blanchard–Kiyotaki demand function:

$$YD_t(i) = \left[\frac{PD_t}{PD_t(i)}\right]^{1/(1-q)} YD_t \tag{7.7}$$

Each individual firm is using a Cobb–Douglas production function with constant returns to scale:

$$YD_t\,(i)\;B_t \cdot LD_t\,(i)^{\beta_1} \cdot HK_{t-1}(i)^{\beta_2}, \qquad \beta_1, \beta_2 > 0, \qquad \beta_1 + \beta_2 = 1 \tag{7.8}$$

where B_t is the total factor productivity, $LD_t(i)$ is the labour input and $HK_t(i)$ is home capital input, both the last two being provided by the domestic households. We assume that DOFs do not have access to international capital markets. Again, it is assumed that it takes one period to install capital equipment.

Each DOF maximises the present value of future profits

$$\sum_{t=0}^{\infty} \rho^t \Pi D(i)_t,$$

where ρ is the discount factor and the current-period profit function is as follows:

$$\Pi D(i)_t = PD(i)_t \cdot YD(i)_t - WD_t \cdot LD(i)_t - PF_{t-1} \cdot HK(i)_{t-1} \cdot RHK_{t-1} + PF_t \cdot HK(i)_{t-1} \cdot (1-\delta) \quad (7.9)$$

This is similar to the problem faced by the foreign-owned firms. However, note that the DOFs are able to set their own prices.

Assuming symmetric equilibrium in the domestically-owned sector, where all individual firms charge the same price and employ the same labour and capital inputs, the first-order conditions for the sector as a whole can be written as:

$$q \cdot PD_t \cdot \beta_1 \cdot \frac{YD_t}{LD_t} - WD_t = 0 \quad (7.10)$$

and

$$\frac{q \cdot \beta_2 \cdot E_t\left[\dfrac{PD_{t+1}}{PF_{t+1}} \dfrac{PF_{t+1}}{PF_t} YD_{t+1}\right]}{HK_t} - RHK_t + E_t\left[\frac{PF_{t+1}}{PF_t}\right] \cdot (1-\delta) = 0 \quad (7.11)$$

$$\Pi D_t = PD_t \cdot YD_t - WD_t \cdot LD_t - PF_{t-1} \cdot HK_{t-1} \cdot RHK_{t-1} + PF_t \cdot HK_{t-1} \cdot (1-\delta) \quad (7.12)$$

7.3.3 *Price stickiness*

It is assumed that prices in the domestically-owned sector are sticky because some DOFs set their prices in advance. Following Calvo (1983), each DOF faces a constant probability λ of altering its price in each period. The probability λ is independent of whether that firm's price was fixed last period.[8]

It can be shown (see, for example, Walsh 1998) that the aggregate price level within the domestically owned sector will be given by:

$$PD_t^q = \lambda PD_t\,(c)^q + (1-\lambda)\,PD_{t-1}^q \tag{7.13}$$

where $PD_t(c)$ denotes the price set at t by those firms that adjust their price. $PD_t(c)$ is governed by:[9]

$$PD_t\,(c) = (1-\rho(1-\lambda))\,qPD_t(eq) + \rho(1-\lambda)\,PD_{t+1}(c) \tag{7.14}$$

where $PD_t(eq)$ is the market-clearing price; related to unit labour costs by equation (10).

7.3.4 Households

The preferences of the infinitely lived representative household are given by:

$$U_t = E_0 \sum_{t=0}^{\infty} \rho^t \cdot U_t(C_t) \tag{7.15}$$

where U_t is the overall utility, ρ is the discount factor and C_t is an aggregate consumption index of domestically produced goods and imported goods. Following Carroll *et al.* (1995), Fuhrer (1998) and McCallum and Nelson (1998), let us assume that households exhibit habit persistence and U_t is given by:

$$U_t = \frac{1}{1-\sigma}\left(\frac{C_t}{C_{t-1}^{\xi}}\right)^{1-\sigma} \tag{7.16}$$

It is assumed that households consume both goods produced by the DOFs and goods imported from abroad. The elasticity of substitution between the two goods is unity. This gives us the following expressions for the aggregate consumption index and the price deflator, respectively:

$$C_t = \frac{CD_t^{\omega} \cdot CI_t^{1-\omega}}{\omega^{\omega} \cdot (1-\omega)^{1-\omega}} \tag{7.17}$$

$$P_t = PD_t^{\omega} \cdot PF_t^{1-\omega} \tag{7.18}$$

where ω is the share of domestic goods in the consumption basket. The price of domestically-produced goods is PD_t, while the price of imported goods is PF_t. The demand for domestic and imported goods are given by:

$$CD_t = \omega \cdot \left(\frac{PD_t}{P_t} \right)^{-1} C_t \tag{7.19}$$

$$CI_t = (1-\omega) \cdot \left(\frac{PF_t}{P_t} \right)^{-1} C_t \tag{7.20}$$

Households maximise their utility subject to the following budget constraint:

$$P_t \cdot C_t + PF_t \cdot HK_t = WD_t \cdot LD_t + WF_t \cdot LF_t + HK_{t-1} \cdot PF_{t-1} \cdot RHK_{t-1} + \Pi D_t \tag{7.21}$$

The left-hand side is the sum of nominal consumption and current-period lending to domestically-owned firms. The first two terms on the right-hand side are labour income received from working with the DOFs and the FOFs, respectively. The third expression is the interest-augmented value of the capital that was lent to DOFs the period before. The final term stands for the revenues coming from the (nominal) profits of the domestically-owned firms.

The first-order conditions of utility maximisation are given by the budget constraint and the Euler condition for utility, which in this case is:

$$P_t \frac{\partial U}{\partial C_t} = E_t[P_{t+1}] \cdot (1 + RHK_t) \cdot \rho \cdot \frac{\partial U}{\partial C_{t+1}} \tag{7.22}$$

Note that for our utility function, $\partial U / \partial C_t$ is given by:

$$\frac{\partial U}{\partial C_t} = \frac{(1-\sigma)U_t}{C_t} - \rho\sigma \frac{(1-\sigma)U_{t+1}}{C_{t+1}} \tag{7.23}$$

Therefore the Euler equation can be written as:

$$\left[\frac{U_t}{C_t} - \rho\xi \frac{U_{t+1}}{C_{t+1}} \right] = E_t \left[\frac{P_{t+1}}{P_t} \right] \cdot (1 + RHK_t) \cdot \rho \cdot \left[\frac{U_{t+1}}{C_{t+1}} - \rho\xi \frac{U_{t+2}}{C_{t+2}} \right] \tag{7.24}$$

By substituting the one-period utility function for U_t, U_{t+1} and U_{t+2}, respectively, it is possible to obtain the Euler equation in terms of current and future levels of the consumption index.

7.3.5 Market-clearing conditions

To establish the links between the different agents within the economy, the following additional assumptions were made:

$$WD_t = WF_t \tag{7.25}$$

$$LD_t + LF_t = L_t \tag{7.26}$$

$$YD_t = CD_t \tag{7.27}$$

Equation (7.25) states that the labour market is competitive and that wages in the two sectors are equal. Equation (7.26) is a full-employment condition ensuring that labour demand of the two sectors equals the labour supply treated as an exogenous factor (and assumed to be constant). Equation (7.27) is the market-clearing condition of the goods produced by the domestically-owned firms. Aggregate output Y_t will be defined as the sum of the sectoral nominal outputs deflated by the CPI:

$$Y_t = \frac{PF_t YF_t + PD_t YD_t}{P_t} \tag{7.28}$$

7.3.6 Links with the international capital markets

The world real interest rate, RWR_t, is treated as exogenous. The world nominal interest rate is defined given exogenous world prices, PW as follows:

$$RW_t = \frac{RWR_t}{PW_{t+1}/PW_t} \tag{7.29}$$

The exchange rate is assumed to be subject to a forward-looking version of the uncovered interest parity (UIP) augmented with an exogenous risk premium $PREM_t$:[10]

$$S_t = \frac{RW_t}{RFK_t} \cdot E(S_{t+1}) \cdot PREM_t \tag{7.30}$$

If UIP is assumed to hold, monetary policy cannot determine both the exchange rate and the interest rate: setting one instrument will determine the other. Therefore equivalent monetary policy strategies can be formulated both as exchange rate rules or as interest rate rules.

7.3.7 Financial flows within the economy and the balance of payments

Figure 7.4 depicts the financial flows between the different agents of the economy. It also allows us to derive the balance of payments for the economy, once we group all the financial flows that occur between a domestic agent and the rest of the world (items *a, b, c, d, f, g, h, o, p, q* in Figure 7.4). The balance of payments thus derived comprises three basic elements: net flows of consumption goods ($NFCG_t$), net flows of capital

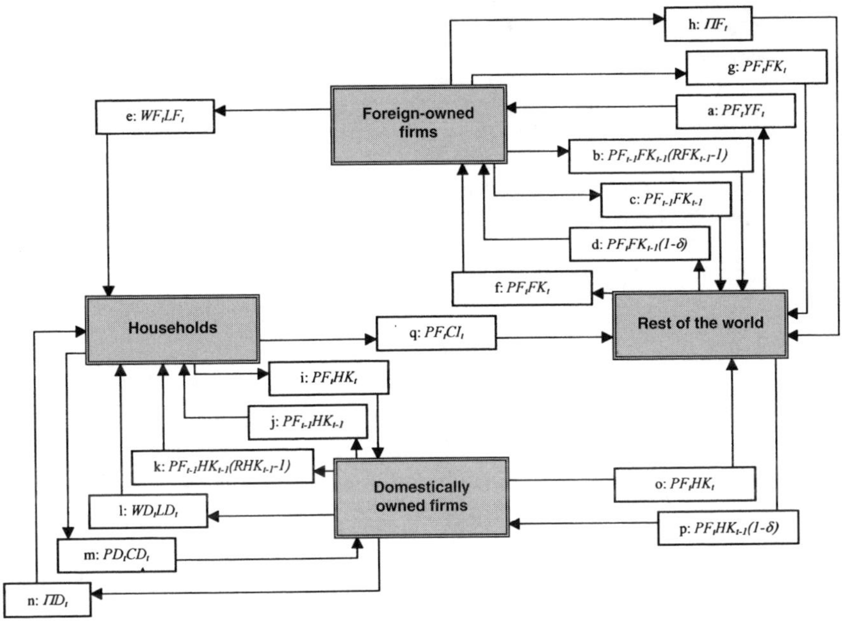

Figure 7.4 Financial flows within the economy (expressed in domestic currency)

Key: a: Sales income of foreign-owned firms
b: Interest payments on previous-period loans from abroad
c: Redemption of previous-period loans from abroad
d: Income from sales of used capital equipment
e: Payroll of foreign-owned sector
f: Loans from abroad financing capital used in next period
g: Purchases of capital goods for next period
h: Transfer of profits
i: Loans from households to domestic firms
j: Redemption of previous period loans from households
k: Interest payments on previous period loans from households
l: Payroll of domestic sector
m: Sales income of domestic firms (consumption of domestic goods)
n: Transfer of profits
o: Purchases of capital equipment from abroad
p: Income from sales of used capital equipment
q: Import consumption

goods ($NFKG_t$), and interest payments and profits (IPP_t). These three items sum up to the current account (CA_t) and a capital account (KA_t).

Net flows of consumption goods are given by the nominal difference between the output of the foreign-owned sector and the consumption of imported goods:

$$NFCG_t = PF_t \cdot YF_t - PF_t \cdot CI_t \tag{7.31}$$

Flows of capital goods for both sectors are given by the difference between the revenues from selling used capital and the costs of new capital goods purchased for the next period:

$$NFKG_t = PF_t \cdot FK_{t-1}\,(1-\delta) - PF_t \cdot FK_t + PF_t \cdot HK_{t-1}\,(1-\delta) - PF_t \cdot HK_t \tag{7.32}$$

The balance of interest payments and profits in our case involve only the remittances of the foreign-owned sector:

$$IPP_t = -PF_{t-1} \cdot FK_{t-1}(RHK_{t-1} - 1) - \Pi F_t \tag{7.33}$$

The balance of the current account is given by:

$$CA_t = NFCG_t + NFKG_t + IPP_t \tag{7.34}$$

Finally, the capital account balance is equal to the change in the capital invested in the foreign-owned sector:

$$KA_t = PF_t FK_t - PF_{t-1} FK_{t-1} \tag{7.35}$$

The structure of the model guarantees that the balance of payments is always in equilibrium, thus the current account is always financed by the capital account. In a non-inflationary steady state with zero productivity growth, both the capital account and the current account are zero.

7.3.8 A profit-based measure of external competitiveness

As presented in Section 7.2.7, the current account measure derived above is a mirror image of capital flows to the foreign-owned sector: a current account deficit always represents an increase of foreign investment in production. In the model there exists no agent – such as the government – that could borrow from abroad for purposes of consumption. As a consequence, the current account measure does not adequately describe the external debt constraint on monetary policy, namely the short-term trade-off between disinflation and temporary imbalances of the external position, as the economy is by definition always in a state where current account imbalances are financed by investment in the foreign-owned sector. Another measure of the external position and competitiveness is needed, therefore, to formulate the dilemma that monetary policy faces.

The measure of external competitiveness that we adopt is a version of the profit-based real exchange rate suggested by Lipschitz and McDonald (1992), Marsh and Tokarick (1994) and Kovács (1998). The idea behind this measure is that the competitiveness of an economy or a sector depends on the share of income going to capital: (the inverse of) the share of labour cost in value added. [11] The higher the labour share in value added, the less profitable it is to produce in the given economy/ sector. Such measures of competitiveness are defined for both sectors as the following:

$$COMPF_t = \frac{(PF_t \cdot YF_t)/(WF_t \cdot LF_t)}{(PF_{ss} \cdot YF_{ss})/(WF_{ss} \cdot LF_{ss})} \quad (7.36)$$

and

$$COMPD_t = \frac{(PD_t \cdot YD_t)/(WD_t \cdot LD_t)}{(PD_{ss} \cdot YD_{ss})/(WD_{ss} \cdot LD_{ss})} \quad (7.37)$$

where the index *ss* denotes the steady-state level of the given variables. $COMPF_t$ increases whenever the share of labour cost in value added is declining, reflecting a temporary increase in profitability in the foreign-owned sector relative to its steady-state level. $COMPD_t$ is a similar measure of profitability in the domestically-owned sector. Our measure of *external* competitiveness shall be defined as the relative competitiveness measure of the traded and non-traded sectors (or in our set-up, the foreign-owned and the domestically-owned sectors):

$$EXT_t = \frac{COMPF_t}{COMPD_t} \quad (7.38)$$

An increase in EXT_t means that it is more profitable to carry out production in the foreign-owned sector than in the domestically-owned sector. Resources would then be drawn to the foreign-owned sector, reflecting an enhanced ability to repay external debt. In simulations, we shall introduce EXT_t as an objective in the monetary policy rule besides the deviation of the rate of inflation from the target. The aim is to reflect the short-run disinflation–competitiveness dilemma of monetary policy in a country with high external debt.

7.4 Calibration

The model was calibrated to quarterly data. The parameters of the production functions were chosen to conform to studies of the Hungarian data. Following Valentinyi (2000), we used the parameters of Halpern and Körösi (1998), who estimated static and dynamic Cobb–Douglas production functions for groups of Hungarian enterprises differentiated by their ownership structure. α_1 and α_2, the factor shares in the foreign-owned sector, were set to 0.65 and 0.35, respectively, while β_1 and β_2, the factor shares in the domestically-owned sector, were set to 0.76 and 0.24.

The parameter q was set to 0.9, taken from the international literature. The parameter λ, reflecting the sluggishness of the prices in the domestically-owned sector, was set to 0.25 in the base line. We can find a slight empirical support for this base line: Tóth and Vincze (1998) provide a table on the frequency of price revisions for Hungarian firms. They found that those firms that produce for the domestic market mainly revisit their prices once a year. This is in line with setting λ ατ0.25.

As to the utility function, the standard structural parameters used in the literature were assumed. The subjective discount factor ρ was set to 0.99 for one quarter. For the other parameters of the utility function, two parameter sets were tried. One parameter set ($\sigma = 0.2$, $\xi = 0$) represents the case without habit persistence, the other ($\sigma = -6.11$, $\xi = 0.8$) stands for the case where habit persistence is present. For the latter the parameter set estimated by Fuhrer (1998) was used. The domestic share of consumption ω was set to 0.75 to match the actual data in Hungary.

7.5 The properties of the model

In this section we outline the results of some basic simulations and describe the main properties of the model. A rule describing monetary policy is needed. For the baseline simulations, an exchange-rate targeting rule, similar to the rule suggested by McCallum (1999), will be used. McCallum investigates the properties of a policy rule where the level of the exchange rate set by monetary policy is a function of inflation and output gap. We replace the output term in the rule with the relative profitability of the foreign-owned sector, as we wish to simulate a monetary policy that aims to keep the external balance in equilibrium instead of smoothing aggregate output.[12] The policy rule takes the following form (lower-case letters denote natural logarithms):

$$s_t = s_{t-1} - \phi_1(p_t - p_{t-1}) - \phi_2(ext_t - ext^*) \tag{7.39}$$

where ext^* denotes the long-run equilibrium level of external competitiveness (and equals zero in this case, as *EXT* is defined relative to the steady-state levels). The parameters ϕ_1 and ϕ_2 are set to 0.5 and 0.25, respectively, for the baseline simulations.

It is important to emphasise that equation (7.39) is not intended to capture the properties of the crawling-peg regime that was in place in Hungary until May 2001. First, the crawling-peg system was a strategy that was implemented to bring down high or moderate inflation to a level consistent with price stability, therefore it is difficult to interpret its properties in basic simulations where the initial values of the variables correspond to a no-inflation steady state. Also, as with any real world monetary policy, it is reasonable to assume that the crawling peg as it was in Hungary contained state-dependent and asymmetric elements. As the reaction of monetary policy should depend on the type and the direction of shocks, it is difficult to describe with a simple rule. Equation (7.39) is nothing more than a simple instrument rule for demonstrational purposes, but it enables us to explore the properties of the model assuming a monetary authority that intends to smooth both inflation and external competitiveness.[13] Furthermore the model can be solved for other policy rules as well, for example with rules that attempt to proxy the inflation-targeting regime introduced in June 2001.

The starting point for the simulations[14] was a steady state with no inflation and zero growth in the exogenous variables. Shocks were applied from period 1 onwards. It was assumed that all shocks were unexpected when they occurred.

To solve the model, terminal conditions have to be specified. As our shocks are temporary, and hence autonomous in the sense of Chiang (1992), we can suppose that the endogenous variables gravitate back towards their steady state over the long run. Therefore we could specify the terminal conditions as

$$\lim_{t\to\infty} X_t/X_{t-1} = 0 \qquad 7.40)$$

for all endogenous variables.

Figure 7.5 shows the impulse responses of the key variables for a permanent 1 per cent productivity increase in the foreign-owned sector.[15] Higher productivity in the foreign-owned sector leads to a high increase in output due to higher exports (*YF*), and also results in a temporary rise in the relative profitability measure (*EXT*). It also pushes up wages in both sectors, resulting in an inflationary pressure due to the Balassa–Samuelson effect. As the monetary policy rule includes a zero-inflation target, the inflationary pressure is somewhat counteracted by the appreciating path of the exchange rate (*S*). The temporary current account deficit (*CA*) is due to the inflows of capital to the foreign-owned sector. As a result of the higher wage income of households, both consumption and savings rise. However, as households and domestic firms have no access to external capital markets, the accumulation of capital takes a considerable time.

Figure 7.6 plots the values of the same variables for a 100 basis point increase in the risk premium (in yearly terms).[16] The risk premium shock

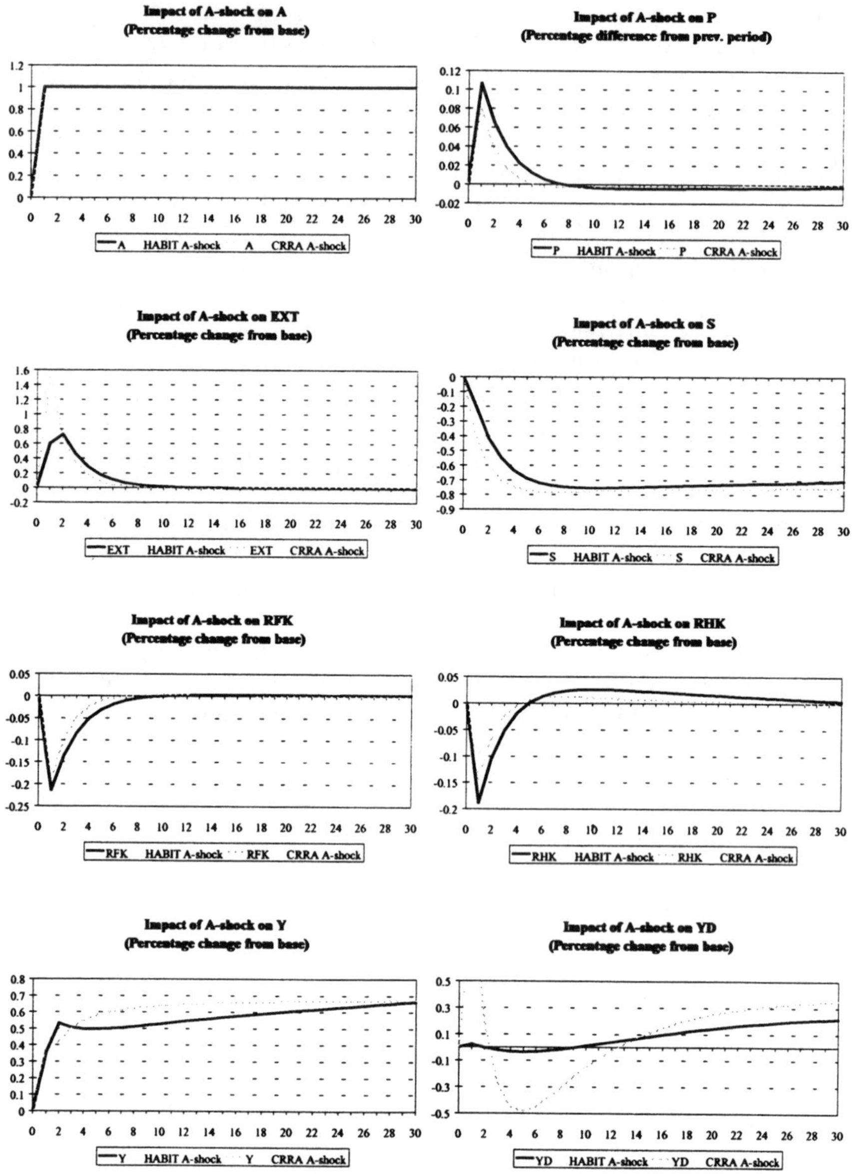

Figure 7.5 Baseline impulse responses, productivity shock.

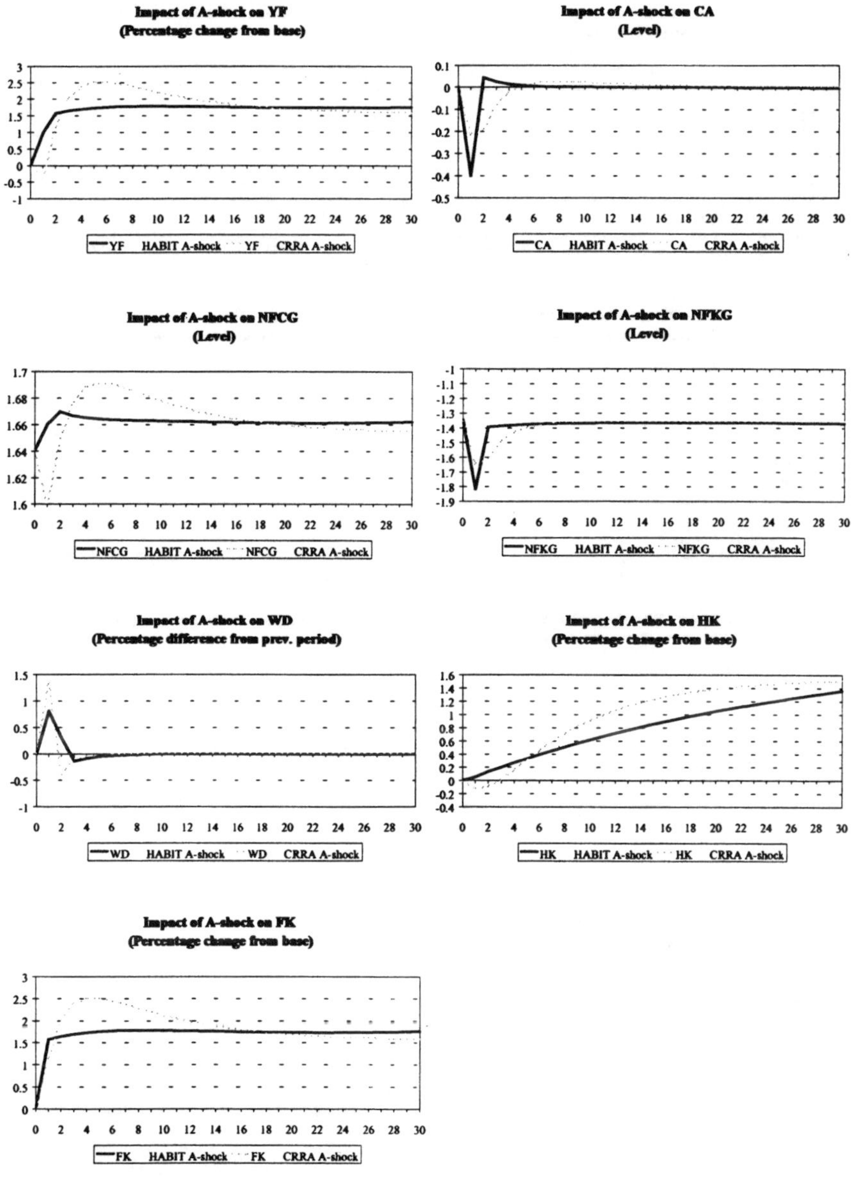

Figure 7.5 Continued.

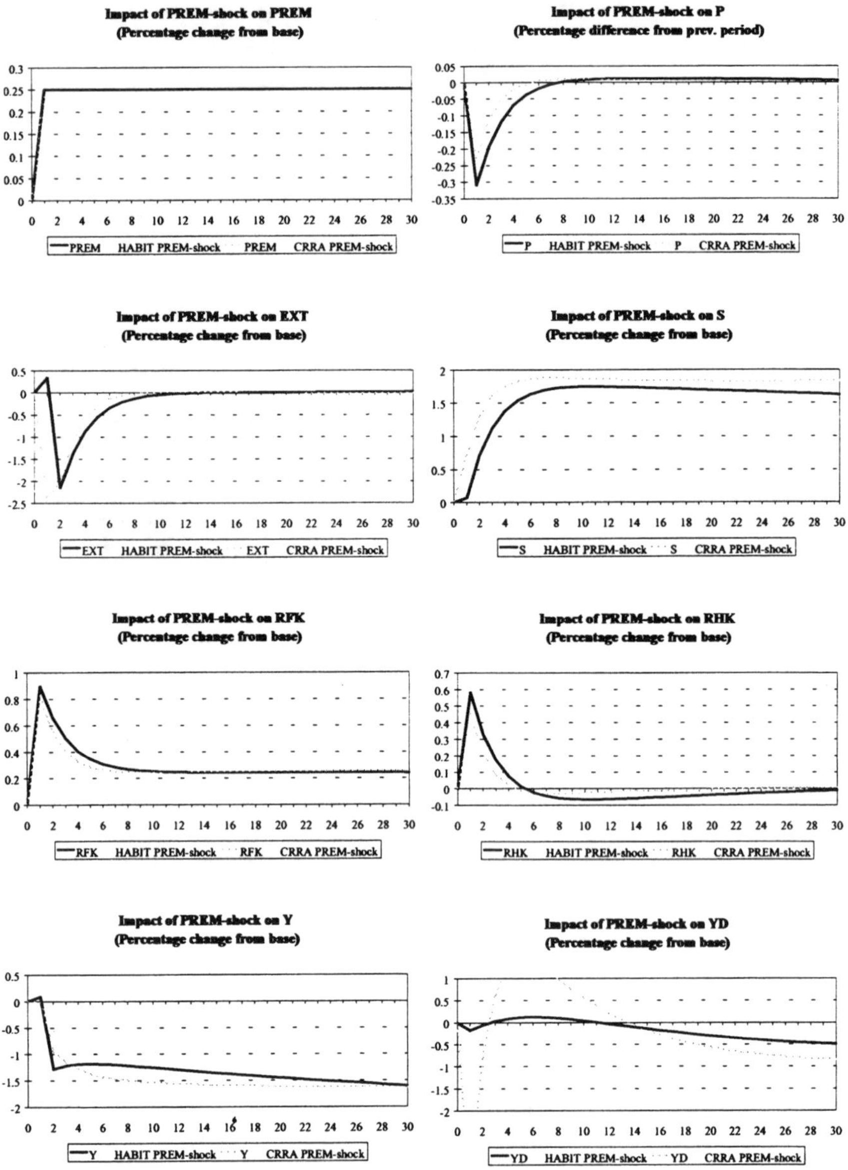

Figure 7.6 Baseline impulse responses, risk premium shock.

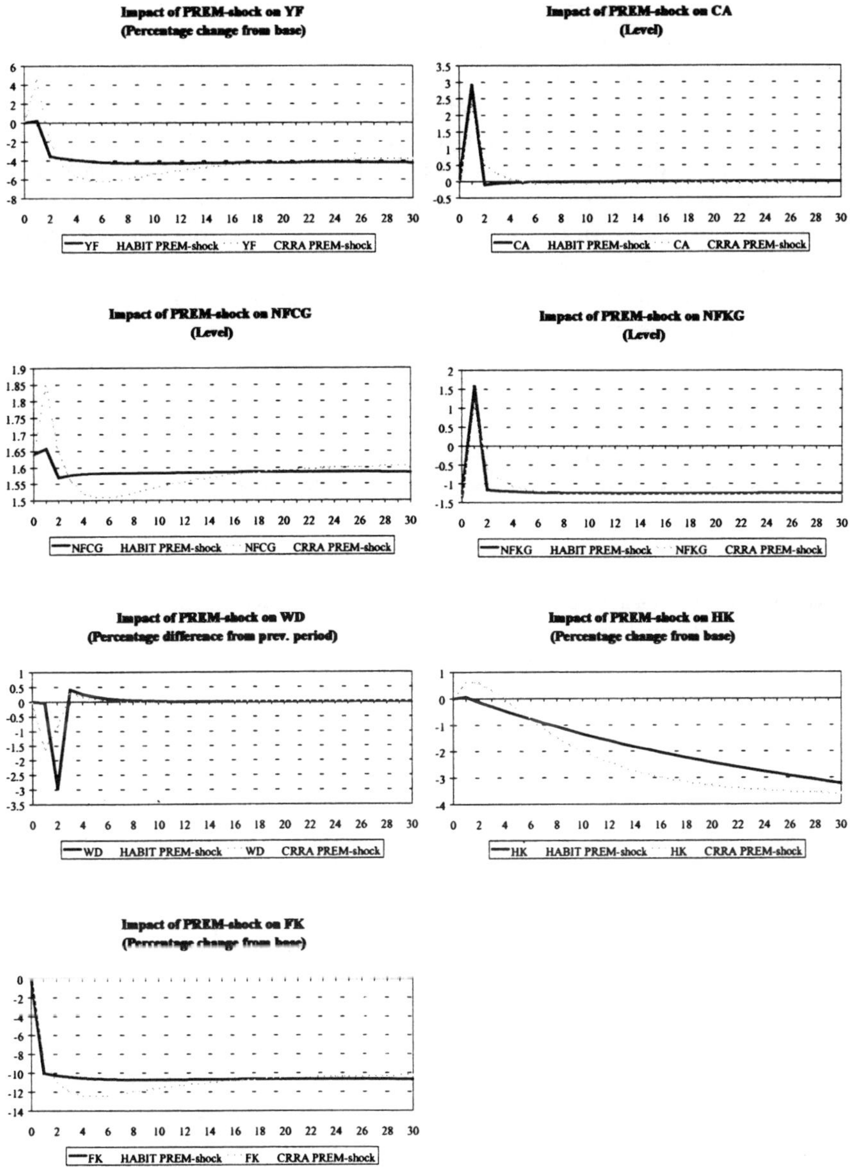

Figure 7.6 Continued.

leads to an almost immediate deterioration in output growth due to lower exports. The measure of relative profitability declines sharply. However, it is alleviated to some extent by the depreciation of the currency, as monetary policy loosens in response to the loss in competitiveness. The increase in the risk premium puts downward pressure on the price level, which is counteracted somewhat by the depreciation of the exchange rate. The overall impact of the shock is a slight decline in the price level. The current account surplus is due to an outflow of capital goods, resulting from the running down of the capital stock in both sectors. As in the case of the productivity shock, the change in capital stock takes place almost immediately in the foreign-owned sector, while in the domestically-owned sector it takes longer.

The simulation also allows for a comparison between the two different specifications of the utility function of consumers. Figure 7.7 shows the difference when we allow for habit persistence. As with other real variables, the consumption path generated by the habit formation model seems smoother and more plausible. This is consistent with Fuhrer's (1998) findings on habit persistence in the United States.

7.6 Short-run trade-off between disinflation and external competitiveness

Can the model capture the specific dilemma of a country with a high external debt, that is the trade-off between faster disinflation and temporary gains in external competitiveness? The question is tackled here in the case of both a temporary rise in foreign-owned firms' productivity and a shock to the risk premium.

The productivity shock in the foreign-owned sector leads to an increase in wages, pushing up costs in the domestically-owned sector and creating

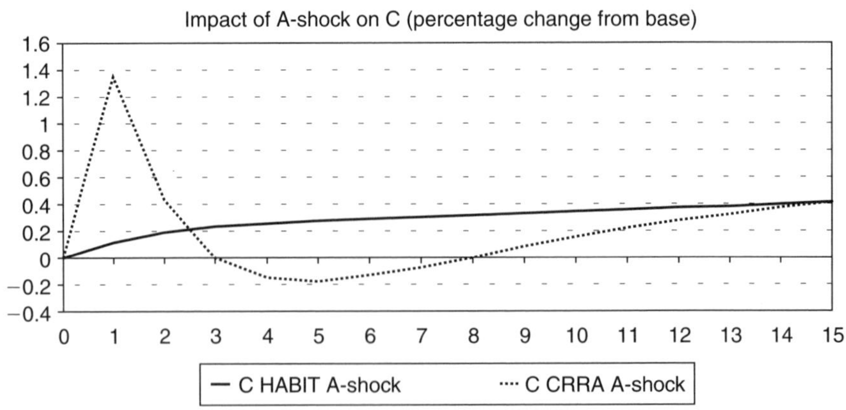

Figure 7.7 Response of consumption to a productivity shock, with and without habit persistence.

inflationary pressure through rises in the prices of its products. On the other hand, the increase in productivity results in a temporary gain in the relative profitability of the foreign-owned sector, as it takes time for the domestic sector to reach the market-clearing level of prices. The monetary authority is able to reduce the inflationary impact of the productivity shock by setting the path of the exchange rate to allow for an appreciation. However, this can only be done in detriment to the gain in relative profitability. This trade-off will be explored by using a simplified version of the rule described by equation (7.39):

$$s_t = s_{t-1} - \phi_1(p_t - p_{t-1}) \tag{7.41}$$

By choosing the value of ϕ_1, the monetary authority can decide how much inflationary pressure it wishes to accommodate. A value of 0 corresponds to a fixed exchange rate regime, where the inflation is fully accommodated, whilst higher values correspond to more anti-inflationary regimes.

Simulation results with different ϕ_1 values are plotted on Figure 7.8. To measure the trade-off, the short-term (eight-quarter) cumulated increase in price level (*P*) is plotted against the short-term cumulative gain in relative profitability (*EXT*). The trade-off is apparent in the fact that for higher values of ϕ_1 the inflationary impact of the shock is smaller, but at the cost of a smaller gain in external competitiveness.

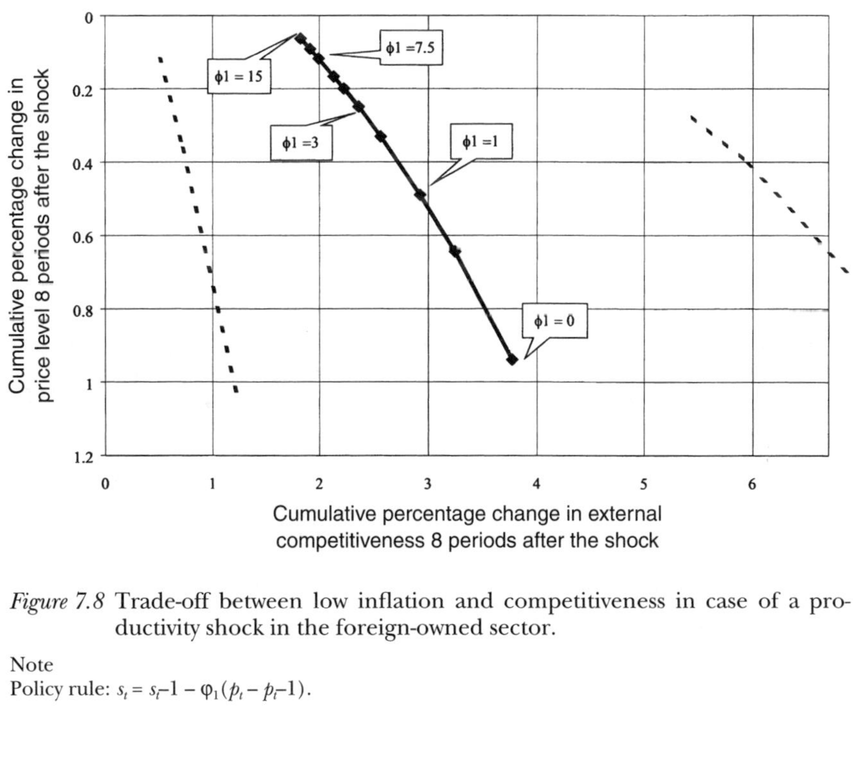

Figure 7.8 Trade-off between low inflation and competitiveness in case of a productivity shock in the foreign-owned sector.

Note
Policy rule: $s_t = s_t{-}1 - \varphi_1(p_t - p_t{-}1)$.

In the case of a risk premium shock, the monetary policy trade-off is slightly different. An increase in the risk premium results in a temporary deterioration of external competitiveness due to the higher capital costs in the foreign-owned sector. The lower profitability in the foreign-owned sector pushes the wages downwards, passing through to falls in the price level in the domestically-owned sector. Monetary policy in this case is able to alleviate the loss of competitiveness by allowing for a depreciation in the currency, but only at the cost of higher-than-otherwise inflation. Policy preferences regarding this trade-off can be approximated with the following rule:

$$s_t = s_{t-1} - \phi_2(ext_t - ext^*) \tag{7.42}$$

By choosing the value of ϕ_2, the monetary authority can decide how much deterioration of the external balance it wishes to accommodate. $\phi_2 = 0$ represents the fixed exchange rate, whilst higher values indicate attempts to smooth temporary fluctuations in external competitiveness.

Simulation results are shown in Figure 7.9. As in the case of the productivity shock, the short-term cumulated increase in price level (*P*) is plotted against the short-term increase in external competitiveness (*EXT*) for different ϕ_2 values. Once again, a trade-off is clearly present. With fixed exchange rates, the inflation becomes negative while competitiveness

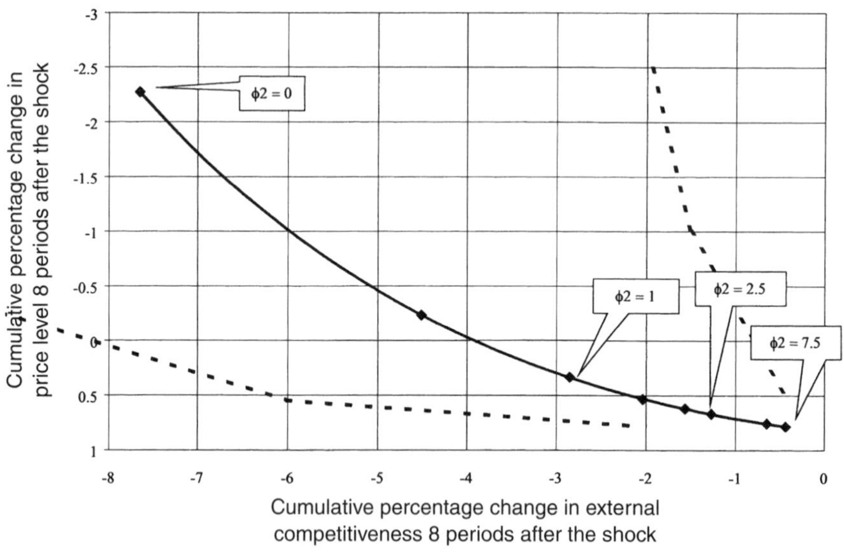

Figure 7.9 Trade-off between low inflation and competitiveness in case of a risk premium shock.

Note
Policy rule: $s_t = s_t{-}1 - \varphi_2(ext_t - ext^*)$.

deteriorates significantly. However, by allowing for a depreciation of the exchange rate, the monetary policy can alleviate the loss of relative profitability, although only by generating positive inflation.

What is interesting is that the nature of the trade-off depends heavily on the stickiness of the prices in the domestically-owned sector. Dotted lines on both charts present the nature of the trade-off for alternative specifications of the price-sluggishness parameter λ. Beyond the baseline simulation with $\lambda = 0.25$, the two dotted lines plot the results for $\lambda = 0.5$ and $\lambda = 0.125$. It can be seen that the faster the price adjustment, the steeper the curve describing the trade-off. The efficiency of monetary policy in affecting external competitiveness therefore depends crucially on the extent of nominal rigidities. The true extent of rigidities is an empirical issue, and can even vary historically. However, for 'plausible' values of λ, the trade-off seems to be important in Hungary.

7.7 Conclusions and directions of further research

A small dynamic general equilibrium model was constructed to describe some properties of the transmission of monetary policy in Hungary. Important characteristics of the Hungarian economy – the high degree of trade openness, sectoral differences in productivity growth, the difference in access to capital markets of foreign-owned and domestically-owned firms, the low level of monetisation of households and the fact that monetary policy reacts to external competitiveness as well as inflation – were taken into account. Simulations with the model showed that it is able to reproduce some of the stylised features of the Hungarian economy. Furthermore, experiments highlighted the importance of the trade-off between low inflation and short-term external competitiveness of the economy. The sensitivity analysis also quantified the role of nominal rigidities in determining the nature of this trade-off.

Further research is needed, however, to refine the model's structure and calibration to enable it to tackle more general issues surrounding monetary policy in Hungary. First, more validation is necessary to confront the simulation results of the model with the dynamics of real data. The monetary policy rule could also be improved: a more complex formulation, allowing reactions to distinguish the source of the shock, would be more realistic and interesting.

Finally, the introduction of government as an autonomous agent in the model could be another useful refinement, as it would allow more realistic simulation of current account dynamics. This change would also open up the possibility of partially endogenising the risk premium and of tackling questions related to policy co-ordination (see Şahinbeyoğlu (2000)). Furthermore, it would allow for a more subtle treatment of the linkage between domestic and foreign capital markets.

Acknowledgment

I am heavily indebted to Lavan Mahadeva for his help. I also wish to thank Joseph Djivre, Javier Gómez, Juan Manuel Julio, András Kármán, Zsolt Kondrát, Bojan Markovic, Tomasz Łyziak, Gulbin Sahinbeyoglu, Peter Sinclair, Chang Shu, Gabriel Sterne, Sándor Valkovszky, Balázs Világi and János Vincze for the helpful discussions and comments on the earlier versions. I am also grateful to Stephen Wright for discussing the paper at the CCBS/UK Money, Macro and Finance Group Workshop on 4 September 2000, and for providing great ideas about potential future developments of the model presented here. Richard Hammerman provided excellent research assistance. The views expressed here are those of the author and do not necessarily represent those of the National Bank of Hungary.

Notes

1 Although this paper was originally written during the crawling-peg regime that was maintained by the National Bank of Hungary until May 2001, most of its conclusions apply also to the inflation-targeting regime that was introduced afterwards assuming that the risk premium is exogenous.

2 For a more detailed description of these issues, see, for example, Neményi (2000).

3 Some items of the capital account – e.g. capital flows with a maturity shorter that 1 year and interest and exchange rate derivatives – were subject to capital controls in Hungary until June 2001. However, experience showed that even that level of liberalisation was enough to put the (premium-augmented) UIP condition into play.

4 Lane (2000) examines the effects of monetary policy on the current account in a dynamic general equilibrium framework and shows that in a dynamic general equilibrium framework the sign of the reaction depends on some key parameters of the representative household's utility function, namely the relative size of the intertemporal elasticity of substitution and the intratemporal elasticity of substitution between tradables and non-tradables.

5 This effect is exacerbated by the fact that many of these firms are producing for export markets, and therefore borrowing in foreign currency is a natural hedge for them.

6 Basu and Taylor (1999) give a thorough overview of the role of labour market assumptions in business cycle models.

7 RFK_t denotes a 'gross' interest rate $(1 + r)$.

8 Although not included in this model for the sake of simplicity, empirical evidence generally confirms that the presence of intermediate goods can be an important factor that magnifies the real effects of price stickiness. Basu (1994) provides a model where intermediate goods – modelled within an input–output structure – significantly afffect output dynamics.

9 In keeping with, for example, Ascari (2000), we assume that risk-averse agents can pool resources and insure themselves against the consequences of shocks. That means that there are no distributional complications arising from the staggered pricing decisions.

10 Treating the risk premium as an exogenous factor is an important abstraction from reality. Obviously, monetary policy itself affects the risk premium, therefore different monetary rules would imply different paths for the risk premium

(Vincze 2000). However, to keep the model tractable, this simplification had to be made.

11 It is worth mentioning that Galí and Gertler (1999) and Galí (2000b) have recently argued that fluctuation in the real marginal cost is a theoretically well-founded and empirically good measure of excess demand. They suggest its use as an alternative to the conventional output gap. The measure of external competitiveness introduced here is consistent with this line of thought.

12 Csajbók and Varró (2000) estimate a policy rule describing the behaviour of the National Bank of Hungary and express the policy variable in terms of deviations of inflation and external balance. They use the current account balance as a measure of external equilibrium.

13 Svensson (1999) discusses extensively the problems related to the representation of monetary policy with simple instrument rules.

14 Solutions were calculated by assuming model-consistent rational expectations and using the Fair–Taylor algorithm. Calculations were carried out using Win-Solve 3.41. Simulations carried out using Stacked Newton solution methods reported near-identical results.

15 Solid lines represent the habit persistence solutions, while dotted lines are the solutions obtained with the conventional CRRA utility function.

16 As in the model, all interest rates are expressed in quarterly terms. A 100 basis point increase isequivalent to a 25 basis point increase in quarterly terms, as plotted in Figure 7.4.2.

8 Monetary transmission mechanism in Poland

Tomasz Łyziak

8.1 Introduction

In order for a central bank to be effective in achieving its monetary goals, central bankers should have a sound understanding of the channels of transmission of monetary policy into output and inflation. This is particularly true in the case of Poland's inflation-targeting regime, implemented in 1998, because of its emphasis on requiring the central bank to provide quantified explanations of the state of the economy.

The monetary transmission mechanism in Poland has been in a continual state of rapid evolution during the transition from socialism. These repeated structural breaks, when combined with the constraint of a short time series, have made it difficult to establish firm empirical estimates of parameters. For example, Christoffersen and Wiscott (1999: 29) claim that the lack of a firm statistical linkage between falling inflation and a tightening of monetary policy via short-term interest rates is not surprising, given that both inflation and interest rates have been falling nearly monotonically in Poland over the past years. This is an example of a 'price puzzle', a phenomenon that also afflicts developed country data (Christiano *et al.* 1998: 30–1), but the steeper disinflation in transition economies makes it more problematic to overcome and impedes the extraction of detailed information on the factors that determine inflation.

This chapter presents a small-scale macroeconomic model of the Polish economy. Similar to models by Svensson (2000), McCallum and Nelson (1999) and Batini and Haldane (1999), this model is designed to provide a stylised representation of the monetary transmission channels that is broadly consistent with both economic theory and the unique features of the Polish economy. The core equations of the model are as follows: an aggregate demand curve, a reduced-form monetary base function, a relationship that determines prices given wages and one that determines wages given prices, an uncovered interest rate parity (UIP) equation for the exchange rate, and a policy rule for setting interest rates. The model emphasises one specific aspect of monetary transmission in Poland: it allows for and estimates a credit channel (more precisely, a bank-lending channel) that could *a priori* be considered to act as a supplement to traditional interest rate channels in Poland.

The chapter is organised as follows. Section 8.2 lays out the theory concerning the bank-lending channel, and section 8.3 links the theory to the Polish context, in part by highlighting the stylised facts on the operation of the bank-lending channel in Poland. Section 8.4 presents and interprets our estimations of the small structural model's equations, while section 8.5 presents the interest rate impulse responses of selected variables. Finally, section 8.6 provides a conclusion to our study.

8.2 The bank-lending channel – theoretical underpinnings

According to the traditional money view, monetary policy influences inflation through the real interest-rate channel (Figure 8.1). A monetary-policy tightening leads to a temporary rise in real interest rates. Investment in inventories and capital goods and private-sector consumption all fall. Lower aggregate demand puts downward pressure on prices such that GDP is pushed below its potential level.

The credit view of monetary policy stresses that banks should be distinguished from other financial intermediaries because they are better placed to deal with certain types of borrowers, particularly small enterprises and households. These borrowers have limited direct access to other sources of finance, such as equity (Walsh 1998: 286). Changes in monetary-policy stance not only generate adjustments in interest rates but also affect both sides of the banking-sector balance sheet. A monetary contraction restricts sources of reservable liquidity, by price or quantity (Hall 2001: 9). If banks are not able to offset a decline in reserves, they have to reduce their assets, among which is the supply of bank loans. As a result of monetary-policy tightening, credit allocated to bank-dependent borrowers may fall. As these agents have no other source of financing, a fall in real volume of credit may lead them to cut their consumption and investment spending (see Hubbard 1994: Mishkin 1995).

According to this view.[1] the bank-lending channel is not a separate, independent alternative to the traditional interest-rate channel, but rather a set of supplementary factors that amplify and propagate it (see Ramey 1993: 1–2; Bernanke and Gertler 1995: 28). In estimating the aggregate demand curve of the Polish model, we aim to allow for both interest-rate channel and credit channel (bank-lending channel) effects, as in

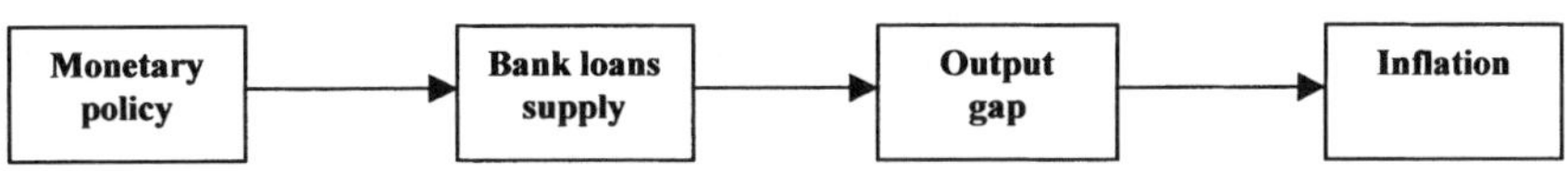

Figure 8.1 The bank-lending channel.

Bernanke and Blinder (1988). Standard IS curve models limit the effects of monetary policy on output and inflation to their impact through the real interest rate (see Nelson 2000; Meltzer 2001).

In a standard monetary framework there are only two categories of bank assets, namely money and a representative interest-bearing asset. The Bernanke and Blinder set-up further divides the interest-bearing assets into bonds and bank loans. Banks hold bonds (B), loans (L) and reserves (R) as assets. Deposits (D) are banks' liabilities. All of these quantities are expressed in nominal terms. The representative bank's balance sheet can therefore be written as:

$$B + L + R = D \tag{8.1}$$

It is assumed that reserves are held only to meet a strict legal reserve requirement and that they are a proportion (r^r) of deposits, i.e.

$$R^d = r^r \cdot D \tag{8.2}$$

Banks choose their relative holdings of bonds and loans according to interest rates on these two instruments. These two assets are not necessarily perfect substitutes. The demand for bonds as a share of banks' non-reserve deposits, $b = B/(1 - r^r)\,D$, depends positively on the yield on bonds, i^B, inversely on the interest rate on loans, i^L, and positively on the reserve requirement ratio $(1 - r^r)$:

$$B = b(i^B, i^L)\cdot(1-r^r)\cdot D \qquad \frac{\partial b}{\partial i^B} \geq 0, \qquad \frac{\partial b}{\partial i^L} \leq 0 \tag{8.3}$$

The supply of loans as a share of non-reserve deposits, l^s, is related positively to the interest rate on loans and inversely to the yield on bonds:

$$L^s = l^s(i^L, i^B)\cdot(1-r^r)\cdot D, \qquad \frac{\partial l^s}{\partial i^L} \geq 0, \qquad \frac{\partial l^s}{\partial i^B} \leq 0 \tag{8.4}$$

The demand for loans is assumed to depend on the interest rate for loans and on the value of economic activity (Y):

$$L^d = l^d(i^L, Y) \qquad \frac{\partial l^d}{\partial i^L} \leq 0, \qquad \frac{\partial l^d}{\partial Y} \geq 0 \tag{8.5}$$

Loan supply is equal to loan demand, implying:

$$l^d(i^L, Y) = l^s(i^L, i^B)\cdot(l-r^r)\cdot D = l^s(i^L, i^B)\cdot\left(\frac{1-r^r}{r^r}\right)\cdot R^s \tag{8.6}$$

where R^s denotes reserves supply determined by a central bank. With a few additional assumptions about the pass theory of consumer prices and asset prices, the above equation can be solved for the real interest rate on loans as a function of the real yield on bonds and the real amount of reserves supplied:

$$r^L = \phi\left(r^B, \frac{Y}{P}, \frac{R}{P}\right) \quad \frac{\partial\phi}{\partial r^B} \geq 0, \frac{\partial\phi}{\partial Y/P} \geq 0, \frac{\partial\phi}{\partial R/P} \leq 0 \tag{8.7}$$

If we place the loans' market equilibrium condition (8.7) into the general formula of the IS curve linking output demand to interest rates on loans and bonds:

$$\frac{Y}{P} = Y(r^L, r^B) \quad \frac{\partial Y}{\partial r^B} \leq 0, \frac{\partial Y}{\partial r^L} \leq 0 \tag{8.8}$$

we obtain a modified aggregate demand relationship as follows:

$$\frac{Y}{P} = Y\left(r^B, \phi\left(r^B, \frac{Y}{P}, \frac{R}{P}\right)\right) \tag{8.9}$$

Equation (8.9) is called the CC curve (for 'commodities and credit') by Bernanke and Blinder (1988: 436). According to the CC curve, monetary policy has an effect on output demand both through the interest-rate channel and also via the bank-lending channel. Changes in monetary policy generate an adjustment in the bond rate (i^B), which influences the level of economic activity. This interest rate effect is a combination of the traditional interest rate channel and an indirect effect feeding through the real interest rate on loans. The supply of reserves in real terms (R^s/P) directly affects the supply of bank loans through the bank-lending channel.

Reserves supply is assumed to be proportional to reserve money (M^0/P). The loan market's equilibrium condition (6) rewritten in terms of reserve money looks as follows:

$$l^d(i^L, Y) = l^s(i^L, i^B) \cdot (1 - r^r) \cdot D = l^s(i^L, i^B) \cdot \left(\frac{1 - r^r}{c + r^r}\right) \cdot M^0 \tag{8.10}$$

where c indicates the ratio of cash in circulation to deposits.

8.3 The Polish monetary transmission mechanism: the bank-lending channel in Poland – what do the stylised facts tell us?

There are two prerequisites that theory tells us must be fulfilled for the bank-lending channel to operate. First, borrowers (at least some of them) should not be able to fully substitute bank credit for other sources of finance. Second, banks should not be able to shield their loan portfolios from changes in monetary policy; in other words, monetary policy actions (generating changes in the monetary base) should influence the banks' supply of loans (see Watson 1999: 9 or Ramey 1993: 3).

In Poland as with other transitional economies, capital markets are relatively shallow and banks compose the sole or major source of external funds for domestically-owned companies. On these grounds alone, the existence of a bank-lending channel would seem highly probable (Hoggarth 1996: 10). Despite the gradual development of a capital market in Poland, banks continue to be the most important financial intermediaries for most firms. The corporate bonds market does not practically exist and the commercial paper market is fairly shallow. In March 2000 commercial bonds stood only for 1.2 per cent and commercial papers for 5.8 per cent of total bank credit to enterprises. The equity market is accessible only to a limited group of enterprises, and does not play a key role in raising funds (National Bank of Poland 1999:.46).

A National Bank of Poland monthly survey of companies[2] shows that the share of firms using bank credit grew from about 80 per cent in 1995 to almost 88 per cent in 1998 and more than 85 per cent in 1999. The majority of these firms were not able to finance both investment and current activity without bank credit. In 1998 as many as 77.4 per cent of enterprises were entirely or almost entirely dependent on banks as a source of financing for current activity, with the shares for the two previous years being approximately the same (Figure 8.2). Investment activity is similarly dependent on bank credit. As Figure 8.3 shows, only a very small percentage (about 6 per cent) of surveyed enterprises claimed complete financial independence from bank credit for investment financing in 1998.

It should be noted, however, that Polish enterprises' internal sources of financing (i.e. retained profits) continue to be more important than all combined external sources. The share of bank credit in GDP is quite low, although it grew from nearly 20 per cent in 1993 to about 27 per cent in 1999 (see National Bank of Poland 2000a: 95–9). Moreover, the sizeable disparity between domestic and foreign interest rates, together with underestimation of exchange rate risk, has heightened corporate interest in accessing foreign loans: in the first quarter of 2000 the share of outstanding external indebtedness of the non-government and non-banking sector[3] in total bank credit to enterprises reached 17.7 per cent.

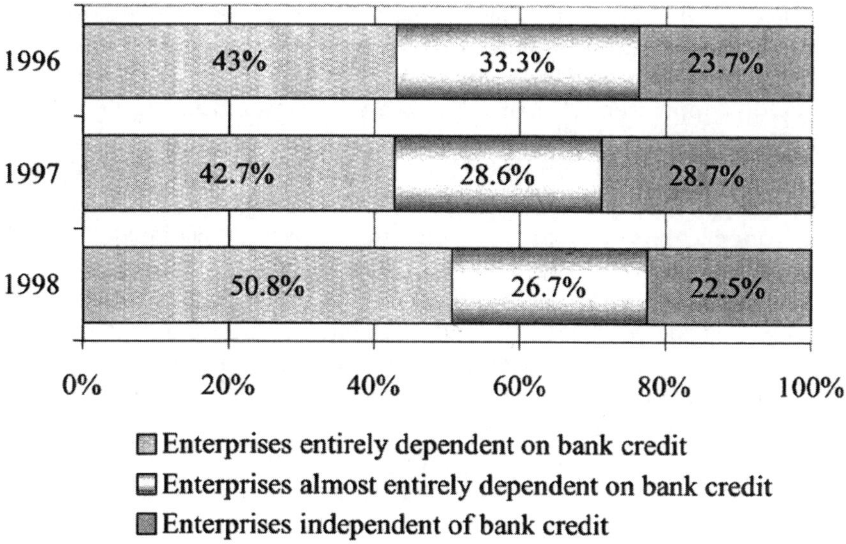

Figure 8.2 Dependence on bank credit for current activity financing.

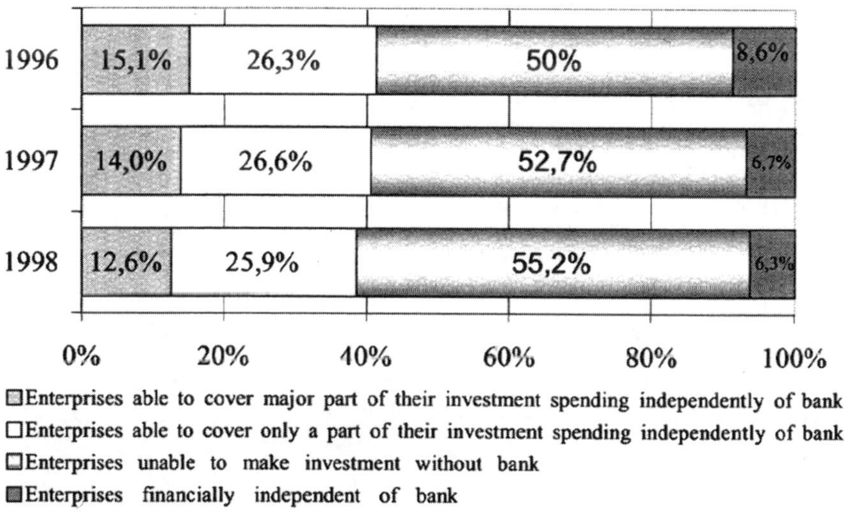

Figure 8.3 Dependence on bank credit for investment activity financing.

Despite the relative importance of internal finance, we have enough evidence to conclude that a majority of Polish enterprises depend on bank credit for financing both their current and their investment activity. The first condition for a bank-leading channel is satisfied for Poland's firms: if the credit supply were reduced, it appears firms would not to be able to fully finance their spending from other sources.

Turning to the second condition of the bank-leading channel, that monetary policy must have the power to shape bank loans supply, available evidence seems to indicate that the impact of National Bank of Poland monetary policy on credit supply is, if anything, weak. The main reason is that Polish banks hold large amounts of treasury bills in their portfolios; in the years 1995–99, bills amounted to an average of 19.7 per cent of total assets. Banks are hence able to straightforwardly implement buffer-stock behaviour. In response to a tighter monetary policy, they reduce the growth in treasury portfolios (their most liquid assets) by more than the growth in their loan portfolios without raising rates (Łyziak 2000a; see also Garvetsen and Swank 1998 for buffer-stock behaviour evidenced in the Netherlands).

An excessive level of banks' holdings of central bank debt is often referred to as an excess liquidity problem. The main source of excess liquidity, a phenomenon occurring in Poland since 1994, was the increase of the central bank's reserves between in 1994 and 1998, when they grew by about $23 billion (Figure 8.4). The increase in reserves resulted from factors over which the National Bank of Poland had no direct influence in terms of volume, such as income earned on the privatisation of state

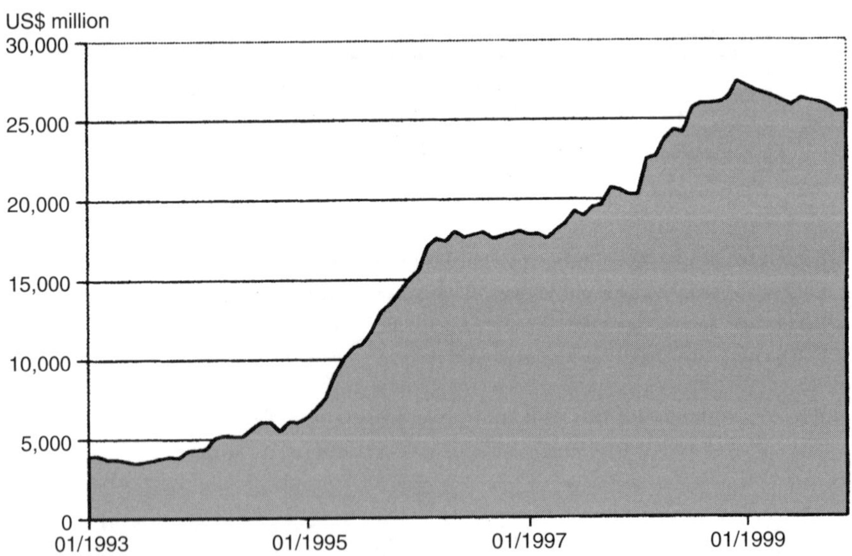

Figure 8.4 Gross official reserves, 1993–99.

enterprises, credits taken abroad by the public sector and direct investments (National Bank of Poland 1999: 36).

The excess liquidity problem made commercial banks less dependent on the central bank, which – instead of playing the role of the lender of last resort – had to absorb excess liquidity from the market. The problem was reflected in the direction and size of open market operations as conducted in recent years in Poland. As is evident from Figure 8.5, the issue of NBP bills served as the primary vehicle for open market operations in recent years. It should be noted that in 1997 the National Bank of Poland temporarily accepted personal deposits. The implementation of this exceptional instrument of monetary policy was due to a limited impact of changes in official base rates on banks' lending and deposit rates (National Bank of Poland 1998: 22).

Another important factor lessening the impact of National Bank of Poland monetary policy actions on credit supply was the extent of state ownership in the Polish banking sector, which was most significant prior to 1999. In Table 8.1, we can see that between 1993 and 1999 banks with majority public-sector interest accounted for almost 60 per cent on average of total assets of the banking sector, falling from over 80 per cent in 1993 to under 24 per cent in 1999.

The dominant position of state-owned banks meant that the influence of monetary policy on bank credit supply was diminished. State-owned banks enjoyed softer budget constraints. regulatory privileges, customer loyalty, and more extensive branch networks than privately-owned institutions. These advantages explain the public perception that such banks

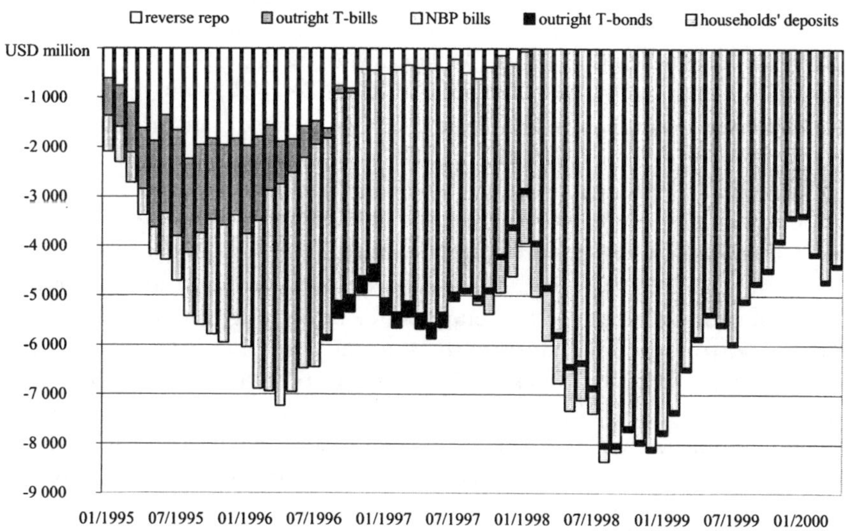

Figure 8.5 Average daily stock of open market operations (source: O*BOP*).

Table 8.1 Structure of the Polish banking system, 1993–99 (share of banking-sector total assets) (in percent)

	1993	*1994*	*1995*	*1996*	*1997*	*1998*	*1999*	2000 (*Sep.*)
Banks with majority public-sector interest:	80.4	76.1	68.3	66.5	49.3	45.9	23.9	23.5
of which: directly owned by Treasury	*76.1*	*70.8*	*63.0*	*51.1*	*38.2*	*36.7*	*22.1*	*21.8*
Banks with majority private-sector interest:	13.0	18.6	26.9	28.9	46.2	49.8	71.8	72.4
of which with majority Polish equity	*10.4*	*15.4*	*22.7*	*15.1*	*30.9*	*33.2*	*24.6*	*3.3*
of which with majority foreign equity	*2.6*	*3.2*	*4.2*	*1.4*	*15.3*	*16.6*	*47.2*	*69.1*
Co-operative banks	6.6	5.3	4.8	4.6	4.5	4.3	4.2	4.1

Source: National Bank of Poland 2000b: 27; National Bank of Poland 2000c: 25.

were 'too state-owned to fail'.[4] Public confidence in public vs private banks is indicated in the results of the OBOP surveys, summarised in Figure 8.6. 'Different institutions and organisations can enjoy different degrees of public trust. Do you personally trust private (state) banks?')

Specific features of the relationship between banks and borrowers, such as provision of credit lines and privileges accorded to 'big' clients, can also explain why the bank-lending channel may not operate in Poland. By the 'credit lines phenomenon', we refer to the situation in which banks are more willing to extend credit to borrowers with whom they have worked before. Such practices help banks to minimise the risk generated either by information asymmetry or by the fact that immediate reduction of their loans supply could make borrowers unable to meet previous liabilities.[5] Although it is not possible to detect such a relationship directly, there is evidence suggesting that it does exist. Studies of the credit debt of enterprises in 1996 and 1997, for example, show that companies tended to maintain a similar (positive or negative) change in credit debt in both years, or made similar changes in its level in the opposite direction (contracting–repaying).

As far as the privileged situation of 'big' clients is concerned, the evidence from the United Kingdom (Dale and Haldane 1995) as well as from the United States (Gertler and Gilchrist 1993; Gilchrist and Zakrajšek 1995) suggests that whilst monetary policy tightening initially leads high-quality borrowers to demand more credit at prevailing interest rates, the borrowers for whom bank credit is a non-substitutable source of external financing are faced with a decline in the volume of loans supplied to them. It appears that Polish banks display a similar pattern of behaviour. In 1996–97, when National Bank of Poland monetary policy was restrictive, 'big' borrowers (defined as firms whose debt exceeded 0.0001 per cent of the total credit in the economy) kept a relatively constant level of credit debt, whilst 'small' borrowers faced a sharp fall in credit (usually it

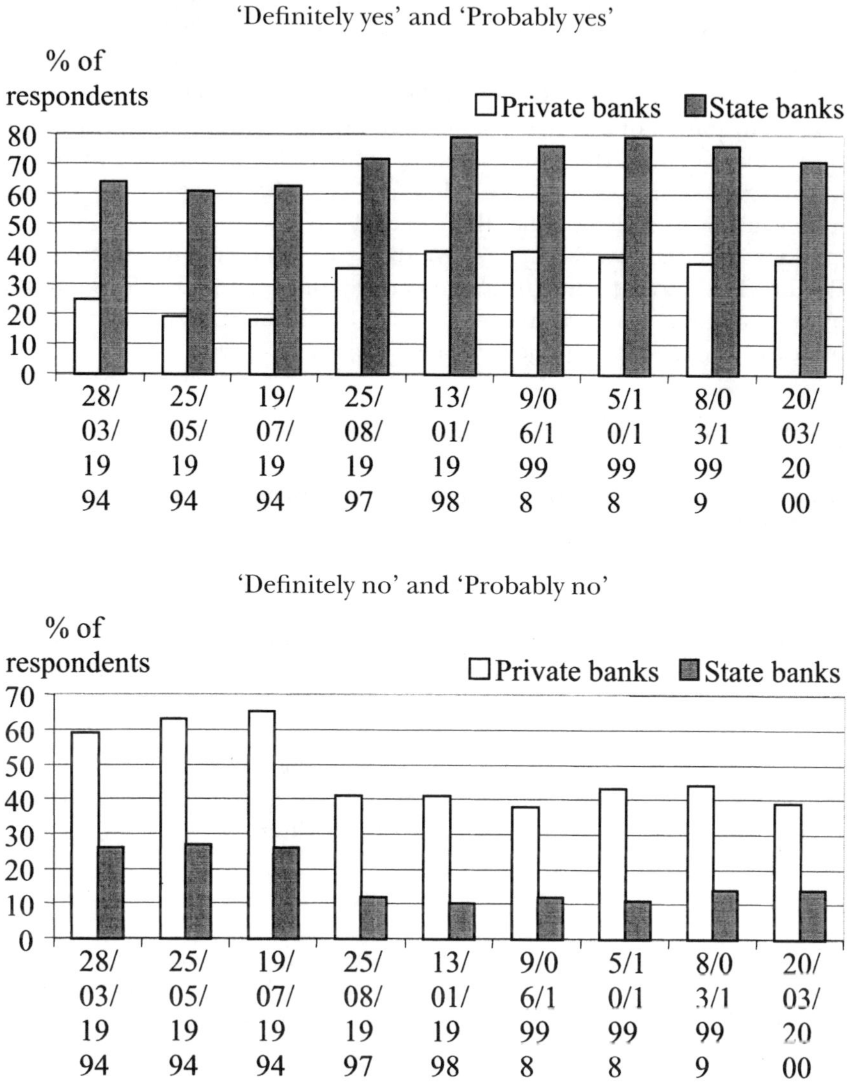

Figure 8.6 Public perception of state versus private banks (percentage of respondents choosing selected answers to survey question.

was reduced to zero). The aggregate results may be that total bank credit is not immediately affected by a monetary policy contraction.

Some of the factors that act to weaken the impact of monetary policy on bank loans supply, such as the excess liquidity problem, should be expected to diminish in the near future. However, the structural shift towards replacing state ownership with foreign ownership in the banking sector (see Table 8.1) appears to have only slightly increased the potency of the bank-lending channel. Opiela (1998) has estimated that the most sensitive aspect of the credit channel is private bank behaviour. State-owned banks and foreign banks have access to funds that are less dependent on monetary policy. On the other hand, banks continue to be the dominant source of external financing in Poland, and there appears to be no reason why this, the principal factor linking bank loans supply to the output gap, should not still be relevant. Our brief survey of the stylised facts leads us to conclude that there is evidence of structural changes that can act to either weaken or strengthen the bank-lending channel in Poland. The current strength of the bank-lending channel and its importance in coming years will therefore have to be gauged from our econometric estimates of the monetary sector and the IS curve.

8.4 Small-scale model of monetary transmission in Poland

8.4.1 Aggregate demand curve – interest-rate channel and credit-channel effects

The aggregate demand curve estimated here is based on the Bernanke and Blinder (1988) specification, as described in section 8.1. Because of the large treasury securities portfolio held by Polish banks, average quarterly yields on treasury bills with 1-year maturity are used as the bank loans' opportunity cost in the CC curve. The dependent variable is the GDP output gap ($y - y^*$), used as a measure of economic activity. In the absence of alternatives, the Hodrick-Prescott filter procedure was used to measure potential output and hence the output gap. The final version of the CC curve form used in the model can be written as:

$$y - y^* = \zeta_0 + \zeta_1 \cdot (M^0 - M^{*0}) - \zeta_2 \cdot r^{TB} + \varepsilon \tag{8.11}$$

where M^0 stands for the real reserve money supply (minus its potential value) and r^{TB} stands for the real, *ex-post* yields on 1-year treasury bills. Our preferred estimate of the CC curve was as follows (standard errors in parentheses):

$$y_t - y_t^* = 0.008 + \underset{(0.145)}{0.435} \cdot (y_{t-2} - y_{t-2}^*) + \underset{(0.098)}{0.284} \cdot \left[\left(y_{t-1} - y_{t-1}^*\right) - \left(y_{t-2} - y_{t-2}^*\right)\right] + \underset{(0.055)}{0.114} \cdot \left(M_{t-1}^0 - M_{t-1}^{*0}\right) - 0.650 \cdot r_{t-3}^{TB} \tag{8.12}$$

The coefficient on the real interest rate (–0.65) was imposed *a priori* on the basis of different estimations and by comparison with other countries' estimates (Taylor 1993a: 85–93). Free estimates of this parameter yielded similar values but without acceptable levels of significance. Imposing the value on this coefficient did little to alter the other elasticities in the equation.

The real exchange rate (or a direct measure of the foreign demand gap) would normally be expected to appear among the explanatory variables in the CC curve. The real exchange rate, however, is not statistically significant for Polish output. This finding could be due to low price elasticities on imports and exports in Poland[6] as well as to the fact that Poland is only a moderately open economy (Table 8.2).

At first glance the estimations seem to indicate that both channels of monetary transmission, i.e the interest-rate channel and the bank-lending channel, function in Poland. However, the monetary base coefficient in the CC curve may not exclusively reflect the impact of growth in the monetary base on the output gap via the supply of bank credit. A high correlation between output and money base may be due rather to the role that foreign direct inflows play in determining both in Poland.

To begin our explanation, we note that the monetary base in Poland has been affected by capital inflows as the National Bank of Poland has followed a policy of partially sterilised interventions. Figure 8.7 shows that there have been periods (in 1994 in 1997, and at the start of 1998) when

Table 8.2. Degree of openness: Czech Republic, Hungary and Poland in 1998

	Czech Republic (%)	*Hungary (%)*	*Poland (%)*
Exports-to-GDP ratio	60.0	50.6	25.7
Imports-to-GDP ratio	61.4	52.7	31.0

Source: J. Neményi 2000: 3.

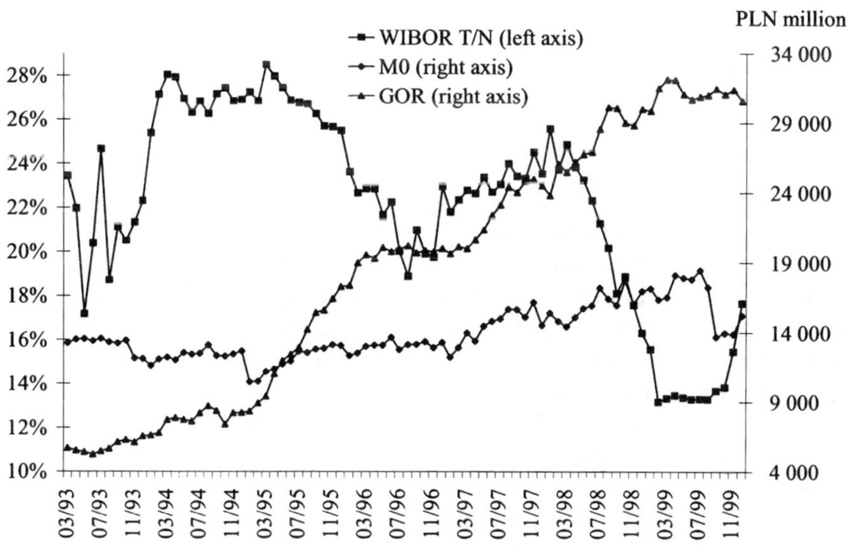

Figure 8.7 WIBOR T/N, monetary base and gross official reserves.

Poland faced vast increases in official reserves due to capital inflows. Although the WIBOR T/N (Tomorrow Next Warsaw Interbank Offer Rate) has increased in these phases, reflecting some sterilisation (and hence monetary policy tightening) of the capital inflows, there has been net increase in the monetary base (M0).

A large part of capital inflows in Poland has come in the form of foreign direct investment (FDI). The share was 71.6 per cent in 1997, 74.8 per cent in 1998 and 58 per cent in 1999. These FDI flows, which arose mainly because of the privatisation process (National Bank of Poland 2000a: 116) have been important for growth in Polish output, especially in the later 1990s. One piece of evidence is that labour productivity gains have been particularly strong in those manufacturing sectors with a high contribution of foreign direct investment to overall capital formation (De Broeck and Koen 2000: 11).

Our estimate of the coefficient of real money base in the CC curve may therefore only indicate that monetary policy and output were caused by the same underlying phenomenon. That is especially likely if the FDI flows represented long-run productivity improvements at home relative to abroad. If so, and the very simple measures of potential output and potential money base demand that we used may not have captured this supply-side shock component, the correlation between our detrended series for the output gap and the real money base reflects fundamental productivity improvements rather than the monetary channel that we want to model.

This explanation based on FDI flows recognises that capital flows are important for monetary aggregates while at the same time implying that the National Bank of Poland's influence on commercial banks' balance sheets may be more limited than face-value estimates suggest.

Another feature of the Polish CC curve is a lagged response of the output gap to changes in interest rates. Other studies corroborate these estimates. For example, vector autoregression estimates have shown that, depending on the measures of demand pressure (real GDP gap or industrial output gap) and of interest rate (yields on treasury bills with 1-year maturity or interbank interest rates), the fall in the output gap takes place four to six quarters after an interest rate shock (Kokoszczyński 1999).

Why might credit demand – and, as a consequence, the output gap – be so insensitive in timing to interest rate changes in Poland? It may be that the less than fully developed nature of the Polish banking system, combined with its state of excess liquidity, make it less effective as a transmitter of monetary policy impulses to the economy than other countries' banking systems. The privileged position of 'big' borrowers, discussed previously, may have consequences not only for the operation of the bank-lending channel, but for the interest rate channel as well. Figure 8.8 clearly demonstrates that minimum interest rates on loans (offered by commercial banks to their best clients) are less sensitive to changes in National Bank of Poland monetary policy as measured by changes in the

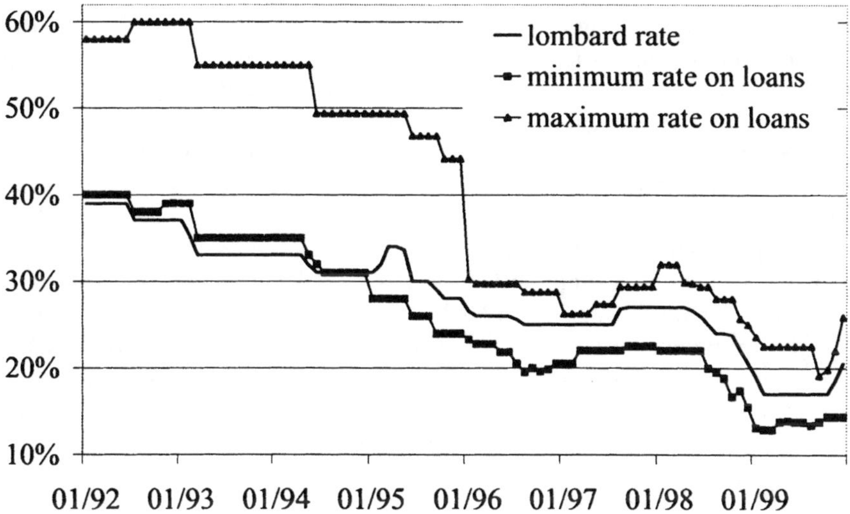

Figure 8.8 Minimum and maximum interest rates on loans in commercial banks and the NBP Lombard rate.

Lombard rate[7] than are maximum interest rates on loans, especially when monetary policy tightening is analysed.

It should also be remembered that the introduction of the market economy constituted a new lesson in Poland, and there may have been an ongoing 'learning process' regarding financial decisions. Also, in Poland, as in other transitional economies, consumers' preferences and tastes have gradually inclined towards Western patterns (Table 8.3). This trend may have increased the propensity to consume over time. Both these factors would make credit demand and, as a consequence, the output gap, less sensitive to interest rate changes.

Table 8.3 Shifting consumption patterns – percentage of households equipped with selected durable goods in the United Kingdom and in Poland

Goods	*UK*	*Poland*
Passenger car	70.0	44.5
Colour TV	96.6	93.9
Personal computer	29.0	10.2
Refrigerator & freezer	90.0	98.7
Microwave oven	77.0	11.2
VCR	84.0	55.8
Compact disc player	63.0	7.9
Washing machine and spin dryer	91.0	97.9
Dishwasher	22.0	1.1

Source: National Bank of Poland 2000a: 95.

8.4.2 Monetary base curve

The monetary base curve should be interpreted as a reduced form of the money market equilibrium condition, one that takes account of both demand and supply determinants of the monetary base.

In theory the demand for real money balances is a function of economic activity and the opportunity costs of holding money, that is, a nominal interest rate. The traditional approach presupposes that monetary authorities exogenously determine money supply (Stevenson *et al.* 1988: 8). This hypothesis, however, even as far as the reserve money is concerned, seems implausible both from a theoretical and an empirical point of view (see Goodhart 1994: 1424–36).

The monetary base can be expressed as a sum of three components: the monetary base supply for banks (M_b^{0S}), the monetary base supply for government (M_g^{0S}) and the monetary base supply for foreign agents in domestic currency (M_f^{0S}) (Onado 1992: 79–80):

$$M^{0S} = M_b^{0S} + M_g^{0S} + M_f^{0S} \tag{8.13}$$

The 1997 Constitution prohibits direct budget financing by the National Bank of Poland. Therefore, the monetary base supply for government can be excluded from the above written equation:

$$M^{0S} = M_b^{0S} + M_f^{0S} \tag{8.14}$$

While the money supply for banks can be directly determined by the central bank (mainly through the use of reserve requirements), reserve money for foreign agents is moulded by foreign demand for domestic money balances and is affected by monetary policy only through the nominal exchange rate. The huge capital inflows experienced in Poland have led to an increase of gross official reserves. These capital inflow shocks have made it difficult to ascertain the relationship between interest rates and the quantity of reserve money (Bruni *et al.* 1996: 328).

The WIBOR T/N interest rate that appears in the LM curve is treated as the National Bank of Poland's policy variable in our model, although, at the time of writing, the National Bank of Poland uses three main instruments: the Lombard rate, open market operations and reserve requirements. The Lombard rate is a last resort rate, which stabilises the 'ceiling' interest rate in the market. Open market operations – nowadays in the form of sales of NBP bills with 28-day maturity – stabilise the 'floor' market interest rate. Reserve requirements influence the long-term liquidity position of the Polish banking sector and smooth the volatility of market interest rates.

Since the main interest rates of the National Bank of Poland (Lombard rate and rediscount rate) are changed rather seldom and the excess liquidity problem lessens their importance in the monetary transmission mechanism, they could be ruled out as policy variables. From the beginning of 1994 till the end of 1995, the NBP targeted a WIBOR T/N rate to stabilise the market, sterilise capital inflows and keep consistent with the exchange rate policy based on the crawling-peg system. At the beginning of 1996 a monetary base growth target was announced, but the strict emphasis was put on the crawling peg, and because of this the interest rate policy was still very important. Interest rates dominated as an instrument even after the crawling peg was allowed to fluctuate within a wider band in May 1996 (Szpunar 1998: 28). During 1997, when monetary base growth targets were not announced but still in place, the WIBOR continued to be emphasised unofficially. In the summer of 1998 the Monetary Policy Council approved a direct inflation-targeting strategy and indicated that the yield on 28-day NBP bills would be the main instrument. The Council influences the 1-month interbank market rate (WIBOR 1M) and, through that, the loan interest rates in banks. Therefore, starting from 1998 it may have been more appropriate to treat the WIBOR 1M (and not the WIBOR T/N) as the central bank's policy variable. Differences between these rates in terms of their quarterly averages appear to be so small, however, that using WIBOR T/N in this role seems to be an acceptable compromise. Another reason for treating WIBOR T/N as the policy variable is that our estimates of interest rate equations confirmed that factors not connected with monetary policy have little influence on WIBOR T/N; in other words, the NBP can effectively control WIBOR T/N.[8]

The estimates of the money base curve were as follows (standard errors in parentheses):

$$M_t^0 = -0.496 + \underset{(0.047)}{0.652} \cdot M_{t-1}^0 + (1-0.652) \cdot Y_{t-1} - \underset{(0.456)}{0.900} \cdot i_t + \underset{(0.226)}{0.546} \cdot r_t^r + \underset{(0.037)}{0.117} \cdot \Delta gr_{t-1} + - \underset{(0.01)}{0.079} \cdot dum_{9501} - \underset{(0.022)}{0.084} \cdot dum_{9904} \quad (8.15)$$

The set of explanatory variables consist of the log of real GDP, Y, the nominal WIBOR T/N, i, the required reserve ratio, r^r, and the proportionate change in gross official reserves in real terms, Δgr. Gross official reserves can be treated as exogenous with respect to monetary policy as implemented by the National Bank of Poland, since, as already noted, a large part of reserves' increases was connected with factors independent of monetary policy, such as income on state enterprise privatisation, credits taken abroad by the public sector and direct investments. There are also dummy variables in the monetary base curve, capturing the denomination change in the zloty in January 1995, dum_{9501}, and the Y2K problem dum_{9904}.

Equation (8.15) illustrates that the influence of National Bank of Poland monetary policy on the monetary base is constrained. The coefficient of the policy interest rate is fairly low. This fact becomes evident when we compare the interest rate's long-run impact on the monetary base in Poland with analogous measures in other countries.[9] The monetary base in Poland is even less sensitive to changes in interest rates than narrow money aggregates in the United States, Canada, Italy and the United Kingdom (Table 8.4). We would suggest that this insensitivity reflects the presence of excess liquidity in the Polish banking system.

8.4.3 The Phillips curve

The production technology of our small structural model of the Polish monetary transmission mechanism takes the form of a constant elasticity of substitution (CES) function. Domestic goods are not assumed to be completely independent of foreign goods. According to Asteriou *et al.* (2000), the price equation can be written as:

$$p = \mu_0 + w - \frac{1}{\sigma} \cdot (q - n) - \frac{\sigma - 1}{\sigma} \cdot a + \mu_1 \cdot (p - p^*) + \mu_2 \cdot \rho + \mu_3 \cdot \text{var} \quad (8.16)$$

where p is the price, p^* is competitors' prices, w is the wage, $(q - n)$ is productivity, a is technical progress.[10] ρ is an index of demand and *var* is the level of uncertainty.[11] All variables are in logs.

The price equation, wage equation and inflation expectations formation process are estimated as a system:

$$\begin{aligned} p_t - p_{t-1} = \alpha_0 + \alpha_1 \cdot \left[w_{t-1} - \alpha_2 \cdot (y_{t-1} - l_{t-1}) - \left(p_{t-1}^{Ger} - ne_{t-1} \right) \right] + \\ \alpha_3 \cdot \left[p_{t-1} - \left(p_{t-1}^{Ger} - ne_{t-1} \right) \right] + \alpha_4 \cdot (fp_t - p_t) + \alpha_5 \cdot \left(y_{t-3} - y_{t-3}^* \right) + \\ \alpha_6 \cdot \left(\frac{1 - \gamma_2}{\gamma_1} \cdot \Pi_{t/t-1}^e \right) \end{aligned} \quad (8.17)$$

Table 8.4 Long-run coefficients in the LM curve in selected countries

Country	*Monetary aggregate (M)*	*Coefficients of*		*Long-run coefficient on i*
		M(–1)	*Interest rate (i)*	
USA	M1	0,953	–0,224	–4,77
Canada	M1	0,937	–0,511	–8,11
France	M1	0,683	–0,316	–1,00
Germany	M1	0,697	–0,646	–2,13
Italy	M1	0,895	–0,387	–3,69
Japan	M1	0,750	–0,479	–1,92
UK	M1	0,916	–0,778	–9,26
Poland	M0	0,652	–0,900	–2,59

Source: Taylor 1993a: 95 and author's calculations.

$$w_t - w_{t-1} = \beta_0 + \beta_1 \cdot [(p_{t-1} - w_{t-1}) + \alpha_2 (y_{t-1} - l_{t-1})] \\ + \beta_4 \cdot e_t + \beta_5 \cdot dum_{9901} \quad (8.18)$$

$$\Pi^e_{t+1/t} = \gamma_0 + \gamma_1 \cdot (p_{t+1} - p_t) + \gamma_2 \cdot \Pi^e_{t/t-1} \quad (8.19)$$

where p_t is the price level (log) in period t, y is the real GDP (log), $(y - y^*)$ is the output gap, w is wage level (log), l is employment (log) and $\Pi^e_{t+1/t}$ is the individual expectation (at time t) of inflation in period $t + 1$. There is also a term for the log level of net food prices: $(fp - p)$, that is, the difference between food price level and overall price level. The nominal effective exchange rate, ne, and German export prices (in Euros, log), p^{Ger}, also enter the price equation. These variables capture important features of the Polish price-setting mechanism. First, the fact that a large share of the CPI is food prices makes inflation sensitive to food supply shocks,[12] and second, the economy is moderately open. It should be noted that the difference between p^{Ger} and ne is import prices in domestic currency, denoted as p^{imp}, while the difference between p and p^{imp} is the real exchange rate, e.

The expected inflation data in this study derived from directly observed responses to a survey question.[13] Figure 8.9 plots the raw data.

A quantified expectations series is derived from these qualitative survey responses with the use of a technique pioneered by Carlson and Parkin (1975). The estimations point to a long-run constant bias in inflationary expectations, as presented in Figure 8.10. Although we have evidence that

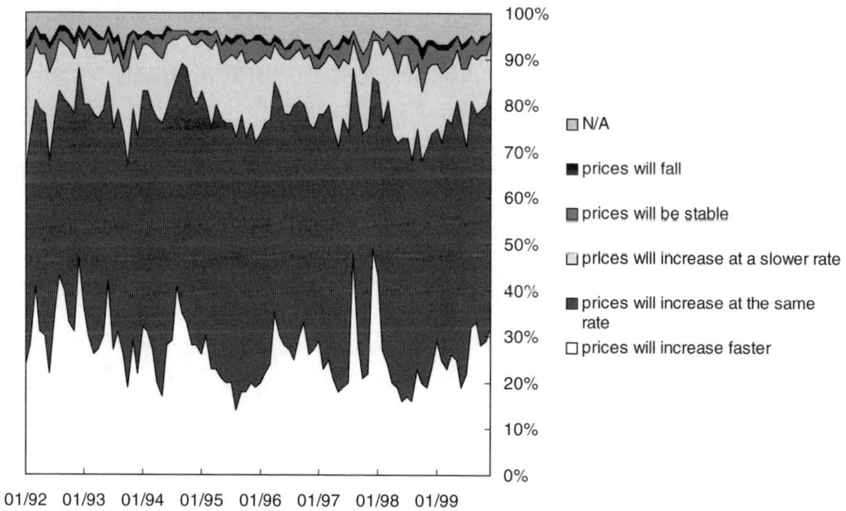

Figure 8.9 Structure of answers to survey question concerning price movements over the next 12 months: 'Do you expect, in comparison with current events, prices over next 12 months: (1) will increase faster; (2) will increase at the same rate; (3) will increase at a slower rate; (4) will be stable; (5) will fall; (6) I don't know'

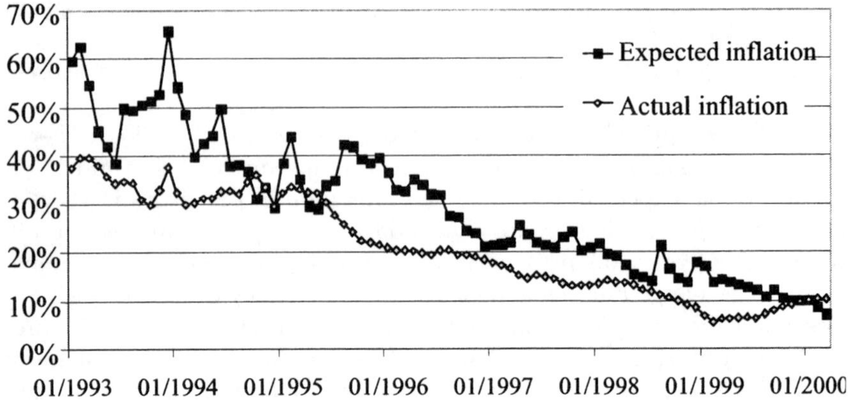

Figure 8.10 Individuals' inflationary expectations and actual inflation. For each month: expected inflation indicates the CPI year-to-yearly change expected a year before, estimated by adjusted Carlson and Parkin probability method; actual inflation shows the actual CPI yearly change.

inflation expectations in Poland and other countries are not fully rational, there are good reasons to believe that this bias indicates a quantification error, and we need to correct for that.[14]

To offset the bias in the Carlson and Parkin method, we take our mismeasured inflation expectations series and adjust it by a constant so that in the long run, actual inflation is equal to our new expected inflation series. The indicator of inflationary expectations used in the price curve, $1 - \gamma_2/\gamma_1 \cdot \Pi^e_{t+1/t}$, is the adjusted unbiased measure of individuals' expectation (at time t) of inflation in period $t + 1$, calculated as a long-run solution of the inflationary expectations equation.

The estimation results of the inflationary expectations equation and the price equation are given below (standard errors in parentheses; see also Appendix to this chapter):

$$\Pi^e_{t+1/t} = -0.005 + \underset{(0.187)}{0.370} \cdot (p_{t+1} - p_t) + \underset{(0.132)}{0.756} \cdot \Pi^e_{t/t-1} \tag{8.20}$$

$$\begin{aligned} p_t - p_{t-1} = {} & -0.518 + \underset{(0.024)}{0.096} \cdot \left[w_{t-1} - \underset{(0.029)}{0.411} \cdot (y_{t-1} - l_{t-1}) - \left(p^{Ger}_{t-1} - ne_{t-1} \right) \right] \\ & + -\underset{(0.027)}{0.098} \cdot \left[p_{t-1} - \left(p^{Ger}_{t-1} - ne_{t-1} \right) \right] + \underset{(0.047)}{0.175} \cdot (fp_t - p_t) \\ & + \underset{(0.035)}{0.091} \cdot \left(y_{t-3} - y^*_{t-3} \right) + \underset{(0.297)}{0.977} \cdot \left(0.659 \cdot \Pi^e_{t/t-1} \right) \end{aligned} \tag{8.21}$$

The dynamic homogeneity property and the restriction of a unit coefficient on inflationary expectations (adjusted) in the Phillips curve are jointly accepted: the Wald statistic $\chi^2 = 0.006$. The impact of the output gap on inflation, apart from through the mark-up of prices on labour costs, is fairly weak (see, for example, Kokoszczyński 1999), and so inflationary expectations emerge as a very commanding determinant of price changes. One may conclude that they compose an important cause of inflation inertia in Poland, and determine to some extent the efficiency of the monetary policy (National Bank of Poland 1998: 20).

The wage equation can be written in the following way (standard errors in parentheses):

$$w_t - w_{t-1} = 3.953 + \underset{(0.056)}{0.714} \cdot \left[\left(p_{t-1} - w_{t-1} \right) + \underset{(0.029)}{0.411} \cdot \left(y_{t-1} - l_{t-1} \right) \right]$$
$$- \underset{(0.050)}{0.108} \cdot e_t + \underset{(0.011)}{0.152} \cdot dum_{9901} \qquad (8.22)$$

The dummy variable dum_{9901} is used to reflect the structural break in the wage time-series occuring in 1999. From this year on, average gross monthly wages and salaries have been increased by the mandatory premium for social security.

The estimates demonstrate that wages in Poland are flexible: they are procyclical and adjust quickly to changes in productivity and – especially – to price movements. They react to variations in the real exchange rate, i.e. depreciation of the domestic currency (fall in *e*) leads to the expansion of real wages. This in turn means that changes in the nominal exchange rate affect inflation not only through import prices but also indirectly, through their impact on wage setting.

The quick adjustment of wages to changes in the price level could result in part from the strong indexation mechanisms existing in Poland particularly before 1998, although indexation could equally well explain inflation inertia. Wages in the public sector are determined by the Tripartite Commission, which consists of representatives of the government, the employers' association and trade unions. If consensus is not reached within the Commission, the government decides the size of wage increases.[15] The public-sector wage norm has not been effective in constraining wage growth, and actual wage growth routinely exceeds the Tripartite Commission's norm, which has served as a floor rather than a ceiling for wage increases. Although wage-setting in the private sector is decentralised, excessive wage growth in the public sector puts pressure on private-sector employers to match the wage increases:

> The collective bargaining system (…) allowed for wage growth irrespective of the financial condition of the enterprises concerned. Wage rises were brought about by powerful workforce pressure, frequently bearing no relationship to company financial performance, with the result that wage growth indices established during collective bargaining were constantly overshot.
>
> (National Bank of Poland 2000a: 134)

It is assumed that labour supply is proportional to income, when both are measured relative to their potential values. This relationship can be captured as:

$$(l_t - l_t^*) = \eta_0 + (y_t - y_t^*) \tag{8.23}$$

where η_0 is a constant.[16]

8.4.4 Remaining equations

To close the small-scale macroeconomic model, we need two additional structural equations: uncovered interest rate parity (UIP) and the monetary policy rule.

Uncovered interest rate parity relates expected change in the exchange rate between domestic and foreign currency to differences in their interest rates and a risk premium. For simulation purposes we will ignore the risk premium component, assuming that it is exogenous with respect to monetary policy actions. Hence the UIP condition can be written in real terms as follows:

$$e_t - e_{t+1} = r_t^{TB} - r_t^{f\,TB} \tag{8.24}$$

where e denotes real exchange rate, while r^{TB} and $r^{f\,TB}$ denote real yields on 1-year domestic and foreign treasury bills, respectively.

In the model it is supposed that monetary policy operates in accordance with the Taylor rule, i.e. the short-term real interest rate is set in response to inflation and output gap measures. The basic form of the monetary policy rule can be written as:

$$r_t = 0.5 \cdot (y_t - y_t^*) + 0.5 \cdot (\Pi_{t+4} - \Pi^{tar}) \tag{8.25}$$

where r denotes the real short-term interest rate controlled by monetary policy (WIBOR T/N), $y - y^*$ denotes the output gap, Π is the annual inflation rate and Π^{tar} is the corresponding target.

There are two interest rates in the model: the NBP monetary policy rate (WIBOR T/N) and yields on treasury bills with 1 year maturity. These are related to each other, as bills of different maturities become perfect substitutes in the long-run. The relationship between them is estimated as follows (standard errors in parentheses):

$$\Delta i_t^{TB} = 0.002 + \underset{(0.126)}{1.055} \cdot \Delta i_t - \underset{(0.054)}{0.338} \cdot i_{t-1}^{TB} + \underset{(0.082)}{0.271} \cdot i_{t-1} \tag{8.26}$$

where i^{TB} is the (nominal) yield on treasury bills and i is the monetary policy rate.

8.5 Relative importance of different transmission channels

We ran a simulation of the passthrough of a monetary policy shock on this small structural model of the monetary transmission mechanism in Poland.[17] The purpose of these exercises is to characterise the strength and speed of monetary transmission in Poland as well as to separate the effects of different monetary transmission channels, focusing on the bank-lending channel.

The first simulation demonstrates the total impact of a 1 per cent change in the nominal short-term interbank interest rate (WIBOR T/N) on selected variables, namely the output gap, inflation, the monetary base and the real exchange rate. Reactions of these variables to the interest rate shock are presented in Figure 8.11.

As can be seen in the figure, the real exchange rate reacts immediately, appreciating by over 0.51 per cent in the first quarter, 0.48 per cent in the second quarter and 0.46 per cent in the third quarter after the interest rate shock. The exchange rate appreciation leads to the fall in inflation, amounting to 0.03 per cent in the fourth quarter following the shock. The output gap is affected by the change in interest rates with a three-quarter delay; the maximum reaction, equal to 0.32 per cent, takes place in the sixth and seventh quarters. At the same time the output gap reacts to the gradual fall in the monetary base, which amounts to around 0.37 per cent in the second quarter, 0.47 per cent in the third quarter and 0.55 per cent in the fourth quarter following the impulse.

The reduction in demand pressure affects inflation with a delay, and only slightly – inflation falls by 0.06 per cent in the ninth quarter after the shock.

Inflation responds to interest rates through various channels. In the

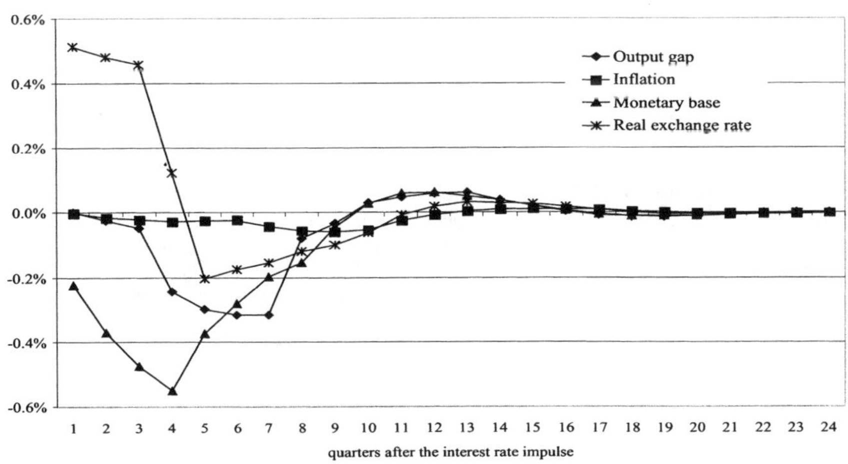

Figure 8.11 Response functions to the interest rate impulse (of 1 per cent).

subsequent simulation we attempt to separate these channels. Any method of distinguishing channels relies on arbitrary assumptions. Our approach was the following: the response of inflation to interest rate shock was estimated with the reserve money fixed, (that is, with the bank-lending channel turned off) and then again with this channel switched on. The difference between the two simulations roughly indicates the effects of the bank-lending channel. Second, we fixed both the reserve money and the exchange rate, and thus obtained an estimate of the transmission solely through the intertemporal substitution of consumption and investment. The results are presented in Figure 8.12.

The most immediate effects of the rise in the interest rate on inflation are transmitted by the exchange-rate channel. In fact, until the third quarter following the shock, the exchange-rate channel constitutes the only mechanism in the model through which the monetary policy influences inflation. Over longer horizons the fall in the output gap, resulting from the operation of the interest-rate channel and additional effects of the bank-lending channel, produces a second dip in inflation.

The bank-lending channel is moderately significant: in the ninth quarter after the shock the fall in inflation, amounting to 0.06 per cent, can be split into 0.05 per cent reflecting interest-rate channel effects and 0.01 per cent reflecting bank-lending channel effects. Even then, it should be stressed that the weight of the bank-lending channel may be overestimated due to an excessively high coefficient in the demand curve, as discussed earlier. The relative importance of all analysed – channels of monetary transmission in subsequent quarters is shown in Figure 8.13.

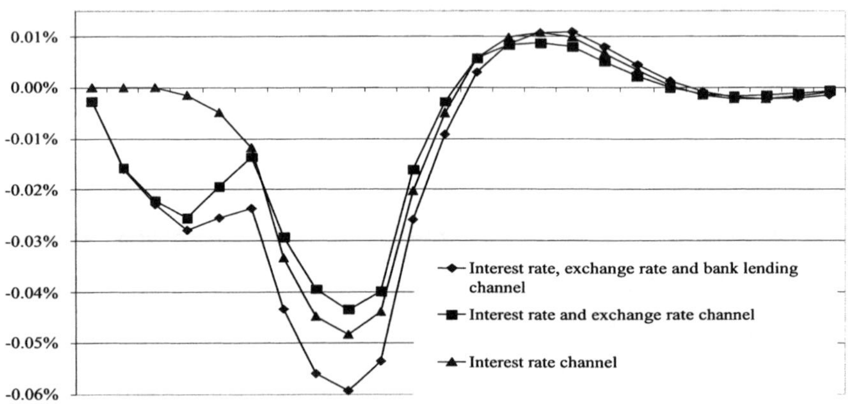

Figure 8.12 Interest rate impulse – effects of different monetary transmission channels on inflation.

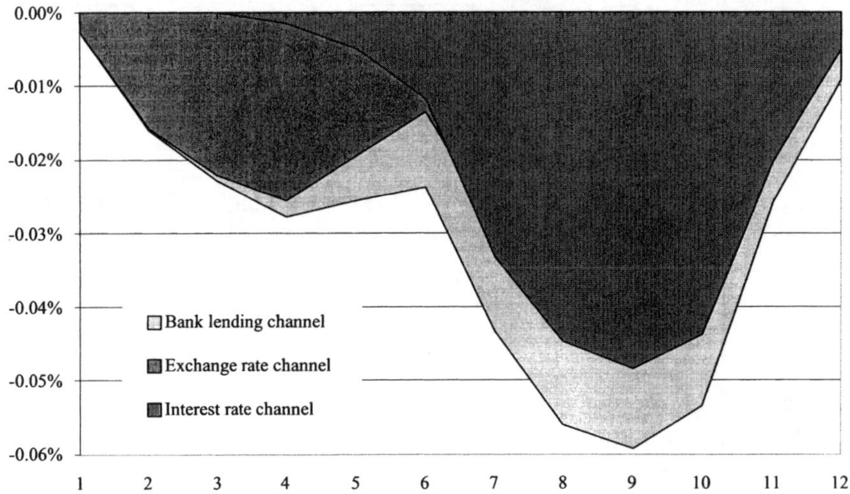

Figure 8.13 Interest rate impulse – relative importance of different channels of monetary transmission.

8.6 Conclusions

The small structural macroeconomic model presented in this chapter summarises the main channels of the monetary transmission mechanism in Poland – the interest-rate channel, the exchange-rate channel and the bank-lending channel – and also the role of inflationary expectations in the transmission process. The model serves not as a comprehensive description of the economy, but rather attempts to explain some features of monetary transmission in Poland and to verify the usefulness of selected theoretical concepts in capturing these characteristics. The structure of the model as well as the results presented in this paper are rather preliminary. Subsequent works should be focused in particular on reformulating the model in terms of more appropriate measures of output gap, inflation and inflationary expectations.

As presented in Figure 8.14, the model presupposes that monetary policy acts to achieve its final purpose – price stability – through several channels. Changes in interbank short-term interest rates, influenced considerably by the National Bank of Poland, have an impact on other interest rates, such as interest rates on loans or yields on treasury bills, which determine the level of economic activity – the traditional interest-rate channel. Moreover, changes in interest rates evoke exchange rate adjustments, which affect inflation immediately through import prices and indirectly through wage-setting – the exchange-rate channel.[18] Special attention is devoted in this paper to the bank-lending channel, which is

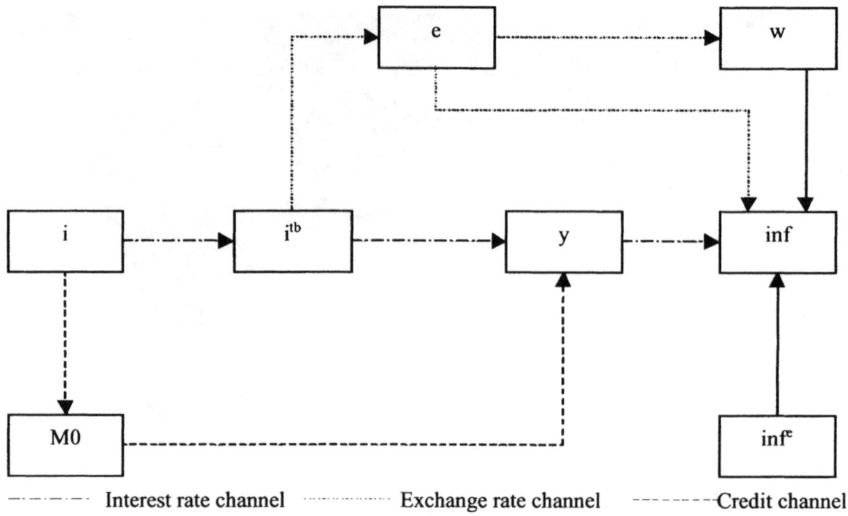

Figure 8.14 Monetary transmission mechanism as described by the model.

incorporated in the aggregate demand curve using Bernanke and Blinder's (1988) approach. The most interesting feature of such an IS curve is that it utilises the real monetary base as a proxy for the bank-lending channel.

Estimation results indicate that the exchange-rate channel is the quickest way by which the National Bank of Poland may affect inflation, although exchange-rate effects on inflation are not very strong. It should be pointed out that real appreciation of the exchange rate constituted an essential pillar of the Polish disinflation process, even if the use of the exchange-rate channel was constrained by the objective of maintaining international competitiveness.

The effectiveness of the interest-rate channel of monetary transmission appears to be constrained: the output gap is moderately sensitive to changes in interest rates, but its response is delayed in time, while the linkage between inflation and the output gap is very weak.

The statistical significance of reserve money in the demand curve would suggest that the quantity of bank credit in the economy is determined not solely by credit demand, but by the performance of banks' balance sheets as well. According to this view, a decline in reserve money supply, which reduces banks' liabilities, would result in a corresponding adjustment on the asset side, including the amount of credit on offer. It must be stressed, however, that Poland has experienced huge capital inflows that were treated with sterilised interventions. Both money base and output were affected by these inflows and so the estimated effect of the real monetary base on output, a measurement included in the Bernanke and Blinder (1988) approach, would seem to be spurious for Poland.

The legacy of these inflows has been an excess liquidity problem in the Polish banking system, which has meant that especially the monetary base but also broader monetary aggregates have been to some extent uncontrollable by the National Bank of Poland (see Lutkowski 2000; Bruni *et al.* 1996; 328). Curbing of the growth in gross official reserves, the main source of structural excess liquidity, began at the end of 1998. The National Bank of Poland will gradually gain more power to influence the reserve money supply. As a result, given the banking-centred structure of Polish business financing and the relatively slow development of the commercial paper and bond markets, it may be expected that in the near future monetary policy will be able to utilise the bank-lending channel to a larger extent.

Appendix: estimation results

Table 8.5 Demand curve (Equation 21)
Dependent Variable: $y-y^{*}$+0.65*rtb(−3)
Method: Least Squares
Sample(adjusted):1994:3 1999:4
Included observations: 22 after adjusting endpoints
Newey–West HAC Standard Errors & Covariance (lag truncation = 2)

Variable	*Coefficient*	*Std error*	*t-Statistic*	*Probability*
C	0.007991	0.004914	1.626336	0.1213
M0(−2)	0.113722	0.054767	2.076471	0.0524
y(−2)−y*(−2)	0.434899	0.145533	2.988314	0.0079
[y(−1)−y*(−1)]-[y(−2)-y*(−2)]	0.283910	0.098099	2.894106	0.0097

R-squared	0.265180	Mean dependent var,	0.005880
Adjusted R-squared	0.142710	S.D. dependent var,	0.026391
S.E. of regression	0.024435	Akaike info criterion	−4.422599
Sum squared resid.	0.010748	Schwarz criterion	−4.224228
Log likelihood	52.64859	F-statistic	2.165260
Durbin–Watson stat.	2.156269	Prob. (F-statistic)	0.127541
JB-statistic	24.36198		
Prob. (JB-statistic)	0.000005		
Breusch–Godfrey serial correlation LM test (one lag included)			
F-statistic	2.025750	Probability	0.172746
Obs*R-squared	2.342431	Probability	0.125893
Breusch–Godfrey serial correlation LM test (two lags included)			
F-statistic	0.961687	Probability	0.403275
Obs*R-squared	2.360841	Probability	0.307150
Breusch–Godfrey serial correlation LM test (three lags included)			
F-statistic	1.135013	Probability	0.366672
Obs*R-squared	4.070128	Probability	0.253991
Breusch–Godfrey serial correlation LM test (four lags included)			
F-statistic	1.011649	Probability	0.434507
Obs*R-squared	4.933069	Probability	0.294234
Ramsey RESET Test (number of fitted terms: one)			
F-statistic	0.176173	Probability	0.679940
Log likelihood ratio	0.226814	Probability	0.633897
Ramsey RESET Test (number of fitted terms: two)			
F-statistic	0.611872	Probability	0.554548
Log likelihood ratio	1.621402	Probability	0.444546
Ramsey RESET Test (number of fitted terms: three)			
F-statistic	1.061619	Probability	0.394684
Log likelihood ratio	4.235856	Probability	0.237096
Ramsey RESET Test (number of fitted terms: four)			
F-statistic	1.296530	Probability	0.318570
Log likelihood ratio	6.932854	Probability	0.139479

Table 8.6 Monetary base curve (Equation 8.15)
Dependent Variable: M0
Method: Least Squares
Sample(adjusted): 1993:3 1999:4
Included observations: 26 after adjusting endpoints
Newey–West HAC Standard Errors & Covariance (lag truncation = 2)
M0=C(1)+C(2)*M0(–1)+(1–C(2))*y(–1)+C(3)*i+C(4)*rr++C(5)*d(gr(–1))+C(6)*dum9904

	Coefficient	*Std error*	*t-Statistic*	*Probability*
C(1)	–0.495805	0.093930	–5.278427	0.0000
C(2)	0.652269	0.047032	13.86848	0.0000
C(3)	–0.900541	0.456496	–1.972726	0.0633
C(4)	0.546523	0.226031	2.417909	0.0258
C(5)	0.117538	0.037302	3.151012	0.0053
C(6)	–0.078905	0.009638	–8.187120	0.0000
C(7)	–0.083799	0.022347	–3.749906	0.0014

R-squared	0.980995	Mean dependent var.	9.130423
Adjusted R-squared	0.974994	S.D. dependent var.	0.131594
S.E. of regression	0.020809	Akaike info criterion	–4.682022
Sum squared resid.	0.008228	Schwarz criterion	–4.343304
Log likelihood	67.86629	Durbin–Watson stat.	1.863286
JB-statistic	0.670523		
Prob.(JB-statistic)	0.715151		
Breusch–Godfrey serial correlation LM test (one lag included)			
F-statistic	0.075259	Probability	0.786952
Obs*R-squared	0.108255	Probability	0.742140
Breusch–Godfrey serial correlation LM test (two lags included):			
F-statistic	0.250457	Probability	0.781268
Obs*R-squared	0.744175	Probability	0.689294
Breusch–Godfrey Serial Correlation LM Test (three lags included):			
F-statistic	0.417035	Probability	0.743175
Obs*R-squared	1.885601	Probability	0.596487
Breusch–Godfrey Serial Correlation LM Test (four lags included).			
F-statistic	1.094648	Probability	0.394699
Obs*R-squared	5.874697	Probability	0.208703

Table 8.7 System: Phillips curve (equation 8.17), wage equation (equation 8.18), inflation expectations equation (equation 8.19)
Method: Three-Stage Least Squares Sample: 1992:2 2000:4
Instruments: w(–1) y(–1)–1(–1) p(–1) pimp(–1) fp/p y(–3)–y*(–3) dum9901 y–1 pimp y(–2)–y*(–2) y(–1)–y* (–1) y–y* inf(–1) c
Convergence achieved after: 1 weight matrix, 6 total coef. iterations

	Coefficient	*Std error*	*t-Statistic*	*Probability*
c1	0.976927	0.296566	3.294130	0.0016
c2	0.756541	0.131847	5.738014	0.0000
c3	0.369816	0.186580	1.982074	0.0515
c4	–0.518267	0.130358	–3.975736	0.0002
c5	0.096325	0.024085	3.999368	0.0002
c6	0.410574	0.028853	14.22972	0.0000
c7	–0.098434	0.027390	–3.593850	0.0006
c8	0.174769	0.046975	3.720460	0.0004
c9	0.090624	0.034615	2.618035	0.0109
c10	3.953298	0.293490	13.46994	0.0000
c11	0.714516	0.056256	12.70112	0.0000
c12	0.151954	0.010738	14.15122	0.0000
c13	–0.107707	0.049836	–2.161245	0.0341
c14	–0.004563	0.004250	–1.073583	0.2867

Determinant residual covariance2.53E-13

Equation: p=p(–1)+c1((1–c2)/c3)*infexp/4+c4+c5*[w(–1)–c6* (y(–1)–1(–1)) + –pimp(–1)]+c7*(p(–1)-pimp(–1))+c8*fp/p+c9*(y(–3)–y*(–3))*
Observations: 28

R-squared	0.999680	Mean dependent var.	0.718893
Adjusted R-squared	0.999546	S.D. dependent var.	0.359747
S.E. of regression	0.007666	Sum squared resid.	0.001117
Durbin–Watson stat.	2.415727		

Equation: w=w(–1)+c10+c11[(p(–1)–w(–1))+c6*(y(–1)–1(–1))] + +c12*dum9901+ c13*(p–pimp)*
Observations: 28

R-squared	0.999439	Mean dependent var.	6.797214
Adjusted R-squared	0.999341	S.D. dependent var.	0.491746
S.E. of regression	0.012622	Sum squared resid.	0.003664
Durbin–Watson stat.	1.755972		

*Equation: infexp(+1)=c14+c3*inf(+1)+c2*infexp*
Observations: 27

R-squared	0.884652	Mean dependent var.	0.057241
Adjusted R-squared	0.875039	S.D. dependent var.	0.029474
S.E. of regression	0.010419	Sum squared resid.	0.002605
Durbin–Watson stat.	2.141977		

Wald test

Null Hypothesis:	c1=1		
Chi-square	0.006053	Probability	0.937987

Table 8.8 Interbank interest rates and yields on Treasury bills (equation 8.26)
Dependent Variable: itb-itb(–1)
Sample(adjusted): 1994:1 1999:4
Method: Least Squares
Included observations: 24 after adjusting endpoints

Variable	*Coefficient*	*Std error*	*t-Statistic*	*Probability*
C	0.002363	0.002231	1.059179	0.3021
i–i(–1)	1.054841	0.126489	8.339380	0.0000
itb(–1)	–0.337897	0.053979	–6.259772	0.0000
i(–1)	0.270876	0.081685	3.316103	0.0034

R-squared	0.826989	Mean dependent var.	–0.001958
Adjusted R-squared	0.801037	S.D. dependent var.	0.004027
S.E. of regression	0.001796	Akaike info criterion	–9.655287
Sum squared resid.	6.45E–05	Schwarz criterion	–9.458945
Log likelihood	119.8634	F-statistic	31.86651
Durbin–Watson stat.	2.026026	Prob. (F-statistic)	0.000000
JB-statistic	0.797470		
Prob.(JB-statistic)	0.671169		
Breusch–Godfrey serial correlation LM test (one lag included)			
F-statistic	0.050136	Probability	0.825216
Obs*R-squared	0.063163	Probability	0.801564
Breusch–Godfrey serial correlation LM test (two lags included)			
F-statistic	0.089842	Probability	0.914483
Obs*R-squared	0.237212	Probability	0.888158
Breusch–Godfrey serial correlation LM test (three lags included)			
F-statistic	0.059421	Probability	0.980376
Obs*R-squared	0.249052	Probability	0.969307
Breusch–Godfrey serial correlation LM test (four lags included)			
F-statistic	0.445294	Probability	0.774248
Obs*R-squared	2.404129	Probability	0.661881
Ramsey RESET test (number of fitted terms: one)			
F-statistic	0.178049	Probability	0.677791
Log likelihood ratio	0.223855	Probability	0.636118
Ramsey RESET test (number of fitted terms: two)			
F-statistic	0.100244	Probability	0.905118
Log likelihood ratio	0.265839	Probability	0.875536
Ramsey RESET Test (number of fitted terms: three)			
F-statistic	0.948388	Probability	0.439338
Log likelihood ratio	3.713928	Probability	0.294058
Ramsey RESET Test (number of fitted terms: four)			
F-statistic	0.852671	Probability	0.512712
Log likelihood ratio	4.637634	Probability	0.326538

Acknowledgment

The preliminary version of this paper was written during the Centre for Central Banking Studies (CCBS) Academic Project on Transmission Mechanisms and Monetary Policy Implementation. I would like to thank Professor Peter Sinclair, Director of the CCBS, as well as all the CCBS team for their hospitality. I am particularly obliged to Dr Lavan Mahadeva and Gabriel Sterne, whose suggestions and day-to-day support essentially contributed to the paper. I highly appreciate many valuable comments on the earlier version received from Professor David Gowland as well as helpful conversations with Alastair Cunningham and Anthony Yates. I am also grateful to Dr Piotr Boguszewski, Joseph Djivre, Áron Gereben, Dr Javier Gómez, Glenn Hoggarth, Juan Manuel Julio, Dr Ryszard Kokoszczyński, Bojan Marković, Jacek Osiński, Gulbin Şahinbeyoğlu and Ewa Wróbel for fruitful discussions and suggestions. I would like to express my gratitude to Richard Hammerman for excellent research assistance. Any errors are of course mine. The views expressed in the paper are mine and do not necessarily reflect those of the National Bank of Poland.

Notes

1 The European Central Bank interprets the operation of the bank-lending channel in the following way: 'An increase in short-term interest rates is usually accompanied by a reduction in the growth of overnight deposits. This can lead banks to reduce their supply of loans, in particular if banks cannot easily replace those deposits with other liabilities. Bank-dependent borrowers such as small and medium-sized enterprises and households could then face a squeeze in their borrowing possibilities.' See ECB (2000).

2 The survey's results are presented annually in the Statistics Department's reports. The authors underline that the sample is not fully representative, reflecting mainly medium and large Polish enterprises' performance. See Boguszewski *et al.* (1997, 1998, 1999).

3 This category contains loans from direct investors (intercompany loans), debt securities and other investment (trade credits and loans).

4 All the banks in Poland have an obligatory partial guarantee resulting from their membership of the deposit protection scheme. Until the end of 1999, three of the four largest, state-owned banks had an explicit full guarantee, this was a way of protecting state-owned banks and improving their competitiveness with domestic and foreign banks. In the years 1994–98, fully guaranteed banks had about 20 per cent of the banking system capital and 35 per cent of the banking system assets. Other state-owned banks had an implicit guarantee associated simply with the state ownership. Opiela (1999) underlines that Polish state banks with guarantees paid a lower deposit rate than private banks. Moreover, according to Nikiel and Opiela (1998), deposits in state banks were less interest-rate sensitive when interest rates on deposits were lowered but more interest-rate sensitive when interest rates on deposits were increased. Thus fully guaranteed banks had an advantage over partially guaranteed banks in raising time deposit funds, which were subject to lower reserve requirements than demand deposits. Thus, during a period of monetary policy tightening, banks

with a full guarantee were able more easily to raise their funds than banks with a partial guarantee.

5 The latter explanation could have been most relevant during the initial years of transformation. Until the end of 1994 the share of bad credits in their total sum was sizeable, eventually resulting in a rationing and a decrease of total credit in real terms. The ratio of irregular (loss) classifications to gross claims was 30.1 per cent (16.7 per cent) in 1993, 27.9 per cent (16.7 per cent) in 1994, and in December 1999, 12.9 per cent {4.6 per cent}. Data source: National Bank of Poland (2000b): 34.

6 VAR models show that the response of the output gap to changes in the nominal effective exchange rate, although consistent with the theory, is not statistically significant, only the response of the industrial output gap in three-dimensional VAR, including non-foodstuffs CPI, the industrial output gap and the nominal effective exchange rate, is significant within the first three quarters after the nominal effective exchange rate shock.

See Kokoszczyński (1999), models Z.I.5.4.1. – Z.I.5.5.3.

7 At present the National Bank of Poland uses three main instruments: the lombard rate, open market operations and reserve requirements. The lombard rate is a last resort rate, which stabilises the 'ceiling' interest rate in the market. Open market operations – nowadays in a form of sales of NBP bills with 28-day maturity – stabilise the 'floor' market interest rate. Reserve requirements influence the long-term liquidity position of the Polish banking sector and smooth the volatility of market interest rates.

8 For instance, Opiela (1998) compares two time series: change of the real WIBOR T/N and residuals of the regression in which the dependent variable is the change of real WIBOR T/N and the independent variables are time trend and retail sale of commodities (instead of real GDP which is not available with monthly frequency). They appear to be very similar, which suggests that monetary policy is the main factor influencing WIBOR T/N.

9 It should be noted that long-run coefficients describe the reaction of different money aggregates to changes in interest rates: for Poland we use the monetary base aggregate, while for other countries we use a narrow money (M1). Despite this fact, our findings still support the hypothesis of a relatively weaker monetary base's reaction to monetary policy actions in Poland, since the respective reactions of monetary base to changes in interest rates in other countries should be even deeper than the reaction of broader money aggregates.

10 Technical progress is modelled by a time trend.

11 Under the special case of Cobb–Douglas technology, σ would be unity, and the term, $w - 1/\sigma \cdot (q - n) - (\sigma - 1)/\sigma \cdot a$, appearing in the CES function, may be replaced by the unit labour cost.

12 Food prices represent around 34 per cent of the whole CPI basket. They lead to a high seasonality of inflation, which, however, is excluded from the model by operating on seasonally adjusted time series.

13 The Demoskop survey, used in the National Bank of Poland for quantifying individuals' inflationary expectations, is carried out at the beginning of each month. The sample consists of 1000 representatives. The question is designed in a qualitative way, e.g. the respondents do not give precise quantitative answers regarding inflation in future, but declare the expected direction of change, comparing their foresights with current price movements. They respond to the following question: 'Do you expect, in comparison with current events, prices over next 12 months: (1) will increase faster; (2) will increase at the same rate; (3) will increase at a slower rate; (4) will be stable; (5) will fall; (6) I don't know'.

14 There are two types of measurement errors associated with surveys of inflation-

ary expectations, survey errors and quantification errors. The first category contains errors covering the extent to which the sample of respondents is statistically not fully representative as well as those resulting from possible misunderstanding of the survey's question and options of answer. Quantification errors, on the other hand, reflect the procedure of quantification – in our case, the errors that may have been generated by the assumptions of an adjusted Carlson and Parkin (1975) method. For details concerning the adjusted Carlson and Parkin method as implemented to quantify individuals' inflationary expectations in Poland, see Łyziak (2000b).

15 In the years 1995–2000, agreements were reached only in 1995 and 1996, the government determined wage growth in 1997–2000.

16 This relationship would follow a general equilibrium model where households trade off leisure and consumption and output is Cobb–Douglas. See, for example; Blanchard and Kiyotaki; (1987).

17 Winsolve 3.41 and 3.50 software was used.

18 This is a constrained version of the exchange rate channel, which excludes the indirect effect of the exchange rate through net exports.

9 Monetary transmission mechanism in Turkey

A view from a high-inflation environment

Gülbin Şahinbeyoğlu

9.1 Introduction

This chapter examines the basic features of the monetary transmission mechanism in Turkey using a small aggregate macroeconomic model. The core equations of the model consist of aggregate demand, wage-and price-setting, uncovered interest rate parity and a monetary policy rule, as well as more unique features of the Turkish monetary transmission. The model describes how agents set wages and prices in a high inflation economy. Changes in exchange rates and interest rates are the primary references informing expectations, and wages and prices adjust very quickly compared to economies such as the United Kingdom. Another idiosyncratic feature of Turkey is the importance of high levels of government debt. Following Flood and Marion (1996) and Werner (1996), we explicitly model the relationship between fiscal and monetary policy found in Turkey by allowing for a currency risk premium that depends on the expected future share of Turkish lira – denominated government debt in GDP. The results show that if monetary and fiscal policy are not co-ordinated, the monetary transmission mechanism is weak and unstable because of the effect of interest rates on the secondary balance and the exchange rate risk premium. These results underline the importance of the recent commitment by the government to achieve primary surpluses in Turkey's new disinflation programme.

9.2 Monetary and fiscal policy

Price stability has become the primary criterion for judging the success of monetary policy in recent years. A key issue is whether the choice of monetary policy, aimed at how best to achieve a target rate of inflation, can be separated from other aspects of government policy, especially fiscal policy decisions. By the separation of monetary and fiscal policy, we refer to the situation in which institutions make no provision to ensure that the optimal path of inflation (and output) pursued by the monetary authority is similar to that pursued by the fiscal authority. Separation occurs either when the objectives of the two authorities are not formally required to be similar or when the two bodies can set their instruments independently of each other. The alternative scenario of co-ordination implies some formal process by which consensus is reached over what shocks are hitting the economy and what they imply for the instruments of policy choice: the interest rate and the fiscal deficit.

Many economists, for example Woodford (1998), have pointed out that the case for policy separation is not unequivocal and depends, in particular, on whether and to what extent fiscal policy has an impact on inflation determination and monetary policy affects the government budget deficit. Even in countries like the United States and the United Kingdom, fiscal and monetary policy can be linked. First, monetary policy can influence the real value of outstanding government debt through its effects on the price level and bond prices, and thus the cost of debt servicing. Second, when 'Ricardian equivalence' does not hold, and the fiscal policy impact on aggregate demand is non-neutral, fiscal shocks change the level of aggregate demand. If the government budget is not expected to adjust according to a Ricardian rule, then both the time-path and the composition of the public debt can have consequences for price inflation, and a central bank charged with maintaining price stability cannot be wholly indifferent to the determination of fiscal policy.

Fiscal–monetary linkages can be more pervasive in indebted, less developed countries. That is especially true when the risk premium on a large outstanding sovereign or private-sector debt is sensitive to macroeconomic conditions (Mishkin 2000b). The main theme of this chapter is to examine the consequences of the separation of fiscal and monetary policies, using heavily indebted Turkey as a case study. We explore this issue by placing the monetary transmission mechanism in Turkey in the framework of a small-scale macroeconomic model. The key equations of the model are an aggregate demand relationship, wage- and price-setting equations, an interest rate parity condition and a rule for debt dynamics. The fiscal and monetary policy rules are distinct equations and are not restricted to targeting the same welfare-maximising combination of inflation and output volatility. This separation of targets indicates that the policies are separate. Also crucial to our story is that debt dynamics are allowed to affect the risk premium in the uncovered interest rate parity condition for the Turkish exchange rate. How best to formalise the co-ordination that this chapter makes a case for is left as an interesting topic for future research.

Fiscal and monetary policy coordination would feature as a main theme in any survey of Turkey's recent monetary history.[1] To set the background, in the first half of the 1990s, public finances deteriorated markedly and political uncertainty intensified in Turkey. As capital flows were largely unrestricted, this turn of events led to the financial crisis of early 1994, characterised by a marked devaluation, triple-digit inflation and a deep recession (Figure 9.1).

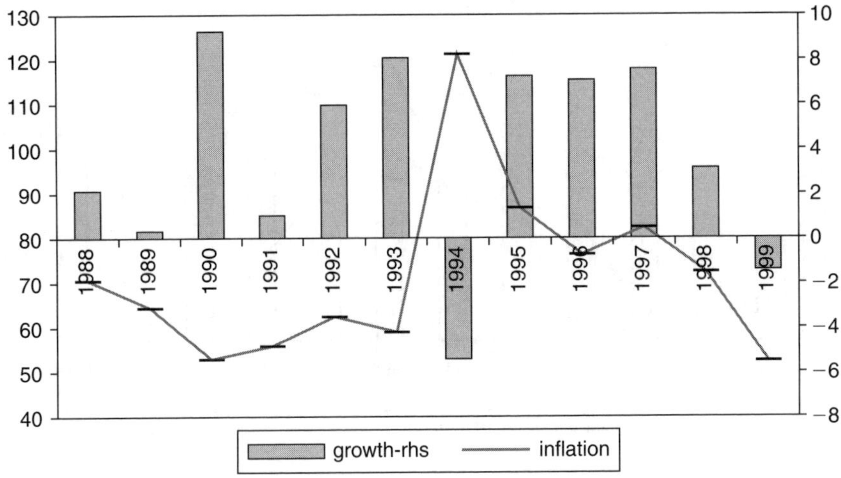

Figure 9.1 Annual inflation and GDP growth (per cent).

The financial crisis of early 1994 shaped the policies of the second half of the 1990s. In its aftermath, measures were taken to gradually reduce political influence on monetary policy and enhance its coordination with fiscal policy. The Central Bank of Turkey, along with the Treasury, built up credibility through transparent, predictable policies. Nonetheless, the fiscal deficit and the inflation rate continued to increase. High and chronic inflation and large public-sector financing requirements, in the context of a fully liberalised exchange rate regime, imposed significant constraints on the central bank's policy options and left little room for policy manoeuvre.[2] The central bank focused on maintaining real interest rate stability and a competitive exchange rate rather than more traditional goals such as price stability (Figure 9.2; see also Daniel and Üçer 1999).

The deterioration in the fiscal position resulted from both substantially negative primary budget balances and high and rising interest rates. Between 1995 and 1999, the public-sector borrowing requirement increased more than two fold; more than 90 per cent of the deficit was financed through domestic borrowing. Meanwhile, real interest rates increased to above 50 per cent (Figure 9.2).

Yet the deteriorating fiscal position has itself been one of the main causes of high real interest rates in Turkey in recent years. This association between fiscal deficits and real interest rate was actually strengthened by the withdrawal of central bank financing of the government debt in the second half of the 1990s.[3]

The fact that the high budget deficits were mainly financed through domestic borrowing could also have been significant (Figure 9.3). Under

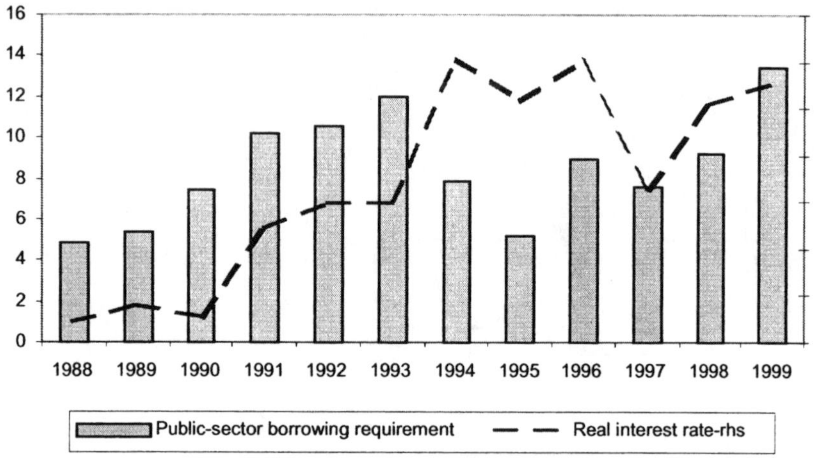

Figure 9.2 PSBR and real interest rate.

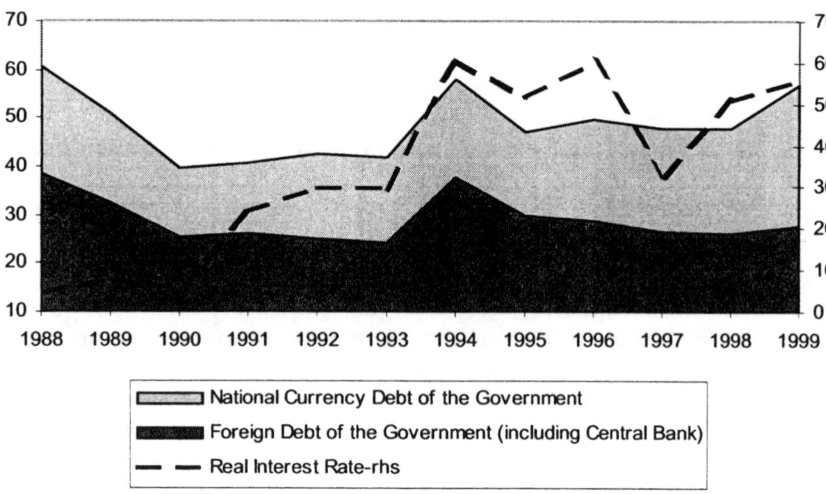

Figure 9.3 Foreign and domestic debt/GNP and real annual interest rate (per cent).

perfect capital markets and when domestic and foreign currency–denominated assets are perfect substitutes, differences in the composition of debt does not matter. However, if risk premia or financial market frictions make bonds imperfect substitutes, then there should be an optimal balance between domestic and external finance that minimises the risk premium, in the light of the overall monetary and fiscal policy stance and market conditions. An excessive reliance on domestic financing would seem to have eroded market confidence in the sustainability of the fiscal stance. A consequence of these factors taken together was that the risk premium on Turkish lira, for example, as proxied by the *ex post* uncovered interest rate parity (UIP) residual, rose steadily over the 1990s to culminate in very high real interest rates (Figure 9.4).[4]

In an effort to control the underlying factors that gave rise to its high-inflation environment, a medium-term disinflation programme was proposed for Turkey for the period 2000–02. The programme aimed to break inflationary inertia through co-ordinating a greater fiscal discipline and pursuing a target path to lower inflation. The inflation rate was set to decline from 65 per cent at the end of 1999 to 25 per cent by the end of 2000, and to single digits by the end of 2002. The most important and unique component of the programme, as originally proposed in 2000, was a nominal anchor provided by a forward-looking commitment to the exchange rate. The exchange rate has a strong impact on prices via expectations formation and imported inflation. The programme also provided for a pre announced exit strategy from the crawling-band regime by mid–2001 for details, see Erçel 1999).

Our main interest in the programme is to explain why it emphasised the need for coordination. A crucial feature was that the system of monetary policy targets was to be supported by a strong fiscal adjustment: a planned increase in the primary surplus that would be associated with greater privatisation proceeds. Also important in the strategy was an incomes policy that linked the increase in government-sector wages and the minimum wage to targeted inflation. Finally, in common with previous policies, a guiding rule for the conduct of monetary policy was to create domestic liabilities in return for foreign exchange assets, and so reduce the proportion of external debt.

The rest of this chapter is organised as follows. In section 9.3 we

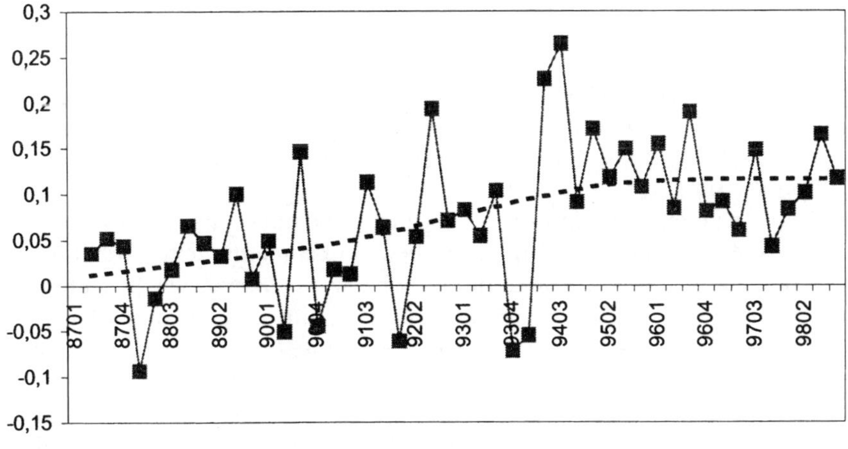

Figure 9.4 Ex post UIP residual.

provide a framework for discussing the determination of real interest rate and the relationship between debt dynamics and the exchange rate risk premium. In section 9.4 we present the key equations of the model and discuss how the Turkish economy is portrayed by the model's impulse responses. Section 9.5 is devoted to the simulation results, while section 9.6 provides a conclusion.

9.3 Debt dynamics, the real interest rates and policy coordination

In this section we aim to provide a framework for our results by explaining how high real interest rates in Turkey are linked to the coordination of monetary and fiscal policy.

The factors that determine the real interest rate in countries in general can be grouped under five broad headings (see also Chadha and Dimsdale 1999):

1 Changes in the real interest rate can arise from structural changes related to savings or investment behaviour. For example, a demographic shift or an altered tax regime can change real rates. A change in policy preferences can have consequences through its effect on public savings, too. For example, an increase in the targeted public debt relative to GDP will require agents to adjust their portfolios to hold more government securities. The real yield on government bonds should rise in order to encourage this shift in asset portfolios.
2 Similarly, changes in the current and expected future profitability of production arising from technical progress or improved market efficiency can result in a shift in investment and consumption behaviour to the extent that they raise lifetime incomes.
3 Monetary factors can matter too. The Fisher identity describes how values for nominal interest rates and inflation imply a real rate of interest. However, the adjustment of nominal rates and inflation to levels that are consistent with long-run interest rates is likely to be slow because of sticky prices, and therefore changes in monetary conditions can be expected to have persistent effects on real interest rates in the short run.
4 Financial market microstructure can also be important, especially when it is related to macroeconomic policy. Governments facing large budget deficits may attempt to reduce their cost of borrowing by imposing restrictions on other borrowers. Hence, the deregulation of capital markets will tend to raise the real interest rate towards the market level.
5 Finally, investors' perceptions of risk have an effect on the real rate of return via a risk premium. As suggested by Chadha and Dimsdale (1999) and Agenor and Montiel (1996), large budget deficits tend to have a positive impact on real rates of interest if they raise risk premia.

A simple model illustrates how the combination of monetary and fiscal decisions determines real interest rates through these different channels (see also Moalla-Fetini 2000).

Government debt at time t is determined by the identity (9.1):

$$\Delta D_G^{PR} + \Delta D_G^{CB} + \Delta D_G^{FX} = I_G^{PR} + I_G^{CB} + I_G^{FX} + TR_{CB}^{G} + P_G \tag{9.1}$$

where Δ is the first difference operator ($\Delta x_t = x_t - x_{t-1}$), and D_G^{PR}, D_G^{CB}, and D_G^{FX}, are the stocks of government bonds held by the private sector, the central bank and the foreign sector, respectively. I_G^{PR}, I_G^{CB}, and I_G^{FX} are corresponding interest payments earned on government bonds by the private sector, the central bank and the foreign sector, respectively. TR_{CB}^{P} is transfers of profit from the central bank to the government, and P_G is the government's primary balance of payments.

The central bank's balance sheet can be written as:

$$\Delta C_{CB}^{PR} + \Delta C_{CB}^{FX} + \Delta D_G^{CB} = \Delta M + \Delta NW \tag{9.2}$$

where C_{CB}^{PR} is claims on the private sector, C_{CB}^{FX} is claims on the foreign sector and M is base money. NW is the central bank's net worth, given by:

$$\Delta NW = I_{CB}^{PR} + I_{CB}^{FX} + I_G^{CB} - TR_{CB}^{G} - OP \tag{9.3}$$

where I_{CB}^{PR} is interest receipts of the central bank on private sector credits, I_{CB}^{FX} is the interest receipts of the central bank on net foreign assets and OP is the operating cost of the central bank.

By substituting (9.2) and (9.3) into (9.1), we get the following expression:

$$\Delta D + \Delta M = -P + OP + IP \tag{9.4}$$

where the net debt of the consolidated government/central bank is given by:

$$\Delta D = \Delta D_G^{PR} + \Delta D_G^{FX} - \Delta C_{CB}^{PR} - \Delta C_{CB}^{FX} \tag{9.5}$$

and interest payments on net debt are:

$$IP = I_G^{PR} + I_G^{FX} - I_{CB}^{PR} - I_{CB}^{FX} \tag{9.6}$$

The consolidated government/central bank budget constraint, equation (9.4), indicates that the sum of the primary deficit and interest payments to the private and foreign sectors should be financed either through bond issuance or money creation.

The first point to note is that the relative weights of the alternative sources of financing of an increase in the deficit depends on the decisions made by the fiscal and monetary authorities, and whether these are separated or co-ordinated. If more money is created to finance a greater deficit, and that deficit is unsustainable, then higher inflation would result, at the gain of a lower level of nominal net debt of the consolidated government/central bank.

Fry (1997) describes three alternative frameworks for monetary and fiscal policy coordination. In the first, the central bank determines the change in reserve money, providing a partial financing of the government's deficit, and the remaining deficit is set in the light of the other available sources. It is imperative under this schema that the deficit is made consistent with the central bank's objectives. In the second framework, the deficit is predetermined, and the central bank increases reserve money to finance the whole deficit. In the third, the change in reserve money and the deficit are set independently, leaving the change in government debt as the residual. This third alternative is possible only if interest rates are allowed to rise to ensure all debt is sold.

According to our definition, only the last type of framework represents a separation of monetary and fiscal policy, and it is this framework that we incorporate in the model. We are assuming that under this third option, there is no institution to guarantee that the change in reserve money as set by the central bank and the deficit as set by the fiscal authority are consistent with one another, having the same targeted path for inflation and output. The former two frameworks necessarily give rise to a co-ordinated policy: under the first the deficit and monetary instruments are in line with the central bank's objective, whilst under the second the fiscal authority's preferences and beliefs dominate, even if high inflation results.

Debt dynamics are of particular concern when the debt is unsustainable. This situation can be captured by setting the real interest rate higher than the growth rate of the economy adjusted for preferences (see also Fry 1997). Following previous notation, let the stock of real government debt follow a time path that is expressed as

$$TD_t = TD_{t-1} * (1 + r_t) + P_t \qquad (9.7)$$

where the sum of domestic debt and foreign debt in real terms is given by $TD_t = DD_t + FD_t^* e_t$, and r_t denotes the domestic real rate (and also the foreign interest rates, for simplicity). The prices of goods and assets move together. Both sides of equation (9.7) can be divided by real gross domestic product (GDP), which grows at a rate per cent and rearranged as follows:

$$\Delta td = p + \left[\frac{(1+r)}{(1+\gamma)} - 1 \right] td \qquad (9.8)$$

where td is the ratio of government debt to GDP and p is the government's primary balance as a ratio of GDP, which equals government expenditure on goods and services g minus tax revenue t, also expressed as ratios to GDP. Finally, equation (9.8) can be expressed in continuously compounded form:

$$dtd = p + (r - \gamma)^{td} \tag{9.9}$$

Equation (9.9) indicates that when the real interest rate exceeds the real growth rate, the debt-to-GDP ratio rises unless the government runs a primary surplus ($p < 0$). To avoid explosive expansion of debt, the government must spend less on goods and services, g, than its tax revenue, t; it must run a primary surplus. By setting $dtd = 0$ in equation (9.9), the required primary surplus for long-run solvency can be expressed as:

$$-p = (r - \gamma)^{td} \tag{9.10}$$

In the short or medium run, a country that has a greater potential to grow faster than its lending partners can borrow from them and increase its debt. However, again here there is an implicit sustainable path for real interest rates which dictates that long-run solvency must be expected to be achieved over some horizon when growth rates converge (Obstfeld and Rogoff 1996).

Expectations as to the sustainability of debt would then have implications for the sustainable real interest rate. In this chapter we focus on how expectations of the impact of fiscal and monetary policies through debt dynamics feed through to the risk premium on the interest rate paid on the debt. This is in contrast to the plentiful past research that discusses the monetisation of debt in the presence of large public deficits. Excess deficits do not lead automatically to monetisation in our model, since we assume that the central bank can issue more domestic-currency bonds than are necessary to fund the deficit, providing the bank wants higher interest rates. Another key assumption is that the demand for foreign-currency denominated bonds is entirely exogenous.[5] In this set-up, the central bank can choose only one among four possible policy options: to control the exchange rate, the interest rate, nominal bond issues or the money supply. Our base-line specification establishes a monetary policy rule that targets the interest rate as the instrument, leaving the remaining three variables to be determined by market forces.

Following the insights of Flood and Marion (1996) and Werner (1996), we explicitly model the impact of an increasing debt burden on real interest rates by formally relating a currency risk premium to the share of Turkish lira denominated debt in GDP.

9.4 Model dynamics and stylised facts

We developed a small aggregate model to describe the Turkish monetary transmission mechanism. The model comprises equations for aggregate demand, wage- and price-setting, debt dynamics and uncovered interest rate parity, and fiscal and monetary policy rules. In this section, the form and estimates of these key equations are presented and the underlying factors determining the dynamics discussed. Fiscal fundamentals, the monetary policy reaction and the formation of expectations all turn out to play a crucial part.

9.4.1 The model

The framework of the model is given by equations (9.11) through (9.18). Each equation is discussed separately in the sections that follow (see also Table 9.1).

Table 9.1 Model parameters

	Equation/Values	
	IS curve	
α_1	–0.12	Real interest rate response
α_2	0.10	Real exchange rate response
α_3	1.38	Autoregressive element
α_4	–0.66	Autoregressive element
Wage-setting		
β_1	0.21	Unit labour productivity
β_2	–0.24	Autoregressive element
Price-setting		
χ_1	–0.18	Autoregressive element
χ_2	0.23	Nominal exchange rate response
χ_3	0.09	Nominal exchange rate response
χ_4	0.11	Unit labour cost
χ_5	1.00*	Inflation expectations response
Risk premium		
φ_1	0.10*	Response to domestic currency debt GDP ratio
φ_2	0.60*	Autoregressive element
Monetary policy rule		
δ_0	0.50*	Feedback parameter
Fiscal policy rule		
ζ_1	–0.10*	Feedback parameter
ζ_2	0.30*	Autoregressive element

Note
* Calibrated parameters.

Aggregate demand:

$$y_t = \alpha_1 ir_t + \alpha_2(er_t - er_{t-1}) + \alpha_3 y_{t-1} + \alpha_4 y_{t-2} + \varepsilon_{1t} \tag{9.11}$$

Wage- and price-setting:

$$\Delta w_t = \beta_1(yt_{t-1} - l_{t-1} + pc_{t-1}) + \beta_2 w_{t-1} + \varepsilon_{2t} \tag{9.12}$$

$$\pi_t = \chi_1\, pc_{t-1} + \chi_2\, \Delta e_t + \chi_3 e_{t-1} + \chi_4\, (w_{t-1} - yt_{t-1} + l_{t-1}) + \chi_5 E\pi_{t+1} + \varepsilon_{3t} \tag{9.13}$$

Government debt identity:

$$\begin{aligned} d_t = -fd_t \exp(e_t) + p_t + ((1 + i_t)\, d_{t-1} + \\ (1 + if_t)\, fd_{t-1} \exp(e_{t-1}))1/(1 + y_t - y_{t-1})1/(1 + \pi_t) \end{aligned} \tag{9.14}$$

Interest rate parity condition:

$$er_t = irf_t - ir_t + er_{t+1} + q_t \tag{9.15}$$

Risk premium:

$$q_t = \phi_1 d_{t+4} + \phi_2 q_{t-1} \tag{9.16}$$

Fiscal policy rule:

$$p_t = \varsigma_1 d_t + \varsigma_2 p_{t-1} \tag{9.17}$$

Monetary policy rule:

$$i_t = \pi_{t+1} + q_t + ir_{ft} + \delta_0(\pi_t - \pi^*) + (1 - \delta_0)\, y_t + \varepsilon_{8t} \tag{9.18}$$

where all variables, except interest rates and the shares in GNP, are expressed in logs. The variable y is the output gap defined as the difference between output and potential output, potential output being the level at which output would be if prices were flexible.

y, w and 1 denote total output, nominal wage rate and employment, respectively; i and ir are nominal and real domestic interest rates, respectively; and irf represents real foreign interest rate. Inflation rate and price level are represented by π and pc, respectively, and π^* denotes the inflation target. er and e denote the real and nominal exchange rate, respectively. In the debt identity equation, d and fd denote the shares of domestic-currency and foreign-currency denominated bonds in GNP, respectively, and p represents the primary balance. q is the time-varying risk premium. E denotes the mathematical expectations operator, and Δ is the first difference operator. *Exp* points to the exponential function of the variables.

9.4.2 Aggregate demand – IS equation

The aggregate demand equation (9.11) describes the dynamic relationship between real output, the real interest rate and the real exchange rate. The equation suggests that the current levels of real interest rate and real exchange rate affect the current level of output. The real interest rate should have a negative impact, $\alpha_1 < 0$, since a rise in real interest rates reduces investment spending due to the higher cost of capital and encourages savings. A real depreciation of domestic currency (an increase in *er*) makes domestic goods cheaper than foreign goods, thereby causing an increase in net exports. Hence, as was estimated, the real exchange rate enters the output equation with a positive coefficient, $\alpha_2 > 0$. Output also depends on its lagged values, indicating that output is to some extent predetermined.[6]

The results of estimating equation (9.11) with Turkish data reveal that current real exchange rate and real interest rate levels are significant in explaining the output gap.[7] The coefficients can be considered low, for both variables ($\alpha_1 = -0.12$, $\alpha_2 = 0.10$), although they have the expected signs.[8] The weak impact of real exchange rate on output could reflect the inelasticity of real trade flows to prices. As suggested by Ghosh (2000), Turkish trade activity elasticities are higher than price elasticities.[9] Estimates of the long-run export price elasticity range between 0.5 and 1.3, whereas short-run price elasticity is estimated to be around 0.4. For the import demand equation, estimation results indicate a long-run price elasticity ranging from 0.05 to 0.5, with short-run price elasticity estimated to be 0.7.

The relatively weak response of output to the changes in real exchange rate and real interest rate indicates weakness in the power of short-run monetary policy actions on the level of output. The first and second lags of output are highly significant with estimated coefficients of $\alpha_3 = 1.38$ and $\alpha_2 = -0.66$, respectively, suggesting that output is persistent and depends heavily on its lagged values (Appendix, Table 9.2).

9.4.3 Wage- and price-setting

The wage–price mechanism estimated in the model consists of two equations, (9.12) and (9.13), that describe how wages and mark-ups, defined as prices over unit labour costs, are set, respectively. The wage equation describes how nominal wages are set as a function of unit labour productivity and past inflation. The mark-up equation is the implicit supply curve of the firm.[10]

Estimations of equation (9.12) reveal that past inflation is a key determinant of wage-setting behaviour in Turkey. Nominal wages, however, are quick to adjust to changes in the price level. The strong and quick passthrough is characteristic of a high-inflation environment where nominal wages need to be continually reset either by indexation or by frequent re negotiation.[11]

In equation (9.13), pricing behaviour is defined as mark-up over unit labour costs. As with the wage equation, a speedy passthrough of nominal changes is apparent: past inflation is not significant in explaining current inflation, but future inflation is. This could explain why both output gap measures were estimated to be insignificant in the Phillips curve; in a high-inflation environment, the gap between actual and potential output is short-lived, and it is difficult to pick up its inflationary implications on quarterly data.

The coefficient in the inflation expectations term is estimated to be equal to unity. However changes in the nominal exchange rate are also significant in affecting price-setting behaviour in Turkey. Taken together these coeffficients violate the dynamic homogeneity property, although static homogeneity is preserved. The importance of these foreign exchange rate changes reflects both external influences on the cost of production and the relative prices of final goods in the inflation basket. Turkey has a relatively open economy with a trade volume of almost 45 per cent of GNP; of which 60 per cent of total imports are intermediary goods and 12 per cent are consumer goods. Meanwhile, almost 50 per cent of the goods in the consumer price index basket are tradable goods (Appendix, Table 9.3).

9.4.4 Expectations formation

In a chronically inflationary environment, agents have an incentive to adjust their expectations more rapidly in response to available information (Figure 9.5). The long history of high and volatile inflation in Turkey, an experience of unsuccessful disinflationary programmes and a

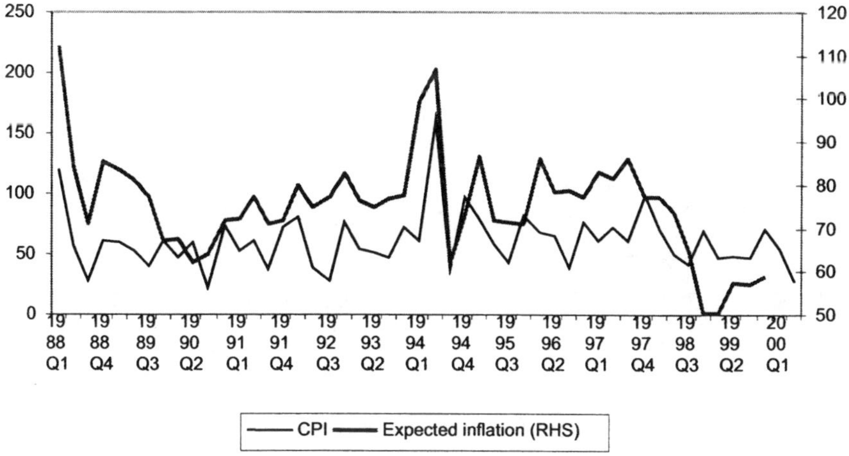

Figure 9.5 Annual CPI inflation and business expectations (quarterly changes).

continuous depreciation of the domestic currency have led agents to form their expectations based on timely data such as changes in interest rates and the exchange rate, as shown in Figure 9.6. Inflationary expectations data derived by the quantification of the business tendency survey exhibit a close relationship to both consumer and wholesale price inflation.[12,13]

Figures 9.5 and 9.6 illustrate the annual CPI inflation and business expectations, and the inflation expectations and references, respectively.

In the case of Turkey, rising real interest rates have become both the cause and the consequence of high-inflation expectations. When there are persistently high and unsustainable levels of public debt, markets become sceptical about the ability of the monetary authorities to pursue a non-inflationary policy. A policy of contraction can worsen the debt dynamics as higher interest rates increase the debt stock and raise the possibility that future debt will be monetised. Because agents anticipate this outcome and incorporate it in their expectations of inflation and interest rates, the disinflationary policy leads to higher real interest rates, slower growth and higher inflation. In the framework of the model, inflationary expectations are assumed to be model-consistent, such that debt sustainability can impact inflation through expectations.

9.4.5 *The monetary and fiscal policy rules*

Monetary policy implementation in the second half of the 1990s can be summarised as having provided stability in financial markets, especially the foreign exchange market. Policy strategy was to control the growth in net domestic assets and create domestic liabilities in return for increases

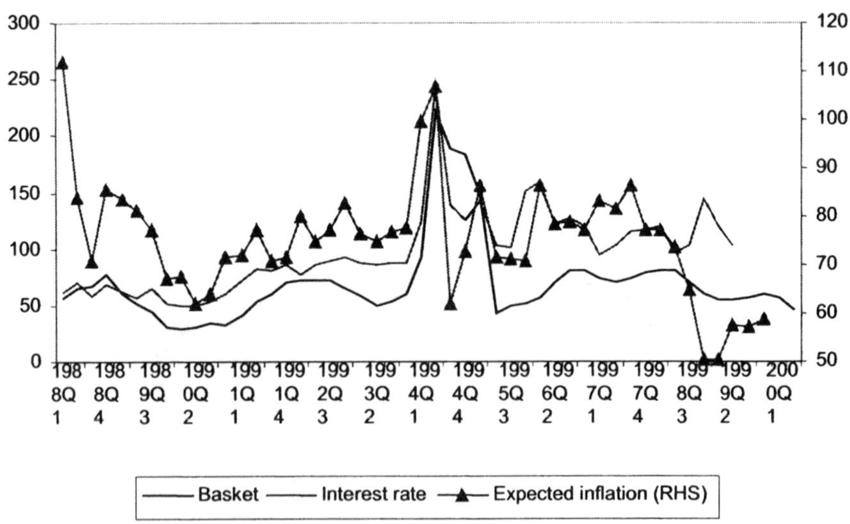

Figure 9.6 Inflation expectations and references (quarterly changes).

in foreign assets. The Central Bank of Turkey announced that it would control the depreciation of the Turkish lira in line with the targeted inflation rate. This policy, aimed at achieving a smooth pattern in the real value of the exchange basket, was named the 'real exchange rate rule', using interventions.[14] The trade-off was the Bank's loss of control over the money supply. The Bank did attempt to control reserve money via the sterilised intervention that offset the liquidity implications of the foreign exchange operations; however, as is common with sterilised interventions, this move had implications for interest rates.

In contrast to this constant real exchange rate policy, and more in keeping with the Central Bank of Turkey's recent shift towards an inflation-targeting regime, the monetary policy rule equation (9.18) makes the real exchange rate change consistent with the divergence of the actual inflation rate from the targeted level and the change in output gap.[15] The feedback parameter is set at $\delta_0 = 0.50$ initially, as suggested by the Taylor rule. Alternative values for the feedback parameter are used to explore the implications of greater or lesser anti-inflation activism. The results of the experiment are reported in section 9.4.

We have captured fiscal policy by a simple rule that returns the primary surplus as a percentage of GDP to its long-run equilibrium gradually. Although more sophisticated rules are more plausible, our intent was only to explore the implications of a fiscal policy rule that is independent of monetary policy. Given that we do not model, for example, productivity shocks, this simple rule seems to serve our purpose.

9.4.6 Uncovered interest rate parity condition

As a departure from the standard small structural monetary policy model, we include the government debt identity in the model and link it to interest rates by modelling a risk premium on Turkish debt that is a function of the expected future domestic debt-to-GDP ratio. Equation (9.14) determines the debt accumulation at time t as a percentage of GDP. Equation (9.15) is the uncovered interest rate parity condition that determines expected real exchange rate depreciation as a function of the domestic and foreign real interest rate differential and a risk premium. The risk premium is linked to domestic currency – denominated debt by equation (9.16). The response of the risk premium to domestic currency debt-to-GDP ratio, ϕ_1, is set at 0.1, and the autoregressive component, ϕ_2, is set to 0.6.

9.5 Simulations

Using baseline parameterisation, we compare and interpret the model's responses to two basic experiments, a fiscal shock and a monetary policy shock. As a third exercise, we compare three alternative experiments of different monetary policy rules.[16]

9.5.1 Experiment 1 – an increase in government spending

The first experiment is of an unanticipated 1 percentage point increase in net government spending: an increase of 1 per cent in the primary deficit-to GDP ratio in quarters five to eight.

The expansion in government spending increases total output at the time of the shock. However, the rise in output quickly reverses; the effect becomes ever more contractionary as real interest rates rise. Real interest rates rise because the 1 per cent increase in the primary deficit is financed through more issuance of domestic debt: the domestic debt-to-GDP ratio rises from its baseline level of 0.30 per cent to 0.35 per cent. That expansion of debt pushes up the risk premium and causes the nominal exchange rate to depreciate. The higher foreign prices in domestic currency terms onto the inflation rate, moving it to above 0.3 per cent on a quarterly basis.

The risk premium is not the only influence on exchange rates. Monetary policy shifts the nominal exchange rate (or, equivalently, interest rates) in response to higher expected inflation. Tighter policy reverberates back onto the secondary deficit, and these higher interest rate payments engender substantial persistence of the total domestic debt. That keeps the risk premium high, putting pressure on the exchange rate to depreciate and setting off further monetary policy reactions. Although all variables return to their initial equilibria quite quickly, the impulse responses reveal that the path towards equilibrium is somewhat bumpy. For example, the real exchange rate appreciates at a level of 0.1 per cent and then depreciates at the same level (Figure 9.7). Also note that the increase in government spending eventually crowds out private-sector spending through its effect on real interest rates.

9.5.2 Experiment 2 – an increase in interest rates

The second experiment is an unanticipated monetary policy shock: a 1 percentage point increase in the nominal interest rate (in annual terms) spread through quarters five to eight. As should be expected, there is also an initial appreciation of the domestic currency of over 3 per cent through UIP. The inflation rate initially declines by almost 1 per cent on a quarterly basis, as the passthrough in Turkey is quick. The increase in nominal interest rates leads immediately to a parallel increase in real interest rates. The higher real interest rates constrain output and lead to a recession, but the response of output to the contractionary monetary policy is relatively short-lived.

However, unlike in a standard model, the increase in the nominal interest rate here leads to an expansion of the domestic debt-to-GDP ratio by increasing the burden of interest rate payments. The secondary balance, the share of interest rate payments in the government deficit, rises as a response to increasing interest rates (Figure 9.8). The domestic debt-to-

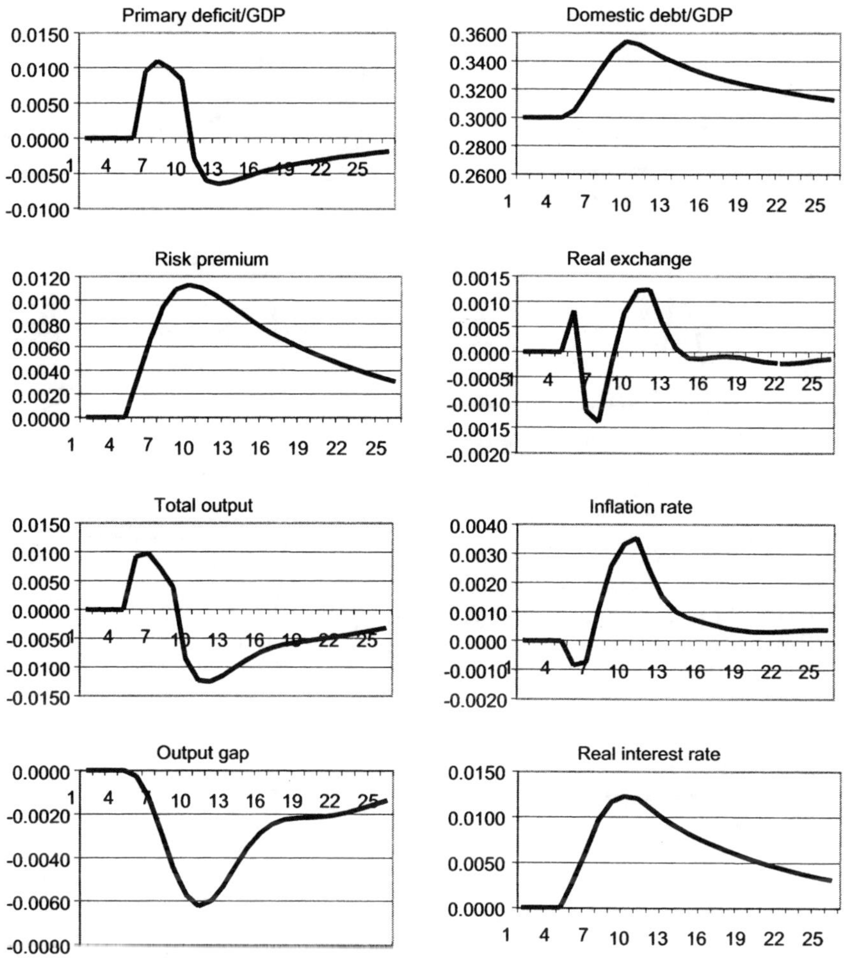

Figure 9.7 Experiment 1 – an increase in government spending.

GDP ratio increases to 0.32 from the baseline level of 0.30. The expanding domestic debt raises the risk premium to almost 0.3 per cent. Monetary policy reacts, raising the real interest rate to a peak of 1.3 per cent.

9.5.3 Experiment 3 – the monetary policy rule

As a third experiment, we compare simulation results under different monetary policy rules by solving with alternative values of the feedback parameter, δ_0, as 0.2, 0.5 and 0.9, respectively.

The fiscal shock analysed in the first experiment was an unanticipated 1 per cent increase in government spending proxied by an increase of 1 per

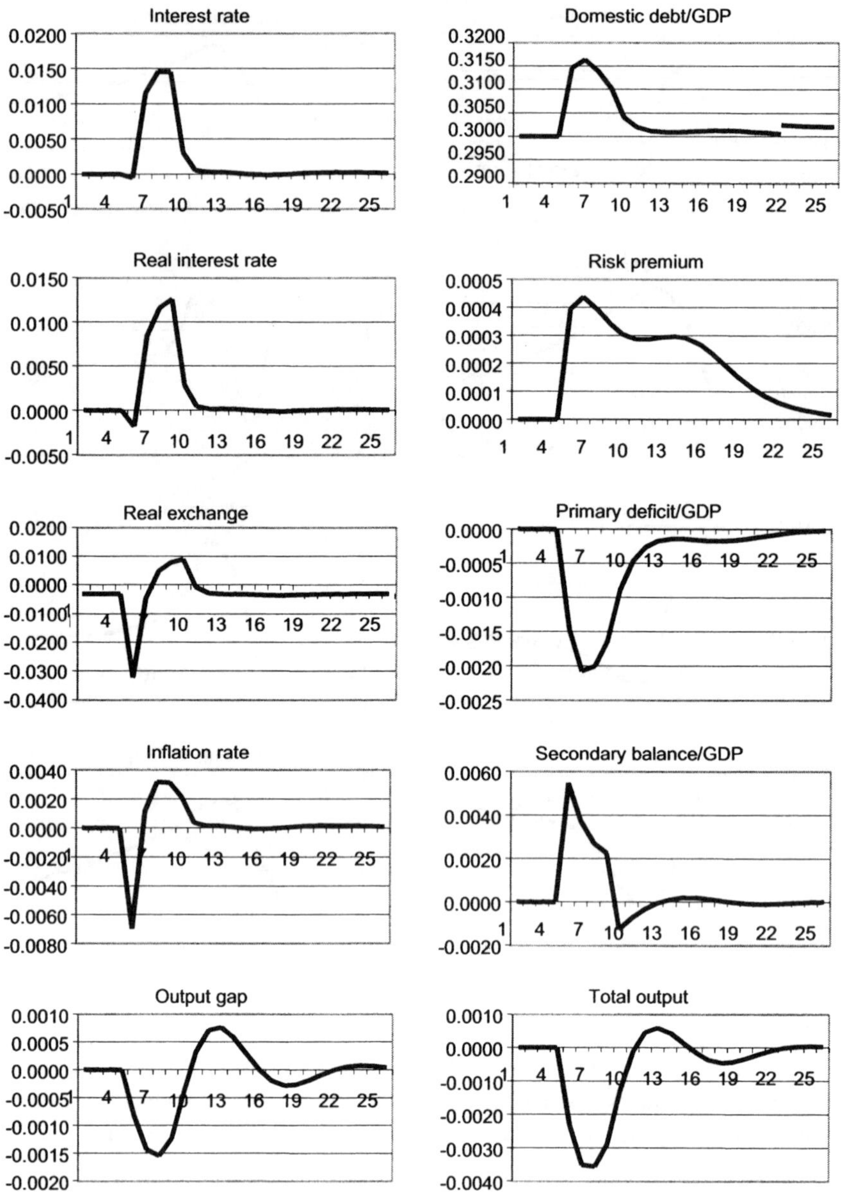

Figure 9.8 Experiment 2 – an increase in interest rates.

cent in primary deficit in quarters five to eight. The simulation results reveal that the stronger the anti-inflationary weight in the central bank's objectives, the more volatile the inflation rate and the exchange rate become. When the monetary authority is most anti-inflationary, $\delta_0 = 0.9$, inflation stabilisation occurs rapidly but at the cost of a very volatile real exchange rate.

These results show that in the absence of co-ordination of monetary and fiscal policies, the monetary authority has to face a trade-off between market stability (measured by real exchange rate volatility) and price stability. Unless fiscal policy and monetary policy are somehow co-ordinated, any contractionary stance by the monetary authority will feed into government debt through an expansion in secondary deficit and will result in higher real interest rates, higher appreciation of domestic currency and more volatile price changes (Figure 9.9).

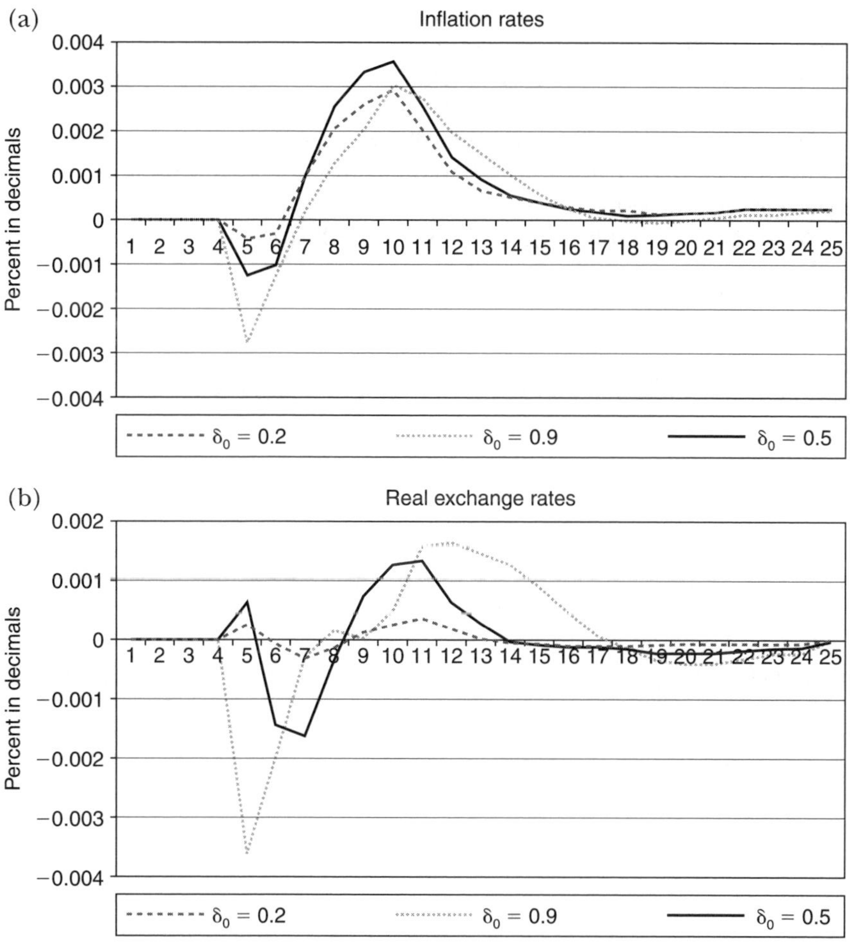

Figure 9.9 Experiment 3 – the monetary policy rule.

9.6 Conclusion

The primary aim of this study was to analyse the basic features of the monetary transmission mechanism in Turkey using a small aggregate macroeconomic model that provides a broad and stylised representation of the whole economy. The estimation results of the core equations of the model suggest that wages and prices are very quick to adjust and inflationary expectations are more important to price-setting behaviour in a highly inflationary environment that in more stable economies such as that of the United Kingdom.

Large and persistent deficits and a heavy reliance on domestic financing are important factors in explaining high real interest rates. High real interest rate levels have become both the cause and the result of high inflation, and have weakened the monetary policy transmission mechanism. In the absence of policy co-ordination between the monetary and fiscal authorities, an anti-inflationary monetary policy will feed into government debt by raising the exchange rate risk premium and increasing debt servicing costs, adding to the volatility of exchange rates.

Simulations using our model highlighted the desirability for monetary or fiscal policy co-ordination in Turkey, although we have not explained how that should best be achieved.

However, our results explain how a long history of high and chronic inflation and large public-sector financing requirements with a fully liberalised exchange rate regime have constrained the Central Bank of Turkey, at times forcing it to maintain market stability and a competitive exchange rate rather than pursuing more orthodox goals such as price stability. The results from this study emphasise the importance of the recent commitment by the Turkish government to achieve primary surpluses in its new disinflation programme.

Appendix

Table 9.2 Estimation results of aggregate demand equation Dependent Variable:y
Equation (3.11). Method: Least Squares
Sample (adjusted): 1987:3 1999:2
Included observations: 48 after adjusting endpoints

Variable	*Coefficient*	*Std error*	*t-Statistic*	*Probability*
C	0.00	0.11	–0.01	1.00
ir	–0.12	0.03	–3.72	0.00
er	0.10	0.03	3.40	0.00
y(–1)	1.37	0.10	13.47	0.00
y(–2)	–0.66	0.10	–6.77	0.00

R-squared	0.89	Mean dependent var.	0.19
Adjusted R-squared	0.89	S.D. dependent var.	2.28
S.E. of regression	0.77	Akaike info. criterion	2.42
Sum squared resid.	25.58	Schwarz criterion	2.61
Log likelihood	–53.01	F-statistic	91.54
Durbin–Watson stat.	2.19	Prob.(F-statistic)	0.00
Breusch–Godfrey serial correlation LM test (one lag included)			
F-statistic	2.14	Probability	0.15
Obs*R-squared	2.33	Probability	0.13
Breusch–Godfrey serial correlation LM test (two lags included)			
F-statistic	1.68	Probability	0.20
Obs*R-squared	3.63	Probability	0.16
Breusch–Godfrey serial correlation LM test (three lags included)			
F-statistic	1.11	Probability	0.36
Obs*R-squared	3.68	Probability	0.30
Breusch–Godfrey serial correlation LM test (four lags included)			
F-statistic	0.95	Probability	0.44
Obs*R-squared	4.27	Probability	0.37
Ramsey RESET test (number of fitted terms = one)			
F-statistic	0.01	Probability	0.91
Log likelihood ratio	0.02	Probability	0.90
Ramsey RESET test (number of fitted terms = two)			
F-statistic	0.52	Probability	0.60
Log likelihood ratio	1.21	Probability	0.55
Ramsey RESET test (number of fitted terms = three)			
F-statistic	0.50	Probability	0.69
Log likelihood ratio	1.75	Probability	0.63
Ramsey RESET test: (number of fitted terms = four)			
F-statistic	1.16	Probability	0.34
Log likelihood ratio	5.38	Probability	0.25
Jarque–Bera	0.60		

Table 9.3 Estimation results of wage–price system System: Wage–price setting Equations (3.12), (3.13) and corrections to inflation expectations.
Estimation Method: Iterative Three-Stage Least Squares
Sample: 1990:1 2000:2
Instruments: LW(–1) LY(–1)–LL(–1) LCPI(–1) LIMP D(LIMP) LY-LL C

	Coefficient	*Std error*	*t-Statistic*	*Probability*
C(1)	–0.91	0.39	–2.32	0.02
C(2)	–0.23	0.08	–2.79	0.01
C(3)	0.21	0.08	2.74	0.01
C(11)	–0.22	0.26	–0.84	0.41
C(12)	–0.20	0.08	–2.40	0.02
C(13)	0.23	0.06	4.14	0.00
C(14)	0.10	0.04	2.30	0.02
C(15)	0.13	0.06	2.15	0.03
C(24)	0.57	0.23	2.47	0.02
C(25)	0.64	0.34	1.89	0.06
C(26)	–0.01	0.03	–0.44	0.66

*Equation: D(LW)=C(1)+C(2)*LW(–1)+C(3)*(LY(–1)–LL(–1)+LCPI(–1))*
Observations: 40

R-squared	0.17	Mean dependent var.	0.15
Adjusted R-squared	0.13	S.D. dependent var.	0.06
S.E. of regression	0.06	Sum squared resid.	0.12
Durbin–Watson stat.	2.18		

*Equation: D(LCPI)=C(11)+C(12)*LCPI(–1)+C(13)*D(LIMP)+C(14)*LIMP (–1+C(15)*(LW(–1)+LL(–1)–LY(–1))+(1–C(24))*EXPINF/(C(25))*
Observations: 40

R-squared	0.55	Mean dependent var.	0.14
Adjusted R-squared	0.47	S.D. dependent var.	0.05
S.E. of regression	0.04	Sum squared resid.	0.04
Durbin–Watson stat.	2.51		

*Equation: EXPINF(+1)=C(26)+C(25)*D(LCPI(+1))+C(24)*EXPINF*
Observations: 39

R-squared	–0.10	Mean dependent var.	0.19
Adjusted R-squared	–0.16	S.D. dependent var.	0.03
S.E. of regression	0.03	Sum squared resid.	0.03
Durbin–Watson stat.	2.31		

Wald test
Null Hypothesis: (1-C(24)/C(25))=1

Chi-square	0.69	Probability	0.41

Acknowledgment

The initial version of this study was prepared for the CCBS/Money and Finance Group conference on Analysing the Transmission Mechanism in Diverse Economies, 4 September 2000. I am indebted to Lavan Mahadeva and Gabriel Sterne, whose advice and support on the design and solution of the model was invaluable. I thank Ernur Demir Abaan, Joseph Djivre,

Prasanna Gai, Pablo García, Glenn Hoggarth and Ahmet Kipici for their helpful comments, Áron Gereben, Javier Gómez, Juan Manuel Julio, Tomasz Łyziak and Bojan Markovic for their cooperation and Richard Hammerman for his excellent research assistance. Any errors, are of course, mine. The views expressed here are those of the author and are not necessarily those of the Central Bank of the Republic of Turkey.

Notes

1 Özatay (1997) analyses the importance of fiscal and monetary policy coordination in achieving price stability in Turkey during the period 1977–95.
2 The public-sector borrowing requirement increased from around 5 per cent in the late 1980s to 13 per cent of GNP in 1999.
3 In 1989, the use of the short-term advance facility by the Treasury was limited to 15 per cent of budgetary expenditure and the practice of using the rediscount facility as a tool of selective credit policy ended. The Central Bank Act was revised in October 1995. Short-term advances to the Treasury were not to exceed 12 per cent of the current budget appropriations, and this rate was specified as 10 per cent and 6 per cent for 1996 and 1997, respectively, and 3 per cent thereafter.
4 In the second half of 1990s, consolidated budget expenditures increased to 36 per cent of GNP from 17 per cent, while revenues increased to 24 per cent from 14 per cent resulting in a widening budget deficit. The share of interest rate payments in GNP rose sharply over the period, and by the end of 1999 interest payments consisted of almost 40 per cent of total consolidated budget expenditures. In line with government financing strategy, interest payments on domestic and foreign borrowing composed 13 per cent and 1 per cent of GNP, respectively.
5 This set of assumptions could be replaced by modelling how an excessive proportion of external debt creates a risk premium above world rates. Issuing foreign currency debt beyond a given proportion of GDP increases the lender's risk of unexpected devaluations leading to default. This increased risk raises the premium on domestic currency rates paid by the borrowers over world interest rates on loans made elsewhere.
6 Batini and Haldane (1999) include a forward-looking term of $E_t y_{t-1}$. A positive and significant term indicates that monetary policy can affect output today by affecting future expectations of output.
7 The output gap measures are based on Yalçin (2000). He derives two output gap measures for Turkey, one based on a production function estimate and the other on an HP filtering method. Both measures yield similar results in the aggregate output equation.
8 Batini and Haldane (1999) set the real interest rate and real exchange rate elasticities to 0.5 and 0.2, respectively.
9 Şahinbeyoğlu and Ulaşan (1999) also show that export demand is price inelastic in Turkey.
10 Following Łyziak (2000a), direct measures of expected inflation appear in the Phillips curve. Taking into account the need to correct long-run bias resulting both from the survey and the quantification method exploited, the series is adjusted in order to impose the condition that long-run actual inflation is equal to expected inflation (see Appendix, Table 9.3).
11 In recent years, public sector wages have been set bi-annually while the minimum wage is set on an annual basis.

12 Kypycy (2000) quantifies the qualitative responses from quarterly tendency surveys of price expectations of Turkish manufacturing industry.

13 In their analysis of leading indicators of inflation in Turkey, Kalkan *et al.* (1998) find evidence of granger causality running from inflation to various interest rates, reflecting the importance of inflation expectations in determining market rates.

14 The exchange rate basket comprises 1 US dollar and 1.5 Deutsche Mark (0.77 euro).

15 In the framework of the model, the real exchange rate is determined by the uncovered interest rate parity (UIP) condition. In order to avoid double specification of the real exchange rate, we insert the UIP identity in the monetary policy rule equation. Due to this notation, nominal interest rate changes are treated as monetary policy shocks.

16 The model is solved using the Winsolve software package and uses Stacked-Newton solution algorithms.

Part 3

Transparency and market expectations

10 Measures of monetary policy transparency and the transmission mechanism

Richhild Moessner, Toni Gravelle and Peter Sinclair

10.1 Introduction

Over the past 10 years, a number of central banks have endeavoured to make their monetary policy actions more transparent to the public. These central banks include the Reserve Bank of New Zealand, the Bank of Canada, the Bank of England and the Swedish Riksbank. In all these, greater transparency efforts were associated with the adoption of inflation targeting as a new policy regime. The Federal Reserve has also improved its communication over the past 10 years (see Blinder *et al.* 2001). The European Central Bank is still too young for meaningful judgements to be made about changes in its communication policies.

Section 10.1 of this chapter starts with summarising the relevance of transparency for the monetary policy transmission mechanism. We then present a measure for quantifying differences in the transparency of monetary policy using financial market and economic data, and discuss the limitations to our approach. Our approach is based on comparing the reactions of short-term market interest rates to both official interest rate decisions and surprises in macroeconomic data releases across countries. We consider market reactions to both domestic and international macroeconomic data releases, since open economies are affected by international economic developments. We also discuss how this approach may be used to help to identify some of the shocks to which financial market participants react. The method and data are described in more detail in sections 10.2 and 10.3. In section 10.4, we first compare market reactions to official interest rate decisions in the United Kingdom before and after the creation of the Monetary Policy Committee (MPC) in 1997, in order to study whether perceptions of transparency have changed with granting the Bank of England operational independence. We then study financial market reactions to official interest rate decisions and economic data surprises in the United Kingdom and the United States. The results for the United Kingdom, the United States and Canada are compared, drawing on the results for Canada presented in Gravelle and Moessner (2001). Finally, Section 10.5 concludes.

There are different definitions of monetary policy transparency. In this chapter, we define monetary policy as being transparent if the public can anticipate the central bank's official interest rate decisions correctly, based on their knowledge of the central bank's monetary policy reaction function. The monetary policy reaction function is conditional on a set of variables, such as macroeconomic news and changes in asset prices. If signalling by the monetary authority of the magnitude of the next interest rate change, for example via speeches, allows market participants to anticipate the next decisions correctly without an understanding of the reasons for these decisions, then we cannot call monetary policy transparent. Our definition of transparency, which is based on the predictability of monetary policy, differs from one based on the institutional arrangements for communicating monetary policy.

Our approach consists in studying the reactions of market interest rates to official interest rate decisions and macroeconomic news, rather than estimating a full structural model for the determinants of changes in market interest rates. Within our simple framework, we omit other variables which are likely to be important for explaining changes in market interest rates, such as the exchange rate, and whose importance is likely to differ across countries. These considerations lead us to conclude that our measure is likely to be better suited for comparing the transparency of monetary policy over time for one particular country, rather than comparing it across countries for a particular time period. However, we did not have a sufficiently long time series of surprises in macroeconomic variables available to allow us to perform such a comparison over time for individual countries. In this chapter, we focus on the responses of short-maturity market interest rates to economic news (including both official interest rate decisions and surprises in macroeconomic data releases), in order to study differences in perceptions of monetary policy transparency across countries. The chapter does not provide an investigation of the effect of monetary policy transparency on credibility, however. Monetary policy is credible if the public believe that the central bank will achieve its professed intended outcome. For inflation targeting regimes, the outcome is the inflation target. In that case, credibility may be measured by the difference between the public's inflation expectations and the inflation target. In order to investigate perceptions of both transparency and credibility, it would be necessary to consider the reactions of long-maturity forward market interest rates to monetary policy decisions (see Haldane and Read 2000), and economic data releases.

10.1.1 Relevance of transparency for the transmission mechanism

The degree of monetary policy transparency has an effect on the monetary policy transmission mechanism, and hence on the monetary policy outcome. This is mainly because transparency can influence the public's expectations, which play an important role in the transmission mechanism of monetary policy. For example, the public's inflation expectations influence the level of real interest rates (which equal the nominal interest rates minus the expected inflation rates), and therefore determine the impact of any specific level of nominal interest rates. Real interest rates matter since investment and savings decisions by rational agents are based on real, rather than nominal, interest rates (see Bank of England 1999b). Inflation expectations also influence price- and wage-setting, and thereby affect actual inflation in later periods.

An overview of the possible benefits and adverse effects of monetary policy transparency is presented in Blinder *et al.* (2001). There, the aim of transparency is stated as providing the public with a clear view of the central bank's objectives, of its methods (including which economic data are selected and how they are interpreted, and which models are used for forecasting), and of its procedures, including the arguments put forward and the degree of uncertainty in decision-making. Weighing the theoretical and empirical case for and against transparency, Blinder *et al.* (2001) come out in its favour.

Transparency may have the following benefits. First, it can make monetary policy more efficient (see Blinder *et al.* 2001, and references therein). Monetary policy is most effective if market participants correctly anticipate it, since the central bank only controls short-term interest rates, but monetary policy also affects the economy via the impact on longer-term interest rates (as well as asset prices and exchange rates). Short- and long-term interest rates are linked via market expectations. The central bank can shape these expectations by communicating its policy in a transparent fashion, and hence make its monetary policy more efficient. By reducing the scope for misinterpretation of its policy actions, these market expectations, which depend in part on expected future monetary policy, may become more stable and predictable (see Blinder 1998; Blinder *et al.* 2001). This may lead to greater stability in financial markets (see Chadha and Nolan 1999; Geraats 2000). However, it may also increase financial market volatility, if markets trade on every piece of information in the policy debate (Chadha and Nolan 2002a).

Second, transparency may make it easier for central banks to build their credibility (see Tarkka and Mayes 1999; Geraats 2000; Blinder *et al.* 2001). This is especially important for young central banks, which have as yet no historic record to draw credibility from, or for central banks with a record of high inflation in the past (see Geraats 2000). By showing the public that they apply a strategy for achieving their monetary policy goal, central banks can alleviate their credibility problems without having to wait for the monetary policy outcome to be established after the lags of monetary policy (see Tarkka and Mayes 1999), which may be of up to around 1 or 2 years' duration, or even longer. This is particularly important if the economy undergoes structural change, making the transmission mechanism more uncertain, for example in the euro area and the Czech Republic (see Tarkka and Mayes 1999). Greater credibility is beneficial since it reduces the inflation bias[1] (Geraats 2000) and the cost and need of disinflationary policies (see Tarkka and Mayes 1999). Transparency is also likely to strengthen the channel of the transmission mechanism affecting the real economy via price- and wage-setting, which partly depends on the private sector's expectations (see Clarida *et al.* 1998; Blinder *et al.* 2001). Some survey evidence for the perceived importance of transparency for establishing credibility is provided by Blinder (2000), who conducted a survey of central bankers and academic economists. In one of his questions, respondents were asked to rank seven factors in order of importance in establishing a central bank's credibility. For both groups, transparency came fourth in this ranking.

Third, transparency may give a central bank greater flexibility to respond to economic shocks, contributing to greater stability of the economy, since the central bank's actions are better understood as responses to shocks, and are less likely to lead to a loss of credibility (Geraats 2000). Also, the cost of policy changes may be reduced with greater transparency. If economic conditions change, requiring a reversal of monetary policy, the public can better understand, and perhaps even anticipate, the policy reversal, which may then take place without a loss of credibility to the central bank (see Blinder *et al.* 2001).

Fourth, greater transparency about the economic data and forecasting models used by the central bank ('economic transparency', a concept which does not include transparency about policy preferences) can reduce the inflation bias of a central bank's monetary policy (see Geraats 2001). Geraats (2001) obtains this result in a theoretical model of monetary policy which assumes a sequence of events where the central bank first sets its monetary policy target, then economic shocks happen, subsequently the central bank sets its monetary policy instrument, and finally the public's inflation expectations are formed. This sequence of events reflects an implicit assumption of the existence of lags in monetary policy. The public has the opportunity to respond to the monetary policy actions by revising their inflation expectations, and thereby the public can affect the monetary policy outcome. Consequently, the central bank needs to incorporate the effect of its policy actions on the public's expectations. Therefore, the response of private-sector expectations forms an integral part of the transmission mechanism within Geraats' model. Geraats finds that economic transparency can eliminate the inflation bias, while precommitment may not be able to. However, Geraats finds that greater transparency about the central bank's policy preferences may worsen the inflation bias. By contrast, previous influential models of monetary policy by Kydland and Prescott (1977), and developed further by Barro and Gordon (1983), found that the inflation bias can only be eliminated if the central bank can precommit to its monetary policy action, and is not allowed discretionary policy. These models assume a sequence of events where the central bank sets its monetary policy instrument only after the public has formed its inflation expectations, and that there are no shocks.

Finally, transparency increases the democratic accountability of monetary policy, since the public have sufficient information to understand the policy regime, to check whether the central bank's actions match the policy regime, and to judge the central bank's performance (see Geraats 2000; Mishkin 2000a; Blinder *et al.* 2001).

A discussion of the main arguments against transparency is given in Blinder *et al.* (2001) (see also Kydland and Prescott 1977; Cukierman and Meltzer 1986; Cukierman 2000). Welfare effects of monetary policy transparency are also discussed in Buiter (1999), Issing (2000), and Morris and Shin (2000).

10.1.2 Measures of monetary policy transparency

This chapter presents a measure of transparency which is based on the extent to which monetary policy is fully anticipated by a subset of the public, namely financial market participants, and is in that particular sense 'transparent'. By studying financial market reactions to economic news, including both official interest rate decisions and economic data releases, we try to quantify how perceptions about the transparency of monetary policy by financial market participants differ across countries. Arguably, financial market participants are a well-informed segment of the public on monetary policy matters, since they commit money to trades in financial instruments, whose pay-offs depend in part on the outcome of monetary policy decisions. Our approach is different from one which measures transparency based on the arrangements for communicating monetary policy, such as the publication of inflation forecasts and of the minutes of monetary policy meetings. It allows for the possibility that the central bank's transparency efforts are not understood or believed by the public. This may happen, for example, if the public finds the communication confusing, or if the central bank is thought to have an incentive for misleading the public, and its policy is not considered to be credible (see Tarkka and Mayes 1999). A central bank with a high score for transparency based on the arrangements for communicating its policy, may therefore have either a high or a low score based on our measure, depending on how far its transparency efforts allow the public to anticipate its actions. Our approach therefore provides information complementary to the former measures. While there has recently been increasing theoretical work on the effects of monetary policy transparency, there has been more limited empirical work on measuring transparency. Recent empirical work on the degree of transparency of different central banks, based on the arrangements for communicating monetary policy, includes a survey of central banks to measure several different characteristics of their monetary policy frameworks, including transparency (see Fry *et al.* 2000). Using results from this survey, Chortareas *et al.* (2002) construct an index of transparency based on the details of central banks' published forecasts. Using this index of transparency, they find that, for inflation and money targeting – but not for exchange-rate targeting – central banks, an increase in the detail that central banks include in their published forecasts is associated with lower average inflation.

Recent empirical work on measuring monetary policy transparency, based on studying financial market reactions to official interest rate decisions, includes Cook and Hahn (1989) for the United States; Dale (1993), Haldane and Read (2000) and Clare and Courtenay (2001) for the United Kingdom; Muller and Zelmer (1999) for Canada; and Hardy (1996) for Germany. Haldane and Read (2000) show that greater monetary policy transparency, i.e. a reduction in the markets' uncertainty about the monetary authority's reaction function, implies that short-maturity market interest rates will react less to monetary policy changes since they are better able to anticipate them. However, by only looking at market reactions to monetary policy decisions, it cannot be distinguished whether a smaller reaction is due to a better understanding of the monetary policy reaction function, or whether it is due to other factors, including the following: signalling of the next policy decision by the central bank, e.g. via speeches, without revealing any information about the monetary policy reaction function; a delayed transmission of interest rate changes along the yield curve; or market imperfections, for example during financial market crises.

If market participants have a better knowledge of the central bank's reaction function, markets should react more fully to news about the state of the economy, in particular macroeconomic data releases, which enter in part into the monetary authority's reaction function. Therefore, markets should react to macroeconomic announcements they view as important to the monetary authority's reaction function and that are unanticipated.

According to the expectation theory of the term structure of interest rates, nominal money market interest rates and government bond yields reflect an average of future official interest rates expected over the periods of the maturities of the interest rate contracts. For spot interest rates the relevant period ranges from the present to the maturity of the contract. For forward interest rates, the relevant period ranges from the date in the future at which the forward interest rate contract starts, to the maturity date of the contract.[2] If the official interest rate is changed unexpectedly by the monetary authority (for example, increased by 100 basis points) and if the official rate is expected to be left unchanged for some time subsequently (for example, for a period of 6 months), spot and forward interest rate contracts maturing up to 6 months ahead should increase by 100 basis points on the day of the official interest rate decision, according to this theory, reflecting the higher level of official interest rates expected over that period. If the official interest rate is expected to be reduced again by 100 basis points to its original level in 6 months' time, then forward interest rates starting more than 6 months ahead should remain unchanged, and spot interest rates with maturities of more than 6 months should rise by less than 100 basis points. If macroeconomic data releases, combined with an understanding of the monetary authority's reaction function, lead market participants to partly anticipate the official interest rate decision, then short-term market interest rates would rise ahead of the date of that decision, for example on the dates of the releases of stronger-than-expected economic data. The official interest rate decision itself would then lead to changes in short-term market interest rates of less than 100 basis points upon its publication, having already been partly anticipated.

It is therefore useful to look also at the reactions of short-term market interest rates to macroeconomic news, and to study the relative explanatory power across countries of macroeconomic news and official interest rate decisions for daily market interest rate changes. In countries where monetary policy is more transparent, short-term market interest rates should react more strongly to macroeconomic news which is considered to be important in the central bank's reaction function, anticipating future interest rate changes. Consequently, macroeconomic news should have greater explanatory power for daily yield changes, relative to monetary policy decisions, than in countries where there is less transparency. Conversely, in countries where monetary policy is less transparent, short-term market interest rates should react more strongly to monetary policy decisions, and less to macroeconomic news, with market participants not being able to anticipate future interest rate changes as well as in countries with greater transparency. For less transparent regimes, monetary policy decisions should therefore have greater explanatory power for daily yield changes, relative to macroeconomic news. In section 10.4.4 we also discuss some limitations to this approach, which are mainly due to the omission of surprises in variables besides official interest rate decisions and macroeconomic data which are likely to be important in explaining changes in market interest rates.

Note that the macroeconomic variables deemed important in the monetary authority's reaction function may change over time, depending in part on the monetary policy regime. For example, if a central bank targets the money supply, rather than inflation, then monetary aggregates are expected to play a relatively greater role (see Campbell and Lewis 1998; Fleming and Remolona 1999).

Official interest rate decisions, and their accompanying statements, may reveal information about changes in the monetary authority's reaction function, for example about a different emphasis placed on various kinds of domestic or international macroeconomic news in the decisions. Market interest rate responses on the days of official interest rate decisions may therefore also reflect an improved understanding of the monetary policy reaction function for the future.

Nominal market interest rates are the sum of real interest rates and inflation expectations, expected over the period of the maturity of the interest rate contracts. For long-maturity spot and forward government bond yields, changes in inflation expectations can have a significant impact on these yields, which may offset the impact of changes in expectations of real interest rates over the period of the contract. As shown in Haldane and Read (2000), if monetary policy is not yet fully credible and acquiring greater credibility, long-maturity forward rates are expected to react with a negative coefficient to changes in official interest rates, since higher short-term real (and hence nominal) interest rates can lead to lower inflation expectations, and therefore lower long-maturity nominal interest rates. Changes in long-maturity yields therefore reflect perceptions of both transparency and credibility, and may in turn provide information on both.

There is a long line of research investigating the reactions of financial asset prices to data releases, including that by Ulrich and Wachtel (1984), Goodhart and Smith (1985), Fleming and Remolona (1997) who provide a review of some of this literature; Fleming and Remolona (1999), who examine US Treasury price movements in reaction to the release of data such as inflation, GDP and employment; and Campbell and Lewis (1998), who examine Australian asset price reactions to US and domestic macroeconomic announcements. Recent work on the reactions of sterling yields to macroeconomic news includes that by Brooke *et al.* (1999) and Joyce and Read (1999), both of which consider daily data, and Clare and Courtenay (2001), who study intra-day data.

10.1.3 Identification of shocks to which financial markets react

As mentioned in the previous section, transparency might give central banks greater flexibility to respond to economic shocks. By studying financial market reactions to macroeconomic news, we can attempt to identify the shocks to which market participants react. Those economic indicators which have the largest and most significant coefficients in the regressions of daily yield changes on economic news can be identified as the most important kinds, for a given frequency of release. By comparing the regression results for yields of different maturities, it is possible to identify at which time horizons different shocks are considered to be most important. In turn, this provides information about which shocks the central bank is perceived to attach most importance to in its reaction function. We consider the impact of surprises in both UK and US economic data releases on financial market interest rates, since monetary policy in open economies is expected to be influenced by international developments. Results for the United Kingdom and the United States are presented in section 10.4.

10.2 Methods

10.2.1 Market reactions to monetary policy decisions

To assess the reaction of sterling market interest rates to official interest rate decisions, we follow the methodology of Haldane and Read (2000) in regressing daily yield changes on changes in official interest rates:

$$\Delta Y_t = \alpha + \Sigma_{j=1}^{J} \beta_j \Delta Y_{t-j} + \gamma \Delta r_t^{off} + \varepsilon_t \qquad (10.1)$$

where ΔY_t are daily money market interest rate or government bond yield changes at close of business on day *t*, Δr_t^{off} are changes in official interest rates, and the sum runs over the number, *J*, of lags of the daily yield changes.

In section 10.4.1, we study the impact of official interest rate decisions on sterling yields of different maturities, to gain insights into the transparency of monetary policy, and we test for the presence of a regime change of market reactions with the introduction of the MPC and the Bank of England's operational independence in monetary policy.

This approach only considers market reactions to *actual* changes in official interest rates, rather than to *surprises* in these interest rate decisions. If markets are efficient, they should only react to the surprise components of the decisions. This approach is different from the approach adopted for reactions to macroeconomic news, where we regress on surprises in data releases (see section 10.2.2). We only consider market reactions on dates when the monetary authority met and decided to change the official interest rate. On days when the monetary authorities met and decided *not* to change interest rates, the actual change is equal to zero, and does not contribute to the regression result. However, market participants may well have expected a non-zero change on such a day, which is expected to lead to a change in market interest rates in efficient markets; this effect would be captured by regressing on the surprise component of the interest rate decision. For a pre-announced schedule of official interest rate decision meetings, as in the case of the UK after the adoption of inflation targeting, no-change observations can usefully be included. However, for countries without a pre-announced schedule of monetary policy meetings, it is not possible to include 'no-change' decisions. It would therefore provide additional insight to study market reactions to the surprise component of interest rate decisions in the United Kingdom. However, we did not have a consistent time series of survey-based market expectations of official interest rate decisions available for the United Kingdom. Kuttner (2001) estimates the impact of monetary policy decisions on market interest rates using data from the federal funds futures market to separate changes in the target federal funds rate into anticipated and unanticipated components. However, it is not possible to use this method here, since there does not exist an analogous futures contract in the United Kingdom.

The coefficients in all the regressions in this chapter are estimated by ordinary least squares (OLS), with the standard errors calculated using a Newey–West adjusted covariance matrix, which yields consistent estimates in the presence of both heteroscedasticity and autocorrelation (Newey and West 1987).

10.2.2 Market reactions to macroeconomic news

To assess the impact of macroeconomic announcements on sterling and dollar market interest rates, we use a time-series event-study methodology following Joyce and Read (1999), and estimate the following model for market interest rates of different maturities:

$$\Delta Y_t = \alpha + \Sigma_{i=1}^{N} \beta_i \, (X_{i,t} - X_{i,t}^e) + \varepsilon_t, \tag{10.2}$$

where the sum runs over the number, N, of macroeconomic announcement variables, ΔY_t is the daily yield change at close of business on day t, and $X_{i,t}$ is the actual macroeconomic announcement, while $X_{i,t}^e$ is the expected value of that announcement. Thus $(X_{i,t} - X_{i,t}^e)$ is the unanticipated component, or surprise of the macroeconomic data release. The surprises of the data releases are normalised by the standard deviation of the surprise over the period considered (January 1995 to September 1999), for better comparability of the coefficients. In this study we examine reactions of sterling and dollar yields to surprises in the release of 10 UK and 11 US macroeconomic indicators. The variable for the surprise, $(X_{i,t} - X_{i,t}^e)$, is set to zero on days when there was no release of indicator i.

If the monetary authority's reaction function is better understood by market participants, we would expect the coefficients β_i to be larger and more significant for those indicators which are perceived as being more important variables in the monetary authority's reaction function, for a given frequency of release, and the set of macroeconomic news variables to have large explanatory power for daily yield changes. However, for macroeconomic indicators released at different frequencies, a comparison of their perceived importance in the reaction function cannot be made in this way, since for example monthly indicators would contain more news than quarterly data. In this study, we consider 18 monthly macroeconomic indicators, and 3 quarterly indicators, as described in Section 10.3.3.

10.2.3 Impact of macroeconomic news and monetary policy decisions

To determine the relative explanatory power across countries for yield changes of macroeconomic news and monetary policy decisions, we also perform an event study of sterling and dollar yield curve responses to both kinds of announcements:

$$\Delta Y_t = \alpha + \Sigma_{i=1}^{N} \beta_i (X_{i,t} - X_{i,t}^{e}) + \gamma \Delta r_t^{off} + \varepsilon_t \quad (10.3)$$

where the sum runs over domestic and/or US macroeconomic surprises, and the official interest rate decisions include domestic and/or US ones. Again, the surprises of the data releases are normalised by the standard deviation of the surprise over the period considered.

The relative explanatory power across countries can be quantified by comparing the adjusted R^2 of the regressions where only macroeconomic news variables are included, with the adjusted R^2 of the regressions where both macroeconomic news variables and official interest rate changes are included.

10.3 Data

10.3.1 Financial assets

We consider the reaction of the following sterling and dollar market interest rates to macroeconomic news announcements and monetary policy decisions: the front two short sterling contracts traded on LIFFE,[3] the front two eurodollar contracts traded on the Chicago Mercantile Exchange, and yields on 2-, 5-, and 10-year benchmark government bonds. Short sterling futures are futures contracts on 3-month sterling Libor interest rates. Similarly, eurodollar futures are futures contracts on 3-month dollar deposit rates. These futures contracts have fixed expiry dates, with the most liquid contracts expiring four times a year, in mid-March, mid-June, mid-September and mid-December.

In this chapter we consider heavily traded interest rate instruments, namely money market interest rate futures, and benchmark government bond yields, which tend to react quickly to economic news. We chose interest rate futures, rather than short-term cash deposit interest rates, since the latter appear more sluggish. This is for example suggested by Granger causality tests, which indicate that daily changes in rates implied by money market futures contracts Granger-cause daily changes in deposit rates, but not vice versa. As mentioned in the introduction, it would be interesting also to consider the reactions of long-maturity forward, rather than spot, interest rates, in order to be able to study differences in both the transparency and the credibility of monetary policy across countries. Within the expectation hypothesis of the term structure of interest rates, forward interest rates are easier to interpret theoretically than spot rates, since they reflect current market expectations of short-term interest rates over a certain period in the future. By contrast, spot interest rates reflect an average of expectations of short-term interest rates between the present and the maturity date of the contract. One disadvantage of the money market futures contracts and benchmark government bond yields used here is that these contracts have fixed expiry dates, so that their maturities vary over time. By contrast, constant-maturity forward and spot interest rates can be derived by estimating government bond yield curves (see, for example, Anderson and Sleath 1999), which are theoretically more attractive to use. However, using long-term forward interest rates, estimated by fitting a yield curve to available government bond prices, has the disadvantage that the interest rates obtained in this way are not directly traded in the market and are therefore likely to exhibit less sensitive reactions to economic news. The estimation of forward interest rates from government bond prices introduces some noise, since the yield curve estimation involves numerical interpolation of government bond prices between the discrete maturities where bonds are available. Also, less liquid government bonds, whose prices may be affected by special factors and be less responsive to economic news, are included in the estimation. Since the financial market reactions to surprises in individual macroeconomic data releases can be rather small for the daily yield changes used here, we opted for those financial market interest rates which are expected to contain the least amount of noise, and thus provide the highest signal-to-noise ratio.

We use close-of-business rather than intra-day financial market data in this study, in part because we would like to capture the effects that are important enough to persist over a whole day, but chiefly since this allows us to carry out comparisons with a wider range of asset prices. Using daily instead of intra-day asset price data might give rise to the problem that other influences on the same day (which may or may not constitute 'news') may offset or reinforce the impact of the news item being studied. However, there is no reason to believe that other news released on the same day should be systematically correlated with the news item being studied, so biases seem unlikely.

10.3.2 Official interest rate decisions

For official interest rate decisions in the United Kingdom, we use the Bank of England's official interest rate as announced by the MPC following their monthly policy meetings. Prior to the establishment of the MPC, we used the Bank's official interest rate announced by the Bank after the meetings between the Chancellor of the Exchequer and the Governor of the Bank of England, rather than the UK commercial banks' base rate as in Haldane and Read (2000). For changes in official interest rate decisions in the US, we use the federal funds target rate changes. The Canadian study uses the Bank of Canada's target overnight rate as the official rate.

10.3.3 Macroeconomic announcements

To assess the response of financial asset prices to macroeconomic announcement surprises, we need a measure of the market's expectation of these variables in question. The expectations are measured using median survey expectations from survey data contained in the Money Market Services (MMS) database for several series of UK and US macroeconomic data releases. The MMS survey expectations are based on telephone surveys of market participants, which are normally conducted about 1–2 weeks before the data releases. Surprises in economic data releases are then measured as the actual data release minus the median survey expectation. Consequently, there exists a lag between the date of the survey expectations and the date of publication of the data. News arriving between the survey and publication date is therefore not included in the survey expectations, whereas it is included in the market interest rates (if markets are efficient). Moreover, if the distribution of respondents' best-guess point-forecasts is asymmetric, the median expectations may be inferior to the mean expectations as a measure of surprise. Also, individuals' distributions may themselves be asymmetric. Our results may therefore be distorted by these effects. In the Appendix to this chapter, we test whether the sterling yield responses to macroeconomic surprises are efficient.

From a large set of economic indicators contained in the MMS database, we use data on actual releases and median survey expectations of the following 10 UK macroeconomic announcements between January 1995 and August 1999:

1. RPIX inflation (year-on-year percentage changes)
2. Average earnings (year-on-year percentage changes of 3-month averages)
3. monthly changes in unemployment (in thousands)
4. Industrial production (month-on-month percentage changes)
5. Retail sales (year-on-year percentage changes)
6. Producer price index (input prices) (year-on-year percentage changes)
7. GDP (National Accounts release, year-on-year percentage changes)
8. Current account balance (in £ bns)
9. Visible trade balance (in £ bns)
10. Public sector borrowing requirement (PSBR) (in £ bns).

All but two of these indicators are released monthly: GDP and the current account balance are released quarterly.

Table 10.1 presents summary statistics for the UK macroeconomic data releases and the median survey expectations from the MMS database. The standard deviations are used to normalise the surprises of the economic data releases in the regressions reported below. The mean surprises are in general small compared with the standard deviation of the surprises.

We also investigate the impact on sterling and dollar market interest rates of the following 11 US macroeconomic announcements contained in the MMS database, between January 1995 and October 1999:

1 Monthly changes in non-farm payrolls (NFP) (in thousands)
2 The National Association of Purchasing Managers' index (NAPM)
3 CPI (month-on-month percentage changes)
4 PPI (month-on-month percentage changes)
5 The unemployment rate (as a percentage of the labour force)
6 Average hourly earnings (month-on-month percentage changes)
7 Industrial production (month-on-month percentage changes)
8 Total trade balance in goods and services (in $ bns)
9 Retail sales (percentage changes of values in $ bns on a month ago)
10 Gross domestic product (final numbers, quarter-on-quarter percentage changes)
11 Housing starts (private residential real estate activity in millions of units).

All the indicators are released monthly, except for the quarterly GDP figures. Summary statistics are presented in Table 10.2. This set of US indicators is also selected by Gravelle and Moessner (2001), and is based in part on the study by Fleming and Remolona (1999) on the impact of US indicators on US fixed-income markets.

Table 10.1 Summary statistics of releases between 2 January 1995 and 31 August 1999 for UK macroeconomic announcements

	Actual		*Median forecast*		*Surprise*	
	Mean	*St. dev.*	*Mean*	*St. dev.*	*Mean*	*St. dev.*
RPIX	2.70	0.45	2.73	0.24	0.02	0.14
Average earnings	4.14	0.59	4.13	0.56	0.01	0.24
Unemployment	–21.84	21.13	–15.13	13.52	–6.72	16.74
Industrial production	0.02	0.60	0.21	0.25	–0.19	0.53
Retail sales	3.02	1.76	3.12	1.54	–0.10	0.85
PPI	–2.11	7.50	–1.91	7.12	–0.20	1.03
GDP	2.68	0.87	2.61	0.88	0.07	0.22
Current Account	–0.26	1.38	–0.81	1.05	0.55	1.27
Visible trade	–1.24	0.60	–1.22	0.50	–0.02	0.26
PSBR	1.34	4.67	1.61	3.92	–0.27	1.43

Table 10.2 Summary statistics of releases between 2 January 1995 and 1 October 1999 for US macroeconomic announcements

	Actual		*Median forecast*		*Surprise*	
	Mean	*St. dev.*	*Mean*	*St. dev.*	*Mean*	*St. dev.*
USNFP	196.73	148.10	191.82	56.18	4.91	127.93
USNAPM	51.72	3.65	51.99	3.33	–0.26	2.07
USCPI	0.20	0.13	0.22	0.09	–0.03	0.10
USPPI	0.09	0.31	0.15	0.17	–0.07	0.23
USUNEMP	5.00	0.52	5.04	0.51	–0.04	0.14
USHRLYE	0.30	0.25	0.28	0.08	0.02	0.23
USINDP	0.27	0.49	0.19	0.35	0.08	0.25
USTRDGS	–11.74	3.82	–11.49	3.27	–0.25	1.68
USRSL	0.27	0.40	0.37	0.31	–0.10	0.30
USGDPF	3.51	1.61	3.50	1.54	0.01	0.27
USHSES	1.50	0.14	1.49	0.12	0.01	0.07

10.4 Yield curve reactions to official interest rate decisions and macroeconomic news

In this section, we first examine sterling yield curve responses to monetary policy decisions, and to domestic macroeconomic news separately. In particular, based on the reactions of market interest rates to official interest rate decisions, we investigate whether the introduction of operational independence for the Bank of England and creation of the Monetary Policy Committee in May 1997 have increased the transparency of monetary policy.[4] We then study the reactions of sterling and dollar yields to both UK and US macroeconomic news, as well as official interest rate decisions in the two countries. We go on to compare the results for the United Kingdom, the United States and Canada (drawing on results for Canada from Gravelle and Moessner 2001), in order to draw out the implications for the differences in the perceptions of monetary policy transparency in the three countries.

10.4.1 Sterling yield curve reactions to official interest rate decisions

Together with the introduction of Bank independence, measures to enhance the transparency of monetary policy were adopted. This subsection aims to quantify whether the monetary authority's reaction function has become better understood by market participants due to the changes in the way monetary policy was conducted and communicated to the public. These measures included the publication of the votes on official interest rates of each MPC member, and the publication of the minutes of the deliberations of the monetary policy committee soon after the meetings (originally the MPC minutes were published 6 weeks after the MPC meetings, and this lag was later shortened to 2 weeks). Also, the inflation target was made explicitly symmetrical in 1997, with the Governor of the Bank of England being required to write an open letter to the Chancellor of the Exchequer if inflation is more than 1 percentage point above or below the target.

The enhanced transparency measures with establishment of the MPC came in addition to the already existing transparency measures introduced after inflation-targeting was adopted in October 1992. These earlier transparency measures included the formal scheduling and publicising of the monthly monetary policy decision-making process (including dates of meetings for setting official interest rates, the publication of the Bank of England's quarterly *Inflation Report*, the publication of press releases at the time of official interest rate changes, and the publication of the minutes of the monthly monetary policy meetings (see King 1994; Haldane and Read 2000).

As shown in Haldane and Read (2000), the introduction of an inflation target in 1992 and the introduction of these transparency measures increased the markets' ability to anticipate changes in monetary policy. In this subsection, we investigate whether the additional transparency measures introduced in 1997 with Bank independence helped to further improve the markets' understanding of the monetary authority's reaction function.

We estimate equation (10.1) separately for the periods pre- and post-Bank of England independence, starting in January 1993, including three lags of the dependent variables, the market interest rates. Results are presented in Tables 10.3 and 10.4. At all maturities, the value of the coefficient γ for changes in the official interest rates fell post-Bank independence. Up to 5 years' maturity, R^2 also fell in the second period. This indicates that official interest rate decisions came as less of a surprise, and had less explanatory power after Bank independence. This is consistent with the view that monetary policy has become more transparent. The

Table 10.3 UK asset price response to domestic interest rate changes pre-BoE independence, January 1993 to May 1997

Asset	γ	*p-value*	*S. E.*	R^2	*Adj.* R^2	*DW.*
Front futures contract	0.359203	*0.0024*	0.117852	0.1018	0.098	1.96
Second futures contract	0.323168	*0.0010*	0.098049	0.0633	0.060	1.97
2-year yield	0.262807	*0.0024*	0.086365	0.0438	0.040	1.99
5-year yield	0.132126	*0.0456*	0.066008	0.0101	0.006	2.02
10-year yield	0.046642	*ns*	0.064381	0.0055	0.002	2.02

Notes
The first number is the coefficient, and the second number is the significance level. Estimated using Newey–West adjusted covariance matrix; ns stands for not significant at the 5% level. Adj. R^2 stands for adjusted R^2, and S.E. for standard error. DW is the Durbin–Watson statistic.

Table 10.4 UK asset price response to domestic interest rate changes post-BoE independence, June 1997 to August 2000

Asset	γ	*p-value*	*S.E.*	R^2	*Adj.* R^2	*DW*
Front futures contract	0.221652	*0.0088*	0.084359	0.0612	0.056	2.00
Second futures contract	0.199292	*0.0403*	0.097024	0.0363	0.031	2.00
2-year yield	0.088771	*ns*	0.062612	0.0099	0.005	2.01
5-year yield	0.006543	*ns*	0.065029	0.0020	–0.003	2.01
10-year yield	–0.079584	*ns*	0.053394	0.0067	0.002	2.01

Notes
The first number is the coefficient, and the second number is the significance level. Estimated using Newey–West adjusted covariance matrix; ns stands for not significant at the 5% level. Adj. R^2 stands for adjusted R^2, and S.E. for standard error. DW is the Durbin–Watson statistic.

coefficients for official interest rate changes fell from about 0.3 in the first period to about 0.2 in the second period for the front two short sterling futures contracts. The coefficients of the 2- and 5-year gilt yields also fell in the second period, and ceased to be significant. Figure 10.1 shows the coefficient of changes in official interest rates, γ, as a function of maturity before and after Bank of England independence, together with 95 per cent confidence intervals (calculated by multiplying the standard errors by a factor of 1.96, i.e. assuming a large sample). As shown in Figure 10.1, the 95 per cent confidence intervals for γ overlap for the two periods, and we can therefore not conclude that the change in the level of the coefficients was significant at the 5 per cent significance level.

The results are consistent with the results of Clare and Courtenay (2001), who found that, while sterling interest rate futures prices reacted more strongly after Bank independence over a short window (5 minutes)

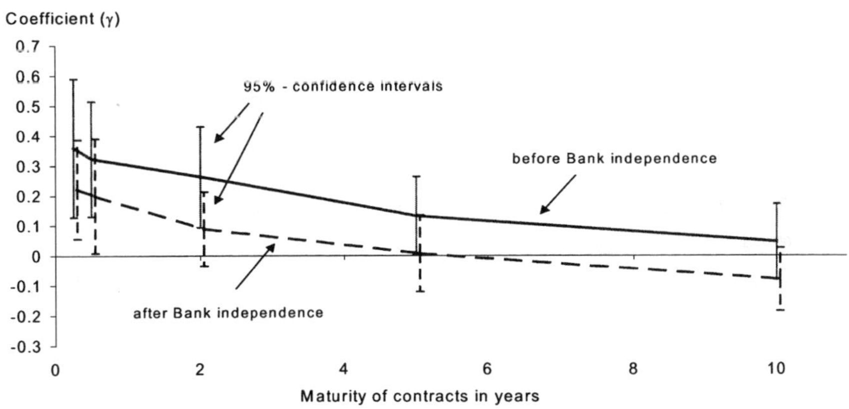

Figure 10.1 Coefficients (γ) of changes in market interest rates to changes in the Bank of England's official interest rate.

around interest rate decisions, the cumulative response over a longer window (1 hour) was smaller than before, i.e. yield curve reactions were dampened.[5]

The coefficients decrease at all maturities post Bank of England independence. This might imply that the credibility as well as the transparency of monetary policy has increased with Bank independence. As Haldane and Read (2000) show, the reaction of the term structure of interest rates may be used to infer information about the market's perception of both the transparency and credibility of monetary policy: a dampened reaction to monetary policy decisions of forward interest rates at short maturities is consistent with an increase in monetary policy transparency, while a dampened reaction to monetary policy decisions of forward rates at long maturities is consistent with an increase in monetary policy credibility. However, we only consider long-term *spot* yields here, so that the interpretation of reactions of long-maturity interest rates in terms of monetary policy credibility is not as straightforward. It would be interesting to repeat this study for long-term forward interest rates, in order to learn more about changes in monetary policy credibility.

We also estimated the long-run relation between changes in the Bank's official rate and changes in market interest rates, for the front short sterling contract. We estimated the long-run relation using a fully modified unrestricted error correction model estimator (see Phillips and Hansen 1990; Inder 1993). This involves regressing the current change in market interest rates on a constant term, the current change in the official rate, and current and lagged differences in changes in the market and official interest rates (we included 10 lags). The long-run relation is then given by the coefficient, θ, for the current change in the market interest rate on the current change in the Bank's official interest rate. The equation was estimated by two-stage least squares, using all the independent variables as instrumental variables, except for the current difference in the change in the market and in the official rate. The results for the periods before and after operational independence of the Bank of England are presented in Table 10.5. We find that the long-run coefficient also decreases with the introduction of operational independence.

10.4.2 Sterling yield curve reactions to surprises in UK macroeconomic indicators

In this section we investigate whether the monetary authority's reaction function is sufficiently transparent to market participants that short-term market interest rates react to surprises in some of the macroeconomic indicators, which might be considered to be important in the monetary policy reaction function, partly anticipating the next official interest rate decision. We regress changes in sterling yields on a constant and the surprise measures of the 10 UK macroeconomic announcements, as

Table 10.5 Long-run response of the front short sterling yield to official interest rate changes before and after BoE independence

Period	θ	*p-value*	*S. E.*	R^2	*Adj. R^2*	*DW.*
Before independence: Jan 1993 to May 1997	0.4224	0.0002	0.1138	0.3365	0.3161	2.01
After independence: Jun 1997 to Aug 2000	0.3529	0.0032	0.1194	–0.0014	–0.0362	2.01
Whole period: Jan 1993 to Aug 2000	0.3948	0.0000	0.0809	0.2382	0.2260	2.00

Notes
The first number is the long-run coefficient, and the second number is the significance level. Estimated using a fully modified unrestricted ECM estimator, including 10 lags. Adj. R^2 stands for adjusted R^2, and S.E. for standard error. DW is the Durbin–Watson statistic.

described in section 10.2.2. The results of estimating equation (10.2) for the five different interest rate contracts over the sample of January 1995 to August 1999 are reported in Table 10.6. We report only the coefficients that are significant at the 5 per cent level, and some regression statistics.

Among the monthly indicators, the shocks to which financial market participants have reacted most can be identified from Table 10.6 as retail and producer price inflation, labour market data (including average earnings and unemployment), industrial production and retail sales. As noted above, the significance of the regression coefficients is not a good measure for the relative importance of macroeconomic data released at different frequencies. Also note that daily changes in market interest rates do not just react to the economic indicators reported in Table 10.6, where results are only reported that are significant at the 5 per cent level – they also react to surprises in other data releases, albeit at significance levels lower than 5 per cent. Also, daily yield changes are likely to be less sensitive to some data surprises than intra-day changes, if other important news is released on the same day. Moreover, the survey expectations for some indicators may be less reliable, and reflect the whole market's expectations to a lesser extent.

The short end of the sterling yield curve is significantly affected (at the 5 per cent level) by a larger number of UK indicators than the long end. The same six indicators affect the front two short sterling contracts (namely RPIX, PPI, average earnings, unemployment, industrial production and retail sales). Four of these indicators significantly affect the 2-year benchmark bond yield. Only two UK indicators, namely PPI and average earnings, affect both the 5- and 10-year benchmark bond yields. Average earnings and PPI affect all five maturities, and they have the highest significance levels at all maturities, with average earnings being the more significant of the two, again at all maturities. RPIX, the inflation index tar-

Table 10.6 UK asset price response to domestic macroeconomic surprises: 2 January 1995–1 October 1999

Asset	*Significant surprises*	*R^2 (Adj. R^2)*	*DW*
Front futures contract	RPIX(0.019472, *0.0390*); PPI(0.017757, *0.0002*); AVE(0.026096, *0.0001*); Unemp(–0.017024, *0.0051*); Indp(0.015235, *0.0228*); Rsale(0.023743, *0.0004*);	0.063 (0.055)	1.97
Second futures contract	RPIX(0.027505, *0.0208*); PPI(0.024659, *0.0011*); AVE(0.035707, *0.0000*); Unemp(–0.018407, *0.0191*); Indp(0.018368, *0.0109*); Rsale(0.027641, *0.0013*);	0.062 (0.054)	1.90
2-year yield	RPIX(0.021136, *0.0445*); PPI(0.018226, *0.0198*); AVE(0.025819, *0.0048*); Rsale (0.021327, *0.0253*);	0.029 (0.021)	1.92
5-year yield	PPI(0.019027, *0.0173*); AVE(0.033025, *0.0000*);	0.034 (0.026)	1.92
10-year yield	PPI(0.017365, *0.0066*); AVE(0.022040, *0.0018*);	0.021 (0.013)	1.99

Notes
First number in parentheses is coefficient, second number in italics represents significance level. Estimated using Newey–West adjusted covariance matrix. Adjusted R^2 (Adj. R^2) are presented in the brackets below the R^2 measures.

geted by the Bank of England, is significant for the front three maturities. The explanatory power of UK macroeconomic news for changes in UK yields decreases with maturity of the interest rate contracts, as measured by R^2, which is 0.06 at the short end and 0.02 at the long end.

In the Appendix to this chapter, we test whether sterling fixed income markets react efficiently to domestic macroeconomic data releases, and find that over the period considered here, sterling fixed income markets tend to react to surprises, rather than to expected values, as measured by MMS survey expectations, of UK macroeconomic data releases.

10.4.3 Sterling and dollar yield curve responses to surprises in US and UK macroeconomic indicators

Small open economies are affected by international economic developments and capital flows. It is therefore relevant to study the possible influence of international economic events on the financial markets of open economies. A study using intra-day asset price data has shown that Australian fixed income markets are significantly affected by US macroeconomic news (Campbell and Lewis 1998). Another study, using daily data, has shown that sterling money market interest rate futures and 10-year UK government bond yields react significantly to surprises in some US macroeconomic indicators (Brooke *et al.* 1999).

It is also interesting to see whether the kinds of US economic indicators, which exert an influence on financial markets internationally (e.g. in the UK), are actually the same indicators that affect the domestic US financial markets, and the financial markets of other open economies. Gravelle and Moessner (2001) present results for the impact of US macroeconomic news on Canadian and US fixed income markets; for comparison, we also present the impact of US indicators on the United States below.

US macroeconomic announcements only

First we consider the impact of the US indicators separately. As shown in Table 10.7, among the 11 US macroeconomic surprises considered in this study, the following indicators affected UK yields significantly (at the 5 per cent level): non-farm payrolls, NAPM, industrial production, retail sales, hourly earnings, GDP and CPI. These results suggest that UK financial market participants consider international economic developments to be important in the MPC's reaction function. The three labour market statistics non-farm payrolls, unemployment and hourly earnings are released at the same time. The US indicators affecting UK yields are a subset of those affecting US yields, except for US GDP, which affects the United Kingdom only (at the 5 per cent level).

The explanatory power of US indicators for UK yield changes, as measured by R^2, increases slightly with the maturity of the interest rate contracts, from about 0.04 at the shortest to about 0.05 at the longest maturity. This is in contrast to US yields, where the explanatory power of US (i.e. domestic) indicators decreases with maturity. As shown in Table 10.6, domestic UK macroeconomic indicators have greater explanatory power at shorter maturities, and there is a greater number of significant ones. This indicates that shorter maturities are dominated to a greater extent by domestic, relative to international, macroeconomic news than longer maturities. NAPM affects UK yields at all maturities, and it has the highest significance levels among the US indicators. This is not surprising, as NAPM tends to be a good predictor of US GDP.

Some of the release dates of UK and US indicators may be overlapping, which can lead to spuriously significant results for some indicators. By regressing on surprises, rather than actual levels, of the indicators, we should be able to disentangle to some extent the reactions to different indicators even if they are released on the same date, if the surprises are orthogonal to each other. However, if the surprises are correlated to some

Table 10.7 Asset price response to US macroeconomic surprises: 2 January 1995–1 October 1999 (Newey–West regressions, skipped observations)

Asset	*Significant surprises, UK*	R^2 *(Adj.* R^2*)*	*Significant surprises, US*	R^2 *(Adj.* R^2*)*
Front futures contract	USNFP(0.020646, *0.0306*); USNAPM(0.023520, *0.0000*); USCPI(0.013597, *0.0326*); USINDP(0.012956, *0.0017*); USGDPF(0.018852, *0.0457*);	0.0381 (0.029)	USNFP(0.043526, *0.0001*); USNAPM(0.019380, *0.0012*); USCPI(0.016148, *0.0054*); USPPI(0.007799, *0.0458*); USINDP(0.018084, *0.0058*); USRSALE(0.023584, *0.0080*)	0.1494 (0.1413)
Second futures contract	USNFP(0.033648, *0.0104*); USNAPM(0.033093, *0.0000*); USCPI(0.019709, *0.0226*); USINDP(0.017133, *0.0030*)	0.0455 (0.036)	na	
2-year yield	USNAPM(0.024095, *0.0005*); USCPI(0.017922, *0.0356*); USINDP(0.015353, *0.0180*)	0.0276 (0.028)	USNFP(0.059271, *0.0001*); USNAPM(0.028961, *0.0000*); USCPI(0.020369, *0.0346*); USINDP(0.015304, *0.0164*); USUNEMP(–0.023452, *0.0279*)	0.1013 (0.0926)

5-year yield	USNAPM(0.032176, *0.0000*); USINDP(0.014603, *0.0027*); USRSALE(0.022125, *0.0118*)	0.0425 (0.033)	USNFP(0.057774, *0.0001*); USNAPM(0.032341, *0.0000*); USUNEMP(–0.018875, *0.0481*); USHRLYE(0.023315, *0.0357*)	0.0958 (0.0870)
10-year yield	USNAPM(0.036805, *0.0000*); USINDP(0.012104, *0.0107*); USGDFF(0.036058, *0.0279*); USRSALE(0.026012, *0.0094*); USHRLYE(0.020715, *0.0444*)	0.0529 (0.044)	USNFP(0.049067, *0.0006*); USNAPM(0.032729, *0.0000*)	0.0840 (0.0751)

Notes
First number in parentheses is coefficient; second numbers in italics represent significance level. Adjusted R^2 (Adj. R^2) are presented in the brackets next to the R^2 measures.

extent, for example because the positions in the business cycles in the two countries are believed to be quite similar, then the market reactions to two data releases cannot be cleanly separated. Therefore, as previously mentioned, by estimating asset reaction with only UK or US macroeconomic surprises a significant coefficient for a UK (or US) indicator may be spurious since the estimation may be biased due to an omitted variable problem.

Combining UK and US surprises

We now turn to examining the sensitivity of sterling and dollar market interest rates when the set of UK and US indicators are combined (in equation (10.2)). To check for the robustness of our results, given the possible occurrence of coinciding release dates, we investigate the yield curve response by regressing on both UK and US announcement surprises at the same time (results are reported in Table 10.8).

Including both UK and US macroeconomic announcement surprises in the regressions alters the results for the significance of the surprise variables on UK yields in the following way. Only in two instances is there a change in the significance of UK indicators for UK yields: RPIX becomes insignificant for the 2-year yield, and global visible trade becomes significant for the 10-year bond yield. No additional US indicator becomes significant for any of the UK yields. In three instances, a US indicator loses its significance: US CPI is no longer significant at the 5 per cent level for the front and second short sterling contracts and the 2-year bond yield; the remaining results are unchanged. This may indicate that excluding UK indicators in regressions on US indicators leads to spurious significance of some US indicators, due to omitting important variables in the regression, leading to a bias in some coefficient estimates. However, US CPI remains significant at the 10 per cent level in the three instances, so that any possible bias when omitting UK indicators is likely to be small.

Among the UK indicators, only the current account has a significant effect on US yields, and only at maturities up to 2 years. We think that this significance is very likely to be spurious. Regressing US yields on UK indicators, which are not expected to be significant for US yields, may provide us with an indication of the amount of noise (or spuriously significant results) present in our method. The only change in the significance of US indicators on US yields is that US retail sales becomes significant for all three bond yields.

The addition of US indicators in the regressions of UK yields demonstrates that US and UK indicators together have explanatory power for UK yield changes above that of UK indicators alone, and it provides a measure for the extent of international influences on financial markets in the UK.

In the presence of both UK and US macroeconomic indicators as explanatory variables, we again find that at short maturities more UK indicators than US ones affect UK yields. whereas at long maturities more US indicators than UK ones affect UK yields (at a 5 per cent significance level). At short maturities, combining UK and US macroeconomic announcement surprises leads to a greater increase in explanatory power (in terms of the adjusted R^2) over the case of considering the impact of US indicators only, than over the case of including UK indicators only. This implies that UK macroeconomic indicators play a greater role in explaining short-term UK market interest rate changes than US indicators.

Together with our previous results that the explanatory power (in terms of adjusted R^2) of UK macroeconomic announcement surprises only on UK yields decreases with maturity, while the explanatory power of US indicators only on UK yields increases with maturity (see Tables 10.6, 10.7), the results of this section suggest that international influences, relative to domestic ones, are larger at long than at short maturities. We also test whether sterling fixed income markets react efficiently to US macroeconomic announcement surprises, rather than to the expected values in these indicators (see Appendix).

10.4.4 Measures of transparency in international comparison

In this section, we estimate equation (10.3) for UK and US yields, including UK and US macroeconomic surprises as well as UK and US monetary policy decisions, in order to quantity the differences across these countries in the importance of macroeconomic news relative to official interest rate decisions for explaining yield curve changes. For the UK, we find that in the presence of UK and US macroeconomic indicators, the coefficient for the domestic interest rate changes are significant for the front two short sterling contracts and the 2-year gilt yield (see Table 10.9). US monetary policy decisions are not significant for UK yields, in contrast to the US macroeconomic indicators. The addition of UK official interest rate decisions increases the explanatory power of the regressions for UK yields at short maturities, but less so at long maturities (as can be seen by comparing the values of the adjusted R^2 in Table 10.9 with those presented in Table 10.6).

For the nearest interest rate futures contract, the coefficient for domestic official interest rate changes in the regressions on both macroeconomic news and official interest rate changes is largest for Canada, followed by the United Kingdom and the United States (the results for Canada are presented in Gravelle and Moessner 2001). These results might suggest differing degrees of the predictability of monetary policy in the three countries. However, these results are based on regressions which omit surprises in other variables that are likely to be important for explaining changes in market interest rates, such as the exchange rate, rather than on a full structural model. The omission of such additional

Table 10.8 Asset price response to UK and US macroeconomic surprises: 2 January 1995 – 1 October 1999

Asset	*Significant surprises, UK*	R^2 *(Adj.* R^2*)*	*Signifiant surprises, US*	R^2 *(Adj.* R^2*)*
Front futures contract	RPIX(0.018146, *0.0480*) PPI(0.017877, *0.0002*) AVE(0.023756, *0.0005*) Unemp(–0.017129, *0.0047*) Indp(0.014612, *0.0251*) Rsale(0.024236, *0.0003*) USNFP(0.020896, *0.0285*) USNAPM(0.023737, *0.0000*) USINDP(0.011091, *0.0093*) USGDPF(0.020360, *0.0218*)	0.098 (0.081)	Curr Acc (–0.021181, *0.0090*) USNFP(0.043629, *0.0001*) USNAPM(0.019900, *0.0011*) USCPI(0.016964, *0.0038*) USPPI(0.008637, *0.0223*) USINDP(0.018106, *0.0059*) USRSALE (0.023464, *0.0081*)	0.165 (0.150)
Second futures contract	RPIX(0.025678, *0.0251*) PPI(0.024841, *0.0011*) AVE(0.032678, *0.0001*) Unemp(–0.018719, *0.0158*) Indp(0.017683, *0.0110*) Rsale(0.027804, *0.0010*) USNFP(0.033952, *0.0096*) USNAPM(0.033584, *0.0000*) USINDP(0.014667, *0.0144*)	0.103 (0.087)	na	

2-year yield	PPI(0.018415, *0.0192*)	0.054 (0.037)	Curr Acc(–0.032943, *0.0469*)	0.111 (0.094)
	AVE(0.022189, *0.0208*)			
	Rsale(0.021315, *0.0261*)			
	USNAPM(0.024890, *0.0005*)		USNFP(0.059390, *0.0001*)	
	USINDP(0.013482, *0.0421*)		USNAPM(0.029838, *0.0000*)	
			USCPI(0.020120, *0.026*)	
			USINDP(0.015020, *0.0166*)	
			USRSALE(0.036300, *0.0013*)	
			USUnemp(–0.023441, *0.0297*)	
5-year yield	PPI(0.019204, *0.0168*)	0.075 (0.058)		0.101 (0.084)
	AVE(0.030052, *0.0001*)			
	USNAPM(0.033374, *0.0000*)		USNFP (0.057923, *0.0001*)	
	USINDP(0.012383, *0.0134*)		USNAPM(0.033009, *0.0000*)	
	USRSALE(0.021468, *0.0171*)		USRSALE(0.042245, *0.0000*)	
			USHRLYE(0.023431, *0.0359*	
10-year yield	PPI (0.017532, *0.0063*)	0.073 (0.057)		0.088 (0.071)
	AVE(0.020381, *0.0037*)			
	Glob Vis Trade (0.020673, *0.0418*)			
	USNAFM(0.038076, *0.0000*)		USNFP(0.049247, *0.0006*)	
	USINDP(0.010577, *0.0258*)		USNAPM(0.033281, *0.0000*)	
	USRSALE(0.025250, *0.0126*)		USRSALE(0.038173, *0.0000*)	
	USGDPF(0.035908, *0.0315*)			
	USHRLYE(0.020679, *0.0457*)			

Notes
First number in parentheses is coefficient; second numbers in italics represent significance level. Adjusted R^2 (Adj. R^2) are presented in the brackets next to the R^2 measures.

Table 10.9 Asset price response when UK and US monetary policy changes are included (in addition to UK and US macroeconomic surprises): 2 January 1995–1 October 1999 (Newey–West regressions, skipped observations)

Asset	*Domestic monetary policy coefficient, UK*	*R^2 (Adj. R^2)*	*Domestic monetary policy coefficient, US*	*R^2 (Adj. R^2)*
Front futures contract	0.255977 (*0.0027*)	0.152 (0.135)	0.175829 (*0.0017*)	0.183 (0.166)
Second futures contract	0.258983 (*0.0054*)	0.136 (0.119)	na	
2-year yield	0.152693 (*0.0208*)	0.065 (0.047)	0.349048 (*0.0012*)	0.136 (0.118)
5-year yield	0.064371 (*ns*)	0.076 (0.058)	0.328685 (*0.0020*)	0.122 (0.104)
10-year yield	–0.030957 (*ns*)	0.074 (0.056)	0.260490 (*0.0033*)	0.102 (0.083)

Notes
Regression coefficient, and significance level (in brackets); ns stands for not significant at the 5%-level. Adjusted R^2 (Adj. R^2) are presented in the brackets next to the R^2 measures.

important variables will lead to biased estimates of the coefficients for official interest rate changes. When the surprises of other relevant variables are included in the regressions, the coefficients for official interest rate changes may be significantly modified, so that it is not easy to compare the results across countries directly. The importance of omitted variables, and the associated bias, is likely to differ across countries. In particular, the importance of the exchange rate is very likely to be larger for open economies such as Canada and the United Kingdom.

For the nearest interest rate futures contract, the additional explanatory power of official interest rate decisions, on top of domestic and US macroeconomic news, is largest for Canada,[6] followed by the United Kingdom and the United States. When adding changes in official interest rates to the regressions on macroeconomic news variables, the adjusted R^2 rises by 0.15 to 0.2 for Canada, by 0.06 to 0.14 for the United Kingdom, and by 0.02 to 0.17 for the United States. The explanatory power of domestic and US macroeconomic news, as measured by the adjusted R^2, is smallest for Canada, and larger for the United Kingdom and the United States. These results might also be thought to indicate differing perceptions of transparency in the three countries. However, we do not estimate a full structural model, and the omission of surprises in other important variables in the regressions will lead to a lower adjusted R^2 than would otherwise be the case. The importance of omitted variables is very likely to differ across countries, leading to differences in their adjusted R^2. In particular, as mentioned above, surprises in the exchange rate and competitiveness are likely to be more important for Canada and the United Kingdom, whose economies are more open, than for the United States. If the surprises in all other important variables were included, the results for the adjusted R^2 due to domestic and US macroeconomic news, and the additional explanatory power of official interest rate changes, might change significantly. It is therefore not easy to compare the results across countries. Moreover, underlying fundamentals, such as equilibrium real interest rates, may differ in variability across countries, which would also lead to differences in the values for the adjusted R^2. It might therefore be more promising to compare these measures of transparency for a single country over time, rather than to compare them across countries.

An understanding of the authorities' monetary policy reaction function by the public may be inherently more difficult to achieve in open economies with inflation targets, whose domestic economic activity is likely to be more strongly influenced by exchange rate fluctuations, than in closed economies with inflation targets, where exchange rate changes have a smaller impact. Since exchange rate movements can be difficult to predict, and are sometimes not directly related to fundamental economic factors, the greater impact of the exchange rate on open economies may impede a better understanding of the monetary policy reaction function of inflation targeting central banks in open economies. Also, the absence of fixed meeting dates, as in the case of Canada over the period studied here (see Gravelle and Moessner 2001), is likely to make it harder for financial market participants correctly to anticipate monetary policy decisions.

10.5 Conclusions

In this chapter we have considered yield curve reactions to monetary policy decisions and macroeconomic news in an international context, and presented a possible measure for quantifying the differences in the transparency of monetary policy across countries, using financial market and economic data. It is interesting to try to measure differences in monetary policy transparency, since transparency can influence the public's expectations, which play an important role in the transmission mechanism of monetary policy, and can thus affect its outcome. For example, greater transparency may make monetary policy more efficient, help to build a monetary authority's credibility, and reduce the inflation bias.

We found that yields of the nearest two short sterling futures contracts and three benchmark gilt yields reacted less strongly to changes in the Bank of England's official interest rate after Bank independence, compared with the previous period. However, the changes in coefficients are not significant at the 5 per cent level at any maturity. This suggests, but doesn't provide statistically significant evidence (partly due to the short sample period after establishment of the MPC), that monetary policy has become more transparent with the granting of independence to the Bank of England. Haldane and Read (2000) found a larger and statistically significant dampening of yield curve surprises to official interest rate changes with the introduction of inflation targeting in 1992 and the accompanying transparency measures (e.g. publication of the *Inflation Report* and a pre-announced schedule of monetary policy meetings). These earlier efforts to achieve greater transparency may have had a first order impact on the market's understanding of the monetary policy reaction function, while the changes introduced in 1997 may only have marginally increased further the understanding of the monetary policy reaction function. It would be interesting to update this study in a couple of years' time once more data are available for the post-Bank independence period.

The dampened reaction to official interest rate decisions in the United Kingdom after 1997 might, however, also have been due to factors other than a better understanding by market participants of the monetary policy reaction function. For example, during the financial market turbulence in the wake of the Russian debt default and collapse of LTCM in 1998, there might have been a delayed transmission of interest rate changes along the yield curve, as market prices were affected to a greater extent by risk premia in a more volatile environment, possibly leading to dampened yield curve reactions to official rate changes.

We described a measure for comparing the degree of monetary policy transparency across countries, based on how transparent monetary policy is perceived to be by financial market participants, rather than on the arrangements for communication by the monetary authorities. Our approach consisted in comparing short-term market interest rate reactions to both official interest rate decisions and surprises in domestic and international macroeconomic data releases across countries. This allowed for the possibility that a monetary authority's communications are perceived as confusing or misleading, and it allowed investigation of which kinds of shocks financial market participants react to. We also discussed some limitations of our approach.

We found that between 1995 and 1999, the coefficient for domestic official interest rate changes, when regressing on both macroeconomic news and official interest rate changes, was largest for Canada, followed by the United Kingdom and the United States, for the nearest interest rate futures contract. Moreover, the additional explanatory power of official interest rate decisions, on top of domestic and US macroeconomic news, was largest for Canada, followed by the United Kingdom and the United States. Thirdly, the explanatory power of domestic and US macroeconomic news, as measured by the adjusted R^2, was smallest for Canada, and larger for the United Kingdom and the United States. These results might be thought to indicate differing perceptions of monetary policy transparency in the three countries. However, as discussed in section 10.4.4, these results are likely to be affected by the omission of surprises in other variables which are likely to be important for explaining changes in market interest rates. The inclusion of such variables might significantly change these results, so that it is difficult to draw conclusions about the perception of monetary policy transparency across the three countries. In particular, surprises in the exchange rate are very likely to be more important for the open economies of Canada and the United Kingdom than for the United States.

It would be interesting to update this study, since financial market participants were very likely still learning about the Monetary Policy Committee's reaction function in the 2 years following its creation in 1997. This would also allow us to study the impact of reductions in official interest rates between scheduled meetings in 2001. Moreover, updating this study may provide a sufficiently long time period for investigating changes in the measures of transparency for individual countries over time.

There are some other caveats to our results. Our approach for comparing monetary policy transparency across countries involves studying market interest rate reactions to surprises in macroeconomic data releases, as measured by the difference between the actual data out-turns and median survey expectations. The results therefore depend on the timeliness and representativeness of the surveys, which may differ between countries, and which may depend in part on the degree of development of a country's financial markets. The results also depend on the speed of the response of market interest rates to news, which may be faster for countries with more developed financial markets, and slower in times of financial market crises. Moreover, we considered the response of daily changes in market interest rates to news, which may give rise to errors due to several news items being released on the same day, whose surprise components may be correlated. It would therefore be interesting to apply a similar approach to the one used here to intra-day financial market data.

We found a significant reaction of UK yields to a number of US macroeconomic indicators, which indicates that international influences are considered to be important in the MPC's monetary policy reaction function. This is as might be expected for an open economy, for which international economic developments are important.

In this chapter we considered heavily traded interest rate contracts, namely money market interest rate futures and benchmark government bond yields, in order to work with market interest rates which respond quickly to news. It would be interesting also to consider the reactions of long-maturity forward, rather than spot, interest rates derived from yield curves estimated from government bond prices, in order to study differences in the perceptions of both the transparency and credibility of monetary policy across countries.

Appendix

Are sterling market reactions to UK macroeconomic data releases efficient?

In the Appendix we investigate whether sterling fixed income markets react efficiently to macroeconomic news. We also perform these tests as a check on the quality of the data on median survey expectations used in this paper, and in order to see whether revisions of past macroeconomic data, which occur at the same time as the release of new data, might have a large impact.

In order to test if yields react efficiently, we estimate the following regression:

$$\Delta Y_t = \alpha + \Sigma_{i=1}^{N} \lambda_i X_{i,t}^{e} + \Sigma_{i=1}^{N} \beta_i \left(X_{i,t} - X_{i,t}^{e}\right) + \varepsilon_t, \tag{10.4}$$

which is the regression in equation (10.1) with the additional inclusion of the median survey expectations of macroeconomic indicators as explanatory variables. If markets are efficient, we should see a significant reaction only to surprises in the data releases, but not to their expected values. Both the actual and expected values of the indicators are normalised by the standard deviation of the surprise over the period considered (2 January 1995 to 1 October 1999), for better comparability of the coefficients.

Table 10.10 shows the results for the coefficients and their significance levels; all coefficients are shown, not just those which are significant at the 5 per cent level. None of the median survey expectations is significant at the 5 per cent level over this period for any of the yields, while the indicator surprises which are significant at 5 per cent are broadly unchanged when adding expected values to the regression: for the front futures yield, the same indicators are significant as in the absence of the expected values in the regressions, as can be seen by comparing with the results in Table 10.5; for the second futures contract, five of the six indicator surprises remain significant at 5 per cent when adding the expected values in the regression (unemployment is no longer significant); for the 2-year gilt yield, three of the four indicator surprises remain significant (PPI drops out); for the 5-year gilt yield, the same two indicator surprises, plus in addition RPIX, are significant at 5 per cent; finally, for the 10-year yield, the same two indicators remain significant when adding expected values in the regression.

We can therefore conclude that over the period considered here, sterling fixed income markets tend to react to surprises, rather than to expected values, as measured by MMS survey expectations, of domestic macroeconomic data releases.

Are sterling market reactions to US macroeconomic data releases efficient?

We also test whether sterling fixed income markets react efficiently to US macroeconomic announcement surprises, rather than to the expected values in these indicators, by estimating equation (10.4) for US macroeconomic indicators. Results are reported in Table 10.11. For the nearest two short sterling futures contracts, the expected values of none of the US indicators are significant at the 5 per cent level. Moreover, the same US indicators are significant at the 5 per cent level when adding the median survey expectations to the regression, as can be seen by comparing with the results reported in Table 10.6 (and the p-value for CPI increases to 0.053, just slightly above the 5 per cent limit).

However, for gilt yields at 2-, 5- and 10-year maturity, the expected values of one US indicator (GDP), two indicators (GDP and retail sales) and three indicators (GDP, retail sales and NAPM), respectively, are significant at the 5 per cent level. Note that GDP is quarterly data, so that the rather small sample size might lead to spurious results, for both median survey expectations and announcement surprises. When comparing with Table 10.6, we can see that, for the gilt yields, the changes when adding median survey expectations in the regression are the following: at 2 years, the surprise in CPI is no longer significant; at 5 years, the surprise

Table 10.10 Reactions of UK yields to expected values and surprises of UK macroeconomic announcements: 2 January 1995–1 October 1999 (Newey–West regressions, skipped observations)

	Front futures yield	*Adj.* R^2: 0.057	*2nd futures yield*	*Adj.* R^2: 0.059
	λ_i	β_i	λ_i	β_i
RPIX	–0.000184 (0.6479)	0.019824* (0.0300)	–0.000222 (0.6463)	0.028043* (0.0137)
AVE	0.000160 (0.7835)	0.026008* (0.0000)	8.40E-05 (0.9097)	0.035486* (0.0000)
Unemp	–0.008204 (0.2680)	–0.014145* (0.0340)	–0.012352 (0.1842)	–0.015387 (0.0737)
Indp	–0.007117 (0.3875)	0.014298* (0.0275)	–0.014105 (0.1624)	0.016718* (0.0181)
Rsale	–0.000395 (0.7835)	0.024190* (0.0008)	–0.001730 (0.3421)	0.027746* (0.0028)
PPI	0.000791 (0.3164)	0.015486* (0.0003)	0.001312 (0.2241)	0.020946* (0.0027)
GDPF	0.002154 (0.1676)	0.001335 (0.9056)	0.003298 (0.0967)	0.004946 (0.7607)
Curr Acc	0.016077 (0.1788)	–0.017860 (0.2235)	0.017331 (0.3534)	–0.029166 (0.1866)
GVTrade	–0.001562 (0.1438)	0.000820 (0.8988)	–0.001995 (0.1787)	0.004264 (0.6410)
PSBR	–0.000719 (0.6474)	–0.002791 (0.6700)	–0.002387 (0.3035)	–0.000430 (0.9649)
	2-year yield	*Adj.* R^2: 0.023	*5-year yield*	*Adj.* R^2: 0.027
RPIX	–0.000116 (0.8111)	0.021540* (0.0327)	–0.000280 (0.5209)	0.022346* (0.0418)
AVE	–0.000284 (0.7175)	0.025815* (0.0039)	–0.000150 (0.8515)	0.032918* (0.0000)
Unemp	–0.006147 (0.5428)	–0.011634 (0.1895)	–0.012861 (0.1866)	–0.008263 (0.3242)
Indp	–0.007170 (0.5477)	0.007163 (0.2956)	–0.008727 (0.4798)	0.002293 (0.7145)
Rsale	–0.002785 (0.1341)	0.020168* (0.0365)	–0.002097 (0.2450)	0.014870 (0.1382)
PPI	0.002390 (0.0611)	0.012445 (0.1493)	0.001092 (0.3262)	0.016146* (0.0445)
GDPF	0.000445 (0.8728)	0.003646 (0.8626)	0.002756 (0.1266)	0.008857 (0.5620)
Curr Acc	0.038745 (0.3898)	0.024264 (0.6742)	–0.007027 (0.7818)	–0.034846 (0.1941)
GVTrade	–0.001626 (0.2544)	0.010447 (0.2717)	–0.001025 (0.5047)	0.018691 (0.0917)
PSBR	–0.001355 (0.6084)	0.003241 (0.7543)	–0.001354 (0.5969)	0.005662 (0.5666)

	10-year yield	*Adj. R^2*: 0.014
RPIX	–0.000466 (0.2532)	0.013190 (0.1470)
AVE	0.000124 (0.8359)	0.021699* (0.0006)
Unemp	–0.012570 (0.1683)	0.002778 (0.7048)
Indp	–0.002178 (0.8725)	0.001019 (0.8637)
Rsale	–0.001149 (0.5267)	0.006492 (0.5295)
PPI	0.001362 (0.2143)	0.014123* (0.0301)
GDPF	0.002196 (0.2195)	0.013446 (0.3585)
Curr Acc	–0.011517 (0.6370)	–0.034047 (0.1754)
GVTrade	–0.000512 (0.7564)	0.019927 (0.0761)
PSBR	–0.002578 (0.2678)	0.010230 (0.2284)

Notes

First number is coefficient, second is significance level.; Adj. R^2 stands for adjusted R^2.

* denotes significance at 5% level.

Table 10.11 Reactions of UK yields to expected values and surprises of US macroeconomic announcements: 2 January 1995–1 October 1999 (Newey–West regressions, skipped observation)

	Front futures yield	*Adj. R^2*: 0.027	*2nd futures yield*	*Adj. R^2*: 0.035
	λ_i	β_i	λ_i	β_i
NFP	0.013377 (0.3716)	0.019155* (0.0398)	0.018833 (0.3515)	0.031793* (0.0134)
NAPM	–0.000214 (0.2561)	0.022536* (0.0000)	–0.000129 (0.6483)	0.031520* (0.0000)
Indp	–0.000725 (0.8321)	0.012711* (0.0158)	–0.000805 (0.8704)	0.017100* (0.0193)
Rsale	–0.001773 (0.7018)	0.007441 (0.4652)	–0.003216 (0.5749)	0.010522 (0.3733)
GDP	–0.000715 (0.2567)	0.020288* (0.0487)	–0.001193 (0.1759)	0.020345 (0.1981)
CPI	–0.000253 (0.9398)	0.013477 (0.0529)	–0.001317 (0.7607)	0.018790 (0.0526)
PPI	0.008813 (0.2352)	0.004666 (0.3517)	0.010920 (0.2604)	0.006984 (0.2957)
Unemp	–0.000592 (0.4387)	–0.007669 (0.4029)	–0.001323 (0.1955)	–0.003914 (0.7305)
Hrlye	–0.007635 (0.7169)	0.000938 (0.8887)	0.003417 (0.8959)	0.003462 (0.7192)
Trdgs	–0.000179 (0.8019)	–0.003813 (0.3901)	0.000335 (0.7366)	–0.008905 (0.2094)
Hses	0.000346 (0.2186)	–0.002614 (0.6493)	0.000364 (0.3291)	0.001425 (0.8434)
	2-year yield	*Adj. R^2*: 0.016	*5-year yield*	*Adj. R^2*: 0.041
NFP	0.013576 (0.4759)	0.010894 (0.4534)	–0.009167 (0.6886)	0.026457 (0.0746)
NAPM	–0.000184 (0.5324)	0.023732* (0.0006)	–0.000478 (0.1530)	0.030738* (0.0000)
Indp	–0.000527 (0.9262)	0.015607* (0.0467)	–0.002066 (0.6830)	0.015366* (0.0032)
Rsale	–0.008629 (0.0765)	0.011921 (0.1426)	–0.011660* (0.0153)	0.017939* (0.0329)
GDP	–0.001706* (0.0107)	0.025778 (0.0601)	–0.003262* (0.0262)	0.045790* (0.0452)
CPI	–0.000220 (0.9589)	0.016350 (0.0858)	0.001180 (0.7993)	0.017316 (0.0997)
PPI	0.009342 (0.3451)	0.009897 (0.1537)	0.009690 (0.3312)	0.004691 (0.5343)
Unemp	–0.000141 (0.8925)	–0.004096 (0.6385)	0.000191 (0.8623)	0.002102 (0.8143)
Hrlye	–0.016588 (0.4827)	–0.005489 (0.6531)	–0.005755 (0.8195)	0.010517 (0.3124)
Trdgs	0.000502 (0.6396)	–0.013037 (0.1139)	0.001665 (0.0953)	–0.006301 (0.3836)
Hses	3.32E-05 (0.9316)	0.002963 (0.6927)	4.54E-05 (0.9083)	–0.000430 (0.9556)

	10-year yield	*Adj. R^2*: 0.055
NFP	–0.011436 (0.6015)	0.027716* (0.0473)
NAPM	–0.000647* (0.0418)	0.035180* (0.0000)
Indp	–0.000239 (0.9580)	0.012111* (0.0097)
Rsale	–0.013946* (0.0061)	0.020456* (0.0278)
GDP	–0.003164* (0.0040)	0.042318* (0.0028)
CPI	0.000677 (0.8841)	0.010286 (0.3313)
PPI	0.008967 (0.3950)	0.002922 (0.6835)
Unemp	0.000550 (0.5957)	0.005110 (0.5395)
Hrlye	–0.006126 (0.7758)	0.018558 (0.0538)
Trdgs	0.002020* (0.0443)	–0.006615 (0.3540)
Hses	–9.69E-05 (0.7758)	0.005249 (0.4125)

Notes
First number is coefficient, second is significance level.; Adj. R^2 stands for adjusted R^2.
* denotes significance at 5%-level.

in GDP becomes significant; and at 10 years, NFP becomes significant (and the p-value for hourly earnings surprises rises slightly above 0.05 to 0.054).

We therefore find that the nearest money market futures contracts react efficiently to UK and US macroeconomic data releases. Gilt yields seem to react more efficiently to UK than to US macroeconomic data releases, over the period of January 1995 to October 1999 considered here, since none of the median survey expectations of UK indicators is significant at the 5 per cent level, while some of those for US indicators are.

Acknowledgment

The views expressed are those of the authors and do not necessarily reflect those of the Bank of Canada or the Bank of England. We would like to thank Bill Allen, Peter Andrews, Charlie Bean, Andrew Clare, Roger Clews, Charles Goodhart, Andy Haldane, Neal Hatch, Lavan Mahadeva, Vicky Read, Clifford Smout, Gabriel Sterne, and participants of the CCBS conference on Financial Market Monitoring and Market Reaction to Economic Events on 27 November 2000 for useful discussions and helpful comments. We would also like to thank Dan Huynh for excellent research assistance.

Notes

1 The inflation bias is an incentive on the part of the monetary authority to create surprise inflation, in order to achieve higher output.

2 In practice, the prices of market interest rate contracts also include risk premia, for example due to credit and liquidity risk.

3 The front contract is defined as the contract with the nearest expiry date, except for the months where contracts expire; on the first day of these months, we already switch to the contract with the next-but-one expiry date. The second front contract is defined in a similar way.

4 The sample period for the data on market expectations of macroeconomic indicators used in this study is around 3 years shorter than that for official interest rate decisions. We therefore studied market reactions separately in the two periods before and after Bank independence in 1997 only for the reactions to official interest rate decisions, but not to macroeconomic data surprises. If a longer sample of macroeconomic survey expectations had been available, it would also have been interesting to study whether market reactions to macroeconomic surprises have changed with the creation of the MPC.

5 Note that Clare and Courtenay consider all MPC decisions since Bank independence, but only those monetary policy meetings before where a decision to change the Bank's official rate was made, while we only consider those meetings where a decision for a change in the Bank's official rate was made both before and after May 1997.

6 For Canada, the additional explanatory power of official interest rate decisions is largest, even though we only added the domestic official interest rate decisions, not the domestic and US ones as for the UK.

Part 4

Monetary policymakers' perspectives

11 Central Bank Governors' Symposium, 2001, Bank of England discussant's comments

Governor of the Bank of Barbados

Marion Williams

First I would like to congratulate the authors on this interesting study. Given the short time that I have I would then like to offer a few insights as to how the transmission mechanism operates in an emerging market in countries such as Barbados. My first point is that in our environment, monetary policymakers may have to keep their eye on more than one intermediate objective. The ultimate goal is economic and financial stability, but central banks may have to take a more active role in creating a stable environment for the development of sound financial markets as well as in stabilising short-run movements in inflation. For example, the Bank of Barbados mission statement explains that we are charged with promoting monetary stability; promoting a sound financial structure; fostering development of the money and capital markets; and channelling commercial bank credit into productive activities and fostering credit and exchange conditions conducive to the orderly and sustained economic development of Barbados.

The point is that in small open emerging market economies such as ours, multiple objectives may need to be pursued in order for us to direct the economy towards the most favourable paths for the development of growth and inflation. Of course the priority placed on each objective can shift from time to time depending on the circumstance in which the economy finds itself. Take the balance between inflation and exchange rate stability. If there is a difficulty with inflation as public sector wages rise out of control; then inflation becomes the most important priority. If exchange rate stability is severely threatened then it may become the more important factor. Generally speaking, most developing countries have to juggle these objectives simultaneously.

I also wanted to comment on the question raised in Mahadeva and Sinclair's paper[1] of whether the IMF monetary model approach, in its traditional form, is still relevant as a monetary policy model for developing countries. I would say that this framework is not as relevant as it used to be for several reasons. First the financial system has become more liberalised as the banking system is being integrated with consumers and producers, both through direct lending and through financial intermediaries such as insurance companies, pension funds and so on.

In addition there seems to be a misperception that transmission of monetary policy is principally a domestic affair. That seems to me to be out of date: the transmission mechanism now has a crucial global dimension. For example, domestic residents have access to foreign currency accounts overseas and can interact with global equity markets. In our discussions, when we refer to changes in asset prices we no longer refer to only domestic prices.

So I do believe that there needs to be some modification to the traditional approach to reflect these changes. And already many countries are thinking of adapting their approach to modelling their transmission mechanism, not necessarily because they are explicitly rejecting the former IMF model, but because in practical terms they recognise that the type of banking system which had been emphasised in this set-up is no longer as relevant as it has been in the past.

Note

1 See Chapters 1–5 of this volume.

12 Central Bank Governor's Symposium, 2001, Bank of England discussant's comments

Governor of the Bank of Canada

David Dodge

It is a special honour to be here today to make these comments as I am very much a new boy, having come to the bank only 4 months ago. While I used to teach money and banking and international finance, for the last two decades I have been at Treasury or working on microeconomic issues so I still come at the issues being discussed today very much still as an outsider. And in that regard, I found the paper extremely useful.

I was also struck by the tremendous degree of uncertainty that remains with respect to the monetary transmission mechanism and hence the much greater difficulty that we have as central bankers in dealing with the transmission mechanism than I had in Treasury in dealing with the impact of fiscal policy. This uncertainty is all the greater when one must deal with the challenges of very large flows of trade and capital movements.

What I shall do briefly is to make a few short comments on the paper before us[1] and then turn to the role of uncertainty in the transmission mechanism.

The model of the monetary transmission mechanism described in the paper by Mahadeva and Sinclair conforms quite closely to the views of the Bank of Canada, as described in a number of our publications. Their paper, quite correctly, emphasizes the importance of trying to understand the transmission mechanism and the complexity of the task. Our Quarterly Projection Model operationalizes many of the concepts discussed by Mahadeva and Sinclair, and is used extensively at the Bank of Canada for policy advice and forecasting. Many of you may be familiar with this model, and I'm certain that many of the central banks represented here have similar models designed to describe their economies.

One potential element of the transmission mechanism that was downplayed in the Mahadeva–Sinclair paper was the role of financial variables such as money and credit. Finding a role for money and credit can be difficult, although many of the stories we tell are based on these variables. Much work has already been done to try to understand the relationship between money and output or inflation. The theoretical links are well established, but the empirical relationships are often weak and unstable. We need to push our knowledge of the money and credit channels of policy further in order to determine just exactly how important they are for the transmission mechanism. Central bank policy is also often evaluated based on observed growth rates of money and credit, so we need to be prepared to respond to these commentaries. Work on the credit channel of monetary policy is receiving increasing attention in the literature. Many of our economies have experienced credit crunches in the past during which financial institutions became quite unwilling to make loans to certain sectors of the economy. These events may be episodic in nature, but they need to be understood so that policy can properly respond if, and when, they do occur.

There have even been those who have argued that the United States and Canada might have been moving into a credit crunch earlier this year. When we observe the weak credit growth we have had in 2001, we need something to help us understand whether it is caused by supply-side or demand-side effects. Only a fully articulated model of the transmission mechanism that includes supply and demand decisions about credit can do that. This is not easy. And this will always remain to some extent a judgement call.

Now let me turn to another key problem: the role of uncertainty. Uncertainty in our models – whether it be represented by simple confidence bands around our forecasts or something more complex – makes policy more difficult. Under uncertainty, it becomes harder in the first instance to interpret or understand what is actually happening in the economy and then to determine what the impact of a policy action would be. Uncertainty affects the lives and decisions of households and firms by raising risk premiums, reducing consumption and investment, and creating inefficient allocations of investment. All this is because it becomes more difficult to anticipate the future. Much work has been done on the conduct of monetary policy under uncertainty, but more is needed to enhance our understanding of how central banks should operate when in such circumstances.

I would like to take a moment to discuss how we conduct policy at the Bank of Canada and how we deal with uncertainty. When designing the framework within which policy is formulated, it is important to build in features that help to reduce uncertainty for households, for firms, and, ultimately, for ourselves as central bankers. Our most important tool for achieving this is our official inflation-control agreement with the government, which was just renewed a few weeks ago. We have extended our target range of 1–3 percent for another 5 years, to give Canadians greater assurance that the low inflation experienced in the 1990s will continue. We have had inflation-control targets bands in place now for just over a decade, and they have proven to be effective in anchoring inflation expectations. We must have an understandable anchor. The narrowing spread between survey measures of inflation expectations and our announced targets is evidence of improved central bank credibility and reduced

ORDER NUMBER

PO NYAATP08

BOOK NUMBER

9763678

BAY NUMBER

2063-8

AUTHOR	Mahadeva, L (ed)
TITLE	How Monetary Policy Works (Central Bank Governor's Symposium) (Volume 4)

uncertainty in the economy. Low stable and predictable inflation is our mantra. After 10 years, the expectation of 2 percent inflation has become well anchored. Even as energy prices are pushing inflation well above target, as yet we can see no evidence that expectations have shifted.

The question which faces us internally is how to go about dealing in uncertainty about future in an open economy with a floating exchange rate. The Bank of Canada recently adopted a new process based on eight fixed announcement dates each year for decisions on changes in our key policy instrument, the target for the overnight rate.

There are four key inputs into the decision process leading up to these action dates.

First, we produce a base case projection using QPM, our main quarterly projection model. A number of risk scenarios are also typically included in the projection exercise. These scenarios make alternative assumptions about possible movements of key exogenous variables (such as US interest rates or output, world oil prices). The purpose is to help us assess risks to the base case projection. Second, projections and current information are gleaned from monetary, credit, and financial variables. Third, information is derived from talking to CEOs and CFOs, which includes a survey of business intentions and sentiment and a GDP projection based on these interviews and other regional information. Fourth, we incorporate financial markets' information at home and abroad on credit conditions.

Our internal uncertainty is reduced but not eliminated by this process of comparing the evidence from each of these sources. So key to dealing with market and public uncertainty is communication to markets, to the public and to government, in particular the Department of Finance.

The communication strategy of the Bank of Canada is designed to be open and transparent so as further to reduce the uncertainty faced by the public. We publish regular reports to share our view on the functioning of the economy, on the current state of the economy, and on our projection of the path for inflation as it moves back to the target midpoint. We also keep the Department of Finance well briefed about our thinking.

In sum, I applaud the efforts of Mahadeva, Sinclair, and the other authors who contributed to this work. I urge them and others to continue with this valuable work, to help us expand our knowledge of the transmission mechanism, and thus reduce the degree of uncertainty we face.

Note

1 See Chapters 1–5 of this volume.

13 Central Bank Governors' Symposium, 2001, Bank of England discussant's comments

Governor of the Bank of India

Bimal Jalan

One advantage of being the fifth speaker and the third discussant is that I don't have to add very much to what has been already said. I don't have much to add by way of either theory or policy to what Mahadeva and Sinclair[1] have told us. They have been entirely fair and reasonable in taking stock of the current state of knowledge on this subject, outlining the present consensus on what a central bank should do and what it cannot or should not try to achieve. In the area of policy, I am particularly impressed by two of their observations:

First, despite all the theory and all the straightforward monetary management rules, the real world is very different. (This point was also emphasised by Governor Dodge.) This is because, as they say:

- the past is imperfectly reported;
- the future is unknowable;
- and key relationships linking economic variables rarely stand still.

If we don't know what is actually happening today (the recent substantial revision of GDP numbers for the last quarter in US is a good reminder), and if we don't know what is likely to happen next quarter – how do we decide on small monetary policy changes of a quarter per cent or half-a-per cent in short-term rates when these changes are going to be transmitted and affect output/inflation 12 to 18 months from now? The chances of being right in certain situations are as strong as those of being wrong. The lesson here is not that we should, therefore, shut up shop – but that expectations from the central bank have to be modest and we have to work at it to make it so. Central banks have to be prepared to change course fast if the earlier decision happens to be wrong.

A second important policy point highlighted by Sinclair and Mahadeva, with which I also fully agree is that:

- Different monetary strategies will work best in different environments – there is no universally successful technique for monetary policymaking. This is an interesting observation because of the current penchant for universal monetary rules, universally valid institutional structures, and universal financial standards and codes.

The Mahadeva–Sinclair paper has many more insights, but I won't go into all of them. But these two findings – imperfect knowledge and the importance of local conditions in monetary policymaking – are, to me, extremely significant.

So much on what they said. Let me make three additional points for whatever they are worth – as an observer of Indian monetary policy developments, and as a participant in monetary policymaking in an emerging or developing economy:

As I watch the process of policymaking in several countries and regions, with global impact, I cannot help feeling that – despite much greater transparency in sharing information and the process of decision-making in central banks – there is some dissonance between what we say we do, and what we *actually* do. Ask any prominent central banker today and he or she is likely to tell the public that:

- he or she is not worried about exchange rates unless it affects inflation;
- he or she is not worried about growth, but only about inflation – growth or employment is not a central bank's job;
- and he or she is not worried about asset prices unless it affects inflation.

Yet let us look at the monetary policymaking in the last few years, and ask ourselves: how many of monetary policy changes have been because of concern only about potential inflation and how many have been in response to other concerns – e.g. growth or exchange rate? I am sure that we will find that most central banks, though not all, have responded to these other concerns at one time or another, even though the underlying inflation rate was satisfactory.

This is because ultimately, governments and central banks have to respond to the primary concern of the people, and the principal economic problem facing their countries during particular periods of time. When growth is good, productivity and wages are rising in step, external conditions are favourable and inflation is low – there is obviously no problem or conflict, and everyone involved in policymaking can concentrate on the objective of keeping things going as they are. Central banks can do what they know best – inflation control; government can keep fiscal deficit under control; and businesses can go about doing their business in expanding markets.

But what happens when things are not so good, or there is a conflict between the goal of preventing inflation from going up in future, say, 18 months later, by half a percentage point over a low target of 2 or 2.5 per cent, and a sharp downturn in industry here and now? This is when the real problem arises – partly because of transmission lags in the effect of monetary policy and uncertain projections about future outcomes.

So my first point is that we can, in the interest of greater transparency and greater credibility, say: yes, in normal times, our primary concern is potential inflation. But we keep the broader picture in view – and if there is a problem in respect of growth/exchange rate, and the inflationary situation is benign, where monetary policy can play a role, we will take action.

My second point relates to the relations between central bank and government. A conventional wisdom now, with which I agree 100 per cent, is that central bank should have *instrumental independence*, and it is best if the powers, responsibility and accountability of a central bank are enshrined in the stature. This is good and desirable as far as it goes. But I also believe that, in a democracy, a central bank can do its job much better if there is a convergence of views between the government and central bank on what is the most important problem of the day and what should be done about it. This is not, of course, to put in doubt whether, in a particular phase of the domestic business cycle or international economy, monetary policy can play a role in meeting the country's objectives in terms of stabilisation of markets, unemployment or exchange rate. My main message here is that it is useful for credibility – especially during difficult periods – if there is confidence that central bank and government are talking to each other, and not talking or acting at cross-purposes.

I would like to make a third and final point on monetary policymaking in an emerging market context. The two points that I mentioned just now – the need to take into account more than one objective (particularly to sustain growth and to maintain orderly conditions in foreign exchange markets), and need for harmonious relationship with government – are even more important in emerging market economies. Given the importance of rural population, high poverty, dependence on agriculture, etc., people expect more from government and other public authorities, including central banks. At the same time, a large part of the economy is non-monetised, which makes the transmission channels and mechanisms of monetary policy less amenable to small changes.

Emerging financial markets, except a few, are typically thin, where expectations and a few large intermediaries can exert a disproportionate influence in determining financial market prices. Expectations are also more volatile – the monetary literature has highlighted the importance of so-called 'volatility premium' in emerging market economies. In addition, they also suffer from 'financial fragility' – where unexpected development or contagion can have a very large impact on financial stability.

The reality of the emerging market situation makes it important first, to build safety nets (e.g. high foreign exchange reserves); to second, to avoid risk-taking in financial markets; third, to be aware of the need for quick response and flexibility in case of unexpected developments; fourth, to support the gradual development of financial markets along sound links; and above all, to pursue a sound fiscal and macroeconomic policy for sustained high growth with stability.

Note

1 See Chapters 1–5 of this volume.

14 Volatility of foreign financial flows and the monetary transmission mechanism

Evidence from Slovenia

Velimir Bole

14.1 Introduction

In transitional economies, shallow intermediation of loanable funds and sizeable foreign financial flows increase the volatility of exchange and interest rate dynamics as well as money and credit growth. However, while the influence of openness, unsettled institutional structure and foreign financial flows on the monetary transmission mechanism is not in question, it is far from clear how these factors propagate and amplify (or reduce) the effects of standard channels of the monetary policy transmission mechanism.

As transitional economies are small and open, the exchange rate and forex market interventions have a crucial role in the monetary transmission mechanisms. The standard exchange rate channel works through its effect on net exports, by changing the price competitiveness of domestic goods, as well as through effects on net flows of foreign capital, by changing the attractiveness of financial instruments offered by domestic banks.[1] In transitional economies, an exchange rate channel may be significantly influenced by the transition economy's peculiarities, since the openness and incomplete institutional set-up constrain interventions in the exchange rate and forex market aiming at the harmful consequences of volatile foreign financial flows.

Volatile foreign financial flows can also activate a credit channel of the monetary policy transmission mechanism in an open, small economy. Volatile foreign financial flows intensify the volatility of bank's and other agents' liquidity, especially if financial (bank) intermediation fragility is enhanced by its shallowness.[2] Such volatility in banks' liquidity also causes swings in the supply of intermediate credits and, therefore, in the availability of loanable funds for different segments of economic agents. Corresponding swings in the external finance premium could differ from borrower to borrower (see, for example, Bernanke and Gertler 1995). Availability of loanable funds is therefore not only time-dependent, but could also differ significantly among segments of agents; some of them could be even subject to credit rationing.[3]

The bank-lending channel effects could therefore be propagated and modified by the standard exchange-rate channel effects in open transition economies facing an unsettled financial structure and volatile foreign financial flows.[4] Other interventions (apart from the exchange rate) of monetary policy designed to neutralize and contain major swings in forex flows could similarly propagate and modify the bank-lending channel effects, by changing the size and volatility of foreign financial flows.[5]

The sections below present empirical evidence to corroborate specific characteristics of the credit channel of the monetary policy transmission mechanism. Rationing of bank credits to some segments of borrowers is the main characteristic studied, so that key analysed factors of the transmission mechanism could be classified under 'bank lending view' factors.[6] The interplay of standard exchange-rate (and other forex interventions) channel effects and credit channel effects is also documented. Empirical evidence is presented for Slovenia, in the period of transition.

The structure of the rest of the chapter is as follows. The second section presents evidence on the volatility of foreign exchange flows, and a focal episode of analysis is determined. Elements of the bank-lending channel are documented in the section 14.3. Primary as well as more formal evidence is presented, to show that credit rationing is taking place for some segments of borrowers in the focal episode. In section 14.4, the mechanism of credit rationing is analysed. Vanishing foreign exchange flows activate an interplay between exchange rate and bank-lending channel effects; section 14.5 chapter is devoted to this interplay of effects. Section 14.6 summarizes the findings.

14.2 Foreign financial flows and the focal episode

14.2.1 Forex flows volatility

Between 1992 and 1999, the volatility of foreign exchange flows was mainly caused by swings in capital flows, since the current account deviated considerably from zero only at the very beginning and end of the period.

Figure 14.1 shows net capital flows and the current-account balance expressed in percentages of GDP.[7] The volume and the structure of the foreign exchange inflows were highly volatile. Long-term swings as well as short-term fluctuations were present. In some quarters, changes amounted to around 10 per cent of (quarterly) GDP.

Many of the factors causing changes in capital flows could be classified among the 'push factors' which are exogenous to monetary policy.[8] Current-account dynamics were determined more by monetary policy; the only important exceptions were the deterioration in the balance of services after 1997, and the drop in the balance of trade in 1999.[9]

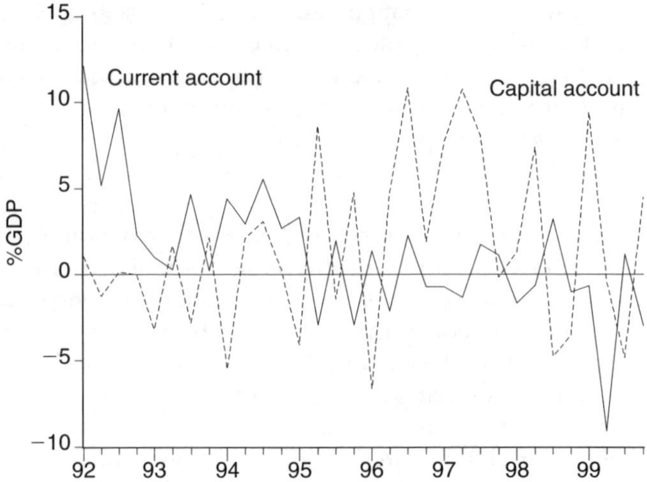

Figure 14.1 Balance of payments (source: Monthly Bulletin BS; own calculations).

14.2.2 Monetization on the retail forex market

Monetization on the retail forex market may be defined by net foreign exchange bought by the banking sector (including central and commercial banks) from the non-banking sector.[10] In comparison with components of the balance of payments, monetization on the retail forex market enables additional insights into the monetary policy transmission mechanism effects of foreign financial flows. There are at least three reasons why those additional insights are especially valuable in studying the effects of credit and exchange-rate channels of the monetary policy transmission mechanism.

First, currency substitution remains substantial in Slovenia.[11] Timing and size of changes in some components of capital inflow (e.g. capital inflow through the household sector[12]) therefore only weakly correspond to the changes in 'atolar parts' of the bank balance sheets. Besides, there is significant difference between the timing of changes in the balance of payments items and corresponding forex flows. The size and dynamics of (net) monetization (as a cash flow concept) have a more direct impact on the bank credit supply than components of the balance of payments, as they directly affect the 'tolar' part of bank balance sheets.

Second, because of the managed floating exchange rate regime and significant currency substitution, the exchange rate was explicitly driven by monetization on the retail forex market and not by pure changes in the balance of payments items, in the studied period. Only net monetization directly reflected the balance between demand and supply on the retail forex market (see, for example, Bole 1997).

Third, the importance of monetization (in comparison with balance of payments items) is also corroborated by the very timing of the launch of new instruments for containing and neutralizing foreign financial inflows.[13] Indeed, all these instruments were launched in periods when monetization on the retail forex market attained peak values (see Bank of Slovenia Annual Reports, and Bole 1999a). Thus, monetization on the retail forex market could actually figure in the (revealed preference) reaction function of the monetary authority. In Figure 14.2, monetization on the retail forex market is given in percentages of quarterly GDP. Dates of launching new instruments for containing and neutralising foreign financial inflows are marked by a star.

In Figure 14.2, the dynamics of monetization illustrate, even more clearly than components of the balance of payments, that the studied period (1992–99) covers three major swings in net forex flows. Swings in net monetization on the retail foreign exchange market were considerable. In all three periods of low monetization, net forex bought from the non-banking sector dropped to zero, or even reached negative values. In other periods, net monetization on the retail foreign exchange market was much higher, in 1992 and 1994 average values exceeded almost 10 per cent, and in 1997 5 percent of broad money.

The drop in monetization at the beginning of the downward phase of swings in monetization was also very fast. In all three swings, a considerable

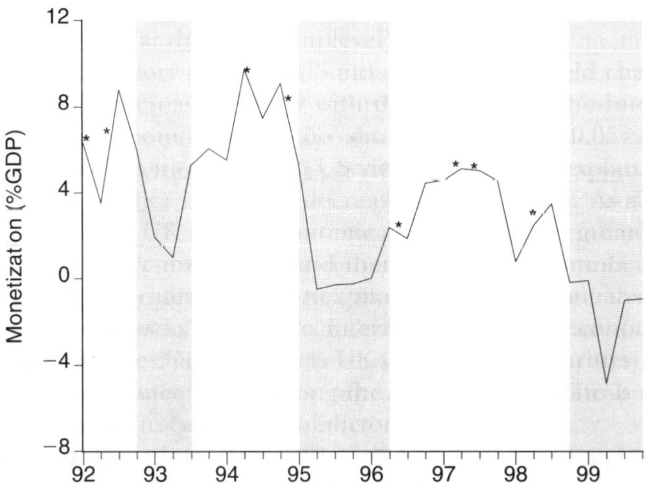

Figure 14.2 Monetization on the retail forex market (source: Monthly Bulletin BS; own calculations).

Note
* Launching of new measure (instrument).

drop in monetization of more than 4.5 per cent of quarterly GDP took place in a period not longer than one quarter.

14.2.3 The low monetization phase as focal episode

The very volatility in the external variables[14] uncovered the studied characteristics of the credit channel of the monetary policy transmission mechanism. Thus focal episode of the analysis has to be determined by phases in swings of the foreign financial flows.

In Slovenia, the bulk of foreign capital inflow to the private sector went through foreign bank credits, so large drops of net foreign financial inflow would have to coincide with the cutting of credit supply from abroad and (*all things equal*) also with an increase in demand for credits from other (domestic) sources.

Falling monetization caused domestic bank credits to rocket. The increase in demand for credit from domestic sources, triggered by the cutting of credit supply from abroad, was accompanied by the increase in domestic bank credit supply driven by an increase in non-borrowed reserves of banks. Falling monetization squeezed money and, because of the unchanged base money supply, also increased bank liquidity.[15] The corresponding acceleration of domestic bank credits was so strong that credit growth even endangered the soundness of the banking system (see Bole 1999b for summary of the mechanism). Taking into account the familiar argument that 'tightening of monetary policy may have a strong effect on the real sector when credit is already tight but a weak effect when credit is initially plentiful' (see Blinder 1987), periods of sizeable and rapidly falling monetization could be appropriate for studying the monetary policy transmission mechanism. In the first stage of low monetization periods, when sources of foreign credit were drying up, policy intervention in the supply of (bank) credit would have to have a much greater effect than in other phases of forex flows. The behaviour of financial variables crucial for bank credit markets therefore has to be studied in periods of low monetization.[16]

To define a focal episode, first the periods of 'high monetization' have to be identified. Such periods encompass, heuristically speaking, those periods in which the Central Bank explicitly increases (through additional measures[17]) efforts to mitigate the adverse effects of high net forex inflows (of huge monetization on the retail forex market).

The term 'low monetization phase' indicates periods in which monetization on a retail forex market fell considerably (in comparison with the nearest 'intervention' periods) or even became negative. More formally, the 'low monetization phase' is defined by periods between two consecutive troughs in cycles of monetization; that is by periods in which monetization was smaller than half the difference between the nearest 'intervention' peak monetization and the nearest low point of the corresponding monetization cycle.[18] In Figure 14.2, periods of the low monetization phase are shadowed. According to the definition, the low monetization phase encompasses the periods 1992/Q4–1993/Q4, 1995/Q1–1996/Q2 and 1998/Q4. The defined low monetization phase is the focal episode for the present analysis of a monetary transmission mechanism.

14.3 Bank credit rationing-evidence

14.3.1 Bank lending channel-descriptive analysis

A key element of the credit channel is the external finance premium (the difference between the cost of external funds and funds generated internally). According to the way monetary policy affects an external finance premium, two variants of a credit channel are distinguished: the balance sheet view and bank lending view (see Bernanke and Gertler 1995). In the case of the bank lending view, an external finance premium reflects asymmetries on the credit markets, and therefore potential adverse selection contamination of the credit market. Equilibrium on such a market usually involves restrictions (and not price adjustment) on the size of credits, known as credit rationing (see, for example, Stiglitz and Weiss 1981).

As already summarized, a drop in forex net inflows accelerated bank credit growth. As banks were unable to manage either credit risks or increased maturity mismatch, when credit supply considerably accelerated, a significant drop in foreign financial flows also endangered the soundness of the banking system in Slovenia (see, for example, Bole 1999b).

The effects of volatile foreign financial flows were not confined to the banking sector. The rapid increase in bank credits in the low monetization phase not only jeopardized banking soundness but also reduced(!) the liquidity of the business sector. Increased domestic bank credit supply replaced the falling loanable funds inflow from abroad, but the increased volume of bank credits was not channelled uniformly across banking clients. Differences in the external finance premium among segments of economic agents increased considerably, so that some segments were actually rationed out of the bank credit market. The divergence in liquidity between different sectors increased considerably.

The scale of rationing is illustrated in Figure 14.3. Two graphs are given: the first presents net monetization on the retail forex market (in percentages of GDP), and the second the business sector share in the change in total net bank credits.[19]

The second graph illustrates that in the later stage of all three periods of a low monetization phase, growth of bank credits to the business sector fell considerably behind the growth of overall banking credits. In the high monetization phase, increments in bank credits to the business sector

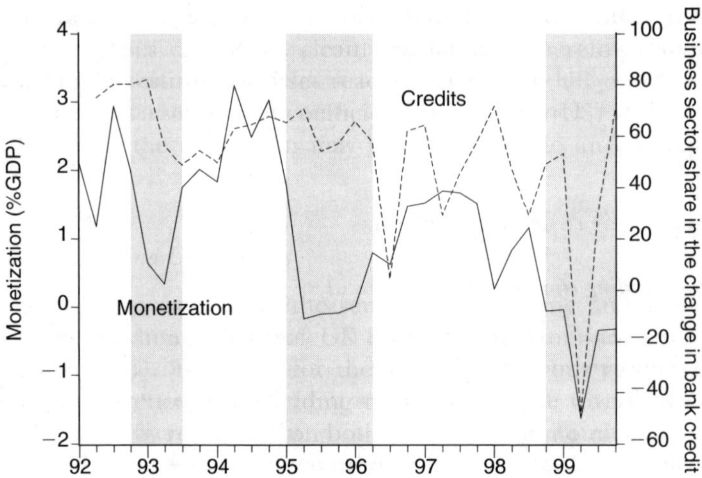

Figure 14.3 Monetization and increment in credits to the business sector (source: Monthly Bulletin BS; own calculations).

(non-financial corporations) attained more than 60 per cent of total bank credit increments. In the low monetization phase, increments in bank credits to the business sector fell to around 50 per cent of increments in total bank credits in 1993, to almost zero (nominal stagnation of domestic bank credits to the business sector) in 1996, and even to negative values (nominal shrinking of credits to the business sector) in 1999. Explanation of illustrated rationing is given in the following section.

14.3.2 Liquidity of the business sector

To ascertain that the fall in the business sector share in the bank credit change actually affected the real performance of the economy, it is necessary to document that this fall was not caused by changes in the credit demand structure and (or) that it was not offset by accessing alternative domestic sources of credit.

Being rationed out from the bank credit market in the low monetization phase, the business sector could have offset the relative fall in bank credits only by accessing alternative domestic sources of credit. Indeed, as illustrated in Figure 14.1, swings in the current account balance have been considerably smaller and less systematic than swings in monetization, so alternative credit sources only of domestic (and not foreign) provenance could be important. However, the supply of alternative domestic credit instruments was limited mainly to trade credit, while the possibility of using other capital market instruments was almost negligible. Trade credit, however, could not alleviate the drop in funding of a whole business sector.

If the business sector was not able completely to offset the corresponding (relative) squeeze in loanable funds in the low monetization phase, rationing of the credit supply to the business sector must have serious real effects.[20] To illustrate such effects, and therefore to document that enterprises were not able to gain additional access to other (non-bank) credit, Figure 14.4 presents the assessed liquidity position of enterprises and broad money (in percentages of GDP). Data on the assessed liquidity position of enterprises are from regular quarterly surveys made by the Chamber of Commerce (survey data on liquidity position are available from the middle of 1993). Survey data on assessed liquidity position are calculated using Munich IFO Institute methodology.[21]

According to the judgement of management, the liquidity position of enterprises was seriously affected in the periods of a low monetization phase. The deterioration was greatest in 1999, when in net terms more than 40 per cent of enterprises assessed their liquidity position as 'bad'. In 1995, assessed liquidity of the business sector was also affected, in net terms, for at least 10 per cent of enterprises. The graph of broad money illustrates that there was no aggregate deterioration in liquidity in the periods of a low monetization phase.

14.3.3 Statistical evidence

The following two statistical experiments document the statistical significance of the low monetization phase effects on business sector credits.

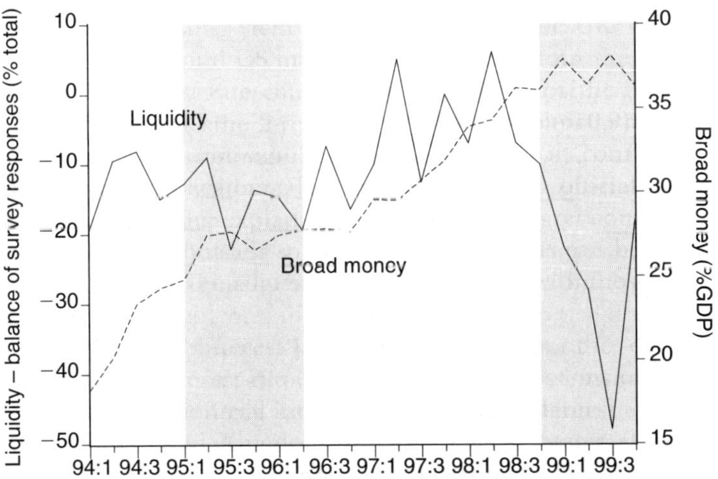

Figure 14.4 Liquidity* of the business sector and broad money (source: Monthly Bulletin BS; 'Business Expectations of Enterprises', Chamber of Commerce; own calculations).

Note
* Balance of survey responses on assessed liquidity (IFO methodology).

First, univariate autoregression of domestic bank credit increments is estimated, using a dummy for the low monetization phase periods as an exogenous variable. An autoregression is estimated for the following dependent variables: increment in credits to the business sector (per unit of GDP), increment in credits to other (non-business) sectors (per unit of GDP) and increment in credits to the business sector (per unit of total bank credit increment). In the estimated equations, the order of autoregression is 3, while the exogenous dummy is distributed over three lags using the linear Almon weighting polynomial. All equations are estimated using quarterly data for the period 1992/Q1–1999/Q4. Variables used in estimation are checked for unit root; in all cases ADF statistics were significant at 5 per cent statistical significance.[22] Key statistics of estimated autoregression are presented in Table 14.1 (see Appendix to this chapter). The statistical significance of estimated equations as well as *t*-statistics of the sum of coefficients at distributed lags of a low monetization phase dummy are given.

The autoregression of business sector share in the bank credit change confirms the significance of the low monetization phase effects; the equation and negative sum of coefficients at lags for the low monetization dummy are significant at a 0.05 level of significance. The equation for change in the bank credits to the business sector is significant at 0.05 and the sum of the low monetization dummy is negative, but not significant. The equation for change in bank credits to other (non-business) segments is not significant, the sum of coefficients at lags of the low monetization dummy is positive and not significant.

The cycling of increments in credits to the business sector (per unit of total credit increments) could result from cyclical movements of the economy, independent of foreign financial flows. Such movements of the economy could change the structure of credit demand and therefore also effective bank credit supply. To examine the significance of the low monetization phase effects, when controlling for variables of standard business cycling, we also estimate a simple VAR model (of order one) encompassing such business cycling. Three endogenous variables are used in the model: (relative) increment in credits to the business sector; GDP growth rate; and wage bill (per unit of GDP).[23] A dummy for a low monetization phase is used as an exogenous variable. Because the ADF test denies unit root presence for all mentioned variables, a standard VAR model is estimated. Parameters of the model are given in Table 14.2. (see Appendix)

In Figure 14.5, a twelve-quarters response to the impulse of a low monetization period is illustrated for the increment in credits to the business sector (in percentages of total bank credits increment). The simulated impulse of the low monetization period is six quarters long.[24] Although parsimonious criteria (Schwartz) as well as the short time series (32 quarters) used in the analysis are in favour of the lowest possible order of the

VAR model, an impulse response function is given for VAR of orders one and two.[25] In Figure 14.5, a one standard deviation error band is added in each case.

The simulated impulse of the low monetization period significantly cut the business sector share in the bank credit change. Peak values of decline, of over one standard deviation, are attained one quarter after the impulse of the low monetization period disappears. Just two quarters after the low monetization impulse starts, a relative increment in credits to the business sector drops by more than half of its standard deviation. The responses of relative credit increments are essentially the same for both VAR models.

14.4 Bank credit rationing-mechanism

14.4.1 The role of information capital and collateral – hypothetical explanation

As documented, in the low monetization phase, considerable acceleration of bank credit growth was triggered by vanishing foreign financial flows. In banks, acceleration of credit growth caused not only maturity mismatch but also a deterioration of claims quality. The strong acceleration of credit growth increased the agency problem considerably, especially in smaller banks (see Bole 1999b). Facing the fast-growing number and volume of credits, smaller banks had no capacities to keep the quality of screening and monitoring unchanged.

So, despite the high minimum capital requirement for a full bank licence and strong average capital adequacy,[26] the quality of collateral became a much more important condition for keeping the pace of credit

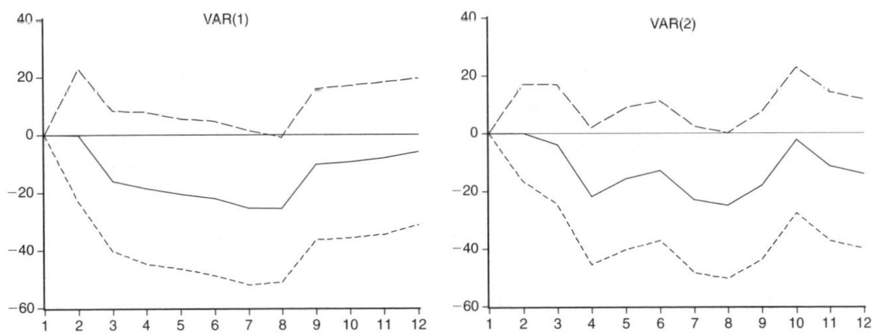

Figure 14.5 Responses of relative credit increment to low monetization period impulse (source: own calculations).

Note
* Business sector share in the bank credit change.

growth, after falling monetization triggered significant credit acceleration. Because of much lower information capital, for smaller banks, solvency and especially liquidity of collateral were crucial.

The quality of available collateral differed considerably among the main segments of bank clients. Short-term (consumer) credits to the household sector were, in principle, insured by insurance companies, if the client was already a customer of the bank and was employed in a solvent enterprise. Long-term credits to the household sector (housing loans) were usually collateralized additionally by mortgage. Other (non-bank) financial organizations offered, liquid collateral (government bonds, commercial papers, bonds and stocks of blue chip enterprises, etc.). Enterprises from the business sector (non-financial corporations) had much less liquid collateral, mainly immovable assets, for which the market was almost illiquid.

Bigger and older banks had disproportionately larger information capital. They were able to forecast the net worth of clients more accurately, because they had a long business track record of their clients, knew their suppliers and customers, knew their product niches, etc. Older and bigger banks also had an advantage in estimating the net worth of potential new clients by knowing the performance of their existing clients, being active on similar buying or selling markets, and by knowing their own clients who had business relationships with potential new clients. Therefore, existing information capital enabled bigger and older banks to mitigate an adverse selection problem with new clients more efficiently than smaller banks (see Bole 1999b).

Many of the potential new clients from the business sector were among the better performing enterprises from the tradable sector (and exporters), so the low monetization phase was an opportunity to obtain new clients and keep them for longer periods. By getting new clients from the business sector in a low monetization phase, bigger banks and banks with strong capital adequacy facilitated an increase in their market share; that is, they crowded out other (foreign and domestic) suppliers of credit in the long run.

Therefore, it could be expected that in the low monetization phase, smaller banks, banks with small information capital or banks with a relatively low capital adequacy ratio would step up credits predominantly to the household sector and to other (non-bank) financial institutions. Meanwhile, banks with larger information capital and stronger capital adequacy would not channel an increase in credits mainly to the household sector and to other (non-bank) financial institutions, at least not at the expense of growth of credits to the business sector.

14.4.2 Statistical evidence

The previous hypothetical explanation of the credit rationing mechanism stresses the role of fast credit growth and factors determining costs of deterioration in expected credit solvency. The most important factors would have to be information capital, quality of collateral and capital adequacy. Identified factors of bank credit rationing are tested by the model:

$$rBC_{it} = a_0 + (a_1 + a_2{}^*LMP_{it})^*rOC_{it} + (a_{3v} + a_4{}^*LMP_{it})^*CA_{it-1} + (a_5 + a_6{}^*LMP_{it})^*BS_{it-1} + u_{it} \qquad (14.1)$$

The subscripts i and t indicate the bank and year respectively. The meaning of variables in the model is as follows: rBC and rOC denote a rate of growth of credits to the business sector and to other sectors respectively; CA stands for capital adequacy and BS for the size of balance sheet; LMP is the dummy variable for the low monetization phase. Parameters at the dummy for a low monetization phase enable a testing of the significance of the low monetization modification effects on growth of credits to the business sector for the following factors: credit rationing (a_2), capital adequacy ratio (a_4), and the size of bank (a_6). It is supposed that the information capital of a bank is correlated with the relative size of its balance sheets. Therefore, the significance of a_6 could indicate the low monetization modification effect of information capital on bank credit growth (information capital effect on rationing). The significance of the high monetization effect of capital adequacy, balance sheet and growth of credits to other sectors on the growth of credits to the business sector could be evaluated through testing the significance of parameters a_1, a_3 and a_5.

The model is estimated on a panel date for the period 1993–99. Because capital adequacy data are not available for shorter periods than years, bank-year panel data are used. Because periods of a low monetization phase do not fit completely to calendar years, central years are used. All data on individual banks used in the analysis are from the Central Bank internal database.

Credit growth rates are defined as December over December growth rates of corresponding credits for every particular bank. Capital adequacy is expressed in percentages, and the size of a balance sheet in percentages of the banking sector average size; timing of both variables is the end of the year. In the sample, for a particular year, all banks are included that were active at least in that (particular) year and in the year before. Because of mergers, bankruptcies and establishing of new banks, the panel is not balanced.

Model (1) is estimated by using the fixed effects method.[27] Results are presented in Table 14.3 (see Appendix). In the first column a whole sample is used. Since in 1993 two big banks had entered the rehabilitation status, their capital adequacy and balance sheet figures were drastically changed and their business behaviour regulated in the middle of 1993; in the second column of the table estimates are given for a 'clean' sample of the period 1994–99.

In Table 14.3, parameter estimates and corresponding *t*-statistics (in brackets) are given. Estimates and *t*-statistics are given also for yearly fixed effects. The number of observations and adjusted R^2 are given at the bottom of Table 14.3.

In the first column, the effect of low monetization on rationing of credits to the business sector is significant at 0.05. Estimates also confirm the expected positive effect of capital adequacy. Capital adequacy mitigates rationing significantly at 0.05, in the low monetization phase. The sign of the balance sheet size is as expected (positive), but the estimate of the low monetization modification of information capital effect is not significant. Only fixed effects for 1996 and 1999 are significant at 0.05. In high monetization phases, the credit activity of banks channelled to business sector is positively (and significantly) correlated with credit activity channelled to other sectors (a_1 is positive and significant); the capital adequacy and balance sheet are not significant for the periods of high monetization.

Figures in the second column of Table 14.3 (period 1994–99) further corroborate the results for the whole sample. Low monetization modification of credit rationing effect and capital adequacy effect are again highly significant, but low monetization modification of balance sheet (information capital) effect is also significant, at least at the 0.10 level (*t*-statistic is equal to 1.8). The effect of the high monetization phase is additionally confirmed, too. Adjusted R^2 is also considerably higher (0.32) for the 'clean' sample.

14.5 Interplay of exchange rate and credit channel

14.5.1 Exchange rate and credit channel – descriptive analysis

The Bank of Slovenia manages the exchange rate. As is documented elsewhere, it has massively intervened on the forex market to contain and neutralize the effects of considerable swings in forex flows on exchange rate appreciation and volatility. Forex interventions of the Central Bank were concentrated in high monetization periods (see, for example, Bank of Slovenia Annual Reports; Bole 1999a).

In the low monetization phase, the exchange rate was allowed to float relatively freely. The Central Bank was using only limited forex interventions since the demand and supply of forex roughly balanced. Nevertheless, depreciation pressures increased, in the later stage of all periods of a low monetization phase, as a considerable and systematic drop in monetization fed foreign exchange depreciation expectations.

To illustrate the dynamics of an exchange rate in the periods of low

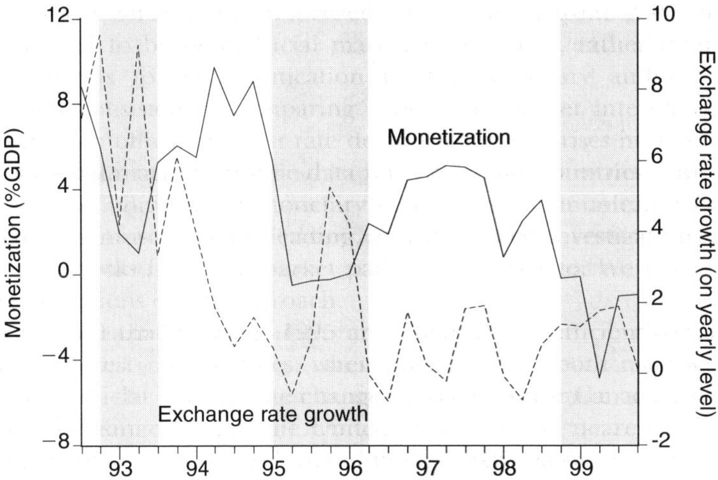

Figure 14.6 Monetization and exchange rate growth (source: Monthly Bulletin BS; own calculations).

monetization and corresponding dynamics of credit rationing, Figure 14.6 gives monetization in terms of GDP and growth rates of an exchange rate (for DM).

Comparison of different periods of a low monetization phase illustrates the potential effect of an exchange rate on the rationing of bank credits to the business sector (see Figure 14.6). The period 1999 is compared with the periods 1993 and 1995–96. Contrary to what the Central Bank did in the first two periods of a low monetization phase (1993 and 1995–96), in 1999, it not only stopped sterilized forex intervention (as it had done in previous periods of low monetization) but also launched heavy opposite intervention, to prevent exchange rate depreciation.[28] Figure 14.6 suggests that in 1999, a stable nominal exchange rate (in the period of large demonetization on the retail forex market[29]) was behind much stronger rationing of the credits to the business sector, in comparison with the previous periods of a low monetization phase.

Descriptive evidence shows that, in the low monetization phase, expected depreciation of an exchange rate had to play a crucial role for credit channel effects. Increased expectations of depreciation stimulated demand for investment goods and consumer durables (such as cars).[30] An accelerated build-up of exchange rate depreciation expectations therefore gave an additional push to the credit demand.

Demand for credit to purchase investment goods and consumer durables mitigated once exchange rate expectations were realized. Such credit demand weakening effectively curbed further acceleration of bank credits (see Bole 1999b). However, accelerated depreciation (in the later stage of low monetization phase periods) coincided not only with mitigating credit demand but also with diminishing credit rationing of bank credits to the business sector.

14.5.2 Statistical evidence

To give some more formal evidence on the effects of the exchange rate interventions in the low monetization phase, VAR analysis is conducted. Using a simple three-dimensional VAR model, responses to the exchange rate shock are studied through standard Choleski decomposition (see, for example, Christians *et al.* 1998).

It is already documented that in the monetization peaks the Central Bank as a rule increased its forex intervention efforts by launching new instruments for neutralizing and containing the costs of large foreign financial inflows. Therefore it is assumed that monetization enters the reaction function of the monetary authority. We assume also that in conducting exchange rate policy, the Central Bank took care regarding the size of credit rationing.

Taking into account such assumptions, the analysed VAR model includes three endogenous variables: monetization (in percentages of GDP); the ratio of an increment in the credits to business sector with total credits increment; and the growth rate of an exchange rate. The rank of variables exogeneity in the experiment is determined by the following order of variables: monetization, relative increment in the credits, and exchange rate growth. The alternative ordering of monetization and relative increment in credits is checked also.

It is well documented that, in the 1990s, capital flows were driven mostly by push factors.[31] Therefore, net foreign financial flows (in percentages of GDP) are added as an exogenous variable to the model. In the opposite case, exogenous impulses (coming from international capital markets) influencing volatility of the monetization variable would not have been explained by the model. The foreign financial flows variable (in percentages of GDP) enters the model in first difference.

A model is estimated for the period 1992/Q1 to 1999/Q4. Both the small number of pieces of information and parsimonious criteria (Schwartz) are in favour of the smallest (first) order of VAR model. All variables in the model were tested for the presence of a unit root; the ADF test was significant for all of them at least at the 0.05 level of significance. An estimated model is presented in Table 14.4 (see Appendix); parameter estimates, *t*-statistics and adjusted R^2 are given. Impulse response function of monetization and relative increments in the credits are illustrated in Figure 14.7.

The impulse of a one standard deviation to the exchange rate growth would already push monetization up in the second quarter. The peak impact on monetization (per unit of GDP) exceeds 21 per cent of the

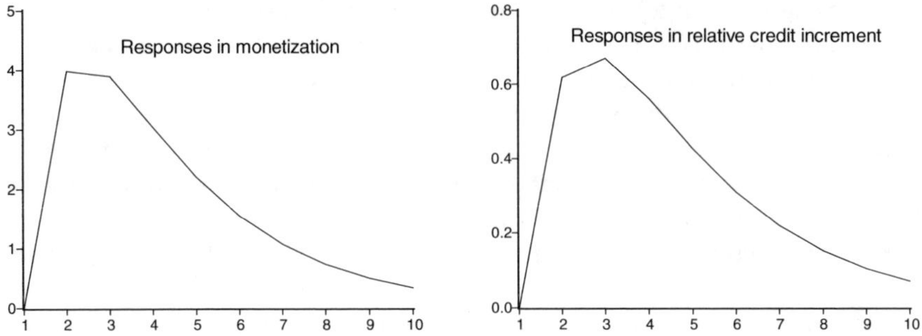

Figure 14.7 Responses to impulse in exchange rate growth (source: Own calculations).

Note
a Monetization on the retail forex market (in percentages of GDP).
b Business sector share in the bank credit change.

standard deviation of the monetization variable; it would be attained three quarters after a shock to the exchange rate policy. The response of relative increments in credits to the business sector follows a similar timescale. Peak value, of around 20 per cent of standard deviation, is attained in the third quarter after impulse to the exchange rate growth path. A cumulative increase in relative credit increments in eight quarters would attain slightly less than 75 per cent of standard deviation of a relative increment in credits to the business sector. Taking into account average values of both variables in the studied period, an impulse to the exchange rate of 1 per cent would in the peak quarter increase the business sector share in the bank credit change by 1.5 percentage points.

14.6 Conclusions

This chapter tackles specific bank-lending channel effects activated by the volatility of foreign financial flows. Empirical evidence is presented for Slovenia, in the period of transition (1992–99).

Large swings in foreign financial flows caused considerable volatility of bank credit growth. Aside from banking soundness, volatility of the bank credit supply also crucially affected the bank-lending channel of the monetary policy.

Monetization of foreign exchange on the retail forex market identifies appropriately the changes in the monetary policy environment that are decisive for specific credit rationing effects, triggered by foreign financial flows.

Swings in monetization on the retail forex market caused not only cyclical movement in bank credits, but also cyclical segmentation of the borrowers. In the low monetization phase, credits to the business sector (non-financial corporations) were rationed. Real costs of rationing were significant, because alternative (non-bank) domestic credit sources were scarce. Trade credit was the only more important alternative, but it was of negligible relevance for mitigating rationing of a whole business sector.

In the low monetization phase, uncertainty with regard to borrowers' creditworthiness is pinpointed as the main factor behind rationing of bank credit to the business sector. On the segment of the credit market where information asymmetries are less important (credits with qualitative liquid collateral) and therefore a smaller entry barrier, the majority of banks were active when falling monetization accelerated credit demand. The opposite happened on the segment of the credit market where information asymmetries are important and therefore entry barriers much higher; on that segment, only banks with high information capital or strong capital adequacy were active.

In the low monetization phase, therefore, banks with larger information capital (bigger banks) and banks with higher capital adequacy were not increasing credit supply to the household sector and to other (non-bank) financial institutions at the cost of curbing credit supply to the business sector. Smaller banks and banks with a lower capital adequacy ratio increased credit supply predominantly to the household sector and to other financial institutions; borrowers from those two sectors had better (more liquid) collateral than the business sector. In the low monetization phase, delayed (or even absent) depreciation of the exchange rate increased rationing of the credits to the business sector.

Three differences from the bank-lending channel known in literature are important. First, the studied 'channel' amplifies and propagates the exchange rate and other forex intervention effects of the monetary policy transmission mechanism, and not interest rate effects as the conventional bank-lending channel does. Secondly, the segmentation of the business sector versus other borrowers is highlighted, and not the small versus large enterprises segmentation known from literature. Thirdly, only a specific segment of banks is identified as active in rationing business sector credits.

Appendix: Statistical tables

Table 14.1 Low monetization phase effects[a]

Dependent variable	*F-significancy*	*t-statistics*[b]
Increment in credits to other sectors (% GDP)	0.245	0.20
Increment in credits to the business sector (% GDP)	0.042*	–0.96
Relative increment in credits to the business sector[c]	0.036*	–2.02*

Source: Time series data are from Monthly Bulletin BS; own calculations.

Notes

a The tested model is $y_t = c_0 + 3b_k y_{t-k} + 3a_k\, dum_{t-k}$; tests significant at 95% are marked by (*).

b t-statistics of the sum of coefficients a_k at Almon distributed low monetization dummy dum_t

c Increment in credits to the business sector in percentages of total bank credits increment.

Table 14.2 VAR model: business cycles and low monetization effects

	Lag	*Credits*	*GDP*	*Wage bill*
Intercept	–	–80.19 (–1.2)	–39.10 (–3.4)	3.429 (2.9)
Credits[a]	1	–0.007 (–0.03)	–0.027 (–0.8)	0.005 (1.3)
GDP[b]	1	1.188 (1.6)	–0.405 (–3.0)	0.031 (2.2)
Wage bill[c]	1	17.34 (1.9)	6.000 (3.8)	0.518 (3.2)
Low monetization[d]	1	–17.07 (–1.9)	0.379 (0.2)	–0.132 (–0.8)
R^2		0.26	0.52	0.54

Source: Time series data are from Monthly Bulletin BS; own calculations.

Notes
a Increment in credits to the business sector in percentages of total credits increment.
b Growth rate of GDP.
c Wage bill per unit of GDP.
d Dummy for low monetization phase.

Table 14.3 Growth of credits to the business sector[a] (Factors of credit rationing[b])

	Sample 1993–99	*Sample 1994–99*
Intercept	47.299 (3.1)	35.594 (2.9)
Credits to other sectors		
a_1	0.214 (3.1)	0.214 (3.9)
a_2	–0.170 (–2.1)	–0.286 (–4.0)
Balance sheet		
a_5	–0.028 (–0.8)	–0.028 (–1.0)
a_6	0.024 (0.5)	0.075 (1.8)
Capital adequacy		
a_3	–0.079 (–0.3)	–0.079 (–0.4)
a_4	0.850 (2.0)	1.314 (3.6)
Fixed effects		
1994	–11.70 (–0.5)	
1995	–9.749 (–0.6)	–8.207 (–0.4)
1996	–38.00 (–2.2)	–39.64 (–2.1)
1997	–32.54 (–1.6)	–20.8 (–1.8)
1998	–25.15 (–1.2)	–13.45 (–1.1)
1999	–61.08 (–3.7)	–57.71 (–3.4)
R^2	0.21	0.32
No observations	175	150

Source: The Bank of Slovenia internal data.

Notes
a Panel (bank-year) data analysis.
b For every factor, first parameter indicates the effect of high monetization phase and second parameter the effect of low monetization modification.

Table 14.4 VAR model: exchange rate effects

	Lag	*Monetization*	*Credits*	*Exchange rate*
Intercept	–	1.433 (1.3)	34.73 (3.9)	0.789 (0.8)
Monetization[a]	1	0.752 (4.7)	2.304 (1.8)	0.023 (0.2)
Credits[b]	1	–0.029 (–1.3)	0.095 (0.5)	0.0004 (0.02)
Exchange rate[c]	1	0.293 (1.9)	1.887 (1.5)	0.524 (3.8)
Capital flow[d]	1	0.016 (0.2)	–1.616 (–2.9)	–0.0018 (–0.03)
R^2	–	0.53	0.43	0.41

Notes
a Monetization in percentages of GDP.
b Business sector share in the bank credit change.
c Growth rate of exchange rate (DEM).
d Increment in net capital flow (in percentages of GDP).

Notes

1 In this last-mentioned variant of the exchange rate channel, obviously an interest rate channel is involved too (see, for example, Mishkin 1995).
2 On different sources of liquidity constraints, and policy affecting spending by altering liquidity limitation, see Tobin (1978).
3 As is well known, even in the most developed economies, imperfections are a central feature of intermediation of loanable funds, so that, for example, bank credit allocation is made more by quantity rationing rather than price adjustment.
4 Some authors already interpret the credit channel only as a propagation and amplification of the standard interest rate channel effects. For them, the credit channel is not a genuine channel of the monetary transmission mechanism (see, for example, Bernanke and Gertler 1995, Meltzer 1995).
5 For the overview of possible policy measures to contain and neutralize foreign financial flows, see Calvo *et al.* (1994).
6 On a 'credit view' ('balance sheet' versus 'bank lending view') discussion (see, for example, Bernanke and Gertler 1995, Meltzer and Mishkin 1995). A theoretical foundation of credit rationing and informational asymmetries on the credit market are given in the classical paper by Stiglitz and Weiss (1981). On quantitative importance of credit rationing factors in transmission mechanism, see McCallum (1991).
7 Standard balance of payments data are used.
8 On 'push factors' of foreign financial flows see, for example, Fernandez-Arias and Montiel 1996; on factors of foreign financial flows in Slovenia, see Bole 1999a.
9 In 1997, shuttle trading fell significantly after Italy introduced lower prices of gasoline in the parts of Italy near the border with Slovenia. In 1999Q2, deterioration of balance of trade was caused by speculative increase in imports before introduction of VAT in July 1999.
10 Foreign-exchange trading among banks is usually dubbed as a wholesale trading on foreign-exchange markets; see, for example, Bingham (1994). By analogy, foreign-exchange transactions between banks and their clients from nonbanking sector can be classified in retail part of the foreign exchange market (see also Bole 1999a).
11 In 1999, forex deposits still encompassed 28 per cent of M3 (see Monthly Bulletin, Bank of Slovenia).

12 As detected in the balance of payments item 'currency and deposits of other sectors'.

13 Different instruments of monetary policy were used to mitigate effects of excessive net capital inflows. In June 1994, for example, even derivatives (Central Bank bills with warrant) were launched to combat huge acceleration of capital inflows through the household sector. For details on instruments used, see Bole (1999a).

14 In Slovenia, crucial external variables were push factors of foreign financial flows. However, cross-exchange rates of foreign currencies (especially between the US$, German mark and Italian lira), and economic activity in the EU (especially industrial production in Germany) were also important.

15 The operative target of the Central Bank was base money; the money rule included the volume of transactions, interest rate, inflation and financial wealth variables (see Bole 1997).

16 In limiting the analysis to a focal episode, the basic strategy of the analysis is similar to the idea in the well-known paper on the credit channel for the US economy (see Romer and Romer 1990). However, contrary to the methodology of that paper, in the present analysis the focal episode is determined by explicit policymaker actions. In the aforementioned paper, the focal episode is determined by 'words spoken in its boardroom and not its actions' (see comments by Friedman 1990).

17 The Central Bank exercised sterilized foreign exchange intervention systematically in the whole studied period, but in the periods of extreme increase of foreign financial inflows, as a rule it launched additional measures for containing and neutralizing foreign financial inflows (see Bank of Slovenia Annual Report, and Bole (1999a).

18 Defining 'intervention' peaks by launching new policy measures for containing and neutralizing forex inflows, the seriousness of possible objections to the 'objectivity' of chosen focal episode is diminished (see, for example, Friedman 1990; Romer and Romer 1990).

19 Credits to non-financial corporations are denoted as credits to the business sector.

20 The argument that 'tightening of monetary policy has strong effects on the real sector when the credit is already tight and weak effects when credit is initially plentiful' is well known (see Blinder 1987).

21 See *Business Expectations of Enterprises* (in Slovenian), Chamber of Commerce, Ljubljana, 2000.

22 Corresponding results are available from the author upon request.

23 A wage-bill variable is included in the studied VAR model because the bulk of the bank credits to non-business sectors present credits to the household sector. At the end of 1999, credits to the household sector represented 77 per cent of total credits to non-business sectors; see Monthly Bulletin BS.

24 Average length of actual low monetization periods was 5.4 quarters.

25 Estimated parameters of VAR with order two are available from the author upon request.

26 After 1995, the minimum capital requirement for a full license was 60 million Deutsche Marks. In the studied period, capital adequacy was smoothly declining; in 1999, it attained 13.9 per cent.

27 Observing that a considerable correlation of time error component with yearly averages of growth rates of credits to other sectors as well as yearly averages of capital adequacies could exist, consistency of parameter estimates is secured using fixed effects estimation.

28 Because of inflation fears at the introduction of VAT in July 1999, the Central

Bank intervened to curb depreciation pressures on the forex market, driven by a substantial fall in monetization on the retail foreign exchange market.

29 Through forex operations on the retail forex market around 17 per cent of M1 was withdrawn in 1999.

30 Investment goods in the business sector and consumer durables are mostly imported goods or pure tradable goods.

31 See, for example, Fernandez-Arias and Montiel 1997. On factors affecting foreign financial flows in Slovenia, see, for example, Bole (1999a).

15 The monetary transmission mechanism in South Africa

Daleen Smal and Shaun de Jager

15.1 Introduction

Central banks often have to act or react in response to actual, perceived or anticipated events. In the ever-changing internationalised economy, the South African monetary authorities have increasingly become exposed to numerous challenges in their efforts to achieve domestic price and financial market stability. Throughout the world, most central bank policy initiatives have been aimed at achieving and maintaining price stability and the South African Reserve Bank is no exception to this rule. In this regard, the Bank's primary objective remains protecting the value of the currency so as to achieve balanced and sustainable economic growth over the long term. This objective has become entrenched in the Bank's monetary policy formulation and implementation procedures, and it has been articulated in both the Constitution of the Republic of South Africa, Act No. 108 of 1996, and in the South African Reserve Bank Act, Act No. 90 of 1989.

When the central bank decides on a route or action to be taken, it sets in motion a series of economic events. The sequence of events starts with the initial influence on the financial markets, which in turn slowly works its way through to changes in current expenditure levels (especially private consumption and investment). Changes in domestic demand influence the current production levels, wages and employment, and in the process eventually lead to a change in the domestic prices, i.e. the rate of inflation. Economists refer to this chain of developments as the 'transmission mechanism of monetary policy'.

Since there are long lags in the transmission mechanism (i.e. between monetary policy initiatives and the rate of inflation), the chain of events emanating from a change in the Reserve Bank's repurchase rate needs to be studied and analysed conclusively. The study of these intricate links between the key economic variables will ensure that correct policy measures are taken now to affect a specific outcome in future. The purpose of this chapter is therefore to give a short description of monetary policy developments and how the monetary transmission mechanism has evolved in South Africa over the past two decades. Specific reference will also be made to the new inflation-targeting monetary policy framework. Sections 15.3 and 15.4 refer to the various channels of the monetary transmission mechanism, and section 15.5 considers the use of a macro-econometric model in an effort to describe the monetary policy initiative and the time lags before its impact on the domestic economy and inflation.

15.2 Monetary policy in South Africa over the past two decades

The De Kock Commission of Inquiry into the Monetary System and Monetary Policy in South Africa (De Kock 1985) originally laid the foundation for monetary policy implementation during the 1980s. The report proposed a monetary policy model firmly directed towards the overall objective of maintaining a stable financial environment, which was very much in line with the actions taken in most developing countries during that time. Most central banks viewed a stable financial environment as a precondition for low rates of domestic price increases, i.e. a rate of inflation that would have no material effects on the decision-making processes of all the participants in the economy.

The monetarist approach to monetary policy in South Africa during the 1980s did not imply that the central bank was absolutely resolute in its policy initiatives. On the contrary, it did have sympathy for national objectives such as the generation of economic growth, the creation of job opportunities and the improvement in the living conditions of the average citizen. However, it was believed that maximum economic development could only be achieved and sustained in an environment in which the financial conditions were stable (Stals 1997). The De Kock report summarises its findings by stating that higher rates of inflation will impede real growth and employment in the long run, and that balance of payments objectives, growth and employment can best be supported by maintaining a climate of reasonable domestic price stability (De Kock 1985: A10).

The strategy recommended by the De Kock Commission and followed by the South African Reserve Bank in its pursuance of protecting the value of the currency was initially based on monetary targeting. This strategy essentially anchored monetary policy decisions to changes in the growth rate of the domestic M3 money supply. Broad money supply targets were announced for the first time in the second half of 1985 for the period starting in the last quarter of 1985. In the first quarter of each subsequent year, a target for M3 growth was announced. Figure 15.1 illustrates the target ranges, later referred to as 'guidelines', and the actual growth in the M3 money supply. M3 growth was brought within the target range in 1992 and undershot the target range in 1993. The target was substantially overshot in subsequent years before declining again to fall within the target range in February 1999 (Casteleijn 2000).

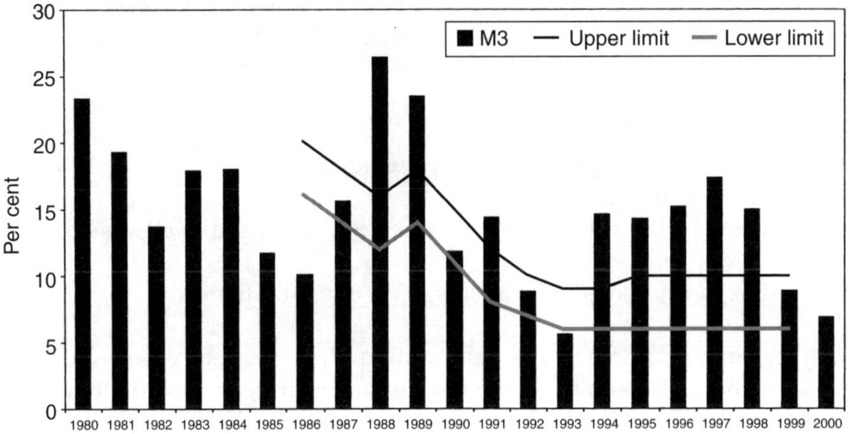

Figure 15.1 M3 money supply growth and the M3 target ranges.

The relationship between M3 and the demand for goods and services was significantly changed by the growing integration of global financial markets, the liberalisation of the South African capital market, the relaxation of exchange controls, and financial deepening in the form of the extension of banking services to the previously unbanked. Van der Merwe (1997) notes that the pursuance of price stability was made even more difficult by the fact that the complex transmission mechanism of monetary policy had become distorted by these changing world conditions. The relationship between changes in interest rates, money supply and the inflation rate had now become far more obscure under these liberalised conditions than in the period in which South Africa was to a great extent isolated from external foreign influences. As a result of the increased volume of international capital flows, the effect of changing domestic interest rates began to reflect the change in the external value of the rand, i.e. the exchange rate. This had the ultimate effect that longer time lags had become discernible between the policy change and its desired impact on the real economy and inflation.

It was essentially these changes in the transmission mechanism of monetary policy that eventually affected the credibility of the money supply as the intermediate guideline of monetary policy. As international capital flows and developments in domestic financial markets began to obscure the transmission mechanism of monetary policy, it became apparent that the change in the money supply had become a less reliable indicator of underlying inflation, and therefore also a less reliable anchor for monetary policy.

The South African Reserve Bank accordingly started to move away from formally targeting the money supply and began using a far broader range of economic indicators for the determination of its policy actions, called the eclectic approach to monetary policy decision-making. According to Stals (1997), the wider range of indicators included in this approach consisted of:

- changes in bank credit extension;
- the overall liquidity in the banking system;
- the level of the yield curve;
- changes in the official foreign reserves and in the exchange rate of the rand; and
- actual and expected movements in the rate of inflation.

At the time, many countries had shifted their monetary policy efforts towards inflation targeting as a means of ensuring price and financial market stability. Stals (1998) commented that South Africa should also gradually move towards a similar situation and that, in the absence of a predetermined inflation target, the Bank should strive to bring inflation down to the average rate of inflation in South Africa's major trading-partner countries, i.e. inflation rates of between 1 per cent and 5 per cent.

The repurchase rate (repo) system (for further detail, see Stals 1998; Van der Merwe 1998) was introduced on 9 March 1998 in an effort to ensure that financial instruments would become more flexible and that interest rates would react more quickly and sensitively to the periodic changes in the underlying financial market conditions. The repo rate is considered far more transparent than the previous method of accommodation in that it continuously signals the Bank's policy intentions, i.e. through the regular disclosure of the amount of liquidity that the Bank is prepared to make available on a daily tendering basis to the banking institutions. The most important signal is the amount of liquidity provided by the Bank.

The Minister of Finance announced on 23 February 2000 that inflation targeting would be the new monetary policy framework in South Africa, and that the government had decided to set an inflation target range of 3 to 6 per cent for the year 2002. The primary objective of monetary policy would still remain the protection of the value of the currency in order to obtain balanced and sustainable economic growth in the country.

Monetary policy is forward-looking, because of the long lags (from about 18–24 months) that monetary policy initiatives take to make their mark on inflation (Mboweni 2000a: 67). Although the adoption of this framework implies that the central bank must remain resolute in its efforts to achieve the target, it does not necessarily mean that the monetary authorities are left without any form of discretion. The Bank will accordingly monitor domestic economic developments closely in order to determine the origin and likely impact of any subversive shock or impediment to its ultimate goal in achieving the target. Allowance will be made for serious supply shocks. If such shocks do occur, the public will be informed of the likely consequences for the attainment of the inflation target.

The monetary policy stance will also be communicated regularly to the public. A monetary policy statement is released after every meeting of the Monetary Policy Committee. A Monetary Policy Forum, which meets twice a year in the major centres of South Africa, has also been established for ongoing discussions on monetary policy. In addition, a Monetary Policy Review is published twice a year to increase transparency in the application of monetary policy.

Figure 15.2 shows the size of the quarterly changes in the South African Reserve Bank's official discount rate relative to the number of changes of that particular magnitude since 1980. The modal event is for the Reserve Bank not to change its interest rate, in line with other central banks worldwide (Sinclair 2004; chapter 2 in this volume). From the Figure it can be deduced that when South African official rates do change, the changes are usually between 100 and 200 basis points, measured over one quarter. This is similar to the quarterly changes in central bank rates observed in OECD countries. This compares to the quarterly changes of at least 300 basis points in central bank rates in much of Latin America and the transition countries. By contrast, many African and Asian countries appear loath to change their central bank interest rates at all (Sinclair 2004; chapter 2 in this volume). Given that these changes refer to nominal interest rates, it is important to take the levels of inflation in the various regions into consideration when analysing the magnitude of change.

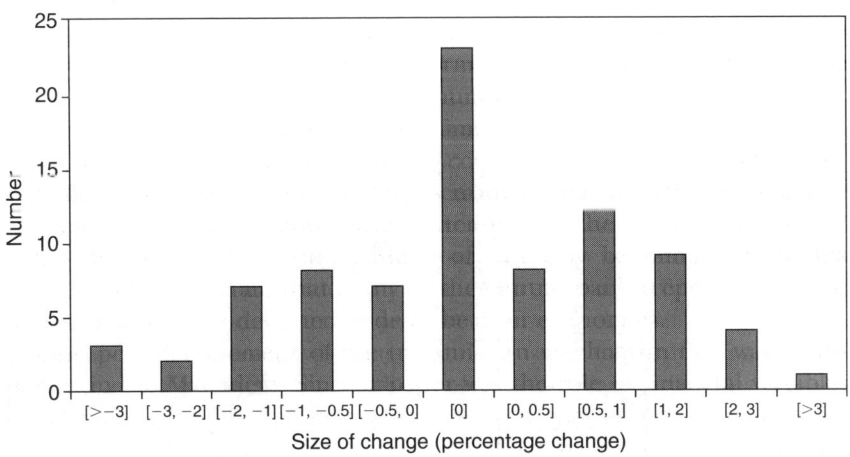

Figure 15.2 Change in central bank interest rate.

15.3 The monetary transmission mechanism

When the Reserve Bank decides to influence the change in the repurchase rate, it sets in motion a series of economic events. Economists refer to this chain of developments as the 'transmission mechanism of monetary policy'. The main links in the transmission mechanism of monetary policy, depicted in the flow chart in Figure 15.3, can be briefly described as follows: the main instrument for monetary policy is the repurchase (or repo) rate. The repo rate has direct effects on other variables in the economy, such as other interest rates, the exchange rate, money and credit, other asset prices and decisions on spending and investment. Thus, changes in the repo rate affect the demand for and supply of goods and services. The pressure of demand relative to the supply capacity of the economy is a key factor influencing domestic inflationary pressures. Inflation is, amongst others, the result of pressures originating in the labour market and/or the market for goods and services as well as a result of imported inflation, which is influenced by exchange-rate movements.

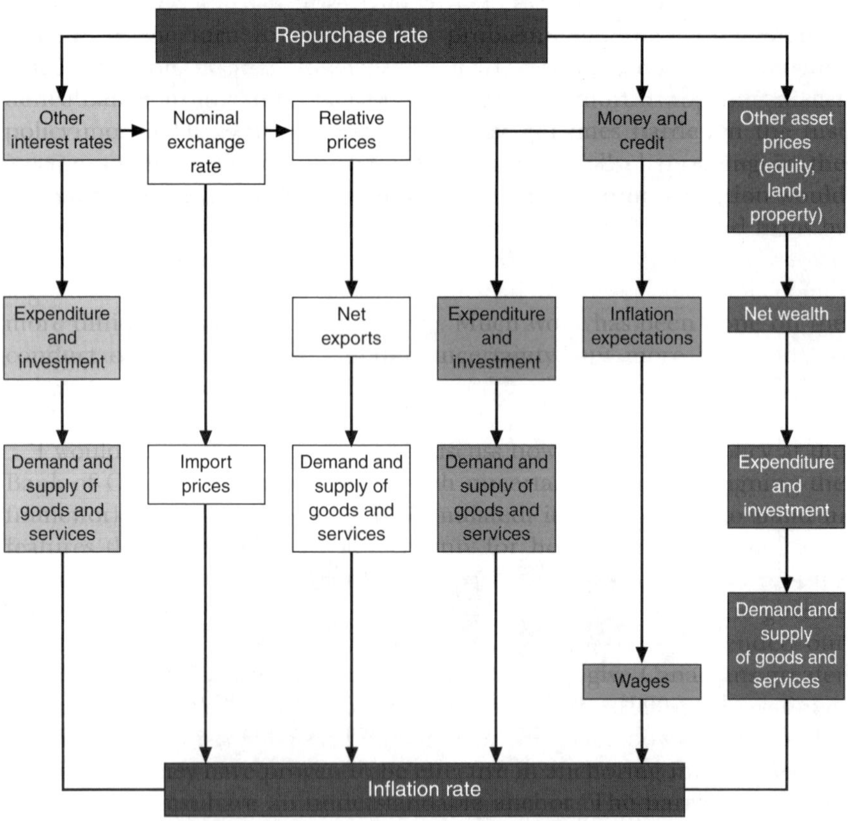

Figure 15.3 Monetary policy transmission mechanism.

The size of the change in any central bank's interest rate is not a good indication of the likely impact of monetary policy on that economy. If market interest rates, the exchange rate of the rand, credit or other asset prices do not respond meaningfully to changes in the official interest rate, monetary policy will have little effect on the economy – i.e. the channels are blocked or not fully functional (*The Economist*, 30 June 2001: 70).

Central banks change interest rates to stabilise the economy in the face of shocks. However, it should be noted that if successful stabilisation is achieved, the trend in inflation and output would remain fairly stable, whereas the trend in interest rates would be more volatile. This is because the interest rate was used as an instrument to affect the stability in output and inflation in the first place, so that in hindsight (*ex post*), the link between interest rates, output and inflation becomes somewhat ambiguous. It is hence often erroneously inferred that monetary policy instruments are powerless and unnecessary in a stable economy. Boivin and Giannoni (2002) conclude that what appears to be a decline in the impact of monetary policy is in fact testimony to the improvement in the conduct of monetary policy since the 1980s. Central banks now respond more quickly to changing economic expectations, thus smoothing out the effect of interest rate shocks and reducing the variability of output and inflation.

There are long lags in the transmission mechanism (i.e. between a change in the monetary policy stance and the rate of inflation), and it is important to note that these lags differ from country to country and also within the same country from time to time. The asymmetries in monetary policy transmission are in a large part attributable to the differences in the financial structures, which in turn are due to differences in the legal structures, in countries (Cecchetti 1999). In general, it is accepted that the lag varies between 12 and 24 months, but with rapid financial market innovations and globalisation, this lag may change.

15.4 A graphical exploration of channels in monetary policy transmission

Through economic research, various models were developed to explore and better understand the channels through which monetary policy affects aggregate demand and ultimately inflation. This section briefly describes some of the channels, or transmission mechanisms, using the categories provided by Mishkin (1995) – namely an interest rate channel, other asset price channels and a credit channel.

15.4.1 Interest rate channel

The interest rate impact, i.e. changes in the repo rate, influences the interest rates on retail financial products. Soon after the official rate is changed, domestic banks are inclined to adjust their lending rates, usually, but not necessarily, by the same amount as the policy change. Mahadeva and Sinclair (2001) explore the econometric link between official interest rates and interest rates on loans and deposits in a number of countries. They estimate the long-run effect of official interest rates on deposit rates as 0.935 for South Africa, also finding coefficients close to unitary for the United Kingdom, Germany and Switzerland. Coefficients significantly less than unitary indicate some form of imperfect competition among retail banks, thus weakening the transmission channel via deposit rates to household savings. On loan rates, the long-run relationship for South Africa was estimated as 1.006. Figure 15.4 shows the relationship between the Reserve Bank discount rate, the prime overdraft rate of commercial banks and the interest rate on fixed deposits. It is clear that these rates move in tandem.

Firms and individuals respond to the change in interest rates by altering their investment and spending patterns. As a result, consumer spending (C), fixed capital formation (I) and real output (y) start to respond. It is precisely through this channel that demand pressures feed through changes in the output gap to inflation.

Following the simple, yet adequate, framework of Mishkin (1995), the interest rate channel can be presented as follows:

$$\downarrow \text{repo} \rightarrow \downarrow \text{interest rates} \rightarrow (\uparrow \text{I}, \uparrow \text{C}) \rightarrow \uparrow \text{y} \tag{15.1}$$

Figure 15.5 shows the changes in real private consumption expenditure, real fixed capital formation and the real prime rate of banks.

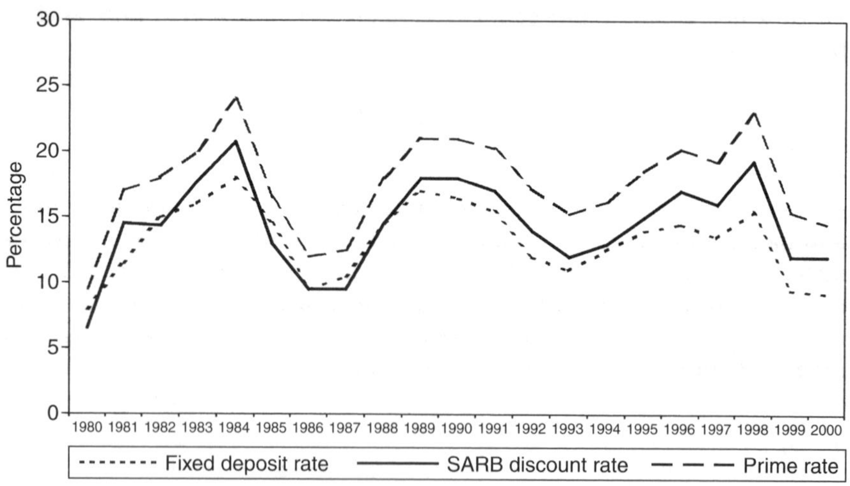

Figure 15.4 Nominal interest rates.

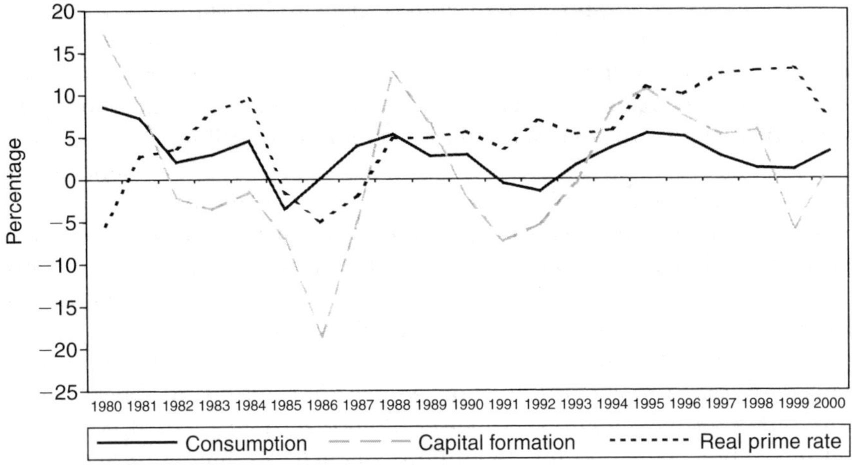

Figure 15.5 Real private cosumption expenditure, real fixed capital formation and real prime rate.

15.4.2 Other asset price channels

Other relative asset prices and real wealth are also channels for transmitting monetary effects through the economy. Two other asset prices, those on foreign exchange and equities, in addition to bond prices, act as channels for the transmission of monetary effects.

When South African real interest rates fall, deposits denominated in rand become less attractive than deposits denominated in foreign currencies and the rand depreciates. The lower value of the rand (ER) makes foreign goods more expensive than domestic goods, causing a rise in net exports (NX) and hence in aggregate output. The schematic illustration of the exchange rate channel is:

$$\downarrow \text{repo} \rightarrow \downarrow \text{interest rates} \rightarrow \downarrow \text{ER} \rightarrow \uparrow \text{NX} \rightarrow \uparrow \text{y} \tag{15.2}$$

Figure 15.6 shows the net exports of goods and services as a percentage of gross domestic product and the real prime rate.

A further important consequence of the depreciation of the rand is that it directly increases the cost of imported goods and therefore has a positive effect on the domestic price level, and hence on inflation.

Monetary policy can also affect the economy through its effect on the valuation of equities. As monetary policy is relaxed, the public finds it has more money to spend and one potential place for spending this money is the stock market. The higher demand for stocks leads to a subsequent rise in their prices. Combining higher equity prices with higher investment

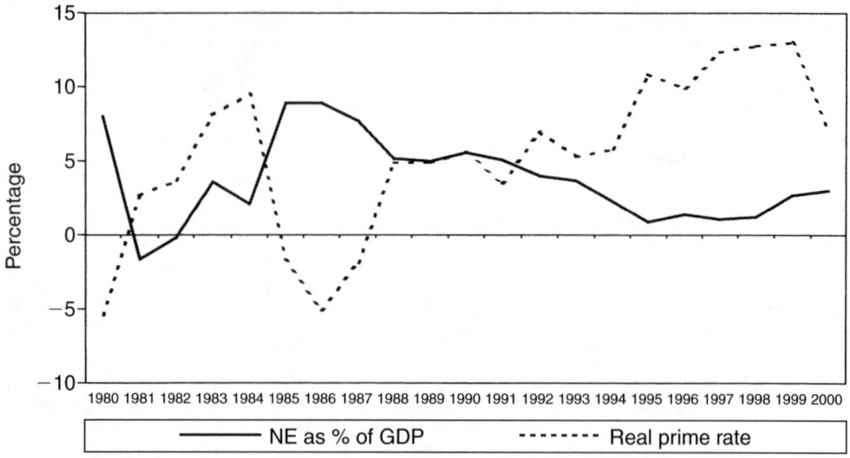

Figure 15.6 Net exports as percentage of GDP and the real prime rate.

spending leads to the following schematic transmission of monetary policy:

$$\downarrow \text{repo} \rightarrow \uparrow \text{equity prices} \rightarrow \uparrow \text{I} \rightarrow \uparrow \text{y} \tag{15.3}$$

For households, wealth is an important component of their lifetime resources. Portfolios consisting of common stocks and property form a major part of an individual's wealth. Monetary policy has the ability to influence the balance sheets of consumers, i.e. their wealth. Relaxing monetary policy will result in an increase in equity and property prices, thereby increasing the lifetime resources of consumers and consequently raising their consumption. Schematically this transmission channel is as follows:

$$\downarrow \text{repo} \rightarrow \uparrow \text{prices on equity, housing, land} \rightarrow \uparrow \text{C} \rightarrow \uparrow \text{y} \tag{15.4}$$

As Mishkin (1995) pointed out, this can be a powerful channel that adds substantially to the potency of monetary policy.

15.4.3 Credit channel

The third channel relates to asymmetric information in financial markets, and works first through effects on bank lending, and secondly through effects on the balance sheets of firms and households.

Certain borrowers will not have access to credit markets unless they borrow from banks. Expansionary monetary policy increases bank reserves and bank deposits, thus increasing the amount of loans available. This increase in loans will cause investment and consumer spending to rise. Schematically, the monetary policy effect is represented as:

$$\downarrow\text{repo} \rightarrow \uparrow\text{bank deposits} \rightarrow \uparrow\text{bank loans} \rightarrow \uparrow\text{I}, \uparrow\text{C} \rightarrow \uparrow\text{y} \qquad (15.5)$$

An important implication is that monetary policy through this channel will have a greater effect on those more dependent on bank loans, such as smaller firms, since larger firms have recourse to obtaining funds by issuing new share capital. As circumstances and restrictive regulatory frameworks change to allow banks greater ability to raise funds, the potency of this channel will be reduced (Mishkin 1995).

The balance sheet channel also arises from asymmetric information in credit markets. The higher net worth of firms and households leads to more collateral available for loans, and the banks' potential losses from adverse selection becomes lower. This, coupled with the improvement in the cash flow situation of firms and individuals, can be represented in the following schematic illustration for the balance sheet channel of monetary policy tansmission:

$$\downarrow\text{repo} \rightarrow \uparrow\text{price expectations}, \uparrow\text{cash flow} \rightarrow \downarrow\text{adverse selection},$$
$$\downarrow\text{moral hazard} \rightarrow \uparrow\text{lending} \rightarrow \uparrow\text{I}, \uparrow\text{C} \rightarrow \uparrow\text{y} \qquad (15.6)$$

15.5 Illustration of the monetary transmission mechanism by means of a model

The aim of this section is to illustrate the possible macroeconomic impacts of a change in monetary policy. In reality, the economy is continually affected by various external influences and disturbances, and the aim of monetary policy is to return the economy to a state of equilibrium rather than to disturb it. The actual outcome of a change in the policy stance therefore also depends on the prevailing domestic and foreign economic circumstances. These factors include the extent that the change in policy adjustment was anticipated, current business and consumer confidence, the fiscal policy stance, the state of the global economy, and the credibility of the monetary authorities. All these factors (either separately or in combination with one another) have the capacity to influence the eventual magnitude and time-path of the monetary policy response, i.e. the monetary policy transmission mechanism.

A small macroeconometric model, incorporating as fully as possible the channels described, has been developed in an attempt to illustrate the transmission mechanism of monetary policy in South Africa. The repurchase rate is shocked by an increase of 100 basis points from its baseline scenario during the very first year of the 3-year simulation period in order to illustrate graphically the change and time lag of the response. The results of the model have been categorised by means of the following two alternative scenarios:

1 A 1 percentage point increase in the repurchase rate;
2 A 1 percentage point increase in the repurchase rate, with a Taylor-type monetary policy reaction function added to the model.

In both scenarios, the repo rate is increased by 100 basis points from its baseline level and then kept unchanged for a period of four quarters. The first scenario makes provision for the interest rate differential and purchasing power parity to play a role in the trend in the real exchange rate. The second scenario depicts a situation in which the real exchange rate still reflects the change in the interest rate and inflation differentials, but has the added feature that the repo rate also adjusts to the change in domestic inflation and output by means of a Taylor-type rule.

Taylor (1993a) developed the rule as a suitable formulation to set nominal interest rates in reference to a change in domestic growth (or the output gap) and the deviation in the current rate of inflation from the rate specified in the inflation target. The adapted Taylor rule in this analysis is similar to the one used by the Bank of England (Bank of England, 1999a: 30), and is specified as follows:

$$i = r + inf_t + a_1 (inf_t - inf_t^*) + a_2 (y_t - y_t^*) \tag{15.7}$$

The adapted Taylor rule therefore implies that nominal interest rates (i) are a function of the equilibrium real interest rate (r), the current rate of inflation (inf_t), current inflation less the inflation target ($inf_t - inf_t^*$), and the output gap specified as the excess of actual output over potential output ($y_t - y_t^*$). In this simple rule, the responsiveness of nominal interest rates to the deviation of inflation from target, and the output gap is determined by the weights a_1 and a_2 and both are usually set at 0.5 (see Bank of England, 1999a: 35).

The results show that in both scenarios, the initial impact of the raised level of the interest rate will be to lower real domestic demand (consumption and investment expenditure in particular), and consequently real GDP output. In addition, since the exchange rate is endogenous in the model, the rising repo rate alters the interest rate parity differential between domestic and foreign interest rates, and in this way serves as a means to attract foreign funds. These capital inflows cause the exchange rate of the rand to appreciate and the relative price of imported goods to decline. Figures 15.7 and 15.8 show the effect of the initial change in the repo rate and the responses that this caused.

Figure 15.7 shows the 100 basis point adjustment to the repo rate over the first four quarters, and how the repo rate reverts back to the baseline level as from the fifth quarter of the simulation period. The Taylor rule

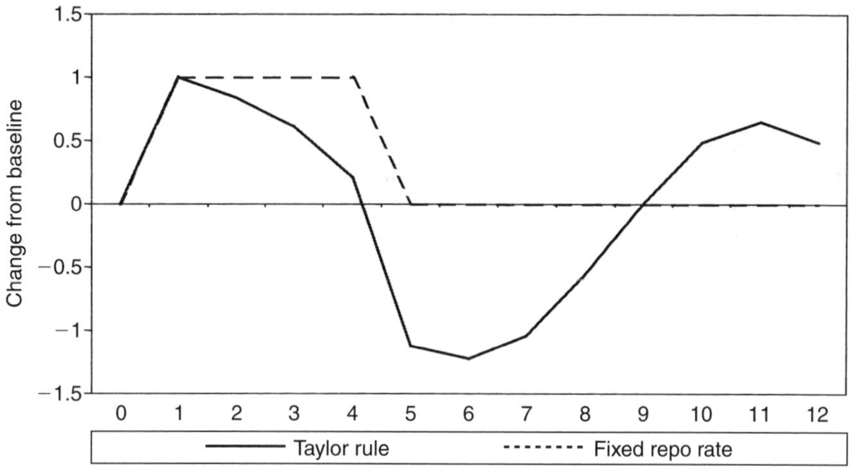

Figure 15.7 The simulated adjustments to the repurchase rate.

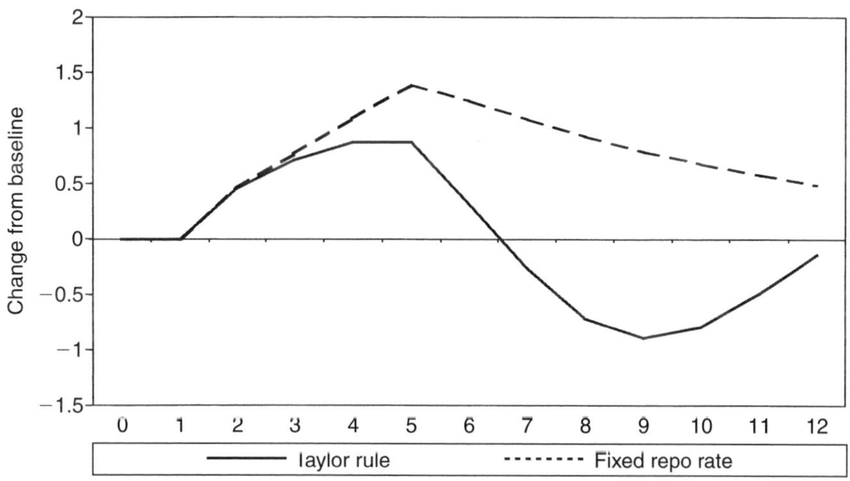

Figure 15.8 The simulated results related to the real exchange rate.

scenario differs, in that once the repo rate has been raised and growth and inflation start to decline, there is scope for the repo rate to be reduced, so that as from the fifth quarter to the ninth quarter the repo rate remains below the baseline level.

Figure 15.8 shows how the real exchange rate reacts to the change in the repo rate (i.e. the interest rate differential) as well as to the change in purchasing-power parity. The figure shows that in both scenarios the depreciation reaches a peak after five quarters before returning to the baseline level. After undershooting the baseline level, the rising levels of output and inflation towards the end of the simulation period (caused by the reduced level of the Taylor-rule-adjusted repo rate), essentially mean that the inflation disparity is negated after approximately 3 years.

The dual effects of the interest rate and the exchange rate on economic activity are illustrated in Figure 15.9 and 15.10. Figure 15.9 depicts the change in the real domestic demand or gross domestic expenditure, and Figure 15.10 tracks the trend in the real gross domestic product or output. The trends are fairly similar. Domestic demand responds directly to the raised level of interest rates (specifically on household consumption

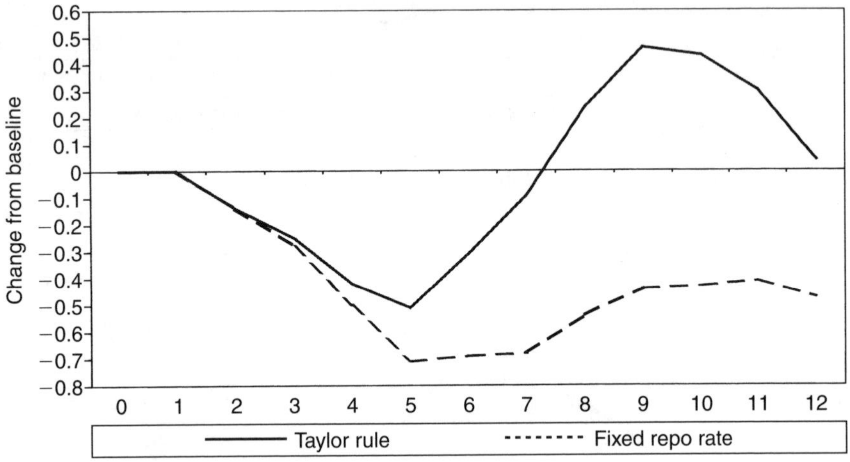

Figure 15.9 The simulated results related to real gross domestic demand.

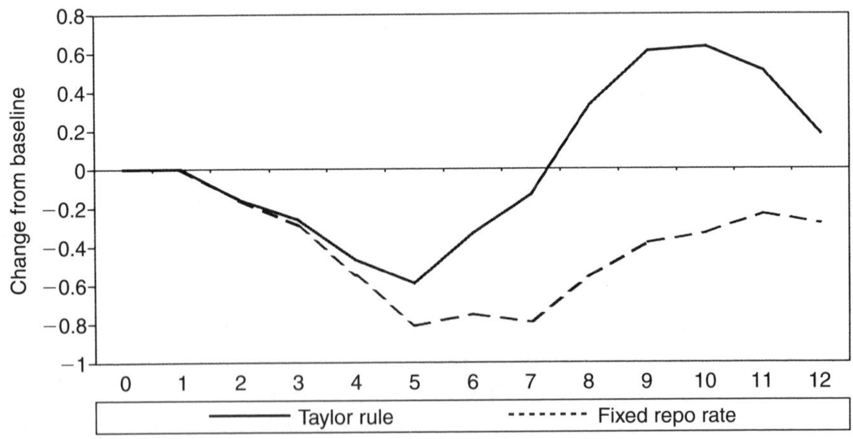

Figure 15.10 The simulated results related to real gross domestic product.

and private investment expenditure), and real output growth reflects both the decline in demand and in net exports, due to the effects of the appreciation of the real exchange rate.

Real demand and GDP output growth both start to fall after the initial policy adjustment, reaching a maximum decline after five quarters. From this point on, economic activity starts to return smoothly to base.

Figure 15.11 shows that the Taylor rule and fixed repo rate scenarios reach their peak after a period of six to eight quarters, or 18 to 24 months. This suggests that it would take approximately 2 years for an interest rate adjustment to have its maximum effect on inflation.

However, it should be stressed that this simulation exercise is purely illustrative. The assumption that the policy change is reversed after 1 year means that the results cannot be used to infer how much the interest rate needs to be adjusted in order to achieve a desired reduction of inflation over a specific period of time.

The results of the two simulations nevertheless prove that any change in the official interest rate takes time to achieve its full impact on the economy and inflation. Empirical evidence in the major industrialised countries of the world suggests that it takes on average up to 1 year for the response to a monetary policy change to have its peak effect on demand and production. In addition, it takes up to a further year for these activity changes to have their greatest impact on the inflation rate (Bank of England 1999a: 9). However, these average time lags tend to vary between economies and remain uncertain between different points in time. In particular, they depend on many other factors such as the state of business and consumer confidence, the stage of the business cycle, current events in the world economy and expectations about the future trend in inflation. These other influences remain beyond the direct control of the

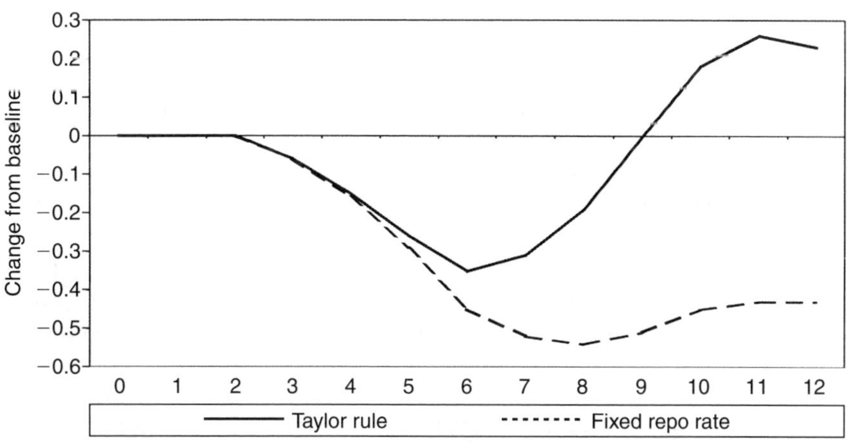

Figure 15.11 The simulated results related to rate of inflation.

monetary authorities, but combine with slow adjustments to ensure that the impact of monetary policy is subject to long, variable and uncertain lags (Bank of England 1999a).

15.6 Concluding remarks

The purpose of this study was to define and illustrate the various channels of the monetary transmission mechanism in South Africa. In order to ascertain the importance of the link between interest rates, the real economy and inflation, it is imperative to understand the perceptions and decision-making processes of the monetary authorities at a particular time. To this end, provision has been made to explain briefly the various monetary policy regimes since the mid-1980s, i.e. with specific reference to the time lags in which it was believed that inflation would react suitably to the monetary policy initiative. Only in the year 2000, when South Africa adopted an inflation-targeting monetary policy framework, did the importance of the time lags and magnitude changes of key economic variables begin to gain more prominence.

The results of simulations with a macroeconometric model support the notion that there are long time lags between a change in interest rates and the impact on the real economy, and that in some instances this impact will only be felt after a period of between four to six quarters. Fluctuations in the real economy influence the output gap, so that as the gap between actual and potential economic activity adjusts, inflationary pressures will start to change. However, the effects of the change in real output will only start to affect inflation after a further three to four quarters, with the result that the monetary policy transmission mechanism can be expected to have an impact on inflation after a period of between 12 and 24 months, with the full impact taking at least 2 years.

It should be noted that these results are somewhat ambiguous, and therefore it is dangerous to infer that a specific interest rate adjustment is needed now to bring inflation down by a certain magnitude 2 years hence. The impact of the interest rate is not universal, and may even vary between two different periods of time. Reasons for the possible variations in the impact can be attributed to other external factors, such as the current perception of the economy, business and consumer sentiment, the state of the global economy, the extent that the interest rate adjustment was anticipated, and the structure and functioning of the financial market. Unfortunately, it is difficult to make provision for many of these factors in the structure of a model, as they merely represent perceptions and are accordingly difficult to quantify in the context of a model. The specification for any model therefore reflects a judgement between complexity and simplicity, and there will always be the age-old argument that certain aspects can be evaluated and appraised better by utilising a different type of model or different model structure.

Acknowledgment

The assistance of M. Mashiane is gratefully acknowledged. However, the views expressed are those of the authors and not necessarily those of the South African Reserve Bank.

16 What do we know about the channels of monetary transmission in transition economies?

Hungary's experience under the exchange rate targeting regime

Judit Neményi

16.1 Introduction[1]

Economists may agree that monetary policy affects inflation and real economic activity, but their views on the chain of reactions from monetary policy impulses (the transmission mechanism) differ considerably. Transition economies represent a special group of emerging markets, that of countries transforming a centrally planned (directed) structure into a market-oriented economy. Even in the more advanced Associated Countries[2] (ACs), our knowledge about the monetary transmission mechanism is limited. These countries are characterised by permanent structural, institutional and behavioural changes, imposing 'excess' disturbance on the transmission process, compared to more developed countries. The effectiveness of different transmission channels must be largely determined by the state and evolution of financial systems and market segments. These structural changes should make both perception and reaction lags, and elasticities, vary over the transition period. Therefore, the empirical verification of any stable parameter model seems to be a *priori* a dubious venture, or at best very difficult, in view of the technical problems involved.[3]

This chapter tries to show what seems to work and what doesn't, and where the 'black holes' of the transmission process we would like to explore are. As the relevance of different transmission channels is not independent of a country's characteristics and of the type of monetary regime chosen, we will take a look at Hungary's development, but with a view to more general conclusions. Section 16.2 briefly reviews factors impeding of monetary transmission in ACs. Section 16.3 deals with the problems of an appropriate regime choice in Hungary, which is a key issue from the standpoint of credibility. In Section 16.4, constraints on interest rate policy under the exchange rate targeting regime are discussed. The channels of transmission are highlighted through stylised facts in section 16.5, and the results and failures of the empirical investigations of the transmission mechanism in Hungary enable us to draw some general conclusions in section 16.6.

16.2 Impeding factors of monetary transmission in transition economies

The effectiveness of transmission in the transitional economies has largely been determined by the level of development of their market economies. Having more or less completed the most painful phase of economic transformation by 2000, the advanced ACs now entered the period of convergence leading to accession to the European Union (EU). While the transition period was intended to create market conditions by restructuring the centrally planned economies, the convergence period is aimed at closing the gap between the levels of development of the EU and the transition economies.

How transmission functions is often far from clear even in developed countries, so it is no surprise that in the 'transitional world' monetary policymakers face increasingly high uncertainty about the final outcome of the chain reaction induced by their decisions. Several factors hindering monetary transmission are present, and not only in the early phase of the transition. The advanced ACs also show great differences in the reforms already implemented to establish market conditions. The most important 'blocks' of factors that should be taken into account when analysing transmission channels can be summarised as follows, (see Begg 1998):

1 Consistency of the present and expected macroeconomic 'policy mix' (fiscal, monetary and exchange rate policies), and the credibility of (past and future) economic policy.
2 The appropriate selection of a monetary regime, its transparency and the credibility of monetary policy.
3 Sound policies attuned to microeconomic conditions, such as privatisation, which are prerequisites for making the transmission more efficient.
4 Establishing deep, liquid money and capital markets and their prudential regulation and supervision.
5 New problems might arise in monetary transmission from emerging market turmoil and contagion. Increased uncertainty stemming from abroad is an additional factor motivating the actor (both domestic and non-resident) to modify change strategy and behaviour. This makes the final outcome of the monetary policy steps harder to predict.

Despite their common features, the ACs present quite different pictures in terms of the stage of their microstructures (see Table 16.1) as well as their macroeconomic indicators (Table 16.2), both of which reflect the ability of the candidates to meet the requirements for EU (EMU) membership.[4]

Table 16.1 Indicators of market economy in the Czech Republic, Hungary and Poland (per cent)

	Integration to the European Union		*Openness**		*Market economy*	*Vulnerability**		*Monetisation**
	Exports to EU/Total	*Imports from EU/Total*	*Exports/GDP*	*Imports/GDP*	*Private sector/ GDP*	*Public Debt/ GDP*	*Current account/ GDP*	*Broad Money/G DP*
Czech Republic								
1993	58.6	55.6	–	–	65*	19.2	0.3	71.9
1998	63.9	60.4	60.0	61.4	75	27.5	–1.9	70.3
Hungary								
1993	71.2	56.7	–	–	55*	90.8	–5.0	52.9
1998	72.2	64.5	50.6	52.7	80	62.7	–4.3	42.3
Poland								
1993	75.5	69.7	–	–	55*	108.9	–0.7	35.9
1998	70.4	67.1	25.7	31.0	65	43.0	–4.5	42.0

Source: OECD reports.

Note
* In 1994.

Table 16.2 Main macroeconomic indicators in the Czech Republic, Hungary and Poland (1994–99)

	Gross domestic product (% change)						*Current account balance (% of GDP)*					
	1994	*1995*	*1996*	*1997*	*1998*	*1999**	*1994*	*1995*	*1996*	*1997*	*1998*	*1999**
Czech R.	3.2	6.4	3.8	0.3	–2.3	–0.5	–2.1	–2.7	–7.6	–6.1	–1.9	–1.2
Hungary	2.9	1.6	1.3	4.6	5.1	4.5	–9.4	–5.6	–3.9	–2.2	–4.8	–4.3
Poland	4.8	7.9	6.1	6.9	4.8	3.6	1.0	0.7	–1.0	–3.1	–4.4	–7.6
	Consumer prices (% change, annual average)						*General government balance (% of GDP)*					
	1994	*1995*	*1996*	*1997*	*1998*	*1999*	*1994*	*1995*	*1996*	*1997*	*1998*	*1999**
Czech R.	10.1	9.1	8.8	8.4	10.7	2.0	2.7	0.8	0.3	–1.2	–1.5	–0.7
Hungary	18.9	28.3	23.5	18.3	14.4	10.0	–9.6	–7.3	–4.6	–5.1	–4.8	–4.4
Poland	33.3	26.8	20.2	15.9	11.7	7.1	–3.2	–3.3	–3.6	–3.3	–3.0	–3.4

Sources: IMF, *International Financial Statistics* and *World Economic Outlook* BIS, *Annual Reports*; National Bank of Hungary, *Annual Reports*; Czech National Bank's website.

Note
* Forecast of the National Bank of Hungary and *The Economist* pool of forecasters.

During the 1990s, and especially after 1995, Hungarian authorities implemented several measures that helped to eliminate the above impediments to the transmission mechanism by coordinating macro- and micro-, fiscal and monetary policies; transforming monetary policy's arsenal in line with the European standards; and restructuring the financial system according to market principles (see Neményi 1996; Haplern and Neményi 2002). The most important lesson Hungarian experience provides us with is this. Sound macro- and microeconomic conditions help to reinforce each other. The timing and sequencing of reforms is also crucial for ensuring that the transformation leads to more efficient operation. This is increasingly true for the steps of market liberalisation: premature attempts at liberalisation should be avoided in order that capital flows contribute to more efficient operation rather than adding to the vulnerability of the country.

In advanced ACs, central banks have carried out a transformation of instruments according to market economic principles. However, the transition from instruments of direct control to a market set-up calls for institutional and economic conditions which permit the central bank to influence short-term money market rates, and create an efficient transmission mechanism through the financial institutions. To this end, most ACs have had to restructure their banking sectors. However, they followed quite different approaches to privatisation and consolidation. The timing and sequencing of restructuring varied across the countries, and therefore the effectiveness of transmission channels in different countries will depend on the state of their financial institutions as well. Finally, efficiency in this context is reflected by the degree of predictability of responses of the non-financial sector to the central bank's impulses.

Establishing credibility has a key role in making the transmission 'clearer' and more powerful in transition countries. It is, nonetheless, a rather lengthy process. Low credibility makes expectations deviate from targets. To increase the chance of a more efficient transmission, the monetary regime should be transparent and should fit with the level of development of an economy and its financial system. Transparency means that the monetary policy objectives are clear, and that instruments are adequate and adequately used. Transparency is of primary importance because it determines whether monetary actions may be seen as unexpected or not. If market participants are 'surprised' by policy actions and/or by their outcome, their expectations for the future will be modified according to the deviation of facts from the targets. Owing to the importance of the credibility issue, section 16.3 outlines the major elements of regime choice.

16.3 Monetary regime choice in transitional economies

> It is unlikely that many emerging-market economies moving toward greater exchange rate flexibility would accept benign neglect of the exchange rate. The exchange rate is the single most important asset price for a small open economy. Policymakers in such countries are understandably reluctant to eschew all foreign-exchange market intervention and subordinate all exchange rate policy to other targets.
>
> Eichengreen *et al.* (1999: 34)

Finding an appropriate monetary and exchange rate regime for supporting transformation and stabilisation has been a key issue for the entire transition period. It is still the most challenging task in the run-up to European Union accession. Strengthening the credibility of the monetary regime is a key factor in making the transmission more predictable under the changing conditions of transition.

Looking ahead, in the medium-run, more advanced ACs, including Hungary, follow two interdependent goals: integration into the world economy, and convergence towards the EU. This can be translated into the double targets of high economic growth and disinflation to achieve price stability. According to the lessons from transition in the early and mid-1990s, this requires a harmonisation of micro- and macroeconomic policies, and a balanced mix of fiscal and monetary policies. Since both the Copenhagen and the Maastricht criteria leave some room for free interpretation, individual countries must find their 'optimum' monetary policy strategies as a means of satisfying the convergence criteria in the medium run on their own. Accordingly, they are free to choose the appropriate monetary and exchange rates regime allowing them to meet convergence criteria on a sustainable basis. Monetary policy has a clear-cut task to fulfil in the run-up to European Union entry and subsequent monetary union membership. Inflation should continue to decline, and the price and exchange rate stability criteria should be satisfied.

There is a vast literature on the problems posed by the various monetary and exchange rate regime choices. Numerous authors deal with the general considerations, and also focus on a number of criteria identifying the structural characteristics of an economy and their interdependence (see, for instance, Eichengreen and Masson 1996). The transition countries have implemented different monetary regimes. The targeting arrangements and instruments in the individual countries have been changed frequently and this has admittedly added to the uncertainty of transmission. However, this was, unavoidable, due to the irreversible transformation these economies have been undergoing (Table 16.3). The more advanced ACs differ widely in the role of the exchange rate in their monetary strategies. This is true not only for the past, but also for the future, as was emphasised at the Helsinki accession strategy meeting,

Table 16.3 Changes in exchange rate regimes in ACs

	Fixed		*Limited flexibility*		*More flexible*	
	Currency Board	*Peg*	*Narrow band*	*Tightly managed*	*Broad band*	*Free float*
Czech Republic		X·········	·········	·········	·········	⇒X
Estonia	X					
Hungary		X·········	⇒X			
Poland			X·········	·········	⇒X·········	⇒X
Slovenia				X		

Source: Exchange Rate Regimes in Selected Advanced Transition Economies: Coping with Transition, Capital Inflow and EU Accession. IMP European I. Department February 2000.

organised by the ECB in November 1999. The Czech Republic and Poland seem to pay no attention to the level and volatility of the exchange rate, aiming at ambitious inflation targets. Slovenia is running a flexible exchange rate regime, but according to the system's track record, it is far from neglecting the movements in the exchange rate. Estonia has a currency board regime.

The monetary arrangements have changed more or less in line with the exchange rate arrangements. In Poland, however, there was a short period when a monetary targeting regime was operated. Since switching to a flexible exchange rate regime, the Czech Republic and Poland have aimed to follow 'pure' inflation targeting based on 'net inflation', and CPI, respectively (see Helsinki documents for the ECB meeting). The openness of the country and the weak transparency of 'net inflation' in the case of the Czech Republic, and the steadily deteriorating external account despite significant (maybe excessive) monetary tightening in Poland, raises some doubts concerning the effectiveness of the selected regimes.[5]

Let us now turn to the main problems involved in a credible regime choice in the case of Hungary. Ever since the beginning of the transition period, monetary policy in Hungary has relied on an exchange rate targeting regime. It started with a fixed[6] exchange rate regime with irregular adjustments of parity. With the aim of promoting stabilisation and gaining credibility, the fixed exchange rate regime of the early 1990s was replaced, in 1995, by a crawling peg system (with a ±2.25 per cent band), based on a pre-announced rate of monthly devaluation. What are the relevant points the Hungarian authorities have given priority to when upholding an exchange rate targeting regime throughout the entire transition period in Hungary? The decision was motivated by concerns about fundamentals and sustainability.

- Hungary is a small, open economy with largely liberalised capital movements, It has already achieved a relatively high level of integration with EU countries.[7] At the start of transition Hungary had 'unbearably' high (public) debt to GDP ratio, and the major part of the outstanding debt was denominated in foreign currency. Under such circumstances, the exchange rate deserved priority.

- Before 1995, exchange rate changes and aggregate price changes could be divorced for non-trivial lengths of time, though – on a disaggregated level – many prices indeed followed quite closely the development of the exchange rate. By the mid-1990s, the process of changing relative prices, largely stemming from the liberalisation of prices and trade and from large-scale privatisation, had been completed. This strengthened the role the exchange rate played in disinflation. Monetary aggregates and prices had shown little coherence, or much less than exchange rates and prices. Money demand was considerably affected by the development of emerging market segments and the supply of new instruments. It was also difficult to establish a relationship between monetary aggregates and domestic demand, and to answer questions about the impact of the monetary variables on domestic demand, net exports and production. Under such conditions the exchange rate channel would have priority over other channels, supporting the arguments in favour of the choice of an exchange rate targeting regime in Hungary. The fixed exchange rate regime – in 1990–95 – proved to be inefficient in establishing credibility, as several factors (e.g. a high inflation differential and the resulting 'excess' real appreciation of the forint, as well as steadily growing budget and current account deficits) continuously fuelled expectations of recurrent devaluation. The crawling peg regime with a preannounced rate of devaluation seemed to be an appropriate means of providing market participants with an anchor in the period of bringing down the high rate of inflation to a single digit level.
- A sound fiscal and monetary policy mix is a prerequisite for any exchange rate regime to function well. Optimality of a given regime can be judged only by taking these policies into account. During the transition in Hungary, swings in domestic demand and net exports appear to be positively correlated with budget deficits. This suggests that fiscal policy changes are indeed the main driving forces of real economic fluctuations in Hungary. The historical development of the saving-investment balance suggests that whenever the monetary, exchange rate and fiscal policies were inconsistent, as in 1992–95, the deterioration of the current account could not be avoided despite significant tightening in monetary policy. The external equilibrium problem could not be solved without fiscal adjustment, as monetary policy was able to counteract the fiscal loosening only to a negligible extent.[8] Failure to harmonise fiscal and monetary policies during the first half of the 1990s reinforced the requirement for a sound fiscal policy as a means of sustaining the narrow-band crawling exchange rate regime.

- It is important to clarify the objection function of the authorities – the priorities they attach to disinflation and to minimising output loss (competitiveness). During the 1990s Hungarian monetary policy followed the ultimate target of reducing inflation under a balance of payments (BoP) constraint. This means that the external equilibrium counted as much as inflation reduction when the targets were set. This is understandable when we recall that there has always been strong correlation between external equilibrium and inflation in Hungary. Whenever the external equilibrium started to worsen (e.g. in 1993–94, mainly due to the fiscal policy dominance), devaluation expectations burst, leading to the realignment of central parity and higher inflation.
- Political and policy aspects also mattered for regime selection. In order to (re)gain credibility, the launch of a stabilisation package and the new economic policy in 1995 inevitably called for a change in the exchange rate regime, though the structural characteristics of the economy changed little. With an obstinately high inflation differential *vis-à-vis* main trading partners, and the legacy of low credibility of a pegged regime with irregular realignments, a crawling regime with gradually reduced monthly rates of devaluation seemed to be appropriate for anchoring. It was transparent and predictable.
- Vulnerability raises the issue of fixity versus flexibility. In shock prone, small open and liberalised countries – even if with healthy fundamentals – a fixed exchange rate arrangement can become risky, leaving room for undesired speculation. As soon as the credibility of stabilisation policies based on some degree of fixity of the exchange rate has gained ground, it becomes essential to find an exit, possibly with soft lending.

Thus, in Hungary, the exchange rate seemed to be the best candidate for an efficient nominal anchor to control inflationary expectations and tradable sector pricing behaviour. It is true that the historical development in the early 1990s did not support this assumption, but the fact that non-monetary sources of inflationary pressure had been largely eliminated tended to improve the chance of a regime organised around the exchange rate target. Efforts at harmonising fiscal and monetary policies supported this regime choice as well. Considering the BoP sensitivity of Hungarian economic development, and the uncertainty about the role of monetary aggregates, exchange rate targeting seemed the only monetary regime that could be used efficiently during the 1990s. Nevertheless, in the period of disinflation, from moderate inflation towards a single-digit rise in the CPI, adoption of a crawling exchange band was preferred to an irregularly adjustable peg, since the still-substantial inflation differential would have undermined the latter's credibility. Nor could the preconditions for an inflation targeting regime be met during the 1990s.

Hungary has maintained a pre-announced crawling band system since March 1995. The National Bank of Hungary (NBH) devalues the central parity of the band relative to a basket every day according to the pre-announced monthly rate of crawl. The rate of depreciation (the crawl of the band) has been set jointly by the government and the NBH, inflation expectations taking into account the economy's adjustability and the improvement in its competitiveness. When setting the inflation target and the exchange rate path, the government and the Bank examined the nature of the shocks affecting the economy. They set objectives after filtering out transitory effects. The path of the exchange rate can only play the role of an effective anchor on expectations if it reflects a credible commitment. This in turn requires the selected nominal path to be conducive to macroeconomic equilibrium. The exchange rate path should therefore be set with an eye on both the expected development of aggregate demand and supply and the flexibility of fiscal and incomes policies. The central bank decisions affect aggregate demand with an uncertain lag. International capital market developments and capital flows also limit the NBH's ability to influence domestic interest rates, given the quasi-fixed (narrow band) exchange rate regime. Thus the disinflation strategy has been built on the co-ordination fiscal and monetary policies. In order to reduce volatility of the exchange rate and prevent large, unexpected movements, the width of the band around the central parity was set relatively narrowly (±2.25 per cent). The central bank has an intervention commitment at the edges, but has reserved the right to intervene within the band if necessary. While the width of the band has been unchanged since the introduction of the crawling regime, the rate of the pre-announced monthly depreciation has been gradually reduced from 1.9 per cent at the outset to 0.3 per cent effective in June 2000.

The NBH could maintain its narrow band despite several speculative shocks that may have generated appreciation above the announced level. The narrow-band policy was quite risky in periods of emerging market crises. Nevertheless, the NBH has regarded the exchange rate relative stability as being crucial for stabilisation policy, and for two main reasons. The first is the inertia of market expectations and behaviours. The more this inertia is present when the exchange rate appreciates significantly above the target, the more the immediate reaction would be felt on the relative prices of tradable to non-tradable goods. This could lead to deterioration in the current account, which should be avoided in a country like Hungary, where the potential threat of any reversal in the external position would again cause problems with creditworthiness. Vulnerability of the emerging domestic sector (more traditional branches of the economy) to unexpected exchange rate movements was taken as the second risk-factor of a more flexible regime in the early stabilisation phase of transition. The multinational sector, which benefited first from the capital inflow, had a less vulnerable profit margin and more favourable access to external borrowing. However, the profitability of the more traditional industries would probably have been hit harder by an unexpected appreciation, and that could result in output loss. It is important to stress that non-market considerations, such as preserving seigniorage through more gradual disinflation, have never played a role when setting the targets.[9]

The disinflation policy Hungary has followed aims at achieving a 'soft landing' in disinflation and avoiding turning points possibly stemming from suppressed inflation. The policy has never targeted more than a 4–5 percentage-point reduction in the inflation. This has been a remarkable achievement, particularly as disinflation has not required large sacrifices in terms of growth. The 'balanced and gradualist' policy Hungary has followed since 1995 has proved successful. Disinflation has been continuous, and in 2000 Hungary entered the fourth consecutive year of relatively high growth. A favourable aspect of this development is that both the external and internal imbalances fell substantially. Today they are considered sustainable (see Table 16.2). In 'peace time' this regime did not differ a lot from an inflation targeting system as the inflation and exchange rate targets were harmonised, but whenever shocks (positive from FDI, or negative from emerging markets contagion) hit the country, the inflation target had no absolute priority over the exchange rate (Figure 16.1).[10]

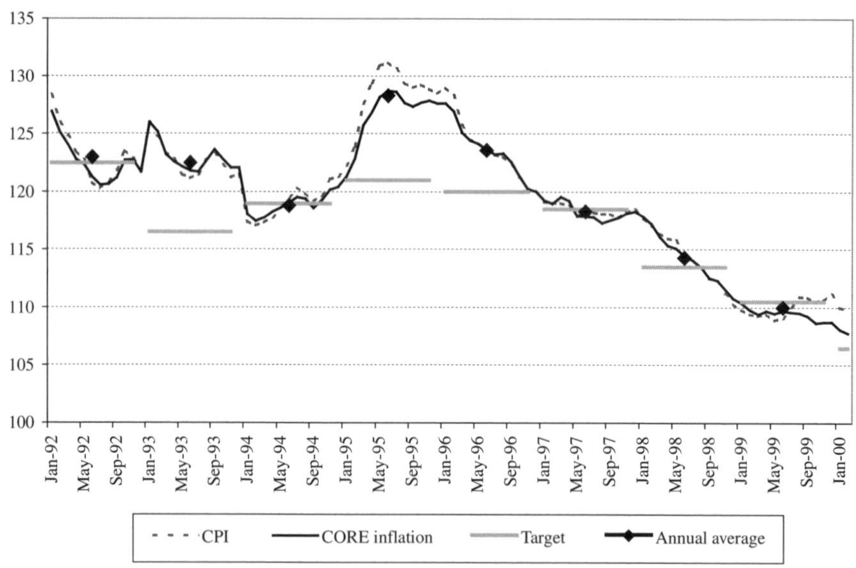

Figure 16.1 CPI, core inflation and inflation targets in Hungary.

16.4 Room for manoeuvre of monetary policy under the pre-announced crawling peg system

Following an exchange rate target does not mean that domestic interest rates do not matter, but the manoeuvring space for interest rate policy is necessarily limited. It is also affected by developments in international capital markets To maintain the credibility of the band, forint yields should be consistent with the open economy uncovered interest rate parity (UIP) conditions:

$$i = i^* + \Delta e^T + \mu = \pi^* + r^* \Delta e^T + \mu = \pi + r \quad (16.1)$$

where i = domestic interest rate; π = domestic inflation; r = domestic real interest rate; $i^* = \pi^* + r^*$ = foreign interest rate; π^* = foreign inflation; r^* = foreign real interest rate; Δe^T = preannounced depreciation of the forint; and μ = required risk premium.

As long as the crawling band is credible (so that market participants are reasonably sure that the central bank will not permit the exchange rate to leave its band) and capital movements are largely liberalised, domestic interest rates cannot deviate, over a longer period, from the sum of foreign interest rates, the expected (pre-announced) rate of depreciation and investors' required risk premium on forint-denominated instruments. As the financial system works with an imperfect substitutability, and taking into account the inherent uncertainties stemming from the lack of full credibility, monetary policy can be said to have some degree of independence in Hungary. Rearranging equation (16.1) for the difference in real interest rates shows that the domestic real interest rates can exceed the foreign real interest rates to the extent that the required risk premium is higher than the real appreciation of the domestic currency. As the real exchange rate has had an appreciating trend (the Balassa–Samuelson effect), the central bank could tighten monetary conditions if the required risk premium allowed. Foreign tightening (that is the increase in r^*) may help domestic monetary policy import 'severity'. Moreover, the still existing short-term capital control[11] can also help to cope with the pressures stemming from speculative inflows.

There is historical evidence that the risk premium can be very high and volatile in emerging markets. This may, paradoxically, increase the level of independence of monetary policy in shock-prone countries with exchange rate targets. Whenever – in response to domestic shocks – monetary policy attempted to keep domestic interest rates at a higher level than that strictly consistent with the required risk premium, this at once attracted interest-sensitive capital inflows. The capital inflow caused the nominal exchange rate to stick to the upper edge of the band, forcing the central bank to intervene to protect the band. Under the current system in Hungary, intervention in the foreign exchange market is automatically sterilised. Excess liquidity received by the internal financial sector is absorbed by the central bank's sterilisation instruments. Whenever the required risk premium declined, the need for an exit strategy from the narrow band regime became a key issue.

The required interest premium has equally been influenced by country-specific, regional and global factors. Country-specific risk is related to the economic performance, reflected by macroeconomic indicators, and includes both default and currency risks. Country-specific risk would be the major component of the high interest differential prevalent following the implementation of the adjustment package, until the new regime became more credible for the markets. During the recent crises hitting emerging markets, however, the Hungarian economy happened to meet the undesirable effects of contagion (the spread of a crisis across the region not justified by fundamentals).

Sterilisation is of course costly, as the interest paid on the central bank's sterilisation instruments is higher than the interest received on the currency purchased plus the rate of depreciation. Sterilisation costs show up in the profit and loss account of the central bank. Nevertheless, a cost-benefit calculation of sterilisation should take account of the fact that a more flexible exchange rate regime, implying greater volatility of exchange rate (thus reducing need for sterilisation), would entail a greater currency risk premium and higher interest rates on the full outstanding stock of public debt. This latter, in turn, could easily far exceed the sterilisation costs incurred under the crawling peg system.

The development of an interest differential on Hungarian forint-denominated assets reflects strengthening credibility of the narrow-band exchange rate regime, and the underlying economic policy. Actually, this occurred surprisingly quickly following the implementation of the adjustment package in 1995. From early 1996 the risk premium on domestic-currency denominated assets was considerably much lower in Hungary than in Poland or in the Czech Republic, where disinflation was based more on monetary restrictions and/or more volatile exchange rates (Figure 16.2).

The fact that, under the current exchange rate, targeting system sterilisation could entail fiscal costs does not necessarily imply that, in an effort to curb speculative capital flows, monetary policy should make instant adjustments in domestic interest rates in the wake of changes in required risk premium. This appears desirable. Volatility in the risk premium would spread to domestic interest rates, and cause the exchange rate to fluctuate within the band. This, in turn, would increase uncertainty in the markets and entail a decline in investment and output losses in the longer run. The NBH's interest rate policy has been guided by the intention of following permanent changes in the required interest premium. For the purpose of smoothing domestic interest rates, the Bank followed its sterilised intervention policy and managed the temporary fluctuations in the risk premium at the expense of sterilisation costs.

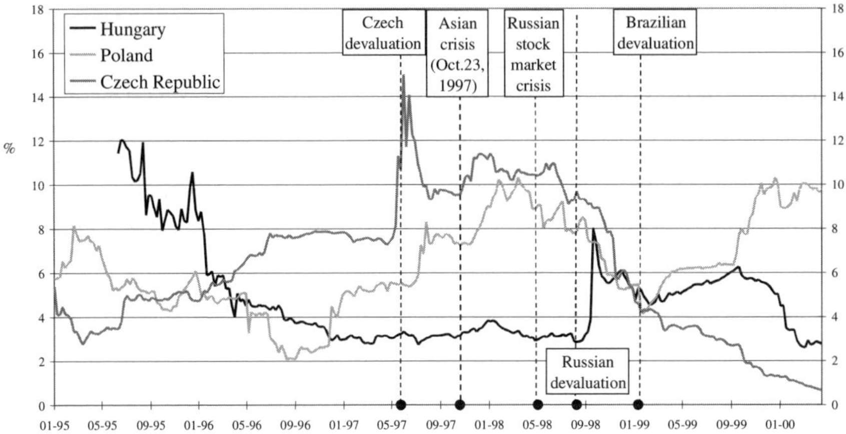

Figure 16.2 Interest rate premia, January 1995–21 April 2000.

Note
No adjustment for exchange rate changes is made for the Czech Republic where the currency was either fixed of floating.

All in all, interest rate policy requires careful balancing. On the one hand, interest rates should be consistent with the path of domestic (dis)inflation. On the other hand, they should not cause a surge in short-term speculative capital inflows. Caution is required, as capital movements tend to follow a 'one-way street'. Stronger inflows, induced by favourable conditions, can easily swing over into long-term outflows should the slightest uncertainty appear, and at the current phase of economic development it is unquestionably in Hungary's interest to attract foreign capital.

Since 1995, interest rates have not always been perfectly in line with parity conditions. This is reflected by the volume of central bank foreign exchange intervention. The main lesson of this period is that a sustained deviation from uncovered interest rate parity (including the risk premium) would entail unbearable or at least increasing costs, and not that an independent policy is inconceivable. Any combination of desired interest and exchange rate policy determines the level of capital flows that might or might not be acceptable from the reserve management point of view and/or taking into account sterilisation cost. To answer the question of how efficiently this policy could promote stabilisation efforts and what the 'size' of monetary policy steps should be. Section 16.5 presents more details about the different transmission channels.

16.5 The transmission channels in the preannounced crawling peg system

Hungary's exchange-rate targeting arrangement, where the disinflation strategy is based on the anchoring role of the pre-announced exchange-rate path, creates several peculiarities for the monetary transmission mechanism. The main task of interest rate policy has been to defend the band in a credible manner. However, even if the central bank is committed to an exchange rate target, domestic interest rates are not completely pre-determined (as shown above). They have non-negligible effects on domestic economic development via the interest-rate and balance-sheet channels.

The policy of sterilised intervention, followed by the NBH since 1996, has brought about significant changes in the operation of monetary policy transmission. Before 1995, the NBH had influenced market interest rates through the marginal costs of borrowing (by active repo and by open market purchases of government securities). Under the crawling peg regime, the Bank offered financial institutions alternative investment instruments (deposit facilities and/or sterilisation bonds). Due to the excess liquidity sterilised by short-term central bank instruments, this regime has the disadvantage that the effectiveness of transmission between the central bank reference interest rate and banking interest rates is determined by the arbitrage opportunities.

It is important to see that in this regime money plays no traditional leading indicator role. The NBH supplies whatever quantity of money is demanded at the given interest rate. This does not mean that we should disregard the path of monetary aggregates. On the contrary, by the analysis of the demand for money we can obtain important information regarding the development of markets and instruments, and the portfolio decisions of investors. Nevertheless, the monetary aggregates may have no predictive power over the other determinants of inflation.[12] In the short run, market interest rates are the most important policy variable.

While transmission via the exchange-rate channel should be relatively rapid and efficient, the intensity and timespan of interest-rate transmission are much less predictable. The greatest efficiency could be assigned to the exchange-rate channels operating via the direct influence of the preannounced exchange-rate path over the CPI, and the exchange rate expectations. The exchange-rate channel, working through the real exchange rate effect on the demand for domestic goods, seems to play a lesser role in the control of inflation. The central bank focuses on short-term nominal interest rates. The central bank's actions then influence market yields along with a 10-year horizon of government securities yield curve and banking interest rates. The short-term interest rates also translate into short- and longer-run real interest rates through changes in inflation and exchange rate expectations. This in turn results in adjusting market participants' decisions and in changing target variables (domestic demand and inflation). The most important characteristic that should be taken into account when analysing transmission channels in transition economies (including Hungary) is that the financing structures of these countries have been subject to fundamental transformation during the transition and convergence period. In this respect, in Hungary we expect that from the 'negligible' leverage position of the mid-1990s the private sector demand for credit will show a steadily growing future path, partly independently of domestic monetary conditions, until a credit-to-capital ratio typical of more advanced economies is achieved. This undoubtedly adds to the uncertainty of transmission via interest-rate and credit channels.

Unfortunately, to gain more precise information about elasticities and lags of transmission we can hardly rely on conventional empirical analysis, as, due to the shortness of time series, most of the econometric estimations fail at reliability statistical tests.[13] It might be suspected that the empirical analysis based on disaggregated and/or panel data might yield more relevant assessment of different channels. This will be one of the directions where we would like to extend our investigation in the future.

16.5.1 The exchange rate as a nominal anchor

The exchange-rate path has directly acted as a nominal anchor through the pricing of tradables (predominantly industrial goods), which account for about 30 per cent of the domestic consumer basket. The forint exchange rate and foreign inflation have a decisive influence on the domestic pricing of such products. At the same time, the pre-announced rate of devaluation, by affecting expectations, has also helped exchange rate policy to contribute indirectly to the steady decline in inflation. The pricing strategies of the market participants and wage negotiations have become increasingly consistent with the inflation target in recent years (Figure 16.3).

The credibility of the crawling regime, as well as the anchoring role of the exchange rate, have been significantly enhanced since its introduction. This is reflected by two facts. First, the tradable pricing followed quite closely the preannounced devaluation, even when the nominal effective exchange rate path deviated from the target devaluation, either because of the exchange rate movements within the band or because of cross-exchange rate changes. Secondly, the low interest differential on Hungarian forint-denominated assets now prevailing reflects the growing credibility of the exchange rate commitment (Figure 16.2)

Until 1998, the crawling band system had practically been operating as a quasi-fixed crawling peg. The NBH intervened exclusively at the upper of the band. In 1998, first the general elections then the Russian crises provoked a significant increase in the required premium on

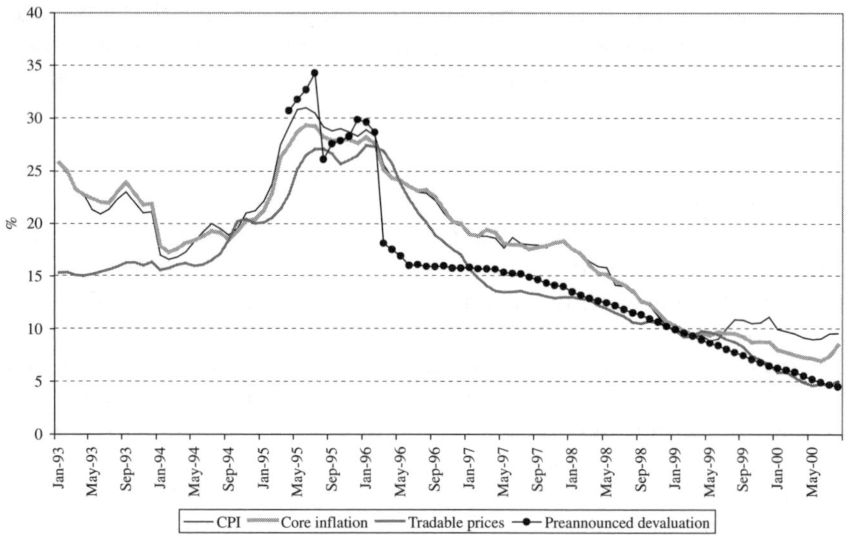

Figure 16.3 Inflation and exchange rate in Hungary.

forint-denominated assets. The exchange rate left the upper edge of the band, and finally the NBH had to sell some 2 billion USD to defend the band. As the market turmoil calmed down, given strong fundamentals for the Hungarian economy, the forint strengthened again with a somewhat higher volatility than in the pre-crises period. (Figure 16.4).

In catching-up economies (including transition countries), the equilibrium real exchange rate (on a CPI basis) may be expected to appreciate in the medium run. This would reflect the permanently higher productivity of the tradable sector *vis-à-vis* both the non-tradable sector and Hungary's main trading partners (the Balassa–Samuelson effect). The two sectors compete for the same factors of production (labour and capital), and the factor incomes (wages and incomes from capital) can be supposed to level out between the two sectors. The service sector often displays slower productivity growth; it can only offer the same wage rates as other sectors with no loss of profit if its prices increase at a higher rate than the tradable sector's, where prices are set in accordance with the exchange rate. Against this background, price increases of services remain permanently above tradables price inflation, resulting in the long-term appreciation of the real exchange rate (Figure 16.5).

When setting the pre-announced crawl, Hungarian authorities were aware of this feature of the country.[14] The pre-announced devaluation was always set lower than the steadily decreasing (target) inflation differential relative to the industrial countries. Thus the crawl was an 'active' device in the disinflation process. However, taking into account the inertia of expec-

Figure 16.4 Real effective exchange rates of the Forint (1994 = 100).

Note
Higher value indicates real appreciation. The unit labor cost and the profit based indices are calculated from value added figures.

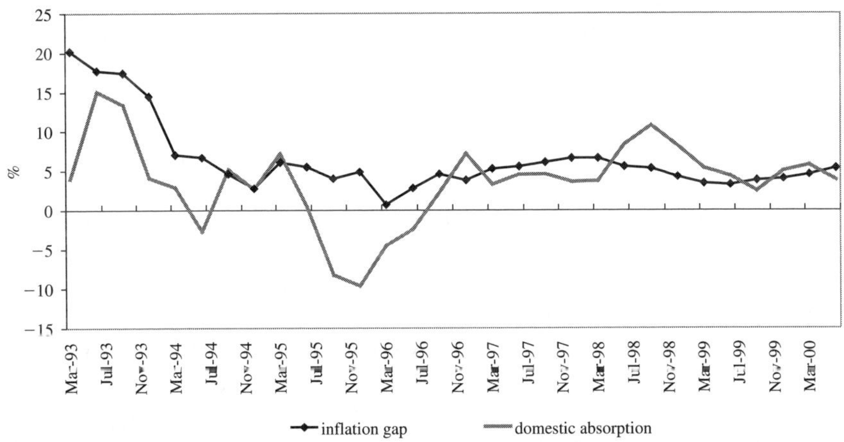

Figure 16.5 Growth of domestic absorption (y- o- y) and the non-tradable tradable inflation gap.

tations, the slope of the band was never set 'too steep' in order to avoid 'undesirable' appreciation of the exchange rate even in the short run, which would imply 'more than equilibrium' real appreciation of the forint.

The past few years have also witnessed considerable productivity growth in the service sector, attributable to strong inflows of foreign direct investment. The information technology explosion is likely to bring about a sharp improvement in the productivity of services as well. Recent developments indicate that it takes a relatively short time for Hungarian companies to pass through cost increases (caused, for instance, by exchange rate changes) to prices. The Hungarian economy seems to be affected by nominal rigidity to a decreasing extent. Wage increases out of line with productivity growth are rarely observed, so the trend in the real effective exchange rate based on unit labour costs improved, then stabilised from 1996 onwards. Nevertheless, structural rigidities (for example in the labour markets) merit special attention ... While the trend of the real exchange rate is predominantly influenced by structural factors (such as relative rises in productivity), deviations from the real appreciating trend seem to correlate with swings in domestic demand.

16.5.2 Monetary conditions

Converging economies are interested in having sufficiently high real interest rates in order to fulfil the task of stabilisation. High real interest rates might, however, result in a surge in excessive capital inflows of interest arbitraging character. The use of the exchange rate as a shock absorber, by shifting to a more flexible exchange rate regime when the credibility of the stabilisation policy has already gained ground, is the usual policy remedy for this problem. Yet recent experience in various emerging markets has yet to provide us with convincing evidence about the expedience of such policy.[15] The appropriate mix of monetary conditions in transition economies is still therefore an open issue.

In Hungary, monetary policy has benefited from the rather narrow 'manoeuvring space' the band and the parity conditions provide. While in the medium run the trend of the real exchange rate is determined mostly by the structural characteristics of the country, this does not preclude short-run deviations from the real exchange rate trend;[16] provided that the fiscal and external conditions for real and nominal convergence were met, monetary policy could reduce interest rate, according to the fall in the required risk premium. However, whenever the soundness of the fiscal stance was in doubt – and this showed up in the worsening of the current account – the monetary authorities were reluctant to reduce interest rates, and tried to maintain higher real interest rates, even at the expense of capital inflows and sterilisation. Whenever the central bank interest rate policy was dominated by domestic conditions and the prevailing interest rates were higher than determined by the parity conditions, central bank foreign exchange intervention was substantial, implying that the actual interest rate differential must have been higher than the required risk premium. (Figure 16.6)

When calculating monetary conditions, we rely on short-term, forward-looking indicators of both the real exchange and interest rates, computed with inflation forecasts and pre-announced devaluation (Figure 16.7). As

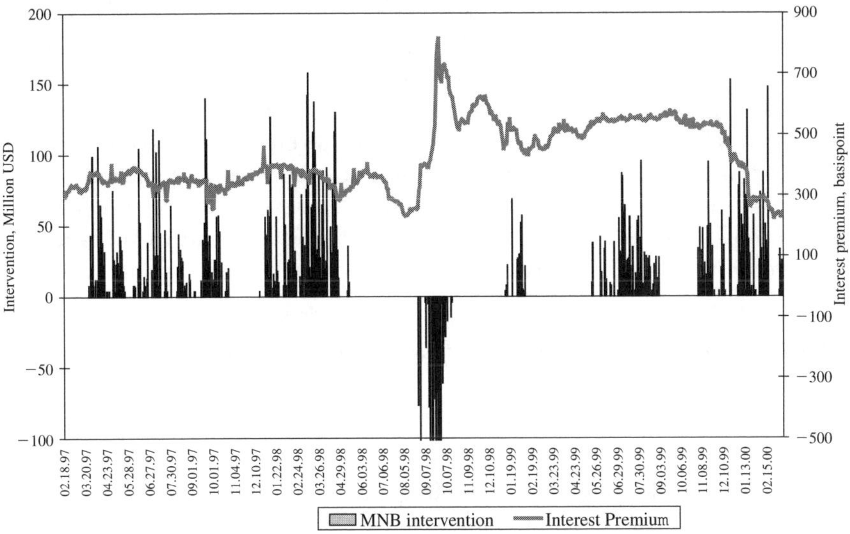

Figure 16.6 Central bank intervention and interest premium on TB-3m.

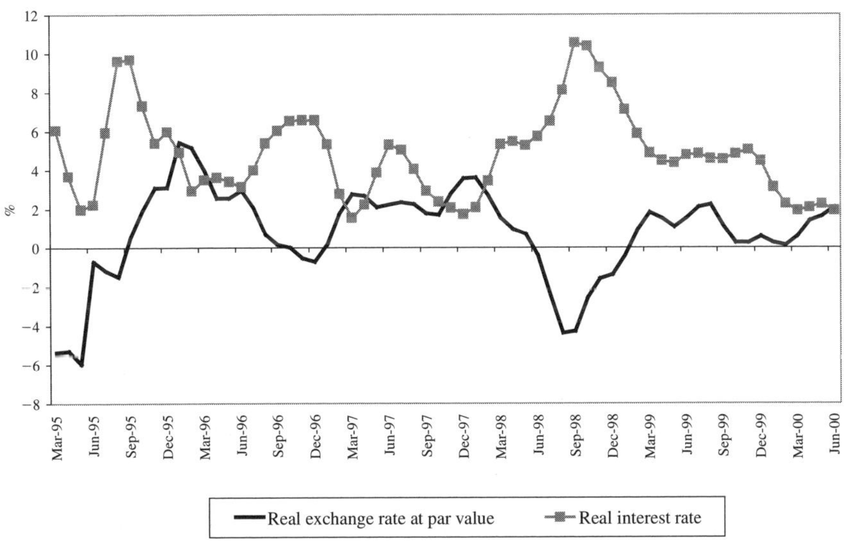

Figure 16.7 Monetary conditions.

Note

The real interest rate is calculated on the basis of three-month Tbill's yield with forward-looking inflation. The real exchange rate here is not identical with REER's on Figure 16.4. It shows the ratio of preannounced exchange rate changes for 3 months and forward-looking inflation.

monetary policy decisions could not be based upon econometric empirical evidence, the monetary policymaking has relied upon a rather '*ad hoc*' combination of the effects of real exchange rate and real interest rates, with a permanent 'adjustment' of weights comparing targets with the outcome. The NBH could not construct an empirically based MCI.[17] Observations about the operation of the different channels suggest that real exchange and interest rates cannot be taken as perfect substitutes for monetary restriction in Hungary. Despite these difficulties, the central bank could apparently react both to domestic shocks and to shifts in the risk premium of external origin, by adjusting the monetary policy mix.

16.5.3 Central bank interest rates and the government securities yields

The NBH intervenes at the shortest end of the yield curve and lets the market set the appropriate interest rates and yields for longer maturities. The central bank's instruments conform to international standards, and appear appropriate even for handling unexpected events. Since March 1996, the sole 'instrumental' central bank rate has been the interest rate on the reverse repo (later the interest rate on the 1-month, 2-week deposit facility). The active and reverse repo (O/N) rates provide a 'tunnel' for the market interest rates (Figure 16.9). At times of liquidity shortages, inter-bank rates are close to the reporate. At times of excess liquidity, inter-bank rates come close to the central bank deposit rate. The interest rate of the 2-week deposit facility is the most important reference rate of the NBH influencing the short-term 3-month treasury bill (TB) yields, which in turn affect deposit and/or credit rates in the banking sector. (Figure 16.8). During the transition period the NBH gradually ceased to intervene at multiple points of the yield curve, leaving more room for market forces (see Nemény 1996).

The changes in the central bank posted rate show up almost immediately in the yield of short-term TBs, provoking response by the banking sector. The rapidity and intensity of response, however, depends on several factors (see Világi and Vincze 1997; Árvai 1998): whether banks are liquidity constrained and whether they are interested in buying government securities rather than lending to enterprises, how the households' behaviour changes, income, wealth and liquidity effects and so on. Experience since 1996 shows that changes in the NBH's repo rates quickly feed through to the commercial banks' deposit and lending rates, even allowing for short intervals when banks tried to shield their clientele from the effect of drastic changes (Figure 16.9). The present system the NBH operates, based on its passive side instruments, might be somewhat less efficient, due to the large amount of sterilisation stock at the central bank.

The market yield curve on the 10-year horizon (see Csajbók and Neményi 1998) is determined by longer-term market expectations and the risk premium (the currency and liquidity risk) (Figure 16.10). The

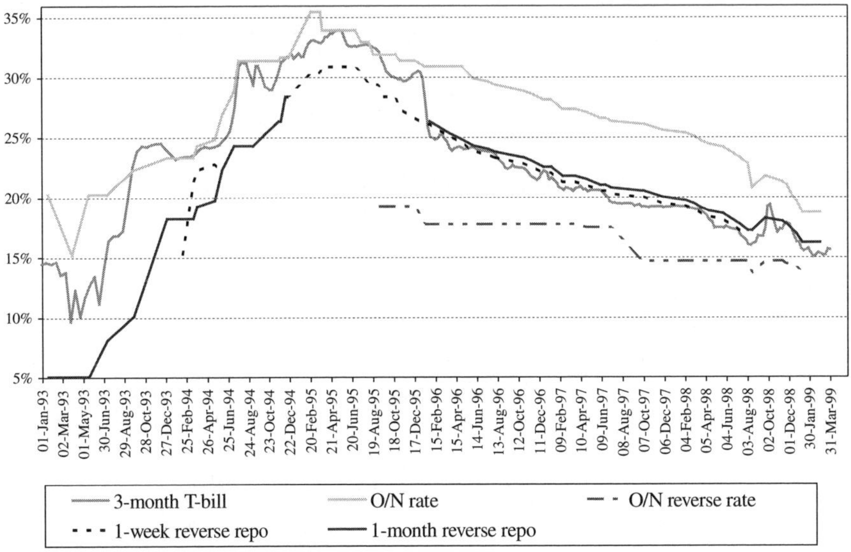

Figure 16.8 Active and reverse repo rates.

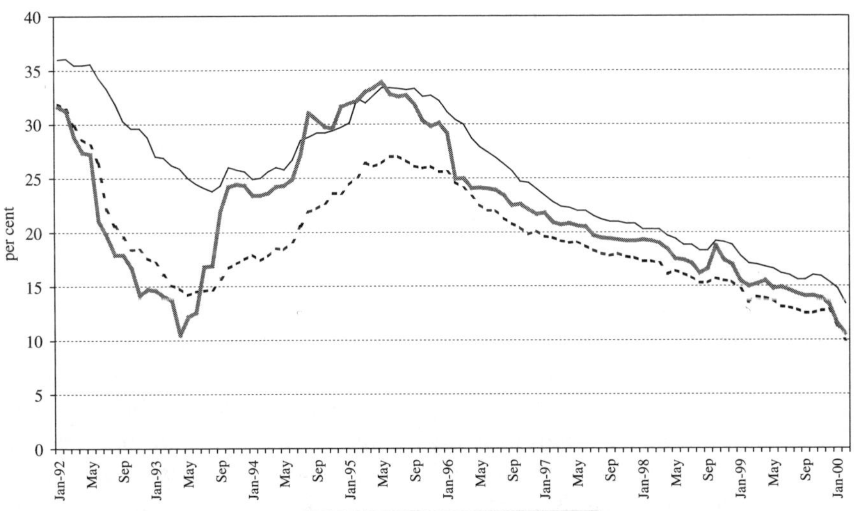

Figure 16.9 Corporate credit rates, household deposit rates and TB-3m yields.

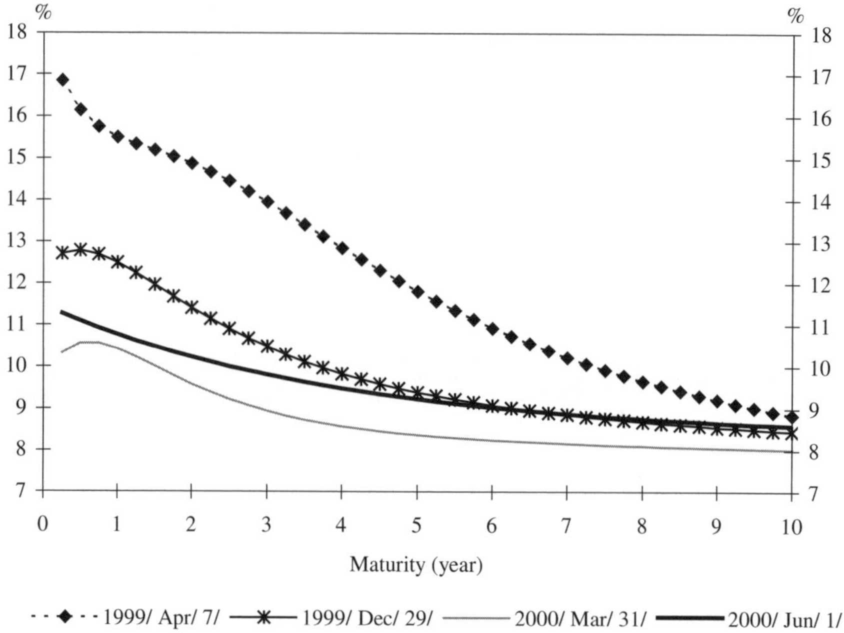

Figure 16.10 Zero coupon yield curves.

government securities market has been increasingly playing the role of benchmark (lowest risk) assets in Hungary, providing market participants with instruments for portfolio and liquidity management. Moreover, the yield curve determined in the government securities market could be used efficiently in policy decisions, reflecting market evaluation on the economic prospects and credibility of policy. However, extracting information from market yields needs much circumspection because swings and shifts in the yield curve might hide very different underlying explanatory factors (more details can be found in Reports on Inflation, published by NBH). In the first decade of transition, Hungary belonged to the group of double-digit, moderate inflation countries pursuing continuous disinflation. As the trend of inflation is declining, the central bank has, shocks aside, displayed an interest rate with a continuously falling path as well. The market yield curve also has a negative slope. One possible explanation is that changes in the slope and shifts in the curve reflect changing expectations, taking the premium as constant. However, the premium can rarely be taken as constant. Yield curve analysis therefore needs to consider both the external and the internal factors on which the investors' decisions are based (see more in Csajbók (1998)). Very often when, following a forward-looking policy or for smoothing the short-term risk premium volatility, the central bank was cautious in lowering interest rates it was not interpreted as a sign of a stronger anti-inflationary commitment, but as evidence that inflation could exceed the 'target'. Looking ahead, an additional problem may emerge in extracting information from the yield curve: once price stability is attained, the curve could twist to give the positive slope typical of stable economies.

16.5.4 The interest-rate and credit channels

The traditional interest-rate channel is supposed to work through real interest rates influencing consumers' and investors' decisions. In a disinflating country, however, the determination of real interest rates is not so clear cut. Expectations may well deviate from the policy targets, especially if market participants' confidence has previously been undermined by surprise inflation. That is what happened in Hungary in 1995. In the earlier phases of transition, inflation expectations were backward-looking and required special circumspection regarding interest decisions. In the more advanced phase of stabilisation, the forward-looking view began to strengthen.

After 1995, market interest rates have followed the central bank signals quite closely, Budget borrowing needs fell significantly. The credibility of the crawling exchange rate regime was strengthened. Nevertheless, as we will see, the efficacy of interest and credit channels has been limited by several transitional factors related to emerging markets and structural changes.

Analysis of interest and credit channels, given the regime changes and shortness of time series, can unfortunately rely only on stylised facts and

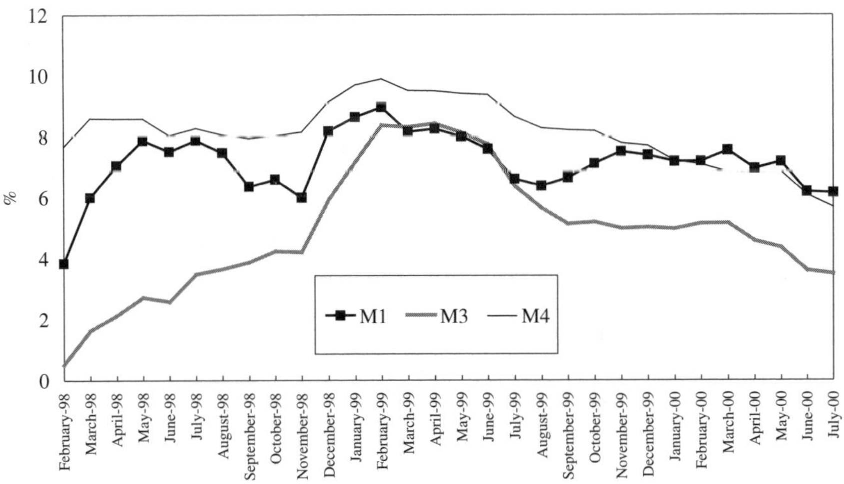

Figure 16.11 Real growth of monetary aggregates.

partial investigations. These suggest that neither households nor enterprises have been very sensitive to the interest rate changes in Hungary, excluding the period when real interest rates fell to a negative range due to policy mistakes (1993). Households' financial savings have been apparently more influenced by other factors. These include, as precautionary moves, the appearance of new, long-term saving instruments and, later on, money illusion related to falling inflation, equity prices, housing market development etc. The resumption of growth and the rise in the real incomes of households, experienced since 1997, allowed rising consumer spending. Savings have been subject to income and wealth effects. The shifts in the government yield curve as well as the rise (and fall) in equity and real estate prices undoubtedly caused both immediate and longer-run effects. Moreover, the rapid growth of non-bank financial intermediaries raises the question of how much the expansion of disintermediation may lessen the effectiveness of traditional channels and instruments of monetary control.

How can monetary policy influence money aggregates under such transitional conditions? What can be said about the relationship between money aggregates and inflation? The instability of demand for money is quite obvious under transitional circumstances. In a recent empirical study, the path of narrow money (M1) of households in Hungary could be described by a buffer-stock type model using household transactions, short-term real interest rates and a proxy for the financial innovations as explanatory variables. As expected, narrow money proved to be weakly exogenous to inflation, which allows the conclusion that a relatively high increase in cash and sight deposits does not necessarily lead to an upsurge in inflation. Recently, M1 and also M4 (which includes households' and corporations' holding of government securities) manifested quite rapid real growth. However, disaggregating these into household and corporate sector money holdings reveals that this is mainly due to the high liquidity of profitable enterprises. Some household savings were diverted into mutual funds and pension funds.

The credit channels (lending and balance sheet) do not suggest further optimism concerning the power of monetary policy. Inside the 'black box' there has been substantial transformation in both the financial and the corporate sectors. In early transition, the transitional collapse of the corporate sector[18] significantly restricted the commercial banks' lending. The high spreads prevalent between lending and borrowing interest rates could be explained by factors other than client risk, and high mandatory reserve requirements and operation costs. These factors are still hindering transmission, although much less than earlier on in the transition period. [19] The risk of lending reduced as corporate sector profitability improved, due to the changes in ownership (privatisation and FDI), and as a consequence of macroeconomic adjustment in 1995. Nevertheless, few firms performed well. This aggravated the asymmetric information problem, since there are a number of new (mainly small and medium-sized) firms with no track record. The mandatory reserve regulation came closer to international-standards, yet, in the period of strong capital inflows from 1995 onwards, the need to sterilise the excess liquidity did not allow the central bank to reduce the reserve ratio substantially. It was 12 per cent in 2000. Solving the bad debt problem and privatising, the restructuring of the banking sector helped to reduce operating costs, which have, however, still remained above international levels. Having improved their capital adequacy ratios, the banks can now take on higher risk. On the other hand, the banks are well aware of the fact that the best clients have direct access to external funding. Consequently, whenever monetary tightening occurs it only curbs those sections of corporate borrowing which are less internationalised.

The structure of corporate finance has a marked bearing on the transmission mechanism, and so do changes in the financing facilities available for Hungarian enterprises. In Hungary, the 'inherited' financing structure has not weakened transmission via credit channels. In the corporate sector, the average debt to equity ratio was very low at the beginning of the transition and it started to increase quite slowly. The leverage (bank credit to the total (book) value assets of enterprises) was around 12–14 per cent in 1994–96 (see Csermely and Vincze 1999; Table 16.4). During the 1990s, Hungary received substantial foreign direct investment funds through privatisation and greenfield investments. In addition, the 1995 adjustment assigned primary importance to restoring tradables profitability. All this resulted in an increasing share of retained earnings in corporate finance.

The stock of household credit was very low, too (see Table 16.4). Recently, households' liquidity constraints have been relaxed by the

Table 16.4 The role of credit in financing

	1995	*1996*	*1997*	*1998*	*1999*
Hungary					
Corporate loans/GDP (%)	18.6	18.6	20.3	20.4	21.6
Total (foreign + domestic) corporate credit/GDP (%)	29.3	28.5	29.9	30.6	33.4
Household loans					
as per cent of GDP	6.12	4.63	4.40	3.86	4.28
as per cent of disposable income	8.90	6.60	5.30	5.40	5.50
Loans total/GDP					
Czech Republic	–	–	59.53	55.90	
Poland	–	–	22.21	23.40	22.99
Slovenia	–	–	29.65	32.05	
Hungary	–	–	24.70	24.30	25.90

Source: National Bank of Hungary, Banking Department.

expansion of consumer credits, which started rapidly from a very, low level in 1998. As real rates of interest on consumer loans are very large, around 15 per cent, the fast growth of household credit may be ascribed to convergence toward a market economy financing structure, leaving little room for influence by central bank action (Figure 16.12).

The 'other' asset prices (i.e. other than interest and exchange rates) have been playing an increasingly important role in consumers' and corporations' decisions. The financial assets share of gross household savings is liable to vary, as may the allocation of savings between different financial instruments. These decisions may then lead to changes in the share of banking deposits in the households' portfolios. The development of Stock Exchange prices (BUX) seems to be strongly influenced by international conditions (see Figures 16.13). Housing and land prices may be expected to rise over the longer term, as the EU accession process develops. Through the wealth effect, these developments may contribute to a rise in consumer spending. Any monetary expansion accommodating the underlying demand for credit may itself contribute to some growth in domestic demand. Nevertheless, it is very unlikely that, by increasing interest rates, the central bank can significantly curb the domestic demand boom induced by other asset price channels, since part of the upsurge in demand for credit can be expected independent of the pricing of loans (at least in the current phase of the development of these market sectors).

The corporate sector is increasingly integrated into the global economy. The internationalised part of the corporate sector (multinational and foreign-owned companies) has improved access to external financing facilities independent of domestic monetary conditions. In consequence, whenever domestic monetary conditions were tightened, there was a shift in the clientele of the domestic banking sector towards

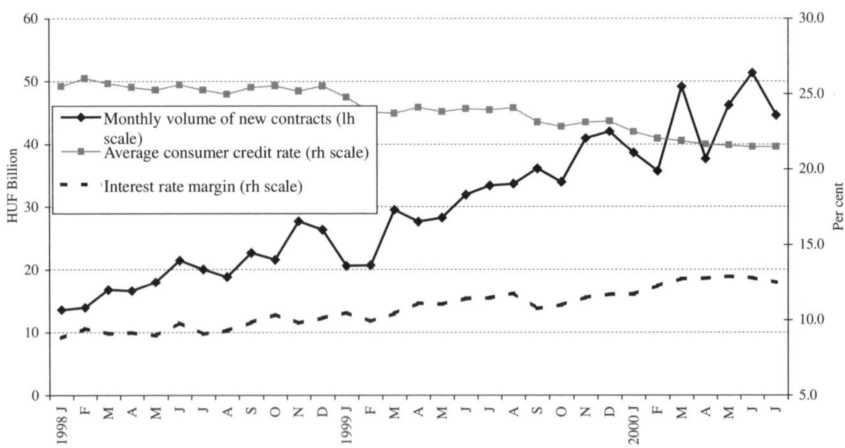

Figure 16.12 Households borrowing.

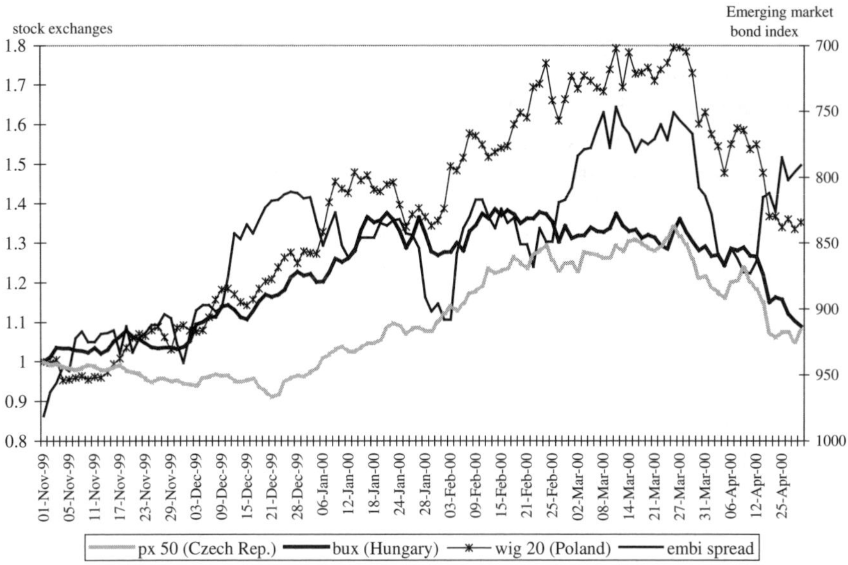

Figure 16.13 Indices of stock exchanges in central Europe and emerging market risk.

riskier enterprises and branches (SMSEs, owned by resident), exacerbating moral hazard and adverse selection problems. This makes the banks cautious. In addition to the high cost of borrowing, which reduces the demand for credit, this may explain why lending by domestic banks to corporations has remained moderate throughout the transition. A simple analysis based on corporate lending data reveals two tendencies. First, the major part of the corporate sector's stock of credit has been increasingly denominated in foreign currency, with a substantial proportion of loans borrowed abroad. That element in corporate debt is mostly attributable to foreign-owned companies with intensive export activity, which use foreign exchange borrowing against currency risk. Second, monetary policy tightening appeared to be capable of influencing the borrowing activity and investments decisions of the more traditional sectors.

16.6 Conclusions

Hungary's experience during the first decade of the transition to a market economy allows us to derive some general conclusions concerning monetary transmission in transitional economies. These are as much suggestions for further analysis as conclusions. It would be interesting to see whether Hungarian perceptions apply in other more advanced ACs or in countries in an earlier phase of transition. Our assessment, however, is not free from contradictions, mainly because, for lack of a sufficiently long transitional track record, we cannot really rely on the empirical verification of different assumptions. One of the most important questions to be investigated is the timing and the scale that monetary policy should react with, in order to achieve a more effective policy within the limited room for manoeuvre. Hungarian lessons are not unambiguous here.

Our limited knowledge about the transmission suggests that uncertainty about the impact of interest rate changes on inflation and output gives rise to rather cautious and less aggressive monetary policy responses.[20] Considering the events of the low credibility phase of transition in Hungary, there is no doubt that 'very ambitious' actions almost always failed. [21] This is why, following the 1995 adjustment, Hungarian monetary policy embarked on a more cautious course, in order to increase credibility. In addition, more recent experience points to a relatively weak responsiveness of market participants to real interest rates. This may be true of other emerging and transforming economies as well. In the stabilisation phase, monetary measures cannot substitute for necessary adjustment in fiscal and structural policies. In the subsequent, more 'equilibrated', phase of development, accompanied by a lower rate of inflation, monetary easing (tightening) seems to be quite ineffective in promoting (curbing) the economic activity. Making monetary policy more predictable may be preferable to aggressive monetary steps, at least in response to shocks of domestic origin.

The Hungarian experience also seems to reinforce Leiderman's assessment based on Israel's lessons from the Russian crisis management. He said:

> ...once Brainard's one-period framework is extended to a multi-period dynamic setup, and once various forms of uncertainty are considered, various relations may emerge, including that which suggests that uncertainty should lead to more aggressive monetary policy responses, quite in contrast to Brainard's result.
>
> (Leiderman 2002: 2)

In Hungary this happened when the Russian shock had an intensive, contagious impact on country-specific risk, notwithstanding the strong fundamentals. An aggressive increase of interest rate was unavoidable at that time, because the credibility of the narrow band had temporarily weakened.

Thus, when we try to determine the 'optimum' dose of monetary policy measures, we have to take into account both the type of the shock as well as the type and credibility of the monetary regime in a country. At this point, it helps to consider what Hausmann (1999:8) has to say about Latin American countries:

> As country risk increases, interest rates should go up more in floaters than in fixers, with countries following intermediate regimes falling in between. This is an indication that in floating regimes country risk has a greater effect on expectations of depreciation, which then amplify the impact on domestic interest rates. Therefore, ceteris paribus, floating regimes exhibit greater transmission of external volatility to both the exchange rate and the domestic interest rate.

Sharing this view, Hungarian authorities have always attempted to find an 'optimum' mix of exchange rate commitment and monetary tightening.

Hungary's case underlines the fact that for monetary transmission to be effective in restructuring economies, the most important thing is to find an appropriate and credible monetary regime, chosen and designed as part of a consistent macropolicy framework. It is very unlikely that the monetary and exchange rate arrangements can remain unchanged throughout the transition and convergence periods.

Transitional economies cannot completely disregard the evolution of their exchange rate. The exchange rate is the most important asset price, even if it is not used as an intermediate target. It does not make much difference whether the exchange rate regime is fixed, narrow-band or floating: should fiscal support be missing, monetary policy cannot do much, and stabilisation is bound to fail sooner or later. It is always important to identify the source of the transition and convergence problems, and to select those that come under monetary policy responsibility. The effectiveness of monetary policy can be enhanced provided that the other policies responsible for improving the operation of the economy are applied.

Macro- and microeconomic factors are equally important and interrelated. Microeconomic restructuring makes stabilisation irreversible. Stable macroeconomic indicators are necessary for successful privatisation and avoiding or mitigating market disturbances.

In small markets, liberalisation may be helpful for market development and deepening, but early liberalisation is dangerous. The development of capital markets (especially government securities markets) is essential for improving the transmission of monetary policy.

Emerging market contagion should be treated as exogenous. Higher reserves and costs associated with 'defence' might impede the convergence of the ACs, or make it costlier.

Concerning the effectiveness of transmission, Hungarian lessons are somewhat special, due to the exchange rate targeting monetary regime prevalent in Hungary and the policy of sterilised intervention the NBH has followed since 1995. It follows from this that the direct channel of the nominal exchange rate to CPI inflation has been the strongest, while the effectiveness of channels working via the real exchange rate and real interest rates has been hampered by special transitional factors. While the costs of the policy of sterilised intervention appear lower than would theoretically be expected, the large volume of sterilised (excess) liquidity would make the transmission less effective.

The way monetary transmission functions can differ sharply from one country to another. This is even true of more advanced ACs, depending on the level of market (financial sector) development, country characteristics (such as openness, integration, and product and export structure) and the inherited structures of finance. Even if the central bank's signals seem to affect the market yields and banking interest rates quickly, several factors diminish the effect of monetary policy on private sector decisions. In this regard, the transformation of the inherited financing structure dominates the whole transition and convergence period. Following a relatively high growth path, in Hungary, household and corporate debt can be expected to increase, and demand for credit will probably be largely determined by this 'equilibrium' process. Both the traditional interest-rate channel and the lending channel seem to be losing importance. Therefore, this will change only if the present abundant liquidity position of the corporate sector is trimmed. As the most rapidly growing part of the corporate sector has direct access to funding from the international markets, domestic monetary conditions are binding only for financing the 'traditional or emerging' activities. This is perhaps the weakest point of monetary transmission.

Notes

1 This chapter was first prepared for the Workshop on the Transmission Mechanism of Monetary Policy, held on 19–23 June 2000 at the Bank of England.

2 The Czech Republic, Estonia, Hungary, Poland and Slovenia entered EU membership negotiation in 1998 and have gained accession, in May 2004, since the time of writing.

3 Shortness of time series, and regime and behaviour changes.

4 A detailed comparison of all the transition countries-transformation to market economies is presented in Svejnar (1999).

5 It has to be noted, however, that the track record is still too short to give any firm verdict.

6 The forint has been pegged to a basket whose composition was changed several times during the 1990s. Since 1 January 2000, the basket has been weighted 100 per cent on the euro.

7 The export/GDP and import/GDP ratios are above 50 per cent; only the short-term capital restriction remains to be liberalised, and more than 80 per cent of exports and imports are conducted with EU member states.

8 Fiscal adjustment involved first transparency, then cutting PSBR according to equilibrium requirements and reducing debt ratio to a sustainable level. The problem of fiscal foundation of convergence is discussed in Halpern and Neményi (1999).

9 In Hungary, seigniorage has not been a substantial source of finance for the budget (see Barabás *et al.* 1998, 1999).

10 Inflation and exchange rate targeting can be consistent, according to Leider-

man and Svensson (1995: 1); 'as long as it is clear that the inflation target has priority if a conflict arises.'

11 Short-term borrowing abroad and derivatives have not yet been liberalised, and non-residents are not allowed to buy treasury bills.

12 This is explained by the quasi-fixed exchange rate regime Hungary uses, but it can also be found in other, more developed, countries owning more flexible regimes. Svensson (1999:3), reviewing the different transmission channels in order to build up a forward-looking model for small open economies, concluded: 'In this view of transmission, it is apparent that perhaps somewhat paradoxically and heretically, money only plays a minor role. For instance, many models, including central bank models, do not even specify a demand function for money.'

13 Following an exchange rate targeting regime over the whole transition period we prepared empirical estimations covering the 1990s. They confirmed the view that the period of crawling peg can be taken as 'homogenous' in the sense that a systemic relationship between basic instrumental and target variables cannot be rejected *a priori*. In the previous (before 1995) regime the relationship between policymaking and market actions had a more *ad hoc* character, which eroded the anchoring role of the exchange rate as well.

14 In case of Hungary the annual average equilibrium real appreciation was estimated as 2–3 per cent (see Simon and Kovács 1998).

15 See experience in Latin American countries (Hausmann 1999), Israel (Leiderman 1999), and Poland.

16 The short-term volatility, however, can be different in the different regimes; see Darvas and Szapáry (2000: Table 3).

17 All the problems presented in Eika *et al.* (1996) are present.

18 The external shocks (CMEA crises) were amplified by an excessively severe bankruptcy law implemented in 1992, which required financial sector restructuring according to international standards in 1993–96.

19 The restructuring and privatisation of the banking sector helped to remove the most important distorting factors.

20 See Brainard (1967) and Leiderman (1999), who raised the question of whether this proposal needs revision, considering the new uncertainties the transitional economy faces

21 The sudden fall of interest rates in 1993 led to a loss of domestic savings as the ambitious inflation target was not credible. The unusual size increase in interest rates could not solve the credibility problem stemming from unsustainable fundamentals in 1994.

17 Goals and instruments of monetary policy

Past, present and future

Charles Freedman

17.1 Introduction

It is difficult to try to peer into the future and assess what central banks might look like in, say, 25 years. Of course, the advantage of looking that far ahead is that I will not be held accountable for my forecast since I will have long since left the central banking business. But, more seriously, looking forward this far does raise interesting questions. What responsibilities are fundamental to central banking and will always be with us? Will central banks continue to have supervisory responsibilities, or will these increasingly be passed on to independent agencies? What will be the role of central banks in promoting financial stability? What are the best ways of carrying out the various central bank responsibilities? How is the relationship between government and central bank likely to evolve over time? How will central banks communicate with the public and the markets? etc., etc.

What I would like to do today is to focus mainly on the monetary policy responsibilities of central banks and to frame the presentation in terms of the following schematic outline of how central banks conduct monetary policy:

Instrument → Anchor or intermediate target → Goal

For example, in Canada today, starting at the right, one can think of the goal of monetary policy as the maintenance of a low rate of inflation, the anchor as the inflation-control target (and, more precisely, the intermediate target as the forecast rate of inflation six to eight quarters in the future), and the instrument as the overnight rate of interest. In every country, a decision must be made regarding these three elements of the monetary policy framework. And all three of them have seen changes over time in response to broad macroeconomic developments (such as the 'great inflation' of the 1970s), to structural changes in the economy (such as the reduction or elimination of exchange controls), and to advances in our theoretical understanding of the macro-economy (such as the modelling of expectations formation).

It may be helpful in trying to look forward to begin by looking backward and analysing the factors behind the changes that have brought us to our current situation. The perspective that I will take is to try to understand what, if anything, the developments over the last quarter-century tell us about what might happen over the next 25 years or so. In light of the schematic outline I just presented, this leads me to three specific questions about the future of monetary policy.

1 What will be the future goal or goals of monetary policy?
2 What will be the anchor or intermediate targets used to achieve these goals?
3 What will be the instrument of monetary policy? Indeed, will the central bank have the instruments to achieve these goals? An important element in addressing this question will be to examine whether the expansion of electronic money will diminish or eliminate the capacity of central banks to carry out their responsibilities, as some have argued.

There are two other questions of interest about monetary policy that I will also address very briefly, but time constraints prevent me from discussing at length:

1 What is likely to happen to the independence and accountability of central banks?
2 How will transparency and communications issues evolve?

It will not surprise you to learn that my perspective on these matters has been shaped by my experience over the past quarter century at the Bank of Canada, as well as by participation in international groups, such as BIS committees, which has allowed me to compare and contrast how various central banks have responded to developments. While most of my experience has been with the central banks of industrialized countries, I have also discussed the relevant issues with staff of the central banks of emerging economies, both bilaterally and in the context of IMF presentations that I have made. It is important to recognize that there will always be some differences in approach to policy depending on the nature of a country's economy, its stage of development, and its history and culture. Nonetheless, there are also important elements of uniformity and, indeed, of convergence that we have seen and will likely continue to see.

17.2 Goals of monetary policy

Central banks have always been in the forefront of those that promote low inflation or price stability as *a* or *the* goal of monetary policy. And this goal has long been recognized as the best contribution that monetary policy can make to the achievement of a well-functioning economy, one in which the path of output is relatively stable and potential output posts a solid rate of growth.

Having said that, I would note that there have been significant changes over time in the views of the economics profession over the precise way in which inflation and real economic outcomes interact. In the heyday of Keynesianism, it was commonly argued that there was a negatively-sloped long-run Phillips curve (in unemployment – inflation space) and hence that there was a trade-off between unemployment (or output relative to capacity) and the rate of inflation. This led many economists to argue that the role of monetary policy was to aim for the rate of inflation and rate of unemployment that gave the optimal outcome on this trade-off curve. Optimality in this case presumably came from minimizing the loss function (of the public or the government) that contained inflation and unemployment as its arguments.

The theoretical insights of the late 1960s (by Friedman and by Phelps) and the inflationary and stagflationary experience of the 1970s led to broad acceptance of the view that there was either no *long-run* trade-off between output and inflation, or that high inflation led to lower and not higher output in the long run. Within central banks (as opposed to some proponents of rational expectations in the academic community), there continued to be the view that in the *short run*, there was a cyclical relationship between output or unemployment and inflation, such that pressures of demand on capacity led to upward movement in inflation, and weak levels of activity relative to capacity led to downward pressures on inflation. The short-run trade-off and the long-run absence of a trade-off were reconciled by the adjustment of inflationary expectations. Thus, a change in inflation that was deemed likely to persist led to a corresponding change in inflation expectations by the markets and the public, and the new rate of inflation could be maintained only if output returned to capacity or unemployment returned to the non-accelerating inflation rate of unemployment (NAIRU).

What is the current view on these matters? Let me begin with the way in which monetary policy might affect longer-term growth and then turn to the way that it relates to short-run or cyclical developments.

The long-run relationship between the rate of inflation and the growth of capacity output is central to the decision regarding the level of inflation that the central bank should aim for. It is now generally accepted that high rates of inflation are not conducive to good growth performance. They make it more difficult for savers and investors to make good economic decisions, divert resources away from productive uses to providing protection against inflation, result in inefficiencies from the interaction of inflation and the tax system, etc.

While high inflation rates are clearly unfavourable for growth, there is an ongoing debate as to whether moderate inflation, on the one hand, or low inflation or price stability, on the other hand, provides the best environment for economic growth. The argument for moderate inflation focuses on the role of inflation in 'greasing the wheels' of the economy. In particular, some economists have raised the possibility that downward wage rigidity, the zero lower bound for nominal interest rates and the deleterious effects on the economy of a possible deflationary outcome would argue for aiming at a target rate of inflation that might be termed 'moderate' (say 3 to 5 per cent), rather than low (say 2 per cent or lower).

The current view in the central banks of industrialized countries is that these criticisms are overstated; that even with inflation at 2 per cent or somewhat lower, the economy is capable of functioning well and achieving good growth outcomes. Thus, the average rate of CPI inflation in the second half of the 1990s in the G-7 countries was just under 2 per cent, while their average growth rate was just over 3 per cent. (For the G-7 excluding Japan, the numbers were 2.2 per cent inflation and 3.5 per cent output growth.)

A remarkable change has also taken place in recent years in the attitude toward inflation in many emerging and developing countries. While developing countries in Asia had long aimed for low inflation, monetary policy in Latin American countries had in many cases resulted in rates of inflation ranging from high to very high, along with periods of hyperinflation when the authorities totally lost control. The move towards moderate to low rates of inflation in emerging and developing countries has reflected a consensus that good economic performance is most likely to be achieved by avoiding high rates of inflation and aiming for moderate to low rates of inflation.

Of course, solid macroeconomic policies (both monetary and fiscal) are a necessary but not sufficient condition to achieve good economic performance. Appropriate policies must also be put in place to promote an educated labour force, labour market flexibility, openness to international trade, competition in markets, etc. But without the underpinnings of a sound macroeconomic framework, countries are unlikely to achieve robust economic growth over time.

Let me now turn from the long-run relationship between output and inflation to their short-run or cyclical relationship. As noted above, the central bank consensus continues to be that there is a *short-run* relationship between output relative to capacity (the gap) and inflation (relative to expectations). However, since inflation expectations will adjust to actual inflation, this relationship does not allow the central bank to choose a point on a trade-off curve.

In current thinking, the focus of attention is on the trade-off between inflation variability and output variability. Thus, if a central bank followed a policy approach of adjusting its instrument so as to try to keep the rate of inflation very close to its desired level over an overly short term, it would have to accept considerable variability in output. However, if the central bank was less aggressive in keeping inflation near its target over the very short run, output variability would be less, while inflation variability would be greater. In this environment, policymakers can choose the point on the trade-off curve between output variability and inflation variability by the way that they structure their policy rule. Moreover, the choice of monetary policy rule may result in the entire variability trade-off curve shifting towards or away from the origin.

This perspective involves a view of the economy as being buffeted by a series of unpredictable shocks and the central bank setting a rule that would result in outcomes that involve some variability of inflation (around the preferred level) and some variability of output around capacity. In practice, the way that central banks in most industrialized countries behave involves focusing on maintaining the rate of inflation at some low level and returning it gradually to that level following a shock. An overly rapid return to the desired inflation rate leads to very high output and instrument variability, while an excessively slow return results in overly high inflation variability. Thus, aiming at a given low rate of inflation and responding appropriately to shocks allows the central bank to contribute to reasonably good cyclical performance in response to unforeseen shocks.

What does the way in which views have changed over the past quarter-century indicate about monetary policy goals over the next quarter-century? I would expect that the maintenance of low inflation, or perhaps even price stability, will be the primary goal of monetary policy in the future. I base that judgment on the expectation that the high inflation experience of the period between the mid-1960s and the 1980s will continue to be seen as an aberration that had unfortunate economic and social consequences, and that the perceived 'normal' state of the economy will be one in which inflation is largely absent.

There are, however, a couple of risks to this projection regarding the future goal of policy. The first is that the achievement of low inflation outcomes will lead to a replay of the economic and intellectual environment of the first two decades of the post-war period. That is, after a long period of low inflation or price stability, expectations become so well-anchored that even in periods in which the economy is pressing against or exceeding capacity the upward movement in inflation is relatively limited. The authorities are then encouraged to pursue overly stimulative policies (since such policies do not initially seem to result in much additional inflation), which eventually would cause inflation to rise and the anchor of low inflation expectations to be loosened and then lost. The entire inflation episode would then be repeated before there was again recognition of the importance of preventing inflation from taking off. To prevent such an outcome, the authorities must always remain vigilant about inflation outbreaks and, as part of their communications strategy, focus on the costs of inflation and the benefits of maintaining low inflation and price stability.

A second possible risk to the forecast that low inflation will continue to be the primary goal of monetary policy would be the spread of the so-called 'Japanese disease' to other countries. Japan has found itself for the past decade in a situation in which, following the collapse of the late 1980s of the asset price bubble, inflation has been near and at times below zero, economic growth has been very low, and the authorities have not been able to overcome the interaction of problems in the financial sector and uncertainty-induced low expenditures by Japanese households and businesses. There are two potential lessons to be drawn from the Japanese experience. One, which is widely accepted, is that policy must be aimed at avoiding getting into Japanese-type problems in the first place. The implication is that the low-inflation policy must be conducted symmetrically. That is, central banks must act expeditiously not only to prevent inflation from accelerating when demand presses against capacity, but also to prevent inflation from declining below its desired level when the economy is weakening and putting downward pressure on inflation. A second possible lesson, which is not as widely accepted, is that central banks should try extraordinary measures if they arrive at a Japanese-style situation.

Just as theoretical analysis interacted with the realities of high inflation in the latter half of the 1960s and in the 1970s to change the views of the economics profession about the costs and benefits of inflation, it is possible that theoretical and empirical analysis might play a similar role in the future. One area that would benefit from further analysis and could potentially have important policy implications would be the quantification of the benefits of a shift from moderate to low inflation and from low inflation to price stability. While many of the linkages between inflation reduction and the long-term benefits of increased output and economic welfare are widely recognized, it has not proven easy to quantify these benefits at low rates of inflation.

Another characteristic of monetary policy that has begun to be the subject of study is whether the authorities should aim at a goal for the rate of inflation or at a goal for the price level. In the case of a low inflation goal, bygones are bygones and the central bank does not take into account past overshoots or undershoots of the policy goal in conducting policy. In contrast, a price-level goal (whether aimed at a zero rate of increase or a positive rate of increase of prices) does take into account past overshoots or undershoots of inflation in conducting policy. Thus, for example, if the goal was to achieve a price level that increased 2 per cent per year, an inflation outcome of 3 per cent in 1 year would necessitate targeting less than 2 per cent inflation for a subsequent period until the price level returned to its target path. While preliminary research in a one-good model has shown that a policy of aiming for a price-level goal may have a number of positive attributes in theory, it is too early to judge whether this would be the case in practice. In particular, most of the analyses done thus far have not dealt with permanent shocks to labour productivity, the real equilibrium exchange rate or real energy prices.

To sum up this section, my expectation is that central banks will continue to pursue a low inflation or price stability objective as their contribution to a well-functioning economy. Achieving such an objective will underpin longer-term economic growth and reduce the amplitude of cyclical fluctuations. Moreover, emphasizing low inflation as a means to an end and not as an end in itself in their communications strategy will help central banks to generate support for low inflation as the goal of monetary policy.

17.3 Anchors and intermediate targets for monetary policy

Given that the goal of monetary policy is to achieve or maintain a low rate of inflation or price stability, how would a central bank go about achieving it? The typical answer to this question is the adoption by the central bank of a nominal anchor or intermediate target. Over the years, three principal kinds of nominal anchor have been used by central banks as a way of focusing the conduct of policy and tying down or anchoring the expectations of the public – targeting monetary aggregates, fixing the exchange rate, and targeting the forecast rate of inflation within the framework of an inflation-targeting regime.

Twenty-five years ago, most industrialized countries had just entered a period of targeting monetary aggregates. This was done in the context of trying to bring down the rate of inflation from the high level that it had reached in the early 1970s to the much lower level that was believed to be necessary for good economic performance. The intent of the policy was gradually to bring down the targeted rate of growth of some measure of money (narrow in some countries, broad in others) from a high starting point to a much lower level and thereby wring inflation out of the system.

There were different views of the mechanism at work that would link the deceleration of money growth to a decline in price inflation. The more monetarist view focused on a direct causal link between money growth and the rate of inflation. The typical view in central banking circles, in contrast, was that the mechanism operated through more traditional, structural relationships. Thus, too high a rate of inflation (i.e. one that was higher than consistent with the targeted growth rate of money) would result in a rise in the rate of growth of money demanded above the target rate, leading the central bank to raise policy interest rates. This would lead to a rise in short-term market interest rates, and, to a lesser extent, long-term interest rates, and this in turn would slow the growth of aggregate demand (relative to capacity) and feed into lower inflation.

Essential to this sequence of events were two preconditions. The first was stability in the demand for money. This was necessary so that the appropriate signal would be forthcoming regarding the pace of growth of nominal aggregate demand and the needed change in interest rates. Second, the response of interest rates to the deviation between money and targeted money had to exert appropriate effects on demand and inflation. If the relationship of money demand to interest rates was too elastic, then an excessively high rate of expansion of aggregate demand would give rise to only small increases in interest rates (because that was all that was needed to return money growth to its targeted rate), which might not be sufficient to effect a slower growth of aggregate demand very quickly (or at all).

By the mid-1980s, just 10 years later, most countries had abandoned monetary targets or had significantly downgraded the role of the monetary aggregates. The main reason was that the money-demand relationship had proved unstable. While this instability was initially attributed to the deregulation of financial institutions and markets that was then going on in many countries, it occurred also in some countries that had deregulated much earlier. In those countries, the instability seemed to be related to innovations initiated by financial institutions in which they changed the characteristics of the various financial instruments and services that they offered to the public. As experience in many countries has subsequently shown, these kinds of innovations have continued apace and have lessened the information content of the monetary aggregates to the extent that they cannot bear the weight of being a formal target for monetary policy. It should be noted nonetheless that, in some countries, monetary aggregates continue to play a role in the conduct of policy because they bring some information to the assessment of the current economic and inflation situation. Even in these countries, however, they are usually only one of a number of variables feeding into the outlook for the economy and inflation. And formal monetary targets have not yet totally disappeared. For some countries with a *de jure* or *de facto* floating exchange rate regime, and unsophisticated domestic financial markets in particular, they continue to provide a useful nominal anchor.

In the context of a financial sector that is continuously innovating, I do not expect monetary targeting (or credit targeting, which had an academic following for a brief period) to be much used in the future as an intermediate target for monetary policy.

For many countries, especially smaller ones, the nominal anchor 25 or 30 years ago was a fixed exchange rate to a larger neighbour or to a major trading partner. If a country on a fixed exchange rate did not make periodic changes in the value of the parity of its peg, it would achieve a rate of inflation close to that of the country to which its currency was pegged. Hence, one way of achieving low inflation was to peg to a currency whose monetary authority had a history of maintaining a low rate of inflation.

As financial markets became more open and as private capital flows expanded in size, the adjustable peg regime became increasingly difficult to manage. And the tendency has been to move in one of two directions – on the one hand, to a hard fix in the form of a monetary union or the use of some other country's currency (dollarization or euroization), and, on the other hand, to a floating exchange rate regime.

For the country operating under a monetary union or dollarization the question of how to achieve low inflation is resolved, provided that the central bank of the monetary union or the country whose currency is being used is itself able to conduct policy to deliver a low rate of inflation. Of course, the central banks of countries entering into a monetary union will find their role in monetary policy much reduced. They will presumably have input into the monetary policy deliberations of the monetary union's central bank, and have a vote in setting the policy rate of interest. And to carry out this role effectively they will have to maintain a competent research and analysis unit. Moreover, they may well continue to have responsibilities in operational areas (e.g. payments system) and in supervision. But I anticipate that they will increasingly look like the regional Federal Reserve banks in the United States.

In recent years an increasing number of countries have either chosen or been forced to adopt floating exchange rates. In the context of a floating exchange rate regime and without stable monetary aggregates, what can serve as the nominal anchor for the central bank? The tendency over the past decade among a number of countries has been to move to an inflation-targeting regime.

What has been the overall experience of the industrialized countries with inflation targets? First, those with targets moved from being in the relatively high-inflation group of countries to being in the low-inflation group, and they achieved this in a fairly short time. Second, as these countries achieved their announced goals over time, financial markets adjusted their longer-term inflation expectations and built these expectations into longer-term interest rates. The risk premia that compensate investors for inflation uncertainty declined or vanished. Moreover, participants in product and labour markets adjusted their expectations of future rates of inflation downward as the inflation targets were achieved. At the same time, inflation expectations became partly linked to the target and were less sensitive to movements of inflation away from the target. Third, despite these adjustments, one cannot find improvements in the sacrifice ratio in the data of the countries with inflation targets. Fourth, the targets have been extremely helpful in explaining central bank actions (and, sometimes, inactions) to the financial markets and the public. Fifth, the forecast of inflation has effectively become the intermediate target of policy in countries with inflation targets, and the framework for the analysis of new economic information has shifted to its effect on inflation 1 to 2 years into the future; in other words, the framework has become more forward-looking. Moreover, by focusing on bringing the rate of inflation back to the target over a 1- to 2-year horizon when it deviates from the target, the policy approach results in relatively low variability of both output and inflation. Sixth, according to the staff at a number of central banks with inflation targets, the quality of monetary policy discussions within the central bank has been significantly improved by the introduction of explicit targets.

With the success of inflation targets in containing inflation in industrial countries, a number of emerging-market economies have either adopted or are considering adopting inflation targets as the centerpiece of their monetary policy framework. Included in this group are Brazil, Chile, the Czech Republic, Hungary, Indonesia, Mexico, Peru, Poland, South Africa, South Korea and Thailand.

The best way to think of the inflation-targeting approach to the conduct of policy is to treat the central bank as targeting the forecast of inflation a few quarters out. Thus, when there are pressures of demand on capacity that are judged likely to lead to upward pressure on inflation relative to target in the future, the central bank will act to raise interest rates. And, when the economy is weak, with demand below the economy's productive capacity, there would be downward pressure on future inflation relative to its target, and the central bank would counter this by lowering interest rates, thereby supporting the economy.

A useful way of characterizing this approach more formally is to think of the central bank as minimizing a quadratic loss function whose arguments are the deviation of inflation from its target and the deviation of output from capacity. By acting to return inflation to its target, not as quickly as is technically feasible but more gradually, monetary policy both achieves the longer-run goal of hitting the inflation target and minimizes the variability of output around capacity.

Of course, there are a number of other important issues related to the implementation of inflation targets, I would note in passing, that have been discussed in detail in the literature. Which measure of inflation should be chosen? How does the targeting arrangement deal with various kinds of supply shocks? Should the target be point or a range? If the rate of inflation is outside the target range, how should the central bank be held accountable?

A key element of the inflation-targeting regime is the way that the floating exchange rate fits into the framework. When the central bank acts to raise or lower interest rates, the exchange rate is likely to appreciate or depreciate in consequence. This exchange rate movement acts in concert with the interest rate movement to bring inflation back toward the target, both via its direct impact on prices and, more importantly, via its indirect effect through aggregate demand. But how should the central bank respond in this framework to exchange rate movements that have been induced by factors other than interest rate changes? The answer is that appropriate response of interest rates to an exchange rate movement will depend on the cause of the movement and what it indicates about the future direction of aggregate demand and inflation. If the exchange rate movement appears to be in response to a shock associated with a strengthening or weakening of aggregate demand and hence future inflation (for example, a shock in the terms of trade), the central bank should not try to offset the equilibrating nature of the exchange rate movement by an interest rate adjustment. However, if the source of the exchange rate movement is a portfolio adjustment by investors that is not associated with a 'real' shock, the central bank may adjust interest rates to offset the aggregate demand effects of the exchange rate movement.

If the central bank is successful in achieving the initial inflation targets it will gain credibility, and this increase in credibility in turn will allow it to take advantage of one of the major benefits of inflation targets; the way in which they can anchor inflation expectations. Increased credibility and well-anchored inflation expectations give the central bank increased room to manoeuvre following temporary shocks, since the behaviour of the public and of markets will continue for some time to be based on expectations that the central bank will maintain control over inflation. However, it is important to emphasize that if the central bank does not take action to counter more persistent pressures, credibility will suffer and the anchor will begin to disappear. As noted earlier, the central bank must always be vigilant about the risks of sustained inflation pressures.

So what is the prognosis for nominal anchors in the future? Unlike monetary aggregate targeting, which was always potentially vulnerable to the possibility of instability in the relationship between money and inflation, the other two principal anchors, the exchange rate and the inflation target, are not subject to that kind of problem. Hence they both have the capability of lasting longer than did the monetary aggregate targets as the intermediate target or anchor for controlling inflation.

I also believe that the movement away from the classic fixed peg rate that we have seen in the 1990s will continue. That is, I would predict that over time there will be more truly hard fixes than today, more inflation-targeting floaters and fewer soft fixes. Countries that deem it appropriate to their circumstances to fix their exchange rate will move either to a monetary union or to the use of another country's currency and that will serve as their anchor. The large countries and those intermediate-sized countries for whom this type of arrangement is viewed as inappropriate will maintain floating exchange rate regimes.[1] I expect that the nominal anchor for most countries with a floating exchange rate will be an explicit commitment to a target rate of inflation (as in the current inflation-targeting countries). A few countries will be able to rely on an implicit commitment to low inflation (as in the United States).

One final word on this subject. David Laidler (1999) has emphasized the importance of a country having a coherent monetary order. By this he means a set of arrangements whereby: (i) monetary policy has a well-defined goal; (ii) the authorities charged with achieving that goal have the powers needed to achieve it; (iii) private sector agents, or at least a representative majority of them, understand that goal, expect it to be pursued, and base their own actions on that expectation; and (iv) the relevant policymaking authorities are accountable to the electorate both for their choice of policy goals and for their performance in pursuing them. It is important to keep in mind in assessing different possible arrangements how different parts of the set of arrangements mutually reinforce each other and that, for example, simply opting for a floating exchange rate regime does not provide a coherent monetary order without the other elements of the package, most importantly the nominal anchor.

17.4 Instruments for the implementation of monetary policy

While the choice of goals and of nominal anchors (or intermediate targets) of policy has been limited to a small number of options, the way in which monetary policy has been implemented has differed greatly across countries. In large part this was a result of countries having different histories, resulting in different kinds of financial institutions, laws, practices and traditions. Since central banks made use of the arrangements bequeathed them by history to implement policy, this has resulted in various kinds of mechanisms evolving over time.

In spite of all the differences in the details of the way policy was implemented, two basic types of arrangements could be discerned even 25 years ago. One involved mechanisms whereby the central bank could influence or control a short-term interest rate in the expectation that changes in this rate would feed into other (market) interest rates and the exchange rate, and thereby affect spending and ultimately inflation. In other words, these central banks operated on the traditional transmission mechanism via their influence on the 1-day interest rate or some other short-term rate of interest (such as a 2-week repo rate), although the way they did this was not always transparent. The focus was on affecting the behaviour of lenders, borrowers and financial institutions through changes in the rates of interest facing them in markets.

The other approach involved quantitative measures that directly impinged on the ability of banks to extend credit and/or to expand the money supply. While most common in developing countries, they were also used in earlier periods in many industrialized countries. For example, in France the 'encadrement du crédit' set quantitative limits on credit growth at banks, while in England the 'corset' in effect imposed progressive taxes on the growth of banks' interest-bearing liabilities. Quantitative restrictions played the key role in policy implementation in developing countries because of the preponderant role of banks and the absence of well-developed domestic financial markets in these countries. Central banks would therefore affect nominal spending through measures directly impacting on the rate of growth of bank balance sheets.

In comparing the situation 25 years ago and today, two major trends stand out, both involving forms of convergence. First, more countries are focusing on the use of mechanisms to influence short-term interest rates in their implementation of policy and fewer are relying on quantitative measures. I would attribute this shift away from quantitative mechanisms and towards interest rate mechanisms to the development of financial markets (albeit limited in many of the developing countries) and the gradual elimination of controls of all sorts.

Second, countries that use changes in the short-term interest rate as the centrepiece of their approach to policy implementation have simplified the mechanisms used to influence the rate and have become more transparent regarding their target for that rate. This increased simplicity and transparency can be attributed mainly to changes in the way financial institutions behave and, relatedly, to changes in central bank views about how policy can be most effectively carried out.

In earlier years, even in many countries that relied on influencing interest rates as their primary mechanism of policy implementation, the arrangements involved an element of moral suasion or traditional practices. For example, in Canada, while there were arrangements for the chartered banks to borrow from the Bank of Canada, it was considered inappropriate for the banks to avail themselves of this type of borrowing overly often, and frequent recourse to this type of borrowing was frowned upon by the authorities. The entire implementation system was based on this 'code of conduct', which led to banks wanting to maintain a cushion of excess reserves with the Bank of Canada, permitting the central bank to influence the overnight rate of interest by changes in the amount of excess reserves provided.

Over time, it became increasingly difficult in Canada to rely upon this type of moral suasion as banks increasingly focused on their 'bottom line' and became less inclined to play by the 'rules of the game'. The Bank of Canada therefore moved to a system that relied upon cost incentives to get the banks to behave in a way that allowed it to have the desired degree of influence on the overnight interest rate.

Until the mid-1990s, although the Bank of Canada adjusted the supply of reserves or settlement balances to achieve its desired level for the overnight rate, the market was left to draw inferences about the target rate from the actual behaviour of the rate. Now the Bank of Canada and many other central banks explicitly announce the target rate at which they are aiming. The increased transparency in this area relates to the view that markets function better if they have a more complete understanding of what the central bank is trying to do.

What about the future? I would expect that explicit targeting of a short-term interest rate as the preferred approach to policy implementation will become almost universal, as will transparency about the policy rate objective. The technical mechanisms behind the way central banks affect the supply of reserves or settlement balances will continue to vary across countries as a result of different institutional practices, but for all practical purposes the end result will be very similar.

One challenge to this view that central banks will be able to influence the overnight rate in the future in much the same way as they are currently doing has come from Ben Friedman of Harvard University, who has questioned whether in a world of electronic money (e-money) central banks will be able to maintain their influence over short-term interest rates and through them on aggregate demand and inflation (Friedman 1999).

Effectively, what has been crucial in the past for the ability of central banks to influence the behaviour of short-term interest rates has been the combination of the monopoly power of the central bank over the supply of reserves or settlement balances, and its ability to impose terms and conditions related to the excess or shortfall of reserves or settlement balances. Together, these have determined the incentives for banks to adjust their balance sheets in response to central bank actions. What Friedman questions is whether the spread of e-money will affect central bank balance sheets and/or the mechanism for the settlement of payments in such a way as to erode this monopoly power of central banks.

My own view[2] is that although they are often the result of legal requirements, the arrangements by which the central bank controls the supply of, and conditions pertaining to, reserves and settlement balances also reflect the advantages of the central bank as the provider of the mechanism to settle payments imbalances among banks. These advantages include the riskless character of the central bank and its ability to act as lender of last resort. These characteristics give the central bank a comparative advantage in providing the settlement mechanism, making it very unlikely that other mechanisms, including variants of electronic money, will supplant the current types of arrangements for the foreseeable future.

Let me expand on this position by examining two types of e-money, stored value cards (SVCs) and network money, which could potentially compete with the two kinds of central bank liabilities, bank notes and the reserves or settlement balances of banks.

SVCs are prepaid cards in which funds are stored in electronic form on a computer chip (or integrated circuit) embedded in the card. A number of SVC schemes have been developed, with Mondex, Visa Cash and Proton among the best known brand names internationally. In prepaid software products or network money products, funds are stored in electronic form on devices such as the hard disk of a computer and are transferred over communications networks such as the Internet. These products are at a far earlier stage of development than the SVCs.

Could SVCs totally replace bank notes in the foreseeable future? Such an outcome seems unlikely. History suggests that a variety of payment media can co-exist. What seems to happen is that a form of specialization occurs, with different types of payments being made by different types of payment media. Most of the SVCs issued to date have relatively low limits, and the experience thus far suggests that their principal use will be for small-value face-to- face purchases. One would therefore expect SVCs to have only a small and gradual impact on the demand for bank notes, and hence on central bank balance sheets.

A recent survey by the Bank of International Settlements (2000), based on 1999 data, supports these judgements. The average value of purchases using SVCs is less than US$10 for most card-based products; in very few cases is it above US$25. The float outstanding (which is the counterpart to central banks' currency outstanding) is typically small, and in no case does it appear to exceed US$75 million.

However, let us assume for purposes of argument that the extreme outcome does occur, that SVCs displace bank notes (and coins) entirely, and that the major item on the liability side of the central bank's balance sheet therefore disappears entirely. Is the central bank capable of influencing the very short-term interest rate in such an environment? I would answer that it could, but that some of the techniques used by central banks to influence the policy rate might have to be significantly altered.

Assume that the settlement of payment imbalances continues to take place on the books of the central bank. One way for the central bank to implement policy in this environment would be to try to reproduce the type of arrangements that it uses in the current environment. To do this, the central bank could issue interest-bearing central bank bills. With the proceeds of the bill issue, the central bank could purchase government debt. If the central bank were to issue appreciable amounts of these bills, its balance sheet would, on the surface, not look very different from the present (although perhaps smaller), and it could conduct open-market operations in government debt as it currently does.

Rather than the central bank attempting to replicate the current system, in which it has a sizeable balance sheet and uses open-market operations to influence the very short-term interest rate, the emphasis in the hypothesized environment might shift to a corridor system for the overnight interest rate such as the one currently used in Canada. The Bank of Canada sets a band for the overnight rate of interest by providing standing facilities in which it is prepared to accept overnight deposits at a certain rate of interest and to extend overnight loans at a higher rate of interest. With such an arrangement, the terms and conditions surrounding the holding and borrowing of settlement balances are central to the influence that the central bank has on the policy rate, and changes in the size of the balance sheet play at most a supporting role. In such a case, the displacement of bank notes by SVCs would have little or no influence on the ability of the central bank to implement monetary policy.

Thus, there are a number of ways in which a central bank could implement monetary policy in a world where SVCs entirely replace bank notes, but in which settlement continues to take place on the books of the central bank.

What about the possibility that network money or some other mechanism could replace adjustments in the central bank balance sheet as an arrangement for settling payments imbalances? The Bank for International Settlements survey referred to earlier indicates that, at least to date, there are relatively few network-based products in operation and all of these are very small. Nonetheless, it is worth examining the argument that in the future network money or some other mechanism could replace the central bank balance sheet as the locus for settling payments imbalances.

There are at least three reasons why the central bank has become the locus of settlement for payments imbalances among banks. First, the central bank is risk-free since it cannot fail. Second, the central bank is able to act as lender of last resort (in some cases by providing standing facilities), so that ordinary shortfalls in payments can easily be met, and it can also provide emergency lending assistance in the event of a serious liquidity problem. The third reason is historical. In the past, the central bank imposed reserve requirements on banks but permitted them to meet those requirements on average over a period of time. When banks had to hold balances at the central bank to meet reserve requirements, those balances could efficiently do double duty in serving as settlement balances as well.

There are alternative ways to settle imbalances, and banks could, in principle, use one of these as the mechanism for settlement. For example, one bank could act as the settlement agent for all other banks. Thus, all other banks would hold settlement balances and/or take loans from that settlement bank to settle imbalances. Effectively, the settlement bank would act as a central bank. However, this mechanism has several drawbacks. Since the settlement bank is not risk-free, the other banks could potentially be taking on considerable risks in holding funds with it. Also, the settlement bank might be taking on undesired risk in extending credit to banks with shortfalls. Moreover, the other banks would likely be uncomfortable about the competitive advantage one of their number would gain by being treated as the equivalent of the central bank.

Another arrangement for settlement could involve banks transferring riskless instruments, such as treasury bills, among each other to settle payments imbalances. While feasible, this arrangement also has drawbacks relative to a system in which banks transfer settlement balances at the central bank. First, and perhaps most important, there is no lender of last resort to provide credit in the event of a shortfall. This approach would therefore require the banks to hold very large amounts of treasury bills to avoid a situation where an unusually large payment outflow puts a bank in a position where it cannot meet its obligations. Second, because banks have to pay a higher rate on term deposits than they receive on treasury bills, the cost of holding treasury bills to cover settlement imbalances could be significant, especially in comparison with systems in which the central bank offers near-market overnight interest rates on deposits, or where the arrangements are structured so that only small amounts of deposits have to be held by banks. Third, if government debt declines, there could be a shortage of the riskless securities needed for end-of-day settlement.

For all these reasons, I conclude that banks will continue to use the transfer of settlement balances at the central bank as an efficient and relatively inexpensive way of settling imbalances (assuming that the arrangements involve either very low settlement balances or the remuneration of settlement balances at near-market rates of interest).

I would go one step further and argue that, even in the extremely unlikely case that the spread of SVCs led to the elimination of bank notes and that the development of network money permitted alternative settlement services to be offered that effectively competed with central bank services, central banks would very likely be able to continue to influence the policy rate. Of course, the techniques used by central banks to implement policy would have to adjust to changes in the institutional environment.

One possibility would involve the central bank insisting on settlement of its own transactions on its own balance sheet and refusing to settle on the alternative mechanisms. This type of arrangement would be strengthened if the central bank continued to act as banker for the government.

A second possibility would involve a situation in which the central bank continued to establish a corridor for the overnight interest rate by providing standby facilities in which it was prepared to accept overnight deposits at a certain rate of interest and to extend overnight loans at a higher rate of interest. If market rates of interest were tending to decline below the central bank's deposit rate, market participants would choose to hold overnight deposits with the central bank. The central bank could accept payment for the deposit in marketable assets, which would then remain on its balance sheet. Conversely, if the overnight rate were tending to increase above the top of the band, borrowing institutions would turn to the central bank for funds. The central bank would fund these loans by issuing its own liabilities (either marketable paper or deposits on its books), which would be held by the borrowing or other institutions.

In short, the attributes of central banks would very likely allow them to continue to exert an influence over the very short-term interest rate, and hence would give them the lever necessary to affect spending and inflation even if e-money were able to displace both bank notes and central bank settlement services.)

17.5 Independence and accountability, transparency and communications

I would like to add a few thoughts on these important and interesting aspects of central banking, which have seen major changes in the last 25 years.

Central banks in many countries have been given increased independence in recent years. The basic factor driving this development has been the widespread acceptance of the view that a monetary policy aimed at low inflation is best achieved by giving the central bank the responsibility for conducting monetary policy.

It is important to distinguish between instrument independence and goal independence. In the former, the objective of policy is set by government or Parliament and the central bank is authorized to take whatever actions are necessary to achieve the objective that has been set. In the latter, the central bank has the authority to set the goal of policy, and in practice it typically also has the power to implement policy to achieve that goal.

If one examines the situation today, there is a range of arrangements across countries, even among independent central banks. At one end of the spectrum, the Bank of England has instrument independence but the goal of $2\frac{1}{2}$ per cent inflation is set by the Chancellor. At the other end, the ECB determines the rate of inflation that it is aiming to achieve, albeit in the context of a treaty that sets price stability as its mandate. In between, in New Zealand and Canada the target for inflation involves a joint agreement by the government and the central bank.

There is continuing debate in the literature as to how efficacious central bank independence is in achieving low inflation and output stability. One reason for the difficulty in reaching definitive conclusions in this area is that it is hard to measure independence, since there are both formal and informal characteristics to the relationship between the central bank and the government and it is only the former that are readily measurable. A second factor behind the debate is that it is hard to pin down the direction of causation. The argument is that countries that are averse to inflation are also more likely to make their central banks independent. Hence, it has been argued that central bank independence is the result of the desire for low inflation and not a separate causal factor in achieving such an outcome.

In central banking circles, it is strongly (and I believe correctly) believed that independence *does* contribute to the achievement of low inflation. Requiring a group of experts independent of government to take appropriate actions to achieve the objective of low inflation removes or at least insulates the interest rate decision-making process from short-term political pressures. And this is of benefit both to the central bank and to the government.

Along with independence comes accountability, and transparency and communications make an important contribution to accountability. In addition, the current view is that transparency and communications enable monetary policy to be conducted more effectively.

One of the most striking changes in recent years in central banking practices has been the movement to increased transparency. Twenty-five years ago, the typical attitude among central banks was to say little and let actions speak for themselves. Surprising markets was the order of the day. Today, in contrast, most central banks have a communications strategy that focuses on making a wide range of information available to markets and to the public. This enhanced transparency typically involves making explicit the objective of monetary policy, clarifying the views of the central bank on the transmission mechanism, and explaining the current outlook of the central bank regarding output and inflation. Central banks use monetary policy reports, inflation reports, press releases on fixed meeting dates, minutes of meetings of the monetary policy committee, speeches, and articles in their review or bulletin to communicate their views on these matters.

There are a number of benefits that accrue from increased transparency. The public will be more inclined to support the policy objective and approach if they understand it better, and the actions of employers and employees in setting prices and wages will be more consistent with the achievement of the goal of low inflation in an environment where the central bank objective and strategy are both clear and credible. The actions of central banks in adjusting the very short-term interest rate will be transferred more smoothly across financial markets if market participants understand the rationale for the central bank action and their views are broadly in line with those of the central bank. Indeed, in my view, the best situation is one in which markets are generally able to anticipate central bank actions because they interpret the implications of newly-released data for the output and inflation outlook in a similar way to the central bank and comprehend the way in which the changed outlook will influence the central bank's views on the need to adjust interest rates.

17.6 Concluding remarks

The past 25 years have been very eventful for central banks. And while I believe that many of the trends over that period will continue to be important for the way monetary policy is conducted, unforeseen developments may well lead to outcomes that we cannot anticipate at this time. This means that the formulation and implementation of monetary policy and its transmission mechanism will long continue to be interesting subjects of study for academics, and that central banking will continue to provide a fascinating career for practitioners.

Acknowledgment

The author would like to thank Paul Jenkins and David Longworth for comments on an earlier draft of this paper. The views expressed in this paper are those of the author and should not be attributed to the Bank of Canada.

Notes

1 Countries' decisions not to enter a monetary union or dollarize might be based on a concern that the large country to which they might tie their fortunes would conduct an overly inflationary monetary policy or because their economic structure differs from that of the potential partner country, leaving them vulnerable to idiosyncratic shocks, or because their trade patterns are such that linking to a single currency results in excessive swings in competitiveness when there are sharp movements in major countries' exchange rates.

2 The rest of this section draws heavily on Freedman (2000).

18 Monetary policy and the supply side

John Vickers

18.1 Introduction

To come from the Bank of England to speak to the Society of Business Economists is to be a nominal economist among real economists. Businesses like yours and those who work in them are the real economy – the supply side – the workings of which ultimately determine the paths of real economic variables such as output growth, employment and productivity. The Bank's paramount monetary policy objective of price stability, on the other hand, concerns (the rate of inflation of) a nominal variable – the general price level or, inversely, the purchasing power of money. The MPC pursues that objective by determining the terms of supply for money itself.

Interactions between the real and nominal sides of the economy are my subject this evening. I want to discuss some possible implications for inflation–and hence for monetary policy – of some current developments on the supply side, in particular the ongoing revolution in information and communications technology.

Views on the relationship between inflation and the real economy have shifted substantially over the years. Long ago, in the age of the Paleo paradigm, it was believed that there was a trade-off such that higher real activity could be sustained at the expense of higher inflation. That view having collapsed under the weight of both theory and facts – a rare and thus devastating combination – the current conventional (and correct) wisdom is that higher inflation cannot increase real activity sustainably. So the best that monetary policy can do for the real economy is to secure and maintain actual and expected price stability.

Recently, moreover, a view has gained ground that special supply-side developments can ease the task of monetary policy – in particular, that current technological and competitive developments are helping, or will very soon help, to suppress inflation. Then the prospect would be higher growth together with *lower* inflation. (And indeed in the Necro paradigm inflation is dead.)

Assessing this view involves answering two questions:

1 What are the implications for growth of current and prospective supply-side developments?
2 What do these developments mean for inflation, and hence for monetary policy that targets inflation?

18.2 Information technology and economic growth

Twenty years ago I worked for IBM on a competition law case. The question was whether IBM possessed, and was abusing, a dominant position in the computer hardware industry. A similar antitrust case had been brought against IBM by the US government long before – when President Johnson's term of office was drawing to its close in January 1969. The fact that the computer industry was large enough to see major antitrust litigation more than 30 years ago shows that the large-scale commercial exploitation of information technology (IT) is far from new.

Since then the costs of computing power have gone on falling dramatically, the personal computer has become pervasive in home as well as office, the accessibility and capability of IT have been enormously enhanced by ever-improving user-friendly software, and, spurred by falling telecommunications costs, computer networking has exploded. And now there is the Internet.

These developments – the Internet above all – are self-evidently amazing. They hold out the prospect of substantial productivity gains in the years to come, just as IT has for many years past. Developments in IT might also help to sharpen competition, as new forms of business organisation challenge older ones, and by improving price transparency generally. But what does all this add up to in macroeconomic terms?

Ironically, just as the IT revolution was getting underway, measured productivity growth in the United States and elsewhere slowed down. Table 18.1 shows Jorgenson and Stiroh's (1999) analysis of US economic growth from 1948 to 1996. In the golden age from 1948 to 1973, estimated annual output growth was 4 per cent, and labour productivity growth – the growth of output per unit of labour – was 3 per cent. Total factor productivity (TFP) growth – i.e. allowing also for capital and consumer durable inputs, which grew strongly over the period – was, on these estimates, a little under $1\frac{1}{2}$ per cent. In the 1973–96 period, by contrast, output growth slowed to about $2\frac{3}{4}$ per cent despite a rise in labour input growth, productivity growth fell to around $1\frac{1}{2}$ per cent (less in the early 1990s), and TFP growth was less than $\frac{1}{2}$ per cent.

This slowdown, which forms the background to the late-1990s US growth spurt, is the Solow productivity paradox. Robert Solow quipped in 1987 that 'you can see the computer age everywhere but in the productivity statistics'. Various explanations have been put forward for the paradox of a productivity slowdown in the age of IT.

Table 18.1 Sources of US Economic growth 1948–96

	Growth rate		
	1948–73	*1973–90*	*1990–96*
Outputs			
Total output	4.020	2.857	2.363
Non-computer	3.978	2.650	1.980
Computer outputs	0.042	0.207	0.384
Inputs:			
Capital services	1.073	0.954	0.632
Non-computers	1.049	0.845	0.510
Computers	0.025	0.109	0.123
Consumers' durables	0.550	0.426	0.282
Non-computers	0.550	0.414	0.242
Computers	0.000	0.012	0.040
Labour input	1.006	1.145	1.219
Aggregate total factor	1.391	0.335	0.231

Source: Jorgenson and Stiroh, 1999.
(This analysis is based on data available prior to the comprehensive National Accounts revisions of October.)

Note
Contribution of inputs and outputs are real growth rates weighted by average, nominal shares. All average annual.

The first possibility is measurement problems (see Griliches 1994). The balance of economic activity in developed economies has increasingly shifted towards service sectors whose output is hard to measure. If the under-recording of 'true' output has increased since the early 1970s – which is something we ultimately have to guess at – then the slowdown in productivity growth will have been overstated by the official figures. (Relatedly, inflation in the 'true' cost of living may have been overstated by available price indices. But inflation targets for monetary policy can be based only on available indices.)

Second, since it is only recently that computers have become a large part of the capital stock, perhaps one should not have expected a major IT contribution to growth much before now. On Jorgenson and Stiroh's estimates in Table 18.1, computer outputs accounted for about 0.4 per cent of annual US growth in 1990–96, and computer inputs contributed less than 0.2 per cent to growth. Computers by then accounted for as much as a fifth of the contribution to growth of capital services, reflecting the vast shift towards IT investment prompted by the sharp declines in IT equipment prices that reflect the dramatic technological advances made by the computer industry. But the gains to IT investment have, on these figures, accrued to computer producers and their customers, rather than generating externalities in the form of TFP growth.

Third, it could be that an IT-based acceleration in productivity has just got underway in the US and is just around the corner in other countries such as the UK. Ten years ago Paul David (1990) suggested, on the basis of the historical experience of electrification in the US, that it was too soon to be disappointed that the computer revolution had not yet led to a discernible acceleration of economy-wide productivity. Commercial electricity generation began in the 1880s, but did not have a substantial measurable impact on US productivity until the 1920s.

The diffusion of general-purpose technologies such as electricity and IT can take a long time and be arduous processes insofar as scarce resources are absorbed in the associated processes of economic restructuring. As David (2000) puts it:

> For these changes to be set in place typically requires decades, rather than years. Moreover, while they are underway there is no guarantee that their dominant effects upon macroeconomic performance will be positive ones.

And he notes the limits to historical analogy. While history may teach that an instant productivity pay-off is not to be expected and that its absence is not inconsistent with a large eventual pay-off, it cannot foretell the time-path of such gains. That said, David is cautiously optimistic that, relative to the experience of the past two decades, the future may well bring a resurgence of TFP growth resulting from the exploitation of IT.

Is that what we are seeing in the US right now? Figures 18.1 and 18.2 show the level and growth rate of US non-farm business labour productivity since 1970. Since 1996, annual productivity growth has averaged about

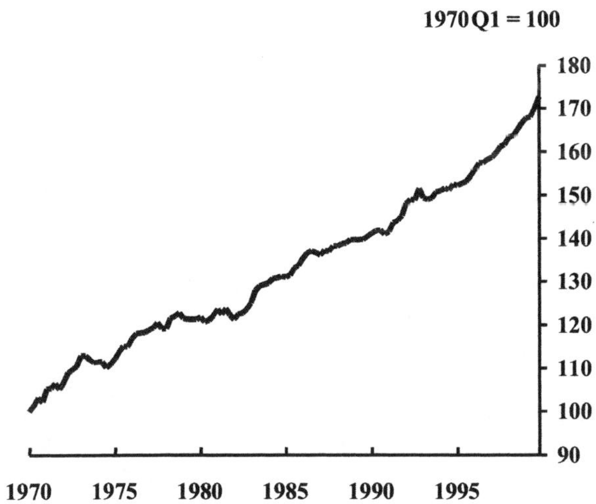

Figure 18.1 US non-farm business sector labour productivity (source: Primark Datastream).

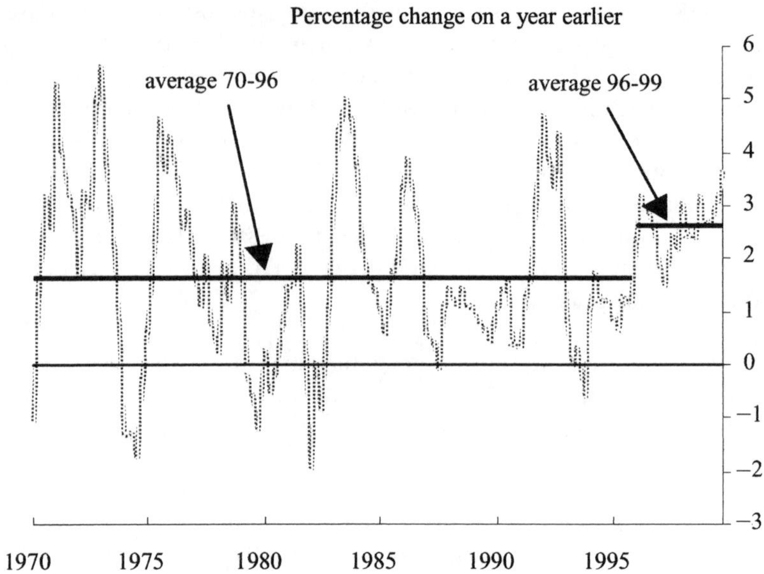

Figure 18.2 US non-farm business sector labour productivity (source: Primark Datastream).

$2\frac{1}{2}$ per cent, 1 percentage point higher than over the 1973–96 period. This is undoubtedly impressive, but is it evidence at last of a substantial broad-based productivity impact of IT across the economy as a whole?

Robert Gordon (1999) is doubtful. His decomposition of the US productivity growth recovery accounts for all of it in terms of three factors:

1 The normal cyclical rise in productivity that typically occurs in economic upswings;
2 Large productivity gains in the computer industry itself;
3 Improvements in inflation measures that have had the effect of increasing measured productivity growth.

This is not to deny the good productivity news. Rather, it is to locate it, as far as (2) is concerned, in the computer-producing sector of the US economy, and not generally across the economy.

Oliner and Sichel (2000), however, reach a somewhat different view from their analysis of the recent data. Unlike Gordon, they do not attempt to distinguish between cyclical and trend movements in productivity. Of the 1 per cent rise in US labour productivity growth between the first and the second half of the 1990s, Oliner and Sichel attribute $\frac{1}{2}$ per cent to the increasing use of IT capital throughout the non-farm business sector, and another $\frac{1}{4}$ per cent to advances in the technology for producing computers. On this view, IT is most of the story behind the recent acceleration in US productivity.

So far I have dwelt on the US evidence because it has been so extensively debated, because productivity there has recently picked up so sharply, and because the US is the country that has been at the leading edge of the IT revolution since its commercial inception, (but let us not forget the intellectual forefathers of IT, such as Charles Babbage and Alan Turing). What are the implications for us in the UK?

Annual labour productivity growth over the past 40 years in the UK has been about 2 per cent on average – see Figure 18.3. Since 1996, however, just as productivity growth in the US picked up, it has been not much above 1 per cent in the UK. It would be pessimistic to have as one's central expectation a persistence of 1 per cent or so productivity growth in the period ahead, though uncertainty and volatility in the data mean that 1 per cent, like 3 per cent, is an entirely possible outcome. In good part because of the strength of business investment in the late 1990s (see Figure 18.4) – probably a growing share of which has been in IT – a more likely outcome would seem to be a rise in productivity growth, perhaps to around its longer-run trend rate of about 2 per cent. (Together with annual labour force growth of near $\frac{1}{2}$ per cent, this would imply a central expectation for output growth of around $2\frac{1}{2}$ per cent.) Anyhow, that is what all the MPC members have assumed as the central case in

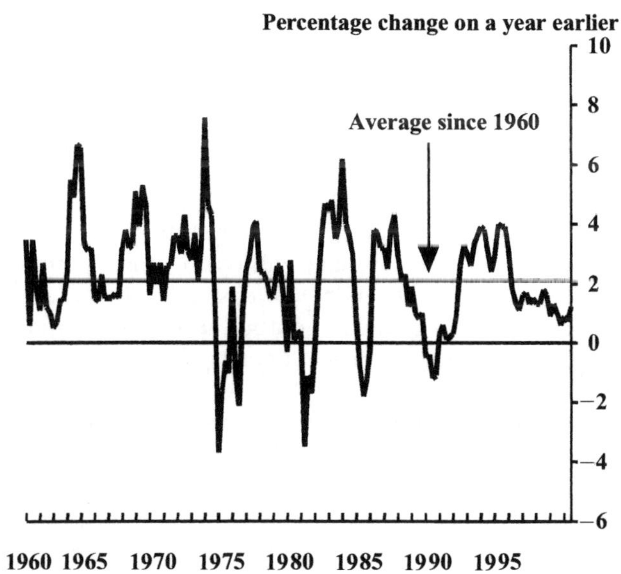

Figure 18.3 UK labour productivity (GDP per person employed) (source: ONS and Bank of England).

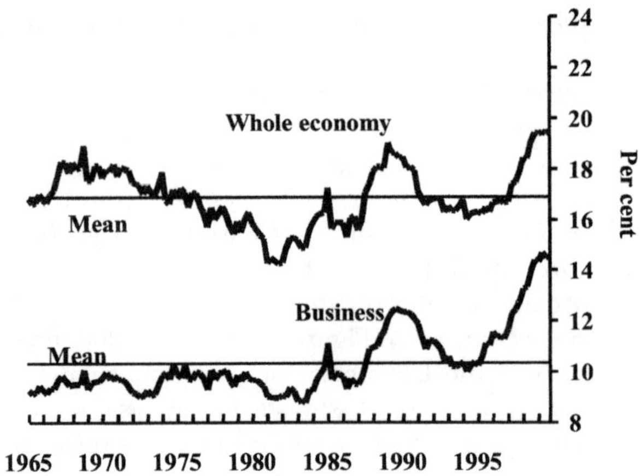

Figure 18.4 Investment as a share of GDP (source: ONS and Bank of England).

Note
At constant prices.

recent projections. (We have also assumed a further decline in the stock/output ratio, which business-to-business e-commerce may help to bring about.)

Higher productivity growth than that is entirely possible – as is less – but 2 per cent is not far short of the $2\frac{1}{2}$ per cent productivity growth that the US has experienced in the remarkable recent years. And although it is growing rapidly in the UK, the IT sector, which appears to have experienced especially sharp productivity gains, is a larger part of the US economy.

Is 2 per cent annual productivity growth large or small in broader historical terms? From a long-run perspective it is quite large. No historical knowledge is needed to show this. If it had grown at that rate since 1066, output per head would then have been one hundred-millionth of its current level. Even with 1 per cent annual productivity growth, output per head would have been an impossible 10,000 times smaller then than now.

Estimates of the trend rate of growth of output in the British industrial revolution show a slow but steady rise from about 1 per cent in the second half of the eighteenth century to around 2 per cent in the early nineteenth century, then a peak of perhaps $2\frac{1}{2}$ per cent mid-century, before a significant slowing of growth (see Crafts 1998). Allowing for labour force growth, productivity growth was much smaller than these figures, and, according to Crafts, 'total factor productivity growth was apparently very modest during the Industrial Revolution and was less than 1 per cent per year throughout the 19th century'. This despite inventions such as the steam engine, railways, steel and the telegraph – the 'Victorian Internet' discussed in Wadhwani (2000).

But what about the more recent experiences of the post-war golden age of growth in Western Europe, and of the East Asian economies which at times grew at rates close to 10 per cent? In the latter case, a good deal of the spectacular growth performance can be accounted for by demographics, fast capital accumulation, and the seizing of huge technological catch-up opportunities (see Young 1995). Some of those factors are also relevant to the experience of post-war Europe, which shows that high labour productivity growth over an extended period is by no means unprecedented, especially in the presence of strong capital investment, but it is historically rather unusual.

It is nevertheless quite possible that the IT revolution could at some point bring a period of historically unusual productivity growth. For example, it is plausible that the diffusion of Internet technology is and will be much faster than that of previous innovations. But some caveats must be kept in mind.

First, productivity growth does not happen by magic. Without continual innovation, growth would slow, and the main engine of innovation at present is IT. So while IT will no doubt add to productivity growth in the sense that it would be lower without IT, productivity growth without IT might have been lower than average past rates.

Second, other things being equal, the level of innovation must keep rising for productivity growth not to slow down. (The reference to 'other things being equal' is because innovation is by no means the only source of productivity growth. Others include exploitation of scale economies, gains from structural adjustment, and human capital investment.) Loosely speaking, steady growth requires innovation to grow as fast as output. So if the feeling is correct that there is more innovation now than there used to be, it does not necessarily follow that productivity growth will be higher than in the past, because 'a greater number of new things is not necessarily a greater rate of new things' (Triplett 1999).

Third, strong capital accumulation is generally a prerequisite for high labour productivity growth. Gains from IT depend on investment in physical capital and in intangible, but nonetheless important, knowledge capital and human capital. Investment is one way in which the prospect of supply-side improvement may stimulate demand. This is a suitable point to turn to the monetary policy implications of IT.

18.3 Implications for monetary policy

Now let us *assume* that the IT revolution has created an unusual opportunity for a period of substantially higher productivity growth, and perhaps also for a structural intensification of competition. What then are the implications for inflation, and hence for monetary policy?

At first sight this might seem obvious. If costs are falling because of greater productivity, and if prices are if anything decreasing in relation to costs, then the pressure on prices would surely seem to be downwards.

But that is to confuse real and nominal (i.e. money-denominated) variables. Higher productivity means that more output can be produced from given inputs, so the price of output will tend to decrease relative to the prices of inputs. In particular, if competition does not weaken, output prices will fall relative to input prices such as wages. That is to say, wages will rise relative to prices – the real wage will increase. But this, by itself, says nothing about the effect on the level or rate of change of prices, or of nominal wages, or of nominal unit labour costs.

To put the point starkly, one could infer nothing about the path of inflation – movement in the value of money – from knowledge that oranges were getting cheaper in relation to lemons.

Shifts in productivity and competition can certainly affect inflation, but – as Willem Buiter (2000) has emphasised with his customary clarity – the links are by no means straightforward. The simple argument above that rising productivity means downward pressure on prices is at best seriously incomplete.

A full argument must involve monetary variables. Inflation is after all a monetary phenomenon. In that spirit, suppose for a moment that monetary policy involved setting a path for the growth of some monetary aggregate *M*. Holding that path fixed, higher productivity growth would mean lower inflation if velocity – the ratio of nominal demand to *M* – did not shift. Inflation would then have to fall to keep the path of nominal demand the same.

But why would velocity stay the same? Velocity is notoriously variable, at least for most UK monetary aggregates. And it seems quite plausible that IT developments such as e-commerce should increase velocity, at least for narrower monetary aggregates, by facilitating economies in holdings of transactions balances. (Indeed, there has been some speculative discussion recently of a prospect of the ultimate demise of money, though it is interesting that the 1990s were the first decade since at least the 1940s that narrow money velocity *fell* in the UK, perhaps partly because of lower nominal interest rates.) If developments in IT increased both productivity growth and velocity in the thought experiment with a fixed money growth path, then the implications for inflation would be mixed.

However, although monetary quantities are valuable indicator variables, monetary policy in practice involves choosing the (inter-temporal) *price* of money – the short-term nominal interest rate – with the explicit aim in the UK of achieving the inflation target. The question then arises of whether, for a given nominal interest rate path, the arrival of a productivity-boosting supply-side opportunity will tend to increase or decrease inflation. And of whether, by implication, interest rates need to be increased or decreased to keep inflation on target.

In a range of simple macroeconomic models, the dynamics of inflation depend, among other things, on the output gap – actual output minus potential output (see, for example, McCallum and Nelson 1997; Clarida *et al.* 1999; Woodford 1999). A positive output gap tends to go with rising inflation – as demand presses on capacity – and an increasing output gap tends to mean accelerating inflation. The converse applies for negative and falling output gaps.

This sort of framework, which can be built up from microeconomic foundations, offers a simplified but coherent account of how supply-side developments can affect the paths of nominal variables. For example, a positive supply shock – such as unexpectedly higher (total factor) productivity growth, or a fall in the unemployment rate consistent with steady inflation – reduces the output gap and so lowers the path of inflation for a given path of nominal interest rates.

At first sight this might seem to justify the view that the IT revolution, as a positive supply shock, will moderate inflation. After all, we are assuming here that it will raise productivity growth unusually. (Moreover, as Sushil Wadhwani (2000) has stressed, it might also reduce the NAIRU via effects on product market competition and by improving the efficiency of matching people to jobs in the labour market.)

But supply 'shocks' are so called for a reason – they are *unexpected* changes in supply capacity. If the Interest, say, improves productivity (relative to a world without the Internet), that will now hardly be a surprise. An innovation such as the Internet is perhaps better described, when it arrives, as a shock to future productive potential. Once an improvement to the supply-side has come to be anticipated – whether or not it has yet been realised – demand too may be boosted. Then the innovation imparts a demand shock as well as a supply shock. So depending on the links between the supply side and demand, a relevant question is whether the productivity improvement turns out to be more or less than expected. And timing is important, for an anticipated supply-side improvement could boost demand by more than supply in the short term.

Two kinds of demand channel matter. The first, mentioned above, is direct investment demand, without which the supply-side improvement is unlikely to be realised. New technological opportunity creates a high marginal return on investment in new technology and so leads to a surge of investment in capital embodying it. Insofar as the new technology allows extra economies in inventory investment or reduces the marginal return on investment in 'old' technologies, there may be some offset to the expansion in investment demand, but the likely direction of the overall effect seems clear.

Moreover, new technological opportunity may encourage various other forms of investment in the broad economic sense, including training and restructuring of organisations and employment. Investment of this kind may temporarily reduce supply – for example because employees investing in training are not full-time in production activities – rather than being part of investment demand.

The second channel is via increase in consumer demand in anticipation of future income gains. The most prominent aspect of this mechanism concerns stock-market wealth. Stock markets generally rose strongly in the last decade (see Figure 18.5). Especially striking over the past year or so has been the extraordinary rise of IT sector stock prices (see Figure 18.6). (Some stellar performers have yet to make profits, suggesting that the hallmark of exceptional stock market valuation is no longer a very high price/earnings ratio, but an appropriately negative one.) As well as

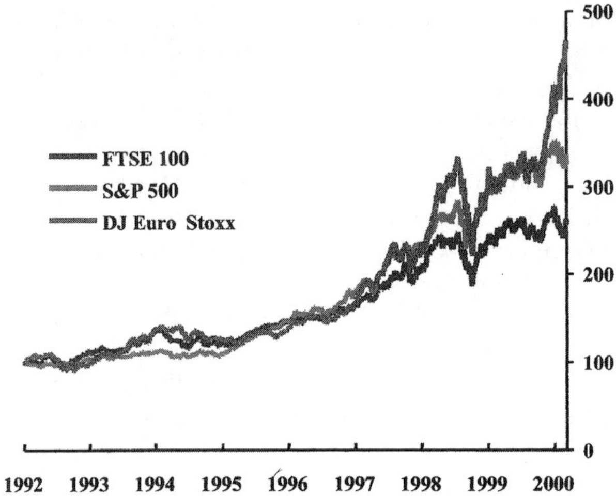

Figure 18.5 Worldwide equity indices, measured in local currency (1/1/92 = 100) (source: Datastream).

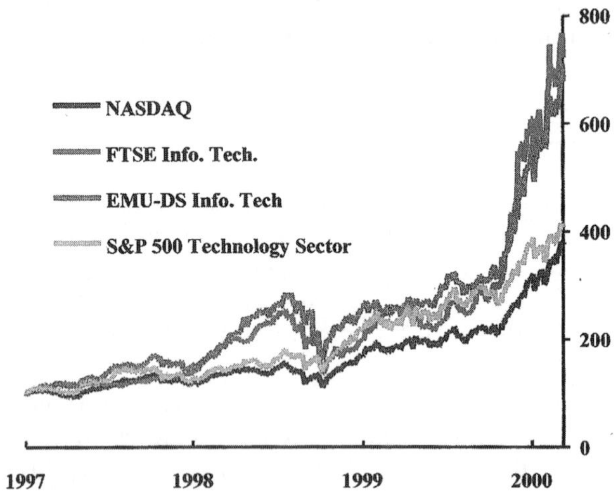

Figure 18.6 Worldwide technology indices, measured in local currency (1/1/97 = 100) (source: Datastream).

stimulating consumption, high stock-market values may also further boost investment by lowering the cost of capital.

Stock-market wealth gains related to IT have been very large in the US. They have been large, but not as large, in the UK because the IT sector is proportionately smaller here – (see the Box on page 10 of the Bank of England's February *Inflation Report*). But of course rises in the US and other overseas stock markets affect demand in the UK via external demand and wealth effects for domestic holders of international stocks.

Current market valuations of IT stocks, if interpreted as reasonable expectations of future dividend flows, imply enormous future profits for IT companies. This accords with the hypothesis that IT is about to bring substantial increases in productivity growth (a good part of which the IT companies will capture). But the general level of current stock prices, relative to the past, sits less easily with the proposition that competition in the economy as a whole, as distinct from particular sectors, is about to be greater than in the past.

Stock-market wealth is the most visible but not the only source of demand stimulus in anticipation of productivity gains. Unusually high productivity growth would certainly be positive for real labour income growth – and hence for human capital wealth – especially if accompanied by a structural increase in competition. (In overall demand terms, a partial offset to the gain to labour income from greater competition would be the corresponding loss to profit income, but share prices should already reflect this in the case of quoted companies.) Once these labour income gains were expected, they would be a stimulus to consumer demand whether or not the expected gains had yet started to come through.

This does not presume that households spend freely out of expected 'permanent income'. Many households are near the limit of borrowing constraints, but many (including savers) are not, especially in an environment of financial liberalisation. And attitudes to risk and uncertainty may limit the spending even of the unconstrained. The point remains, however, that expectations of greater productivity growth and competition, if shared by households, could significantly increase consumer demand through effects on non-financial, as well as financial, wealth.

One way of drawing together these points is by reference to the concept of the *natural rate of interest*, which is defined as the short-term real rate of interest that would prevail in an economy with fully flexible prices (and hence always a zero output gap).

If a new technological opportunity appears unexpectedly, it would be normal in a wide and far-from-perverse range of circumstances for the natural rate of interest to *increase* for a period. The new opportunity increase the marginal return on investment – specifically, on investment to exploit the new technology. The marginal reward for saving – i.e. postponing consumption – must rise correspondingly in order to keep demand in line with potential supply (and the output gap equal to zero).

A standard economic relationship, which is derived from the inter-temporal optimisation behaviour of (unconstrained) consumers, links the real rate of interest positively to the growth rate of consumption. The real rate of interest is higher when consumption growth is higher because the richer I expect to be in the future than now, the more reward I will need to defer some consumption from now to the future. The arrival of a new technological opportunity seems likely to be doubly positive for consumption growth. If exploited it will raise output growth, and, in order to be exploited, it will require substantial investment, and hence saving, in the near term. In that event, in order to bring demand and supply into balance, the natural rate of interest will be higher than if the technological opportunity had not arisen.

This account has, for simplicity, glossed over open-economy aspects. If the new technological opportunity were country-specific and the country small in relation to the world economy, then the effect on the relevant natural rate of interest might be negligible. The happy country could consume ahead of the full realisation of the supply- side improvement, run a trade deficit, and finance itself by borrowing from abroad. The technological opportunities offered by IT are not country-specific, though the rates of diffusion of their benefits are likely to vary, perhaps unpredictably, from place to place.

It is not just a theoretical or perverse possibility that the arrival of a new technological opportunity might, on unchanged real interest rates, increase demand by more than supply in the short term. In his Humphrey–Hawkins testimony to Congress last month, Federal Reserve Board Chairman Alan Greenspan (2000) stated that:

> Accelerating productivity growth entails a matching acceleration in the potential output of goods and services and a corresponding rise in the real incomes available to purchase the new output. The problem is that the pickup in productivity tends to create even greater increase in aggregate demand than in potential aggregate supply.

The prospect of demand increasing by more than supply in the short term is also a feature of some recent analysis of business-to-business (B2B) e-commerce by Brookes and Wahhaj (2000). They estimate that annual growth could be higher by $\frac{1}{4}$ per cent over the next decade on account of B2B. However, imparting a 'B2B shock' in simulations of the IMF's Multimod model of the world economy causes higher inflation and interest rates in a range of industrialised countries in the short term, but not in the long run. Demand boosts from anticipatory rises in equity markets are particularly emphasised by Brookes and Wahhaj, and they judge the US to be the country most susceptible to this effect.

Suppose, then, that prospective productivity gains do tend to cause demand to increase by more than supply in the short term on unchanged real interest rates. Does it follow that actual real interest rates – and therefore nominal interest rates – need to be higher, in step with the higher natural interest rate, in order to keep inflation on target? This requires examination of how the sources of the productivity gains might also shift the relationship between the output gap and inflation.

This question is hard. A full attempt at it, which would involve analysis of the microeconomics of price-setting, is well beyond my scope. But here are some general comments.

First, if short-term nominal inertia is greater for costs than for prices, which I think is plausible in the case of wage costs, then a reduction in price – cost margins would tend temporarily to lower price inflation (for a given output gap path). But the quantitative importance of this point is hard to gauge. The existence, size and phasing of a prospective structural compression of price-cost margins on account of IT are unclear. And just as firms exploiting new technologies compete with others to win customers, so they compete – very evidently – for resources such as skilled employees and investment capital, and in the process put some upward pressure on costs generally.

Second, if the long-run consequence of e-commerce were ever more widespread real-time pricing, then the importance of nominal price stickiness would diminish over time. My bet is that the convenient underpinning institution of central bank money would still survive, but monetary policy would have ever less traction on the real economy. The job for monetary policy would be to set the nominal interest rate equal to the natural rate of interest plus the inflation target. Monetary policy errors would have less effect on the real economy, but with less price stickiness might lead to rather volatile inflation. I am unsure whether monetary policy would be more or less boring in these circumstances.

18.4 Conclusion

On the first question posed – the impact on economic growth potential of current and prospective technological advances – I am a cautious optimist. Prospects seem good for a sustained recovery in UK productivity growth from its subdued level of recent years. It is possible that there will be a leap to a historically high productivity growth rate over the next couple of years – the horizon that matters most in setting monetary policy – but that would be rash to presume. Past growth has stemmed from the exploitation of past innovations, which were no doubt spectacular in their day, just as computers were yesterday and the Internet is today. And history teaches that the lags from innovation to growth tend to be long and variable – more so than for monetary policy. Hence the caution with the optimism. We can but wait and see, so neither an ostrich nor a lemming be.

The second question concerned the implications for inflation. If IT is bringing a supply-side revolution, cannot monetary policy be eased for a while? That simply does not follow. Indeed, the arrival of an unusual supply-side opportunity could easily expand demand by more than supply initially, so that the natural real rate of interest goes up, not down, in the short term. That does not lead me to presume that the IT revolution has upward implications for inflation and nominal interest rates, because other, possibly offsetting, effects could also be at work, for example involving competition. But, equally, I see no strong grounds to presume that the overall effect on inflation is downward. This conclusion might seem like a classic case of 'on the one hand, on the other hand' economics. It is, and that should be no surprise. The supply side cannot be expected to take care of the value of money.

That is the task for monetary policy, and the reason why monetary policy is aimed at price stability, not a growth target. No one knows how the supply-side potential of the economy will grow, or the trajectory of demand in relation to supply. Inflation targeting – especially with a symmetric target – is a framework for a flexible and forward-looking response from monetary policy to these and other uncertainties in the light of unfolding data. Whatever the supply side may have in store, delivering low and stable inflation – and being expected to do so – is how monetary policy can give sustainable growth its best chance.

Acknowledgment

This was originally a Speech to the Society of Business Economists in London on 15 March 2000. I am very grateful for the help I received in preparing this chapter from Andrew Bailey, Hasan Bakhshi, Ian Bond, Willem Buiter, Alec Chrystal, Roger Clews, Nick Crafts, Spencer Dale, Paul David, David England, Phil Evans, Nigel Jenkinson, Mervyn King, Jens Larsen, Ed Nelson, Peter Sinclair and Peter Westaway. Responsibility for the contents is, however, mine alone.

Bibliography

Adams, C. and Coe, D. T. (1990) 'A systems approach to estimating the natural rate of unemployment and potential output for the United States', *International Monetary Fund Staff Papers* 37(2): 232–93.

Agenor, P. R. and Aizenman, J. (1994) 'Macroeconomic adjustment with segmented labour markets', *National Bureau of Economic Research Working Paper* No. 4769.

Agenor, P. R. and Montiel, P. J. (1996) *Development Macroeconomics*, Princeton, NJ: Princeton University Press.

Ahmed, S. (1987) 'Wage stickiness and the non-neutrality of money: a cross-industry analysis', *Journal of Monetary Economics*, 20(1): 25–50.

Alberro, J. (1981) 'The Lucas hypothesis on the Phillips curve: further international evidence'. *Journal of Monetary Economics* 7(2): 239–50.

Allen, C. (1997) 'A survey of flexible functional forms, applied to production analysis', in Allen, C. and Hall, S. (eds.) *Macroeconomic Modelling in a Changing World: Towards a Common Approach. Series in Financial Economics and Quantitative Analysis*, Chichester: Wiley, pp. 17–40.

Allen, F. and Gale, D. (2000) Financial Contagion, *Journal of Political Economy*, 108, pp 1–33.

Allen, S. G. (1992) 'Changes in the cyclical sensitivity of wages in the United States, 1891–1987', *American Economic Review* 82(1): 122–40.

Al-Nowaihi, A. and Stracca, L. (2002) 'Non-standard central bank loss functions, skewed risks, and certainty equivalence', *European Central Bank Working Paper* No. 129.

Alogoskoufis, G. S. and Smith, R. (1991) 'The Phillips Curve, the Persistence of Inflation, and the Lucas Critique: Evidence from Exchange-Rate Regimes', *American Economic Review* 81(5), 1254–75, December.

Amato, J. D. and Gerlach, S. (2001) 'Modelling the Transmission Mechanism of Monetary Policy in Emerging Market Countries Using Prior Information', *Bank for International Settlements Papers* No. 8 (Part 12).

Andersen, T. M. (1994) *Price Rigidity: Causes and Macroeconomic Implications*, Oxford: Oxford University Press.

Andersen, T. M. and Beier, N.C. (2000) 'Noisy Financial Signals and Persistent effects of Nominal Shocks in Open Economies', *CEPR Discussion Paper*, No. 2360.

Anderson, N. and Sleath, J. (1999) 'New estimates of the UK real and nominal yield curves', *Bank of England Quarterly Bulletin*, Vol. 39 (4), p. 384–92.

Aoki, K. (2001) 'Optimal Monetary Policy Responses to Relative Price Changes', *Journal of Monetary Economics*, 48, pages 55–80.
Árvai, Zs. (1998) 'The Interest Rate Transmission Mechanism between Market and Commercial Bank Rates in 1992–1998', *National Bank of Hungary Working Paper*, 1998/10.
Árvai, Zs. and Menczel, P. (2000) *Households' Savings in Hungary between 1995 and 2000*, National Bank of Hungary (in Hungarian).
Ascari, G. (2000) 'Optimising Agents, Staggered Wages and Persistence in the Real Effects of Money Shocks', *Economic Journal*, 110(465), pages 664–86, July.
Asterion, D., Lucas, P., Pain, N. and Price, S. (2000) 'Manufacturing price determination in OECD countries: markups, demand and uncertainty in a dynamic heterogeneous panel,' City University, Department of Economics. Discussion Paper Series, No. 90.
Astley, M. S. and Yates, A. (1999) 'Inflation and real disequilibria', *Bank of England Working Paper* No. 103, December.
Atingi-Ego, M. and Matthews, K. (1996) *Monetary Targeting in the Era of Financial Liberalisation: The Experience of Uganda*, Liverpool: *Liverpool Business School.*
Bailey, M. (1956) 'The welfare cost of inflationary finance.', *Journal of Political Economy*, 64, pages 93–110.
Bakhshi, H. and Yates, A. (1998) 'Are UK Inflation Expectations Rational?', *Bank of England Working Paper*, No. 81.
Baldwin, R. E. (1988) Hysteresis in import prices: the beachhead effect, *American Economic Review*, 78, pp 773–85.
Ball, L. (1994) 'What Determines the Sacrifice Ratio?', In Mankiw, G. (ed.), *Monetary Policy*, Chicago, IL: University of Chicago Press.
Ball, L. (1999) 'Aggregate demand and long-run unemployment', *Brookings Papers on Economic Activity*, 0(2): 189–236.
Ball, L. (2000) Near-Rationality and Inflation in Two Monetary Regimes, *National Bureau of Economic Research Working Paper*, No 7988.
Ball, L. and Mankiw, N. G. (1992) 'Relative-Price Changes as Aggregate Supply Shocks', *National Bureau of Economic Research Working Paper*, No. 4168.
Ball, L. and Mankiw, N. G. (1994a) 'A Sticky-Price Manifesto', *Carnegie–Rochester Conference Series on Public Policy*, 41, pages 127–51.
Ball, L. and Mankiw, N. G. (1994b) 'Asymmetric price Adjustment and Economic Fluctuations', *Economic Journal*, 104(423), pages 247–61, March.
Ball, L. and Mankiw, N. G. (2002) The NAIRU in Theory and Practice, *National Bureau of Economic Research Working Paper*, No 8940, May 2002.
Ball, L. and Romer, D. (1991) 'Real Rigidities and the Nonneutrality of Money' in Mankiw, N.G. and Romer, D. (eds.), *New Keynesian economics*, Volume 1, *Imperfect competition and sticky prices*, Cambridge, MA: MIT Press.
Ball, L., Mankiw, N. G. and Romer, D. (1988) 'The New Keynesian Economics and the Output-Inflation Trade-Off', *Brookings Papers on Economic Activity*, 0(1), pages 1–65.
Bank for International Settlements (1994) *National Differences in Interest Rate Transmission Mechanism*, Basel: BIS.
Bank for International Settlements (1995) *Financial Structure and the Monetary Policy Transmission Mechanism*, Basel: BIS.
Bank for International Settlements (2000) *Survey of Electronic Money Developments*, Basel: BIS.

Bank for International Settlements (2001) Study of the effects of consolidation in the financial services industry, Group of Ten Deputies working party, Taskforce on the effects on monetary policy, Basel: BIS.

Bank of England (1999a) *Economic Models at the Bank of England.*

Bank of England (1999b) 'The transmission mechanism of monetary policy', *Bank of England Quarterly Bulletin Vol.* 39 (2), pages. 161–70.

Bank of England (2000) *Annual Report.*

Bank of Japan (1995) *Financial Stability in a Changing Environment,* Proceedings of the Bank of Japan Conference, 28–29 October 1993, Tokyo: Macmillan Press.

Bank of Thailand (2001) Inflation Report, April. Bangkok: Bank of Thailand.

Barabás, Gy, Hamecz, I. and Neményi, J. (1998) Fiscal Consolidation, Public Debt Containment and Disinflation (Hungary's Experiences in Transition) *National Bank of Hungary Working Paper* 1998/5.

Barabás, Gy, Hamecz, I. and Neményi, J. (1999) Fiscal Deficits and Public Debt during the Transition, in Dethier J-J and L. Bokros (eds), *Public Finance Reform during the Transition, the Experiences of Hungary,* Budapest: The World Bank.

Bårdsen, G. and Fisher, P. G. (1993) The Importance of being Structured, *Norwegian School of Economics and Business Administration Working Paper* 93/02.

Barrell, R., Dury, K. and Hurst, I. (1999) 'Analysing Monetary and Fiscal Policy Regimes Using Deterministic and Stochastic Simulations', *EUI Working Paper,* ECO 99/37(330), Department of Economics, European University Institute.

Barro, R. J. (1992) 'World Interest Rates and Investment', *Scandinavian Journal of Economics,* Vol. 94, No. 2, pages 323–42.

Barro, R. J. (1996) 'Inflation and growth', *Federal Reserve Bank of Saint Louis Review,* Vol. 78, No. 3.

Barro R. J. and Gordon, D. (1983) 'Rules, discretion and reputation in a model of monetary policy', Journal of Monetary Economics, Vol. 12 (1), pages 101–121.

Barro, R. J. and Sala-I-Martin, X. (1990) 'World Real Interest Rates', *National Bureau of Economic Research Macroeconomics Annual,* Boston: MIT Press. NBER.

Basu, S. (1994) 'Intermediate Goods and Business Cycles: Implications for Productivity and Welfare', *National Bureau of Economic Research Working Paper,* No. 4817.

Basu S. (1995) Procyclical Productivity Increasing Returns or Cyclical Utilisation, *National Bureau of Economic Research Working Paper* No. 5336,

Basu, S. and Taylor, A.M. (1999) 'Business Cycles in International Historical Perspective', *National Bureau of Economic Research Working Paper,* No. 7090.

Batini, N. and Haldane, A. G. (1999) 'Forward – Looking Rules for Monetary Policy', in Taylor, J.B. (ed.), *Monetary Policy Rules,* Chicago, IL: University of Chicago Press, or *Bank of England Working Paper* No. 91.

Batini, N. and Nelson, E. (2000) 'Optimal Horizons for Inflation Targeting', *Bank of England Working Paper* No. 119, July.

Batini, N., Harrison, R. and Millard, S. P. (2000a) 'Monetary Policy Rules for an Open Economy', *Computing in Economics and Finance* 361, or *Bank of England Working Paper,* No. 149.

Batini, N., Jackson, B. and Nickell, S. (2000b) Inflation Dynamics and the Labour Share in the UK, *External MPC Unit Working Paper Discussion Paper No 2,* London: Bank of England.

Baumol, W. (1952) 'The transaction demand for cash: an inventory-theoretic approach', Quarterly Journal of Economics 66: 545–56.

Bayoumi, T. (1999) 'Estimating Trade Equations from Aggregate Bilateral Data', *International Monetary Fund Working Paper,* No. 99/74, May.

Bean, C. R. (1981) An econometric model of manufacturing investment in the UK, *Economic Journal,* 91, pp 106–21.

Bean, C. B. (1986) 'The Terms of Trade, Labour Supply and the Current Account', *Economic Journal* 96 (Suppl.): 38–46.

Bean, C. B., Larsen, J. D. J. and Nikolov, K. (2002) Financial Frictions and the Monetary Transmission Mechanism: Theory, Evidence and Policy Implications, *European Central Bank Working Paper Series,* No 113, January 2002.

Begg, D. (1998) Monetary Transmission and Monetary Policy in EU-Associated Countries. Paper prepared for the research project 'Factors Hindering the Efficiency of the Transmission Mechanism of Monetary Policy in ACs' London: *Centre of Economic Policy Research.*

Bell, B. D. (1996) *Wage Curve or Phillips Curve?* Oxford: University of Oxford Institute of Economics & Statistics.

Bergin, P. R. and Feenstra, R. C. (1998) 'Staggered Price Setting and Endogenous Persistence', *National Bureau of Economic Research Working Paper,* No. 6492.

Berk, J. M. (1998) 'Monetary Transmission: What Do We Know and How Can We Use It', *Banca Nazionale del Lavoro Quarterly Review,* 51(205), pages 145–70, June.

Berk, J. M. (1999) 'Measuring Inflation Expectations: A Survey Data Approach', *Applied Economics,* Vol. 31, No. 11, pages 1467–80, November.

Bernanke, B. S. (1983) 'Nonmonetary Effects of the Financial Crisis in the propagation of the Great Depression', *American Economic Review,* Vol. 73, No. 3, pages 257–76, June.

Bernanke, B. S. and Blinder, A. S. (1988) 'Credit, Money and Aggregate Demand', *American Economic Review,* No. 78, pages 435–9, May.

Bernanke, B. S. and Gertler, M. (1995) 'Inside the Black Box: The Credit Channel of Monetary Policy Transmission', *The Journal of Economic Perspectives,* Vol. 9, No. 4, pages 27–48, Fall.

Bernanke, B. S. and Mihov, I. (1995) 'Measuring Monetary Policy', *National Bureau of Economic Research Working Paper,* No. 5145.

Bernanke, B. S. and Mihov, I. (1998) 'The Liquidity Effect and Long-Run Neutrality', *National Bureau of Economic Research working paper,* No. 6608, June.

Bils, M. (1987) 'The Cyclical Behaviour of Marginal Cost and Price', *American Economic Review,* Vol. 77, No. 1, pages 838–55, December.

Bingham, T. R. G. (1994) 'Foreign exhange markets', in *The New Palgrave Dictionary of Money and Finance,* Vol. 2 (P. Newman, M. Milgate and J. Eatwell, eds), New York: The Stockton Press, pp.154–6.

Blanchard, O. J. and Kiyotaki, N. (1987) 'Monopolistic Competition and the Effects of Aggregate Demand', *American Economic Review,* Vol. 77, No. 4, pages 647–66, September.

Blanchard, O. and Quan, D. T. (1989) 'The dynamic effects of aggregate demand and supply', *American Economic Review* 79: 655–73.

Blinder, A. S. (1987) 'Credit Rationing and Effective Supply Failures', Economic Journal, Vol. 97, pages 327–52.

Blinder, A. S. (1998) 'Central Banking in Theory and Monetary regimes', Cambridge MA: MIT Press.

Blinder, A. S. (2000) 'Central Bank Credibility: Why do we care? How do we build it ?', *American Economic Review* Vol. 90, No. 5, pages 1421–31.

Blinder, A., Goodhart, C., Hildebrand, P., Lipton, D. and Wyplosz, C. (2001) 'How do central banks talk?', Report prepared for presentation to the Third Geneva World Conference on the World Economy held on 4, May 2001. Washington. DC: Brookings Institute.

Bogdanski, Jl., Tombini, A. A. and Werlag, S. R. C. (2000) 'Implementing Inflation Targeting in Brazil', *Working Paper Series,* No. 1, Banco Central do Brasil, July. (www.bcb.gov.br/ingles/public/wps/wps1.pdf).

Boguszewski, P., Bolek, A., Puchalska, K. and Kołodziejczyk, D. (1997) Enterprises in 1996 on the basis of surveys and Central Statistical Office data, *Bank i Kredyt,* 9/1997 (in Polish).

Boguszewski, P., Sawicka, A. and Puchalska, K. (1998) Enterprises in 1997 on the basis of researches and Central Statistical Office data, *Bank i Kredyt,* 9/1998 (in Polish).

Boguszewski, P., Sawicka, A., Puchalska, K., Kocięcki, A. and Jankiewicz, Z. (1999) Enterprises' financial performance in 1998 on the basis of surveys and Central Statistical Office data, *Materiały i Studia,* No. 88, National Bank of Poland (in Polish).

Boivin, J. and Giannoni, M. (2001) The monetary transmission mechanism: has it changed? New York: Federal Reserve Bank of New York.

Boivin, J. and Giannoni, M. (2002) Has monetary policy become less powerful?, *Staff Reports* 144, Federal Reserve Bank of New York.

Bole, V. (1997) Stabilization in Slovenia: From High Inflation to Excessive Inflow of Foreign Capital, in Macroeconomic Stabilization in Transition Economies, ed. by Blejer, M.I. and Skreb, M., Cambridge: Cambridge University Press, pages 234–55.

Bole, V. (1999a) 'Financial Flows in a Small Open Economy; the Case of Slovenia', Paper presented at the Conference 'Financial Flows to Transition Economies', IIASA, May 1997, in *The Mixed Blessing of Financial Inflows in Transition Countries in Comparative Perspective,* Gacs, J., Holzmann, R. and Wyzan, M. (eds), Lubjiana: Edward Elgar, pages 195–238.

Bole, V. (1999b) The Conduct of Monetary Policy and Banking Soundness: A Slovenian Episode, in Central Banking, Monetary Policies, and the Implications for Transition Economies, (ed. Blejer, M.I. and Skreb, M.), Lubjiana: Edward Elga pp. 185–212.

Borio, C. E. V. (1996) 'Credit Characteristics and the Monetary Policy Transmission Mechanism in Fourteen Industrial Countries: Facts, Conjectures and Some Econometric Evidence', in *Monetary Policy in A Converging Europe* Alders, K., K. Koedijk, C. Kool and C. Winder (eds), Dordrecht: Kluwer Academic Publishers pages 77–115.

Borio, C. E. V. and Fritz, W. (1995) 'The Response of Short-Term Bank Lending Rates to Policy Rates: A Cross-Country Perspective', *BIS Financial Structure and the Monetary Policy Transmission Mechanism,* Basel: BIS, 106–53.

Boyd, D. and Smith, R. (2002) 'Some econometric issues in measuring the transmission mechanism, with an application to developing countries', in Mahadeva, L. and Sinclair, P. (eds.), *The Theory and Practice of Monetary Transmission in Diverse Economies,* Cambridge: Cambridge University Press.

Brainard, W. (1967) Uncertainty and the Effectiveness of Policy, *American Economic Review,* Vol 57 pages 411–33.

Brayton F., Levin, A., Tryon, R. and Williams, J. C. (1997) 'The Evolution of Macro

Model at the Federal Reserve Board', *Finance and Economics Discussion Paper Series*, No. 1997/29, Federal Board.

Brayton, F., Roberts, J. M. and Williams, J. C. (1999) 'What's happened to the Phillips Curve?' *Finance and Economics Discussion Series Paper* No. 1999–2049, Federal Reserve Board.

Britton, A. (1989) *Policymaking with Macroeconomic Models*, National Institute of Economic and Social Research, Aldershot: Gower.

Britton, E. M., Fisher, P. G. and Whitley, J. D. (1997) 'Comparing the transition mechanism in France, Germany and United Kingdom: Some issues and results', *Bank of England Quarterly Bulletin* 37(2).

Britton, E. and Whitley, J. (1997) 'Comparing the monetary transmission mechanism in France, Germany and the United Kingdom', *Bank of England Quarterly Bulletin*, Vol. 37, No. 2, pages 152–62, May.

Britton, E., Larsen, J. D. J. and Small, I (2000) Imperfect competition and the dynamics of mark-ups, *Bank of England Working Paper*, No 110.

Brooke, M. and Wahhaj, Z. (2000) 'The Shocking Economic Effects of B2B', Goldman Sachs Global Economics Paper no 37.

Brookes, A. M. (1999) 'Monetary Policy and the Reserve Bank Balance Sheet', *Reserve Bank of New Zealand Bulletin*, Vol. 62, No. 4, December.

Brookes, M., Danton, G. and Moessner, R. (1999) 'News and the sterling markets', Bank of England Quarterly Bulletin, November: 374–83.

Bruni, F., Fair, D. E. and O'Brien, R. (eds.) (1996) 'Risk Management in Volatile Financial Markets: Introduction', *Financial and Monetary Policy Studies*, Vol. 32, pages ix–xii, Kluwer Academic Publishers, Dordrecht.

Budd, A., Levine, P. and Smith, P. (1988) 'Real Wage Adjustment and Long-Term Unemployment', in Unemployment, hysteresis and natural rate hypothesis, R. Cross. Oxford: Basil Blackwell Ltd, pages 41–64.

Buiter, W. H. (1995) 'Macroeconomic Policy During a Transition to Monetary Union', *CEPR Discussion Paper*, No. 1222, August.

Buiter, W. H. (1999) 'Alice in Euroland', *CEPR policy paper*, No. 1.

Buiter, W. H. (2000) 'The New Economy and Old Monetary Economics', unpublished paper, Bank of England.

Burkett, P. and Vogel, R. C. (1992) 'Financial Assets, Inflation Hedges, and Capital Utilization in Developing Countries: An Extension of McKinnon's Complementarity Hypothesis', *Quarterly Journal of Economics*, Vol. 107, No. 2, pages 773–84, May.

Caballero, R. J. (1999) 'Aggregate investment', in *Handbooks in Economics*, Vol. 15, *Handbook of Macroeconomics*, Vol. 18 (J.B. Taylor and M. Woodford, eds), Oxford: Elsevier Science.

Calvo, G. A. (1983) 'Staggered Prices in a Utility-Maximizing Framework', *Journal of Monetary Economics*, Vol. 12, No. 3, pages 983–98, September.

Calvo, G. A. and Kahn, M. S. (1994) Money Demand, Bank Credit and Economic Performance in Former Socialist Economies, *International Monetary Fund Working Paper* 94/3 (1994)

Calvo, G. A., Leiderman, L. and Reinhart, C. (1994) The Capital Inflows Problem: Concepts and Issues, *Contemporary Economic Policy*, Vol. 12 (3) pages 54–66.

Campbell, F. and Lewis, E. (1998) 'What moves bond yields in Australia?', *Reserve Bank of Australia Research Discussion Paper* No 9808.

Canova, F. (2000) 'Testing Calibrated General Equilibrium Models', in Mariano,

R., Schuermann, T. and Weeks, M. (eds.), *Simulation-based Inference in Econometrics*, Cambridge University Press, Cambridge, UK.

Canzoneri, M. B. (1980) 'Labor Contracts and Monetary Policy', *Journal of Monetary Economics*, Vol. 6, No. 2, pages 241–55, April.

Canzoneri, M. B. and Dellas, H. (1998) 'Real Interest Rates and Central Bank Operating Procedures', *Journal of Monetary Economics*, Vol. 42, No. 3, pages 471–94, December.

Card, D. (1990) 'Unexpected Inflation, Real Wages and Employment Determination in Union Contracts', *American Economic Review*, Vol. 80, No. 4, pages 669–88, September.

Carlson, J. A. and Parkin, J. M. (1975) 'Inflation Expectations', *Economica*, Vol. 42, No. 166, pages 123–38, May.

Carroll, C. D., Overland, J. and Weil, D. N. (1995) 'Saving and Growth with Habit Formation', *Federal Reserve System Finance and Economics Discussion Series No. 95–42.*

Cartens, A. and Werner, A. (1999) 'México's Monetary Policy Framework under a Floating Exchange Rate Regime', *Documento de Investigación*, 9905, Banco de México. (http://www.banxico.org.mx/gPublicaciones/DocumentosInvestigacion)

Casares, M. and McCallum, B. T. (2000) 'An Optimizing IS-LM Framework with Endogenous Investment', *National Bureau of Economic Research Working Paper*, No. 7908.

Casteleijn, A. J. H. (2000) The viability of implementing an inflation targeting monetary policy framework in South Africa', *South African Reserve Bank Quarterly Bulletin*, No 216, June.

Catao, L. and Rodriguez, S. (2000) 'Banks and Monetary Shocks in Emerging Markets: How far can we go with the "credit view"?', *International Monetary Fund Working Paper*, No. 00/68.

Cecchetti, S. G. (1999) 'Legal Structure, Financial Structure and the Monetary Policy Transmission Mechanism', *National Bureau of Economic Research Working paper*, No. 7151.

Cecchetti, S., Genberg, H., Lipsky, J. and Wadhwani, S. (2000) Asset prices and central bank policy, Geneva reports on the world economy number 2, CEPR.

Chadha, B., Masson, P. and Meredith, G. (1992) 'Models of Inflation and the Costs of Disinflation', *International Monetary Fund Staff Papers*, Vol. 39, No. 2; also in *International Monetary Fund Working Paper*, No. 91/97.

Chadha, J. S. and Dimsdale, N. H. (1999) 'A Long View of Real Rates', *Oxford Review of Economic Policy*, Vol. 15, No. 2, pages 17–45, Summer.

Chadha, J. S. and Nolan, C. (2002a) Inflation Targeting, Transparency and Interest Rate Volatility: Ditching 'Monetary Mystique' in the UK, *Journal of Macroeconomics*, Volume 23, Number 3, Summer.

Chadha, J. S. and Nolan, C. (2002b) 'Supply shocks and the "Natural rate of interest": An exploration' in Mahadeva, L. and Sinclair, P. (eds.), *The Theory and Practice of Monetary Transmission in Diverse Economies*, Cambridge: Cambridge University Press.

Chari, V. V., Jones, L. and Manuelli, R. (1996) 'Inflation, growth and financial intermediation', *Federal Reserve Bank of Saint Louis Review*, Vol. 78, No.3.

Chiang, A. C. (1992) *Elements of Dynamic Optimization*, New York: McGraw-Hill, ch.5.

Chirinko, Robert S. (1980) 'The Real Wage Rate over the Business-Cycle', *Review of Economics and Statistics*, Vol. 62, No. 3, pages 459–61, August.

Chopra, A. (1985) 'The Speed of Adjustment of the Inflation Rate in Developing Countries, A Study of Inertia', *International Monetary Fund Staff Papers*, Vol. 32, No. 4, pages 693–733, December.

Chortareas, G., Stasavage, D. and Sterne, G. (2002) 'Does it pay to be transparent? International evidence from central bank forecasts', *Proceedings of the Twenty-sixth Annual Economic Policy Conference of the Federal Reserve Bank of St Louis*, St Louis: Federal Reserve Bank of St Louis.

Christiano, L. J., Eichenbaum, M. and Evans, C. L. (1996) 'Identification and the Effects of Monetary Policy Shocks', in Blejer, M. I., Eckstein, Z. V. I., Hercowitz, Z. V .I. and Leiderman, L. (eds.), *Financial Factors in Economic Stabilization and Growth*, Cambridge: Cambridge University Press, pages 36–74.

Christiano, L. J., Eichenbaum, M. and Evans, C. L. (1997) 'Sticky Price and Limited Participation Models of Money: A Comparison', *European Economic Review*, Vol. 41, No. 6, pages 1201–49, June.

Christiano, L. J., Eichenbaum, M. and Evans, C. L. (1998) 'Monetary Policy Shocks: What Have We Learned And To What End?', *National Bureau of Economic Research Working Paper*, No. 6400.

Christoffersen, P. F. and Wescott, R. F. (1999) 'Is Poland Ready for Inflation Targeting?', *International Monetary Fund Working Paper*, No. 99/41.

Church, K. B., Sault, J. E., Sgherri, S. and Wallis, K. (2000) 'Comparative Properties of Models of the UK Economy', *National Institute Economic Review*, 0(171), pages 106–22, January.

Clare, A. and Courtenay, R. (2001) 'Assessing the impact of macroeconomic news announcements on securities prices under different monetary policy regimes', *Bank of England Working Paper* No. 125.

Clarida, R., Galí, J. and Gertler, M. (1998) 'Monetary Policy Rules in Practice: Some International Evidence', *European Economic Review* Vol. 42 (6), pages 1033–67.

Clarida, R., Galí, J. and Gertler, M. (1999) 'The science of monetary policy: a new Keynesian perspective', *Journal of Economic Literature*, 37: 1661–707.

Clarida, R., Galí, J. and Gertler, M. (2000) Monetary policy rules and macroeconomic stability: evidence and some theory, *Quarterly Journal of Economics*, 115, pp 147–80.

Coe, D. T. and McDermott, J. C. (1996) 'Does the Gap Model Work in Asia?', *International Monetary Fund Working Paper* WP/96/69, July.

Condon, T., Corbo, V. and De Melo, J. (1995) Productivity Growth, External Shocks, and Capital Inflows in Chile: A General Equilibrium Analysis, *Journal of Policy Modelling*, Volume 7. No 3, Fall 1985, pages 379–406.

Cook, J. and Hahn J., (1989) 'The effect of the changes in the Federal funds target rate on market interest rates in the 1970s', *Journal of Monetary Economics*, 24, 331–51 (1989)

Cooley, T. F. (1997) 'Calibrated Models', *Oxford Review of Economic Policy*, Vol. 13, No. 3, pages 55–70, Autumn.

Cooley, T. F. and Hansen, G. (1989) 'The inflation tax in a real business cycle model', *American Economic Review*, Vol. 79, No. 4, pages 733–48, September.

Corker, C., Beaumont, C., Van Elkan, R. and Iakova, D. (2000) 'Exchange Rate Regimes in selected Advanced Transition Economies – Coping with Transition,

Capital Inflows, and EU Accession', *International Monetary Fund Policy Discussion Paper*, No. 00/3.

Correia, I., Neves, J. C. and Rebelo, S. (1995) Business Cycles in a small open economy, *European Economic Review, 39*, page 1089–113.

Crafts, N. (1998) 'Forging Ahead and Falling Behind: The Rise and Relative Decline of the First Industrial Nation', *Journal of Economic Perspectives*, 12, 193–210.

Crawford, A. (2001) Downward nominal wage rigidity: a review of micro evidence from Canada, Bank of Canada, mimeo.

Cross, R. (ed.) (1995) *The natural rate of unemployment: Reflections on 25 years of the hypothesis*, Cambridge: Cambridge University Press.

Csajbók, A. (1998) Zero-coupon Yield Curve Estimation from a Central Bank Perspective, *National Bank of Hungary Working Paper* 1998/2.

Csajbók, A. (1999) Information in T-Bill Auction bid Distribution, *National Bank of Hungary Working Paper* 1999/6.

Csajbók, A. and Neményi, J. (1998) The Contribution of the Government Securities Market to the Development of Wider Securities Markets in Hungary, in: Capital Market Development in Transition Economies, Paris: OECD.

Csajbók, A. and Varró, L. (2000) Interest rate policy within a crawling band regime? An attempt of estimating a monetary reaction function, National Bank of Hungary, mimeo.

Csermely, Á. (2000) 'Demand for Transaction Money in Hungary', National Bank of Hungary mimeo (in Hungarian).

Csermely, Á. and Varró, L. (1998) The Crawling Band Regime, a Monetary Framework for Gradual Disinflation, The case of Hungary, Prepared for the Workshop on Intermediate Targeting organised by the Bank of England in October 1998.

Csermely, Á. and Varró, L. (2000) 'The crawling band regime: a monetary framework for gradual disinflation', National Bank of Hungary, mimeo.

Csermely, Á. and Vincze, J. (1999) Leverage and Foreign Ownership in Hungary, *National Bank of Hungary Working Paper 1999/1*

Cufer, U., Mahadeva, L. and Sterne, G. (2000) 'Specifying an inflation target: the case of administered prices and other candidates for exclusion' in Mahadeva L. and Sterne G. (eds.), *Monetary Policy Frameworks in a Global Context*, London: Routledge.

Cukierman, A., (2000) 'Accountability, Credibility, Transparency and Stabilisation Policy in the Eurosystem', *Tel Aviv University* (unpublished).

Cukierman, A. and Meltzer, A., (1986) 'A Theory of Ambiguity, Credibility, and Inflation under Discretion and Asymmetric Information', *Econometrica*, Vol. 54, pages 1099–128.

Dale, S. (1993) 'The effect of changes in Official UK rates on Market Interest Rates since 1987', *The Manchester School*, Vol. 61, pages 76–94.

Dale, S. and Haldane, A.G. (1995) 'Interest Rates and the Channels of Monetary Transmission: Some Sectoral Estimates', *European Economic Review*, Vol. 39, No. 9, pages 1611–26, December.

Daniel, J. and Üçer, M. (1999) 'Turkey: Monetary Policy from the 1980s to Now', Emerging Markets Economics Research, Boston: Credit Suisse First.

Darvas, Zs and Szapáry, Gs (2000) Financial Contagion under Different Exchange rate Regimes, *National Bank of Hungary Working Paper* 1999/10.

David, P. (1990) 'The Dynamo and the Computer: An Historical Perspective on

the Productivity Paradox', *American Economic Review Papers and Proceedings*, 80, 355–61.
David, P. (2000) 'Understanding Digital Technology's Evolution and the Path of Measured Productivity Growth: Present and Future in the Mirror of the Past', forthcoming in Brynolfson, E., and Kahin, B., eds, *Understanding the Digital Economy*, Boston: MIT Press.
Debelle, G. and Laxton, D. (1996) 'Is the Phillips Curve Really a Curve? Some Evidence for Canada, the United Kingdom, and the United States', *International Monetary Fund Working paper*, No. 96/111.
De Broeck, M. and Koen, V. (2000) 'The "Soaring Eagle": Anatomy of the Polish Take-Off in the 1990s', *International Monetary Fund Working Paper*, No. 00/6.
De Broeck, M., Krajnyak, K. and Lorie, H. (1997) 'Explaining and Forecasting the Velocity of Money in Transition Economies, with Special Reference to the Baltics, Russia and other Countries of the Former Soviet Union, *International Monetary Fund Working Paper*, No. 97/08.
De Fiore, F. (1998) 'The Transmission of Monetary Policy in Israel', *IMF Working Papers*, 98/114, IMF.
De Gregorio, J. (1993) 'Inflation, taxation and long-run growth', *Journal of Monetary Economics*, 31, pages 271–98.
De Kock, G.P.C. (1985). *The monetary system and monetary policy in South Africa, Final report to the Commission of Enquiry into the Monetary System and Monetary Policy in South Africa*, Government Printers, Pretoria.
Derviz, A. (1999) 'Generalized Asset Return Parity and the Exchange Rate in a Financially Open Economy', *Bulletin of the Czech Econometric Society*, 6, pages 67–102.
Dethier, J-J and Bokros, L. (1998) Public Finance Reform during the Transition, the Experiences of Hungary, Washington, DC: *The World Bank*.
Devereux, M. B. and Lane, P. R. (2000) 'Exchange Rate Flexibility and Monetary Policy Choices for Emerging Market Economies' (unpublished).
Devereux, M. B. (2002) '*Monetary Policy, Exchange Rate Flexibility, and Exchange Rate Pass-through*' Toranto: Bank of Canada.
Dickey, D. A. and Fuller, W. A. (1981) 'Likelihood Ratio Statistics for Autoregressive Time Series with a Unit Root', *Econometrica*, Vol. 49, No. 4 pages 1057–72, June.
Diebold, F. X., Ohanian, L. E. and Berkowitz, J. (1998) 'Dynamic Equilibrium Economies: A Framework for Comparing Models and Data', *Federal Reserve Bank of Minneapolis Staff Reports*, No. 243.
Dixit, A. K. (1989a) Hysteresis, import penetration and exchange rate pass-through, *Quarterly Journal of Economics*, 104, pp 205–24.
Dixit, A. K. (1989b) Entry and exit decisions under uncertainty, *Journal of Political Economy*, 97, pp 620–38.
Dornbusch, R. and Fischer, S. (1992) 'Inflación Moderada', *Ensayos sobre Política Económica*, Junio: Banco de la República.
Drew, A. and Hunt, B. (1998) The Forecasting and Policy System: preparing economic projections, *Reserve Bank of New Zealand Working* Paper, no G98/7.
Dufour, J. M. (1982) 'Generalised Chow Tests for Structural Change: A Coordinate Free Approach', *International Economic Review*, Vol. 23, No. 3, pages 565–75, October.
Easton, B. and Patterson, K. (1987) 'Interest rates in five macroeconomic models of the UK: Survey, analysis and simulation', *Economic Modelling* 4(1): 19–64.

Edwards, S. (1983) 'The Short-Run Relation Between Growth and Inflation in Latin America: Comment', *The American Economic Review*, Vol. 73, No. 3.

Eichengreen, B. and Masson, P. (1996) Exit Strategies – Policy Options for Countries Seeking Greater Exchange Rate Flexibility, *International Monetary Fund Occasional Paper* No 168.

Eichengreen, B., Masson, P., Savastro, M. and Sharma, S. (1999) Transition Strategies and Nominal Anchors on the Road of Greater Exchange rate Flexibility. *Princeton Essays in International Economics* 213, Princeton, NJ: Princeton University, Dept of Economics.

Eijffinger, S., Schaling, E. and Verhagen, W. (1998) 'The Term Structure of Interest Rates and Inflation Forecast Targeting', *Tilburg: – Centre for Economic Research Discussion Paper*, No. 9885, August.

Eika, K., Ericsson, N. R. and Nymoen, R. (1996) Hazard in Implementing a Monetary Conditions Index. *Federal Reserve Bank International Finance Discussion Papers*, No. 568.

Ekeland, I. and Schein Kman, J. A. (1986) 'Transversality conditions for some infinite horizon discrete time optimization problems', *Mathematics of Operational Research*, 11: 216–29.

Elliott, J., Kwack, S. Y. and Tavlas, G. S. (1986) An econometric model of the Kenyan Economy, *Economic Modelling* 3(1): 2–30.

Engle, R. F. (1982) 'A General Approach to Lagrange Multiplier Model Diagnostics', *Journal of Econometrics*, Vol. 20, No. 1, pages 83–104, October.

Erçel, G. (1999) 'Disinflation Program for the Year 2000: Implementation of Exchange and Monetary Policy', *The Central Bank of the Republic of Turkey* (also available at http://www.tcmb.gov.tr).

European Central Bank (2000) *Monthly Bulletin*, July.

Fackler, J. S. and Rogers, J. H. (1995) 'Output, Inflation and Stabilization: a Counterfactual Analysis', *Journal of International Money and Finance*, Vol. 14, No. 5, pages 619–40.

Fair, R. C. (1994) *Testing Macroeconometric Models*, Cambridge, MA: Harvard University Press.

Faust, J. (1998) 'The Robustness of Identified VAR Conclusions about Money', *Carnegie-Rochester Conference Series on Public Policy*, 49(0), pages 207–44, December.

Faust, J. and Rogers, J.H. (1999) 'Monetary Policy's Role in Exchange Rate Behaviour', *International Finance Discussion Papers*, No. 652, November.

Faust, J. and Svensson, L.E.O. (1999) 'The Equilibrium Degree of Transparency and Control in Monetary Policy', *International Finance Discussion Paper*, No. 651, Federal Reserve System.

Favero, C. A. and Maffezzoli, M (2001) 'Calibration', in Favero, C.A. (ed.) *Applied Macroeconometrics*, New York: Oxford University Press, Ch. 8.

Favero, C. A., Giavazzi, F. and Flabbi, L. (1999) 'The Transmission Mechanism of Monetary Policy in Europe: Evidence from the Banks' Balance Sheets', *CEPR Discussion paper*, No. 2303.

Ferenczi, B. (1999) 'Labour Market Developments in Hungary from a Central Bank Perspective: Stylised Facts', *National Bank of Hungary Working Paper*, 1999/5.

Fernandez-Arias, E. and Montiel, P. J. (1996) The Surge in Capital Inflows to Developing Countries: an Analytical Overview, *The World Bank Economic Review*, Vol.10, pages 51–77.

Fischer, S. (1981). 'Relative shocks, relative price variability and Inflation,' *Brooking Papers on Economic Activity*, No 2, pages 381–441.

Fischer, S. (1988) 'Real Balances, the Exchange Rate, and Indexation: Real Variables in Disinflation', *The Quarterly Journal of Economics*, Vol. 103, No. 1, pages 27–49, February.

Fischer, S. (1993) 'The role of macroeconomic factors in growth', *Journal of Monetary Economics*, Vol. 32, No. 3, pages 485–512.

Fischer, S., Sahay, R. and Vegh, C. (1998) 'How Far is Eastern Europe from Brussels?', *International Monetary Fund Working Paper*, No. 98/53.

Fleming, M. and Remolona, E. (1997) 'What moves the bond market?', *FRBNY Economic Policy Review*, Dec 1997, pp. 31–50.

Fleming, M. and Remolona, E. (1999) 'The term structure of announcement effects', *BIS Working Papers*, June 1999.

Flood, R. P. and Marion, N. P. (1996) 'Speculative Attacks: Fundamentals and Self-fulfilling Prophecies', *National Bureau of Economic Research Working Paper*, No. 5789.

Fortin, P. (1991) 'The Phillips Curve, Macroeconomic Policy, and the Welfare of Canadians', *Canadian Journal of Economics*, Vol. 24, No. 4, pages 774–803, November.

Freedman, C. (2000) 'Monetary policy implementation: past, present and future – will the advent of electronic money lead to the devise of central banking?', *International Finance* 3: 211–27.

Friedman, B. M. (1990) Comments and Discussion on (Romer, C. and Romer, D.) New Evidence on the Monetary Transmission Mechanism, *Brookings Papers on Economic Activity*, pages 204–9.

Friedman, B. M. (1995) 'Does the Monetary Policy Affect Real Economic Activity? Why Do We Still Ask this Question?', *National Bureau of Economic Research Working Paper*, No. 5212, August.

Friedman, B. M. (1999). 'The future of monetary policy: the central bank as an army with only a Signal Corps?, *International Finance* 2:231–8.

Friedman, M. (1968) The Role of Monetary Policy, *American Economic Review*, Vol 58, March, pp 1–17.

Friedman, M. (1980) Memorandum to U.K. Treasury and Civil Service Committee on 'Enquiry into Monetary Policy,' 11 June 1980. In Great Britain, *House of Commons (1979–80)*, 720, part 1 (July 1980): 55–61.

Fry, M., Julius, D., Mahadeva, L., Roger, S. and Sterne, G. (2000) 'Key Issues in the Choice of Monetary Policy Framework' in Mahadeva, L. and Sterne, G. (eds.), *Monetary Frameworks in a Global Context*, London: Routledge.

Fry, M. J. (1997) *Emancipating the Banking system and Developing Markets for Government Debt*, Routledge, London.

Fry, M. J. and Lilien, D. M. (1986) 'Monetary Policy Responses to Exogenous Shocks', *American Economic Review*, Vol. 76, No. 2, pages 79–83, May.

Fuhrer, J. C. (1998) 'An Optimising Model For Monetary Policy Analysis: Can Habit Formation Help?', *Reserve Bank of Australia Research Discussion Paper*, No. 9812.

Fuller, W. A. (1976) *Introduction to Statistical Time Series*, Wiley, New York.

Galí, J. (2000a) 'New Perspectives on Monetary Policy, Inflation and the Business Cycle', *CEPR Discussion Paper* No 3210.

Galí, J. (2000b) 'The Return of the Phillips Curve and other recent Developments in Business Cycle Theory', *Spanish Economic Review, 2000.*

Galí, J. and Gertler, M. (1999) 'Inflation Dynamics: A Structural Econometric Analysis', *Journal of Monetary Economics*, 44, No. 2, pages 195–222, October.

Galí, J., Gertler, M. and Lopez-Salido, J. D. (2001) 'European Inflation Dynamics', *European Economic Review*, Vol. 45, No. 7, pages 1237–70, June.

García, J. and Montes, G. (1988) 'Coffee Boom, Government Expenditure and Agricultural Prices: The Colombian Experience', *IFPRI Research Report*, 68.

Garretsen, H. and Swank, J. (1998) 'The Transmission of Interest Rate Changes and the Role of Bank Balance Sheets: A VAR-Analysis for Netherlands', *Journal of Macroeconomics*, Vol. 20, No. 2, pages 325–39.

Geraats, P. (2000) 'Why Adopt Transparency? The Publication of Central Bank Forecasts', *UC Berkeley Discussion Paper*. Berkeley, CA: University of California.

Geraats, P. (2001) Precommitment, Transparency and Monetary Policy', Bundesbank Discussion Paper 12/01, September.

Gereben, A. (2000) 'The Interbank Money Market in Hungary: Lessons from the Period between September 1998 and March 1999', *National Bank of Hungary Occasional Paper*, No. 7.

Gertler, M. and Gilchrist, S. G. (1993) 'The Role of Credit Market Imperfections in the Monetary Transmission Mechanism: Arguments and Evidence', *Scandinavian Journal of Economics*, Vol. 95, No. 1, pages 43–64.

Gertler, M. and Gilchrist, S. G. (1994) Monetary Policy, Business, and the Behavior of Small Manufacturing Firms, *The Quarterly Journal of Economics*, Vol. 109, pages 309–40.

Ghosh, A. R. (2000) 'Turkey's External Current Account', *International Monetary Fund Staff Country Report*, No. 00/14, Washington, DC: International Monetary Fund.

Gilchrist, S. G. and Zakrajšek, E. (1995) 'The Importance of Credit for Macroeconomic Activity', in Peek, J. and Rosengren, E.S. (eds.), *Is Bank Lending Important for the Transmission of Monetary Policy?*', Boston, MA: Federal Reserve Bank of Boston: Conference Series, No. 39.

Giovannini, A. (1985) 'Saving and the real interest rate in LDCs'. *Journal of Development Economics* 18(2–3): 197–217.

Gómez, J. (2000) 'Wage indexation, inflation inertia and the cost of disinflation', Banco de la República, mimeo.

Gómez, J. and Julio, J. M. (2000) 'Transmission mechanisms and inflation targeting: the case of Colombia's disinflation', *Borradoresde Economia 168*, Banco de la República de Colombia.

Goodhart, C. A. E. (1994) 'What should Central Banks Do? What should be their Macroeconomic Objectives and Operations?', *Economic Journal*, 104(427), pages 1424–36, November.

Goodhart, C. A. E. and Smith, R. (1985) 'The impact of news on financial markets in the United Kingdom', *Journal of Money, Credit and Banking*, Vol. 17, No. 4, Nov 1985.

Gordon, R. (1990) What is New-Keynesian Economics?' Journal of Economic Literature, Vol XXVIII (September 1990) pages 1115–71.

Gordon, R. (1997) 'The time-varying NAIRU and its implications for monetary policy', *Journal of Economic Perspectives* Vol. 11: 11–32.

Gordon, R. (1999) 'Has the "New Economy" rendered the productivity slowdown obsolete?', Working Paper, Chicago: Northwestern University.

Gourieroux, C. and Montfort, A. (1990) *Time Series and Dynamic Models*, Cambridge: Cambridge University Press.

Grandmont, J.-M. (1989) 'Keynesian Issues and Economic Theory', CEPREMAP Working Paper No 8907.

Granger, C. W. J. and Pesaran, M. H. (2000) 'Economic and Statistical Measures of Forecast Accuracy', *DAE University of Cambridge Working Paper*, No. 9910.

Gravelle, T. and Moessner, R. (2001) 'Reactions of Canadian Interest Rates to Macroeconomic Announcements: Implications for Monetary Policy Transparency', *Bank of Canada Working paper* 2001–5.

Gray, J. A. (1978) 'On Indexation and Contract Length', *Journal of Political Economy*, Vol. 86, No. 1, pages 1–18, February.

Gray, J. A. and Kandil, M. (1991) 'Is Price Flexibility Stabilizing? A Broader Perspective', *Journal of Money, Credit and Banking*, Vol. 23, No. 1, pages 1–12, February.

Gray, J. A., Kandil, M. and Spencer, D. E. (1992) 'Does Contractual Wage Rigidity Play a Role in Determining Real Activity?', *Southern Economic Journal*, Vol. 58, No. 4, pages 1042–57, April.

Green, C. and V. Murinde, (1993) The Potency of Stabilization Policy in Developing Economies: Kenya, Tanzania and Uganda', *Journal of Policy Modelling*, Volume 15, 4, pages 427–62.

Greenspan, A. (2000) Testimony before the US House of Representatives Committee on Banking and Financial Services, 17 February.

Griliches, Z. (1994) 'Productivity, R&D, and the data constraint', *American Economic Review*, 84, 1–23.

Gurney, A., Henry, H. and Pesaran, B. (1989) The Exchange Rate and External Trade, in Britton, A (ed.), *Policymaking with Macroeconomic Models*, National Institute of Economic and Social Research. Aldershot: Gower, pages 9–31.

Hagemann, R. (1999) 'The Structural Budget Balance: The International Monetary Fund's Methodology', *International Monetary Fund Working Paper*, No. 99/95, July.

Haldane A. and Read, V. (2000) 'Monetary policy surprises and the yield curve', *Bank of England Working Paper* No. 106, January 2000.

Hall, S. (2001) 'Credit channel effects in the monetary transmission mechanism'. *Bank of England Quarterly Bulletin*, Winter 2001.

Halpern, L. and Kőrösi, G. (1998) 'Corporate performance in the transition: econometric analysis of Hungarian exporting firms, 1985–1994', in *Hungary: Towards a Market Economy* (L. Halpern and C. Wyplosz, eds), Cambridge: Cambridge University Press. pp. 192–215.

Halpern, L. and Neményi, J. (2002) Fiscal foundation of the Convergence to the EU, Hungary towards European Accession, Paper prepared for the Fifth Dubrovnik Conference on Transition Economies 'Ten Years of Transition: What Have We Learned and What Lies Ahead', organised by the National Bank of Croatia, June 23–25, 1999. Boston: MIT Press.

Haltmaier, J. T. (1996) 'Inflation-adjusted potential output', *International Finance Discussion Papers, Board of Governors of the Federal Reserve System*, No 561, August 1996.

Hamecz, I. J., Vincze and Zsoldos, I. (1998) 'The nature of Hungarian inflation' in Halpern, L. and Wyplosz, C. (eds.), *Hungary: Towards a Market Economy*, Cambridge University Press, Cambridge.

Hanson, J. A. (1980) 'The Short-Run Relation between Growth and Inflation in Latin America: A Quasi- Rational or Consistent Expectations Approach', *American Economic Review*, Vol. 70, No. 5, pages 972–89, December.

Hardy, D. (1996) 'Market Reaction to Changes in German Official Interest Rates', *Deutsche Bundesbank Discussion Paper* No. 4.

Harvey, A. and Jaeger, A. (1993) 'Detrending, Stylised facts and the Business Cycle', *Journal of Applied Econometrics*, Vol. 8, No. 3, pages 231–47, July–September.

Hausmann, R. (1999) Latin America: No firework, no crisis? Paper presented in Vienna Conference in November 1999 on Financial Crisis. Vienna: Austrian National Bank.

Heffernan, S. A. (1997) Modelling British interest rate adjustment: an error correction approach, *Economica*, 64, pp 211–31.

Hendry, D. (1984) Econometric modelling of house prices in the United Kingdom, in *Econometrics and Quantitative Economics*, eds. D. Hendry and K. Wallace, Blackwell, Oxford, pp 135–172.

Hendry, D. (2001) Modelling UK inflation, 1875–1991, Nuffield College, University of Oxford, mimeo.

Hendry, D. F. and Clements, M. P. (1994) 'On a Theory of Intercept Corrections in Macroeconometric Forecasting', in Holly, S. (ed.), *Money, inflation and employment: Essays in honour of James Ball*, Oxford: Edward Elgar, pages 160–82.

Hendry, D. F. and Mizon, G. E. (2000) 'On Selecting Policy Analysis Models by Forecast Accuracy', in Atkinson, A. B., Glennerster, H. G. and Stern, N. H. (eds.), *Putting Economics to Work: Volume in Honour of Michio Morishima*, London: London School of Economics: STICERD.

Hess, G. D. and Shin, K. (1999) 'Some International Evidence on Output-Inflation Tradeoffs', *Macroeconomic Dynamics*, Vol. 3, No. 2, pages 187–203, June.

Hogan, V. (1998) 'Explaining the Recent Behaviour of Inflation and Unemployment in the United States', *International Monetary Fund Working Paper*, No. 98/145.

Hoggarth, G. (1996) 'Introduction to Monetary Policy', *Handbooks in Central Banking*, No. 1, Centre for Central Banking Studies, Bank of England.

Hoover, K. D. (2001) *Causality in Macroeconomics*, Cambridge: Cambridge University Press.

Hubbard, R. G. (1994) 'Is there a "Credit Channel" for Monetary Policy?', *National Bureau of Economic Research Working Paper*, No. 4977.

Hughes, A. J. and Fisher, P. G. (1990) 'Practitioners' Corner, On Economic Structures and model solution Methods: Or should Econometricians Use Network Methods for Model Solutions?', *Oxford Bulletin of Economics and Statistics*, Vol. 52, No. 3.

Imrohoroglu, A. (1989) 'The welfare cost of inflation under imperfect insurance', *University of Southern California Mimeo.*

Inder, B. (1993) 'Estimating Long-Run Relationships in Economics', *Journal of Econometrics*, Vol. 57, pp. 53–68 (1993)

International Monetary Fund Institute (1996) Financial Programming and Policy: The Case of Sri Lanka, *International Monetary Fund Institute*, May 26, 1996.

Ireland, P. N. (2000) 'Money's role in the monetary business cycle', unpublished manuscript, Boston College.

Isard, P. (2000) 'The role of MULTIMOD in the International Monetary Fund's Policy Analysis', *International Monetary Fund Policy Discussion Paper* PDP/00/5.

Issing, O. (2000) 'The Eurosystem: Transparent and Accountable or Willem in Euroland', *CEPR Policy Paper* No. 2.

Jadresic, E. (1996) 'Wage indexation and the Cost of Disinflation', *International Monetary Fund Working Paper*, No. 96/48.

Jadresic, E. (1999) Inflation Targeting and Output Stability, *International Monetary Fund Working Paper*: 99/61, April 1999.

Jones, L. and Manuelli, R. (1995) 'Growth and the effects of inflation', *Journal of Economic Dynamics and Control*, 19, pages 1405–28.

Jorgenson, D., and Stiroh, K. (1999) 'Information Technology and Growth', *American Economic Review Papers and Proceedings*, 89, 109–22.

Joyce, M. and Read, V. (1999) 'Asset price reactions to RPI announcements', *Bank of England Working Paper* No. 94, March 1999.

Joyce, M. and Wren-Lewis, S. (1990) *The Role of the Real Exchange Rate and Capacity Utilisation in Convergence to the NAIRU*, London: Bank of England.

Julius, D. (2000) *New Trends in a New Economy*? London: Bank of England.

Jung, W. S. (1985) 'Output-Inflation Tradeoffs in Industrial and Developing Countries', Journal of Macroeconomics, Winter 1985, Vol 7. No 1, pages 101–13.

Junguito, R. (1998) 'Costos y Beneficios de la Inflation'. Presented at the Banco de la República Conference on: 'Why is it Important to Decrease Inflation and How to do it', Bogota, Banco de la República.

Juselius, K. and Macdonald, R. (2000) *International Parity Relationships Between Germany and the United States: A Joint Modelling Approach*, Discussion Papers 00–10. Copenhagen: University of Copenhagen.

Kakes, J. J. (2000). Identifying the mechanism: is there a bank lending channel of monetary transmission in the Netherlands?, *Applied Economics Letters*, Vol 7, pages 63–67.

Kalkan, M., Kipici, A. and Peker, A. (1998) 'Leading Indicators of Inflation in Turkey', in Üçer, E.M. (ed.), *Macroeconomic Analysis of Turkey: Essays on Current Issues*, The Central Bank of the Republic of Turkey, Ankara.

Kamin, S., Turner, P. and van 't dack, J. (1998) 'The transmission mechanism of monetary policy in emerging market economies: an overview', *BIS Policy Papers*, (03a), January (available at http://www.bis.org/publ/plcy03a.pdf).

Kandil, M. (1991a) 'The Changing Cyclical Variability of Economic Activity in the United States: A Sectoral Investigation', *Journal of Macroeconomics*, Vol. 13, No. 1, pages 25–45.

Kandil, M. (1991b) 'Variations in the Response of Real Output to Aggregate Demand Shocks: A Cross-Industry Analysis', *The Review of Economics and Statistics*, Vol. 73, No. 3, pages 480–8, August.

Kandil, M. (1995a) 'Cyclical Fluctuations Across Industries of the United States: Evidence and Implications', *Journal of Economics and Business*, Vol. 47, No. 1, pages 17–37, February.

Kandil, M. (1995b) 'Asymmetric Nominal Flexibility and Economic Fluctuations', *Southern Economic Journal*, Vol. 61, No. 3, pages 674–95, January.

Kandil, M. (1996a) 'Sticky-Wage or Sticky-Price? Analysis of the Cyclical Behaviour of the Real Wage', *Southern Economic Journal*, Vol. 63, No. 2, pages 440–59, October.

Kandil, M. (1997) 'What Differentiates Industrial Business Cycles? A Cross-Country Investigation', *Applied Economics*, Vol. 29, No. 2, pages 197–212, February.

Kandil, M. (1999a) 'Industrial Output Variability and Real Wage Fluctuations: Determinants and Implications', *Economic Inquiry*, Vol. 37, No. 3, pages 452–72, July.

Kandil, M. (2000a) 'Demand shift across U.S. industries and the stabilizing function of nominal wage and flexibility', *Applied Economics*, Vol. 32, No. 4, pages 441–58, March./docinves/doc9905/doc9905.pdf).

Kandil, M. (2000b) 'Wage Flexibility and Economic Performance: evidence across Industrial Countries', *International Monetary Fund Working Paper*, No. 00/137.

Kandil, M. and Woods, J. G. (1995) 'A Cross-Industry Examination of the Lucas Misperceptions Model', *Journal of Macroeconomics*, Vol. 17, No. 1, pages 55–76, Winter.

Kandil, M. and Woods, J. G. (1997) 'Cyclical Comovements in Industrial Labor and Product Markets: Theory and Evidence', *Economic Inquiry*, Vol. 35. No. 4, pages 725–44, October.

Kashyap, A. and Stein, J. C. (1997) 'What Do a Million Banks Have to Say About the Transmission of Monetary Policy?', *National Bureau of Economic Research Working Paper*, No. 6056, June.

Kent, C. and Lowe, P. (1997) Asset price bubbles and monetary policy, research discussion paper 9709, Reserve Bank of Australia.

Kelly, C. M. (1985) 'A Cautionary Note on the Interpretation of Long-Run Equilibrium Solutions in Conventional Macro Models', *Economic Journal*, 95(380), pages 1078–86, December.

Kganetsano T. A., Mahadeva, L. and Masalila K. S. (2002) 'An Inflation Modelling Framework for Botswana', Bank of Botswana mimeo.

Kiley, M. T. (1996) The Lead of Output Over Inflation in Sticky price Models, *Board of Governors of the Federal Reserve System Finance and Economics, Discussion Series*, 96/23, August.

Killick, T. and Malik, M. (1992) 'Country Experiences with International Monetary Fund Programmes in the 1980's', *World Economy*, Vol. 15, No. 5, pages 599–632, September.

Kim, Benjamin, J. C. (1988) 'Real Wage Response to Monetary Shocks: A Disaggregated Analysis', *Journal of Macroeconomics*, Vol. 10, No. 2, pages 183–200, Spring.

King, M. A. (1994) 'Monetary Policy in the UK', *Fiscal Studies*, Vol. 15, pages 109–29.

Kipici, A. (2000) *Determination of Inflationary Expectations*, The Central Bank of the Republic of Turkey, Ankara.

Kiyotaki, N. and Moore, J. H. (1997) Credit Cycles, *Journal of Political Economy*, 105, pp 211–48.

Kokoszczyński, R. (ed.) (1999) Monetary Transmission Mechanism: Overview of Main Theories and Specification of the Transmission in Poland, *Materialy i Studia*, No. 91, National Bank of Poland (in Polish).

Kormendi, R. C. and Meguire, P. G. (1984) 'Cross-Regime Evidence of Macroeconomic Rationality', *Journal of Political Economy*, Vol. 92, No. 5, pages 875–908, October.

Kovács, M. A. (1998) 'The Information Content of Real Exchange Rate Indicators', *National Bank of Hungary Working Paper*, No. 1998/8.

Kovács, M. and Simon, A. (1998) 'The components of the real exchange rate in Hungary', National Bank of Hungary working paper, No. 1998/3.

Kuttner, K. N. (1994) 'Estimating Potential Output as a Latent Variable', *Journal of Business and Economic Statistics*, Volume 12. No 3, pages 361–7 July 1994.

Kuttner, K. N. (2001) 'Monetary Policy Surprises and Interest Rates: Evidence

from the Fed Funds Futures Markets', *Journal of Monetary Economics*, Vol 47: 523–44 (2001).
Kydland, F. and Prescott, F. (1977) 'Rules rather than discretion: The inconsistency of optimal plans', *Journal of Political Economy* Vol. 85(3), pp. 473–91 (1977)
Laidler, D. (1999) The Exchange Rate Regime and Canada's Monetary Order. Bank of Canada Working Paper No. 99–7.
Lane, P. R. (2000) 'Money Shocks and the Current Account', in Calvo, G., Dornbusch, R. and Obstfeld, M. (eds.), *Money, Factor Mobility and Trade: Essays in Honor of Robert Mundell*, Cambridge, MA: MIT Press.
Laubach, T. and Williams J. C. (2001) 'Measuring the Natural Rate of Interest', *The Federal Reserve Board, Finance And Economics Series*, No 2001–56.
Leyard, R., Nickell, S. and Jackman, R. (1991) *Unemployment: Macroeconomic Performance and the Labour Market*, Oxford: Oxford University Press.
Lee, K. C., Pesaran, M. H. and Pierse, R. G. (1990) 'Testing for Aggregation Bias in Linear Models', *Economic Journal*, 100(400), Supplement, pages 137–50.
Leiderman, L. (1998) Monetary Policy and Disinflation in Israel. *The Bank of Israel Discussion Papers No. 04/1998*
Leiderman, L. (1999) Monetary Policy under Uncertainty – some Lessons from Israel. Paper for the conference on 'Monetary Policy under Uncertainty' organised by ECB at Frankfurt in December, 1999 Frankfurt: European Central Bank.
Leiderman, L. and Svensson L. E. O. (1995) *Inflation Targets*, Centre for Economic Policy Research, London.
Levine, R. and Renelt, D. (1992) 'A sensitivity analysis of cross-country growth regressions', *American Economic Review*, Vol. 82, No. 4, pages 942–63.
Lipschitz, L. and McDonald, D. (1992) 'Real Exchange Rates and Competitiveness: A Clarification of Concepts, and Some Measurements for Europe', *Empirica*, 19 (1): 37–69.
López, M. (2000) 'Seignorage and the Welfare Cost of Inflation in Colombia', *Ensayos sobre Política Económica*, forthcoming.
Lucas, R. E. (1972) 'Expectations and the Neutrality of Money,' Journal of Economic Theory, 4, page 103–24.
Lucas, R. E. (1973) 'Some International Evidence on Output-Inflation Trade-Offs', *American Economic Review*, Vol. 63, No. 3, pages 326–34, June.
Lucas, R. E. (1987) *Models of Business Cycles*, Basil Blackwell.
Lucas, R. E. (1994) 'On the welfare cost of inflations'. *Working Papers in Applied Economic Theory* 94–07, Federal Reserve Bank of San Francisco.
Lucas, R. G. (2000) 'Inflation and Welfare', *Econometrica* **68(2)**: 247–74.
Lutkowski, K. (2000) Are we threatened with a wave of inflation?, *Magazyn Finansowy*, No. 112 (728) (in Polish).
Łyziak, T. (2000a) 'Monetary Transmission Mechanism in Poland, Theoretical Concepts vs. Evidence', National Bank of Poland, Warsaw.
Łyziak, T. (2000b) 'Badanie oczekiwań inflacyjnych podmiotów indywidualnych na podstawie ankiet jakościowych [Individuals' inflationary expectations – a qualitative questionnaire survey]', *Bank i Kredyt*, 6/2000, National Bank of Poland, or: 'Inflationary expectations' quantification on the basis of qualitative surveys', typescript.
Łyziak, T. (2000c) 'commercial bank assets under the influence of central bank policy instruments. An overview of operation of the credit channel of monetary

transmission in Poland, 1995–1999, *Bank i Kredyt*, 3/2000, National Bank of Poland (in Polish).

Mackie, D., Miles, D. and Taylor, C. (1989) 'The impact of Monetary Policy on Inflation: Modelling the UK Experience, 1978–86, in Britton, A. (ed.), *Policymaking with Macroeconomic Models*, National Institute of Economics and Social Research. Aldershot: Gower, pages 151–85.

Maclennan, D., Muellbauer, J. and Stephens, M. (1998) 'Asymmetries in Housing and Financial Market Institutions and EMU', *Oxford Review of Economic Policy*, Vol. 14, No.3.

Mahadeva, L. and Sinclair, P. J. N. S (eds.) (2002) *The Theory and Practice of Monetary Transmission in Diverse Economies*, Cambridge: Cambridge University Press.

Mahadeva, L. and Šmidková, K. (2000) 'What Is the Optimal Disinflation Path to Be Targeted in the Czech Economy?', *Czech Economic Association Conference 2000: Papers and Proceedings Prague – November 2000* (http://www.financeauver.org/20001 1en.htm).

Mahadeva, L. and Sterne, G. (eds.) (2000) *Monetary Policy Frameworks in a Global Context*, Routledge, London.

Mahadeva, L. and Sterne, G. (2002) 'The Role of Short-run Inflation Targets and Forecasts in Disinflation', Bank of England Working Paper No. 167, October.

Mair, V. H. (2000) The Columbia Anthology of Traditional Chinese Literature, New York: Columbia University Press.

Mankiw N. G. and Reis, R. (2001) Sticky Information Versus Sticky Prices: A Proposal to Replace the New Keynesian Phillips Curve, *National Bureau of Economic Research Working Paper No 8290*, May 2001.

Mankiw, N. G. and Romer, D. (eds.) (1991a) 'Imperfect Competition and Sticky Prices, *New Keynesian economics* Vol. 2, Cambridge, MA: MIT Press.

Mankiw, N. G. and Romer, D. (eds.) (1991b) 'Coordination failures and real rigidities', in *New Keynesian economics* Vol. 2, Cambridge, MA: MIT Press.

Mankiw, N. G. (2001) The Inexorable and Mysterious Trade-off between Inflation and Unemployment, *Economic Journal*, 111, May 2001, C45–C61.

Manning, A. (1993) 'Wage Bargaining and the Phillips Curve: The Identification and Specification of Aggregate Wage Equations', *Economic Journal*, 103(416), pages 98–118, January.

Marsh, I. W. and Tokarick, P. (1994) 'Competitiveness Indicators: A Theoretical and Empirical Assessment', *International Monetary Fund Working Paper*, 94/29.

Masson, P. R., Savastano, M. A. and Sharma, S. (1997) 'The Scope for Inflation Targeting in Developing Countries', *International Monetary Fund Working Paper*, No. 97/130.

Mavroeidis, S. (2002) Identification and mis-specification issues in forward-looking models, unpublished manuscript.

Mboweni, T. T. (2000a). *A new Monetary Policy Framework*, Appendix to the statement issued by Mr T.T. Mboweni, Governor of the South African Reserve Bank, 6 April, also published as a statement in the *South African Reserve Bank Quarterly Bulletin*, No 216, June.

Mboweni, T. T. (2000b). *The monetary policy stance*, Statement issued by Mr T.T. Mboweni, Governor of the South African Reserve Bank at a meeting of the Portfolio Committee on Finance, Cape Town, on 19 April, also published as a statement in the *South African Reserve Bank Quarterly Bulletin*, No 216, June.

McCallum, B. T. (1976) 'Rational Expectations and the Natural Rate Hypothesis: Some Consistent Estimates', *Econometrica*, Vol. 44, No. 1, January.

McCallum, B. T. (1986a) 'Some Issues Concerning Interest Rate Pegging, Price Level Determinacy, and the Real Bills Doctrine', *Journal of Monetary Economics*, Vol. 17, No. 1, pages 135–60, January.

McCallum, B. T. (1986b) On 'Real' and 'Sticky-Price' Theories of the Business Cycle, *Journal of Money, Credit and Banking*, pages 397–414.

McCallum, B. T. (1991) Credit Rationing and the Monetary Transmission Mechanism, *American Economic Review*, Vol. 81, pages 946–51.

McCallum, B. T. (1992) 'Real Business Cycle Theories', in Vercelli, A. and Dimitri, N. (eds.), *Macroeconomics: A survey of research strategies*, Oxford: Oxford University Press, pages 167–82.

McCallum, B. T. (1994) A reconsideration of the uncovered interest parity relationship, *Journal of Monetary Economics*, 33, pp 105–32.

McCallum, B. T. (1999) 'Analysis of the Monetary Transmission Mechanism', *National Bureau of Economic Research Working Paper*, No. 7395.

McCallum, B. T. (2000a) 'Theoretical Analysis Regarding a Zero Lower Bound on Nominal Interest Rates', *National Bureau of Economic Research Working Paper*, No. 7877.

McCallum, B. T. (2000b) 'Inflation Targeting and the Liquidity Trap', Fourth Annual Conference of the Central Bank of Chile, mimeo.

McCallum, B. T. (2001) 'Should monetary policy respond strongly to output gaps?', *American Economic Review Papers and Proceedings* 91 (May 2001), 258–62 and *National Bureau of Economic Research Working Paper* No. 8226.

McCallum, B. and Nelson, E. (1997) 'An Optimizing IS-LM Specification for Monetary Policy and Business Cycle Analysis', National Bureau of Economic Research Working Paper No. 5875.

McCallum, B. T. and Nelson, E. (1998) 'Nominal Income Targeting in an Open-economy Optimizing Model', *National Bureau of Economic Research Working Paper*, No. 6675, August.

McCallum, B. T. and Nelson, E. (1999) 'An Optimizing IS-LM Specification for Monetary Policy ànd Business Cycle Analysis', *Journal of Money, Credit and Banking*, Vol. 31, No. 3, Part 1, pages 296–316, August.

McKibbin, W. J. and Vines, D. (2001) 'Modelling Reality: The need for both intertemporal optimization and stickiness in models for policy-making', *Oxford Review of Economic Policy* Vol. 16 N4.

Meltzer, A. H. (1995) Monetary, Credit and (Other) Transmission Processes: A Monetarist Perspective, *Journal of Economic Perspectives*, Vol. 9, pages 49–72.

Meltzer, A. H. (2001) 'The Transmission Process', in *The Monetary Transmission Process: Recent Developments and Lessons for Europe*, edited by the Deutsche Bundesbank, Basingstoke: Palgrave Publishers.

Menczel, P. (2000) 'What do the savings show?', *Bankszemle*, 2000/8 (in Hungarian).

Meredith, G. (1999) 'REPMOD: A Smaller Sibling for Multimod', *International Monetary Fund Working Paper*, No. 99/08, January.

Meredith, G. (2002) Uncovered Interest Parity and the Monetary Transmission Mechanism, in *Monetary Transmission in Diverse economies*, eds. L. Mahadeva and P. Sinclair, Cambridge: Cambridge University Press, 208–36.

Miller, M. H., Edison, H. J. and Luangaram, P. (2000) Asset bubbles, leverage and 'lifeboats': elements of the East Asian crisis, *Economic Journal*, 110, pp 309–34.

Mishkin, F. S. (1995) 'Symposium on the Monetary Transmission Mechanism', *Journal of Economic Perspectives*, Vol. 9, No. 4, pages 3–10, Fall.

Mishkin, F. S. (1998). *The economics of money, banking, and financial markets*, New York: Columbia University: Addison Wesley Longman, Inc.

Mishkin, F. S. (2000a) 'What Should Central Banks Do?' *Federal Reserve Bank of St. Louis Review* (November/December): 1–13 (2000)

Mishkin, F. S. (2000b) 'Inflation Targeting in Emerging Market Countries', *National Bureau of Economic Research Working paper*, No. 7618.

Mishkin, F. S. and Savastano, M. A. (2000) 'Monetary Policy Strategies for Latin America', *National Bureau of Economic Research Working paper*, No. 7616.

Moalla-Fetini, R. (2000) Inflation as a Fiscal Problem, *International Monetary Fund Staff Country Report*, No. 00/14, Washington: International Monetary Fund (also available at http://www.imf.org).

Modigliani, M. (1971) Monetary policy and consumption, in *Consumer spending and money policy: the linkages*, Boston: Federal Reserve Bank, pages 9–84.

Mohanty, M. S. and Klau, M. (2000) What deterrmines inflation in emerging market economies?, Basel: BIS.

Montiel, P. J. (1991) 'The Transmission Mechanism for Monetary Policy in Developing Countries', *International Monetary Fund Staff Papers*, Vol. 38, No. 1.

Montiel, P. J. and Ostry, J. D. (1991) 'Macroeconomic Implications of Real Exchange Rate Targeting in Developing Countries', *International Monetary Fund Staff Papers*, Vol. 38, No. 4.

Morris, S. and Shin, H., (2000) 'Social Value of Public Information', *American Economic Review* 52 (5), December 2002, pages 1521–34.

Morsink, J. and Bayoumi, T. (1999). A peek inside the Black Box: the monetary transmission mechanism in Japan, *International Monetary Fund Working Paper*, No 137 (WP/99/137), Asia and Pacific Department, International Monetary Fund, October.

Muellbauer, J. (1994) 'The Assessment: Consumer Expenditure', *Oxford Review of Economic Policy*, Vol. 10, No. 2.

Muellbauer J. and Lattimore, R. (1995) 'The Consumption Function: A Theoretical and Empirical Overview', in Pesaran, M.H. and Wickens, M.R. (eds.), *Handbook of Applied Econometrics – Macroeconomies*, Oxford: Blackwell Press.

Muller, P. and Zelmer, M. (1999) 'Greater transparency in monetary policy: impact on financial markets', *Bank of Canada Technical Report* No. 86, August 1999.

Mundell, R. A. (1999) 'Exchange rate arrangements during the transition economies', in M. Škreb and M. Blejer (eds) Proceedings of the Third Dubrovnik Conference on the Balance of Payment, Exchange Rates and Competitiveness in Transition Economies, Dubrovnik 25–27 June. Dordrecht: Kluwer Academic Publishers.

Mundlak, Y., Cavallo, D. and Domenech, R. (1990) 'Effects of Macroeconomic Policies on Sectoral Prices', *The World Bank Economic Review*, Vol. 4, No. 1.

Mussa, M. and Savastano, M. A. (1999) *The IMF Approach to Economic Stabilization* IMF Working Paper WP/99/104 July 1999.

National Bank of Hungary (1998) Reports on Inflation, November 1998.

National Bank of Hungary (1999) Reports on Inflation, April 1999.

National Bank of Poland (1998) *Medium-Term Strategy of Monetary Policy (1999–2003)*, http://www.nbp.pl.

National Bank of Poland (1999) *Inflation Report 1998*, http://www.nbp.pl.

National Bank of Poland (2000a) *Inflation Report 1999*, http://www.nbp.pl.

National Bank of Poland (2000b) *Summary Evaluation of the Financial Situation of Polish Banks 1999.* General Inspectorate of Banking Supervision.

National Bank of Poland (2000c) *Summary Evaluation of Financial Situation of Polish Banks in Period: January–September 2000*, General Inspectorate of Banking Supervision (in Polish).

Neiss, K. S. and Nelson, E. (2001) The real interest gap as an inflation indicator, *Bank of England Working Paper No 130*

Neiss, K. S. and Nelson, E. (2002) Inflation Dynamics, Marginal Cost, and the Output Gap: Evidence from three Countries. Proceedings (March) Federal Reserve Bank of San Francisco. San Francisco: Federal Reserve Bank.

Nelson, R. (1989) On the Measurement of Capacity utilisation, *The Journal of Industrial Economics*, March 1989, Volume XXXVIII, no 3.

Nelson, E. (2000) 'Direct Effects of Monetary base on Aggregate Demand: Theory and Evidence', *Bank of England Working Paper No 122*

Nelson, C. R. and Plosser, C. I. (1982) 'Trends and Random Walks in Macroeconomic Time Series', *Journal of Monetary Economics*, Vol. 10, No. 2, pages 139–62, September.

Neményi, J. (1996) Monetary Policy in Transition (the case of Hungary), in Proceedings of the Conference: Where Do We Stand with the Monetary Transformation in Central and Eastern Europe – Strategies, Instruments and Transmission Mechanism, Vienna: Austrian National Bank.

Neményi, J. (1997) Capital Inflow, Macroeconomic Equilibrium, The Public Debt and The Profit and Loss of the National Bank of Hungary, Acta Oeconomica, vol.48, No.3–4, pp. 241–70.

Newey W. and West K., (1987) 'A Simple Positive Semi-Definite, Heteroskedasticity and Autocorrelation Consistent Covariance Matrix', *Econometrica*, Vol. 55, pages 703–8.

Nickell, S. (1988) 'The Supply Side and Macroeconomic Modelling', in Bryant, R., Henderson, D.W., Holtharn, G., Hooper, P. and Symansky. S.A. eds *Empirical Economics for Interdependent Economies*, Brookings Institution, Washington DC, pages 202–217.

Nickell, S. (1996) 'Inflation and the UK Labour Market' in Jenkinson, Tim (ed.), *Readings in Macroeconomics*, Oxford: Oxford University Press: 141–8.

Nikiel, E. M. and Opiela, T. P. (1998) Interest Elasticity of Time Deposits in Poland: Its Influence on the Cost and Future Competitiveness of Commercial Banks', in Polański Z. [ed.], *Rynek Pieniężny w Polsce w Drugiej Poełowie Lat Dziewięédziesiątych: Stan i Perspektywy, Economic Transformation Series*, No. 96, Gdansk Institute for Market Economics, Warsaw (in Polish).

Nickell, S. and Quintini, G. (2002) The recent performance of the UK labour market, *Oxford Review of Economic Policy*, 18, 2002, pp 202–20.

Obstfeld, M. (1982) Can We Sterilize? Theory and Evidence, *American Economic Review: Papers and Proceedings*, 72 (No. 2, May), pages 45–50.

Obstfeld, M. and Rogoff, K. (1999) 'New Directions for Stochastic Open Economy Models', *National Bureau of Economic Research Working Paper*, No. 7313.

Oliner, S. and Sichel, D. (2000) 'The Resurgence of Growth in the Late 1990s: Is Information Technology the Story?', Paper given at the conference on Structural Change and Monetary Policy at the Federal Reserve Bank of San Francisco, 3–4 March. San Francisco: Federal Reserve Bank of San Francisco.

Onado, M. (1992) *Economics of Financial Systems*, Bologna: *il Mulino.*

Opiela, T. P. (1998) 'Credit channel of monetary transmission in Poland: the role of ownership structure and banks' balance sheets', *Bank i Kredyt*, 6/1998, National Bank of Poland (in Polish).

Opiela T. P. (1999) 'Monetary Policy and Bank Lending in Poland: The Role of Government Deposit Guarantees', unpublished manuscript.

Orphanides, A., Porter, R. D., Reifschneider, D., Tetlow, R., and Finan, F. (1999) 'Errors in the Measurement of the Output Gap and the Design of Monetary Policy', *Federal Reserve Board Finance and Economics Discussion Series* No. 1999–2045, August.

Osiński, J. (1999) 'Monetary policy of the National Bank of Poland in years 1993–1997. Experience and opportunities for using related conclusions in the future', *Bank i Kredyt*, 7–8/1999 (in Polish).

Özatay, F. (1997) 'Sustainability of Fiscal Deficits, Monetary Policy, and Inflation Stabilization: The Case of Turkey', *Journal of Policy Modelling*, 19(6), pages 661–81.

Pagan, A. (1984) 'Econometric Issues in the Analysis of Regressions with Generated Regressors', *International Economic Review*, Vol. 25, No. 1, pages 221–47, February.

Pagan, A. (1986) 'Two Stage and Related Estimators and Their Applications', *Review of Economic Studies*, Vol. 53, No. 4, pages 517–38, August.

Pagan, A. (2000) 'Econometric Analysis of Turning Points', *paper presented to the ESRC Macro Study Group at the Institute for Fiscal Studies, London, 25 February 2000.*

Peel, D. A. and Chappell, D. (1981) 'Rational Expectations and Wage and Price Inflexibility: A Note', *Scandinavian Journal of Economics*, Vol. 83, No. 1, pages 115–20.

Peermans, G. and Smets, F. (2002) Are the effects of monetary policy in the euro area greater in recessions than in booms? in *Monetary Transmission in Diverse Economies*, eds. L. Mahadeva and P. Sinclair, Cambridge: Cambridge University Press, pp 28–48.

Perera N. (1984) Exogenous Shocks and Macroeconomic Policies in LDCs: A Study of Sri Lanka with an Econometric Model, Journal of Policy Modelling, Vol 16, No 3, pp. 335–45.

Pesaran, M. H. (1987) *The Limits to Rational Expectations*, Oxford: Basil Blackwell.

Pesaran, H. M. and Smith, R. P. (1999) 'Structural Analysis of Cointegrating Vars', in McAleer, M. and Oxley, L. *Practical Issues in Cointegration Analysis*, Oxford: Blackwell.

Pesaran, M. H., Shin, Y. and Smith, R. (1996) 'Testing for the "Existence of a Long-run Relationship"', Cambridge Working Papers in Economics 9622, Department of Applied Economics, University of Cambridge.

Phelps, E. S. (1994) *Structural Slumps: The Modern Equilibrium Theory of Unemployment, Interest and Assets*, Cambridge, MA: Harvard University Press.

Phelps, E. S. and Winter Jr., S. G. (1970) 'Optimal Price Policy under Atomistic Competition', in E.S. Phelps (ed.), *Microeconomic Foundations of Employment and Inflation Theory*, New York: Norton.

Phillips, A. W. H. (1958) 'The Relation Between Unemployment and the Rate of

Change of Money Wage Rates in the United Kingdom, 1861–1957', *Economica*, Oxford: Blackwell.

Phillips, P. and Hansen B. (1990) 'Statistical Inference in Instrumental Variables Regressions with I(1) processes', *Review of Economic Studies*, Vol. 57, pages 99–125.

Pirttilä, J. (2000) 'Fiscal Policy and Structural Reforms in Transition Economies: An Empirical Analysis', *Bank of Finland Discussion paper*, No.5, Institute for Economies in Transition.

Poterba, J. (2000) Stock market wealth and consumption, *Journal of Economic Perspectives*, 14, pp 99–118.

Prachowny, M. F. J (1992) 'Okuns' Law: Theoretical Foundations and Revised Estimates', *The Review Of Economics and Statistics*, 75(2): 331–5.

Polak, J. J. (1998) 'The International Monetary Fund Monetary Model At 40', *Economic Modelling* 15(3): 395–410, July.

Quah, D. (1992) 'The Relative Importance of Permanent and Transitory Components: Identification and Some Theoretical Bounds', *Econometrica* 60(1): 107–18, January.

Quah, D. T. (1995) 'Business Cycle Empirics: Calibration and Estimation, An Introduction', *Economic Journal*, 105, pages 1594–647.

Ramey, V. A. (1993) 'How Important Is the Credit Channel in the Transmission of Monetary Policy?', *National Bureau of Economic Research Working Paper*, No. 4285.

Roberts, J. M. (1995) 'New Keynesian economics and the Phillips curve', *Journal of Money, Credit, and Banking* Vol. 27: 975–84.

Roberts, J. M. (1997) 'Is Inflation Sticky?', *Journal of Monetary Economics*, Vol. 39, No. 2, pages 173–96, July.

Roberts, J. M. (1998) *Inflation Expectations and the Transmission of Monetary Policy*, http://www.federalreserve.gov/pubs/feds/1998/199843.

Romer, C. and Romer, D. (1990) New Evidence on the Monetary Transmission Mechanism, *Brookings Papers on Economic Activity*, Vol 1 pages 149–98.

Rotemburg J. J. and Woodford, M. (1991) 'Markups and the Business Cycle' in Blanchard, O. J. and Fischer, S. (eds.), *National Bureau of Economic Research Macroeconomics Annual*. Boston: NBER.

Rotemberg, J. J. and Woodford, M. (1998) 'An Optimization-based Econometric Framework for the Evaluation of Monetary Policy: Expanded Version', *National Bureau of Economic Research Technical Working Paper*, No. 233.

Rudd, J. and K. Whelan (2002) 'New Tests of the New-Keynesian Phillips Curve?', *Federal Reserve Board, Finance and Economics Discussion Series* No 2002–30.

Rudebush, Glenn D. and Svensson, Lars E. O. (1998) 'Policy Rules for Inflation Targeting', *National Bureau of Economic Research Working Paper*, No. 6512, April.

Sachs, J. (1980) 'The Changing Cyclical Behaviour of Wages and Prices: 1890–1976', *American Economic Review*, Vol. 70, No. 1, pages 78–90, March.

Şahinbeyoğlu, G. (2000) 'Monetary Transmission Mechanism: A View from a High Inflationary Environment', *Paper prepared for the CCBS/BoE Money, Macro and Finance Group Workshop on Analysing the Transmission Mechanisms in Diverse Economies, 4 September 2000*. Ankara: Central Bank of Turkey.

Şahinbeyoğlu, G. and Ulaşan, B. (1999) 'An Empirical Examination of the Structural Stability of Export Demand Function: The Case of Turkey', *The Central Bank of the Republic of Turkey: Discussion Paper*, No. 9907.

Sargent, T. (1982) The Ends of Four Big Inflations, in *Inflation: Causes and Effects*, ed. R.E. Hall, Cambridge (Massachusetts), National Bureau of Economic Research, pp 41–97.

Sargent, T. J. (1999) *The conquest of American inflation*, Princeton, NJ: Princeton University Press.

Sargent, T. J. and Wallace, N. (1975) '"Rational" Expectations, the Optimal Monetary Instrument and the Optimal Money Supply Rule', Minnesota, MN: University of Minnesota.

Sbordone, A. (1998) Prices and Unit Labour Costs: A New Test of Price Stickiness, *IIES Seminar Paper 653*, Stockholm University.

Sbordone, A. (2002) Prices and Unit Labour Costs: A New Test of Price Stickiness, *Journal Of Monetary Economics* 49, pages 265–92.

Senhadji, A. and Montenegro, C. (1998) 'Time Series Analysis of Export Demand Equations: A Cross-Country Analysis', *International Monetary Fund Working Paper*, No. 98/149.

Shadman-Mehta, F. (1996) Does Modern Econometrics replicate the Phillips Curve?, Université Catholique de Louvain, Institut de Recherches Economiques et Sociales (IRES), Discussion Paper 1996015.

Sidrausky, M. (1967) Inflation and Economic Growth', *Journal of Political Economy* 75: 798–810.

Sims, C. A. (1992) 'Interpreting the Macroeconomic Time Series Facts: The Effects of Monetary Policy', *European Economic Review*, 36(5), pages 975–1000, June.

Sims C. A. (2001) *Implications of Rational Inattention*, Princeton, NJ: Princeton University.

Sjaastad, L. (1998) 'On exchange rates, nominal and real', *Journal of International Money and Finance*, Vol. 17, No. 3.

Smets, F. and Wouters, R. (2002) 'An Estimated Stochastic Dynamic General Equilibrium Model of the Euro Area', *European Central Bank Working Paper*, August 2002, no 171.

Smidkova, K. (1999) 'Menove-rozhodovaci proces: nejistota a role prognoz', Seminar proceedings, Czech Economic Society, Prague.

Soderlind, P. (1999) 'Solution and Estimation of RE Macromodels with Optimal Policy', *European Economic Review*, Vol. 43, No.'s 4–6, pages 813–23, April.

Soderstrom, P. and Sargent, T. (2002) http://hem.passagen.se/ulfsoder/ConquestIntroEng.pdf.

South Africa, Republic (1989) South African Reserve Bank Act, Act No 90 of 1989, Pretoria: Government Printers.

South Africa, Republic (1996) Constitution of the Republic of South Africa, Act No. 108 of 1996, Pretoria: Government Printers.

Sriram, S. S. (1999) 'Survey of Literature on Demand for Money: Theoretical and Empirical Work with Special Reference to Error-Correction Models', *International Monetary Fund Working Paper*, No. 99/64, May.

Stals, C. L. (1997) *The effects of the changing financial environment on monetary policy in South Africa*, Address by the Governor of the South African Reserve Bank, Dr C.L. Stals, at the Annual Dinner of the Pretoria Branch of the Economic Society of South Africa, held in Pretoria on 15 May.

Stals, C. L. (1998) *Monetary policy and Reserve Bank accommodation procedures*, Statement issued by Dr C.L. Stals, Governor of the South African Reserve Bank, South African Reserve Bank, 7 March.

Steiner, R. (1997) 'Los Dolares del Narcotrafico', *Cuadernos Fedesrrollo,* 2, Tercer Mundo.

Steinsson, J. (2002) 'Optimal Monetary Policy in an Economy with Inflation Persistence', *Central Bank of Iceland Working Paper,* December 2000.

Sterne, G. and Bayoumi, T. (1995) 'Temporary Cycles or Volatile Trends? Economic Fluctuations in 21 OECD Economies', *Manchester School of Economic and Social Studies* 63(1): 23–51, March.

Stevenson, A., Muscatelli, V. and Gregory, M. (1988) *Macroeconomic Theory and Stabilization Policy,* Totowa, NJ: Barnes and Noble, 406.

Stiglitz, J. E. and Weiss, A. (1981) Credit Rationing in Markets with Imperfect Information, *American Economic Review,* Vol. 71, pages 393–410.

Stiglitz, J. E. and Weiss, A. (1983) Incentive effects of termination, *American Economic Review,* 73, pp 912–27.

Summers, L. H. (1988) 'Should Keynesian Economics dispense with the Phillips Curve?,' in '*Unemployment, Hysteresis and the natural rate hypothesis,* Cross, R. (ed.), Oxford: Blackwell. pages 11–25.

Summers, R. and Heston, A. (1988) 'A new set of international comparisons of a real product and price levels estimates for 130 countries, 1950–1985', *Review of Income and Wealth,* 34, pages 1–25.

Svejnar, J. (1999) Restructuring, Privatisation, Ownership and Governance in Transition Economies. Paper for the Fifth Dubrovnik Conference on Transition Economies 'Ten Years of Transition: What Have We Learned and What Lies Ahead', organised by the National Bank of Croatia, June 23–25, 1999. Dubrovnik National Bank of Croatia.

Svendsen, I. (1996) Empirical Evidence on Expectations, *Økonomiske Doktoravhandlinger,* No. 28, Universitetet I Oslo.

Svensson, L. E. O. (1999) 'Inflation targeting as a monetary policy rule', *Journal of Monetary Economics,* 43, pages 607–54.

Svensson, L. E. O. (2000) 'Open-economy inflation targeting', *Journal of International Economics,* No. 50, No. 1, pages 155–83, February.

Svensson, L. E. O. (2001) 'Independent Review of the Operation of Monetary Policy in New Zealand', *Report to the Minister of Finance,* February.

Szpunar, P. (1998) 'Indirect goals and the effectiveness of monetary policy', *Bank i Kredyt,* 1–2/1998, National Bank of Poland, (in Polish).

Takamaya, A. (1995) *Mathematical Economics,* 2nd edn, Cambridge: Cambridge University Press.

Tarkka, J. and Mayes, D. (1999) 'The Value of Publishing Official Central Bank Forecasts', *Bank of Finland Discussion Paper 22/99.*

Taylor, A. M. (2001) Potential pitfalls for the purchasing-power-parity puzzle? Sampling and specification biases in mean-reversion tests of the law of one price, *Econometrica,* 69, pp 473–98.

Taylor, J. B. (1993a) *Macroeconomic Policy in a World Economy. From Econometric Design to Practical Operation,* W. W. Norton & Company, New York.

Taylor, J. B. (1993b) 'Discretion versus Policy Rules in Practice', *Carnegie-Rochester Conference Series on Public Policy,* 39(0), pages 195–214, December.

Taylor, J. B. (1995) 'The Monetary Transmission Mechanism: An Empirical Framework', *Journal of Economic Perspectives* 9(4): 11–26, Fall.

Taylor, J. B. (2000) Low inflation, pass-through and the pricing power of firms, *European Economic Review,* 44, pp 1389–408.

Taylor, M. P. (1988) 'What Do Investment Managers Know? An Empirical Study of Practitioners' Predictions', *Economica*, 55(218), pages 185–202, May.

Thiessen, G. G. (1996) Uncertainty and the transmission of monetary policy in Canada, Inspired by the Hermes lecture (1995) at Glendon College and published as a volume by the Bank of Canada, *The Transmission Mechanism of Monetary Policy in Canada*, Toronto: Bank of Canada.

Thornton, D. (2000) 'The Relationship between the Federal Funds Rate and the Fed's Federal Funds Rate Target: Is it Open Market or Open Mouth Operations?', *Federal Reserve Bank of St. Louis Working Paper* No. 1999–22B, December (2000).

Tobin, J. (1978) Monetary Policies and the Economy: the Transmission Mechanism, *Southern Economic Journal*, Vol. 44, pages 421–31.

Torres, R. and Martin J. P. (1997) 'Measuring Potential Output in the Seven Major OECD Countries', *OECD Economic Review*, pages 127–49.

Tôth, I. J. and Vincze, J. (1998) 'The Pricing Behaviour of Hungarian Firms', *National Bank of Hungary Working Paper*, No. 1998/7.

Triplett, J. (1999) 'Economic Statistics, the New Economy, and the Productivity Slowdown', *Business Economics*, 34, 13–17.

Turner, D. and Seghezza, E. (1999) 'Testing for a common OECD Phillips curve', *Economics Department Working Paper* No. 219, OECD.

Ueda, K. (2002) 'The Transmission Mechanism of Monetary Policy near Zero Interest Rates: The Japanese Experience, 1998–2000' in Mahadeva, L. and Sinclair, P. (eds.), *Monetary Transmission in Diverse Economies*, Cambridge University press, Cambridge.

Uhlig, H. (1999) 'What are the Effects of Monetary Policy on Output? Results from an Agnostic Identification Procedure', *CEPR Discussion paper Series*, No. 2137.

Ulrich, T. and Wachtel, P. (1984) 'The effects of inflation and money supply announcements on interest rates', *Journal of finance*, Vol. 39, No. 4 (1984)

United Kingdom Parliament (1996) *House of Lord's Select Committee Report*: Monetary Policy Committee of the Bank of England: Chapter 4: The techniques and transmission mechanism of monetary policy, 27 July.

Uribe, J. D. (1994) 'Inflación y Crecimiento Económico en Colombia: 1951–1992', *Borradores Semanales de Economía*, No. 1, Banco de la República.

Valentinyi, Á (2000) 'Economic growth, convergence and fiscal policy in a small open economy', *Közgazdasági Szemle*, XLVII, pages 391–410 (in Hungarian).

Van der Merwe, E. J. (1997) *South African monetary policy: where are we heading?*, Address by Dr E.J. van der Merwe, at the Conference of the Institute for Strategic Studies and the Graduate School of Management of the University of Pretoria, 14 August.

Van der Merwe, E. J. (1998) *Discussion paper on monetary policy operational procedures*, South African Reserve Bank, October.

Van Wijnbergen, S. (1985) 'Macroeconomic Effects of Changes in Bank Interest Rates: Simulation Results for South Korea', *Journal of Development Economics*, 18, pages 541–54, August.

Varian, H. R. (2002) '*Microeconomic Analysis*', 3rd edn, W. W. Norton and Co., London.

Vegh, C. A. (1992) 'Stopping High Inflation: An analytical Overview', *International Monetary Fund Staff Papers*, Vol. 39, No. 3.

Vickers, J. (2000) 'Monetary Policy and the Supply Side', *Bank of England Quarterly Bulletin*, Vol. 40, No. 2, pages 199–206, May.

Világi, B. and Vincze, J. (1998) The interest rate transmission mechanism in Hungary, 1991–1995, in Halpern, L and Wyplosz, C (eds.), *Hungary: Towards a Market Economy*, Cambridge University Press, Cambridge, pp. 54–86.
Villar, L. and Rincón, H. (2000) 'The Colombian Economy in the Nineties: Capital Flows and Foreign Exchange Regimes', *Borradores Semanales de Economía,* 149, Banco de la República.
Vincze, J. (2000) 'The legend of risk premium', unpublished manuscript (in Hungarian).
Wachter, M. (1976) 'The Changing Cyclical Responsiveness of Wage Inflation', *Brookings Papers on Economic Activity,* 1(76), pages 115–59.
Wadhwani, S. (2000) 'The Impact of the Internet on UK Inflation', speech delivered at the London School of Economics, 23 February.
Wallis, K. F. and Whitley, J. D. (1995) 'Sources of Error in Forecasts and Expectations: U.K. Economic Models, 1984–8' in Wallis, K. F., *Time series analysis and macroeconometric modelling: The collected papers of Kenneth F. Wallis. Economists of the Twentieth Century series,* 2nd edn, Brookfield, Vt.: Elgar, 1995: 267–89.
Walsh, C. E. (1998) *Monetary theory and policy,* Cambridge, MA: MIT Press.
Watson, N. (1999) 'Bank-Lending Channel Evidence at the Firm Level', *Banco de Espana,* 9906.
Werner, A. (1996) 'Mexico's Currency Risk Premia in 1992–94: A Closer Look at the Interest Rate Differentials', *International Monetary Fund Working Paper,* No. 96/41.
Whitesell, W. (1997) 'Interest Rates and M2 in an Error Correction Macro Model', *Board of Governors of the Federal Reserve System: Finance and Economics Discussion Series,* 1997–59, December.
Wicksell, K. (1958) 'The influence of the natural rate of interest on commodity prices', in Lindahl, E. (ed) *Knut Wicksell, Selected Papers on Economic Theory,* Cambridge, MA: Harvard University Press, pp. 67–89.
Williams, M. A. and Baumann, M. G. (1986) 'International Evidence on Output-Inflation Tradeoffs: A Bootstrap Analysis', *Economic Letters,* 21, pages 149–53.
Woodford, M. (1998) 'Public Debt and the Price Level', presented at Bank of England conference on Government Debt and Monetary Policy, *June 18–19, 1998.* Princeton, NJ: Princeton University.
Woodford, M. (1999) 'Optimal Monetary Policy Inertia', *Manchester School Supplement,* 1–35.
Woodford, M. (2000) 'A Neo-wicksellian Framework for the analysis of Monetary Policy', at http://www.princeton.edu/~~woodford/.
Woodford, M. (2002) 'Interest and Prices', at http://www.princeton.edu/~~woodford/.
Wouters, R. and Dombrecht, M. (2000) 'Model-based Inflation Forecasts and Monetary Policy Rules', *National Bank of Belgium Working Paper,* No. 1.
Yalçin, C. (2000) 'An Estimation of Output Gap for Turkey' The Central Bank of the Republic of Turkey, Ankara, (in Turkish).
Yates, A. and Chapple B., (1996) What Determines the Short-run Output-Inflation Trade-off, Bank of England Working Paper Series No 53.
Young, A. (1995) 'The Tyranny of Numbers: Confronting the Statistical Realities of the East Asian Growth Experience', *Quarterly Journal of Economics,* 110, 641–80.
Zsoldos, I. (1997) 'Savings and Portfolio Decisions of the Hungarian Households, 1980–1996', *National Bank of Hungary Working Paper,* No. 1997/4.

Index